HANKEY
Man of Secrets
Volume I 1877-1918

by the same author

THE WAR AT SEA (HMSO)

H.M.S. WARSPITE

THE SECRET CAPTURE

THE NAVY AT WAR 1939-1945

THE STRATEGY OF SEA POWER

A MERCHANT FLEET IN WAR 1939-1945

THE ART OF LEADERSHIP

NAVAL POLICY BETWEEN THE WARS
VOL. I 1919-1929
VOL. II 1930-1939

HANKEY MAN OF SECRETS
VOL. I 1877-1918
VOL. II 1919-1931
VOL III 1931-1963

HANKEY

Man of Secrets

Volume I 1877-1918

STEPHEN ROSKILL

COLLINS
St James's Place, London

First published 1970
Reprinted 1978
© S. W. Roskill, 1970
ISBN 0 00 211327 9
Printed in Great Britain
Collins Clear-Type Press
London and Glasgow

Contents

Illustrations

The pictures facing pages 32, 65, 129, 160, 321 are reproduced
by kind permission of the Imperial War Museum, and that facing
page 576 by courtesy of the Beaverbrook Foundation.

Maps

Abbreviations

Adm.	Admiralty document in P.R.O.
Air	Air Ministry document in P.R.O.
BM.	British Museum
Cab.	(Followed by suffix indicating series) Cabinet Minute or Memorandum
C.I.D.	Committee of Imperial Defence
C-in-C	Commander-in-Chief
Cd. ⎫ Cmd. ⎭	Command Papers
CP. and GT.	Cabinet Memoranda in series indicated
E.E.F.	Egyptian Expeditionary Force
F.O.	Foreign Office document in P.R.O.
G.H.Q.	General Headquarters
G.O.C.	General Officer Commanding
H.P.D.C.	Home Ports Defence Committee of C.I.D.
H.S.F.	High Seas Fleet (German)
IC.	International Conference Series in P.R.O.
IWC.	Imperial War Cabinet Series in P.R.O.
M.E.F.	Mediterranean Expeditionary Force
N.M.M.	National Maritime Museum
O.D.C.	Overseas Defence Committee of C.I.D.
P.R.O.	Public Record Office
Parl. Deb.	Parliamentary Debates (Hansard) 4th Series up to 1909, then 5th Series
Q.M.G.	Quartermaster-General
RA	Royal Archives
S.W.C.	Supreme War Council

Acknowledgments

My first acknowledgments are to Adeline, Lady Hankey and to the second Lord Hankey for placing at my disposal without stint or condition the whole of the first Lord Hankey's papers. Lady Hankey kept every letter her husband wrote to her, from his proposal of marriage to the end of his life; and he wrote to her almost every day when they were separated. This remarkable collection has proved an invaluable supplement to the other records of her husband's long life. The present Lord Hankey and his brothers and sister, the Hon. Christopher Hankey, the Hon. Henry Hankey and the Hon. Lady Benn, have given me very valuable recollections of their father, have read the typescript and have offered me many valuable comments and suggestions. Secondly I must thank H.M. the Queen for gracious permission to quote from the letters and papers of her grandfather, King George V, who showed great confidence in Hankey's judgment and discretion. Miss Jane Langton and her colleagues in the Windsor Castle library could not have been more helpful in my research in the Royal Archives.

Sir Basil Liddell Hart has most kindly read the whole typescript, and has placed at my disposal his unrivalled knowledge of World War I and its aftermath, as well as allowing me to exploit his own great collection of letters and papers. I cannot sufficiently thank him for the time and trouble he took on my behalf, and for the kindness and hospitality he and Lady Liddell Hart have invariably shown me on my many visits of enquiry. Mr. A. J. Sylvester and Mr. Lawrence Burgis, who served as Private Secretary to Hankey from 1916 to 1921 and from 1921 to 1937 respectively, have given me most valuable recollections, as has Lord Bridges, who succeeded Hankey as Secretary of the Cabinet in 1938.

I must thank Sir Godfrey Agnew for explaining to me the work of the Privy Council Office and the duties carried out by Hankey in the appointment which Sir Godfrey holds to-day. Professor Sir James Butler gave me the whole of his correspondence with Hankey about his biography of Hankey's close associate Philip Kerr, Lord Lothian.

Mr. Keith Middlemas of the University of Sussex and Mrs. Eirene White very kindly gave me copies of Hankey's letters to Dr. Thomas Jones, his deputy in the Cabinet Secretariat from 1916 to 1930, whose diary and letters Mr. Middlemas has edited for publication. Sir Winston Churchill's daughter, Mrs. Christopher Soames, provided me with full information about her parents' various homes; and Mr. Martin Gilbert of Merton College, Oxford, who has taken over the great task of completing the authorised biography of Sir Winston Churchill, has most kindly provided me with copies of Hankey letters in the vast collection of Churchill papers. Miss Cecil Leslie, Sir Norman Leslie's daughter, and Miss Gertrude Thompson, formerly private secretary to Leslie and to Lord Salter, have helped me to piece together the story of the introduction of convoy in 1917. An unpublished thesis by Mr. Patrick Cosgrave (Cambridge University, 1968) has been useful in disentangling the Balkan imbroglio of 1914–15. His Grace the Duke of Hamilton has generously allowed me to use Hankey's correspondence with Admiral of the Fleet Lord Fisher now in the Lennoxlove papers. Sir Philip Magnus-Allcroft, the biographer of Marquess Curzon, has very kindly found me Hankey correspondence in the Curzon papers. Mr. F. M. P. Maurice and Professor Joan Robinson, son and daughter of General Sir Frederick Maurice, have given me valuable help and advice over the story of the notorious letter published by the General in May 1918 and its aftermath in the "Maurice Debate". Professor A. Temple Patterson of Southampton University, the editor of the papers of Admiral of the Fleet Earl Jellicoe, generously placed at my disposal Hankey material which he had found in the Jellicoe papers, and Mr. John Barnes of the London School of Economics did me the same service with regard to the papers of Admiral of the Fleet Earl Beatty. Finally Mr. Richard Ollard of Collins & Co. has once again given me very valuable editorial advice, and has piloted the book through all the stages of production with exemplary skill and care.

I am indebted to the following Libraries and Museums for access to or copies of papers in their charge:—

The Bodleian Library—Papers of 1st Earl of Oxford and Asquith and of Viscount Milner.
The British Museum—Papers of 1st Earl Jellicoe, 1st Earl Balfour, Lord Robert Cecil and Mr. Philip Noel Baker.
The National Library of Scotland—Papers of Viscount Haldane.
The Public Record Office of Northern Ireland—Papers of 1st Baron Carson,

The University of Capetown—Papers of Field-Marshal J. C. Smuts.

University of London, King's College, Centre for Military Archives—Papers of Field-Marshal Sir William Robertson, General Sir Ernest Swinton and General Lord Ismay.

The Beaverbrook Library—Papers of 1st Earl Lloyd George and Mr. A. Bonar Law.

The University of Birmingham—Papers of Sir Austen Chamberlain.

The National Maritime Museum—Papers of Admirals Sir Alexander Duff and Sir Herbert Richmond, and of Sir W. Graham Greene.

For permission to reproduce unpublished copyright material I am indebted to the following:—

H.M. the Queen—Papers of King George V.

Beaverbrook Newspapers Ltd.—Papers of 1st Earl Lloyd George.

The Right Hon. the Viscount Scarsdale—Papers of Marquess Curzon of Kedleston.

The Right Hon. the Baron Fisher—Papers of Admiral of the Fleet Baron Fisher of Kilverstone.

The Warden and Fellows of New College, Oxford—Papers of 1st Viscount Milner.

The Right Hon. the Earl Balfour—Papers of 1st Earl Balfour.

Mark Bonham Carter, Esq.—Papers of 1st Earl and Countess of Oxford and Asquith and of Sir Maurice Bonham Carter.

The Right Hon. the Baron Birdwood—Papers of Field-Marshal the Baron Birdwood.

Mr. Winston Churchill—Papers of Sir Winston Churchill.

The Right Hon. the Earl of Derby—Papers of 17th Earl of Derby.

The Right Hon. the Baron de Robeck—Papers of Admiral of the Fleet Sir John de Robeck.

The Right Hon. the Viscount Esher—Papers of 2nd Viscount Esher.

Mrs. Milton Gendel—Papers of Edwin Montagu, Esq.

The Right Hon. the Earl Haig—Papers of Field-Marshal Earl Haig.

A. R. B. Haldane, Esq.—Papers of Viscount Haldane.

Henry Borden, Esq.—Papers of Sir Robert Borden.

David McKenna, Esq.—Papers of Reginald McKenna, Esq.

Mrs. George Shield and Mrs. Allen Leeper—Papers of General Sir Ian Hamilton.

The Dowager Lady Hardinge of Penshurst—Papers of 1st Baron Hardinge of Penshurst.

The Right Hon. the Earl Jellicoe—Papers of Admiral of the Fleet Earl Jellicoe.

The Right Hon. the Viscount Long—Papers of 1st Viscount Long.

The Right Hon. the Baron Mottistone—Papers of 1st Baron Mottistone.

General the Right Hon. Baron Robertson—Papers of Field-Marshal Sir William Robertson.

The Right Hon. the Baron Runciman—Papers of 1st Baron Runciman.

The Right Hon. the Marquess of Waterford—Papers of Admiral of the Fleet Lord Charles Beresford.

Laurence Scott, Esq.—Papers of Mr. C. P. Scott.

Mrs. Eirene White—Papers of Dr. Thomas Jones.

Sir Edward Spears—Extracts from his book *Liaison 1914*.

Messrs. Allen & Unwin—Extracts from Lord Hankey's diary published in *The Supreme Command 1914-1918*.

The Right Hon. the Earl Lloyd George has kindly given his approval to publication of certain of his father's letters not held by the Beaverbrook Library.

All quotations from official records in the Public Record Office are Crown Copyright and are reproduced by kind permission of The Controller, Her Majesty's Stationery Office. All letters and documents not given source references are in the Hankey papers. Letters are in typescript unless stated to be "Holograph", meaning that they are written in the hand of the person signing the letter. "Manuscript" indicates that a letter is in some other or unknown hand.

For research assistance I am, as always, deeply indebted to Commander Geoffrey Hare, who has carried the main burden of scrutinising the vast collection of Cabinet records for Hankey material. My most wisely chosen daughter-in-law Julia (Mrs. Nicholas Roskill) a history graduate of Girton College, Cambridge, also helped me with research in the Public Record Office and gave me the hospitality of her home in London—until family responsibilities expectedly caused her to devote her skills and knowledge to a more maternal field. In the heavy work of searching the Cabinet and C.I.D. records Mr. N. E. Evans, Mr. A. J. Norris and Commander Michael Godfrey of the Public Record Office, have all proved most helpful by doing all they could to mitigate the very severe pressure on their department, and the acute congestion from which it has recently suffered. Dr. C. E. Welch, Archivist of Churchill College, has been indefatigable in searching out Hankey letters in the many collections of papers entrusted to the Churchill College Archive Centre. These included the papers of Baron Lloyd of Dolobran, Admiral of the Fleet Baron Keyes, Admiral of the Fleet Sir John de Robeck, Mr. Reginald McKenna, 1st Viscount Weir and 2nd Viscount Esher.

I am most grateful to the Rev. S. B-R. Poole for the great care and thoroughness with which he has carried out the task of indexing the book.

My devoted secretary Miss Edith Eales has typed nearly the whole manuscript—and retyped much of it several times—with unfailing care. She has also dealt most efficiently with the large correspondence in which this work has inevitably involved me. When the load became too heavy even for Miss Eales to carry, and during an illness from which she has now happily made a full recovery, Mrs. Prudence Barker and Mrs. Joan Ashman both afforded me invaluable secretarial assistance. Finally I must again acknowledge my debt to my wife, who has helped above all by the patience and tolerance she has invariably shown, by accepting uncomplainingly the disruption of family life which authorship always seems to entail, and for coping with telephone calls and visitors in a manner both to satisfy the callers and to save me from avoidable interruptions.

STEPHEN ROSKILL

Churchill College, Cambridge
Blounce, South Warnborough, Hants
1967–69

Chapter 1

The Man and his Making

THE career of the first Lord Hankey in public service was without doubt unique, and will almost certainly remain so. After serving in the Royal Marine Artillery at sea and in the Admiralty's department of Naval Intelligence he became Naval Assistant Secretary to the Committee of Imperial Defence early in 1908. Four years later he was appointed Secretary of that body, and after the outbreak of war in August 1914, when the C.I.D. was placed in a state of suspense, he became successively Secretary of the War Council, the Dardanelles Committee and the War Committee, which were in turn the supreme British authority for the direction of the war under Asquith's ministries. When in December 1916 Lloyd George formed the War Cabinet he appointed Hankey as its secretary and he served the War Cabinet and Imperial War Cabinet in that capacity until, in October 1919, the former was dissolved—after having held 650 meetings. Hankey then continued as secretary of peace-time Cabinets under Lloyd George, Bonar Law, Baldwin, Ramsay MacDonald and Neville Chamberlain. In addition he once again acted as secretary of the Committee of Imperial Defence from June 1920 when its first post-war meeting took place. Furthermore in June 1923 he undertook the additional responsibility of Clerk of the Privy Council, and continued to hold all three appointments until he retired at the end of July 1938.

But Hankey's activities were by no means confined to the secretaryship of British Cabinets. During World War I he acted as British secretary to the many Inter-Allied political and military conferences; and he was secretary of the Imperial Conferences of 1921, 1923, 1926 and 1930. At the Paris Peace Conference of 1919 he first served the British Empire Delegation and then became secretary of the famous Council of Four (or of Three during the Italian withdrawal from the conference). In 1921 he went to Washington with Balfour to act as secretary to the British Empire Delegation to the conference which produced the numerous Washington Treaties and Declarations. Though his chief interest always lay in the field of defence he was Secretary-General to the London Conference on Reparations of 1924, and of The Hague Economic Conferences of 1929 and 1930. There is good evidence that at the former his tact broke a complete *impasse* with the French.

Hankey served again as Secretary-General at the conference convened at Lausanne in 1932, which resulted in the final abolition of Reparations. But he would never involve himself in conferences which he considered foredoomed to failure, or whose broad purposes he disapproved. That explains his absence from the ill-prepared "Coolidge" naval conference held at Geneva in 1927; and although he served as Secretary-General to the first London naval conference of 1930 he took no part in the second conference, called to replace the expiring Washington and London naval treaties, in 1935-6.

In 1933 Hankey visited Germany as a private individual and produced a long report on the Nazi movement for his old friend of the Paris 1919 and The Hague 1929 and 1930 conferences Sir Eric Phipps, who had recently been appointed ambassador at Berlin. He sent several copies privately to officials at the Foreign Office. Hankey certainly was not deceived regarding the realities of the Nazi movement—as were some British visitors whom Hitler and his gang delighted to honour in the 1930s. Indeed he described to Phipps the "extraordinary sense of having come back to civilisation" which he experienced on returning to England.

In the year following his tour of Germany Hankey was invited to attend the centenary celebrations at Melbourne, and the Australian and New Zealand governments took the opportunity to seek his advice on defence problems. As he went out by South Africa and returned through Canada the British government commissioned him "to put the Prime Ministers of all the Dominions wise as to our own defence plans". Having recently written the report of the Defence Requirements Sub-Committee of 1933 he had all the relevant facts at his finger tips.

Hankey served in effect as chief adviser on defence up to his retirement. But he was strongly opposed to any fundamental change in the organisation and functions of the Committee of Imperial Defence. and particularly to the creation of a Ministry of Defence. His dislike of the first move in that direction—the appointment of Sir Thomas Inskip as Minister for Co-ordination of Defence in 1936—was symptomatic of this; and although hard evidence is lacking it is probable that this brought about a feeling among at any rate some Ministers that a change was necessary at the head of the Cabinet and C.I.D. Secretariat.

In addition to his prodigious secretarial activities Hankey acted as chairman of many sub-committees of the Cabinet and C.I.D.—notably the Overseas Defence Sub-Committee and the powerfully constituted Defence Requirements Sub-Committee mentioned above.

The vast knowledge and experience which Hankey accumulated during his thirty years at the centre of affairs, aided and reinforced by an astonishing memory and a capacity for work which never ceased to amaze his colleagues and subordinates, not only won him the confidence of Monarchs, Ministers and heads of the fighting services, but made him the repository of innumerable confidences. The description of him as "the man of a million secrets" is no exaggeration; and his extreme discretion never caused anyone who had confided in him to regret it. That he exerted great power and influence is beyond doubt; and it is not surprising that, especially towards the end of his official career, this should have made him some enemies. It is equally true that he relished the exercise of power behind the scenes and invariably exhibited "a matchless tact", which together made him "at once unobtrusive and formidable".[1]

Hankey was, of course, very closely observed by his colleagues and subordinates at 2 Whitehall Gardens; but they only saw a part of the man—and that the official part. Some, while admiring his dedication to his work and the efficiency with which he ran the machinery of government, regarded him not only as an exacting master (which was true enough), but as hard and humourless. Yet that side of his character dissolved as soon as he entered the intimacy of his family circle, where games and music and long walks in the Wealden countryside took priority. Certainly Hankey was extremely fortunate in finding a wife who not only completely understood him, but made his ambitions, hopes, problems and frustrations her own. And the happiness of the Hankey home and family circle derived in large measure from her staunchness of character and capacity for love and sympathy. Yet the affection in which their four children held their father, as well as the respect they felt towards him, gives the lie to those who, with only the office side of Hankey in mind, saw him merely as a rather inhuman machine of computer-like efficiency.

On his retirement Hankey was not only raised to the peerage which

[1] *The Times*. Obituary notice, 28th Jan. 1963.

he had previously declined at least twice, but was sworn a Privy Councillor. He was also the recipient of one of the choicest plums then in the gift of the British government—an official directorship of the Suez Canal Company. Other offers of employment in the world of finance and business soon poured in on him, but directorships of the Royal Insurance Company and of its subsidiary the Nile Insurance Company were the only important ones he accepted.

Shortly before the outbreak of war in 1939 Neville Chamberlain invited Hankey to join his War Cabinet of only seven ministers; and he accepted that heavy burden as Minister without Portfolio. On the fall of Chamberlain and the appointment of Winston Churchill as Prime Minister in June 1940 Hankey's star waned rapidly. His previous experience did not equip him for Ministerial office, and he was not a success in that capacity; furthermore Churchill understandably, if in some cases unfairly, was strongly prejudiced against those who had served his predecessor. Hankey remained in the government, though not in the War Cabinet, as Chancellor of the Duchy of Lancaster for fourteen months, after which Churchill downgraded him to Paymaster-General. In March 1942 he dismissed him from office with an uncharacteristic letter which contained no word of thanks for Hankey's three decades of service under six Prime Ministers. But Hankey was by that time a strong critic of Churchill over the priority given to "strategic bombing". For he knew that the future course, and indeed the outcome of the war depended not on "de-housing" the German people but on winning the Atlantic battle as a preliminary to the invasion of Europe. His criticism of Churchill increased when the "Unconditional Surrender" dogma was adopted so light-heartedly in January 1943 at the Casablanca conference; since Hankey's long memory went back to the total failure of the draconian clauses imposed on Germany by the Treaty of Versailles. He was indeed one of the first to recognise the long-term consequences of "Unconditional Surrender", as he was one of the first to condemn the decision to bring certain German and Japanese political, naval and military leaders to trial as "war criminals". Though he admitted the justice of bringing to trial before an impartial tribunal vested with proper legal jurisdiction the actual perpetrators of atrocities against the population of occupied countries, prisoners of war and those incarcerated in the abominable German concentration camps, he fought a strenuous and ultimately successful campaign against the trial by the victors and imprisonment of statesmen such as Mr. Shigemitsu, one time Japanese ambassador in London and then Foreign Minister, and of ex-enemy service leaders such as Field-Marshal Manstein who had, in his view, merely carried out their duty. This was at the time a thoroughly unpopular stand to take, and Hankey had great difficulty in finding a British publisher to produce his indictment of Unconditional Surrender and of the war crimes trials (*Politics, Trials and Errors*, 1949). That he was inspired wholly by humanitarian motives is shown by the correspondence he conducted with his associates in the campaign, notably George Bell, Bishop of Chichester, Dean Inge, Lord Maugham (a former Lord Chancellor), Montgomery Belgion, R. T. Paget, Q.C. M.P. and the distinguished jurist F. J. P. Veale.

To return to 1940 it is a curious and interesting phenomenon that just when Hankey's star in the centre of the firmament of British public service and government began to wane, a new star should have risen for him in a totally different constellation—that of scientific research and development. In October of that year he was appointed chairman of the Cabinet's Scientific Advisory Committee, and so came into contact with many of Britain's leading scientists. He also travelled the country tirelessly in company with some of them to further his responsibility for the recruitment of the scientists and technologists needed to help the British war effort—notably in the field of Radar training. He won the confidence, and even the affection, of many of the scientists who were associated with him in this work—and such men do not give their confidence and affection lightly. The golden opinions of Hankey received from men such as the late Sir Henry Dale, formerly President of the Royal Society, Lord Todd, Lord Snow, Professor A. V. Hill and others surely indicate the possession of quite remarkable qualities. And Hankey's election as a Fellow of the Royal Society in June 1942, three months after Churchill had dismissed him, suggests that the Society wished to do what it could to mitigate the harshness of his treatment at the hands of the Prime Minister.

Hankey's years of retirement after the end of World War II continued to be immensely busy, and his literary output prodigious. He was engaged on writing his memoirs of World War I, which were banned from publication by three Prime Ministers (Churchill, Attlee and Macmillan) on the recommendation of his successors as Secretary of the Cabinet Sir Edward Bridges and Sir Norman Brook. After seeking the advice of Sir Lionel Heald, a former Attorney-General, regarding the likelihood of prosecution under the Official Secrets Act, and accepting the need to delete some passages, Hankey finally published them in 1961 under the title of *The Supreme Command* 1914–18. He also published his account of the administrative principles which had governed the conduct of Cabinet business and international negotiations during the period of his public service in *Diplomacy by Conference* (1946). His Cambridge Lees Knowles Lectures were published under the title of *Government Control in War* (1945), and his Oxford Romanes Lecture *The Science and Art of Government* (1951) was also printed. Finally he wrote his study of the peace negotiations of 1919, which was published shortly after his death as *The Supreme Control at the Paris Peace Conference* (1963).

After his retirement Hankey was in constant demand as a lecturer or speaker on public occasions, from discussions at Chatham House to the informal gatherings of the small but very distinguished body known as "The Club", founded by Samuel Johnson and Joshua Reynolds in 1764, to which he was delighted to be elected and which he served later as Treasurer. During these years historians, biographers and students flocked to his study, bombarded him with letters requesting his views on some aspect of his long period of public service, and sought his memories of politicians and statesmen in whom they were interested; and almost to the end of his life he granted them interviews or answered their enquiries in his own hand.

In addition to his historical and literary activities Hankey became a commercial (as opposed to British government) director of the Suez Canal Company, and attended the meetings of the Board in Paris or in Egypt with the utmost regularity. In the 1950s he repeatedly warned British Ministers of the results of their policy of concession towards Egyptian nationalism; and when in 1956 his worst fears were realised he wrote a damning indictment of that policy entitled *Catastrophic Disaster*—which he seems never to have attempted to get published.

In the House of Lords he described himself as a "Cross-bencher", frequently took part in debates, and rode some of his hobby horses— such as his campaign against the adulteration of food—hard. But by initiating the legislation which prohibited the use of agene as a whitener in bread he accomplished an unusual feat for a member of the Upper House. He is remembered as a very accurate, careful speaker who always had at his finger tips the facts regarding whatever subject was being debated. But he did not possess the gift of rhetoric, and relied for conviction of his audience on the soundness of his views rather than on dialectical skill.

In the 1950s he and Churchill made up their quarrel, which went back to 1937 and had led to the parting of their ways in 1942. They exchanged copies of their latest historical works, and when Hankey's 80th birthday brought him a stream of congratulatory telegrams and letters Churchill was among those who remembered the occasion.

The crisis in the Middle East of 1956 hit Hankey very hard; for he was an intensely patriotic man—before patriotism became unfashionable. Throughout his life he was utterly convinced that the British Empire was a great force for peace and stability in the world, which no international organisation such as the League of Nations or the United Nations could possibly replace. And, looking at the condition of this world at the end of the 1960s can even the most convinced "internationalist" claim he was wrong? To witness the defeat and humiliation of his country and its fighting services at the hands of the United Nations and those of its erstwhile ally the United States of America, after having participated in Britain's triumphs over the forces of evil in 1918 and again in 1945 was indeed to drink deep of the draught of bitterness. For the first time in his life, except perhaps for a severe attack of the prevalent influenza in 1918, he became seriously ill; and his children are unanimous in the opinion that he was never again the same man. In the following year he was again ill, and his eyesight and hearing now both began to deteriorate; but his courage never failed him, and he continued almost to the end to try and answer letters and enquiries. He died on 25th January 1963 in the local hospital to which he had been taken for an emergency operation, full of years and of honours. The tributes which poured in on his widow and family, from high and low, were almost overwhelming in their quantity and sincerity; and the Press devoted considerable space to the passing of a man whose life and service had been absolutely unique.

No biography of Hankey would be complete which did not lay proper emphasis on his religious convictions. His faith was simple, orthodox and unquestioning. He rarely failed to go to church on a Sunday, he read his Bible every day, and he was not ashamed for it to be known that he said his prayers regularly. In the family his habit of going up to his bedroom to pray immediately after the evening meal, even when there was company, sometimes provoked mirth. "Where's Pop?" might be asked: to which the reply always was "He's gone to say his prayers". The reason for this habit probably was that he wished to make his devotions while he was still wide awake and able to concentrate fully on the purpose in hand. Until 1956 an outstanding feature of his character was his never-failing optimism; and it is difficult not to feel that this derived chiefly from his faith. Furthermore it must have been his faith, combined with the emphasis he always placed on physical fitness, which enabled him to carry burdens and withstand strains which would have brought on a nervous breakdown in 99% of human beings.

In 1915 Hankey began to keep a diary. It comprises four large leather-bound volumes, fitted with strong locks. Up to 1923 he kept it with regularity, but after that year it becomes more spasmodic—probably because on becoming Clerk of the Privy Council he felt that the diary might be regarded as a breach of the "Declaration" corresponding to a Privy Counsellor's oath of secrecy, which the holder of the Clerkship is required to make. However when Ramsay MacDonald first became Prime Minister in 1924 he asked Hankey whether he was still keeping a diary, and on receiving a qualified negative in reply he instructed him to restart it for the benefit of himself and other Ministers. It thus came to pass that during MacDonald's two terms as Prime Minister (1924 and 1929–35) Hankey's diary regained in some degree the continuity and intimacy which distinguished it during the last twenty months of the Asquith and the whole of the Lloyd George ministries. The final entry is dated 31st August 1942.

Hankey never took his diary on any of his numerous trips abroad. It was always kept under lock and key either in his office or at his home. But he kept a record of his official journeys on loose sheets of paper, which he probably intended ultimately to be bound up with the rest of the diary. Unfortunately he never did so, with the result that some of the loose sheets became damaged. It is the intention of the Churchill College Archive Centre to rebind all the diaries with the loose sheets, after repair, inserted in their proper place, so making this historical document as complete as possible, and sufficiently secure for students to make use of it.

Like most diaries Hankey's is, of course, a highly subjective document, and he confided to it his innermost thoughts and feelings at the time of any entry. But he clearly intended that it should be published some day. Indeed on one occasion he wrote that it might be published "after about fifty years". He never allowed his colleagues or subordinates to read his diary; nor in later years did he allow historians access to it—though he quite often gave them information extracted from it, or the gist of entries. He himself printed a proportion of the entries, or parts of the entries, up to the Armistice of November 1918 in *The Supreme Command*; but he plainly felt inhibited against publishing his more candid and critical comments in those volumes. The official objections to his publishing any of it no doubt enhanced the caution he showed over selecting passages for publication. The chief interest in the diary lies, of course, in what it tells us about events behind the scenes of public life. *The Times* farsightedly remarked in the editorial published to mark Hankey's retirement that "One day a later generation may perhaps learn more than even Greville has recorded of contemporary persons and events from the diary which Sir Maurice Hankey is understood to have kept". Thanks to the generosity of Lord Hankey's heirs that day has now arrived.

As regards the accuracy of the diary, frequent checks with the official Cabinet or C.I.D. minutes, have shown that if Hankey said that a meeting was held on a certain day, and such-and-such subjects were discussed, his diary is always confirmed by the minutes. But the latter are of course couched in dry, official language, and are worded with extreme reticence—especially when differences of opinion were expressed. In writing his diary Hankey felt no such inhibitions, and it thus tells us a great deal about the outlook, ambitions and opinions of the persons involved in any discussion or controversy. Though the diary may therefore be accepted as historically accurate, within the limits imposed on any contemporary record, Hankey showed surprising carelessness in his spelling of proper names; and this has in some cases made it difficult to identify with assurance the persons he was referring to.

The existence of the diary presents, however, peculiarly difficult problems for Hankey's biographer. To reprint the passages which he himself published would obviously be redundant; but to print only the excluded entries would leave the reader hopelessly bewildered. The principle here followed has therefore been to include the whole, or nearly the whole, of such entries as are necessary to the reader's understanding of the narrative—regardless of whether part of them was used by Hankey himself.

The diary contains hardly any signs that Hankey made alterations at a later date. Except in a very few cases, where he appears to have corrected a word or two, it stands as he originally wrote it. This, taken with the fact that the published extracts only very rarely differ from the manuscript, make it seem certain that Hankey himself regarded the diary as a reliable record of the events he witnessed. Editing of the diary has been kept to a minimum, such as introducing punctuation and quotation marks where clarity would be improved by doing so, and reducing somewhat Hankey's excessive use of capital letters. Occasionally there are words which have proved impossible to decipher, and in those cases the best guess possible has been made, and question marks in the text indicate that uncertainty exists. The few words which have been inserted, either for clarity or because Hankey inadvertently omitted them, are shown in square brackets.

After Hankey's eldest son Robin entered the Foreign Service in 1927 he began to write him long letters about current affairs and his own work. He asked for those letters to be kept and ultimately to be returned to him—a request with which, fortunately for the biographer, the present Lord Hankey complied. It seems probable that Hankey regarded those letters as in some degree a substitute for his diary, and that he wanted them preserved against the time when a full biography could be written. Certainly the letters fill many gaps in the final volume of the diary.

Another problem that besets Hankey's biographer is the sheer quantity of the material left behind by him. Indeed one may doubt whether any person, with the possible exception of Sir Winston Churchill, has bequeathed to posterity such a vast accumulation of minutes, memoranda, letters and publications. They must in all amount to many millions of words. Furthermore no one, except once again Churchill, was so near to the centre of national and international politics over so long a period. To attempt to condense this material into a single volume appeared to me to deprive the historically-minded public of much that was of the greatest interest. Fortunately my publisher has agreed with my view that it is both justifiable and necessary to devote two volumes to Hankey's life.

Maurice Pascal Alers Hankey was born at Biarritz on Easter Sunday 1877. The second of his Christian names was given to him in accordance with an old French custom. But that year Easter Sunday coincided with All Fools' Day, and his father is alleged to have described the infant as "an April fool but an Easter egg". He considered that his birth on French soil resulted in "a certain partiality for France" which influenced his outlook in both World Wars, and perhaps also his actions at the many international conferences which he attended in between those conflicts.

Maurice Hankey was the fifth child and the third son of Robert Alers Hankey (1838–1906) and Helen Bakewell (1845–1900). Robert was the sixth of the eleven children (seven sons and four daughters) born to John Alers Hankey (1803–72) and Sarah James (1807–85). John's grandfather Thomas Hankey of Fetcham Park in Surrey (1740–93) had a son William (1771–1859) by a Miss Alers who may have been a German governess in his household.[1] It seems fairly certain that Thomas Hankey and Miss Alers were never married, since William's son John Alers Hankey II offered a large reward for the discovery of a marriage certificate—but without success. However on 16th December 1815 the Prince Regent (George IV, 1820) mitigated the stain of illegitimacy by authorising William Alers by Royal Warrant "to assume the surname of Hankey in addition to Alers and to bear the arms of Hankey only with difference".[2] Thus was instituted the long and prolific line of the family of Alers Hankey.

Robert Alers Hankey, Maurice's father, was educated at Rugby School and Trinity College, Cambridge. Maurice, who was 29 when his father died, remembered him as a very serious, studious and deeply religious man. His intellectual gifts were by no means negligible. His favourite reading was sermons, philosophy and history, and at his death he left a large library of theological works. Robert suffered from delicate health, and for that reason he was sent to South Australia, where he set himself up as a sheep farmer. In that arduous and risky enterprise he seems to have shown originality and enterprise. For example Maurice recorded, presumably from his father's reminiscences, that he was one of the first Australian farmers to fence his land into paddocks for grazing purposes. None the less the disastrous experience of several droughts brought him near to ruin, and after ten years' strenuous work his health broke down.

It was in Australia that Robert Alers Hankey met his future wife,

---

[1] In the 16th and 17th centuries the name Alers was fairly common in Bremen where many of them were pastors. Also a Huguenot family, originally "des Aleurs", changed their name to Alers on settling in Brunswick, Germany, and later assumed the title of "von Alers". But no evidence has been found to prove that Miss Alers was descended from either family.
[2] Debrett.

Helen Bakewell of Adelaide (1845–1900). She came of a Scottish family
which had emigrated to Australia in the very early days of colonisation.
William Bakewell, her father, was a member, and later the head of
Bakewell, Stone and Piper of Adelaide, one of the largest firms of
lawyers in South Australia, which still exists.

In 1865 Robert Hankey and his fiancée came back to England to get
married, after which they returned to South Australia where they
continued to farm until his health failed. On his second return home he
retained ownership of some land near Adelaide to which he intended to
go back; but he never did so. According to Maurice he came out of his
Australian venture "rather more than all square".

On their final return to England Robert and Helen settled in
Brighton, firstly at 27 Eaton Place and then at 1 Chesham Place; but
because of Robert's delicate health they usually wintered abroad. As he
got older Robert's habits became increasingly idiosyncratic and his
hypochondria more pronounced. Fortunately for the children Helen
was a remarkable woman, and coped most capably with her trying
husband. Maurice later described her as "saintly but humorous;
charming but serious. She had a great deal of Scotch blood which came
out prominently in her tough fibre." It is a fair assumption that his own
toughness of physique and strength of character came to him from his
mother's side.

Maurice Hankey's education began at a private day school in
Brighton at the age of 7 or 8; but no record of his time in that establishment has come down to us. Towards the end of his life, when he was
making notes for an interview by the B.B.C., he recorded that he
"gained a definite advantage from being a day boarder", because he
returned each evening to "wise and affectionate parents" and a family
in which the reading of what he called "the best books" was a nightly
ritual. Regular church-going was, as in most middle class families of
those days, an undeviating practice. But in the home the strong
preference of Helen Hankey for "Low Church" and her husband's
equally strong adherence to "High Church" practices produced constant arguments in which the children apparently took sides with relish.
The story goes that Maurice used to show his impartiality by arguing
sometimes in favour of the one and sometimes of the other, and that he
would compromise by attending his mother's Low Church in the
morning and his father's High Church in the evening. Later in life,
however, he became as strongly attached to Low Church principles and

practices as his mother had been, and would declaim vigorously against what he called "Popery".

If the young Maurice accepted church going and family prayers unquestioningly he seems to have resented the concurrent Sunday "prohibitions"—as indeed must surely be the case with any lively and intelligent child. At any rate in later life he recalled that he counteracted such prohibitions by developing "a propensity for toy soldiers". With them he evidently fought many imaginative battles—including one he described as "the siege and destruction of Jericho". Perhaps the biblical subject was chosen to forestall parental opposition to such unsabbatical activities.

While at day school Hankey was introduced to the violin. He later declared that his parents intended his elder brother Clement to be the pupil, but Clement had run away when the teacher first appeared. He was therefore hauled out from under the table where he was hiding and received his first lesson under compulsion. Whether the story is apocryphal or not he continued with his violin, in spite of all difficulties, until shortly after he went to sea; and his interest in and love for music lasted all his life. Though his tastes were always rather conventional they were genuine enough for him to make music one of the dominant influences in the lives of his own children.

We have seen how Hankey's toy soldiers stimulated his interest in warfare at a very early age—an interest which, incidentally, the young Winston Churchill developed in the same manner.[1] In addition Hankey developed at this time what he called "a yearning for a life at sea". It was so intense that he described it as "an itch—like being in love". But for some unexplained reason his father vetoed his desire to sit for a naval cadetship, and instead "to his intense chagrin he was packed off to Rugby, the public school furthest from the sea".[2]

In the winter term of 1890 Hankey joined Mr. John Collins's House, and was placed in the form known as Upper Middle I. At the end of his first term he got his remove into the Lower Fifth, where he remained (a source of disappointment to himself and his parents) until 1892. His parents' inclinations towards a military career then resulted in his transfer to the Army Class. He attained the Sixth form of that Class in 1894, thereby gaining prefectorial powers, and left the school in the following year.

[1] See *My Early Life* (Macmillan, 1944) p. 33.
[2] Sir James Marchant (Ed.), *If I had my Time Again* (Odhams Press, 1950) p. 46.

His mother preserved many of the weekly letters he sent home from Rugby. These deal mostly in subjects of perennial interest to school boys, such as the result of school matches, requests for "stodge" (i.e. supplementary food), and pleas for small sums of money—which his father was often reluctant to provide. As a boy Hankey evidently learnt to take good care of his money—a trait which lasted throughout his life and enabled him later to provide for the less fortunate members of his family. Like most schoolboys he showed a lively interest in the macabre; but one can sometimes detect in his letters flashes suggesting strength of character and a determination to organise his life in his own way. His critical faculty also seems to have developed at an early age.

To Hilda Hankey J. Collins House, Rugby. Undated. c. 1890
Dear Hilda,
Thanks very much for your letter. Yesterday a fellow tumbled down in a run and died; he was a small town-lout [day boarder] and was found in the road in what seemed like his last gasp by some fellows: these got him some brandy and put him in a cab and drove him off to the san. but he died before he got there. . . . I had a big row with one of the masters yesterday who set me 1000 lines because I argued the matter out when he gave me an impot unfairly. I don't know that I have ever before seen anyone so utterly lose his temper before. When he had cooled down, he reduced it to only 150. It was that Mr. Steele who hated Hugh and me so much . . .
                                        Your affectionate brother
I just hear that they have had a post-mortem examination of the fellow that died and that his heart was quite sound but there is to be an inquest to-morrow. Don't get in a funk or spread vague rumours as it might give the school a bad name. I will send details as soon as possible.

To Mrs. Robert Hankey Undated. c. 1890.
Dear Ma,
Thank Pa very much for his exceedingly liberal tip. I am sure you can't say I am frittering it away as I have deposited 4s. for potted meat and jam while I have spent 1s.0. on biscuits and have put away 3s. to keep so that if I do run out I shall have more than enough, in a tin box which has two long nails driven write [sic] through it into the bottom of my table draw[er] inside which is a wooden box opening by a secret spring of my own invention and the whole apparatus is kept in my draw[er] which I always keep locked. To this I hope to add 6d. a week. The boy I am in a study with has had a rather rotten hamper sent him only having a lot of sweets etc, not good substantial biscuits . . . There is the supper bell.

To the same. Undated. c. 1890.

Dear Ma,

. . . The other day one of the boys who clean the boots drowned himself in the canal, he did not only clean the boots but is like a butler in the house. There are two of them who had been suspected of stealing money lately, of which 4£ worth has been missed, so Jacky [Mr. Collins] stuck "the lout" in a study to watch them go into the bathroom who saw them steal some money out of a fellow's trouser pocket, then Jacky said he'd bunk [? dismiss] them and the younger one went and committed suicide while the other . . . is in jail. I wonder if Pa would let me get a bat with my purse money . . . The confectioner has got some cakes in.

The next letter, written most unusually in mid-week, was evidently struck off in a state of high indignation with his parents. It is heavily underlined in red ink.

To Mrs. Robert Hankey. Rugby School. Thursday 24th March 1892

Dear Ma,

It has come to my ears this evening that you or Pa, I don't know which, has written to Jacky to say that Tommy[1] has to wait from Monday till Thursday to "take" me home, I write now to say that it is no good him waiting as I have promised to go home with Bischoff and have ordered a cab in conjunction with him, and as we probably should not get another cab if I went with Tommy . . . it is absolutely foolish for him to wait with me . . . [and] I may get the "Rose-rash" [i.e. German measles, of which there had evidently been an epidemic] in which case I suppose he would have to wait a fortnight to "take" me home as if I could not get home by myself. Do you think that I should get lost . . . that you are so anxious for him to wait for me? I hope at least that I know how to take care of myself better than that! Think what a fool I should look when fellows said to me "Why isn't your brother going home like the other Rose-rashers?" and I should have to answer meekly "Because he has got to 'take me home' " I have made full arrangements for going home . . .

Hardly any letters written in 1894–5 from Rugby have survived, but we know that one of the most important decisions in Hankey's life came about through Mr. Collins having a friend whose son had gone into the Royal Marine Artillery. Hankey saw the chance to achieve his ambition of going to sea by following the example of that boy; and he did so in the teeth of what he later described as the "bitter opposition"

[1]The nickname by which Maurice's elder brother Clement, who overlapped with him at Rugby, went at this time.

of his family, who wished him to have another try for Woolwich. The decision once taken—and one can detect in it the determination and strength of character which was to win him great renown later—he began to work really hard. His reward came when, having "battled his way through stiff examinations, red tape and family opposition", he was accepted as a Probationary Second Lieutenant in the Royal Marine Artillery. That was on 1st September 1895, when Hankey was nearly 18½ years old.

Here we may interrupt the chronological story of Hankey's early life by reviewing his physical characteristics on leaving Rugby. He was short in stature—standing only some 5 feet 5 inches in his socks. Indeed his lack of inches would have debarred him from most regiments. The outstanding feature of early photographs is his very high and wide forehead—the effect of which was perhaps enhanced by the fact that his dark, almost black hair was always thin, and began to recede from his forehead at a very early age. His eyes were brown, large and very wide-open. This, together with his expanse of brow, gave his face unmistakable intellectual distinction. His nose was straight and rather long, and the moustache which he cultivated as a young officer and retained throughout his life failed to conceal a kindly mouth and a strong jaw which together suggest firmness of character without any trace of aggressiveness. The tightly fitting R.M.A. tunic and overalls in which he appears in photographs taken at Eastney Barracks emphasise the masculinity of a compact and graceful body on which there was not an ounce of superfluous flesh. Obviously he was in very hard condition—as indeed he always kept himself, even after his work had become mainly sedentary. The smile which appears in some early photographs is gentle without insipidity, and those who knew him well remember how easily he broke into gusts of laughter which seemed to come from deep down in his broad chest. His tenor voice had a military resonance to it—if he chose to raise it—yet it was musical in cadence and intonation. It will be told later how singing was always one of his favourite recreations.

Hankey arrived at the Royal Naval College, Greenwich, at the end of September 1895 to undergo two years of professional education and training. His letters from Greenwich reveal his contentment with his chosen career, his appreciation of the freedom allowed to the students compared with the restrictions of Rugby, and his enjoyment of the relaxed and friendly atmosphere of a famous naval mess. He got on well

Fisher: a photograph
taken at about the time
he first met Hankey

H.M.S. *Irresistible*

Hankey as a young officer

with the instructional staff, with the naval officers at the College, and with his own batch of 18 young Marine officers. At Greenwich Hankey came under the influence of Captain George Aston R.M.A.[1] who held the post of Professor of Fortification (the forerunner to the History chair) in the college. Aston developed a strong admiration for the young officer from his own regiment, and worked hard to promote his interest. Hankey described him as "a very inspiring person. He inculcated into me a principle I have tried to follow—to work for causes. His chief precept was 'Patriotism first, personal ambition nowhere', and he pitched loyalty to the Service tremendously high—which he got right home to me". At Greenwich Hankey also made friends with Commander John Rushworth Jellicoe (later Admiral of the Fleet Earl Jellicoe of Scapa). Both played in the cricket XI, their outlook and intellectual interests were similar or complementary, and their friendship endured until Jellicoe's death in 1935.

Hankey passed out from Greenwich first of his class with the coveted Sword of Honour. In later life he recalled how an old instructor in the German language, whose Goethe Reading Society he had joined, prophesied when they parted for the last time that "Mr. Hankey is to have a great career".

It is interesting to remark that while he was at Greenwich Hankey's handwriting took the form that was to become so familiar in government circles. The irregularities of the schoolboy hand were now left behind, and in its place he developed a bold, upright and extremely individual script. The handwriting of Cabinet papers of the 1920s is clearly recognisable in the Greenwich letters of 1895-7.

In July 1897 Hankey's class moved from Greenwich to Eastney Barracks, Portsmouth, where the young officers were to undergo the second and more professional part of their training. Since all aspects of land as well as sea warfare fell within the compass of the regiment's duties the course included infantry training and musketry, naval gunnery, mines and torpedoes, bridge-building and other aspects of the science of field engineering. But the first requirement was that the subalterns should themselves reach the very high standard in drill for which the marines have always been famous; and to achieve that object they spent many hours on the parade ground. Hankey, who was

[1]Later Major-General Sir George Aston (1861–1938). Admiralty War Staff 1913–14. Commanded expeditions to Ostend and Dunkirk 1914. Served in War Cabinet Secretariat 1918–19.

already developing a strong sense of regimental pride, evidently took that process in good part.

To Mrs. Robert Hankey Eastney Barracks, Portsmouth. May 29th 1898
. . . On Tuesday we celebrated the Queen's birthday here, by a review etc. of all the troops in the garrison; it was fearfully hot and trying in all one's best clothes; however not a single man fell out . . .

There has been a bit of a war scare here, although it does not seem to have reached the newspapers yet; the reason is that the new, and only just completed battleship *Hannibal* . . . was ordered off to Gibraltar at a few hours' notice. Also a cruiser named the *Dido* and two other ships were ordered off independently . . . The whole thing is inexplicable, especially as Goschen[1] has just gone there in the *Terrible*. The story current here . . . is that Russia is supposed to be sympathising with Spain, and it might become necessary to block up the Straits of Gibraltar.[2] . . .

This morning I had to take the Wesleyans to church; I was conducted to a seat near the front, with the only cushion in the Church, and a gorgeously bound book of Worship "for the officer" . . . My appearance entirely upset the whole Sunday School who all wanted to gaze at me all through the service, and had to be compelled to look to the front with a corner of a bible . . . At the conclusion of the Service the Minister came up and shook hands with me and held a long conversation . . . He did not pray for me but only for those who dwell "in the wild and lurid light of the barrack room". Could you rout out some violin duets for me? . . .

To the same. Sunday June 5th 1898
Dear Mama
. . . I don't think I shall be able to come home for some weeks just now as I am very busy over training some men for a competition. We have to march about 12 miles and then do an attack on a position represented by a target, with real bullets, and the squad that scores the most hits wins. It is a competition open to the Navy and Army for a £50 cup and a sum of money . . . The R.M.A. have never won it yet, the *Excellent* [the Gunnery School at

[1]George J. Goschen (1831–1907), 1st Viscount Goschen 1900. First Lord of the Admiralty March 1871–March 1874 and July 1895–Nov. 1900.
[2]In May and June 1898 there were persistent rumours of a Franco-Spanish secret alliance directed against Britain and the U.S.A. The latter had gone to war with Spain in April, and Britain was widely expected to support the U.S.A. In May the concentration of Spanish troops near Gibraltar was reported, and in the same month disturbing rumours of Russian designs on Ceuta reached London. The warship movements referred to by Hankey were doubtless connected with these reports. See A. J. Marder *The Anatomy of British Sea Power 1880–1905* (1940, Reprinted Cass 1964) pp. 310–11.

Portsmouth] having carried it off every time for some years. As no one senior to me seemed keen on taking it up I volunteered . . . I have a very good squad, consisting of 16 men. I am very keen on our winning . . . or at any rate getting the second prize. . . .

Hankey obviously gained greatly in self-confidence while at Eastney. Though known as "the little officer with the bald head" he successfully overcame what he had initially regarded as a serious handicap. His skill at cricket (at which he kept wicket) helped, as did the evident popularity of his musical talent; and the team which he trained for the Navy-Army competition, described above, duly won the cup. Because promotion prospects for young officers depended largely on the results achieved in their examinations at this stage he worked extremely hard in all the specialist courses (gunnery, torpedo, etc.) which he had to undergo. The results must have exceeded his wildest hopes. At Greenwich he had been first of his class by only 9 marks; but in the Portsmouth courses he achieved first place in all the examinations. The confidential report rendered on 22nd December 1898 at the end of his time at Eastney reads "An exceptionally zealous and promising young officer. Physically strong and athletic. Ability very good indeed."[1]

Hankey's success in the Portsmouth courses gained him the choice of the sea-going appointments available to subalterns. His friend Jellicoe, who was going out as Flag Captain on the China Station, pressed him to come to his ship; but instead he chose H.M.S. *Ramillies* (Captain W. des V. Hamilton), the flagship of the Mediterranean Station. The marine officer who went with Jellicoe was killed in the Boxer rebellion. Not for the last time Hankey felt that what he called "Providence" had intervened on his behalf. It was moreover at this time that losses among officers in the Boer War and in the fighting in China caused the government—after a good deal of hesitation—to increase the strength of the R.M.A., thus greatly improving promotion prospects.

By the time he left Eastney Hankey was extremely ambitious, and his new self-confidence had made him realise that he could justifiably set his sights high in the Service. He obviously had the makings of a good regimental officer; but officers whose gifts are limited to regimental

---

[1]Dated 31st Dec. 1897. I am indebted to Colonel R. W. O'N. Collis, R.M. of the office of the Commandant-General, Royal Marines, for finding this and other confidential reports on Hankey, and to the Ministry of Defence for permission to quote them.

interests do not generally achieve high rank and distinction. When he chose the Mediterranean Station Hankey must have realised that it would open new fields and opportunities to him; but there are no indications that, on leaving England for Malta in the British India Steam Navigation Company's liner *Jelunga* shortly before Christmas 1898, he had any idea regarding the direction in which his interests really lay.

Chapter 2

In the Mediterranean Fleet 1900-1901

WHEN he went to sea Hankey continued the custom ingrained in him at Rugby of writing to his mother every Sunday; and indeed he continued to do so right up to the day of her death in 1900. Many of his Mediterranean letters covered 8, 10 or even 12 pages, and contained admirable descriptions of all that he had seen and done.

The first letter of the new series is dated 23rd December 1898 and gave a description of how he had survived the rolling of the *Jelunga* in the Bay of Biscay, though he had to admit that for two days he "felt distinctly uncomfortable". The landfall at Cape Finisterre, a distant view of the lines of Torres Vedras outside Lisbon and the first sight of Gibraltar excited his historical imagination. Four days later he wrote with a touch of pride that "At last we are 'Down the Straits' as the men call the Mediterranean". The weather was glorious, and after passing Gibraltar "the scene was very fine indeed . . . the jagged mountains of Morocco on one side and the bare Spanish hillsides on the other forming a kind of frame, while right in the middle of the Straits the red sun disappeared amid a blaze of colour". Plainly this first overseas voyage was high adventure to the lively young man whose family life and schooling had so far been somewhat restricted. Not only was he intensely observant—of people as well as of places—but he also developed at this time a descriptive gift which even now makes his letters a pleasure to read. Thus on New Year's Eve he sent his mother his "first impressions of Malta", which he began to explore as soon as he had disembarked. To his disappointment he just missed the *Ramillies*, which had left on a cruise to Greece; and the temporary accommodation provided in the old wooden three-decker *Hibernia* he found thoroughly uncongenial. The chief compensation lay in the fact that for several weeks he had little by way of official duties, and could thus devote most of his time and energy to getting to know Malta and its people. However he quickly made the acquaintance of Captain H. F. Mackay, R.M.A., the Intelligence Officer of the Mediterranean Fleet. That introduction was to influence his whole career, since Mackay, no doubt sensing that Hankey possessed unusual qualities of mind and character, soon recruited him to work on an informal basis in his own field; and it was through Intelligence work that Hankey first prised open the door to the great offices he was to hold in his prime. Probably it was this interest that caused him immediately to write home for the books he needed to start on the study of the Italian language—soon to be followed by a similar demand for books on modern Greek.

Many young officers of those days on arriving in Malta, or for that matter at any naval base or overseas garrison town of the colonial Empire, confined their leisure activities to the English club and the sports club with its golf course, race track and polo grounds, and took no trouble whatever to get to know the indigenous people. The narrowness and snobbery of such men, and too often their women-folk as well, sowed seeds of hatred which were to come to a bitter harvest in the mid-20th century. Hankey's approach to the people and the sights of Malta could not have been more different; and it was the outlook and conduct of the British community that quickly aroused his criticism. Though one may reasonably attribute his critical view of his fellow countrymen, at any rate in part, to the intolerance of youth, there was an uncomfortable element of truth in his indictment of their behaviour.

To Mrs. Robert Hankey. Union Club, Malta, 3rd January 1899 (misdated 1898) . . . . I have been continuing my observations of Malta and the Maltese. I think that the latter are a much maligned race. They are cheerful, civil, and most obliging; for instance a common man today saw me trying to decipher the name of a street and at once called out the name. I have failed to see any anti-English feeling expressed, although there is a sort of deadlock now, on account of a split between the Bishop and the Governor . . . I must say though, they are treated with the utmost arrogance and lack of consideration by the British officers of both services, who make the most disparaging and insulting remarks about the Maltese in their hearing . . . I have not yet visited the churches, as I hear it is best to wait for a good light and the weather is abominable. Yesterday I walked to a place called "Citta Vecchia" about 8 miles away, passing through some very pretty gardens en route. The country is rather monotonous, although to a newcomer it is very interesting. Every little village boasts a church that would be an ornament to Trafalgar Square, and the exteriors of the houses are frequently quite imposing. Last night I obtained a free seat at the opera . . . the opera house is very pretty, and the performance was in many respects excellent . . . I went and paid many duty calls this afternoon. The people were mostly at home, and were without exception asses. In fact the specimens of English society here are most objectionable; they [are] not only all asses, but they are all very silly, jabbering, empty-headed, ugly, conceited asses. I shall avoid society . . .

Hankey's period of almost undisturbed sightseeing ended on 18th January when the *Ramillies* entered the Grand Harbour flying the flag of Admiral Sir John Hopkins[1] and he reported onboard her. His first impressions were very favourable. "Everybody in the *Ramillies*' wardroom", he told his sister Hilda, "was most civil and cordial, all coming up and shaking hands, addressing me by name, and afterwards treating me as if I had been a messmate for years . . ." The officer he was relieving told Hankey that he would have "sole charge of the large detachment of about 110 Marines, under the direction of the Major [H. C. Money], no Naval Officer having anything whatsoever to do with them". The last sentence shows that Hankey was not free from the jealous exclusiveness which has so often caused friction between Marine officers and their naval colleagues; and the criticisms of naval officers to which he was soon to give vent must be read with that failing in mind. To his father he wrote "Of course everything onboard the flagship is very spic and span from the 67-ton guns to the handrails". But he evidently soon realised that the price paid for that smartness was far too high, since three days later he described in critical terms the ordeal of "Captain's Sunday rounds". "Today (Sunday)", he wrote to his mother, "is sacred in the Navy to the great fetish 'brass and paintwork' . . . It is said that if a general engagement was imminent, and the future of the Empire was at stake, before clearing for action the brasswork would be polished and the paint touched up. No one can possibly know what cleanliness is until they have seen a warship on Sunday morning".

Here we may introduce a digression on the state of the Royal Navy before Admiral Sir John Fisher[2] took command of the Mediterranean fleet in the autumn of 1899. In his memoirs Hankey dealt with the service's deficiencies with characteristic understatement, merely remarking that "Efficiency . . . was not what it ought to have been", and deploring "the excessive importance attached to 'spit and polish' ".[3]

[1] 1834–1916. C-in-C, Mediterranean, 1896–9.
[2] 1841–1920, Baron Fisher of Kilverstone 1909. First Sea Lord 1904–10 and 1914–15.
[3] *The Supreme Command 1914–18* (2 Vols., Allen & Unwin 1961) Vol. I, pp. 13–14. Henceforth cited as *Supreme Command*.

In truth the defects were widespread and deep-seated. They derived from nearly a century of unchallenged supremacy, from the contempt of the ruling class (which provided the great majority of senior naval officers) for the new technology, of which they were very largely ignorant, from a rooted conservatism which was automatically resistant to changes which did not conform to a largely outworn "tradition", and from an exclusive educational system based on birth and wealth rather than on ability. Though the Navy was of course merely a microcosm of late-Victorian society, which was still largely based on rule by a hereditary aristocracy, the conditions of sea service and the hierarchic naval command structure tended to produce even greater resistance to change and innovation afloat than on shore. Of course there were some officers who, by the time Hankey joined the Mediterranean Fleet, realised that much was wrong and were striving to set it right[1]; but such officers constituted but a small minority, and they were all too often regarded as dangerous cranks. There is a good deal of truth in Professor A. J. Marder's description of the British Navy of the closing years of the 19th century as "in certain respects a drowsy, inefficient, moth-eaten organisation".[2] Nearly a year was, however, to pass before Hankey witnessed the efforts of one man of genius to shake the Navy out of its lethargy.

After her return from the January cruise the *Ramillies* stayed in Malta for nearly three months, part of the time being spent in dry dock. Though Hankey soon began to chafe at the inactivity of his life he flung himself wholeheartedly into the type of activity which had gained him distinction at Eastney—training tug-of-war teams, boats' crews and field guns' crews from his detachment for fleet competitions. He quickly grew to admire the versatility of his men, and at this time he found little to criticise in his naval colleagues. "It is ship life" he told his mother "that makes the Marine more handy and reliant than the soldierman"; and "naval officers as a class are most excellent people".

At about this time he gave up his violin, because he found that the

---

[1]For example Captain (later Admiral Sir) Percy Scott (1853–1924). Inventor of many improvements to naval gunnery. Involved in fracas with Admiral Lord Charles Beresford 1907 over his signal "Paintwork appears to be more in demand than gunnery . . .".
[2]*Fear God and Dread Nought. The Correspondence of Admiral of the Fleet Lord Fisher of Kilverstone*, Vol. I (Cape, 1952) p. 147. Henceforth cited as "Marder: *Fisher*".

only place where he could practise was a stiflingly hot compartment below the water line; but his interest in and enjoyment of music did not flag. In February he witnessed the celebration of the Feast of St. Paul (the patron Saint of Malta) and sent his mother a long description of "all the pomp and splendour of the Church of Rome" on display, which he found "a wonderful sight which I should have been sorry to miss". The procession and High Masses were followed by the Carnival, during which all Malta appeared to be on the streets of Valletta in fancy dress. For this celebration invitations to the Maltese Club were, he said "heartily sought" by the British. "But", he went on, "do the Maltese get invited [to the Union Club] in return? Bless my soul no! The English won't have them to the club dances, and they are never seen onboard a ship or in a Regimental mess". Obviously his sense of courtesy and good manners was outraged by the conduct of his countrymen.

In mid-April, shortly before the *Ramillies* left Malta on her first cruise with Hankey onboard he had his first taste of the type of trouble which can so easily blow up between naval and marine officers. The occasion was the allegedly unjust punishment which the Commander inflicted on some Marines. Hankey at once reported the matter to Major Money, who took strong action and got the punishment rescinded. This caused an explosion both onboard and in a letter written "for home consumption and not to be spread abroad". Hankey roundly accused the executive branch of the Navy, and especially its younger members of "exclusiveness"—the very charge often levelled by the Navy against the Marines! He said that such officers "take no pride in anything creditable that is done by an engineer, a doctor or a marine; they don't realise that we all form part of one great service and ought to be pulling together with one object ... I refer rather to the younger officers of the Navy. The Captain, Commander, Gunnery and Torpedo Lieutenants, who are all representatives of the best and hardest working type of Naval officers, take a lively interest in the doings of the Marines ... I am far from being anti-Naval but I think that the greatest obstacle in the way of a better feeling between the two branches ... is the attitude of the younger Lieutenants". There were certainly grounds for his wrath over the superiority claimed in those days, and for many decades afterwards, by the executive branch of the Navy.

The Torpedo Lieutenant during most of Hankey's time in the *Ramillies* was H. W. Richmond, one of the ablest and most original-minded officers of his generation, but also one of the most intolerant.[1] Though it may well be the case that Hankey found much to admire in Richmond's intellectual gifts there is no evidence that, as Professor Marder has written, "the two were good friends from then [i.e. *Ramillies* days] on".[2] Not once does Hankey mention Richmond in the many letters he wrote from that ship, and although they corresponded frequently after Hankey became secretary of the C.I.D. their letters were confined entirely to naval policy and strategy. Indeed one would expect that while serving in that delicate position Hankey would regard such a stormy petrel as Richmond, who had a great capacity for antagonising senior officers, with a good deal of mistrust, and would avoid embroilment in the clashes of personality in which he was so frequently involved. That conclusion is strongly reinforced by the fact that when in 1917 Richmond showed a keen desire to become Hankey's naval assistant he tactfully but firmly declined to have him.[3]

April 1899 found the *Ramillies* at Palermo, where Hankey at once embarked on very energetic sight-seeing expeditions in the town and the surrounding countryside. He climbed Mount Pellegrino, and went to various receptions—including one by the Duc d'Orléans, the Pretender to the French throne, who "has a palace and keeps up a small court at Palermo". His account of Palermo society might have come straight out of Giuseppe di Lampedusa's brilliantly evocative novel in which the same scenes are described at the very period when the young Hankey witnessed them.[4] Indeed one feels that Lampedusa himself may have been among "the fashion and beauty of Palermo . . . Dukes, Duchesses, Marquises, officers of the Italian army . . . resplendent in their gorgeous light blue uniforms with their breasts glittering with orders" who assembled for the reception at the Orléans' palace.

From Sicily the *Ramillies* returned briefly to Malta and then sailed to various ports on the Greek mainland and in the islands of the Ionian Sea and Aegean. Hankey at once fell head-over-heels in love with the Greek scene and with the people of that country, sending his mother

[1]Later Admiral Sir Herbert Richmond (1871–1946). President Naval War College, 1920–23; C-in-C, East Indies, 1923–5; first Commandant of the Imperial Defence College 1926–8. Vere Harmsworth professor of Imperial and Naval History, Cambridge University 1934–6; Master of Downing College, Cambridge, 1936–46.
[2]*Portrait of an Admiral* (Cape, 1952) p. 375.
[3]*ibid.* pp. 227, 229, 243, 257 and 261.
[4]*The Leopard* (Eng. trans. Collins and Harvill, 1960) and *Two Stories and a Memory* (*idem* 1962).

long and lyrical descriptions of all that he saw. His archaeological investigations alternated with long excursions into the country, which nearly always included climbing the highest available mountain. It is worth remarking that Hankey's companions on these expeditions were, with one exception (Lieutenant Lord Kelburn[1]), nearly always non-executive officers. Plainly he found the company of the despised engineers, doctors and paymasters more congenial than that of the junior executive officers.

To Mrs. Robert Hankey. Platea, 22nd April 1899.
. . . This place is simply ripping; practically it is a huge and almost impenetrable forest, except by a few native paths, for 6 miles in every direction; the nearest village is eight miles away, and the nearest apology for a road 4 or 5 miles off. All round are mountains and every afternoon I do my 8 or 10 miles over them. One splendid walk brings you to a valley containing several good size lakes and this is a favourite picnic place. The climate is ideal and the whole place is very green while the ground is simply covered with wild flowers of every description, mostly unknown to me. . . . The people of course are most picturesque in their white kilts and stockings and curious shoes, their embroidered waistcoats and regular arsenal of arms in the waistbelt; . . . We always received the greatest civility from them, but their dogs are frightful—fierce as wolves and very brave; I nearly had to shoot one but we managed to stone it away. Up in the mountain we saw 3 eagles. I found my Greek was sufficient to procure the necessities of life . . .

A short time later (16th May 1899) he wrote more about his impressions of the Greek people. On a long walk with Kelburn through wild country near Vateka Bay they had stopped in a village to seek refreshment. The peasants brought them "native wine made on the premises which tasted of mixed beer and vinegar [presumably his first experience of Greek resinated wine]; then they brought us some unsweetened coffee which was excellent . . . Such people as there were in this valley were intelligent and wonderfully polite . . .; one day when I was out walking I found a peasant playing a kind of home-made viola; we sat down and listened and after a bit he handed it to me, so I played on it to the great delight of the rustics".

At Nauplia Hankey climbed the 800 steps up to the citadel (which most modern tourists shirk!) not once but twice; and he managed also to visit Argos and Tiryns. To his disappointment Mycenae proved too

[1] 1874–1963. Not Kelbourne as written by Hankey or Kelburne as in Navy Lists. Serving in *Ramillies* 1899. Later Captain R.N. 8th Earl of Glasgow 1915.

far away. Sunrise in the Aegean inspired him to quote "Homer's favourite remark",[1] and at Marathon he remembered his Byron.[2]

Hankey was working for his promotion examination to Captain at this time, and had reluctantly abandoned hope of taking long enough leave to visit Athens. However when he heard that a destroyer was going to Piraeus from Marathon he threw his good intentions to the winds and embarked in her. Athens proved the highlight of the whole cruise. By luck he and his companion met a correspondent of *The Times* named Bell while breakfasting at the Hotel d'Angleterre (now the Grande Bretagne), and "from this point he became our guide, philosopher and friend". They managed to see all the best-known sights in a single day which, bearing in mind that there was no motor transport in those days, showed considerable stamina; and, not content with that, Bell produced an English "antiquarian" named Pritchard from Peterhouse, Cambridge, who guided them round the National Museum. "Never before", commented Hankey, "have I been so interested in a museum or in things artistic". After that they climbed up to the Acropolis again to see the sunset. "Altogether", he ended, "it was a most successful trip"—beginning apparently at 3 a.m. one day and ending at 2 a.m. on the next day but one.

Hankey's enthusiastic Phil-Hellenism was confirmed and strengthened by a visit to Salonika, which was then in Turkish hands. He found nothing to commend in the city or in its Turkish population; but he was able to travel some distance inland and view the scene of the recent fighting between the Greeks and Turks. The Turkish soldiery filled him with contempt on account of their slovenliness and dirtiness—despite the fact that they had very recently given the Greeks a severe drubbing at Larissa. One wonders whether the view Hankey developed at this time of the relative fighting value of the soldiers of the two nations coloured his outlook when in 1915 he became involved in the prolonged controversy over the Gallipoli campaign, and had to advise the government on whether the struggle against the "hopelessly degraded and corrupt Turks", as he described them sixteen years earlier, should be continued.

The summer cruise was not all spent in sight-seeing—though the

[1]Odyssey II. 1. "The rosy-fingered dawn born of the mist appeared" is the translation Hankey used.
[2]"The mountains look on Marathon/ and Marathon looks on the sea". Don Juan XCVI. 3.

amount of leave allowed to the officers seems to have been very generous. On 10th June Hankey wrote from Cos that he had taken some instruction in the working of the Intelligence Department from the Intelligence officer [Major Mackay], and with him had "thoroughly investigated the defences of every place at which we have touched". Mackay had evidently found an apt pupil. In the same letter Hankey forecast the arrival of Admiral Fisher to succeed Hopkins in command of the fleet; but in fact the change did not take place until the autumn. Nor did Hankey's expectation that the *Ramillies* would return home with the relieved Commander-in-Chief prove correct. Hopkins hauled down his flag on 2nd July and the second-in-command Rear-Admiral G. H. U. Noel[1] took command of the fleet during the interim period. This meant that the *Ramillies* became a "private ship"—a change from "being cock of the walk and bossing the whole show" which did not at all appeal to Hankey. One compensation was that, Major Money having gone home with the Admiral and no relief having yet arrived, he found himself temporarily in command of the marine detachment.

After a visit to Sicily, where to Hankey's disgust Noel's flagship the *Theseus* ran aground in thick fog, the fleet cruised to Sardinia and then to Melilla in Spanish Morocco, where the ancient fortifications stimulated Hankey to renewed exploration. In a letter from Gibraltar (28th July 1899) he complained bitterly of the "corruption" indulged in by naval officers through the system of managing the ships' canteens then prevalent. Promotion, he declared, depended chiefly on "the brightness of the ship's paintwork, brass work etc. at the annual inspection"; and the official supply of paint being inadequate, the deficiency was made up by the officers most concerned in the ships' smartness. According to Hankey the necessary extra supplies were furnished by the contractors to whom the management of the canteens was farmed; and because the profit on the canteens accrued from purchases by the men he held that they should have been returned to them, and not expended on paint. It was certainly the case that large profits were made by canteen managers—until all such contracts were transferred to the Navy, Army and Air Force Institute after World War I. Thus he had grounds for complaining that the gifts made to ships' officers were "practically speaking . . . paid out of the pockets of the sailors, marines and stokers". Though his allegations of corruption among officers probably implied more than he meant the system was a bad one, and Hankey's indigna-

[1] 1845–1918. Later Admiral of the Fleet Sir Gerard Noel.

tion over it shows not only his strong sense of integrity and fair dealing but his capacity to probe every cranny of his service's activities. In the same letter he was highly critical of the lack of enthusiasm for war training, and the absence of realism in gunnery practices; and he was equally scathing about the futility of the drills and evolutions carried out by the fleet, which were in fact a relic of the days of masts and yards.

In August 1899 courts martial were convened on the *Theseus*'s officers on account of the grounding mentioned earlier. The constitution of the courts aroused more criticism from Hankey—because they had to consist solely of executive officers, who had "absolutely no training or instruction in law of any kind". He considered that marine officers, who were trained in military law, and officers of the Paymaster branch, who were "specialists in law" should be entitled to sit on courts martial. Once again one feels that, even though he sometimes exaggerated his case, his instinct for reform was soundly based.

From Gibraltar the fleet cruised to the Italian Riviera, and from Leghorn Hankey obtained a few days' leave to visit Florence; but the sights of that city did not inspire him to a lyricism comparable with his brief days in Athens. Indeed he admitted that the paintings and sculpture of Renaissance Italy held no appeal to him after the sights of classical Greece. His experience of Italy made him a fervent supporter of what he called "the continental Sunday"—which he found greatly superior to the highly restrictive sabbatarianism of his own home and of Rugby school. "Everybody goes to Mass in the morning", he told his mother, "and spends the rest of the day in perfectly innocent amusement: everything in Florence is open free on Sunday so that even the poor can enjoy themselves." These views produced a riposte from Mrs. Hankey, and the argument continued for some months; but Hankey refused to moderate, let alone withdraw his opposition to the sabbatarianism in which he had been brought up.

On 5th September he wrote from Aranci Bay in Sardinia "The new admiral—Fisher has just joined the fleet; he is said to be a tremendous scoundrel but I like his looks. He has got Siamese blood in him.[1]" At about the same time Money's relief, Captain R. H. J. Meister, joined the *Ramillies* and Hankey had to revert to his former subordinate position in the marine detachment. Fisher took the fleet quietly back

[1]Presumably Hankey meant Cingalese blood—which was often said of Fisher, though entirely without foundation.

to Malta without in any way showing his hand, or giving any sign of disapproval of the previous régime. No doubt he was getting the feel of his new command before he let loose the full fury of his daemonic energy. None the less Hankey evidently sensed that great changes were imminent. "I fancy the new Admiral, of whom the executive branch can say nothing too bad," he wrote to his mother, "is going to shake them up out of their fools' paradise a bit . . . [he] is very keen on dancing, and in spite of the great heat and the scarcity of ladies is giving a dance next Saturday". A week later he added some more about the dance. "For some unfathomable reason I was the only subaltern of Marines asked . . . I had not seen Admiral Fisher before; he is a queer looking cuss, but very affable, and he capered about all the evening like a junior snotty [midshipman]. I got on rather better than usual . . . I am not usually a very good 'coxswain' at a dance, but I managed to avoid collisions last night".

At the end of September the fleet sailed to the eastern Mediterranean, and Fisher began to give it a shake-up such as it had never before experienced. High speed was regularly used, by night as well as by day, the risk of collisions being accepted; drills and exercises were at last made realistic; and the dominance of "spit and polish" declined almost overnight. Hankey found the process exhilarating—the more so since it exposed the incapacity and inefficiency of which he had already been severely critical.

To Hilda Hankey. Thaso, 26th September 1899.
The new admiral has been making a series of experiments in various forms of night attack by torpedo-boats, which are very interesting. This is the first practical exercise I have seen done out here . . . So far in every case the Captains of the "boats" and "destroyers" have shown the most consummate ignorance of the elements of tactics and common sense that every boat and destroyer must have been destroyed by the guns of the battleships long before getting within range of their torpedoes. This is only typical of the crass conservatism of the Navy that after all these years they have had torpedo-boats in the Mediterranean fleet, . . . they have no plan or idea.

Hankey had passed the examinations for promotion to Captain in July 1899, and it was appropriate that news that his promotion had been gazetted to date from 12th August should have reached him while at Thaso—always one of his favourites among the Greek islands. Though he thus attained his new rank at the very early age of 22 he had to suffer the frustration of continuing to carry out subaltern's duties for some months. The rise in pay pleased him greatly, and for once he threw his customary financial prudence overboard to celebrate the occasion with his messmates. "After all", he wrote to his mother, "these events only occur once or twice in a lifetime, and one who has created a record ought not to be stingy".

The fleet next visited Salonika again, and Hankey's first impressions of the Turks were as fully confirmed as his detestation of their oppression of the Greeks was strengthened. He decided that the only solution to the "Eastern Question" lay in the transfer of all the Aegean islands to the Greeks—which was perhaps a somewhat sweeping generalisation with regard to a problem which was to perplex the statesmen of the world for another half century. Soon after leaving Salonika Hankey received a letter from the C-in-C telling him that he was "directed by the Lords of the Admiralty to express to me their thanks for the 'zeal and energy' which I had displayed in collecting information about certain ports visited during the summer cruise. . . . It is gratifying to learn that they do take some notice of one's efforts". In the last sentence of that letter to his mother (21st October 1899) one remarks for the first time a feature of Hankey's character which was to endure throughout his career—namely his appreciation of praise. Possibly it derived from the psychological effects of the sense of inferiority which as a youngster his small stature had induced. But even after he had become world-famous he was always delighted to receive expressions of approbation from no matter what source; and he carefully preserved all such letters.

Despite the intense activity which Fisher imposed on the fleet Hankey's thoughts at this time were often directed towards the Far East, where the Boxer rebellion was about to explode, and to South Africa, where open hostilities had begun and his own regiment was engaged. He expressed a longing to see active service, and began to have doubts about his wisdom in opting for the Mediterranean station. When he heard that his father had tried to detain his brother Hugh in England, he read his mother a lecture on patriotism and duty.

To Mrs. Robert Hankey 2nd Dec. 1899. Malta.
. . . I was quite disgusted to hear that Pa wanted to detain Hugh; even if he is pro-Boer over the causes of the war, which I myself believe was forced on the Boers, he ought to support his own country while it lasts, and ought to be proud to have a son engaged; I had far rather see a relative of mine killed

in the war than shirk it for any reasons at all. A soldier at all events has no
right to consider the causes of the war, but ought to go where his regiment
is ordered without grumbling, while he has a leg or a horse to move on, and
families and relatives have no right to try and interfere with him . . .

All of which shows that Hankey's vaunted "liberalism" did not, at the
age of 22½, run very deep. He was, alas, to see his preference for a
relative to be killed in action rather than "shirk" his duty fulfilled all
too soon.

The new century was only a few weeks old when Hankey's prospects
brightened considerably. Rear-Admiral Lord Charles Beresford,[1]
probably the most colourful, not to say idiosyncratic officer of his
generation, was appointed second-in-command of the Mediterranean
fleet in place of Noel, and elected to fly his flag in the *Ramillies*. As his
Flag Captain Beresford brought out R. S. Lowry,[2] who came direct
from the Admiralty's Naval Intelligence Department. The executive
officer, no doubt also chosen by Beresford, was Commander the
Hon. H. L. A. Hood,[3] one of the most brilliant younger officers of those
days.

Soon after the *Ramillies* had recommissioned at Malta Lowry, who
had probably encountered Hankey's work in the field of Intelligence
while in N.I.D., invited him to act as unofficial and unpaid Intelligence
Officer to himself and Beresford. Hankey, whose thoughts had already
turned towards a possible career in that line, leapt at the chance. He at
once began to study all the relevant problems of the Mediterranean
station and, knowing that languages would augment his value, he
added Spanish and modern Greek to the Italian and German which he
was already learning. He quickly won the confidence of both Lowry
and Beresford, and was soon acting as Staff Officer to both of them.
This might well have aroused the jealousy of his more senior shipmates,

[1]1846–1919. 1st Baron Beresford 1916. A Lord Commissioner of the Admiralty
1886, resigned 1888. Rear-Admiral, Mediterranean 1900–2; M.P. (Cons.) for
various English and Irish constituencies 1874–1912. C-in-C, Mediterranean Fleet
1905–7 and Channel Fleet 1907–9.
[2]Later Admiral Sir Robert Lowry (1854–1920). Director of Naval Intelligence 1897–1900; President R.N. War College 1907–8. C-in-C, Coast of Scotland
1913–16.
[3]Later Rear-Admiral Hon. Sir Horace Hood (1870–1916). Was in command of the
3rd Battle Cruiser Squadron at the battle of Jutland (31st May 1916) and lost his life
when his flagship the *Invincible* blew up.

and the fact that it does not seem to have done so is a tribute to his tact. Thus began a new phase in Hankey's career—closely under the eye of an Admiral who was expected to achieve the highest rank.

Early in March came the news of his brother Hugh's death in the battle of Paardeburg, and Hankey did his best to write a sympathetic letter to his mother; but his view that the family had been fortunate "to have lost no one all these years", and that it was better that Hugh should be killed rather than that his father's efforts to deter him from going to South Africa should have succeeded cannot have brought her much consolation.

While the *Ramillies* was refitting Hankey devoted a good deal of time to training the marines of his squadron in musketry, and to organising tactical exercises. This work, his Intelligence activities, and his study of languages made the winter weeks in Malta pass very busily; and his admiration for Lowry and Hood grew apace.

To Mrs. Robert Hankey. Union Club, Malta 1st April 1900 [his 23rd birthday]
. . . I wouldn't change with anyone myself. Every day I find my work more interesting and congenial; sometimes I get information of the most secret nature, and I often know of things weeks before the newspapers. For instance I knew of the Russian war preparations mentioned in *The Standard* some weeks ago, though it was then most confidential. You mustn't mention that though . . .

Evidently Hankey had not yet learnt that extreme discretion, for which he was to become famous later, is essential to gaining and keeping the confidence of those who wield the power. When the fleet left Malta on another cruise to his beloved Greece he boasted to Hilda of his capacity to identify foreign merchantmen and men-of-war correctly, and to forecast their movements. Lowry, he remarked, was "very keen about it [Intelligence work] and is continually asking for information which, so far, I have been able to give".

Platea once more sent him into a state of Phil-Hellenic rapture, and Corfu also came fully up to his expectations. His imagination was excited by the crowds who paraded every evening in the town's great square—"women in the national costume . . . men in the picturesque white kilt of the mountaineer with shoes turned up 2 or 3 inches at the toe, officers with great clanking swords . . . Evzones[1] with blue kilts

[1]Light infantry. Now generally applied to the Greek Royal (latterly Presidential) Guards.

and white stockings . . . priests of the Greek Church and Greek Catholic Church, now and then a group of Albanian peasants with regular arsenals in their waist belts . . . All this I witnessed and much more, and was struck with the curious link the town forms between the East and West".

From Corfu the fleet went to Sardinia and Majorca, which Hankey found almost as delightful as the Greek islands, and then to Gibraltar at the beginning of June. Hankey now foretold to his mother (1st June 1900) "I think it quite possible that I may go on the Intelligence Staff of the Admiralty before embarking again . . .". Evidently the stimulus originally applied by Major Mackay and now encouraged by Lowry and Beresford was bringing him nearer to a decision which would shape his whole career.

During the summer cruise of 1900 Fisher offered a prize of a 50-guinea gold cup for an essay on a tactical subject such as the employment of torpedo vessels in attack and defence. Hankey had apparently argued with his messmates that tactical principles were immutable, and applied equally to sea and land warfare; further that the Navy was not properly educated in tactical and strategic matters, having no Manuals in which the principles were set out. He therefore claimed that military men, who were taught tactics and possessed the necessary text books, knew more about the subject than naval officers. This was undoubtedly provocative, and was probably intended to be so. At any rate when Fisher's prize scheme was announced Hankey's opponents challenged him to put his arguments to the test by entering for the competition.

To Hilda Hankey. Aranci Bay, 16th June 1900
. . . I am at present working hard at an essay on Navy tactics for a competition got up by the Commander-in-Chief. As the subject is quite foreign to me, and all the executive people of any use and of any rank, whose profession it is, are in for it, I don't expect to achieve much distinction, but it is good practice. I am thinking of following [this up?] by a paper on "Landing Parties and the training of Marines" . . . Major Clarke, who is at present senior marine officer out here, has just sent in a long letter to the C-in-C embodying all my ideas for the more immediate reforms required out here, and as the C-in-C is enterprising I hope some of them will be permitted . . .

Hankey's proposals regarding the training and employment of Marine officers amounted to making them specialists, fully equal to the

Gunnery, Torpedo and Navigating officers. The marine officers' special subjects were to be land fighting, musketry and what came later to be called "amphibious warfare". Unfortunately he suffered, as have many innovators, from his ideas being many years ahead of his time; and it was not until World War II that Marine Commandos, organised and trained for precisely the purpose Hankey had put forward at the beginning of the century, were actually introduced. Beresford, however, seems to have been impressed by the proposal; since Hankey told his mother (28th June 1900) that "the Second-in-Command is working up a case for the Marines for his next parliamentary campaign,[1] and I have had to collect many statistics for him".

At about this time Hankey began a study of what he called "Warfare on the Littoral". Four completed chapters and two more uncompleted ones have survived in his papers, and they show that he first made a careful historical study of the subject and then began to apply the fruits of that study to his own times. The titles of his chapters "Landings in relation to Strategy", "Information. Peace Reconnaissance", "The selection of a Landing Place", "Permanent Organisation for Landing Parties", "Opposed Landings", "The Landing and Re-embarkation" indicate clearly enough the line of his thought. He worked at this project intermittently for some eight years, and did not finally put it aside until 1908 when his appointment to the secretariat of the Committee of Imperial Defence forced him to abandon it. The draft remains a monument to his industry and application at a time when he was carrying many responsibilities; and he certainly made use of the knowledge acquired in the process of writing it when he came to advise first the Admiralty and then the C.I.D. on the strategic issues which would arise in the event of war with Germany.

Early in July 1900 Fisher took the fleet up the Adriatic—a cruise which Hankey had for some time been looking forward to keenly. It gave him new places to explore and new people and races to study.

To Mrs. Robert Hankey, Fiume [now Rijeka], *15th July 1900*
...Yesterday I had to interpret for the Admiral to the Mayor of Fiume who was offering an address. An Austrian officer who knew a little Italian was translating it into villainous French, which the skipper interpreted to Lord Charles; seeing this I volunteered my services. They have therefore at last realised that I can talk Italian, and the Admiral has given me orders always

[1] In those days an officer on the Active List of the Royal Navy was allowed to sit as a Member of Parliament. See Geoffrey Bennett, *Charlie B* (Peter Dawnay, 1968).

to come in and read the telegrams from the foreign papers to him. . . . I have translated correspondence for the Admiral in Spanish, French, German and Italian during the past week. I shall probably be practically on his staff at Taranto where we are paying an official visit next week . . . We have been hob-nobbing with Austrian dukes and princes, guests of Lord Charles . . .

Thus did his gift for languages, and his assiduity in studying them, gain for Hankey the entry into Beresford's personal entourage.

From Trieste and Fiume Hankey explored the Istrian peninsula, and made excursions into what were then the Austro-Hungarian provinces of Slovenia and Croatia. But the highlight of the Adriatic cruise came when he got leave to go to Budapest for a few days. He wrote enthusiastically to his mother about the architecture, the baths, the music, and the beer of that formerly delightful city, which he considered in all respects far superior to London—though the Danube disappointed him by proving "not blue at all but mud-coloured".

At Taranto intelligence activities took priority over sightseeing—it being "a new port about which they [the Italians] didn't want us or anyone else to know much". While there Beresford sent for Hankey whenever interpreting was needed, pointed at him and said "*parlate Italiano*". "I never had a minute to myself", he wrote to his mother (29th July), "from the day we arrived to the day we left, and during the last four days at sea I have never stopped writing my report". Evidently Italian security precautions did not prevent the active young Intelligence Officer finding out a good deal.

While at Corfu a general signal announced the result of the essay competition. "The judges", wrote Hankey, to his mother "said that after long consideration they had selected the essay of the Hon. Victor Stanley,[1] a senior lieutenant, as the best, but that five others had run him so close that they had decided to publish their names in order that the C-in-C might congratulate them. These five essays were of such equal merit that it was impossible to pick out one for second place, so the names were published alphabetically. Among them were mine and that of Captain Bacon[2] just promoted first [? post] Captain at a very early age on account of his numerous writings on naval matters . . .

[1]Later Admiral the Hon. Sir Victor Stanley (1867–1934).
[2]Later Admiral Sir Reginald Bacon (1863–1947). Retired in 1909 to become Managing Director, Coventry Ordnance Works. Returned to service in World War I and commanded the Dover Patrol 1915–18. A close friend of Admiral Jellicoe and his official biographer.

Moreover all the competitors and all the umpires are invited to a 'banquet' (not a dinner mind you!) on board the flagship to congratulate us, and to give the C-in-C a chance of expressing his thanks etc. etc. . . . I am therefore rather pleased as I had no previous practical or theoretical knowledge of the subject . . . Besides a good many of the younger Lieutenants R.N. had laughed at the idea of a Marine competing with the 'experts' in a Naval subject . . . It strengthens my position very much too among Naval people, and will make my opinion more worthy of consideration with Lord Charles, when he does me the honour to ask it as he has done on several matters . . ."

At this time Hankey launched himself into yet another field of activity—that of journalism. At the end of August he told his sister Hilda that he had "written to the Daily Mail offering to represent them [on Balkan affairs] if . . . I can get Admiralty permission for expenses only. I think it is possible that they might close with me as they have very heavy expenses in Africa and China and all the regular correspondents are employed or wounded . . .". The Daily Mail replied that they would be glad to receive anything he cared to send, and "would pay for what they used at 3 guineas a column". On being shown this reply Captain Lowry was, understandably "a bit startled"; but, added Hankey, he "promised to support me with the Admiralty".

From time to time during the previous six months or so Hankey had expressed some concern over his mother's health; but he seems never to have realised that she was seriously ill. Thus a telegram that she had died on 9th September left him "so dazed with the suddenness of it all that I can scarcely realise that it has really happened". His many letters to her, though they never contained expressions of deep affection, reveal how strong was the bond between them. Certainly he would argue with her, sometimes quite fiercely, over issues such as his preference for the "Continental Sunday" or the ethics of bull-fighting; but it was always to her that he recounted his hopes and ambitions, his successes and frustrations—besides every detail of his daily life.

In October 1900 Hankey discussed his two Admirals in an interesting letter to his father. Beresford he would like to see First Lord of the Admiralty, but as "he is too straight and is not afraid to speak the truth" it was unlikely that he would ever receive such an appointment. "Admiral Fisher", he continued, "is really up-to-date and has a soul above 'spit and polish' and is consequently rather unpopular among his own cloth"; which makes it apparent that Hankey had learnt how to keep on good terms with both Admirals—despite the fact that relations between them had been strained since shortly after Beresford's arrival.[1]

In a letter to Hilda (5th November 1900) describing a visit to Mycenae ("the legendary home of Atreus, father of Agamemnon and Menelaus") he said that he was considering applying for the post of Intelligence Officer to the Mediterranean Fleet in succession to Major Mackay; but he felt he was too junior to hold such an appointment, and was not very anxious to stay on the station for another 3 years. Actually he very soon dropped the idea, and applied instead for the post of Assistant Adjutant at Eastney. He consulted Beresford about this prospect, and the admiral said "If ever you want any appointment at any time where my influence will tell, I will do all I can for you". Captain Lowry forwarded Hankey's application, and Beresford submitted it to Fisher "for favourable consideration". "Captain Hankey", he wrote, "is a most excellent officer and I strongly recommend him for the responsible appointment of Assistant Adjutant". Though Hankey probably did not see these endorsements on his application (which are preserved in the Royal Marine Office's records) he told Hilda "I have therefore obtained my object in staying in this ship—namely of working up an interest". Though that remark has an 18th century ring about it (the young Nelson also assiduously cultivated the "interest" of admirals such as Hood and Jervis) it is a fact that in the late 19th and early 20th centuries a young officer without private means and lacking friends in high places was severely handicapped in the promotion stakes. Thus it was perfectly natural, and proper, for Hankey to use the influence which he had won through merit and hard work. In fact his application to Eastney was turned down—because he was too senior for the post—and in mid-December he told Hilda that he was to stay in the *Ramillies* in command of the marine detachment when Major Clarke went home. "I met Lord Charles at the door of the church [in Malta] where he was waiting to give a bride away to our flag lieutenant" he added. "When I told him I was staying on he said 'I congratulate you and the *Ramillies*', which was a very nice speech". The change

---

[1] *Supreme Command*, I p. 20. Since Hankey was an eyewitness on the occasion when Fisher sent Beresford a tactless, even insulting, signal about the mooring of his flagship in Malta harbour early in 1900 his statement that trouble blew up between the two admirals "soon after Beresford hoisted his flag" in the Mediterranean must be preferred to Professor Marder's statement that they "remained on friendly terms until the autumn of 1906". Marder: *Fisher*, Vol. II, p. 39.

actually took place on Boxing Day, and at the age of 23½ Hankey thus found himself in a post normally held by a much older and more senior officer. Plainly his reputation had spread far beyond the Mediterranean, and he was by this time very favourably regarded in the office of the Adjutant-General of his corps, as well as by his immediate superiors in the fleet.

While at Platea during the next winter cruise news of Queen Victoria's death (22nd January 1901) was received, and the whole fleet went into mourning. Though this severely curtailed the social side of the officers' life Fisher did not allow it to disarrange his cruise programme or put a stop to his training of the fleet for war. The next port of call was Piraeus, whence Hankey got leave to visit Athens again; but this time he preferred the company of Greek friends, and especially the army officers whom he had met on previous visits, to sight-seeing. When it came to mounting him the Greek officers evidently could not resist the temptation of giving a sailor a difficult ride.

To Hilda Hankey. At sea Athens to Salonika, 13th February 1901
. . . On Monday I went on leave and stayed in Athens until Tuesday evening, spending most of my time with my friend Lestos of the Greek artillery. On Monday evening I was in a café with him, and we met a good many interesting people. Among them was the brother of the Queen of Servia, about whose marriage there was a good deal of talk recently. He is in the Greek cavalry and is reckoned the best rider in Greece. . . .
On Tuesday morning I went fairly early to the artillery barracks, where after the permission of Prince Nicholas, the colonel of the regiment had been obtained, I was given a horse. At first they brought an awful brute which required four men to hold it while I mounted, and when I was on it began kicking and trying to bolt, to the great amusement of the officers round, who sang out, "Oh, Mr. sailor your ship is rolling heavily" in Greek; I succeeded in taming it but they would not let me ride it, as they said it would be very wild when we got among the cavalry squadrons drilling, so they turned it over to a riding master and gave me a very nice beast instead. . . .

From Salonika, where they were witnesses of the Turkish persecution of the Bulgarian section of the population, the *Ramillies* went to the lovely harbour of Suda Bay on the north coast of Crete. While there Hankey recorded the rising tension between Fisher and Beresford, which was to have such prolonged and unhappy effects on the Navy. "Admiral Fisher, who is most vindictive", he told Hilda (3rd March 1901), "seizes every opportunity to show his dislike of Beresford, and refused to give him any ships to play with on this cruise, although several are cruising independently in the vicinity . . . Also he refuses to let Beresford take his ship to any decent places". Though Hankey was not unfair in applying the adjective "vindictive" to Fisher, his own experiences scarcely supported the last sentence quoted; but it was natural for him to side with Beresford, to whom he was much closer at that time.

It was at Syracuse during the winter cruise that Hankey had what appears to be his only serious quarrel with Hood, the ship's commander, whom he had earlier admired so warmly. The trouble arose, as one would expect, over an allegedly unjust punishment inflicted by Hood on a marine. Hankey made a highly insubordinate remark about it in the commander's hearing, and he was promptly hauled before the Captain and placed under arrest. Lowry, however, took a lenient view of the incident, and soon released Hankey from arrest, merely suspending him from duty while an enquiry was carried out. The outcome was that Hankey was "logged"[1]—which, by his own account, "can have absolutely no effect on a marine officer". He described the whole fracas —with a good deal of self-justification—in a long letter to Hilda (12th March 1901); but his behaviour was in truth scarcely conducive to the smooth running of the ship. He probably owed more than he was prepared to admit to Hood's forbearance and Lowry's generosity. At any rate he was very soon able to record that "normal relations were restored" with the commander.

At the beginning of the 20th century the full significance of the German Navy Laws of 1898 and 1900 had not yet been realised in Britain, where France and Russia were still regarded as the most likely enemies. Thus the fleet exercises of September 1901, conducted in the approaches to Gibraltar were probably designed to test the effects of the Russian and French fleets concentrating with the object of driving the British out of the Mediterranean as a preliminary to the invasion of the British Isles—on the lines of Napoleon's strategy in the campaign of 1805. Hankey's conclusion on the exercise was that the Medi-

[1]This meant that an entry recording the offence was made in the ship's log, and had to be signed by the offending officer. When the log reached the Admiralty the entry normally was transferred to the officer's record of service. In the case of Hankey, whose record of service has been preserved by the Royal Marine office, this was not done. On the assumption that Captain Lowry forwarded the ship's log with the entry in it, it must have been omitted by decision of the Adjutant-General.

terranean (i.e. the Russo-French) fleet got the best of the encounter, which may well have been the case, since such a combination would have produced a most serious threat to the British position.

At this time Hankey received the following letters from his one-time mentor at Greenwich Major George Aston, who was now serving in the office of the Deputy Adjutant-General, Royal Marines.

14th June 1901. Private
My dear Hankey,
I think you will like to know that your zeal etc. about field training work has been noted in your services by order of the D.A. Genl. [Deputy Adjutant-General].[1]

Yours ever

29th Nov. 1901
My Dear Hankey,
Does butter help you along? The D.A.G. showed your letter of 3rd August (to me about field training etc.) to Lord Selborne's private secretary Admiral Fawkes[2] who replies "Many thanks for letting me see the letter. It is pleasant to see that your fellows . . . are taking so much trouble in the training of their men". I have sung your praises to the D.A.G. which I hope will do you good in the future. I leave the office tomorrow . . . I am wondering where fate will lead me. I don't know whether Holman[3] will be leaving in February—if he does I will write as strongly as you like in your favour to the D.N.I. for the billet.
Let me know that you are keeping well. Adieu.

Yours ever

Send in all the intelligence work you can. If not sent to sea I shall put in for 3 or 4 months to go to France in the spring to work at the lingo.

In 1901 Admiral Fisher offered another prize for an essay, this time on a strategic subject, and Hankey decided to enter again. He evidently worked very hard at it during the summer and autumn, and a newly acquired typewriter enabled him to present it in attractive form. But before the results were known he had contracted Malta fever, and on 4th December he was "surveyed" at the R.N. Hospital, Malta, and

---

[1]The entry in Hankey's record of service reads: "Instruction of Seamen and Marines in camping, entrenching and scouting work. I frequently visited the work done during this course and was much struck by the zeal and ability with which Captain Hankey conducted it. R. S. Lowry, 30th January 1901."
[2]Later Admiral Sir Wilmot H. Fawkes (1846–1926). Private secretary to the First Lord of the Admiralty 1897–9 and 1900–2.
[3]Major H. W. L. Holman R.M.L.I. was then serving in N.I.D.

invalided home "to obviate prolonged illness". The letters he wrote from the Mediterranean had often referred to the high sickness rate in the Fleet from Malta (or "Mediterranean") fever, malaria and other causes; but he evidently held strong hopes that his abstemiousness and constant attention to physical fitness would render him immune to such illnesses, which were at the time very imperfectly understood. In fact Malta fever, which was widespread and could produce very serious consequences, not excluding permanent disablement, derived from the use of unpasteurised goats' milk—though that was not discovered until some four years later. It seems possible that the wildness of the accusations against brother officers, against the whole Navy and against British politicians which Hankey made in his letters to Hilda during the closing months of 1901 arose from the fact that he was already afflicted with the dread disease, but fought against it for some weeks. Be that as it may his time in the *Ramillies* came to an abrupt end. In his record of service Lowry's commendation (dated 1st January 1902) described Hankey as "Most keen and zealous. Has been Intelligence Officer in this ship for two years. Has knowledge of French, Italian and modern Greek. A very good and able officer. Ability very good indeed". Evidently the squall with Hood was entirely forgotten.

After he had returned home the results of the second essay competition were announced, and he must have been pleased to get the letters reproduced below.

From Rear-Admiral Lord Charles Beresford. H.M.S. Ramillies. Dec. 30th 1901 Malta. Holograph
My dear Hankey,
I want to congratulate you very warmly on being number 3 in the race for the prize essay.[1] 1 and 2 only just beat you [and] it took us hours to decide between the 3. We were as *Ramillies* [men] genuinely delighted to see that 2 of the 1st 3 were officers of that ship i.e. Captain Lowry who won the prize and yourself. May every luck attend you. We all miss you very much, but no one more than
Yours very sincerely
From Captain R. S. Lowry. Address and date as above. Holograph.
My dear Hankey,
At the C-in-C's meeting today, the results of the last essays were read out

[1]In later life Hankey stated that he was placed equally second in both of Fisher's essay competitions (*Supreme Command*, I pp. 18–19) but the letters here reproduced make it plain that his memory was at fault.

1. Lowry
2. Majendie—*Renown*
3. Hankey
4. Grant—*Surprise*

I am sorry you have kept the same place as last time, and though immensely pleased at winning myself I would gladly have seen you there.

All 4 essays were very close and Lord C[harles Beresford] tells me he quite thought your essay was mine, as he recognised one or two words in my hand writing . . . Don't you feel flattered! . . .

Hoping you are much better, and with all good wishes for the New Year
Ever yours sincerely

Hankey's first period of sea service thus lasted for almost exactly three years (Dec. 1898–Dec. 1901); and although it ended, through no fault of his own, on what might have proved an ominous note, he had in fact accomplished a very great deal. Quite apart from developing his astonishing gift for languages, his work in a wide variety of fields had brought him to the attention of Fisher and Beresford, to that of highly placed officers in his own corps (through Aston's good offices) and to the Admiralty's Intelligence Department. In their different ways each of these was to exert considerable influence on his career; but it was Fisher's admiration for the versatile, energetic and capable marine officer which was to prove the most powerful influence. From the Mediterranean command, where he had accomplished both a revolution and a renaissance, Fisher went to the Admiralty as Second Sea Lord (June 1902) and then hoisted his flag as Commander-in-Chief, Portsmouth (August 1903). On 21st October 1904 he became First Sea Lord, and held that crucial post until 25th January 1910. Wherever he went a hurricane of reform—most of which was both timely and necessary— was immediately instituted. Unhappily for the Navy his capacity for making enemies was little less remarkable then his reforming zeal; and the chief of the enemies whom he described as "the Adullamites" and "the Syndicate of Discontent" was his old second-in-command of Mediterranean days Lord Charles Beresford. We shall see later how Hankey managed, by extraordinary tact and diplomacy, to retain the friendship of both disputants, and avoided involvement in the schism which split the Navy from top to bottom.

Chapter 3

From the Naval Intelligence Department to the Committee of Imperial Defence 1902-1908

HANKEY'S recovery from Malta fever must have been rapid, since in April 1902 he made what he later described as his "first entry in Whitehall" to join the staff of the Naval Intelligence Department. He has recorded that he owed the appointment to the good offices of Beresford, Aston and Lowry; but it is probably more correct to attribute it to the work he had done in the Intelligence field while on the Mediterranean station, and to his successes in Fisher's essay competitions. According to his memoirs he found much more to admire and much less to criticise in the organisation and working of the Admiralty than in the fleet,[1] which is the opposite to the view generally held by naval officers. Nor does it seem to have occurred to him that the contrast he has drawn between the Admiralty and the fleet was somewhat illogical, since the Admiralty, being responsible for the efficiency of the fleet, cannot escape responsibility for the defects and inefficiency which had produced such strident criticisms when Hankey was serving afloat. Either those criticisms must have been exaggerated or his approval of the Admiralty's organisation and methods showed a blind spot. This author believes the latter to be the more correct assumption—at any rate until the Fisher whirlwind had blown through the musty corridors of Whitehall.

The director of the Intelligence Department when Hankey joined it was Captain R. N. Custance,[2] whom he "did not find a very inspiring Chief" because of "his somewhat suspicious nature". Rather oddly the post given to Hankey was not one for which his previous service and knowledge of languages fitted him. He was required instead to deal with the coast defences of the British Isles, the Dominions, India and

---

[1] *Supreme Command*, I, pp. 23–4.
[2] Later Admiral Sir Reginald Custance (1874–1935). Director of Naval Intelligence 1899–1902. A prolific writer on naval affairs.

the colonies. However his work in that field not only brought him into touch with the holders of the most important Admiralty posts, but led directly to the appointment which was to shape the whole course of his life. An unending stream of papers and letters dealing with every aspect of coast defence all over the world—guns, searchlights, minefields and so on—poured in on him; and he was also required to frame recommendations on important questions of policy, such as the provision of new naval bases and coaling stations, the construction of docks, and the size and equipment of overseas garrisons. He particularly relished devilling for Custance at meetings of the Colonial Defence Committee,[1] and thus gained his first toehold in the Committee of Imperial Defence when that body was founded on the initiative of A. J. Balfour in 1902.[2]

Less than a year after Hankey joined N.I.D. Custance was relieved by Prince Louis of Battenberg,[3] whom he found a much more congenial chief. Unhappily by that time overwork and his dislike of London, where he was sharing an Oxford Street flat with a brother officer, had combined to bring him near to a state of revolt. Though he managed sometimes to get away for short week-ends either to visit his father at Brighton or to stay with other members of his family, such breaks were too brief to refresh his body and mind after the very long hours spent at his Admiralty desk, or to compensate him for the days and nights he had to spend in London.

So great was Hankey's discontent that in the autumn of 1902 he sent in an application to the War Office to join the Macedonian Gendarmerie. This was an international force then in process of formation to protect

[1]At this time the only permanent Sub-Committee of the C.I.D. Originally established in 1878 the Colonial Defence Committee was suspended from 1879 to 1885. In April 1911 it was renamed the Overseas Defence Committee in deference to the susceptibilities of the self-governing Dominions. C.I.D. 74C. Cab. 38/17/23.

[2]The date of the foundation of the Committee of Imperial Defence is often given as 1904, amongst others by Hankey himself (in *The Supreme Command*). However, as the first meeting of the committee took place on 18th Dec. 1902, when its constitution was approved, it is obvious that its foundation must be dated to that year. It was in 1904 that the Committee was first given a permanent secretariat. See N. H. Gibbs, *The Origins of Imperial Defence* (Oxford U.P. 1955) and *List of Papers of the Committee of Imperial Defence to 1914* (H.M.S.O., 1964).

[3]1854–1921. Director of Naval Intelligence 1902–5. Second Sea Lord 1911–12; First Sea Lord 1912–14. Assumed surname of Mountbatten 1917 by Royal Licence and created Marquess of Milford Haven. Father of Admiral of the Fleet Earl Mountbatten of Burma, First Sea Lord 1955–59.

the Macedonian people against the harsh oppression of their Turkish overlords. It may be regarded as an ancestor of the United Nations Organisation's peace-keeping forces of the mid-20th century. Hankey's knowledge of modern Greek, in which he was examined by the Civil Service Commission in January 1903 and passed as a First-Class Interpreter, made his acceptance for the Gendarmerie virtually certain —when the whole pattern of his life was changed by his meeting his future wife. Up to that moment he had taken no interest in girls, and whether at sea or on shore had always shunned social activities. Then, during one of his visits to Brighton shortly before Christmas 1902, he went to a performance of a light opera; and, catching sight of a girl two rows in front of him in the stalls he said to his companion "That is the girl I am going to marry—the girl with the golden hair".[1] He probably already knew that her name was Adeline de Smidt; and from that day to his death there was only one woman in his life.

Adeline's family, originally prominent citizens of Antwerp and Middelburg, became citizens of Cape Colony through the mischance of the convoy in which her great-grandfather Abraham was travelling home from the East Indies being trapped by an English squadron in Saldanha Bay in 1781 during the War of American Independence. However Abraham married wisely and prospered in his new country. His son, of the same name, became owner of the beautiful estates of Groote Schuur (Great Barn) and Westbrooke in the foothills of Table Mountain. Adeline was born to Abraham III by his second marriage, to Gertrude Overbeek, in 1882. In 1879 he sold Groote Schuur, which was later bought by Cecil Rhodes, by whose Will it became the country residence of the Prime Minister of South Africa—as it remains to this day. Westbrooke became the summer residence of the Governor-General of the Union, and is now the seat of the State President. After selling his estates Abraham built a new house nearby, which he named Highstead.

Though the de Smidt family always spoke Dutch or Afrikaans together, they were pro-British in sentiment and wanted their four children to have an English education. Accordingly they came to England in 1890, and settled first near Southampton and then at 18 Chesham Place, Brighton—almost opposite the Hankeys' home at No. 1. Unfortunately soon after his arrival Adeline's father lost all the money received from the sale of the family estates through the collapse

[1]Lady Benn (Hankey's daughter) to the author 1966. She was probably told this story by Hankey's sister Hilda, who must have got it from Hankey himself.

of a South African bank, and was left with only his pension as a former Surveyor-General of Cape Colony.

The straitened circumstances of her family convinced Adeline that she would have to earn her living, and so she determined to get herself a good education. In face of a good deal of parental opposition she was finally accepted by Brighton High School, where she took her School Certificate. She then made up her mind to become an art teacher, and managed to join Brighton Art School to take a two year course for that purpose. It was in her second year there that she met Maurice Hankey.

A few days after their first meeting it froze hard, and he took her skating; and as long as she continued her studies at the Art School he used, if he were in Brighton, to wait for her and take her home by 'bus. By the beginning of 1903 he was writing to her very formally in Italian as "Egregia Signorina", and tactfully correcting (in red ink) her replies in the same language. On 26th February he wrote "Dear Miss de Smidt. Can I have a yarn with you this week-end?"; and Adeline can have had little doubt what the subject of the "yarn" was to be. A few days later he was describing himself as "the happiest man on earth". On 8th March he wrote to Adeline's father, coming straight to the point; "Dear Mr. de Smidt, I am writing to ask your permission to marry Adeline", and enclosing a short *curriculum vitae*, and a statement of his financial circumstances and prospects. Evidently the necessary parental permission was readily forthcoming, for they were married at St. Mark's church, Brighton, on 15th September 1903; and so began an entirely new phase of life for Hankey. All thought of the Macedonian Gendarmerie was banished from his mind, and even London became tolerable. After their honeymoon at Pontresina the young couple found a temporary home in lodgings on Lismore Road in the outskirts of Croydon, which was not then the epitome of "subtopia" into which it has since been "developed". Open country lay not far from their door.

Hankey had indeed won a remarkable woman. Early photographs show her to have possessed great dignity of carriage and demeanour. She was taller than her husband by several inches, and her well-knit slim figure set off a strongly sculptured and highly intelligent face crowned by abundant golden hair. For 60 years she was to be the constant confidant and companion of a husband whose adoration for his wife was only rivalled by the profound love of their children for her.

Adeline Hankey

Tea at The Corner House, Oxted, 1908

Lord Charles Beresford

To them she was always "Mop" or "Moppy", just as Hankey was "Pop"; and although their family did not entirely escape the normal convulsions of adolescence they remained remarkably united—and indeed continue so to this day. On 4th July 1905 a son, Robert Maurice Alers (Robin), was born to Adeline and Maurice at Lismore Road.[1]

To return to the service side of Hankey's life, in January 1905 Prince Louis of Battenberg was succeeded by Rear-Admiral C. L. Ottley[2] as Director of the Admiralty's Intelligence Department. Hankey has described Ottley as "a man of very remarkable culture, with a fluent pen and engaging manner". His service as naval attaché in various European capitals had given him an insight into diplomatic technique and processes which was unusual in a naval officer; and he possessed a pronounced gift for handling politicians as well as senior officers of the fighting services. As we have already seen, Hankey's own gifts were developing along rather similar lines. It is therefore not surprising that he and Ottley soon got on intimate terms, and that the new Director of Intelligence quickly showed complete confidence in the young marine officer who had already made a name for himself in the department by the work he had done in the Mediterranean. As Hankey had by this time shed his responsibility for the home side of local defence, retaining only the supervision of overseas bases, he was able to give more attention to the high-level defence problems then under discussion in the C.I.D., in which Ottley was deeply involved. Ottley often sent Hankey to deputise for him at committee meetings, so extending and widening the latter's knowledge and experience of the problems of the day, and enabling him to meet and make himself known to the principal politicians of both parties. Hankey's service in N.I.D. under Battenberg and Ottley was to prove a valuable apprenticeship for the posts he was to hold later.

In June 1905, as a result of discussions in the C.I.D., the Admiralty and War Office were asked to form a joint committee to review, and if necessary reorganise the defences of the principal naval bases at home and overseas. Hankey had a big hand in drafting the Terms of Reference of this body, and the C.I.D. promptly approved them.[3] General Sir

[1]Now (1968) 2nd Baron Hankey of Chart. Joined Diplomatic Service 1927. Ambassador at Stockholm 1954–60. Permanent U.K. delegate to O.E.E.C. and O.E.C.D. 1960–5.
[2]Later Sir Charles Ottley (1885–1932). Director of Naval Intelligence 1905–7; Secretary of the Committee of Imperial Defence 1907–11.
[3]Terms of Reference and reports of the Owen Committee are in Cab. 16/1.

John Owen was appointed Chairman.[1] For the remainder of 1905 the Owen Committee concerned itself with bases in the British Isles, which did not lie within Hankey's sphere of responsibility; but when in the following year the committee turned to consider the defence of overseas bases he was, despite his comparative youth, an obvious choice to represent the Admiralty on it. However before that happened he was required to divert his energies into quite a different field.

On 8th July 1905 the Admiralty appointed a committee under Admiral Sir Archibald Douglas[2] "to consider certain questions regarding the extension of the new scheme of training for officers of the Navy". This referred to the "Selborne Scheme" of December 1902, which was launched in 1903–5 during Fisher's time as Second Sea Lord and Commander-in-Chief, Portsmouth.[3] The crux of the scheme was the introduction of a system of common entry and training for all officers—engineers and marines as well as those of the executive branch —with consequential improvement in the status of non-executive officers. We saw earlier that this was a matter on which Hankey had developed strong views during his time in the *Ramillies*.He was now given an opportunity to air those views to the Douglas Committee. In his evidence he represented that marine officers should be totally integrated into the Navy, even to the point of carrying out watch-keeping duties at sea. He urged that they should be regarded as specialists, exactly analagous to gunnery and torpedo officers, but specialists in musketry, land fighting and above all in amphibious warfare.[4] He also read to the committee a statement in which he dealt at length with the subject for which he had coined the term "Warfare on the Littoral". This was in essence a proposal to form "Marine Commandos", and had it been accepted it might have advanced that form of employment for the Corps by some 40 years. The committee may, however, be excused for ignoring it, since the subject did not lie within their terms

[1] 1839–1924. President of Ordnance Committee 1902–4; Colonel Commandant, Royal Artillery 1906.
[2] 1842–1913. A Lord of the Admiralty 1899–1902; C-in-C, North America and West Indies 1902–4 and C-in-C, Portsmouth, 1904–7.
[3] Fisher was Second Sea Lord June 1902–August 1903 and C-in-C Portsmouth, August 1903–October 1904 when he became First Sea Lord.
[4] The Douglas Committee's report dated 18th August 1905, was printed as Cd.2841 (1906) but it contains only a part of Hankey's evidence (Questions 640–676). A revised proof of the more important, and more controversial part (Questions 193–267) exists in his papers; but that part was never published.

of reference; nor did they accept the idea of specialist marine officers. Instead they proposed "that we shall have in future only one class of officer in all departments, and, whether performing Engine Room, Marine, Gunnery, Torpedo, or Navigation duties, all will be equal and will be Executive officers".[1] This amounted to a General List for all officers, such as was not to be introduced into the Navy until after World War II.

At the time when Hankey must have been preparing his evidence for the Douglas Committee he resurrected a paper which he had written in 1904 entitled "Advanced Bases for the Fleet". He had originally submitted this to Captain Ballard,[2] whose endorsement of 15th April 1904 "To receive attention when time permits" does not indicate any very great interest. In November of the following year Hankey sent it informally to Colonel Bor[3] in the office of the Adjutant-General, Royal Marines. Bor replied (2nd January 1906) that "It is certainly a good suggestion", and that the Deputy Adjutant-General was willing to support it; but Hankey did not pursue the matter—probably because he was by that time deeply immersed in other matters.

Looking back today at Hankey's ideas of 1904–5, and with all the wisdom of hindsight provided by two world wars to guide us, it seems that his proposal to integrate marine officers fully into the naval service was scarcely practicable; but on all other issues his only fault lay in the fact that he was some 20–40 years ahead of his time. Thus his proposal for an advanced base for the fleet, to be installed and defended by marines, received the sanction of the Board of Admiralty in 1920, when they approved the establishment of a "Mobile Naval Base". Furthermore in World War II marine officers *did* become specialists in amphibious warfare, and the Royal Marine Commandos repeatedly acted as the spearhead of combined operations—as indeed they continue to act at the present time.

On 28th December 1905 Robert Hankey, Maurice's father, died at Brighton at the comparatively early age of 68. During his last years the very arduous work on which Hankey had been engaged while at home, together with the blissful happiness of his marriage, had prevented him

---

[1]Cd. 2841 p. 57 para. 21.
[2]Later Admiral George A. Ballard (1862–1948). Won R.U.S.I. Gold Medal Essay Prizes 1897 and 1899. Admiral of Patrols, East Coast, and Admiral Commanding, Malta, in World War I.
[3]Later General James H. Bor (1857–1914).

seeing very much of his father. Though Hankey always spoke of him with affection, sometimes salted with slightly ironical anecdotes about his idiosyncrasies, his father never occupied a place in his life comparable to that of his mother. On Robert's death the link with the family home of his childhood's days at Brighton was severed by the sale of the house.

To return to the Owen Committee, Hankey represented to the Admiralty that to carry out the second part of its terms of reference properly it was essential to visit at any rate the more important overseas bases. That proposal was accepted, the cruiser *Terrible* was made available, and her captain, G. A. Ballard, became the senior naval representative on the Committee. On 25th July 1906 she sailed from Plymouth for the Far East by way of the Cape of Good Hope. The Owen Committee had of course to take account of the new international situation brought about by the "Entente Cordiale" of 1904 with France, the rising threat from Germany, and also the far-reaching naval reforms recently introduced by Fisher. The latter included a much greater concentration of strength in home waters; and as Germany possessed few overseas bases it was obvious even before the Owen Committee sailed that reductions in the British garrisons were in the wind. This explains why, in Hankey's words, "we were a most unpopular committee"—among the officers serving in those garrisons. But its unpopularity was, for reasons to be explained later, by no means fully justified.

Hankey was granted the rank of temporary Major before the *Terrible* sailed; but although the promotion pleased him it could not make amends for the separation from Adeline. To mitigate it, and to provide a spiritual link between them they had arranged before parting that both would read the same passages from the New Testament each evening. Every Sunday he attended the ship's church services, evidently regarding them as a good deal more than a conventional custom—as had been the case in his *Ramillies* days; and he also made his Communion regularly, knowing that Adeline would be offering the same sacrifice at about the same time. It is indeed plain that the deepening and strengthening of his religious conviction dates to the time of his marriage; for he had written to Adeline a few days before their wedding "I am glad that . . . the foundation and the coping stone of our love were laid in the church; long may the structure last!"

The first of the many long and descriptive letters which Hankey posted from each port of call during the *Terrible*'s cruise illustrates very nicely the technique he adopted to get his ideas adopted.

To Mrs. Hankey. At sea. 28th July 1906

. . . So far I have succeeded in getting my way as regards the Committee's work—not by talking at the meeting, but by insinuating my ideas to each member privately . . . and making him think it is his own. Then I support him at the meeting and we get our way; whereas if I, by far the youngest member, were to spring it on them at the meeting I should probably meet with strong opposition.

Suaviter in modo was a principle he was to develop to a fine art, and to employ successfully with far more august bodies than the Owen Committee.

The *Terrible*'s first port of call was St. Vincent in the Portuguese Cape Verde Islands, to replenish her bunkers. Hankey was shocked by the colonists' virtually complete integration with the native people, and by Portuguese officers of the garrison serving under a Negro commander. "Fancy English officers", he told Adeline (3rd August), "serving under a West African nigger! But that is a peculiarity of the Portuguese, they have always treated native races more or less on an equal footing, I believe, and have even intermarried with them". Although his outlook on racial matters corresponded with that of almost the whole British ruling class of the period, it is curious that he should have regarded the Africans as so greatly inferior to the Maltese, among whom he had, as we saw earlier, made many friends—and in defiance of the social conventions prevailing at that base.

Though the Owen Committee met almost daily while at sea to discuss the principles on which they should work, it was not until they reached Freetown, Sierra Leone, that they had actually to survey the defences of an overseas base. That port also gave Hankey his first impression of the West African tropical scene, which stimulated his gift for descriptive writing and his never-failing delight in new sights and strange peoples. Within 48 hours the Committee had collected all the information and opinions needed and the ship sailed to her next port of call, Ascension Island, where there was a garrison of Marines. "I don't think I should half mind being King of Ascension with you as Queen" he told Adeline (11th August). "It counts as sea service and is indisputably preferable to the separation involved in ordinary time at sea". In addition to visiting the defences and discussing the problems of the garrison (who in fact regarded themselves as very fortunate

people) Hankey had of course to climb the volcanic peak of the island
—where he was amused to find "a farm worked by a dozen English
marines with English cows, English sheep, and English chickens, for
all the world like a farm at Wadhurst [Sussex], only situated in the
middle of the South Atlantic in the tropics". He also visited the "turtle
pound", whose inmates were then, and for many years later, regularly
shipped home in naval store ships for the delectation of the Board of
Admiralty.

St. Helena, at which the *Terrible* called next, pleased Hankey less than
Ascension—possibly because he did not this time manage to shake off
the other members of the committee and explore the island on his own.
Longwood, Napoleon's house of exile after Waterloo until his death,
he found very sad, and considered the treatment accorded by the
British to "the greatest soldier who ever lived" extremely heartless. As
regards the defences, Hankey persuaded the committee to enter a strong
protest against the intention of the government to withdraw the
garrison. Though he urged its retention on strategic grounds, to safeguard the islands from raids from the French west African territories,
he also stressed that the economic effect on the population would be
disastrous—since export of their agricultural produce had become
almost impossible, and the garrison provided the only other means of
livelihood open to them.

On arriving at Simonstown Hankey was welcomed by large numbers
of Adeline's relations. He had to cope with three complete sets of
uncles and aunts—her father's nine brothers and sisters, and the
brothers and sisters of both his wives; and as most of them were
married and had children of their own Hankey's cousins by marriage
were legion. It is hardly surprising that, as he told Adeline, he "got
rather muddled with all the relations and made some stupid mistakes I
fear". However the beauty of Cape Province and the warmth of the
hospitality of his relations by marriage quickly won his heart. With one
of the uncles he visited "the glorious property" of Groote Schuur, and
explored the lovely foothills of Table Mountain. He consoled himself
for the loss of the estates by recalling that if Abraham de Smidt had gone
on living there he would probably never have met Adeline.

The days at Simonstown and Cape Town were not by any means
spent entirely on the social round. Hankey and his fellow commissioners inspected the defences with their usual thoroughness, and the
former was distressed by the apparently complete lack of co-ordination

between the Army's various branches. The coast defence gunners did not know whether the searchlights could illuminate an attacking warship satisfactorily, and the Engineers in charge of the searchlights were totally ignorant of the capabilities of the guns. "This is the great defect of the Army", he wrote. "Each branch disclaims all knowledge of and even despises every other branch, whereas the closest co-operation between the various branches is indispensable to success". No doubt he stored up his experience of inter-service rivalry and jealousy against the day when he would have to mediate in Army-Navy disputes of far greater moment than the discord between the Sappers and Gunners at Simonstown.

In the same letter he made a prophetic forecast regarding his own future. "Remember this trip is a good thing for me and for you" he told Adeline, who was evidently taking their separation hardly. "It adds to my reputation in precisely the direction in which we wish it added to—not as a fighting man but as a sound peace administrator. Imagine, for instance, if I could get the billet which Captain Ottley suggested to me! It would get me into personal contact with all the leading men of the day. In such a case any liberal tendencies would make themselves manifest, and liberals are so rare among naval and military men that it might lead to all sorts of possibilities!" Evidently Ottley had told Hankey before the latter left England that he was likely to succeed Sir George Clarke[1] as secretary of the Committee of Imperial Defence, and had expressed the intention of taking Hankey as his assistant.

During his time in South Africa Hankey discussed the constitutional problems of the day and the future of the Union with his wife's relations. Though their outlook must in general have been pro-British rather than pro-Boer Hankey himself saw further ahead. "Personally", he told Adeline (22nd August) "I hold the extreme view that the ultimate goal of our policy should be the reinstatement of the Boers in the position they occupied before the war . . . As a matter of fact I think the eventual paramountcy of the Dutch in South Africa is bound to come. The English as a race have ceased to increase rapidly here as elsewhere, whereas the Dutch population increases rapidly . . ." At about the time when he penned those words he infuriated General Owen by arguing in favour of "arbitration as the proper means of settling differences between civilised nations in lieu of war"; and he had

[1] 1848–1933. Baron Sydenham of Combe 1913. Secretary, Colonial Defence Committee 1885–92 and of C.I.D. 1904–7. Governor of Bombay 1907–13.

an equally heated dispute with Major W. T. Furse,[1] who represented
the General Staff on the Owen Committee and had tried to convince
Hankey "that the destiny of the British race is to conquer the whole of
the world '*vi et armis*' [by force of arms] and to rule it for ever afterwards". By the age of 29 Hankey had evidently developed advanced
political views—such as were not currently held by service officers of
those days; nor was he afraid to express such views in public.

From the Cape the *Terrible* set course for Mauritius, where Hankey
found his brother Donald in hospital at the hill station of Curepipe in
very poor health from an abscess on the liver, for which he had under-
gone a severe operation. Mauritius was at that time an extremely
unhealthy station, and Donald was fortunate to be invalided home
without his health being permanently impaired. But his condition
caused his brother great anxiety.

As to the defences of the island, Hankey found it difficult to convince
the commander of the garrison that large expenditure on coastal guns
was unjustified, and that the island's security depended on the fleet
maintaining local command of the sea.

To Mrs. Hankey. At sea Mauritius to Singapore, 3rd Sept. 1906
. . . It is really astounding how ignorant *all* military officers are of the very
first principles of Imperial defence and coast defence, which have been
accepted by successive governments of both parties and are in fact incon-
trovertible . . . They all believe that enormous armies are going to be
transported in prodigious fleets over stupendous distances to invade their
own colony. . . . They seem to misunderstand the whole policy of the
Admiralty and the nation, which is to maintain a great superiority of sea
power and bringing war on to the enemy's coastline, instead of frittering
away our money in providing large local defences for our numerous and
scattered possessions . . .

Plainly Hankey was by this time a fully committed adherent to the
"blue water school" of strategy.

At the end of August the *Terrible* set course for Singapore, a passage
involving nearly a fortnight at sea. Though tedious in most respects
the long stretch across the Indian Ocean at least enabled the committee
to make up arrears in the drafting of their report.

To Mrs. Hankey. At sea Singapore to Hong Kong, 14th September
As we were about to enter the harbour [Keppel Harbour, Singapore] early

[1]Later Major-General Sir William T. Furse (1865–1954). Master General of Ordnance 1916.

I had myself called before 6 o'clock and went on deck directly I was dressed, as I was particularly anxious to satisfy myself concerning certain points connected with the defence. . . . The local general [Major-General Inigo R. Jones], a guardsman by the way who knows about as much of fortress defence as the Pope of Rome I should think, was almost double the height of General Owen. They did form a queer couple. One or two of the military officers seemed keen, but some of them were appallingly "tired". I fear they are a slack lot. I am told that even the staff only work from 10 a.m. to 1 p.m. —hardly suitable hours for a professional man I think . . .

Evidently the effect of the heat and high humidity of Singapore on Europeans, which was to contribute so much to the disasters of World War II, did not escape the notice of the observant Hankey. But the harbour and the town, with the crowds of junks and other craft afloat, and the polyglot, bustling people of many races in the streets fascinated him.

The *Terrible* reached Hong Kong in the immediate wake of a violent typhoon which had struck with practically no warning. As a result the harbour was strewn with wrecks, the damage on shore was enormous and the loss of life heavy—especially among the Chinese waterborne population. Hankey lived up on "The Peak"; but his days were so fully taken up by the duties of the committee and the entertainments arranged by the local authorities that his letters are less informative than usual. He admitted that while at Hong Kong he was not quite his usual energetic, exuberant self. This may have been attributable to the climate, to the pomposity of General Owen, whom he now found "almost insufferable", or to the fact that he "was not altogether happy about the committee's decisions with regard to the defence of Hong Kong". Unfortunately he does not enlarge upon what may have been a serious disagreement in the committee, or between them and the local military authorities. A likely clue is, however, to be found in a letter from Vice-Admiral Hedworth Lambton,[1] the C-in-C, China, to the Governor of Hong Kong written some two years later. The Admiral then roundly attacked the Owen Committee's low standard of gun defences for the colony as "a preposterous proposal".[2] His letter

[1] 1856–1929. Later Admiral Sir Hedworth Meux, which name he took in 1911. C-in-C, China, 1908–10 and Portsmouth 1912–16. King George V's nominee for post of First Sea Lord on Prince Louis of Battenberg resigning in Oct. 1914, but Churchill refused to have him appointed.
[2] Letter of 25th Nov. 1908 reproduced in C.I.D. 56C of 7th April 1909. Cab. 38/15/6.

reached the Admiralty, who described such views as "alarmist"; but when the whole issue came before the Colonial Defence Committee in 1909 McKenna, the First Lord, stuck firmly to the scale of defences recommended by the Owen Committee, which, he said, "were strategically sound".[1]

On 25th September Hankey wrote to Adeline "We are now home-ward bound, hurrah". Three days later his high spirits plummeted when the *Terrible* lost her starboard propeller. Her reduced speed meant that she would be at least a week longer on the return journey—a delay which did not at all appeal to our young husband and father.

In a long letter written while the *Terrible* was crawling painfully across the Bay of Bengal Hankey philosophised on his recent experiences. "This Committee has in many ways been very good for me", he wrote (7th October). "I think it has made me much less conceited, for as the youngest member but one . . . I have done little speaking, confining myself mainly to making suggestions to Ballard direct; I have realised, therefore, how unimportant a person I am, and without losing the least confidence in my own judgement I have realised how necessary it is to compromise with conflicting views, to meet people half way, and sometimes even to sacrifice one's own conviction in order to arrive at a unanimous verdict, which alone can carry weight . . ." Shortly after leaving Colombo he soliloquised on his own position and future.

To Mrs. Hankey. At sea Colombo to Aden, 14th October
. . . The fact is I am a man of peace. I have no desire for war or active service, in fact I strongly deprecate either, and though I should do my duty if sent to the front I could not work up much enthusiasm unless I felt sure that our cause was just, and in 99 cases out of 100 wars appear to me unjust and wrong. Under these circumstances I question whether I am justified in remaining in a service in which I am tolerably well paid in peace in order that the country may exact unquestioning obedience and sacrifice from me in war. To me it seems that I am to some extent a humbug and hypocrite in accepting such a position. But if I give it up what am I to do? The inexorable force of circumstances seems to indicate that I must continue as I have begun. If so I shall seek administrative and organising posts, such as I have already held, rather than active billets, in the hope that I may eventually find a stepping stone into some more congenial service. The billet which Captain O. [Ottley] hinted at would suit me down to the ground, but I scarcely like to think it at all probable. . . .

[1]102nd Meeting of C.I.D. on 29th June 1909. *ibid.*

The writer of these two letters was certainly a very different, and far more mature man than the ambitious and thrusting young marine officer of *Ramillies* days, who had lectured his father on "duty" at the time of the South African war, and had reproached himself for missing active service in that conflict or in the Boxer troubles in China. The happiness of his marriage was of course the primary cause of the change.

The ship's stay at Colombo was so short that inspection of the defences was rather rushed; and as usual there was a great deal of entertaining. Hankey again stayed at Government House and greatly enjoyed the company of Sir Henry Blake,[1] the Governor, who had "served in nearly every crown colony and had governed three-fifths of the total population of British crown colonies comprising I don't know how many millions".

From Aden Hankey wrote that he felt "quite hilarious" over the fact that he was within four weeks of home, and that his high spirits seemed to have infected the whole committee, who were on much better terms with each other than had sometimes been the case earlier in the tour. He also told Adeline how he had "discovered the key to the General's temper. I make a point of invariably addressing him as 'Sir John'; this he cannot resist; he has become civility itself in the mess and at committee meetings, and listens to what I have to say with positive deference". Obviously Hankey had discovered that, with some types, a little judicious flattery could oil the wheels of discussion.

In the same letter (20th October) he discussed the proposal of the Liberal government under Campbell Bannerman to reduce the Navy Estimates for 1907. The navy was, he said, "prodigiously strong", having been built "to fight a combination of France and Russia, when these two were the next strongest naval powers. Consequently, owing to the collapse of Russia, we have an enormous preponderance over any two powers. Add to this that political considerations render a combination of France and Germany against us very unlikely for a decade at least and you see that our position is unassailable . . . under these circumstances the Government are quite right in reducing the naval estimates in order that they may go to the [1907] Hague Conference and say to Germany and France that as an earnest of our desire for a cessation of the rivalry in shipbuilding, which is a burden on the taxpayers of all countries, we have reduced our budgets. If they decline

[1] 1848–1918. Governor successively of Bahamas (1884–7), Newfoundland (1887–8), Jamaica (1889–97), Hong Kong (1897–1903) and Ceylon (1903–7).

to follow our lead we have plenty of time to build ships to retain our supremacy . . . It is a real and genuine attempt towards peace . . .".[1] These were unusual views for an officer of a fighting service to hold, and it is interesting to remark that at the time when Hankey expressed them Admiral Fisher was writing in almost identical terms to Tweedmouth, the First Lord.[2]

While in the Red Sea Hankey gave his wife his prescription for keeping fit in a hot climate. In addition to the careful diet which he followed he made it a habit to carry out a daily routine of physical exercises according to McFadden's (later replaced by Müller's) system. This became a life-long practice, in which Adeline apparently joined.

To Mrs. Hankey. At sea Aden to Suez, 23rd October 1906
The heat still continues . . . The other members of the committee cannot sleep at all at night but I have slept perfectly which I attribute to great moderation in meat, alcohol and sugar. I eat mainly fresh and dried fruits and vegetables, and thrive on them, though of course I eat some meat. I drink lime juice and soda and weak cider and soda, the water being now absolutely undrinkable.

Suez brought the disappointment that his projected trip to Cairo had to be cancelled for lack of time. But for the passage through the canal he was on deck continuously observing through his glasses and "taking a great many notes" for "a certain report"—no doubt for N.I.D.— which he was writing. That report, he said, "will show existing theories, which were not based on accurate personal observation but on an examination of a chart to be all wrong". At Port Said he picked up a report that Lord Charles Beresford was to take command of the Channel Fleet and Prince Louis of Battenberg the Mediterranean Fleet early in the following year.[3] "Would not that be splendid?" he asked of Adeline. "He [Prince Louis] is *the* coming man in the Navy; his

[1]On 27th July the Parliamentary Secretary of the Admiralty had announced in the House of Commons that, with the agreement of the Board of Admiralty, only two instead of four *Dreadnought* battleships would be included in the 1907–8 estimates. A third would be added if the Hague Conference failed to agree on a reduction of armaments. These proposals aroused a wave of indignation from the "Big Navy" press, and a good deal of criticism of Fisher, the First Sea Lord.
[2]See Fisher to Tweedmouth, 26th Sept. 1906. Quoted Marder, *Fisher*, II, p. 91.
[3]Only the first of these reports proved correct. Beresford took command of the Channel Fleet in April 1907, but Battenberg returned to the Mediterranean in February of that year as second-in-command to Admiral Sir Charles Drury. Battenberg became C-in-C, Atlantic Fleet, in November 1908.

daughter is married into the Greek Royal Family and he is a great phil-Hellene[1]; I would make myself useful to him by interpreting Greek and generally get the right side of him. Moreover, as [an] ex-D.N.I. he would certainly give his Intelligence Officer every possible encouragement . . ."

From Malta he looked back on the previous three months with some satisfaction.

To Mrs. Hankey. Malta, 25th October 1906
. . . I have been reviewing the work I have done on this trip in my mind. In addition to the ordinary committee work, which has occupied most mornings from 10.30 to 12.30 at sea and all day on shore, as well as a certain number of statistical tables and notes which I have prepared for their use, I have assisted Dumbleton, the secretary,[2] by typewriting preliminary drafts etc. I have sent home a report consisting of 4 or 5 typed sheets of foolscap to the N.I.D. from almost every port touched at. I have drafted the rough of my book and typed nearly two chapters fair. I have dabbled in the elements of navigation . . . and have picked up enough to be of assistance if ever I take up the subject seriously. I have also studied part of the Intelligence of the Mediterranean and have committed to memory the names of our own and the French ships on the station, and have learned to draw rough plans of the armour and guns of the French principal ships, as well as getting a general idea of the strengths of other fleets on the station. Then I have read Mahan's *Life of Nelson*,[3] and the Histories of Lissa,[4] the war between Chile and Peru and the Chilean civil war. Finally I have read two or three novels. On the whole I don't think it is such a bad record . . . You must not take this self-praise too seriously; sometimes I feel that I am a waster and doing no good in the world . . .

The days at Malta were very busy indeed, as the defence system was far more complex than at more remote bases. Moreover the committee

[1]Princess (Victoria) Alice (1885—), elder daughter of Prince Louis, married in 1903 Prince Andrew of Greece. Their only son (b. 1921) is Prince Philip, Duke of Edinburgh, consort of Queen Elizabeth II.
[2]Major H. N. Dumbleton, R.E.
[3]Hankey judged Nelson very harshly at this time—because of his abominable treatment of his wife after the obsession with Lady Hamilton had taken hold of him.
[4]Presumably the battle of Lissa, fought off the island of that name (now Vis) in the Adriatic between the Italian and Austrian fleets on 20th July 1866. This was the first battle fought between modern ironclad fleets. The much publicised sinking of the Italian flagship by ramming led to the false conclusion that the ram would play an important part in future sea warfare. Battleships of all nations were fitted with rams well into the 20th century.

got seriously at loggerheads with the local military authorities who, according to Hankey, "regarded us as the treacherous minions of a radical Government bent on reducing their defences regardless of efficiency". This was extremely unfair, since it was the War Office which had laid down in the Owen Committee's Terms of Reference that the garrison of Malta was to be cut down.[1] However after some stormy encounters between the committee and the senior officers of the garrison, the squabbles were patched up—thanks once more to Hankey's mediation.

While at Malta Hankey met Lord Charles Beresford several times, and his very friendly attitude made Hankey wonder whether he should not seek the appointment of Intelligence Officer in the Channel instead of the Mediterranean fleet. Beresford, however, had evidently not yet made up his mind about his staff, and while Hankey was still deliberating the merits of the two alternatives he heard from London that the issue had been settled for him. He was to be appointed Intelligence Officer to the Mediterranean Fleet. This news was of course at once transmitted to Adeline. At the same time her husband was able to tell her that the cause of the fever which had struck him four years earlier had been discovered, and that the long-endured scourge was already showing signs of abating. The risk of bringing their small son out to Malta was thus greatly reduced. When the *Terrible* sailed for Gibraltar she carried on board at least one very light heart.

From Hankey's personal point of view the experience gained during the tour in the *Terrible* proved very valuable. When in later years the defences of any overseas base were being discussed in high places his remarkable memory enabled him at once to recall exactly what guns, searchlights and other equipment existed in it; and in many cases he could produce out of his head particulars such as anchorage facilities and depth of water as well. It was that capacity which was to earn him such a high reputation as a walking encyclopaedia on defence matters. The only reward for his labour on the Owen Committee was that he was required to relinquish his rank of Acting Major as soon as it was disbanded. It is a curious feature of his career that he never again wore a Major's insignia.

We have seen how Hankey worked on his draft of "Warfare on the Littoral" while in the *Terrible*. It is likely that the strategic principles which he studied in connection with that work, combined with the

[1] W.O. letters 266/910 of 23rd May and 17th June 1906. Cab. 16/1.

interest he had developed earlier in amphibious warfare, caused him to revert to the question of the use of the Marines as the spearhead of combined operations at this time. At any rate in December 1906 he produced papers entitled "Proposals for Developing the Marine Corps as part of a National Striking Force" and "Proposals for improving the Constitution of our Military Striking Force". Though we have no indication of how his seniors reacted to these proposals, they were certainly in accord with Admiral Fisher's view that the most fruitful employment for our small military forces was to take advantage of our sea power by striking suddenly in overseas theatres.

Hankey had not been reunited with his wife and son many days before he heard that Fisher, now First Sea Lord, had decided to form a small and select body to draft in great secrecy the naval war plans. The chairman was to be Captain Ballard, who had been in command of the *Terrible* during the Owen Committee's tour, and he at once applied for Hankey's services as secretary. The Ballard Committee started work at the Naval War College, Portsmouth, in December 1906, and for the next five months Hankey was thus immersed in the strategic problems which would arise in the event of war with Germany. His studies and experience had already convinced him of the susceptibility of that country to economic pressure through blockade—which of course predicated the maintenance of world-wide sea power. Hence arose his conviction that the correct strategy for Britain to adopt in a war with Germany was, firstly, to secure the homeland against invasion; secondly defend British merchant shipping against a renewal of the *guerre de course* which had caused such heavy losses in earlier wars; thirdly apply economic pressure on the enemy mainly though not entirely through blockade; and, lastly, use our military forces in conjunction with sea power to strike at the enemy in overseas theatres at times and places of our own choice. Those views coloured all his thinking and writing from about 1907 onwards. Unfortunately they were not acceptable to the military authorities. The likelihood of invasion and the correct way to defeat such an attempt, together with the need to despatch an expeditionary force to the continent in support of the French, became the subject of acute controversy between the Admiralty and War Office; and Hankey was soon to find himself at the centre of it.

After completing the war plans Hankey was only allowed the briefest of rests, which he and Adeline and their small son spent on a

Sussex farm, before he took up his new appointment. Despite the heavy pressure to which he had been subject while working on the Ballard Committee he had also been grooming himself for his return to Intelligence work in the Mediterranean by reading widely and deeply in the ancient as well as the modern history of the lands bordering on that sea. Though this was in fact only the resumption of an earlier interest, it seems fair to conclude that his knowledge of Mediterranean history, exemplified by his constant use of quotations from the Greek and Latin classics in his published works, dates to this time.[1] Taken with his gift for languages—for by this time he could read and translate French, Italian, German and modern Greek, and could speak all those languages with some fluency—he must have been an altogether exceptional Intelligence Officer. On leaving N.I.D. Ottley wrote of Hankey "This officer performed all his duties in a most satisfactory manner. He has excellent judgement and great aptitude for drafting reports and memoranda on all questions connected with Coast Defences; he is also both accurate and rapid in his work".

Though Hankey has recorded that he found the Intelligence work of the Mediterranean fleet in good order,[2] he soon expanded the scope of activities in that field. Here it is perhaps necessary to explain that in the early 19th century and indeed throughout World War I, the Naval Intelligence Department (or Intelligence Division of the Naval Staff as it became in 1917) was virtually untrammelled in attaining whatever ends the Director and his representatives in the fleet considered necessary. Today, when the Foreign Office exerts a paramount influence over all Intelligence activities, it may seem extraordinary that until about 1919 the D.N.I. should have held virtually all the threads in his own hands, and should himself have decided on the time and manner of using the knowledge that he possessed. Yet such was the case— especially during the time of Admiral Sir Reginald Hall as D.N.I.

[1]Though *The Supreme Command 1914–18* was not published until 1961, by which time Hankey had no doubt much extended his reading, it is interesting to remark that of the 83 chapter headings he used 12 came from the Greek and Latin classics (with Polybius the most quoted), 31 were taken from a very wide range of histories (with Carlyle easily in the lead), and 23 from English poets—in which class Shakespeare with 11 quotations easily outstripped Dante, Bunyan, Milton, Blake, Swinburne, Chaucer and Kipling, none of whom had more than 3. In Hankey's Romanes Lecture (1951) he introduced 6 quotations from Polybius, Plato and Thucydides.

[2]*Supreme Command* I, pp. 42–3.

during World War I.[1] Thus in 1907 Hankey found himself in a very influential post at the centre of a web of activity which already covered all the countries bordering on the Mediterranean, and which he extended well into Asia Minor and the Middle East.

Soon after his arrival he gave a lecture on Intelligence work to selected officers, and called for volunteers to expand his organisation. Those he recruited were, not surprisingly, mostly Marines. But Hankey evidently did not confine his choice of agents to his own corps, or indeed to officers of the fleet. For example on meeting the Anglican bishop of Gibraltar at a luncheon at Admiralty House he assiduously pumped the prelate about his travels over his vast diocese, and even enlisted his services! Nor does the Bishop appear to have been taken aback by what must have seemed to him a somewhat unepiscopal request. To give another example of the scope and range of the activities of Hankey's organisation, in June 1907 he recorded that his chief assistant Captain Gilbert Drage, R.M.L.I. and another officer had penetrated as far as Trebizond on the Black Sea. Unfortunately a piece of wanton carelessness by the Captain of a British warship, who entrusted a letter from Hankey to Drage to the porter of a hotel in Constantinople, despite the fact that he knew it contained secret instructions, went a long way towards destroying Drage's value. In Intelligence parlance he was "blown"; but that episode seems to have been an isolated misfortune to the network operated by Hankey.

Here it may be useful to explain that the common illusion, fostered by the popular press and by imaginative writers, that an Intelligence organisation depends on sensational and daring coups, such as the rifling of the safe of a foreign diplomat or the seduction of officers by beautiful but dissolute women, is far from the truth. In fact such coups are extremely rare, and when they are brought off their effects are often exaggerated. Rather does successful Intelligence work depend on the painstaking collection of small pieces of information from scores of different sources, on classifying them for reliability by comparative processes, and on fitting the pieces together, as with a giant jig-saw puzzle, until a broad and accurate picture finally emerges. Hankey's work in the Mediterranean conformed very precisely to that pattern.

[1]See Sir William James, *The Eyes of the Navy* (Methuen, 1955). Hall's most famous coup was the deciphering of the Zimmerman telegram, and the manner he used it to exert the greatest possible influence in the U.S.A. See B. W. Tuchmann, *The Zimmerman Telegram* (Constable, 1959).

The chief focus of attention was on the Levant, where the Turkish Empire was obviously tottering towards dissolution. Russian eyes were, as in the previous century, fixed covetously on the Dardanelles and Bosphorus, and German industrial penetration of Turkey could obviously be the prelude to military intervention in the event of a collapse of the Sultanate. Hence arose Hankey's decision to concentrate his efforts during the summer cruise of 1907 on surveying the beaches and harbours of Syria and Palestine, which then formed part of the Turkish Empire and lay on the flank of the important land communications from Constantinople and Asia Minor to Egypt.

As always was the case with Hankey his work was facilitated by the excellent relations he established with senior officers, and by the confidence which they showed him. Thus in June he told Adeline "I again had a long yarn with Prince Louis. He tells me all sorts of interesting items of information and talks quite freely and confidentially". During the summer cruise Admiral Drury, the C-in-C, entrusted to him "a very delicate mission to the British Consul at Syra",[1] which "might in certain contingencies be a very important place for us, as it is a great centre of telegraphic communications in the Levant . . . In fact it is quite a little diplomatic mission and I am very pleased at being entrusted with it". Though he was not prepared to take even Adeline entirely into his confidence on this matter one may guess that the Consul at Syra was required to furnish Intelligence about ships passing to and from the Dardanelles, and that the "certain contingencies" were a war with Germany in which Turkey was her ally.

For the summer cruise of 1907 Hankey and his small staff were accommodated in the battleship *Irresistible* (Captain H. P. Williams). This was not a happy choice, and on 24th June he wrote to Adeline that "the last 24 hours have been the most miserable and unfortunate that I have ever spent". The trouble was that the ship was just out of dockyard hands, and was extremely dirty. Hankey was disgusted to find his cabin infested with vermin, and refused point blank to return to it until it had been properly cleaned. None the less he quickly made friends with the Captain, with whom he found common ground through Williams's service as Naval Attaché at St. Petersburgh and

[1]The capital of the island in the Cyclades group now generally referred to as Sciros (not to be confused with Skyros in the Sporades). Sciros is well placed strategically in the central Aegean, and possessed a small dockyard and naval base. It is now the administrative centre of the Cyclades group.

Constantinople. The first port of call was Alexandria, and while there Hankey put the final touches to his organisation for surveying the harbours and beaches of the Levant. He shared out the work between the officers he had recruited, and briefed them all very carefully regarding the information needed.

In addition to preparing for his Intelligence work Hankey managed to fit in a day trip to Cairo. "I went straight to Cook's", he told Adeline, "got a guide . . . and told him that I wanted to see everything in Cairo as well as the Pyramids in 5 hours, and that I would pay him well if he would get me through with a maximum of economy in time and money. Accordingly we started off by tram to the Pyramids . . . [At the end] I gave the guide 8/-".

Changes in the fleet's programme unexpectedly gave Hankey several days in Cyprus, where he joined a party organised for Admirals Drury and Battenberg to go up Mount Troodos (6,300 feet) in carriages and stay several days in the official summer residences of the officials of the colonial government. The scenery and the people delighted him; and of course his Greek, which he found to be far more fluent than that of any of the local British officials, proved invaluable. From Cyprus the *Irresistible* went to Beirut, where Hankey at once plunged into Intelligence work, recruiting British business men, and indeed anyone with reliable local knowledge to help him.

To Mrs. Hankey. H.M.S. *Irresistible at Jaffa, 17th July 1907*
. . . And now I must take up my narrative of Beirut once more. On Monday afternoon I went a walk with the "padre" to a sandy bay a mile or two away where there was a landing place I wanted to see. I was well rewarded, as I found there 60 large lighters which no one had reported before. In order to ascertain the soundings in the vicinity of the beach I had to bathe, though I had no towel! I then went to the station depot and counted all the engines, trucks, carriages etc., and I found about 7/8 of the total rolling stock of the line. As the result of my day's work therefore I had found a rattling good landing place close to the station, and had discovered that if ever we wanted to paralyse the Damascus line we had only to land there, smash down an easy bridge to prevent their steaming off, and then break up the rolling stock, the whole job not taking more than an hour . . . I had visited about 15 miles of coast and reported on all the landing places, roads etc. etc. including the compilation of a very fair map . . .

Changes in the fleet's programme now caused Hankey to leave the *Irresistible*—without any regrets—and to join the battleship *Queen* in order to obtain an Intelligence report on Rhodes, which was, he said "much needed". But he now became very discontented over the attitude of Admiral Drury towards intelligence work and war plans, and swore to Adeline that he would not stay out another year— merely "keeping things going until Ottley's show comes off". . . . "I heard from Clauson[1]", he told Adeline (21st July), "that great efforts are being made to oust Sir G. Clarke in favour of Ottley. There are strong indications that Ottley will cease to be D.N.I. next March, which would suit us very fairly well". The reports he had heard were substantially correct; for Admiral Fisher *was* endeavouring to replace Clarke as Secretary with his own nominee Ottley. Clarke's appointment as Governor of Bombay was announced a short time later. "This means that Ottley will go to the C.I.D.", Hankey told Adeline, "and probably I shall go also. I hope, however, it will not take effect for sometime yet, as I do want to have a winter with you in our little house at Malta". If an appointment came through he would cable to Adeline the single word "Committee" on receipt of which she was to cancel the shipment of her luggage which had already been arranged.

After calling at Smyrna, where Hankey studied the defences closely, the fleet moved into the northern Aegean, where he combined his Intelligence work with long walks on the islands he had always loved. As the results achieved by his subordinates came in he completed his reports on possible landing places in Syria and on the defences of Rhodes. Then he was selected by Admiral Drury to go with him in the hospital ship *Maine* to pay an official visit on the Sultan of Turkey at Constantinople.[2] This delighted Hankey as it gave him the opportunity to study the forts on the Gallipoli peninsula and also to explore a fascinating city which he had not previously visited.

While at Constantinople news of Ottley's appointment as Secretary of the C.I.D. arrived, and Hankey at once wrote to congratulate him,

---

[1]Later Major-General Sir John Clauson (1886–1918). Secretary, Colonial Defence Committee and Assistant Secretary of C.I.D. 1906–11. Lieut.-Governor of Malta 1911–14.

[2]The transfer to the hospital ship was necessary because by the treaty of 1841 the powers had agreed that the Bosphorus and Dardanelles should be closed to all foreign warships while Turkey was at peace. They were each permitted to maintain an unarmed ship known as a "Stationnaire" off Constantinople—which of course acted as rival centres for Intelligence activities. This state of affairs continued until 1923 when, by the Treaty of Lausanne the Straits were declared open to ships of all nations while Turkey was at peace.

diplomatically "mentioning that we have taken a house for the winter". Of course he did not neglect the opportunity to study the defences of the Bosphorus, which he did from a boat with the Military Attaché, and also the Turkish fleet—which aroused his contempt.

The double passage of the Dardanelles set Hankey thinking about the prospect for an attack on the Gallipoli forts, and he has recorded that "we all agreed that they [the Straits] could not be forced by a naval attack, and I reported accordingly to the Admiralty".[1] The C.I.D. had in fact recently received a study entitled "The Possibility of a Joint Naval and Military Attack upon the Dardanelles",[2] in which the General Staff had recommended strongly against "unaided action by the fleet". When the C.I.D. came to consider the reports they came down emphatically against a landing on the Gallipoli peninsula.[3] Hankey remembered these reports and conclusions when, early in 1915, Churchill was pressing for an attack on the Dardanelles. In February of that year he re-circulated the 1906 papers to the War Council, but without effect. It has passed into history that "unaided action by the fleet" was first tried in 1915; and that, after it had failed, an assault landing on the Gallipoli peninsula was belatedly launched in disregard of the conclusions recorded eight years earlier.

After the visit to Constantinople in September 1907 the fleet returned to the Ionian islands, and Hankey again found himself exploring the surroundings of Navarino and Corfu. His love of those places, combined with the prospect of Adeline joining him in the near future, produced a series of lyrical letters; but they also reveal that under Admiral Drury the drive and energy which Fisher had introduced into the fleet's training some eight years earlier had to a great extent lapsed. "Altogether the atmosphere is not very wholesome;" he wrote (15th September), "there is a certain lethargy and slackness about the whole fleet, due to lack of driving power at headquarters, and I don't think I shall do very much good out here". Three weeks later Adeline and Robin arrived at Malta in the liner *Syria*; and the family quickly settled into the pseudo-Mauresque house, grandiosely called "Alhambra", which Hankey had rented and which still stands in the suburb of Sliema.

Despite the reunion with his family Hankey was working harder than

[1] *Supreme Command* I, p. 42.
[2] C.I.D. 92B of 20th December 1906. Cab. 38/12/60.
[3] 96th Meeting on 28th Feb. 1907. Cab. 38/13/12.

ever that autumn; for he was not content to confine his activities to Intelligence. Knowing what he did about the plans made at home for a war with Germany he considered it essential to apply the same principle of strategic studies and departmental co-ordination to the Mediterranean Fleet, and then to integrate the results with the war plans for the home theatre. With the strong support of Prince Louis, now second-in-command of the fleet, he soon accomplished that object. Before the end of the year plans had been made and orders drafted to meet every possible contingency. In fact Hankey constructed a miniature "War Book" for the Mediterranean Fleet, including its shore bases and dock-yards, which was to serve later as a model for the similar book covering every activity—military, naval and economic—of a Britain girding herself for war.

At the same time he turned his attention to the reorganisation of Malta dockyard and its associated supply departments, in which he found a marked lack of proper co-ordination. To put this right demand-ed great tact, since the dockyard officers were mostly civilians, and were very ready to resent the intrusion of a service officer and an outsider into their affairs. However Hankey wisely "obtained the C-in-C's mandate", which could not be gainsaid, and the task was soon completed. At that moment Robin fell seriously ill.

The years of overwork, much of it in bad climates, combined with worry over Robin, now brought its inevitable consequences. In January 1908, at the very moment when he received a telegram ordering him home to take up the post of Naval Assistant Secretary to the C.I.D., Hankey's health broke down. Though Ottley had kept his promise, the welcome news found Hankey "sick, worn out, and Robin too ill to move from Sliema". The doctors forbade taking the child on the long sea voyage to England; and unless the sea was flat calm they would not permit even the 80 mile passage from Malta to Syracuse to take the trans-continental train home. Hankey would not think of leaving his wife and child in Malta, and he felt (probably wrongly) that if he was not home and ready to take up the appointment on the day named in the telegram he would miss his chance. But calm seas are the exception in the Mediterranean in winter. That January the wind howled and the seas lashed the rocky shores of Malta day after day. To take ship was out of the question. At sundown on the last possible day it fell flat calm, and Hankey and his family embarked—to the sad adieux of their faithful Maltese staff. Adeline at once hurried home to be with her father, who was seriously ill; but he died before she had reached him. Hankey, now relieved of his anxiety to get to London as quickly as possible, stopped in Switzerland for a few days. There Robin made a remarkably quick recovery, and at the end of the month the three of them were united again. Adeline's father, whose way of life had always been extravagant, even after the loss of his fortune in the South African bank crash, left his widow nothing but debts. Hankey not only paid the debts but made his mother-in-law an allowance, so that she could live in modest comfort to the day of her death. Considering that, right up to the time when he received the sum of £25,000 from the government as a gratuity at the end of World War I, he himself was never free from financial anxiety this was remarkably generous. The key to his ability to maintain a modest but comfortable house, educate his growing family privately, and at the same time show such generosity to others is almost certainly to be found in Adeline's thrifty management. As Hankey's responsibilities became heavier he left the financial side of his affairs increasingly in her hands; and her children remember with what consummate skill she overcame the chronic shortage of money from which the family suffered right up to 1919.

In 1908 the prospect of several years in England lay ahead; and that, combined with the dissolution of both their family homes through death, made the moment opportune to seek a more permanent home for themselves. After a short search they bought The Corner House in the village of Oxted on the Kent and Surrey borders. It is a plain, white stuccoed two-storey house, probably built in the late 19th or early 20th century. Its advantages were that it was within easy reach of London, had a pleasant garden and—best of all for two such strenuous walkers —it lay on the edge of beautiful country. Its chief disadvantages were that it stood right on a main road where the traffic was rather heavy; and that, although it faced south, it was deprived of much sun by a screen of trees on the opposite side of the road. Such, then, was to be their home for the next four years; and there on 5th February 1909 their second child, a girl who was christened Ursula Helen Alers, was born.[1]

So ended Hankey's direct connection with the Naval Intelligence Department. The record of his service, still preserved in the office of the Commandant-General, Royal Marines, contains a note that he was "Brought to Their Lordships' notice for his conspicuous ability, zeal

[1]Married 1929 Sir John A. Benn, Bart.

and industry during the 5 years he served in the N.I.D. Has proved himself to possess in quite exceptional degree the qualities requisite in an officer called upon to discharge secretarial functions". If Hankey knew about that encomium he must surely have moved into his new and wider field of activity with enhanced confidence in his own capacity and prospects.

Chapter 4

Assistant Secretary, Committee of Imperial Defence 1908-1912

HANKEY'S appointment as Assistant Secretary of the C.I.D. is dated 15th January 1908, and he probably took up his new duty on that day. The offices of the C.I.D. were at the time at No. 2 Whitehall Gardens, which he has described as "a row of comfortable, old fashioned high houses dating from 1808".[1] Whitehall Gardens stood on the south side of Whitehall on the site of the Old Palace of Westminster. It was a *cul-de-sac* to which vehicles could only gain entry between Gwydyr House and Richmond Terrace, both of which still stand. It curved round behind Gwydyr House and Inigo Jones's magnificent Banqueting House, ending approximately level with the east end of the latter. The houses were on the river side of the short street, and looked out through a screen of fine trees, which were the sole remains of the Privy Garden of the Old Palace, on to the back of the Banqueting House and Gwydyr House. At the north end stood what was left of Pembroke House, which by 1908 had been divided into Nos. 6 and 7 Whitehall Gardens. Then came three dignified, bow-fronted houses with stuccoed façades (Nos. 5, 4 and 3), and at the south end stood No. 2, which had a brick façade except on the ground floor. To the south of No. 2 and detached from it stood Montagu House (No. 1). The general effect of the short row was one of harmonious and dignified diversity. At the back of them was a large garden ending in a high wall which screened the houses from the embankment; but the river and its constant traffic of barges, busy tugs and pleasure boats could be seen from the first floor windows.

When Hankey first entered the room on the first floor of No. 2 where the Committee of Imperial Defence met and the secretary worked, it still preserved much of the original Regency period decoration, though the painted wall panels and carved mantelpiece were in the

[1]*Supreme Command*, I, p. 57.

late French style and dated only from the 1840s. Hankey has very reasonably suggested that the friendly and informal atmosphere of the room contributed to the success of the many meetings and conferences held in it.[1] During World War I Nos. 1, 3 and 4 were also taken over to house the greatly expanded staff of the War Cabinet. In 1938 the demolition contractors moved in and in August of that year the Cabinet Office moved to nearby Richmond Terrace. Two years later, after Churchill had become Prime Minister and Minister of Defence, the office moved to Great George Street above the Cabinet war rooms which had been brought into use on the outbreak of World War II. Finally the Cabinet Office moved to its present location at No. 70 Whitehall early in 1964. Rebuilding began on the Whitehall Gardens site in 1939 but was stopped a few months later; it was not resumed until after the victory of the United Nations in 1945. The ground on which the C.I.D. and War Cabinet offices once stood is now burdened with the monotonous bulk of the Ministry of Defence's main building.

As the Committee of Imperial Defence played such a great part in Hankey's life it may be useful here to outline its functions, its membership and the manner in which its work was carried out. In December 1902, when the Committee was established by Balfour, two existing inter-departmental committees, the Colonial Defence Committee and the Joint Military and Naval Committee, became sub-committees of the new body. The Committee on the Reconstitution of the War Office under Lord Esher, which reported in January 1904,[2] was extremely critical of the means whereby defence policy was supposed to be co-ordinated, and as a result of that body's report the C.I.D. was entirely reconstituted in the following May.[3] Thereafter the Prime Minister became the chairman and the only permanent member of the committee, with powers to select all the other members, and a full-time secretariat was provided. Thus was created the body which, with a break during World War I when its work was largely taken over by policy-making bodies such as the War Council, was to be the principal advisory and consultative body on all matters concerned with home and overseas defence right up to the outbreak of World War II in 1939.

It must be emphasised that the C.I.D. never possessed executive functions. All its recommendations went to the Cabinet for approval and then to the departments concerned for the necessary executive action. Numerous sub-committees were set up to consider and formu-

[1] op. cit. p. 58.   [2] Cab. 37/68/12.   [3] Cab. 37/70/66.

late the principles on which defence policy should be based; many intricate problems concerned with special aspects of defence were considered, and detailed plans were prepared to co-ordinate the actions of the naval, military and civil departments in the event of war. Obviously the secretary of the C.I.D. held the keys to virtually all current problems concerned with war and defence policy; and from 1908 to 1939 there were few political problems which were not, in some way or other, connected with those subjects.

The general system by which the business of the C.I.D. was conducted had been established well before Hankey entered its offices, and is probably attributable to its first secretary Sir George Clarke. Unlike the Cabinet, which, until Hankey became its secretary at the end of 1916, kept no record of its deliberations and decisions, the C.I.D.'s records were meticulously organised. Minutes of each meeting, stating clearly and concisely the conclusions reached, were produced and circulated within 24 hours, and were numbered consecutively from the first meeting held on 18th December 1902 to the day when the Defence Committee of World War II took over its functions. The memoranda produced by members of the C.I.D. or submitted to it by departments were kept in five main series, and were numbered consecutively in each series. These deal with Home Defence (Series A), Miscellaneous Subjects (Series B), Colonial Defence (Series C), Indian Defence (Series D) and the Very Secret File of manuscript reports. To the foregoing was added, shortly after Hankey became Secretary, the "War Book" series (lettered W). Each series was enclosed in bindings of different colour clearly titled and dated in gold lettering, so that the secretariat could tell at a glance where any paper that might be required in a hurry could be found.

Between 1904 and 1914 the business of the C.I.D. was conducted chiefly by means of a Standing Sub-Committee, which differed but little in composition from the full C.I.D., and by four permanent sub-committees. These latter were the Colonial (after 1911 Overseas) Defence Sub-Committee, the Home Ports Defence Sub-Committee formed in 1909, the Air Committee and the Committee on the Co-ordination of Departmental Action, colloquially known as the War Book Committee, both of which were created in 1912. In addition a large number of ad hoc sub-committees were formed to deliberate and report on special issues as they arose. The reports produced by those bodies were usually incorporated in one or other of the series of memoranda already described. In 1909 and again in 1911 Imperial Conferences took place in London with representatives of all the self-governing Dominions present, and it fell to the C.I.D. to prepare the agenda for them and to record the decisions reached.

During World War I the C.I.D. was in effect placed in a state of suspension, and its functions were successively assumed by the War Council (formed in November 1914), the Dardanelles Committee (June to October 1915), the War Committee (November 1915 to November 1916) and the War Cabinet from December 1916. The business of those bodies continued, however, to be organised by Hankey, who was secretary to all of them, on the system established for the C.I.D.—that is to say with numbered minutes and consecutive memoranda. Between 1914 and 1918 a large number of new sub-committees was formed, such as the committees on Turkey, on War Policy, the Joint War Air Committee etc. etc.; and most of them were given their own serial numbers of minutes and memoranda with self-evident abbreviated titles. For example the Joint War Air Committee's minutes were numbered J.W.A.C. 1, 2 etc., and its memoranda Air 1, 2 and so on.

During the first years of peace the C.I.D. did not meet as such and its business was conducted by the Standing Defence Sub-Committee, which was served by the normal C.I.D. secretariat. In 1922, however, the government reverted to the earlier system, and the C.I.D. once again became the advisory body of the Cabinet on all defence matters. In the period between the wars many new sub-committees were formed, some of them permanent (such as the Chiefs of Staff Sub-Committee of 1923) and some of them *ad hoc*. Their Minutes and Memoranda were also given self-evident letters, such as C.O.S. for the Chiefs of Staff Sub-Committee, and were numbered consecutively in accordance with the well-tried earlier system.

When the C.I.D. secretariat was established in 1904 two Assistant Secretaries (one military and one naval) were appointed. By the time Hankey became Secretary in 1912 three more assistants had been added. One of the three could be either military or naval, one was nominated by the Secretary of State for the Colonies as secretary of the Overseas Defence Sub-Committee, and the third was nominated by the Secretary of State for India to handle the problems concerned wholly or mainly with the defence of the sub-continent. The secretary, whose appointment was made by the Prime Minister for a period of five years, received a salary of £1,500–£2,000 per annum depending on his age and seniority, and the post was described as "without claim to pension". Hankey was initially paid on the lowest scale for the post.

During World War I the secretariat expanded greatly. Some of the new recruits were navy or army officers, mostly on the Retired Lists of their services, while others were civilians chosen for their special knowledge of some important subject or theatre of war. After World War I the number of assistant secretaries on the "military side" of the Cabinet Secretariat was stabilised at three, one drawn from each fighting service, and all of them were on the Active Lists of their services. Hankey always insisted that in peace time his "military" assistants should be serving officers, because he held that the service departments were thereby kept in proper touch with defence planning and co-ordination on the highest level, and were thus provided with a nucleus of officers experienced in the conduct of such business. The departments agreed with this principle, and always offered Hankey officers of middle rank (Commander R.N. or equivalent) whose abilities held promise that they would reach high command.[1]

Such, then, in brief outline, was the system whereby defence policy was deliberated, formulated and recorded, of which Hankey was the chief executive from 1912 to 1938.[2]

Hankey has stated that when he joined the C.I.D. secretariat the fortunes of the Committee, though on the turn, were at rather a low ebb[3]; and it is a fact that in 1908 only two meetings took place and no more than nine papers reached the Committee. Three years later the number of meetings was eight and the number of papers submitted totalled 50.[4] The period of quiescence arose chiefly from the hostility of Admiral Fisher, who was virtually boycotting the committee, and the retirement of Balfour, who had been one of its strongest supporters. The quiet interlude did, however, give Hankey the chance entirely to recuperate from the strains and stresses of the preceding years which, as we saw earlier, had brought him to the verge of a breakdown. He also seized the opportunity to take some parts of the promotion

[1]See Appendix B.
[2]For more detailed information on the records of the C.I.D. and its secretarial system see the Introduction to *List of Papers of the Committee of Imperial Defence 1914* (H.M.S.O., 1964). For the Cabinet records of World War I see the Introduction to *List of Cabinet Papers 1915 and 1916* (H.M.S.O., 1966).
[3]*Supreme Command* I, p. 52.
[4]*List of Papers of the Committee of Imperial Defence* (H.M.S.O., 1964).

examination for Major's rank, and passed in certain subjects in November 1905 and in March 1909[1]; but he seems never to have completed the examinations, and he certainly never held the rank of major except in an acting capacity while with the Owen Committee. After six comparatively easy months Hankey turned his mind to the problems which in his opinion needed investigation by the C.I.D., and by a process which might be described as the skilled application of Professor Northcote Parkinson's famous "Law",[2] he soon found plenty of work. We will glance briefly at the more important problems investigated between 1909 and 1912.

Shortly before Hankey joined the C.I.D. secretariat a strong subcommittee under Morley[3] had reported on "the Military Requirements of the Empire as affected by the defence of India"[4]; that enquiry was immediately followed by one, also under Morley, into the defence of Egypt and the Sudan. This was concluded in March 1909.[5] The outcome of those two enquiries was that the reorganisation of the Army, which had been initiated by Lord Esher's[6] Committee of 1903-4 and implemented during Haldane's tenure of office as Secretary of State for War,[7] was based on the provision of an expeditionary force of six infantry and one cavalry division, plus a territorial force of 14 infantry divisions and a like number of yeomanry brigades for home defence.

Meanwhile Field-Marshal Lord Roberts,[8] the influential and much respected veteran of the South African war, had been conducting a

---

[1]Record of Hankey's service preserved in R.M. Office, Ministry of Defence.
[2]"Work expands so as to fill the time available for its completion". C. N. Parkinson, *Parkinson's Law or the Pursuit of Progress* (Murray, 1958) p. 4.
[3]John Morley (1838–1923). Viscount 1908. Politician (Lib.) and man of letters. Chief Secretary for Ireland 1892–5; Secretary of State for India 1905–10. Resigned from Asquith's cabinet on decision to enter the European war 1914.
[4]C.I.D. 98D of 1st May and 98th Meeting of C.I.D. on 30th May 1907. Cab. 38/13/20 and 22.
[5]C.I.D. 107B of 11th March and 102nd Meeting on 29th June 1909. Cab. 38/15/5 and 12.
[6]Reginald Baliol Brett, 2nd Viscount Esher (1852–1930). Chairman of War Office Reconstruction Committee 1903–4; member of C.I.D. 1904.
[7]Richard Burdon Haldane, Viscount 1911. Politician (Lib., from 1924 Lab.) (1856–1928); Secretary of State for War 1905–12; Lord Chancellor 1912–15 and again 1924.
[8]1st Earl Roberts 1900 (1832–1914). C-in-C, India, 1885–93 and Ireland 1895–9. Appointed Supreme Commander in South Africa 1899. Field-Marshal 1895. President National Service League 1905.

campaign in favour of "Universal Training"—in other words conscription; and in November 1905 his proposals came before the C.I.D.[1]
Conscription held little appeal to the Liberal governments of Campbell-
Bannerman and Asquith, whose long term of office began at the end of
that year. But the campaign in favour of it spotlighted one of the two
fundamental cleavages between the Admiralty and the War Office—
namely the likelihood of successful invasion of the British Isles in the
event of war with Germany. The other dispute concerned the despatch
of an expeditionary force to the continent. The Admiralty (or "Blue
Water School") view, which was strongly supported by Fisher and
Hankey, was that as long as the navy held command of the sea in home
waters invasion was not a practical operation of war, though raids in
some force might take place. The War Office (or "Bolt from the Blue")
school held that the fleet might be lured away for a sufficient time to
enable a surprise crossing to be carried out by an invasion army. In
November 1909 Asquith, now Prime Minister, accordingly set up a sub-
committee, which was in fact virtually the full C.I.D. under his own
chairmanship, to investigate the issue, and in its report the sub-
committee came down heavily in favour of the Admiralty.[2] In Hankey's
papers there is a long manuscript memorandum setting out his views
on "Compulsory Service". It is undated but a reference in it to Lord
Roberts's speech of 23rd November in the House of Lords[3] enables us
to be confident that it was written at the end of 1908. The supporters of
compulsory service included Lord Milner,[4] Lord Cromer,[5] Mr.
L. C. M. S. Amery[6] and Colonel Charles à Court Repington,[7] the able

[1]C.I.D. 33A of 3rd Nov. 1905. Cab. 38/10/78 and 82.
[2]C.I.D. 44A of 22nd Oct. 1908. Cab. 38/14/11. The committee's conclusions are
quoted in *Supreme Command*, I, p. 68.
[3]Parl. Deb. Lords, Vol. 196, Cols. 1679–1743. Lord Roberts moved to strengthen
the army so that "the most formidable foreign nation would hesitate to attempt a
landing on these shores", and spoke in alarmist terms of the German threat. The
motion was carried by 74–32.
[4]1st Viscount Milner 1902 (1854–1925). High Commissioner for South Africa
1897–1905. Minister without Portfolio in War Cabinet 1916–18. Secretary of State
for War 1918–19 and for Colonies 1919–21.
[5]Evelyn Baring, 1st Earl of Cromer 1901 (1841–1917). Agent and Consul-General
in Egypt 1883–1907. Chairman, Dardanelles Commission, 1916.
[6]1873–1955. Politician (Cons.). Assistant Secretary, War Cabinet 1917. First Lord
of Admiralty 1922–24. Secretary of State for Colonies 1924–29, for Dominions
1925–29 and for India 1940–45.
[7]1858–1925. Military Correspondent of *Morning Post*, then of *The Times* 1904–18.

if none too scrupulous military correspondent of *The Times*. According to Hankey their claims were that, firstly, compulsory service was "indispensable in order to safeguard the country against invasion"; secondly that "it would improve the physique, discipline and morale of the whole nation"; and lastly that "it would be economical". Hankey proceeded to demolish all three arguments with relentless logic tinged with a good deal of irony. The paper was probably not circulated because by the time it was ready the case against conscription had been won. Its interest lies in the fact that it is the first paper on a major national issue which we know to have come from Hankey's pen.

The resolution of the invasion dispute did not of course produce agreement over the expeditionary force, and a new sub-committee, once again under the Prime Minister, was set up to review what was still called, a little oddly, "The Military needs of the Empire"— excluding Egypt and India which had already been investigated. That report was considered on 24th July 1909,[1] and although the C.I.D. decided that "the expediency of sending a military force abroad, or of relying on naval means only, is a matter of policy which can only be determined . . . by the government of the day", they also expressed the view that "the plan to which reference is given by the General Staff is a valuable one", and "all the necessary details" were therefore to be worked out. This was a severe blow to those who, like Fisher and Hankey, considered that the proper use of our military force was to exploit British sea power by striking unexpectedly in overseas theatres of our own choice.

The disagreements over invasion and over the expeditionary force had at least one beneficial effect in high-lighting the virtually complete absence of joint planning between the Admiralty and the War Office— for which Admiral Fisher must carry a large share of the blame. As long ago as July 1905 Balfour had proposed that the C.I.D. should study combined naval and military operations; but nothing had come of it by the time that the Conservative government fell in the following December. A small group of officers of both services did, however, then start to meet in Whitehall Gardens to discuss the subject inform-ally; but Fisher's mistrust of any continental commitment was so obsessive that he withdrew the naval representative and boycotted the sub-committee. Had Balfour's promising opening been followed up,

[1] C.I.D. 109B of 24th July 1909 and 103rd Meeting held same day. Cab. 38/15/15 and /14 respectively.

and the army and navy been forced into proper collaboration over combined operations—as Hankey fervently desired—the story of Gallipoli might well have been totally different, and World War I might now be less remembered for the appalling carnage produced by trench warfare on the western front.

While the invasion and expeditionary force disagreements were still in progress the long-smouldered quarrel between Fisher and Beresford was fanned into a blaze by the latter sending Asquith a letter (dated 2nd April 1909) setting out in full his complaints against the Fisher régime.[1]

Asquith at once appointed a sub-committee of the C.I.D. under his own chairmanship to investigate the charges.[2] We need not here deal with the details of the controversy. Suffice it to say that the proceedings of the sub-committee cover 328 folio pages of print and 245 pages of Appendices, and on the main issues Beresford showed up very badly under Asquith's penetrating examination. Rarely, if ever, can two obstinate and choleric admirals have wasted so much ministerial time. Hankey appears only twice in the transcript of evidence. To a question by Beresford asking whether he had been on a committee about cruisers some 18 months previously he replied in the negative; and to another asking whether he had been present when Beresford had sought some information from the Naval Intelligence Department he replied "No, Sir".[3] Plainly he was maintaining an attitude of strict neutrality. Indeed he himself has described the way in which both protagonists sought his advice, and the lengths to which he went to avoid a confrontation between them in his office.[4] Beresford's accusation about the lack of war plans was easily and triumphantly refuted by Fisher, who produced the documents drafted by the Ballard Committee, of which Hankey had been a member, some two years earlier.[5] But Fisher's obsession with secrecy was so great that the C.I.D. had up to that time been totally unaware of their existence. The sub-committee reported on 12th August 1909 and vindicated the McKenna-Fisher régime at the Admiralty except in two respects. These concerned the failure to take Beresford, as a C-in-C, fully into their confidence, and the lack of a properly organised Naval Staff analogous to that introduced

[1]See Geoffrey Bennett, *Charlie B.* (Peter Dawnay, 1968) pp. 299–306 for a full account.
[2]Cab. 16/9A. The other members were Lord Crewe, Lord Morley, Sir Edward Grey and Mr. Haldane.
[3]*ibid.* pp. 256 and 324. Questions 2262 and 2672 respectively.
[4]*Supreme Command*, I, pp. 71–4.[5]See p. 79.

in the War Office by Haldane. We will return to that subject shortly.

Almost immediately after the conclusion of the Fisher-Beresford enquiry Ottley and Hankey embarked in the Admiralty yacht *Enchantress* for a short cruise in the Irish Sea and Bristol Channel. The party consisted of Reginald McKenna,[1] the First Lord, and his wife, Vincent Baddeley,[2] the private secretary to McKenna and a Mr. Benn whom Hankey described as "the parliamentary secretary".[3] The ostensible purpose of the trip was to inspect the defences of certain west coast ports, but according to Hankey this was camouflage and the real purpose was "because he [McKenna] wanted unbiassed advice on certain questions" from Ottley and himself. Tantalisingly he gives no indication of what those questions were; but it is surely probable that the Admiralty's future attitude to the despatch of the expeditionary force was one of them. McKenna may also have put out feelers about who should replace Fisher as First Sea Lord, since his retirement obviously could not be long deferred.

McKenna undoubtedly considered appointing Admiral Sir William May, who was at the time in command of the Home Fleet, to the office of First Sea Lord; and he gave May the impression that he was to receive the appointment.[4] But his final choice was Sir Arthur K. Wilson,[5] who had been a member of the C.I.D. since April 1909 and had kept aloof from the Fisher-Beresford controversy. The change was announced on 2nd December 1909 and became effective on the following 25th January. It quickly became apparent that McKenna's choice was not a happy one.[6] In particular Wilson, like Fisher before him,

[1] 1863–1943. Politician (Lib.) and banker. President, Board of Education 1907–8 First Lord of Admiralty 1908–11. Home Secretary 1911–15. Chancellor of Exchequer 1915–16. Chairman, Midland Bank from 1919.

[2] Later Sir Vincent Baddeley (1874–1961). Private Secretary to First Lords of the Admiralty 1901–11. Deputy Secretary of Admiralty 1931–5.

[3] Presumably William Wedgwood Benn, 1st Viscount Stansgate 1941 (1877–1960). Politician (Lib., then Lab. from 1927). A Junior Lord of Treasury 1910–15. Secretary of State for India 1929–31 and for Air 1945–6.

[4] *The Life of a Sailor, Memoirs of Admiral of the Fleet Sir William May* pp. 90–1. Privately printed. Copy in N.M.M.

[5] 1842–1921. Comptroller of Navy 1897–1901. Commanded Channel Squadron 1901–3. C-in-C, Home and Channel Fleets 1903–7. 1st Sea Lord 1909–12. Awarded V.C. for great gallantry at second battle of El Teb 1884. Admiral of the Fleet 1907.

[6] See A. J. Marder, *From the Dreadnought to Scapa Flow*, Vol. I (Oxford U.P., 1961) pp. 211–14 regarding Wilson's character and the consequences of his appointment as First Sea Lord. This source is henceforth cited as Marder, *Scapa Flow*.

absolutely refused to accept a properly organised Naval Staff—despite the strong recommendation in favour of it contained in the report on the Beresford enquiry.

Hankey's experience at sea and in Whitehall had convinced him that a naval staff was essential, and he took the matter up very soon after joining the C.I.D. secretariat. His first step was to send to his former Captain, R. S. Lowry, now in charge of the Naval War College at Portsmouth, a memorandum on the organisation of a staff. Lowry however proved dilatory—perhaps because he knew that the whole concept was anathema to Fisher. On 24th November 1908 he wrote to Hankey apologising for the delay in dealing with his paper and telling him that he had sent it on to Fisher—which was not likely to further Hankey's purpose. Three days later Lowry wrote again to Hankey saying that Fisher thanked him for the paper "and will give full consideration to it".[1] During the next year no progress whatever was made; but Hankey continued to work behind the scenes. He apparently gave Graham Greene,[2] the assistant secretary of the Admiralty, his proposals, and in May 1909 he talked the matter over with McKenna and sent him a memorandum entitled "The organization of a Naval War Staff".[3] Then he went to see Fisher about the scheme he had drafted; and he claims that "gradually I persuaded him".[4] That statement, however, requires qualification, since Hankey's copy of the memorandum is heavily amended in his own hand, and the annotations show that Fisher amended and emasculated it drastically. Furthermore another paper by Hankey, entitled "Training of Officers for the War Staff of the Navy at the War College" is endorsed, again in his hand, "Admiral Fisher contemplated the issue of this as a circular to the Fleet, but did not send it as his tenancy of the post of First Sea Lord was just expiring". An undated scrawl by Fisher gives us the clue to what actually happened. "Dear Hankey", he wrote, "First Lord has sent duplicate of enclosed to Esher (as well as your original) and this is an idea of what First Lord will (after Beresford has gone) put before Committee [i.e. C.I.D.]. Please return with any improvements or alterations you can suggest. Kindly show to Ottley if it won't incriminate him. J.F." The enclosure was the emasculated version of Hankey's original scheme for

[1]Lowry to Hankey 24th and 27th Nov. 1908.
[2]Sir William Graham Greene (1857–1950). Assistant Secretary of the Admiralty 1907 and Permanent Secretary 1911–17. Secretary, Ministry of Munitions 1917–20.
[3]Hankey to McKenna 27th May 1909. [4]*Supreme Command*, I, pp. 73–4.

a naval staff. Thus what Fisher actually, and reluctantly, accepted in principle was a good deal less than what Hankey had wanted to see adopted. Moreover little or nothing was done to implement it either during the last six months of Fisher's time as First Sea Lord or under his successor A. K. Wilson.

Hankey took no further action in the matter of a naval staff until Churchill became First Lord in October 1911—probably because he realised that it was hopeless to do so earlier. Then he took the matter up again promptly. On 13th November 1911 Esher, who, as we have seen, knew all about Hankey's proposals of 1908, wrote at length to Churchill on the subject. He sent a copy to Hankey inscribed "Very Secret. For you and Sir Charles [Ottley] to see". Churchill however needed no convincing, and on 1st January 1912 he made a public pronouncement on the subject. With typical grandiloquence he announced that a "Naval War Staff" was to be created, and that "It is to be the means of sifting, developing, and applying the results of history and experiment, and of preserving them as a general stock of reasoned opinion available as an aid and as a guide for all who are called upon to determine, in peace or war, the naval policy of the country".[1] But good intentions do not always produce the desired result, and in fact the so-called Naval War Staff which Churchill conjured into existence was not organised, manned or employed as a staff should be until the end of 1917—nearly a decade after such an organisation had been adopted in the War Office. The results were as baleful during the period which preceded the outbreak of World War I as they proved during that conflict. The pity of it is that Hankey's proposals both for the organisation of a staff and for the training of the officers needed to man it were not accepted *in toto* when he first put them forward. Even Beresford, whose complaints against senior officers of his own service were not by any means always well founded, was on firm ground when in April 1915 he told Asquith that "Although this institution [a naval staff] was strongly recommended by the Committee [of Imperial Defence in August 1909] it was not formed until two years and four months afterwards, a delay which I hold to have been the cause of many avoidable losses in the present war".[2]

---

[1]Reproduced as Appendix to *Statement of the First Lord explanatory of the Navy Estimates, 1912-13.* Cd. 6106.
[2]Beresford to Asquith 15th April 1915. Copy in Kitchener Papers P.R.O. 30/57/72.

On 1st July 1911 the arrival of the German gunboat *Panther* at Agadir in Morocco touched off a first class international crisis, and during the succeeding months the possibility of war with Germany was very real. Interesting light is thrown on Germany's arrogance at this time of tension by a much later entry in Hankey's diary. This records that Lloyd George told him that Count Metternich,[1] the German ambassador, demanded from Sir Edward Grey,[2] the Foreign Secretary, that he (Lloyd George) should be "turned out of the Government", and "Grey at once replied that, if this was his request, the conversation must end".[3]

On 23rd August Asquith called a special meeting of the C.I.D. to consider "Action to be taken in the event of Intervention in a European War" and other matters concerned with the same subject. Hankey realised early on that this would bring to a head the disagreement between the War Office and Admiralty over the despatch of an expeditionary force to the Continent. Accordingly on 15th August he sent a long and cautiously worded letter on the subject to McKenna. "As Admiralty representative on this secretariat", he wrote, "I think I am not exceeding my duty in drawing your attention to the attitude which the Admiralty adopted towards this question when the general policy was discussed in 1909". Obviously he was as yet by no means confident of the propriety of a direct approach to a Minister. After quoting the conclusions reached in the 1909 investigation,[4] he warned McKenna that the War Office was pressing for a decision over the expeditionary force, and that with Esher and Fisher both abroad the Admiralty must look to its laurels. "It is of course notorious that the D.M.O. [Director of Military Operations], General Wilson,[5] who has brought this question to the front", Hankey continued, "has a perfect obsession for military operations on the continent . . . He holds the view, not only that military action is indispensable in order to preserve

[1]Graf Paul Wolff-Metternich zur Gracht (1853–1934). Ambassador to Great Britain 1901–11. Recalled to Germany shortly after the Agadir crisis.
[2]1st Viscount Grey of Fallodon 1916 (1862–1933). Politician (Lib.). Parliamentary Under-Secretary, Foreign Office 1892–5. Foreign Secretary 1905–16. President, League of Nations Union from 1918. Chancellor of Oxford University 1928–33.
[3]Diary 27th August 1918.   [4]See p. 96.
[5]General Sir Henry H. Wilson (1864–1922). Director of Military Operations 1910–14; chief liaison officer at French H.Q.s 1915; C-in-C, Eastern Command 1917; Chief of Imperial General Staff 1918–22. Field-Marshal 1919. Assassinated in London by Sinn Feiners.

the balance of power in Europe, but that we require a conscript army for the purpose. If he can get a decision at this juncture in favour of military action he will endeavour to commit us up to the hilt; and in a few months' time he will prove that with our existing forces we could not have rendered France proper assistance, and will seek to show that without conscription we cannot fulfil our obligations". He went on to suggest that the Admiralty could either "very properly decline before war [breaks out] to say how long it will be before the transport of troops will be feasible; or else they can stick to the line they took in 1908 that the policy of sending an expedition is altogether a wrong one".

Hankey's warnings, and his suggestions, both went unheeded. At the C.I.D. meeting General Wilson gave a polished and expert explanation of the War Office's proposals, to which his Admiralty namesake Admiral A. K. Wilson could only reply with a halting, ill-prepared and utterly unconvincing statement about the merits of a predominantly maritime strategy.[1] Hankey evidently listened to this display of ineptitude with chagrin and apprehension. He was "reluctantly driven to admit that the Senior Service on this occasion had sustained a severe defeat".[2] Churchill was also disturbed by the incompetent display of the Admiralty's representative, and expressed himself strongly on the subject to Lloyd George. "I cannot help feeling uncomfortable about the Admiralty", he wrote. "They are so cocksure, *insouciant* and apathetic . . . I cannot feel much confidence in Wilson's sagacity after his performance the other day".[3] After making full allowance for Churchill's ambition to displace McKenna at the Admiralty there remains a solid foundation for his misgivings.

Despite the failure of the Admiralty to convince the C.I.D. regarding the merits of a maritime strategy Hankey did not throw in the sponge. In November, after the Morocco crisis was over, he wrote a long memorandum setting out cogently the case against committing the six divisions of the expeditionary force to a campaign in which the two chief continental contestants, France and Germany, were able to put ten to twelve times that number of troops in the field. He argued that Britain would thereby sacrifice the possibility of joint military and naval action, such as to seize a base in the Friesian islands or take the offensive in more remote theatres. "If the French army were beaten", he con-

[1] 114th C.I.D. meeting. Cab. 38/19/49.   [2] *Supreme Command*, I, pp. 81–2.
[3] Churchill to Lloyd George 14th Sept. 1911. Lloyd George papers C/3/15/12. See also same to same 5th Sept. *ibid.* C/3/15/9.

cluded, "it is conceivable that a diversion comparable with Moore's raid and retreat to Corunna [Dec. 1808–Jan. 1809] might be useful in order to draw off a portion of the enemy and give France time to recuperate her energies. Or it might be necessary to support the Belgian army . . . or to assist the Danish army in the event of Germany endeavouring to seize the gates of the Baltic. . . . But if the army has been committed to the centre of the campaign at the outset of war, all possibility of influencing the course of the war in one of the manners suggested—a manner which sea power alone can render possible—disappears, and the great advantage of sea power is to a great extent thrown away". The conclusion is inescapable that if Hankey had been able to state the Admiralty's case on 23rd August Henry Wilson would not have enjoyed what amounted to a walk-over.

Thus was Britain committed to full participation in a continental campaign if war should break out with Germany. Speculation on the might-have-beens of history is rarely a profitable indulgence, but it is difficult not to feel that *had* a proper Naval Staff been brought into being in 1908, and *had* Fisher and A. K. Wilson not been so obsessively blind to the need for such a staff, and *had* the Admiralty and War Office been forced by the government to plan the combined operations which Hankey had so long favoured the whole course of the conflict of 1914–18 would have been different.[1] As it was the government merely set up a joint Navy-Army committee, colloquially known as "the High Level Bridge", to co-ordinate the work of the two departments; and Hankey himself recalled many years later that this substitute for a proper joint planning organisation proved "rather a futile body".[2]

The government's desire to put a term to the inter-service quarrel over strategy also contributed to the decision that McKenna and Churchill should exchange offices in October 1911; for Churchill's military outlook and experience made him far more amenable than McKenna to the War Office's strategic view. There is irony in the fact that under the impact of war Churchill quickly became an ardent advocate for the employment of sea power to wage the "warfare on the littoral" whose merits Hankey had argued ever since his first commission in the Mediterranean, but which the Cabinet had rejected in 1911.

[1]This is certainly the view of perhaps the most brilliant military historian and analyst of the 20th century, Captain Sir Basil Liddell Hart. See his *History of the World War 1914–18* (Faber, 1934). Henceforth cited as *Liddell Hart*.
[2]Letter to Viscount Trenchard, 5th Feb. 1954.

Hankey's long and sometimes tempestuous relations with Churchill lend special interest to his early impressions of the new First Lord. In March 1912 he wrote to Fisher ". . . Churchill's estimates speeches [i.e. on introducing the 1912–13 Navy Estimates] have made a profound impression in the country. He is a really great man, but I expect he got his inspiration from you. He is far more brilliant than McKenna, but probably has not such solid qualities. A bit impetuous, but extraordinarily hard working."[1] The experiences of the next half century were to justify that assessment very precisely.

Shortly before Hankey joined the C.I.D. secretariat the service departments had first become aware of the fact that developments in aeronautics were likely to exert profound influence on warfare, and that Britain was falling far behind Germany, France and Italy in the production and employment of both lighter- and heavier-than-air craft. Accordingly in October 1908 Asquith appointed a sub-committee of the C.I.D. under Esher to investigate and report on what was then called, rather quaintly, "aerial navigation". That body reported early in the following year and recommended the construction of a rigid airship, which was to be a charge on the Navy Estimates.[2] In April 1909 the French government proposed that an international conference on aerial navigation should be held in Paris, and preliminary discussions regarding the agenda took place in London. The Foreign Office, believing apparently that the only matters to be considered in Paris were questions such as "the rule of the road" for aircraft, took no part in the preliminary discussions. The result was that the British delegation to the Paris conference, which was led by Admiral Sir Douglas Gamble,[3] was taken by surprise when the German delegates made it clear that they intended to raise far wider issues, including those concerned with aircraft flying over another nation's territories. In June the Standing Sub-Committee of the C.I.D. considered the matter at the urgent instigation of Churchill,[4] and on 20th Hankey wrote to his wife "I had to attend a conference at the House of Commons under Churchill

[1]Hankey to Fisher 24th March 1912. Lennoxlove papers.
[2]C.I.D. 106B of 28th Jan. 1909. Cab. 38/15/3.
[3]1856–1934. Naval adviser to Turkish government 1909–10. Commanded 4th Battle Squadron 1914. Retired 1917. Adviser to Admiralty on the official histories of World War I.
[4]Minutes of Standing Defence Sub-Committee meeting held on 25th June 1910. Cab. 38/19/60.

to discuss a question referred by our delegates at an International
Convention at Paris, as the result of which it was decided to send me
to Paris with a letter and with further verbal explanations . . .". Though
the letter in question has not survived it must have contained instructions to the British delegates to reject outright the German proposals.
The result was that the conference was adjourned *sine die*—a polite
fiction designed to obscure the fact that it had broken down. To us the
incident has special interest since it was the first occasion when Hankey
acted as the official emissary of the British Cabinet.

In July 1910 the General Staff raised to the C.I.D. the general
implications of what they called "the perhaps unwelcome progress of
aerial navigation", and Asquith promptly directed the Standing Sub-
Committee to report on the matter. This led to Esher putting forward
firm proposals for the formation of a corps of aviators and the development of aeronautics,[1] and so to the formation of the Royal Flying
Corps, with Naval and Military Wings, in April 1912. At the same time
an Air Committee was set up as a permanent sub-committee of the
C.I.D.[2] As Hankey became its first, and indeed its only secretary he was
involved in the military and naval implications of aviation from the very
beginning. Progress however remained painfully slow, chiefly because
of the conservatism of the service departments, until Churchill became
First Lord and at once showed a lively interest in the new developments.

The second Hague conference had been convened in 1907 chiefly in
the hope of calling a halt to the naval race between Britain and Germany. Immediately it came to an end, with very little accomplished,
the British government called a conference in London to review the
old and thorny problem of contraband of war. Severe restriction, let
alone abolition, of contraband struck right at the heart of the exercise
of sea power through blockade and economic pressure—to which
Germany was, as Hankey had long realised, extremely vulnerable. The
resulting Declaration of London, which carried still further the
emasculation of "Belligerent Rights" initiated by the Declaration of
Paris of 1856, therefore aroused his strong apprehensions. Despite the
fact that Ottley, his chief, had been one of the British delegates to the
London Conference Hankey did not hesitate to oppose the proposals
to which it had given birth. In a memorandum to Ottley written in

[1]C.I.D. 119B of 6th Oct. 1910. Cab. 38/16/18.
[2]116th Meeting of C.I.D. on 25th April 1912. Cab. 38/20/9.

February 1911 he set out the whole case against the Declaration of London. As he has told at length the story of how that document, which he has castigated as Britain's "crowning folly", came to be accepted as a political measure by the Liberal majority in the House of Commons there is no need to recapitulate his account here.[1] Suffice it to say that the House of Lords threw out the Declaration; yet on the outbreak of war the British government announced its intention of adhering to its terms. Not until two years later were the self-imposed shackles dropped, and a rigorous blockade of Germany established. To us the most interesting aspect of Hankey's outspoken campaign against the Declaration of London is that he not only conducted it in such a manner as to retain Ottley's friendship, but it evidently caused no loss of confidence in him among the members of the Cabinet. At any rate Asquith, on Haldane's recommendation, appointed Hankey secretary of the C.I.D. almost exactly a year after he had circulated papers condemning in forthright terms the policy which the same Cabinet ministers had approved.

In 1910–11, more or less simultaneously with his campaign against the Declaration of London, Hankey was also taking a big hand in the preparation of the agenda for the 1911 Imperial Conference. Thus in July 1910 he circulated to the C.I.D. a "Memorandum on the Officering of the Navies of the Dominions".[2] While he regretfully accepted that the concept of a single Imperial Navy had been decisively rejected by Australia and Canada, he urged very strongly that the officers of the British and Dominion navies should be educated and trained on a common system, and should be regarded as fully interchangeable. This proposal was in fact widely adopted, and as late as World War II "Imperial" officers (as those of the Royal Navy were called in the Dominions) served in Dominion warships as regularly as Dominion officers served in those of the Royal Navy. In May 1911 Hankey provided Asquith with the trade statistics he would need to support his opening statement to the Imperial Conference, and also drafted for McKenna a long paper on the principles of Imperial defence for use when naval matters came to be discussed.

The conference opened on 26th May with Ottley and Hankey acting as secretaries.[3] All went smoothly until naval defence was reached at the

---

[1] *Supreme Command*, I, pp. 66 and 94–101.   [2] Cab. 38/16/14.
[3] 111th Meeting of C.I.D. Cab. 38/18/43.

second meeting on 29th, when McKenna and Sir Wilfred Laurier,[1] the Prime Minister of Canada, engaged in a verbal duel over what happened to Canadian warships if Britain were at war and Canada at peace. Laurier insisted that only the Canadian Parliament could bring his country into a war, and took "very strong exception" to the C.I.D.'s proposal that "In time of war the Admiralty of the United Kingdom will control the whole of the King's Navy".[2] Asquith finally had to adjourn the meeting while the offending paragraph was redrafted, and next day it reappeared in a form acceptable to all the Dominions— though Laurier went on record that "All the nations of Europe today, in my humble opinion, have gone if I may say so, mad"! No doubt Hankey stored away in his memory, for use at future Imperial Conferences, the lessons on Dominion sensitivity regarding any measure which could be held to infringe their sovereign independence.

Of all the preparations for war in which Hankey had a hand between 1908 and 1912 the most important and fruitful probably was the institution of what became known as the Government War Book, and its offshoots the departmental War Books. These ultimately set out in full detail every step that had to be taken both by the central government and by individual departments should a period of strained relations result in the adoption of what was called the "Precautionary Stage", and in the event of war being declared. The basic idea seems to have derived from the Admiralty, since after World War I Hankey wrote to Sir William Graham Greene "It is true that I owe a great deal to my experience at the Admiralty. I got the idea of the War Book, which is the best thing I have done, from your 'W' List, which I believe was largely your child".[3]

In the C.I.D. the story of the War Book appears to begin with a paper from the General Staff in February 1910 entitled "Questions Requiring Inter-Departmental consideration".[4] In effect the General Staff complained of the complete lack of departmental co-operation. In the following November Hankey wrote a paper on the kindred subject

[1] 1841–1929. Canadian lawyer and politician (Lib.). Leader of Liberal Party 1891. Prime Minister of Canada 1896–1911, and the first French Canadian to hold that office.
[2] C.I.D. 82C para. 5 and 112th Meeting. Cab. 38/18/41.
[3] Hankey to Graham Greene 14th August 1919 and 24th January 1923. Graham Greene papers, N.M.M. GEE/13D.
[4] C.I.D. 114B of 22nd Feb. 1910. Cab. 38/16/4.

of "Co-ordination of Departmental Action on the outbreak of War", which the C.I.D. took at its next meeting.[1] In January 1911 the whole issue was placed in the hands of the Standing Sub-Committee under the chairmanship of Sir Arthur Nicolson, the Under-Secretary of State for Foreign Affairs,[2] and in the following December Lord Esher proposed that it should become a permanent sub-committee of the C.I.D.[3] However the correspondence which passed between Esher and Hankey in late 1911 and early 1912 appears to indicate that it was in fact Hankey who initiated this proposal.[4] Be that as it may the "War Book Committee', as this body was generally known, was now placed on a very firm footing, and its first report, which consisted of a printed proof of the War Book and showed the action to be taken by nine departments, was approved in April 1912.[5] In December the Colonial Office was given a memorandum on the subject so that the self-governing Dominions could adopt a parallel system, and in August 1913 the C.I.D. approved the War Book Committee's second report.[6] Finally a progress report was submitted in July 1914—three weeks before the outbreak of war.[7]

Hankey himself has described at some length the processes whereby the War Book Committee came into being, and also the contribution which it made to the state of readiness of the Empire in August 1914. He attributes much of the credit to two assistant secretaries of the C.I.D.—Majors A. Grant Duff and J. A. Longridge—who carried out most of the enormously detailed work.[8] But one may doubt whether, but for Hankey's persistence and vision, the War Book would ever have come into existence.

Up to the time when Fisher's resignation from the Admiralty took

[1]C.I.D. 121B of 4th Nov. 1910. Cab. 38/16/21.
[2]1849–1928. 1st Baron Carnock 1916. Ambassador at St. Petersburg 1906; Under-Secretary of State for Foreign Affairs 1910–16.
[3]Memo. of 12th Dec. 1911. Cab. 38/19/57.
[4]Esher to Hankey 31st Dec. 1911 and 10th April 1912.
[5]C.I.D. W1. Approved at 116th Meeting of C.I.D., Item 2, on 25th April 1912. Cab. 38/20/9.
[6]C.I.D. W2. Approved at 124th Meeting of C.I.D., Item 2, on 5th Aug. 1913. Cab. 38/24/33.
[7]C.I.D. W3. Approved at 128th Meeting of C.I.D., Item 8, on 14th July 1914. Cab. 38/28/35.
[8]Supreme Command, I, pp. 117–23. Both these close associates of Hankey were killed in action, Grant Duff in the Battle of the Aisne 12th September 1914 and Longridge in the Battle of the Somme 18th August 1916.

effect in January 1910 Hankey does not seem to have been on intimate terms with the redoubtable old Admiral. But Fisher was determined to get back to the Admiralty—especially if war should break out; and as he was extremely well versed in the gentle arts of intrigue and lobbying he probably decided that Hankey would be a useful ally. At any rate on 15th April he wrote to invite Hankey to join "a small batchelor's party [sic]" at Kilverstone. That letter started a correspondence which was to last almost to the day of Fisher's death in 1920, and which rapidly developed in intimacy—and in indiscretion. By the beginning of 1911 Fisher's usual mode of address had warmed to "My beloved Hankey", and he was energetically canvassing his claims to succeed Ottley as Secretary of the C.I.D. with Esher, McKenna (through his wife), Churchill and other politicians or ministers. In return he obviously expected to be kept *au courant* with the discussions then in progress in the C.I.D., of which he remained a member. Nor was Hankey in any way reluctant to meet the old Admiral's wishes.

Hankey to Fisher. 2 Whitehall Gardens. 26th January 1911[1]
I should certainly have written yesterday to wish you many happy returns of the day had it not been that I had hoped to see you at the Defence Committee this morning. As however you did not come I am writing to make good the omission. I see from the papers that you are theoretically retired now, but we do not attach the slightest importance to that.[2] If there were a war you would not remain long in retirement, for your country would at once call upon you —like Cincinnatus—to come up to town and run the war. This is the main reason for your continuing to be a member of the Defence Committee. And in peace also, whenever great controversial questions connected with defence arise we shall demand your assistance.

I very nearly ran down to see you about that poisonous Home Defence Memo. which the War Office tried to ram down our throats.[3] After obtaining Admiralty concurrence to its issue as a purely War Office Memo. they had the impudence to alter it in essential particulars, and to try and tack on abominable militarist doctrines, subversive of the whole principles of Imperial Defence. Luckily we bowled it out, and Sir Arthur Wilson took the matter up. After much lobbying we got a resolution passed to-day referring it for re-drafting to the Home Ports Defence Committee, of which Ottley is

[1]Lennoxlove papers.
[2]Fisher's retirement from the Navy was announced exactly twelve months after his resignation from the Admiralty—that is to say on his 70th birthday (26th Jan. 1911).
[3]Presumably C.I.D. 48A of 3rd Nov. 1910, which was taken at the 108th Meeting on 26th Jan. 1911..Cab. 38/16/20 and 17/5. The Minutes on the War Office memorandum are in C.I.D. 49A of 23rd March 1911. Cab. 38/17/15.

Chairman, and I am Secretary. Not only shall we take all the poison out of the Memorandum but also we have by this means established for all time the principle that the C.I.D. (with its affiliated Sub-Ctees.) and not the Imperial General Staff, shall draft these all important General Principles. So all's well that ends well. . . .

We have new Sub-Ctees, starting forthwith on the subject of "Trading with the Enemy" and "The Co-ordination of Departmental Action".[1] Would it not be worth while as a matter of principle, to let your name appear, in order to add weight to the report, even if you don't bother to attend often? The views you outlined on "Co-ordination" in a letter which I have kept, would be invaluable . . .

Yours ever

In February 1911 Fisher and his wife left England for a prolonged stay on the Continent, and the stream of letters to Hankey then rapidly swelled into a flood. Tempting though it is to quote extensively from Fisher's highly individual and idiosyncratic letters, especially as Hankey refused to make them available to Professor A. J. Marder,[2] we cannot here reproduce more than a small selection.

Fisher to Hankey. Grand Hotel National, Lucerne. 21st October 1911. Holograph *Please burn. Very Secret.*
My beloved Hankey,
I have heard indirectly from the Prime Minister that I need not worry about your future prospects as he recognizes your claims and so to stay quiet where you are. I beg you not to build too much on this because no politician has any sense of honour—it is expediency alone that guides every one of them— but still I think it's good enough for us to rest and be thankful at present . . .

When rumours began to circulate that Ottley was likely to leave the C.I.D. to take up the far more lucrative post of managing director of the great armament and shipbuilding firm of Sir W. G. Armstrong Whitworth & Co. at Elswick-on-Tyne Fisher redoubled his efforts. On 9th November he wrote to Esher "to entreat you to *make sure* with the Prime Minister that Hankey succeeds Ottley if there is any chance. This is VERY, VERY secret. But you know Hankey's great value. I feel you are the only one who could see this through, so I write. I

---

[1]Respectively Lord Desart's Sub-Committee, which reported on 30th July 1912 (C.I.D., 160B. Cab. 30/7/12) and Sir Arthur Nicolson's Sub-Committee, whose reports (C.I.D. W1, 2 and 3) were approved on 25th April 1912, 5th April 1913, and 14th July 1914. Cab. 38/20/9, 24/33 and 28/35.

[2]Marder, *Fisher.* Hankey refused Professor Marder's repeated requests for access to this correspondence between 1954 and 1960.

consider it absolutely vital for the future of the C.I.D."[1] Esher
replied "You may rely upon my looking after Hankey, but Ottley is
NOT to leave the C.I.D. It would never do." But Fisher had plenty of
other strings to pull on Hankey's behalf, and at this time he bombarded
Churchill and Asquith with letters pressing the claims of his *protégé*.[2]
Early in the following year Ottley himself wrote to Churchill that he
was "quite convinced that Hankey is the best successor imaginable",
and asked him to read the letter which he enclosed. In it Hankey set out
in modest terms the grounds for his claim to succeed to the secretaryship. After outlining his previous service and experience, and emphasis-
ing his sympathy with Churchill's ideas about a Naval War Staff, he
ended by saying that, in spite of his comparative youth and juniority of
rank, he believed "there are few persons available who have had such
unique opportunities to qualify for it".[3]

Despite his strenuous efforts Fisher evidently entertained doubts
regarding the success of his lobbying.

Fisher to Hankey. Excelsior Hotel, Naples. 22nd February 1912. Holograph
Burn
My beloved Hankey,
. . . I sent you an express letter within a few minutes of getting your last note
to say I had sent a "hot" one to W.C. [Churchill] and written that he could
send it on to the P.M. I am very disturbed. I expect Haldane will be the
deciding factor, and I know he hankers after Slade,[4] but I doubt the P.M.
agreeing as he had the lowest opinion of Slade—he said so!—but Slade
would play up to Haldane. I cannot believe Custance [will be appointed] as
the whole Beresford sub-committee wondered at his maudlin statement on
the Beresford enquiry. Really the very best thing for you would be Ottley

[1]*ibid.* Vol. II, p. 414.
[2]See Fisher to Churchill from Reigate Priory late October 1911 "Please guarantee
Hankey to succeed him [Ottley]", and again from Lucerne 2nd November 1911
"Don't fail me, my dear Winston, in having Hankey put in his [Ottley's] place".
Also to Asquith from Portsmouth 5th November 1911 "If Hankey took his
[Ottley's] place . . . neither you nor the Navy would I believe suffer from the
transfer". All in Churchill papers.
[3]Ottley to Churchill from Office of C.I.D. 17th February 1912 enclosing Hankey to
Churchill of same date. Churchill papers.
[4]Later Admiral Sir Edmond Slade (1859–1928). Director of Naval Intelligence 1907–
9. C-in-C, East Indies, 1912–13. Sent with expert committee to study the Persian oil
fields 1912, which led to the purchase by the British government of a controlling
interest in the Anglo-Persian Oil Company 1913. Thereafter acted as the Admiralty's
adviser on all problems connected with oil.

remaining on—Time is on your side. His going now precipitates and lessens your chances . . . Telegraph to me if you want any further action. I am confident W.C. will do all he can—he promised me this verbally at Plymouth.

Yours in great haste.   F.

In fact it was Haldane, whom Fisher loathed and commonly referred to as "the arch-Jesuit", who had the decisive influence on the selection of Ottley's successor. On the day after the critical interview Hankey sent his wife a vivid account of what passed between them.

To Mrs. Hankey. 19th February 1912.
Haldane sent me word that he would see me at the War Office at 12.30 p.m. He received me most urbanely, and was rather tickled when I told him I had come to blow my own trumpet. He then listened in stolid, imperturbable silence, while I gassed for a quarter of an hour. I put my case very much as I put it to you last night, but in greater detail. I was never at a loss for a word, and am satisfied that I did myself justice. At the end he asked me my age and rank. He then asked how my relations with Grant Duff would be affected. I told him that G.D. had consented to my being given a status superior to his own, and that I thought he would raise no difficulty. As regards age, I reminded him that at my age he was a Q.C. and a leading member of the English bar (!) (having looked the matter up in *Who's Who*[1]), and I said that so far as I knew there was no other profession (including politics) where a man of 35 would be held too young for a high position. He agreed, and said that in his opinion the difficulty of age might be considered as disposed of. I ended by disclaiming any wish to push out Ottley, whom I described as the ideal man for the post. He thanked me very much for my visit, and, without positively promising to support my claim, he gave me the impression that he was distinctly favourable. He said the P.M. was greatly perplexed, and found it difficult to overrule the Treasury; he said he would probably be seeing the P.M. on the question this morning, and indicated that he would lay my case before him. On the whole I am well satisfied. . . .

Hankey's appointment was announced on 1st March. Fisher was of course delighted. "He [Hankey] is Napoleonic and Cromwellian. I've no doubt Reggie [McKenna] urged his suit" he wrote to Mrs. McKenna.[2] And, again, to Esher, "Hankey is better than Ottley. He is Napoleonic!"[3] But he was almost certainly wrong to claim that Hankey owed the appointment to his own or McKenna's efforts. Indeed study of Fisher's vast and explosive correspondence leaves one wondering

[1] cf. *Supreme Command*, I, pp. 54–6.
[2] To Mrs. McKenna 2nd March 1912. Marder, *Fisher*, II, p. 434.
[3] 2nd April 1912. *ibid.* p. 444.

how much the addressees were taken in by his constant and enormous exaggerations. Probably very little.

The saddest disappointment which resulted from Hankey's success was that of his former mentor at Greenwich, General George Aston, who was one of the strongest candidates to succeed Ottley. Hankey has recorded that, on the very day that he was appointed, he and his wife attended a Court ball at Buckingham Palace, where he at once ran into Aston and so had to act as the bearer of ill tidings. Fortunately Aston took it extremely well. In 1931, when Hankey was evidently thinking of writing an autobiography, Aston sent him extracts from his diary entries for 1912. The entry for 1st March reads "A real facer by the morning post—a letter from Hankey to say that Ottley was leaving the C.I.D. and that he [Hankey] succeeded him. Thank goodness that with the help of a few minutes' thought and a talk with xxx I could rise to the occasion and write him a really nice letter of congratulation." Enclosed with the diary extracts was a copy of Hankey's letter of 29th February, written from his home immediately he heard that his appointment was firm, but which Aston had not received at the time of their encounter at the Palace that evening. In that letter Hankey explained how Asquith had tried to retain Ottley by the promise of an immediate increase of salary to £2,000 plus his naval pension, and an extension of his appointment for five years. But, he went on, "Ottley was not satisfied. Elswick's terms were so tremendous that he felt he could not fairly refuse them unless the Govt. would give him practically a life tenure here and a big pension any time after the age of 60." Asquith had even tried to get the Treasury to accept Ottley's terms. Hankey continued "A week ago Ottley heard that the P.M.'s negotiations with the Treasury had failed, and he decided to resign. In writing to resign he did me the great honour to put my name forward as his successor. Many members of the Committee seem to have done the same, some spontaneously and some at Ottley's request . . ." Such a frank explanation of what had happened would have mitigated the disappointment of a much less magnanimous man than George Aston, who remained Hankey's firm friend until his death.

On 27th April 1911 a third child and second son was born to the Hankeys at The Corner House and christened Christopher Alers.[1] This

[1]Private Secretary to Lord Hankey 1939–40. Served World War II in Royal Engineers and Royal Marines. Ministry of Labour 1946. Transferred to Department of Technical Co-operation 1961 and to Ministry of Overseas Development 1964.

increase in their family made it essential to find a larger home, and within a few months they moved to the house near Limpsfield on the Kent-Surrey border which they renamed Highstead in memory of Adeline's South African home. The purchase of that property was made possible by the greater financial security and improved prospects which Hankey had enjoyed since his appointment to the C.I.D. But despite a private income of about £400 per annum he continued to worry about money, and to live with a degree of frugality which did not escape the notice of his office colleagues.[1] But the latter, of course, knew nothing about Hankey's private benefactions—such as the support he gave to his brother Clement after he was "hammered" on the Stock Exchange shortly after the outbreak of war, and the education he provided for the children of the less affluent members of his own and his wife's families.

We have already seen how, at the time when he joined the R.M.A., Hankey adopted a mode of living which can reasonably be described as Spartan. Nor did his marriage lead to any amelioration of his self-discipline and abstemiousness. He always rose early and began the day, winter or summer, with a cold bath, after which he would do his physical exercises. In the 1920s the Hankeys built on to Highstead, and this ritual then took place on the flat roof outside his bedroom, from which he could at the same time enjoy the magnificent view over the Weald. They also built a small loggia in the garden, and if the weather showed the slightest clemency breakfast would be taken there—sometimes to the discomfort of guests who were less immune than Hankey to a biting wind. Though he bought his first motor car at about the time now reached in our story his day's work would none the less often begin with a walk of a couple of miles to Oxted station. He reached the office around 9 a.m., hard on the heels of the clerks and typists, and long before the majority of senior civil servants had arrived in Whitehall. Unless he had guests to entertain or was invited out to lunch he would probably remain at his desk and refresh himself with the modest sandwich and apple which Adeline had put in his brief case. His hours of work were always extremely long, and he would never leave the office until all official papers and correspondence had been dealt with, and there was no longer much likelihood of a sudden call from a Minister.

The hour at which Hankey would return home was always very

[1]Letters to the author from Mr. Lawrence Burgis (see p. 11) and Sir John Hodsoll (Assistant Secretary C.I.D. 1929–35), 1967.

irregular, and he never followed the practice of most government officials in catching a particular train. Adeline thus grew accustomed, especially in wartime, to sudden telephone calls telling her to expect him very late—or not at all. If work demanded it he would stay in London, generally sleeping at the United Service Club; and if he did take a day off it was as likely as not that he would be recalled by telephone. The domestic side of Adeline's life must have been complicated by the irregularity and uncertainty of her husband's hours and movements; but she took it all as part of the public duties to which he was dedicated, and which she therefore shared with him to the full. Though Hankey's extreme emphasis on physical fitness and self-discipline may seem outmoded to a generation brought up to seek happiness through "permissiveness" and a cure for mental ills on the psychiatrist's couch, it is a fact that their marriage was a complete partnership, and that his mode of living enabled him to carry an almost superhuman burden of work and responsibility.

Chapter 5

Secretary of the Committee of Imperial Defence 1912-14

HANKEY's appointment was on the whole well received by the Press. *The Times* regretted Ottley's departure and remarked pontifically that "Captain Hankey has his spurs to win, but those who know him . . . will not doubt that he will win them speedily and wear them with distinction".[1] The only discordant note came from *Truth*, which criticised the appointment on the grounds of Hankey's youth and lack of experience, and considered that "he would be well paid with half the salary which was properly voted for Sir George Clarke and Sir Charles Ottley".[2] Among the congratulations which came to Hankey were letters from Haldane and Colonel J. E. B. Seely,[3] who was about to succeed Haldane at the War Office. "My warmest congratulations", wrote Seely; "You have the most interesting billet in the British Empire and I am quite sure you will do the job quite excellently. Your ears would burn if you knew what Sir John Fisher wrote to me about you. Good luck to you". Such warmth from the head of one of the two great departments of state with which Hankey was bound to be chiefly concerned augured well for the future—especially as the War Office was less likely than the Admiralty to welcome a marine officer in the appointment. As to Haldane's opinion, his biographer has remarked on Hankey's "wisdom, vigilance, imagination and organising ability, coupled with a character of charm and kindness", and has recorded how to the end of Haldane's career he "constantly referred to Hankey's invaluable and imaginative assistance".[4]

[1] *The Times*, 1st March 1912.
[2] *Truth*, 6th March 1912. Actually on appointment Hankey's salary was £1,500 per annum as compared with the £2,000 paid to Ottley.
[3] 1868–1947. 1st Baron Mottistone 1933. Politician (Lib.). Secretary of State for War 1912–14, when he resigned as a result of the "Curragh Mutiny". Deputy Minister of Munitions 1918; Under Secretary of State for Air 1919.
[4] Dudley Sommer, *Haldane of Cloan* (Allen & Unwin, 1960) pp. 254–5.

On 4th May 1912 Hankey was received for the first time by King George V, and that audience marked the beginning of an association between monarch and an official of the government which, for its intimacy and continuity, has no parallel. Within a few months Hankey was able to tell his wife that he had been "nearly an hour with the King, who was very cordial".[1] Despite Esher's endeavours to procure a Knighthood for Hankey in the 1912 birthday honours he was only made a Commander of the Bath,[2] and on 1st July he attended his first investiture at Buckingham Palace.

As the Court Circular records that Hankey was granted seven audiences in 1912–13 the friendship between monarch and official evidently ripened rapidly.[3] Hankey's correspondence with Lord Stamfordham,[4] the King's private secretary, shows that he did all he could to nourish the association. Thus in April 1913 Stamfordham wrote thanking Hankey for a letter and telling him that the King would be glad to receive a summary of the C.I.D.'s proceedings on the invasion issue.[5] It must therefore have been at about this time that Asquith authorised Hankey to give the King, personally or in writing, an account of all discussions in the C.I.D. Though the delegation of the Prime Minister's constitutional authority for advising the King had its dangers, Hankey carried out his part with such skill and tact that it was never called in question.

When Hankey took over the office of secretary he was already assured of the friendship and support of many of the leading politicians —including Haldane, Esher, McKenna and Seely; while Balfour, though in opposition, remained an ardent advocate of the C.I.D. and attended meetings at which important matters, such as invasion, were discussed. It was probably from Balfour that Hankey learnt the art of drafting a formula which would satisfy both parties to a dispute— which he later developed to a fine art. His discretion was inviolable, and it may have been the strain of preserving so many secrets while constantly being interviewed or questioned—in person, by letter and on the telephone—that produced in him a watchful wariness while on

[1]Letter of 5th Dec. 1912.
[2]Esher to Fisher 11th April 1912. Quoted Marder, *Fisher*, II, p. 444 f.n.(1).
[3]*The Times*, Court Circulars for 1912–13.
[4]Arthur John Bigge, 1st Baron Stamfordham 1911 (1849–1931). Assistant Private Secretary to Queen Victoria 1880–95 and Private Secretary 1895–1901. Private Secretary to Prince George (King George V 1910) 1901–31.
[5]Stamfordham to Hankey, 22nd April 1913.

duty. This gave the impression to some of the office staff that he lacked a sense of humour.[1]

Churchill at first showed no very great warmth towards the new secretary, which is not altogether surprising as he was doubtless very much occupied with the affairs of his new department. Moreover he had expressed to Fisher some doubts regarding whether Hankey should be appointed. But, as we shall see shortly, Hankey quickly won him over. With both Asquith and Mrs. Asquith Hankey was soon on very cordial and confidential terms, and in old age the latter recalled with nostalgia her happy memories of the days before and during World War I when Hankey had regularly lunched or dined with them several times a week in intimate privacy.[2]

Hankey's new position resulted in his being immediately launched into the highest society in the land. In June 1912 he twice attended "full-dress dinners" at 10 Downing Street. A short time later Haldane invited him to a big dinner at the Ritz Hotel at which Prince Arthur of Connaught was guest of honour. These were all men's parties, but in the following month Hankey and his wife, who had been presented at Court in March ("Full dress. Feathers and trains"), were summoned to a garden party at Windsor Castle. Adeline was also very soon included in invitations to lunch and dinner by prominent politicians and service men; and Fisher's first invitation to Hankey to the "bachelor's week-end party" at Kilverstone was quickly followed by a similar invitation to both of them. Adeline later recalled the occasion in a letter to Fisher which throws interesting light on the way his mind was working during the months preceding the outbreak of war.

Lady Hankey to Lord Fisher. Highstead, 5th June 1917[3] Holograph
Dear Lord Fisher,
I have looked through letters which Maurice has had from you from time to time and have found the one of which I enclose a copy. Maurice and I were very much struck with your prophecy, when I came across it a few months ago, and I reminded him then of the delightful week-end we spent with you and Lady Fisher at Kilverstone—and of another prophecy you had made there in the rose garden.

[1]Letter of 8th March 1967 to the author from Mr. Lawrence Burgis, private secretary to Hankey 1921–38.
[2]Undated (c. 1943) letter from Lady Oxford and Asquith to Hankey "I often think of the happy days when we saw you often in 10 Downing Street".
[3]Lennoxlove papers.

You announced on the Monday morning that we must take a later train back to town, as you were going to have a long talk with Maurice in the garden, and I was delighted when you invited me to accompany you—an unexpected honour! I remember very well how you spoke of the war that was coming when the Germans had completed the Kiel Canal in 1914, and you were so convinced that submarines would be the determining factor of the future war, and you picked out Jellicoe—I had never heard of him before —as being *the* man who would be fitted to take supreme command of the Navy. I wish I had put down afterwards all the interesting things you said, but that would have been betraying your confidence.

Yours very sincerely,

On 23rd June 1912 Hankey was "placed on the retired list [of the Royal Marine Artillery] at his own request and appointed to the reserve of officers". No doubt he parted with regret from a corps to which he had become devoted; but his retirement was a measure of the confidence he felt in his future in his new field. His star was now hitched irrevocably to the Committee of Imperial Defence.

As soon as Hankey had taken over as Secretary he put in hand a re-definition of the C.I.D.'s constitution and functions, and also drafted a long paper dealing with its future work. The latter brought him into mild conflict with his old friend and supporter Lord Esher, and he described how and why their views diverted in the following letter to Fisher.

Hankey to Fisher. The Corner House, Oxted. 8th May 1912[1]

... He [Esher] is very anxious to do away with *ad hoc* committees and to concentrate everything in a single permanent sub-committee of fixed membership, which would tend to swallow all the defence policy of the country. This will not take place in my time as Secretary! It would be absolutely ruinous. The big permanent officials could not possibly spare the time for the frequent meetings which would be necessary. They would soon tire of it and boycott us. We would be perpetually treading on the toes of the Admiralty and War Office. Instead of having a dozen sub-committees on at once, as now, each with a membership adapted to the subject under consideration, we should be stagnated with work for which the composition of Esher's sub-committee would be totally unsuitable. ...

Of course I am not going to quarrel with him over it, but I am taking the best points of his scheme and applying them to our existing machinery. As you know, we have had a "Co-ordination" sub-committee sitting for over a year. This has done invaluable work, and made a War Book for every

[1]Lennoxlove papers.

Government department . . . This is to be considered at a meeting to be held on the 25th. What we hope to get done is to have the Co-ordination Committee made permanent and put under the joint alternative chairmanship of the First Lord and Secretary of State for War. The first duty will be to keep the War Book up to date. It will also from time to time report as to action that has been taken on past decisions of the C.I.D. Members will also have the right to draw attention to any weak points in our defence organisation. Personally, I hope in time to add Dominion representatives and to get a British Empire War Book. I hope to go privately and at my own expense to Canada this summer, ostensibly to look after some family investments of which I am joint trustee, but *really* to sow the seeds of this scheme, which is worked out in some detail. Please keep this to yourself. I am working it very cautiously through Esher and Harcourt.[1] Haldane is extraordinarily friendly!

On the 25th, besides the Co-ordination Report, we discuss certain ports to be defended on the east coast, and a host of minor questions affecting wireless telegraphy, and details arising out of the Hardinge Report. I dare say we shall have to have another Owen Committee,[2] as the War Office rightly want to effect savings elsewhere to counterbalance the new expenditure on the east coast. If so, I want to get one of my assistants appointed secretary, so as to keep them on the rails. . . .

In July 1912 the C.I.D. held two meetings in quick succession,[3] and the second of them, which took place on 11th, marked Hankey's first official appearance as its Secretary. On 4th the C.I.D. reviewed British naval dispositions in the light of the passing of the new German Navy Amendment Bill (or "Novella"),[4] regarding which Churchill had circulated a somewhat alarmist paper.[5] At the next meeting Robert Borden,[6] the Canadian Prime Minister, and four other Canadian Ministers were present, and the discussion ranged around the whole of "British foreign policy and the international situation". In marked

---

[1]Lewis Harcourt, 1st Viscount Harcourt 1917 (1863–1922). Politician (Lib.). First Commissioner of Works 1905–10 and again 1915–16. Secretary of State for Colonies 1910–15.

[2]See pp. 67–79.

[3]117th and 118th Meetings on 4th and 11th July 1912. Cab. 38/20/26 and 27.

[4]This was the third amendment to the German Navy Law of 14th June 1900; but as it authorised greatly increased strength it was in essence a new law to establish a much higher standard of strength. It was published in Cd. 6117.

[5]C.I.D. 157B of 2nd July 1912. Cab. 38/20/25.

[6]Later Sir Robert Borden (1854–1937). Canadian politician (Cons.). Prime Minister 1911–20. Represented Canada at Paris Peace Conference 1919, at Washington Conference 1921–22 and on League of Nations Council and Assembly.

contrast to his predecessor Sir Wilfred Laurier, Borden had already come out strongly in favour of "one King, one flag, one Empire and one Navy—a powerful navy to vindicate the flag and to maintain the integrity of the Empire"[1]—which, as we have seen, corresponded precisely with the Admiralty's views. However the concept of a single, unified navy was by no means acceptable to all the people of Canada or to the other Dominions, and it was never brought into being. None the less with the darkening of the European horizon after the failure of Haldane's mission to Berlin earlier in the year, such a display of Imperial unity was heartening to the British people—and might have served as a warning to Germany. Before the Canadian Ministers returned home Hankey wrote Borden a farewell letter, and the latter replied in very warm terms, inviting Hankey to visit him if, as then seemed likely, he came to Canada in the following year.

In the same month that Borden and his colleagues attended the C.I.D. meeting Asquith spoke in the House of Commons on the functions and work of the committee in warmly approving terms. Though he regretted Ottley's departure he was "glad to think that we have in his successor, Captain Hankey, a man intimately acquainted with the work of the office, and thoroughly capable of carrying on its traditions."[2] The whole organisation, he pointed out, cost "very little more than £5,000 [per annum]"—which certainly indicated that the country was getting good value for its money.

In August Hankey circulated his paper, mentioned earlier, on the Constitution and Functions of the C.I.D. In it he recapitulated the work of recent years, with which the reader is familiar, and consolidated all recent experience and practice. At about the same time the Air Committee, which had developed out of the discussions on "aerial navigation", was made a permanent sub-committee,[3] and "Representation of the Dominions" on the C.I.D. was carried a step further on the grounds "that there ought to be some opportunity for the constant co-ordination and co-relation of the action of the different parts of the Empire in regard to defence".[4] Early in 1913 the home government's views were communicated to all the Dominions.[5] The broad policy adopted by the

[1] Speech at Royal Colonial Institute reported in *The Times*, 12th July 1912.
[2] Parl. Deb., Commons, Vol. XLI, Col. 1391 (25th July 1912).
[3] C.I.D. 161B of 27th Aug. 1912. Cab. 38/22/34.
[4] C.I.D. 94C of 5th Nov. 1912. Cab. 38/22/36.
[5] Cd. 6560 (Dominions No. 13) of Jan. 1913.

Dominions was not to keep a permanent representative in London to consult with the C.I.D. but for visiting ministers to attend its meetings when matters concerning their countries were to be discussed.

Meanwhile Hankey's paper on the future work of the C.I.D. had run into some trouble with Esher. With the attendance of Dominion representatives in the offing Hankey was perturbed by the fact that "the principal current questions of Foreign and Imperial policy of the day" did not find their way to the C.I.D. unless one of the departments happened to raise such an issue. He pointed out that in fact this procedure was a rare occurrence, and that the great majority of the problems discussed in the C.I.D. were actually raised by the secretariat. Hankey therefore wanted to set up "a new sub-committee, members of which have the privilege and duty of bringing any question affecting Imperial Defence to the notice of the Chairman". Such a proposal obviously cut across departmental responsibilities, and so was almost certain to arouse opposition. Hankey sent a copy of his paper to Esher who at once telegraphed from his Perthshire home "strongly advising" that he should postpone its circulation. But a copy had already gone to the Prime Minister, who had sent it on to Esher. This produced a large number of marginal comments from the latter, many of them critical.[1] An impartial observer might well feel that Hankey's proposals savoured of "empire building" on behalf of the C.I.D., and Esher was probably right to foresee trouble in them. At any rate Hankey evidently decided not to press the matter, and although he held to his view and continued to work to strengthen the powers of the C.I.D. he tactfully withdrew the controversial paper and adopted a less direct approach.

Hankey's first year as secretary of the C.I.D. was busy enough to satisfy even his gluttony for work. The committee met five times in 1912 and four times in the following year to discuss, and in most cases approve, the many papers on various aspects of defence policy and preparations for war which reached it. In June 1913 the Air Committee submitted its first annual report, which initiated the attempt to catch up with the continental powers in the development of the new arm and to create a unified air service.[2] A Bill was drafted to control "aerial navigation" (referred to by Hankey as "my bill") and passed through

---

[1] Copy of Hankey's paper, dated 22nd Nov. 1912, in Asquith papers, Box 108 Folios 148/158.
[2] C.I.D. 179B of 7th June 1913.

all stages in the House of Commons in February. The investigations into the treatment of neutral and enemy merchant ships in the event of war[1] and into the whole field of trading with an enemy nation[2] laid the foundations for the exercise of economic pressure through blockade, and led directly to the appointment of the Committee on the Co-ordination of Departmental Action which produced the famous War Book.[3] Preparations to institute Press and postal censorship in the event of war were put in hand by another sub-committee, under Churchill.[4] The defence of naval bases at home and overseas continued to command a good deal of attention, as did the old question of the likelihood of invasion or of raids in force on the British Isles. Defence schemes were prepared for Australia and New Zealand,[5] and a conference was fore-shadowed in Canada to consider the creation of a War Book for that country and other defence measures.[6]

Early in January 1913 Hankey set off with other members of the C.I.D. to visit the Bristol Channel ports, with the double purpose of assessing their capacity for the loading and despatch of stores and equipment for the expeditionary force and of inspecting their defences. At the end of that month he accompanied Churchill and Asquith, who had most of his family with him, to Dundee where they embarked in the Admiralty yacht *Enchantress*. The real purpose of the visit was to review the effect of the Admiralty's latest ideas with regard to the blockade of the German High Seas Fleet on the defence of naval bases on the east coast of Scotland (Rosyth and Cromarty) and in the Orkneys (Scapa Flow). Early in the century the accepted strategy had been to establish a close blockade of the German fleet's bases, with light forces patrolling the southern North Sea and heavier units in fairly close support. But by 1911 it had become clear that developments in mine warfare and the arrival of the submarine had made this too risky. Accordingly an "observational blockade" was substituted with forces disposed in the central North Sea. But the serious weaknesses inherent in this scheme were soon made apparent by fleet exercises. The final decision, taken only in July 1914, was therefore to establish a "distant blockade" with the main fleet based on Scapa Flow and a much weaker

[1]C.I.D. 120B of 28th Oct. 1910. Cab. 38/16/19.
[2]C.I.D. 160B of 30th July 1912. Cab. 38/20/31.
[3]*Supreme Command*, I, 119–21.   [4]C.I.D. 168B of 22nd Jan. 1913. Cab. 38/23/4.
[5]C.I.D. 99C of 5th April and 102C of 25th April 1913. Cab. 38/23/15 and 38/24/20.
[6]C.I.D. 108C of 11th Feb. 1914. Cab. 38/25/6.

Channel Fleet in the south. These two forces would, it was believed, effectively control the exits from the North Sea to the Atlantic. The distant blockade, however, held little appeal to Churchill, the First Lord, whose philosophy was always to "seek out, hunt and destroy" the enemy; and the late hour at which the decision in favour of a distant blockade was taken had the unfortunate result that when war broke out none of the northern bases was properly defended, and Scapa Flow was virtually defenceless.[1]

Though it thus came to pass that the visit of the Prime Minister and First Lord to the Scottish bases in 1913 produced no clear-cut decisions regarding their defences it gave Hankey an excellent opportunity to observe the methods of Asquith and Churchill at close quarters and to win their confidence.

To Mrs. Hankey. Admiralty Yacht Enchantress. *Dundee, 31st January 1913*
. . . Although I was itching to go ashore I stayed on board this afternoon, as for the first time I found Winston in the mood to talk "shop". I sat in his cabin for the greater part of the afternoon . . . though I made two excursions to the P.M.'s cabin to show him Admiralty papers bearing on C.I.D. questions. Afterwards Winston and I went ashore to look at the local forts and took a brisk walk along the sands, which was very welcome. The P.M. stayed on board all day; he must have been fearfully tired after his speeches at Dundee, of which he had received the freedom the previous day, but did not show fatigue. He is quite genial and most pleasant, but rather quiet. He strikes me as a man who can throw off all worries and cares of office and just enjoy himself quietly. Violet Asquith[2] evidently dotes on her father . . . She is an immensely keen politician and, as I can see, might carry immense weight with her father. She does not want the vote apparently! She wears the most beautiful dresses, and smokes, which latter I don't like. Otherwise she seems to be a very simple living girl and not at all fast—in fact mainly interested in politics . . . I think it quite probable that there will be an Imperial Conference in Vancouver in July or August, but I don't know whether I shall go. They talk of going in a man-of-war through the Panama Canal, but I hope if I go that they won't find room for me but will send me overland as of course I want to take you . . .

To the same. Enchantress. *Rosyth, 1st February 1913*
. . . This morning I gave the P.M. a private and personal lecture on the

[1]See Marder, *Scapa Flow*, I, pp. 368–77 for a full discussion of blockade strategy 1908–14.
[2]1887–1969. Married Sir Maurice Bonham Carter, principal private secretary to Asquith 1915. Later Baroness Asquith of Yarnbury.

subject of the Forth defences, and completely won him and Winston to my point of view. Afterwards we went all round the new [dockyard] works at Rosyth, which was interesting. . . This trip has been most valuable to me. I began very quietly and spoke very little, and did not seem to get on very fast. Now, however, I have worked my way and they keep consulting me on all sorts of points. Prince Louis[1] and Lambert[2], the Civil Lord, arrived to-day, but the former is going back again by train to London to-night.

Hankey's relations with Balfour and with the King also grew closer and more intimate at this time. Thus on 12th February he told Adeline "I had a long visit from Mr. Balfour to-day. He wanted to know the latest news of the Invasion sub-committee". A week later he wrote "I have no time to describe in detail my very cordial interview with the King", because he was just off, after "a desperately busy day" to visit—again with members of the C.I.D.—the industrial cities and ports of the north-west.

From Barrow-in-Furness, where the party visited the great ship building yard of Vickers and pondered the likelihood of a new enemy emulating the raid by John Paul Jones on nearby Whitehaven in 1778 during the War of American Independence, they went on to Glasgow to visit the shipyards and engineering works on the Clyde. Hankey was at once struck by the ease with which an enemy could block the river by sinking a concrete-filled ship in the fairway, and on his return to London drew the attention of the Home Ports Defence Committee to what he regarded as a serious danger.[3]

In the middle of 1913 Hankey became indirectly involved in the notorious "Marconi Scandal", in which Rufus Isaacs (Attorney General), Lloyd George (Chancellor of the Exchequer) and the Master of Elibank (Government Chief Whip) were alleged to have taken advantage of their official positions to speculate in the shares of the American Marconi Company. When the dealings were exposed Asquith appointed a Select Committee to report on the matter, and on 18th–19th June two days of stormy debate took place in the House of

[1]Prince Louis of Battenberg succeeded Admiral Sir Francis Bridgeman as First Sea Lord on 9th Dec. 1912. Though it was Churchill who, as First Lord, selected Bridgeman the two of them proved totally incompatible in office. See Marder, *Scapa Flow*, I, pp. 258–9.
[2]George Lambert, 1st Viscount Lambert 1945 (1866–1958). Politician (Lib. then Lib. Nat. from 1931). Civil Lord of Admiralty 1905–15. Chairman, Parliamentary Liberal Party 1919–21.
[3]C.I.D. 56A of 31st March 1913. Cab. 38/23/14.

Commons.[1] To brief the Prime Minister for the debate Hankey collected all the relevant C.I.D. papers, in which the creation of an Imperial Wireless Chain had been reviewed. The C.I.D. finally recommended that the project should go forward as a matter of urgency,[2] though Herbert Samuel[3] (Postmaster-General) described the Marconi Company's terms as "exorbitant".[4] By the time the debate took place Hankey considered that many of the reasons for urgency had disappeared, but that the strategic merits of the scheme were still valid. His efficiently prepared summary of the story no doubt helped Asquith to handle a critical debate which brought no credit at all to the Liberal Party or to certain of its Ministers and officials. Hankey left no record of his personal feelings with regard to the conduct of those involved, but we know enough of his character to be confident that their actions, and still more their subsequent public evasiveness and equivocations, must have been highly distasteful to him.

On 19th July while Hankey was enjoying one of his rare quiet days at Highstead a telegram came from Churchill inviting him to join the Board of Admiralty in the *Enchantress* to witness the big fleet exercises which were about to take place. These were designed to test the defences of the east coast against invasion. The "Blue" fleet based on Scapa under Admiral Sir George Callaghan represented the British main force, while the "Red" fleet and transports under Vice-Admiral Sir John Jellicoe, operating from the Thames Estuary, represented the Germans. Hankey joined the *Enchantress* in the Firth of Forth, and that evening he "sat up until 1.15 a.m. arguing with Winston and Seely".

To Mrs. Hankey. At sea 25th July 1913
. . . We are cruising northward again behind our [i.e. the Blue] fleet. I am quite unable to fathom why they are making this move, as there is no information to show any corresponding move on the part of the enemy. My opinion of the C-in-C Home Fleet (never high) has not been enhanced by these manœuvres . . . I should like to get back, but Winston has pressed me

[1] See Frances Donaldson, *The Marconi Scandal* (Hart-Davis, 1962) for a full and admirably impartial account of this *cause célèbre*. The White Paper on the subject is Cd. 217 of July 1913.
[2] C.I.D. 128B of 1st June 1911.
[3] 1870–1963. 1st Viscount Samuel 1937. Politician (Lib.). Postmaster-General 1910–14. Chancellor of Duchy of Lancaster 1915–16. Home Secretary 1916 and 1931–32. High Commissioner for Palestine 1920–25. Leader of Liberal Parliamentary Party 1931–35.
[4] Minutes of 115th Meeting of C.I.D. 14th Dec. 1911.

to stay—considers it very important that I should—more especially as it is possible that Asquith may join us to-night . . .

Actually Jellicoe performed brilliantly, and by the rules of the exercise effected a "landing" of more than 40,000 men from his transports in the neighbourhood of Blyth and Sunderland. The manœuvres were cancelled prematurely lest the results should give valuable information to the Germans.[1] Hankey, however, took a more sanguine view of the result of the exercises. In November he told Lord Stamfordham, for the King's benefit, that although an "enemy" force of 107,000 men had reached British shores, 46,000 had been assessed as "drowned or captured", while 18,000 more had gone home without having accomplished anything. Thus the effective force landed was only 43,000, a result which he considered "rather more reassuring . . . than has hitherto been supposed."[2] His presence in the *Enchantress* during the manœuvres evidently made a favourable impression on the First Lord.

Churchill to Hankey. Admiralty, Whitehall. 28th July 1913. Holograph
My dear Hankey,
I am delighted you were able to come and much enjoyed entertaining you.
Now I think we are going to try it over again with a vigorous Blue offensive. Callaghan will be here to-morrow morning and it shall rest with him.[3]

Yours v. sincerely,

In August Hankey returned to Eastney Barracks for a special dinner given in his honour by the Royal Marine Artillery. "I was terrifically 'lionised' last night" he told Adeline. "There was a tremendous turn-up, numbers of retired officers and fellows from ships—in all nearly 60 . . . I had a great ovation. The Commandant made a very amusing and witty speech proposing my health and I replied with a rousing speech on the lines I told you. I was not in the least bit nervous and forgot no point, though I had omitted to bring my notes. My speech made a great effect . . .". A few days later, on arriving at his office Hankey found a note from Churchill asking him to come round to the Admiralty. He found the First Lord "very sick at the poor figure cut by the Admiralty

[1] See Marder, *Scapa Flow*, I, pp. 352–4 regarding the 1912 and 1913 manœuvres and their effect on British strategy and policy.
[2] Hankey to Stamfordham 27th November 1913. RA.GV E 820/11.
[3] The repeat exercise never took place.

at Tuesday's meeting [of the C.I.D.]"[1] "He wants to avoid it happening
again", continued Hankey, "by introducing a rule that members who
intend to oppose a proposal shall circulate their reasons in writing 2 or
3 days before the meeting. This will prevent people like Sir Arthur
Wilson 'queering the pitch' at the last moment and making a surprise
attack. I quite agree with him and shall do what I can to bring it about
—but his real safeguard is not to make preposterous proposals, though
I did *not* tell him so!" The new secretary had evidently not been long in
learning how to exert his influence with discretion; and to assess his
superiors correctly.

As 1913 drew to a close the work of the C.I.D. increased steadily both
in volume and importance. No large new subjects were raised, but the
international situation obviously demanded that finality should be
attained in the many matters already before the main committee and its
sub-committees. Thus on 19th November Hankey wrote to Adeline
"This is proving a desperately heavy day. A very heavy meeting this
morning and a very heavy meeting this afternoon[2]; and I have just been
asked to attend a meeting at 6.30 p.m. of the 'High Level Bridge' . . .
After that a heavy dinner, and a very heavy cold all the time . . .". All
his life Hankey resented catching a cold, which he seems to have
regarded as an unfair infliction on a person who took so much trouble
over his physical fitness.

Meanwhile Admiral Fisher, who had returned home and become
chairman of the Royal Commission on Fuel and Engines, continued to
plot and plan for the recall to office which he regarded as inevitable—
despite the fact that the date he had originally predicted (Trafalgar Day
1912) had long since passed. The stream of letters to Hankey, whereby
he hoped to bring his ideas to the attention of the politicians, continued
unabated.

---

[1] 124th Meeting of C.I.D. on 5th Aug. 1913. The chief subjects discussed were the
report of the Sub-Committee on Co-ordination of Departmental Action (the "War
Book" sub-committee) and the first report of the Air Committee. Cab. 38/24/33.
In the prolonged discussions on the latter Admiral Wilson had strongly attacked
Churchill's proposal to build large rigid airships in emulation of the German
Zeppelins, and a somewhat heated correspondence passed between them. C.I.D.
172B of 19th Feb. 1913. Cab. 38/23/11.
[2] As the full C.I.D. did not meet on 19th Nov. 1913 these must have been meetings
of one or other of its sub-committees.

Hankey and his staff in September 1918
Back Row: Lt. Col. L. Storr; Fleet-Paymaster P. Row; Lt. Col. L. Wilson;
        Capt. L. F. Burgis
Front Row: Thomas Jones; Lt. Col. W. Dally-Jones; Lt. Col. Sir Maurice
        Hankey; Cyril Longhurst; Capt. Clement Jones

The Secretary's Office, C.I.D., 2 Whitehall Gardens

British Troops advancing at the Battle of Albert, July 1916. A shrapnel shell is exploding overhead

The *Iron Duke* opening fire at the Battle of Jutland

Fisher to Hankey. Langham House, Ham Common. 16th May 1913
My beloved Hankey,
I've written a "spiffing" letter to Balfour and sent him enclosed. I send you this copy to keep as it may be handy for you to have it by you. There is a special messenger going on Sunday I think to the *Enchantress* from the Admiralty . . . in case you have anything to send to the P.M.—though I think it would be dangerous with W.C. at his elbow . . .

The enclosure was a typewritten appreciation of the power and influence of submarines. The summary at the end stated that "As submarines grow and become able to keep the sea for longer periods it will become impossible to say when they may *not* be met. They have the power to fight or to evade a fight at will, so that they can pick and choose their prey and can remain a constant and harassing menace to all surface craft . . .". All of which was to come to pass very precisely during the war.

A few days later Fisher was urging Hankey to stress to Balfour and others the deadly power of submarines against transports carrying a military expedition overseas. In Fisher's view our submarines reduced still further the threat of invasion of the British Isles—which he had never regarded at all seriously. Nor did Fisher neglect any opportunity to malign his former opponents—the "syndicate of discontent" who had tried to obstruct his reforms or had supported Beresford in the great quarrel. No doubt he wanted to make sure that none of them held high office or command when the day came for his own return to power.

In December Fisher sent Hankey the printed proof of a secret paper on submarine developments, entitled "The Oil Engine and the Submarine. A contribution to the Consideration of Future Sea Fighting". This very interesting document, which Hankey had evidently helped to prepare, is not mentioned either in Professor Marder's edition of Fisher's letters or in his history of the period leading to World War I.[1] It appears to have survived only in the Hankey papers. Its theme, stated with true Fisherite reiteration, was that "The submarine is the coming type of war vessel for sea fighting"; and the whole argument set out is a striking example both of Fisher's prophetic vision and of his capacity to state a case with force and clarity. His covering letter is typical of his methods of propagating his views and ideas.

[1] Marder, *Fisher*, II and *Scapa Flow*, I.

Fisher to Hankey. Langham House, Ham Common. Dec. 9th 1913
Secret. Burn

Dear Hankey,

Please read enclosed at once. It is all much improved I think since you read bits of it at a time. The only person who has a copy is Winston. He has had it some days and made no reply to me. I believe he is very cross as I declined to go and stay with him in *Enchantress*. I got an urgent telegram from Lord Knollys[1] to dine with him to meet Winston, but I declined as against my will I had to take part in a crisis lately and did not want to be further implicated.

Burn this. Shall I send a copy to Balfour? I am very much afraid of the Oleaginous Serpent who sits on the Woolsack [i.e. Haldane]. He's playing some game!

Yours

Fisher.

The fateful year 1914 opened quietly as far as the C.I.D. was concerned. Only three meetings took place before the outbreak of war, and they were chiefly concerned with finalising items already on its agenda. In February Walter Runciman's sub-committee on the maintenance of supplies in time of war reported,[2] and in April the Standing Sub-Committee rendered its report on the old question of the likelihood of invasion, about which it had been taking evidence since May 1913. Hankey sent to Stamfordham a series of long letters giving an almost blow-by-blow account of the Sub-committee's deliberations, and of the evidence submitted by the large number of witnesses who appeared before it.[3] These letters make it plain that he regarded the claim of Lord Roberts for no less than 510,000 men for home defence as fantastic. Indeed the Committee rejected such a proposal in short order.[4] The conclusions finally reached by the Sub-committee corresponded so closely with those contained in the Balfour and Asquith Committee reports of 1905 and 1908 that one wonders why it was considered necessary, at a time of tension, to cover all the same ground over again.[5] In particular the enquiry of 1913–14 reaffirmed the principle

[1]Francis Knollys, 1st Viscount Knollys 1911 (1837–1924). Private Secretary to Edward VII as Prince of Wales 1870–1901 and as King 1901–10. Private Secretary to George V 1910–13.
[2]C.I.D. 182B of 12th Feb. 1914. Cab. 38/26/7.
[3]Hankey to Stamfordham 2nd May, 10th, 20th and 26th June, 10th and 18th July, 20th and 27th November and 4th December, 1913, and 19th February, 1914. RA. GV E 280/1–13.
[4]C.I.D. 62A of 15th April 1914. Cab. 38/26/13.
[5]See pp. 94–5.

that "so long as our naval supremacy is assured against any reasonably probable combination of powers, invasion is impracticable". On the other hand the possibility of raids in considerable force, totalling some 70,000 men, was recognised; and the committee therefore recommended the retention at home of two divisions of regular troops to strengthen the Territorial forces. Hankey evidently sent General Sir William Robertson,[1] then Director of Military Training in the War Office, an advance copy of the new report on this subject. In acknowledging it Robertson wrote "I think you have done *very* well indeed, and that against a good deal of opposition of different kinds [presumably meaning the Admiralty]. The report contains all that is required from a W.O. point of view."[2] Though Hankey never considered the threat of invasion realistic he handled the soldiers who had so long used it to support their arguments for a greater army, and for conscription, with consummate tact. Balfour also received a copy of the report, and wrote to Hankey that "as it will now stand [it] fairly represents the evidence which has come before us, and I must congratulate you on the admirable way in which you have carried out the difficult and laborious task of drawing it up".[3]

In April 1914 the report on the insurance of shipping in time of war, which had been gestating for almost a year, also reached the C.I.D. It provided a comprehensive scheme for covering ships and cargoes against war risks, and proposed that the State should receive 80% of the premiums and accept 80% of the risks. This aroused a good deal of opposition, especially from the Treasury, and in consequence the scheme was not put into operation until the eve of war. It then quickly proved successful—and extremely profitable to the State. This gave Hankey, who had long foreseen that if trade was not to be disrupted disastrously the risks of wartime operation must be borne mainly by the government, a good deal of satisfaction.[4] On 18th August, by which time the success of the scheme was apparent, Hankey wrote to the King describing the principles involved and the results so far achieved. Lord Stamfordham at once replied thanking him on behalf

---

[1] 1860–1933. Joined Army 1877 and served in the ranks until 1888. Chief of Imperial General Staff Dec. 1915–Jan. 1918, when he "resigned" after prolonged disagreements with Lloyd George. Field-Marshal 1920.
[2] Robertson to Hankey, 3rd March 1914.
[3] Balfour to Hankey, 3rd April 1914.
[4] *Supreme Command*, I, pp. 105–7.

of the monarch and remarking that "It certainly has proved most successful to the State".[1]

In March 1914 the crisis over the possible coercion of Ulster arose out of the government's Home Rule Bill for Ireland. This led to the so-called "Curragh mutiny", when a number of Army officers handed in their resignations rather than take part in the use of force against Ulster. The likely effect of the crisis on national and Imperial defence caused Hankey great anxiety, and he appealed to Balfour to make a non-party intervention.

Hankey to Balfour. 2 Whitehall Gardens, 27th March 1914
Personal and Confidential.
Dear Mr. Balfour,
I daresay when you called yesterday you noticed that I was very reticent with regard to the question which all of us are thinking about to-day. This, of course, was due to my official position. Ever since you left, however, an idea has been forming in my mind which I venture to put before you, though, with the utmost diffidence.

Supposing to-day that the British Empire were confronted with some great and immediate crisis such as an invasion, outbreak of war, or even an ultimatum; in such an event I am convinced that all parties, Conservative, Liberal, Labour, and even Ulstermen and Nationalists would sink their difference in a patriotic desire to meet the common danger.

The danger with which we are now confronted, though less spectacular and requiring more time to operate, is not less serious than those referred to above. . . .

The present situation has already led to the resignation of officers; if prolonged, it will lead to the resignation of more; the supply of officers, already a serious problem, is likely to be even further diminished; and the difficulty is almost bound to affect injuriously the recruiting of soldiers for both the Regular and Auxiliary Forces; not to mention the deplorable effects on discipline. . . .

Is it too much to hope that all parties might be brought to realise that this danger might jeopardise our whole system of Imperial Defence, and is, in fact, as great a gamble as actual war?

Your own position is an unique one. I myself can testify, from personal knowledge, to the remarkable respect and regard which many members of the Government have for you . . . If it were possible for you to talk privately

[1] Stamfordham to Hankey 18th August 1914. RA. GV Q684/1. Hankey estimated that up to the date of his letter the State had profited to the tune of £1½ millions as a result of the War Risks Insurance scheme.

with Mr. Asquith or Lord Haldane without the fact being known (in this office, for example which has an entrance through the garden) approaching the question solely from the point of view of Imperial Defence, and also to discuss the question with Mr. Bonar Law from the same point of view, is it not possible that some compromise on the Home Rule question might yet be arrived at by mutual concession? . . .

It is with the utmost reluctance that I venture to write to you at all about this question, and I am most anxious not to appear in the matter personally at all. It is only owing to the appalling outlook from the point of view of Imperial Defence that I am constrained to write to you, the founder of the Committee of Imperial Defence, to suggest that Imperial Defence should form a bond to unite the different parties to this domestic quarrel, to avert catastrophe, and to provide a spectacle to the Nation, to the Empire, and to the whole World, which would raise our prestige higher than it has ever been before.

Yours sincerely

Balfour to Bonar Law. 28th March 1914[1]
I was at Defence Com. yesterday with Captain Hankey, who after the meeting implored me to do something, if I could, to compromise over Ulster, his view being (not unnaturally) that if no arrangement was effected the Army would be destroyed, and perhaps the Navy also. He seemed to think, poor dear, that if I saw Haldane something might be done towards effecting an arrangement. I gave him no encouragement and went off to the House to hear Asquith's statement.

He seems, however, to have been so bitten with this idea that he spoke to Haldane in the same sense, with the result that Haldane has written me the note which I herewith enclose.

I must own that I wish Hankey had confined himself to Defence Com[ittee] work, which he does excellently, and did not mix himself up with higher politics of which, naturally, he knows but little. I cannot leave Haldane unanswered, and the question is what I ought to say.

Negotiations dragged on until July when a conference of all parties concerned was called at Buckingham Palace under the Speaker of the House of Commons (Lowther). But neither the latest biography of Balfour nor a recent full history of the Curragh incident contains any mention of arbitration on the line proposed by Hankey being discussed at the conference.[2] The Palace conference broke down on 24th July

[1]Balfour papers. B.M. Add. MSS. 49693 pp. 159–60. The note from Haldane referred to here has not survived in the Balfour or Bonar Law papers.
[2]K. Young, *Arthur James Balfour* (Bell, 1963) and A. P. Ryan *Mutiny at the Curragh* (Macmillan, 1956)

after four fruitless meetings—at the time when the whole of Europe was teetering on the brink of war. Our interest in the issue arises chiefly from the fact that Hankey evidently proposed to Haldane, the Lord Chancellor, that the dispute should be referred to independent arbitrators. On 25th Haldane wrote to Hankey "very privately" that such a proposal had been considered at the Buckingham Palace conference, but was "rejected on behalf of Ulster—decisively".[1]

Meanwhile Seely, the Secretary of State for War, had resigned as a result of the "Curragh Mutiny", and many years later Hankey made some interesting comments on the consequences of the appointment of Lord Kitchener in his place. Hankey was remarking on a paper on British strategy in World War I which had been submitted to him by the Naval Staff College.

Hankey to Captain Geoffrey Blake.[2] 2 Whitehall Gardens. 3rd September 1928. Holograph.
Confidential.

. . . Still, when the war came upon us our policy was quite clear—economic pressure plus a small expeditionary force which, if the French and Russians had been efficient, ought to have prevented a disaster.

Then came an extraordinary event. Seely, the S. of S. for War (a much better man than he is given credit for) had got in a mess over the Irish business—resigned, and Asquith at the moment war broke out was holding the Seals provisionally. There was a shout for Kitchener which was irresistible. K. came. Asquith had very wisely made him a member of the C.I.D. years before in order to keep him in touch; but, immersed in the affairs of Egypt, he [Kitchener] had never kept himself *au courant*. He understood sea power but little and started off on the basis of a continental army. There was no-one in the Admiralty to stand up to him.[3] Prince Louis [of Battenberg] was past his prime, a sick man, and hampered by his German connection.[4]

[1]For Haldane's part in the Ulster crisis see Dudley Sommer, *Haldane of Cloan* pp. 295–6.
[2]Later Vice-Admiral Sir Geoffrey Blake (1882–1968). First Member New Sealand Navy Board 1929–32. Fourth Sea Lord 1932–5. Second in Command Mediterranean Fleet 1936–8. Invalided after a boating accident 1938. Recalled and served on Board of Admiralty as additional A.C.N.S. 1940. Flag Officer liaison with U.S. naval forces in Europe 1942–5.
[3]This reads unfairly to Churchill who, as First Lord, certainly was capable of "standing up to" Kitchener. Presumably Hankey was referring only to the Sea Lords.
[4]See p. 152 regarding Battenberg's resignation and his replacement by Lord Fisher

So K. became complete master of the situation. He would listen to no-one, and had no time to read up the previous studies and decisions. The collapse of the French and the failure of the Russian "steam roller" (which only rolled backwards) played into his hands. K., be it said to his credit, never believed in the one or the other. Thus, partly by the play of circumstance . . . and partly by the failure of our Allies our main effort became a military one . . . Personally I deplored the scale on which the new Armies were built up, but looking back I believe it was inevitable—though of course there was much waste of effort . . .

In May the Air Committee rendered its second report to the C.I.D.[1] Though it showed satisfactory progress with heavier-than-air craft the Germans had maintained, and even lengthened their great lead in airships. The basic reason was that the Admiralty, on whom the responsibility for development of airships had been placed, lacked experience in that field, and possessed no designers or engineers capable of emulating the German Zeppelins. Moreover a substantial body of opinion in the Admiralty was not convinced of the value of rigid airships—chiefly because of their vulnerability. War experience was ultimately to justify the sceptics; but for the first two years the Zeppelins caused us a great deal of trouble.

Also in May 1914 the C.I.D. indulged in one of those prognostications of peace which history has so often falsified—that "The Overseas Defence Committee may act on the assumption that the present international situation is likely to continue for the next three to four years . . .".[2] And as late as July Lloyd George told the House of Commons that he saw "distinct signs of a reaction against armaments throughout the world."[3] Such was the sense of urgency with which Britain prepared for World War I.

At the end of June Hankey wrote to Asquith that Churchill had invited him "to attend a Conference of Admirals", which was to meet at Portsmouth or Portland in the following month. He reassured the Prime Minister regarding the secrecy of proceedings which were bound to deal with "many questions which interest the C.I.D.", and explained that "it is always useful to me to get in personal contact with responsible naval and military officers, and to hear what they think. It is also useful to them to hear something of the difficulties of those who have to deal

[1]C.I.D. 190B of 9th May 1914. Cab. 38/26/22.
[2]126th Meeting of 14th May 1914, Item 5. Cab. 38/27/23.
[3]Speech of 23rd July 1914. Quoted Marder, *Scapa Flow*, Vol. I, p. 429.

with these questions as a whole, and to learn how local considerations have to give way before considerations of wider policy".[1] Faced with these cogent and persuasive arguments Asquith readily agreed to Hankey attending the conference. Unfortunately no record of the proceedings has survived.

On 14th July the C.I.D. held its last peace time meeting. The agenda was long, but the preparatory work had been so thoroughly done that all items were quickly disposed of. The final touches were now applied to the War Book by Hankey's able assistant Major Longridge. As the clouds darkened on the European horizon Hankey found himself engaged in constant conferences and consultations with Ministers and departmental heads. He saw very little of his family during those anxious weeks, and certainly did not share in the chauvinistic euphoria which swept the country in the first days of August 1914. Thus on 29th July he wrote to Adeline "The situation is very serious, though I think there is a fair chance of peace. I am thankful the Govt. are taking no chances . . . I am seeing all my organisation—or a great part of it— work out before my eyes. So far everything has gone smoothly . . . I had two or three interviews with the P.M., and I tackled Winston, who was in Nijinski pyjamas. Don't show this to a soul. I may have to stay up again tomorrow. The P.M. has asked me to keep within reach, so I doubt if I can get away. It is all very interesting being behind the scenes . . .". Though his hopes rose and fell with the gravity of the situation his calm detachment prevailed throughout the deepening crisis. Adeline's "cheery letters" were, he assured her, "a great solace and joy"; and despite the fact that the world they had known seemed likely to fall in ruins about them they found comfort in the knowledge that another child would soon be born to them.[2]

To Mrs. Hankey, 4th August 1914. 2 Whitehall Gardens.
. . . There is a Cabinet meeting at midnight to consider the German reply to our ultimatum [to withdraw from Belgium], and it is morally certain that we shall declare war. I have then, so to speak, to press my last button and my War Book will be complete and my work done—though I shall soon find

[1]Hankey to Asquith, 30th June 1914.
[2]Their fourth child, Henry Arthur Alers Hankey, was born on 1st September 1914 —Adeline's 32nd birthday: He was named after Henry Asquith and Arthur Balfour, who were his Godparents. Joined Diplomatic Service 1937. Served in Paris, Madrid, San Francisco and Santiago (Chile) 1939-53. Counsellor and Head of American Department, Foreign Office, 1956; Ambassador at Panama 1966.

other work to do. I think the Germans are going to bother us a bit, but God grant that we may pull through and give them a jolly hammering!

It certainly is appalling that so desperate a war should have been provoked on such miserably inadequate grounds. I now have a bed in my room, and quite frequently lie down for half an hour or so. It keeps me astonishingly fresh and fit. Everyone I meet in all the Departments looks dreadfully "rattled" and nervy, and I must try and get others to adopt the same plan . . . I must go over to Downing Street now. There is just a bare chance that I might get home tomorrow night.

On 2nd August Haldane sent Hankey "a line of warm congratulation on your success with the war organisation and Book. The arrangements appear to me to be working out almost faultlessly. That is something for you to be proud of." Though Hankey had no illusions about Fisher's habit of exaggeration it probably also gave him satisfaction to receive a letter (8th August) in which the old Admiral congratulated him on "the practical proof of the unprecedented success of your War Book". And many other letters on the same theme reached him at this time.

Despite the congratulations which poured in to Hankey on the score of the War Book in August 1914 a memorandum written by him many years later shows that in one respect he was far from satisfied with it.[1] In the autumn of 1922 he had to defend the Cabinet and C.I.D. Secretariat against a very determined take-over bid by the Treasury, instigated by its able and redoubtable Permanent Secretary Sir Warren Fisher.[2] In course of repelling the assault Hankey produced the following indictment of the Treasury's attitude to war preparations generally and to the War Book in particular.

31. In this great work of preparation for war there was only one of the main Departments whose chapter in the War Book was belated and unsatisfactory, and that was the Treasury, the Central Department of Government. Their War Book is on record in the archives of the Committee of Imperial Defence. It is jejune and inadequate. Even on the financial side

[1]Dated 7th Nov. 1922. Hankey published most of Part I of this Memorandum in *Diplomacy by Conference* (Benn, 1946) pp. 69–82. Part II, from which this extract is taken (para. 31) is unpublished.

[2]1879–1948. Civil Servant. Deputy Chairman, Board of Inland Revenue 1914 and Chairman 1918. Permanent Secretary of Treasury and Head of Civil Service 1919–39. Member of Defence Requirements Sub-Committee 1933, of which Hankey was chairman. Special Commissioner for London 1940–42 during air bombardments of World War II.

there was practically no preparation. The only consideration given to the question took place in connection with a prolonged inquiry by the Committee of Imperial Defence into Trading with the Enemy in War. But the Treasury neglected to make any preparation for the serious position which these inquiries showed must result and which in fact did result. If their record on the financial side was bad, as a Central Department of Government it was worse. They made no preparations at all. Even in regard to the preparations of the Committee of Imperial Defence and other Departments they were often obstructive, particularly in the matter of National Insurance of Shipping and Cargoes in Time of War, in which the opposition of the Treasury, which had lasted for about ten years, was only overcome on the eve of war, when the situation was becoming dangerous. As Secretary of the Committee of Imperial Defence before the War, I can say without hesitation that the Treasury was the least helpful of all the Government Departments.

One need feel no surprise that Warren Fisher's proposals came to nothing—except that Hankey himself took over the Clerkship of the Privy Council as a measure of economy.

This is perhaps an appropriate moment to assess the importance of the work of the C.I.D. prior to the outbreak of war in 1914. In his memoirs Hankey made far-reaching claims regarding the Committee's influence and effectiveness,[1] and those claims were reiterated, in some instance with increased emphasis, by Professor F. A. Johnson in his book *Defence by Committee*.[2] As however that work was to a considerable extent based on the long interviews which Hankey granted the author in the early 1950s, and the records of the Cabinet Office were not open to him, his conclusions must surely be viewed with a good deal of caution. For example one chapter of Johnson's work is entitled "Centre of Strategic Planning: 1906–1911"[3]; yet to-day, with all the official and private records open to historical scrutiny the truth seems to be considerably different. Indeed such strategic planning as took place was generally initiated by the Admiralty or the War Office, which departments sometimes placed their plans and purposes before the C.I.D. and at other times acted independently. After the Agadir crisis

[1] *Supreme Command* Chapter V to XV, esp. pp. 48–50. Also *Government Control in War* (Cambridge U.P. 1945) Ch. II.
[2] Oxford U.P. 1960. For a valuable discussion of the limitations of this work see article by John P. Mackintosh *The Role of the Committee of Imperial Defence before 1914* (English Historical Review, Vol. CCCIV, July 1962).
[3] Johnson, *op. cit.*, Chapter III.

of 1911 the attitude of Ministers, and especially of Asquith, Lloyd George and Churchill, towards the C.I.D. changed, and they showed considerably increased interest in defence problems. Yet even after that date the power of decision was still reserved to the Cabinet—or in one notorious case to a small group of Cabinet Ministers.[1] And Asquith's letters to King George V, which constitute the only record of Cabinet or Ministerial discussions at that time, contain no indication that the C.I.D. entered in any way into the picture.[2] Esher was probably the only person near to the seat of power who appreciated the true significance of this weakness in the constitution of the C.I.D. In April 1912 he wrote to Fisher that "They [Ministers] think of St. Helena, or of Borkum, as isolated problems of defence and attack. They never understand that war for us means war all over the world. It will take Hankey all his time to drive such a conception into the heads of sailors or soldiers, quite apart from politicians."[3] In fact, as we have seen, Hankey tried very hard to do exactly what Esher saw to be necessary; but such a task proved beyond the capacity of any person who lacked executive authority. As to the actual preparations of the Navy and Army for war, it is again the case that they were in the main initiated and carried out by the departments themselves. For example the fact that in August 1914 "The Fleet was ready" and at once moved to its war stations must be attributed to the Admiralty under Churchill's dynamic leadership rather than to the C.I.D.

Hankey has extolled the fact that the C.I.D. was never more than an advisory body; yet it is difficult not to conclude that the lack of executive authority was a source of serious weakness. For example had its con-clusions and recommendations been binding it would surely have been unnecessary for the committee repeatedly to review the likelihood of

[1] The "very secret defence meeting" about the Agadir crisis was attended only by Asquith, Grey, McKenna, Lloyd George and Churchill; which caused a good deal of resentment among other members of the Cabinet. See *The Journals and Letters of Reginald, Viscount Esher*. Ed. M. Brett (4 Vols., Nicholson and Watson, 1934–8) III, p. 58. This source is henceforth cited as Esher, *Journals*.

[2] Asquith wrote four "Cabinet Meeting" letters to George V in November 1911, shortly after the Agadir crisis. In only one of them (1st November) is there any mention of defence issues, and that only concerned Morley's protest regarding Anglo-French Staff conversations having taken place "without the previous knowledge and direction of the Cabinet." Haldane explained how the conversations had been initiated in 1906. Cab. 41/33/28–31.

[3] Esher to Fisher, 20th April 1912. Esher, *Journals*, II, p. 88.

invasion between 1905 and 1914; and the complete uncertainty regarding what its functions should be in war would also probably have been eliminated.[1] The simple truth is that up to 1914, and indeed for some years after the outbreak of war, no one realised that the body which directs strategy must have control over the departments which are to carry it out; and the C.I.D. neither directed strategy nor possessed any measure of control over the Admiralty and War Office.

The consequence of the Asquith government putting the C.I.D. into a state of suspended animation on the outbreak of war was that Ministers either had to choose between the advice tendered them on strategic issues by their service experts or become amateur strategists themselves—neither of which was conducive to the adoption of a sound, settled and properly co-ordinated strategy. The responsibility for this state of affairs, which was to bring tragedy in its wake, must of course rest with Asquith and his Cabinet; but Hankey, though he probably appreciated the dangers of an unco-ordinated and ill-planned strategy while his country was yet at peace, and was certainly the first to represent the correct strategic solutions to the problems which arose in 1914–15, did not bring such issues before the C.I.D. or War Council until after the outbreak of war.

If however the power and influence of the C.I.D. were severely circumscribed by its terms of reference it did carry out much useful work—especially after 1911. Thus it provided a valuable forum for the discussion of defence problems with representatives from the Dominions; and it can reasonably be argued that, but for those discussions, the Dominions would not have joined hands with the Mother Country in August 1914 with the promptitude and enthusiasm that they did show. Secondly the C.I.D. did study and report on a very wide range of subjects, from the insurance of shipping to the control of the Press, which would probably require urgent action in the event of war; and nearly all its recommendations were ultimately accepted by the Cabinet or the War Council. Furthermore in the particular case of the "War Book" the C.I.D. contributed vitally to departmental administrative preparedness and inter-departmental co-ordination.

Yet even in the matter of the issues which did come before the

[1]Haldane wanted the C.I.D. made "the centre of executive control" (*An Autobiography*, p. 235); but Esher held that "in war its doors should be closed: yes, at the very first shot". (Esher, *Journals*, II, p. 250). It was in effect the latter view that prevailed.

C.I.D. there are omissions which, with the wisdom of hindsight and of war experience to guide us, now seem surprising; and Hankey himself ignored, or at least played down, those omissions when he came to write his memoirs. Probably the greatest of them was the failure to study the mobilisation of industry and scientific research for war, including the allocation of man power and scarce materials. Indeed the scale and nature of the national effort required in total war entirely escaped its attention. Nor did the C.I.D. ever consider, let alone work out in detail, the high-level administrative machinery needed to replace conventional peace-time procedures. Yet when every allowance has been made for the constitutional disabilities under which the C.I.D. laboured, and its errors and omissions have been admitted, it still remains true to say that but for its efforts, and in particular those of its Secretary, Britain would almost certainly have been even less prepared for war than she was in 1914.

Nowadays the popular view in democratic countries is that war is wholly and irredeemably evil, and that the concept of a "just war", initiated by St. Augustine in the 4th century and developed by St. Thomas Aquinas in the middle ages, has no solid foundation in philosophy or ethics. But such views come perhaps most easily to a nation like the British who, in many centuries, have never suffered invasion nor gone down in utter defeat. Hankey, though he was certainly no chauvinist, believed that war could be forced on an essentially peace-loving people, and that when such a possibility arose it was merely common sense to prepare against it to the best of one's ability. It was to that end that he had laboured so arduously since 1908, when he had joined the C.I.D. secretariat.

On 4th August 1914 Hankey's duty changed from administering and guiding preparations for war to organising the conduct of war in the most efficient manner possible in his capacity as secretary, and indeed expert adviser, to the bodies which took over the C.I.D.'s functions—namely the War Council, Dardanelles Committee, War Committee and, finally, the War Cabinet and Imperial War Cabinet. His acceptance of the premise that the war had been forced on his country by an aggressive and militaristic adversary, though we now know this to have been a considerable over-simplification of historical events, led naturally to his acceptance of the need to wage such a war with strategic imagination, tactical skill, administrative efficiency and patriotic devotion. Between 1914 and 1918 he worked tirelessly with those objects in view;

and although his record is by no means one of unbroken success in getting adopted the measures that he deemed necessary, he did exert great influence on every aspect of the conflict. The next chapters of this biography will therefore not attempt to give a chronological account of the struggle so much as aim to throw light on one man's influence on its course.

Chapter 6

The Test of War. August 1914—May 1915

THE despatch to France of the first four infantry divisions and one cavalry division of the British Expeditionary Force under Field-Marshal Sir John French[1] took place as planned, and by 20th August they were concentrated on the French left near Maubeuge. Two more infantry divisions followed in late August and mid September, but by that time the B.E.F. had retreated from Mons to a position east of Paris, whence it took part in the successful counter-offensive known as the battle of the Marne early in September.

The advance of the German right wing through Belgium and its swing southwards towards Paris left their right flank open to assault from the sea; and thus arose the very situation which Hankey had foreseen when, before the war, he warned the C.I.D. that "if the Army has been committed to the centre of the campaign at the outset of the war, all possibility of influencing the course of the war in one of the manners suggested . . . disappears and the advantage of sea power is to a great extent lost".[2] His opposition to the despatch of the 6th Division to France having proved unavailing all that could be done was to improvise a threat to the exposed German flank. Hankey suggested landing a brigade of Marines at Ostend—which appealed to Lord Kitchener, the Secretary of State for War, and to the Ministers whom Asquith hastily summoned to consider the idea.[3]

[1] 1852–1925. 1st Earl of Ypres 1922. C-in-C, Aldershot Command 1902–7; Inspector-General of Forces 1907; C.I.G.S. 1912. C-in-C, British Expeditionary Force Aug. 1914–Dec. 1915. C-in-C, Home Forces, 1916. Lord Lieutenant of Ireland 1918–21.
[2] See p. 103. Part of this memorandum is reproduced in *Supreme Command*, I, p. 194.
[3] Hankey actually forgot the part he had played in this improvisation until in the 1930s Captain Basil Liddell Hart drew his attention to the entry in Asquith's diary (see *Memories and Reflections*, p. 28) ascribing the idea to him and not to Churchill—as Liddell Hart had written in his history of World War I. Hankey was evidently delighted to have this pointed out to him, and replied "I had for years envisaged such a rôle for my old Corps . . . and in early days went so far as to complete in the

The Marines landed on 27th–28th August under Hankey's former mentor General Aston. Though they were withdrawn four days later the threat to the German rear was real enough to cause alarm at von Kluck's headquarters.[1] Had one or two Divisions of the splendidly trained Regular Army been available to follow up the Marines the German retreat from the Marne might well have become a rout; but the opportunity was missed. In September another, though less favourable chance arose at the time when both contestants, having reached a state of deadlock on the River Aisne, were extending their northern flanks towards the English Channel in "the race for the sea". It was again at Hankey's suggestion that Aston's Marines and a scratch force of soldiers were sent to Dunkirk; but before they could accomplish anything the need to keep the great port of Antwerp open and in Allied hands became paramount, and the Marines were diverted there.

Despite the fact that the importance of Antwerp had been recognised in every war in which Britain had been engaged from the days of Elizabeth I to those of Napoleon, who described it as "a pistol pointed at the heart of England",[2] no consideration had been given to the problem of holding the port until its peril became acute in September 1914. Once again measures for its defence had to be hastily improvised, in which Churchill played the chief part—as he himself has described.[3]

Quite apart from Hankey's awareness of the strategic opportunities lost during the first few weeks of the war he was acutely conscious that decisions had been taken in a very haphazard manner. The Cabinet of some twenty members was far too big to provide clear direction and rapid decision on the multitude of diverse but important issues that arose immediately war broke out. Decisions were actually taken by a few Ministers hastily called together to deal with any emergency; and no proper record of what they had decided was kept. Such a method of conducting business was anathema to Hankey's orderly mind. Yet it was not until the end of November that a War Council, initially con-

---

rough a book on the strategy and tactics of war on the littoral". To Liddell Hart, 3rd December, 1935. Liddell Hart papers. Actually Hankey never completed the book referred to, even "in the rough". See p. 52.

[1] *Liddell Hart*, pp. 112–13.

[2] Michael Lewis, *The Navy of Britain* (Allen & Unwin, 1948), p. 389.

[3] *The World Crisis*, Vol. I (Thornton Butterworth, 1923), pp. 328–59. Henceforth cited as *Churchill*.

sisting of eight members with Hankey as secretary, was formed; and within a few months that body's membership had swelled to thirteen, and all the disadvantages inherent in too large a directing authority recurred.

At the end of September Hankey produced for the C.I.D. a list of all the Cabinet sub-committees in existence, with the names of their chairmen and secretaries. There were then 22 committees; but the number proliferated greatly as the war progressed, and in March 1915 Hankey reported the total as 38.[1] He himself was secretary of Com-mittee No. 1 the "Co-ordinating Committee on Trade and Supplies", of which McKenna, the Home Secretary, was chairman. Hankey recorded that its function was to co-ordinate the work of ten other committees, on six of which he was represented. "Captain Hankey", he wrote, "is charged with the duty of drawing the attention of their respective chairmen to any overlapping".[2] Thus was instituted the process which has been called "Defence by Committee",[3] in which Hankey played a key part right up to the time of his final retirement. Though he is entitled to a large share of the credit for the system's success in smoothing out difficulties and arriving at satisfactory com-promises, he cannot escape responsibility for the defects of a system which tended to produce formulae acceptable to both parties in a disagreement rather than clear-cut decisions, which expended a great deal of time on circumlocutory discussions, and which produced an ever-increasing flood of paper work.

On 23rd October 1914 Hankey's promotion to Lieutenant-Colonel on the retired list was gazetted.[4] Early in the following month he visited Balfour at Whittinghame, and found the society of the Balfour family as congenial as their setting; but his mention of meetings with Scottish Lord Lieutenants in Edinburgh makes it probable that the purpose of his visit was the instruction of those officers regarding their powers and duties in the event of invasion—a subject which Hankey had handled for the C.I.D. before the war.

[1]C.I.D. 214B of 1st March 1915. Cab. 42/2/2.
[2]C.I.D. 197B of 28th Sept. 1914. Cab. 38/28/38.
[3]See the book of that title by F. A. Johnson (Oxford U.P., 1960).
[4]In official papers of World War I Hankey is almost invariably referred to as "Colonel", but that description is actually incorrect. The records of the Royal Marine Office show that he was not promoted to full Colonel on the retired list until 5th Nov. 1929.

Though Balfour was not a member of the government Hankey continued to consult him on issues of policy which had come within his scope as a member of the C.I.D., and they corresponded regularly. Early in December Balfour wrote asking him to give up the "pernicious practice" of writing in his own hand because "it adds enormously to your labours . . . and I cannot see that any compensating advantage is gained by anybody".[1] But Hankey none the less continued to conduct a great deal of his vast correspondence in manuscript. This was probably in part for security reasons; but he also wrote many letters to Ministers late at night after all secretaries and typists had left his office, or from his home during one of his rare days of "rest".

By the end of November, when the War Council was formed, the state of the conflict on the western front was aptly described by Hankey as "remarkable deadlock".[2] He therefore turned his mind to the problem of how the deadlock could be broken—by either strategical or tactical innovations. We will revert to his strategical ideas later, as he did not put them forward until December; but his tactical proposals necessarily involve us in a review of the origins of the armoured fighting vehicle or "tank". A considerable number of persons, including Churchill, General Sir Ernest D. Swinton[3] and Admiral Murray F. Sueter[4] have claimed a large share of the credit for this revolutionary development,[5] and this is not the place to adjudicate on the matter. Hankey evidently had no wish to contest their claims, but he quotes in his memoirs a letter from Swinton written from G.H.Q. France and dated 11th November 1914 in which Swinton discussed what he called "the Caterpillar", and referred to "your [i.e. Hankey's] idea", and mentioned its use "for bursting in against positions *as suggested by*

[1]Balfour to Hankey, 4th Dec. 1914.
[2]Memo. of 28th Dec. 1914. Asquith papers, box 113, folios 42–4.
[3]1868–1951. Soldier and author. Assistant Secretary C.I.D. and War Cabinet 1913–17. Chichele Professor of Military History, Oxford University 1925–39. Wrote sometimes under pseudonym of "Ole-Luk-Oie".
[4]1872–1960. A pioneer of naval aviation and strong supporter of Air Ministry after 1917. Inspecting Captain of Airships 1908–11. Director of Air Department 1911–15. Superintendent of Aircraft Construction 1915–17. Member of Joint War Air Committee 1916–17. Member of Parliament (Cons.) 1921–45.
[5]See E. D. Swinton, *Eyewitness* (Hodder & Stoughton, 1932). Murray Sueter refers to his receiving the thanks of the Army Council for his share in the development of the "caterpillar landship". Churchill tells his story in *The World Crisis*, Vol. I, pp. 319–20 and Vol. II, pp. 71–91. The most balanced account is probably in B. H. Liddell Hart, *The Tanks*, Vol. I (Cassell, 1959), Ch. II.

you" (italics supplied).[1] A long letter sent by Hankey to Liddell Hart many years later, when the latter was working on his history of the Tank, probably puts the matter in fair historical perspective. It is also revealing with regard to Hankey's method of getting what he wanted.

Hankey to Captain B. Liddell Hart. Highstead, 3rd April 1948. Holograph
Dear Liddell Hart,
... Ernie Swinton has described the beginning on October 20th 1914, when he came to my room at the C.I.D. and spoke of the stalemate on the western front, which he attributed to the combined effects of barbed wire and machine guns (*Eyewitness*, p. 81). In that account he says he reminded me of the Holt caterpillar tractor and suggested its adaption to the elaboration of a military machine and I expect he is right. ...

Anyhow, we all agreed that the idea must be developed and tried out, and the question was "how" and "by whom". That was where I came in and I explained the frightful pressure, already beginning, to procure sufficient munitions of war.

We eventually agreed that we must try more than one channel of approach. So it was arranged that Tulloch[2] should follow up the technical side with a view to finding the right people for design and development; Swinton should try and interest G.H.Q. or the General Staff and Technical side with a view to creating a demand; and I should try my hand with the War Office and Ministers.

Swinton did not have much luck at G.H.Q. Nor did I at first. Balfour bit at once, but he was not yet a member of the Government. Asquith was most appreciative and promised full support—if I could get W.O. to play. But that was the rub. M.G.O. [Master General of Ordnance][3] was too over-whelmed with his own job to take it on. Wolfe Murray[4] was not much use and Callwell[5] had not yet enough grip to push a new idea unless egged on by G.H.Q. Lord Kitchener, always a good friend to me, heard me out but said the armoured caterpillars would be shot up by guns. I was stymied.

[1]*Supreme Command*, p. 228. The original of Swinton's letter, written in pencil, is preserved in the Hankey papers.
[2]Captain T. G. Tulloch, R.A., an explosives expert.
[3]Major-General Sir Stanley B. von Donop (1860–1941), Master General of Ordnance and 4th Military Member of Army Council 1913–16.
[4]Lieut.-General Sir James Wolfe Murray (1853–1919). 1st Military Member of Army Council 1914–15; C-in-C, Eastern Command, 1916–17. Hankey later recorded Churchill's description of him as "Sheep Murray". See p. 219.
[5]Major-General Sir Charles E. Callwell (1859–1928). Retired 1909. Returned to serve as Director of Military Operations, War Office, 1914–15. Author of many books on military history.

On Xmas Day 1914 . . . I had an uncontrollable impulse to put on paper an appreciation of the war situation as a whole, which took the whole day . . . After describing the deadlock it passed to a historical review of how similar deadlocks had been broken in previous wars *viz.* by providing special apparatus, or by an attack from some other direction, both methods being discussed at some length.

Under the special apparatus section . . . was [the following]

"(a) Numbers of large, heavy rollers, themselves bullet proof, propelled from behind by motor engines, geared very low, the driving wheels fitted with 'caterpillar' driving gear to grip the ground, the driver's seat armoured, and with a Maxim gun fitted. The object of this device would be to roll down the barbed wire by sheer weight, to give some cover to men creeping up behind, and to support the advance with machine-gun fire." . . .

Well, the "Boxing Day Memo" as it was called in the office, because it took the whole of that day to touch up and get typed, had a great vogue.[1] Asquith sent it to K. (who already had it), and Churchill sent it to Asquith with an appreciative Minute, and it stirred up peoples' minds against the extreme Western front theory and was passed round the War Council.

So far as Tanks were concerned, in spite of the inadequate description of the future weapon, the effect was decisive; for Churchill at once told the Chief Constructor[2] to design and build a Land Ship and set up a Committee to help him. . . .

Thereafter my policy was to back Swinton; to get him on to the development Committee, and eventually into the command.

I was also "selling" Tanks all the time to the small circle of influential people "in the know"—Asquith and his entourage, Balfour, Lord K. (who remained sceptical) and especially McKenna who, as Chancellor of the Exchequer, held the purse strings. . . .

Hankey's other tactical ideas included bullet-proof shields or armour for the use of the infantry, "smoke balls" to screen advancing troops, rockets with lines attached for dragging down barbed wire, and "spring catapults or special pumping apparatus" for throwing oil or petrol into enemy trenches. Another project conceived by his fertile brain at this time was the use of what he called "Greek Fire", or burning oil, in enemy rivers and harbours. He even carried out experiments at Highstead—but the chief results were to burn down a

---

[1] It is actually dated 28th Dec. 1914.
[2] Sir Eustace Tennyson d'Eyncourt (1868–1951). Director of Naval Construction and chief technical adviser, Admiralty 1912–23. Chairman of committee which produced the prototype tank 1915.

hedge in his garden and pollute a local stream. Though large scale, and according to Hankey, promising experiments took place on the River Orwell the idea was, to his lasting regret, dropped because of French apprehensions with regard to reprisals. We will see later how Hankey resurrected it at a critical time for Britain in World War II.

Hankey was absolutely right in recalling in his letter of 1948 to Liddell Hart that World War I had only been in progress for a few weeks when shortage of ammunition and other war materials became acute. In late August he wrote to his old chief Admiral Ottley, then managing director of Armstrongs, asking for his estimate of the munitions position. Ottley replied with a gloomy forecast. The French were, he pointed out, likely to lose various centres of production, and would therefore rely increasingly on Britain; while the Russian position was already known to be deplorable. Ottley wanted "the immediate appointment of an official with plenary powers to commandeer the entire manufacturing potentialities of the Empire, and more particularly of Great Britain".[1] But such a proposal was far in advance of current thought in British government circles. Hankey sent Ottley's letter on to Kitchener; but nothing was done until May 1915 when Lloyd George was appointed Minister of Munitions in the First Coalition government. By that time the position had deteriorated even more than Ottley had foretold.

In the field of strategy Hankey pressed in the same "Boxing Day" paper for the blockade of Germany to be tightened by an extension of "Belligerent Rights" through stricter control of neutral shipping, and for our sea power to be used to attack Turkey. He envisaged a grand Balkan alliance, and considered that three Army Corps could safely be diverted from the western front to support a campaign in that theatre. "This force", he concluded, "in conjunction with Greece and Bulgaria, ought to be sufficient to capture Constantinople". This proposal may be regarded as the inception of the Dardanelles venture, which was to prove so costly to the Allies—though not because the strategy was ill-conceived. Hankey also wanted "more decisive warfare" waged against "the remaining German colonies" in East and South-West Africa; and there one may feel that his enthusiasm for peripheral

[1]Ottley to Hankey 2nd Sept. 1914. Kitchener papers. P.R.O. 30/57/81. Ottley suggested Sir Percy Girouard (1867–1932) as Munitions Overlord. He considered the task far beyond the capacity of the Master-General of Ordnance's department, Girouard became Director-General of Munitions Supply in 1915.

warfare led him astray, since expeditions of that nature were bound to absorb considerable forces, the loss of her colonies could not be fatal to Germany, and as long as British sea power was supreme they were of no use whatever to her—except possibly as bargaining counters in the event of the war going badly for Germany on the continent.

It was obviously Hankey's "Boxing Day Memorandum" that caused Balfour to write at unusual length expressing tactful misgivings with regard to his somewhat over-simplified advocacy of an offensive in south-east Europe.

Balfour to Hankey. Whittinghame, Preston Kirk. Jan. 2nd 1915
My dear Hankey,
. . .
(2) *Your memorandum upon general Military Policy*
I agree, and I fear that everybody must agree, that the notion of driving the Germans back from the west of Belgium to the Rhine by successively assaulting and capturing one line of trenches after another seems a very hopeless affair; and unless some means can be found for breaking their line at some critical point, and threatening their communications, I am unable to see how the deadlock in the west is to be brought to any rapid or satisfactory conclusion. If the Russians are as strong as they profess to be (of which so far I have seen no signs) they ought not to have the same difficulty in an "offensive" on the eastern frontier as we are experiencing on the western; for, when they have satisfactorily disposed of the Austrians, they might be able to do what the Allies cannot do in Flanders or France . . . Put the matter, however, as we like, no dramatic *dénouement* of the present situation seems to be in sight.

So far I am in entire agreement with your Memorandum; and I also agree with all your observations upon new contrivances for facilitating offensive warfare. But I am not sure that I see in your proposals for attacking the enemy elsewhere than in the North of Europe any solution of our difficulties. It is not that I decry the advantages of inducing the Balkan States . . . to make a combined attack upon Turkey. On the contrary I think such a policy would have very valuable results. But the questions involved are, I fear, so difficult that months of preliminary negotiation would be required to allay passions due to events in the past, and to arrange such a division of spoils as would satisfy these jealous little states. And, in addition, there looms before us the menacing question of Constantinople. Who is to own it? And what is to be the international position of the Bosphorus? The solution you propose for the Dardanelles hardly applies to the other end of the Sea of Marmara.

Moreover it must be remembered that Germany is perfectly indifferent to the fate of her Allies except in so far as her own fate is bound up with it.

Were Turkey completely paralysed, the Russians could no doubt bring troops from the Caucasus to Galicia, and we could take troops from Egypt to German East Africa, or to some European theatre of operations. These would be very great advantages, but they would not finish the war.

I agree, however, that from the political and diplomatic point of view it would be desirable to deprive Germany of everything she has to bargain with; and to hit Turkey as hard as we can. But I fear operations like these, however successful must be regarded as merely subsidiary.

Would it be possible to land troops in Montenegro, and thus add strength to the southern menace to Austria? . . . if it were within the range of possibility, it seems to me that it would not only hasten the Austrian *débâcle*, but might have the indirect effect of compelling Italy to take a hand in the game. Such an operation, could it be carried out, would surely have more effect upon the main theatre of operations than anything we can do in Syria or Africa . . .

Yours sincerely

To return to the western front, the story of the despatch of the extemporised and half-trained British force to Antwerp, and of Churchill's part in it, is too well known to require recapitulation here.[1] By 10th October all was over and the fortress surrendered. But the siege had been prolonged by five days, so enabling the Belgian field army to make good its escape down the Flanders coast, and denying to the Germans for the second time the opportunity to achieve a decision in the west. Though the truth was obscured at the time by the flood of criticism to which Churchill was subjected on account of the losses sustained in the defence of Antwerp, today it is plain that the expedition fully justified itself. So ended what Liddell Hart has regretfully described as "the first and last effort in the west to make use of Britain's amphibious power".[2] But Hankey's faith in the effectiveness of such a strategy was in no wise diminished. In Liddell Hart's view his memorandum of 28th December showed "a grasp of grand strategy" which contrasted markedly with "the horizon of most soldiers, especially the highest, [which] was narrowly bounded by tactics".[3]

With the western front reduced to a state of deadlock and the Russian advance in the east shattered by the German victory at Tannenberg at the end of August the focus of attention shifted to the Middle East. The escape of the two German warships *Goeben* and *Breslau* from the

---

[1]See *Churchill*, I, Ch. XV.   [2]*The Real War* (Faber, 1930), p. 81.
[3]*Liddell Hart*, p. 216.

central Mediterranean to Constantinople at the very beginning of the war—through a succession of muddles and errors committed by the local naval commanders and the Admiralty—had very far-reaching effects.[1] The German mission in Constantinople exploited the situation produced by the arrival of their country's warships very skilfully, hostile acts were committed against Russia by the Turks, and an attack was mounted against the Suez Canal. On the last day of October Britain and France declared war on Turkey. Those developments coincided with the recall of Admiral Fisher to the office of First Sea Lord by Churchill; and so was accomplished the "resurrection" for which Fisher had lobbied and intrigued ever since he had left that same office in 1910.

The Churchill-Fisher combination was initially highly successful. Despite his 73 years the Admiral had lost little, if any, of his thrustful dynamism; while Churchill's vigour and strategic insight provided the necessary complementary qualities in the high level committees as well as at the Admiralty. Those two were not likely to accept tamely the continuation of the deadlock in the west. The first fruits of this remarkable association was the naval victory off the Falkland Islands (8th December) whereby the destruction of Admiral Cradock's squadron off Coronel on 1st November was speedily revenged.[2] But Fisher and Churchill also began at once to seek strategic means of breaking the deadlock in the west through exploitation of sea power. Unfortunately a wide divergence of view regarding the theatre of choice soon became apparent. Fisher favoured a landing on the German coast —either in the North Sea or preferably in the Baltic, within 80 miles of Berlin; but neither his naval colleagues nor the military authorities had any use for such ideas. Kitchener at first proposed a landing at Alexandretta to sever the main line of Turkish communications, but soon came round to the conventional military view that all available forces should be allocated to the "main theatre" in the west; while Lloyd George wanted to give all possible support to the Serbians, who had resisted the Austrian invasion most gallantly but were now faced by greatly superior forces. Thus was born the long-lasting controversy between the "Easterners" and the "Westerners". It would, however, be more correct to describe the controversy as between the "Maritime" and the "Continental" schools of strategy—which had in fact been in progress since the early years of the century. Hankey, as we have seen,

[1]See Marder, *Scapa Flow*, II, Ch. II.   [2]*ibid.*, I, Ch. VI.

had always belonged to the maritime school; but there is no evidence that he ever showed any enthusiasm for Fisher's North Sea or Baltic plans—which in fact never got off the ground. In the letter of 1928, part of which was quoted earlier,[1] Hankey described Fisher's ideas and went on to say that "by the time war came conditions had changed. The submarine had developed; the German navies were formidable . . . and our own mining service was contemptible. Nevertheless Fisher, on his return to power, still believed in his plan and built a mass of miscellaneous craft for its *dénouement* in the Baltic. But he could never persuade anyone else in the Navy or out of it to believe in his plan. . . . The fact is that Fisher was too old. He still possessed vision and driving power. But these were accompanied by a senile exaggeration of the defects of his character—head-hunting carried to excess, suspicion, exaggerated desire for power; and in addition he tired easily and shrank from responsibility".[2]

Meanwhile Churchill was becoming increasingly absorbed in the possibilities of an attack on the Dardanelles, and when on 2nd January 1915 the Russians appealed for a "demonstration" against Turkey to relieve pressure on the Caucasus front his opportunity appeared to have come. Unfortunately Churchill's great powers of persuasion now overbore sound judgement. He at once telegraphed to Admiral Carden,[3] who was in command of the naval forces in the eastern Mediterranean, asking whether he considered "the forcing of the Dardanelles by ships alone a practicable operation". Carden's reply was cautious. The straits could not, he said, "be rushed"; but "they might be forced by extended operations with [a] large number of ships". Kitchener having meanwhile declared that no troops could be spared for a combined operation, plans for a purely naval attack were framed. On 13th Churchill brought the matter before the War Council, and Hankey recorded the extraordinary decision "That the Admiralty should also prepare for a naval expedition in February to bombard and take the Gallipoli Peninsula with Constantinople as its objective".[4] A week later Churchill gave

---

[1]To Captain Geoffrey Blake, 3rd September 1928. See p. 134.
[2]Though few will agree that Fisher ever "shrank from responsibility" this letter otherwise sums up his qualities and defects as they were in 1914–15 very fairly.
[3]Later Admiral Sir Sackville H. Carden (1857–1930). Admiral Superintendent, Malta Dockyard, 1912–14. Commanded Eastern Mediterranean squadrons and naval forces in Dardanelles operation Sept. 1914–March 1915.
[4]*Churchill*, p. 111. *Liddell Hart*, p. 218.

orders that the attack should begin as soon as the new battleship *Queen Elizabeth*, by whose 15-inch guns he set great store, had arrived.

To Mrs. Hankey. Committee of Imperial Defence, 2 Whitehall Gardens. 21st Jan. 1915

Shortly after my arrival this morning I was sent for by the P.M. At 10 Downing Street I found Sir Edward Grey and Lloyd George. The Prime Minister said that as Lord Kitchener was away he had sent for me. We then had a very important discussion and some developments are in the air.

There is to be a very important dinner party at Lord K's house this evening, when the developments are to be discussed with a representative of the French Government . . . In the circumstances I feel I ought to be about. I might be wanted early in the evening when a number of preliminary interchanges of personal views will probably take place, or after the dinner party, or first thing tomorrow morning (or most likely not at all!).

In any case I don't like to go home with the telephone down. I hope they will mend it quick . . .

Hankey saw little of his wife and family at this busy and anxious time, but his almost daily letters told Adeline that great events were in the offing.

On 24th January Hankey recirculated to the War Council the paper of 1906 in which the C.I.D. had considered the question of an assault on the Dardanelles, and the General Staff had come down strongly against "unaided action by the fleet".[1] His purpose must surely have been plain to the Ministers concerned. On 2nd February he followed up with a forcefully worded memorandum to Asquith in which he said "I have been immensely impressed with the cumulative effect of the arguments presented [to the War Council] in favour of *military* action in the Dardanelles at the earliest possible date". He developed at length the reasons why that was so, and also stressed the strategic, economic and political advantages which would accrue from opening up the Dardanelles and Bosphorus.[2] Despite the vacillations over the despatch of troops and the general unpreparedness of both army and navy to undertake a large combined operation Hankey was at first optimistic. On 19th February, however, the assault on Gallipoli was opened by a naval bombardment of the outer forts. Then bad weather stopped all operations for five days. During the interlude Fisher, despite the fact that he had at first gone along with Churchill, wrote to Lloyd George

[1] C.I.D. 92B of 20th Dec. 1906. Cab. 38/12/60.
[2] G.8 of 2nd Feb. 1915. Cab. 42/1/30.

that "Rashness in war is Prudence and Prudence in war is Criminal! The Dardanelles [is] futile without soldiers."[1] It is likely that he had been influenced by Hankey's prescient warnings.

Shortly before the naval bombardment of the Gallipoli forts Lloyd George raised for the first time an alternative project which was in the end to play a very large part in Allied military plans and purposes. On 7th February he wrote to Grey, the Foreign Secretary, pressing for an expeditionary force to be sent to Salonika. He said that he had discussed such a project the previous day with Generals French and Robertson, and described the latter as "a shrewd, clear-headed and strong man". No General, he continued, had made "quite the same impression on my mind as Robertson did yesterday". Moreover, according to Lloyd George, he had described the Salonika idea as "good strategy", and had "maintained that view throughout the discussion".[2] Bearing in mind Robertson's firm adherence to the western front strategy later as C.I.G.S., and also Lloyd George's quarrel with him over that very issue, the impression Robertson made on the Chancellor at their first encounter seems as surprising as the General's alleged willingness to adopt a "peripheral strategy". But in truth Lloyd George had addressed himself to the wrong person; for Grey was notoriously ignorant of military operations and strategy, and of their inseparability from the conduct of diplomacy in time of war.[3] The people whom Lloyd George really had to convince regarding the soundness of his proposal were of course Kitchener and his colleagues on the General Staff. To Hankey, who did understand the diplomatic-military relationship, it was only possible to carry out one overseas attack at that time; and if the decision was in favour of Gallipoli all available strength should be concentrated on that object.

To Mrs. Hankey. Committee of Imperial Defence, 2 Whitehall Gardens. Feb. 22nd 1915
Just a line only as it is after 8 p.m. and I am still in the office . . . It has been a very heavy day. I have had to interview Lloyd George, Balfour, Lord

[1]Fisher to Lloyd George 23rd Feb. 1915. Lloyd George papers E/2/15/4.
[2]Lloyd George to Grey, 7th February 1915. *ibid.*
[3]See G. M. Trevelyan, *Grey of Fallodon* (Longmans, Green, 1957), p. 281. "His [Grey's] principal weakness as Foreign Minister was, in my view, that he took no interest in military operations".

Fisher, Sir Edward Troup,[1] Colonel Cochrane, head of War Office secret service, Col. Gorton[2] (who leaves for France), an M.P. home from the front to attack the Press Censorship, as well as my own staff bothering me and a dozen trivial letters to dictate—to say nothing of setting on foot the new "frightfulness" you and I hatched yesterday.[3] Besides all this I have written the Minutes of the last War Council—14 pages of foolscap in my own fist. Yet this is only a sample day. But I thrive on it! . . .

The meeting of the C.I.D. on 23rd February was the first in which the records show Hankey as actually taking full part in a discussion.[4] It was also the last meeting of the Committee as such until June 1920.[5] On 26th February 1916, the day after the naval bombardment of the Gallipoli forts had been resumed, some marines from the warships landed on the peninsula to demolish the guns in the forts abandoned by the Turks. They met with no resistance, and Hankey told his wife that "This affair is going well. The marines were landed and occupied the forts—quite as I had hoped to see". But in truth the bombardments and small scale landings had given the enemy ample warning of our intentions, and they reacted vigorously. "Up to 25th February", remarks the Turkish official account, "it would have been possible to effect a landing at any point on the Peninsula and the capture of the Straits would have been comparatively easy". But no Allied troops had yet arrived, and for nearly three weeks after that crucial date only a somewhat desultory naval bombardment took place. On 11th March the Admiralty, losing patience with Carden, pressed him to take decisive action. But he had in truth never been up to the heavy responsibility which had fortuitously fallen to his lot. He now fell sick and was succeeded by his second-in-command, Vice-Admiral J. M. de Robeck.[6]

Meanwhile in London there was much discussion about the despatch

---

[1] 1857–1941. Civil Servant. Assistant Under-Secretary of State, Home Office, 1903–8 and Permanent Under-Secretary, 1908–22. Chairman of many government committees, 1922–38. Hankey wrote his name as Sir Ernest, obviously in error.

[2] Colonel J. Gorton had served under Hankey in the C.I.D. secretariat.

[3] This must refer to Hankey's experiments with burning oil. See pp. 148–9. He submitted a paper on the subject on 1st May 1915. C.I.D. 217B. Cab. 42/2/16.

[4] Minutes of 132nd Meeting. Cab. 2/3.

[5] 29th June 1920 is the date shown for the 133rd Meeting.

[6] 1862–1928. Admiral of Patrols 1912–14. Commanded naval forces in Gallipoli campaign 1915–16. C-in-C, Mediterranean 1919–22 and British High Commissioner at Constantinople 1919–20. C-in-C, Atlantic Fleet 1922–24. Admiral of the Fleet 1925.

of troops. At a War Council on 3rd March Churchill optimistically calculated that with a Russian army corps from Batum, three Greek and one French division, and the British troops in Egypt and on Lemnos "we should dispose of 120,000 to 140,000 men".[1] At the next meeting a week later, Kitchener managed to make the total strength "available against Constantinople" 128,710 of all ranks.[2] Neither he nor Churchill ever seem to have realised that, even if all the units arrived at the scene of action, which was not at all likely, such a heterogeneous force could not possibly be fit to carry out that most hazardous of operations of war—an opposed landing. Furthermore the possibility of Greek participation was quickly ruled out by the failure of the British *démarche* in Athens. On 6th March King Constantine refused to adopt the policy favoured by his Prime Minister M. Venizelos,[3] and the latter resigned.

On 6th February "Colonel" E. M. House,[4] President Wilson's special emissary, arrived in London and had discussions with Grey on House's favourite scheme for "Freedom of the Seas". The Foreign Secretary, without consulting the Cabinet, led House to suppose that Britain would go a long way to meet his suggestion that if the Germans stopped submarine attacks on merchant ships we would lift the blockade on foodstuffs.[5] House went straight on to Berlin to sound the German government; but they reacted with singular ineptitude by instructing Bernstorff,[6] their ambassador in Washington, to start propaganda in favour of Freedom of the Seas, thus at once giving House's project a Teutonic flavour. Meanwhile the discussions between House and Grey had aroused Hankey's serious misgivings, and on 25th February he sent

---

[1]Cab. 42/2/3. [2]Cab. 42/2/5.

[3]Eleutherios Venizelos (1864–1936). Cretan and Greek politician and nationalist. Prime Minister 1910–March 1915, when he was forced to resign by King Constantine. Re-elected August 1915, but again forced to resign in October. Formed dissident government at Salonika Oct. 1916, and returned to Athens as Prime Minister in June 1917 after abdication of Constantine. Engaged in disastrous war with Turkey 1920–22, leading to his exile. Returned to Greece 1923. Prime Minister again 1928–32 and for a few months in 1933.

[4]1858–1938. Personal adviser to President Woodrow Wilson and, later, to President Franklin Roosevelt. The title of "Colonel" was entirely fictitious and House never held any military rank.

[5]*Supreme Command*, I, pp. 359–68.

[6]Count Johann von Bernstorff (1862–1939). German Diplomat. Ambassador at Washington 1908–17 and at Constantinople 1917–18. The addressee of the notorious "Zimmerman telegram" of 16th Jan. 1917, which precipitated the entry of the U.S.A. into the war.

Asquith a strongly worded memorandum on the subject. "If Germany's 'Achilles heel' is her food supply", he wrote, "it is only common sense that we should devote our efforts to attacking it systematically"; and he pointed out that before the war the C.I.D. had investigated the matter exhaustively, and had approved the policy of "bringing the utmost possible economic pressure to bear on the enemy". He regarded the possible exemption of our merchant ships from submarine attack and the encouragement of American friendliness as altogether too high a price to pay for the abandonment of what was possibly our most powerful weapon.[1]

From 1st March, described by Hankey as "a red letter day for the development of our economic policy",[2] the British government made applicable the famous Order in Council strengthening the blockade in reprisal for German submarine sinkings—an order which the Americans claimed to be illegal[3]; and Asquith informed the Commons that "there is no form of economic pressure to which we do not consider ourselves entitled to resort". None the less House persisted in his efforts, but when at last Lord Crewe, who was acting for the tired and ailing Grey, brought the issue before the Cabinet in May they decided that no change should be made in our blockade policy. On the 7th of that month a German submarine sank the great Cunard liner *Lusitania*, with very heavy loss of life, including many Americans. Though German ineptitude undoubtedly played a part in the frustration of House's purpose, Hankey's prompt action in drawing the Prime Minister's attention to the implications of the suggested change of policy must also have been influential.

At the beginning of March 1915 Hankey decided to start keeping the detailed diary referred to earlier. He wrote on the flyleaf of the first of the four volumes "For a long time I had felt that my association with many interesting people, and my experiences as Secretary of the Committee of Imperial Defence ought not to go entirely unrecorded.

[1]Hankey to Asquith 25th Feb. 1915. Asquith papers, Box 113, folios 170/2. The greater part of this memorandum is printed in *Supreme Command*, I, pp. 366–7.
[2]*Supreme Command*, I, p. 368.
[3]See M. W. N. P. Consett, *The Triumph of Unarmed Forces 1914–18* (Williams and Norgate, 1923), Ch. IV and Appendix II for particulars of this order and for American arguments against its legality. The Order in Council "Framing Reprisals for Restricting Further the Commerce of Germany" (1915, No. 206) was actually signed on 11th March, but it applied to all ships which had sailed on or after 1st March.

Now, as Secretary to the Prime Minister's War Council, I find myself directly associated with the central policy of the great European war. Though regretting that I have not commenced this diary earlier I have decided that no further time should be lost, and that, so far as time permits, I will jot down from time to time any incidents of historical, political, military or personal interest with which I may be personally connected. Adeline has agreed to act as my *amanuensis*. M. P. A. H. 5th March 1915". The entries for the first month are all in Adeline's hand, but on 1st April Hankey took over from her the task of writing up the diary—and he continued to do so, with very few exceptions, right to the day when he closed the last volume. Probably his frequent separations from his wife during the war made it impossible for her to continue as his "amanuensis".

The first diary entry, not quoted in Hankey's memoirs, is interesting.

Diary 4th March 1915
. . . Saw Captain [W. R.] Hall, Admiralty War Staff,[1] who said that negotiations have been opened to bribe the Turks to oust the Germans, as I had proposed earlier. Communications established through Neil Bey, ex-Minister of Justice, with Talaat Bey.[2]

In fact that brief entry records one of the more extraordinary episodes of World War I, the whole truth of which has only recently been revealed.[3] Two British agents George G. Eady and Edwin Whittall were given authority to commit the British government to a payment of up to £4 millions to buy the Turks out of the war. Despite the opening of the bombardment of the Gallipoli forts on 19th February, and the fact that the terms demanded by the British were severe, negotiations were opened, and on 15th March the British agents, both of whom had long experience of Turkey, met the Turkish representatives at Dedeagatch. The negotiations failed because the British government could not give a guarantee that Constantinople would remain in Turkish hands after the war. As Hankey had, early in

[1]1870–1943. Later Admiral Sir Reginald Hall, the brilliantly successful Director of Naval Intelligence 1914–18. In a conflict from which the Admiralty does not in general emerge well Hall's work was the outstanding exception.
[2]Presumably Hankey was referring to Nail Bey who had been Minister of Finance, not Justice, 1911–12 and Talaat Bey who was acting Minister of Finance and Minister of Interior in 1915.
[3]See article "A Ghost from Gallipoli" by Captain G. R. G. Allen. The Royal United Service Institution Journal, Vol. CVIII, No. 630 (May 1963), pp. 137–8.

his career, been deeply immersed in naval intelligence work in the Middle East,[1] and knew Hall well, it seems likely that his claim to have originated a proposal which was not by any means as fantastic as it may now appear was solidly based. For there was in Turkey considerable opposition to the alliance with Germany, and many influential Turks were imbued with feelings of friendship towards Britain. Had the secret negotiations succeeded the whole course of the war would have been altered, with the British fleet steaming up to Constantinople unopposed and the shortest supply route to Russia thereafter open.

The diary also contains some interesting entries, which Hankey did not reproduce, concerning the search for the German cruiser *Dresden*, the sole survivor from von Spee's Asiatic Squadron after the Falkland Island battle (8th Dec. 1914).

Diary 4th March
Hall also told me the *Dresden* [has been] discovered in remote Chilean bay. Churchill had ordered two ships to attack her. Felt very anxious about this; after consulting Mr. Balfour decided it [was] my duty to tell Prime Minister in confidence. Did so. Afraid lest action in neutral waters should embroil us with Chile and alienate other [i.e. neutral] nations.

5th March
The *Dresden* affair was settled. Grey, who knew that the *Dresden* was in Chilean waters though not of the proposed action wrote to Churchill. The matter was apparently settled at a conference between the P.M., Grey and Churchill, from which the P.M. emerged looking rather heated.

The above diary entries must refer to the location of the *Dresden* by cryptographic intelligence on 5th March. Three days later she was sighted and chased by the cruiser *Kent*, but got away. She then hid in the Juan Fernandez group, where on 14th British warships found her. After a brief action she scuttled herself. So ended the last threat from German surface warships to Allied trade.[2]

Diary 12th March 1915
Yesterday saw the King and spent an hour with him. He read me a long letter from the Prince of Wales, written the night before in France and describing an attack near La Bassée. Extremely good and interesting letter accompanied by a map and a tracing to put over the map showing in different

[1]See Chapters II and III.
[2]See Geoffrey Bennet, *Coronel and Falklands* (Batsford, 1962), pp. 169–172, for a full account of the search for and destruction of the *Dresden*.

Evacuating men and guns from Suvla Bay on rafts in daylight,
December 1915

Water-carts waiting to draw rations from the anchorage, probably at
Cape Helles

Cape Helles: probaby view of 'X' beach

Artificial harbour at Cape Helles

coloured chalks the position before the attack and after, and the position they are aiming at. The letter began "Dear Papa". The King very cordial.

Diary 17th March 1915
I should have mentioned that the P.M. talked to me about the attendance of Mr. Bonar Law and Lord Lansdowne at the War Council on 10th. Mr. Bonar Law came to the P.M. two days ago and told him that though they "enjoyed" the meeting . . . it would not be possible for them, for party reasons, to attend in future. If they did so they feared it would weaken their position in the Conservative Party and, as Mr. Bonar Law put it, render their future support of the government less effective. In the end the P.M. instructed me to send them all papers prepared for the War Council, but not to invite their attendance . . . How astonishing is the influence of party politics.

To return to the Dardanelles, on 18th March, the very day that Hall's agents withdrew from Dedeagatch, Admiral de Robeck opened the general attack for which the Admiralty had been pressing. Unfortunately a few days earlier a small Turkish steamer had laid a line of 26 mines undetected in the waters in which the fleet had been seen to manœuvre during the earlier bombardments. That trivial number of mines sank three of the 18 British and French battleships present and seriously damaged a battle-cruiser. The moral effect was more serious than the material and human loss, since all the sunk ships were old and most of their crews were rescued. De Robeck had originally intended to renew the attack, but on 23rd he changed his mind and reported that the fleet could not get through without help from the army.

Meanwhile a tug of war was in progress in Whitehall between "Easterners" and "Westerners"; and Kitchener, who several times changed his mind, did not authorise the despatch of the well-trained 29th Division until 10th March.[1] General Sir Ian Hamilton,[2] who had

[1] An interesting commentary on Kitchener's fitness for the office of Secretary of State for War at this time is to be found in an undated but post-war letter from General Sir A. Murray (Deputy C.I.G.S. March 1915 and C.I.G.S. September–December 1915) to General Sir Ian Hamilton. Murray remarked that his ten months' experience of close contact with Kitchener had convinced him that he was quite unfit to hold high office at a period of acute strain. At the beginning of each week he was, according to Murray, in fairly good shape; but by Fridays, when he vanished to his house at Broome Park until the following Monday, he showed clearly that he was worn out. Ian Hamilton Papers.

[2] General Sir Ian S. M. Hamilton (1853–1947). G.O. C-in-C, Southern Command 1905–9. Adjutant-General and 2nd Military Member of Army Council 1909–10. G.O. C-in-C, Mediterranean and Inspector-General, Overseas Forces 1910–15. Lord Rector of Edinburgh University 1932–35.

been belatedly nominated to command the troops hurried out—
without his staff. On 18th he met de Robeck, and his first decision was
that the loading of the transports which had arrived was so chaotic that
the whole expeditionary force must withdraw to Egypt to sort things
out.

Meanwhile at home Hankey had followed up his pressure for military
action with a long paper optimistically entitled "After the Dardanelles.
The Next Steps", in which he surveyed all the measures needed to reap
the benefits of the success which he still anticipated.[1] On 16th March,
by which time Kitchener had at last agreed to release the 29th Division,[2]
Hankey sent Asquith one of the most prescient papers he ever wrote.
One feels that he, and he alone fully grasped the risks of the undertaking to which the government was now committed. It is in this
context that Liddell Hart has remarked that "Hankey was the only
expert adviser of the British government who had thought out the
foundations of strategy"[3]; while the latest historian of the Gallipoli
campaign has written that "In London only Hankey seems to have had
any premonition of disaster".[4] Very much the same views, though
worded more guardedly, were evidently held by the official historian.[5]
The tragedy was that none of the politicians or service leaders with
whom rested the power to carry out the measures recommended by
Hankey appreciated the import of his warning. In justice to him the
greatest part of his memorandum is reproduced verbatim; but it should
also be recorded that at this time Hankey sought and received the
advice of J. S. Corbett,[6] the naval historian, with whom he had long
been on intimate terms and who now gave him the fruits of his study
of combined operations in earlier wars. Thus it is reasonable to

[1]G.10 of 1st March 1915. Cab. 42/2/1.

[2]On the vacillations over the despatch of this division between 16th Feb., when the
War Council agreed it should go to Lemnos, and 16th March when it actually left, see
Churchill, I, pp. 603–10.

[3]Liddell Hart, p. 226.

[4]Robert Rhodes James, Gallipoli (Batsford, 1965), p. 94. Henceforth cited as James.

[5]C. F. Aspinall Oglander, Gallipoli, Vol. I, pp. 101–2.

[6]Later Sir Julian Corbett (1854–1922). Barrister 1877–82. Lecturer in History at
Naval War College 1903. Author of many works on naval history including Vols.
I–III of Naval Operations, the official naval history of World War I. On 4th Feb. 1915
Corbett replied at length to Hankey's request "for a note on our old attempts at the
Dardanelles". Cab. 42/1/32.

attribute a part of Hankey's prescience to Corbett's historical knowledge and insight.

2 Whitehall Gardens. 16th March 1915
Prime Minister. Secret

1. From the point of view of the War Council the situation as regards the attack on the Dardanelles is far from clear. As recently as the last meeting the War Council were informed by the First Lord that the navy still hoped and expected to get through the Dardanelles without the assistance of military forces. Now, however, as was anticipated by most naval officers who were acquainted with the locality, the fleet is held up by a combination of mines and howitzers. In order to overcome these obstacles, the employment of a considerable land force is contemplated.

2. It must be borne in mind that up to the present time the employment of military forces has been proposed only to clear up the situation *after* the Dardanelles have been forced. Now, therefore . . . we are faced with a new and possibly very formidable operation to be carried out by the land forces.

3. Is it not desirable that the War Council should ascertain definitely the scope of the operations contemplated, and the extent of the preparations made to carry out these operations? In this connection it must be remembered that combined operations require more careful preparations than any other class of military enterprise. All through our history such attacks have failed when the preparations have been inadequate, and the successes are in nearly every case due to the most careful preparation beforehand. It would appear to be the business of the War Council to assure themselves, in the present instance, that these preparations have been thoroughly thought out.

4. It must be remembered also that one of the greatest advantages to be obtained from this class of operation namely that of surprise, has been lost. If a large force of troops had been sent at the very outset, secretly and unobtrusively, and fully equipped with boats and everything they required, so as to be available the moment the outer forts had fallen, it is by no means unlikely that, assisted by judicious feints to confuse the enemy as to their intended objective, they might have captured the plateau overlooking the forts at the Narrows by a *coup-de-main*. Instead of being announced as a mere demonstration, as was contemplated by the War Council, even the first bombardment of the outer forts was announced as an attack, and at no time has any attempt been made to conceal our intention to force the Dardanelles at any cost. Now that the fleet has been held up by the minefields, the enemy knows exactly the point at which our attack must be directed. He has had as much time as he requires to entrench this point, to emplace his artillery, to pour reinforcements on to the land on both sides of the Straits, and to make every sort of preparations. The military enterprise, therefore, will be of a most

formidable nature. It is suggested that the War Council ought to cross-examine the naval and military authorities on the extent of the preparations, and particularly with regard to such points as the following:

(a) The number of troops it is proposed to employ?

(b) The arrangements made for the supply of boats and tugs?

(c) The preparations made for the provision of landing piers, pontoons, etc?

(d) The arrangements for the supply of water and provisions?

(e) The hospital arrangements. Is it contemplated to use nothing but floating hospitals, or will there be field hospitals on shore?

(f) Is it expected that the Dardanelles will be carried by a *coup-de-main*, or is the possibility of siege operations contemplated?

(g) In the latter event, what siege guns will be available, and what arrangements have been made for landing them and their ammunition?

(h) Possibly, it is proposed that the men-of-war should supply the necessary heavy artillery to overcome the enemy's heavy movable artillery. If so, are the military authorities satisfied that the projectiles available in men-of-war are suitable for this purpose . . .?

(i) What arrangements are contemplated for the transport from the landing place to the army, of supplies of ammunition, food, water, etc., over a rough country with very few roads in it. . . .?

5. Unless details such as these, and there are probably others, are fully thought out before the landing takes place, it is conceivable that a serious disaster may occur.

The War Council considered his memorandum, but only perfunctorily, on 19th; and no action was taken.[1] That same day Hankey wrote to Lloyd George, a strong advocate for the despatch of troops, recapitulating all the points he had pressed on the Prime Minister. He wanted "a joint committee to work out the attack on the Dardanelles in detail", and ended by roundly declaring "we cannot afford another fiasco due to inadequate staff preparation.[2] I hope you will back me up in this if you get a chance. We don't want Lord K. and the First Lord on the Committee, just technical people . . . Mr. Balfour would be a good chairman." Finally he added a postscript "The plan this time must be worked out with the precision of our War Book".[3] One may

[1] Cab. 42/2 and 22/1/2.

[2] Hankey was probably here referring to the total failure of the combined operation against Tanga in German East Africa in November 1914. See J. S. Corbett, *Naval Operations*, Vol. I (Longmans, Green, 1920), p. 374.

[3] Hankey to Lloyd George 19th March 1915. Lloyd George papers C/4/19/4.

see in Hankey's proposal for a Joint Committee the genesis of the idea that finally came to fruit in the Chiefs of Staff Committee of 1923. But in 1915 such a proposal was too revolutionary to receive serious consideration—let alone command acceptance. Asquith and Lloyd George were not the only Ministers on whom Hankey pressed his views. At this time he warned Churchill that at the best the landings would be "of extraordinary difficulty"—to which the First Lord optimistically and obstinately riposted "that he could not see that there was any difficulty at all".[1] In a final attempt on 12th April Hankey wrote to Asquith that the military operation "appears . . . to be to a certain extent a gamble upon the supposed shortage of supplies and inferior fighting qualities of the Turkish armies".[2] Unhappily neither the War Council, nor individual Ministers, nor the service departments heeded Hankey's advice and urgings; and the expedition, when it did arrive, had to cope with difficulties and deficiencies of every kind, which could and should have been foreseen and catered for.

It should not be thought that, because the Dardanelles campaign absorbed so much of Hankey's time and efforts during the early months of 1915, he neglected other aspects of the war. Far from this being the case he produced a stream of papers and wrote many letters on other subjects. For example early in the year he corresponded with Balfour and with his old ally on the C.I.D. Lord Esher, who was now serving as head of the British Intelligence organisation in France, on the question of an alternative strategy to break the deadlock in the west.[3] We have already seen how in February he threw his weight strongly against American proposals for "Freedom of the Seas". In the following month he suggested to Asquith that a committee should be set up under a Cabinet Minister "to adjudicate between the importance of Admiralty and War Office claims [for munitions and scarce materials] and to stimulate production of war material by every conceivable means".[4] For this purpose he again proposed that Balfour's services should be requisitioned; but when the Ministry of Munitions was actually set up in May 1915 it was placed under Lloyd George, and Balfour was given the Admiralty. We thus see how Hankey was one of the first to appreciate that the transformation of industry from a peace

---

[1] *James*, p. 94. [2] *ibid.*
[3] Balfour to Hankey 2nd Jan. and Esher to Hankey 24th Feb. 1915.
[4] Hankey to Asquith 6th March 1915. Asquith papers, Box 27, folios 29–30.

to a war basis, and the settlement of conflicting claims for production, necessitated the creation of a new ministry.

Esher wrote long letters to Hankey about once a week at this time, dealing with every aspect of war policy and strategy. He obviously intended them for the Prime Minister's eye as well as Hankey's, and the latter generally sent them on to Asquith with his comments. The suggestion for an Inter-Allied conference put forward in the letter part-quoted below was a valuable one, and was soon acted on—though in a rather different form from that proposed by Esher.

Esher to Hankey. Gouvernement Militaire de Paris. Etat Major Anglaise. 24th Feb. 1915 Holograph

My dear Hankey,

. . . I have seen a good deal of Millerand,[1] who, for so reserved a man, has been singularly forthcoming of late. I wrote to Lord K. the outcome of his talks. He complains that after the exact composition of the forces to be sent out, and the times of their arrival has been settled, neither was adhered to.

Then he suggested a sort of "Round table" to be formed of the Chief of the G[eneral] Staff of *our* W.O., and the Chief of the G.S. here, and some one designated by the Grand Duke[2] to meet occasionally for the purpose of discussing "excentric [sic] attacks". Joffre,[3] he says, is the C-in-C of the armies of the East in France. It is not within his scope to discuss possible attacks elsewhere. I hope Lord K. will take a favourable view of this proposal, but I am not sure . . .

They [the French] are clever enough to see that in case there is no sensible failure of Germany in May, the Allies should be prepared with well thought out, and carefully planned alternative schemes, whether in Holland, Servia, Constantinople or at any imaginable point. It is these alternatives that it is suggested should be discussed at a "round table" . . . Perhaps you will think over this proposal, and if the P.M. has the patience to read this letter, you might invoke his favourable consideration. . . .

[1]Etienne A. Millerand (1859–1943). French politician (Socialist). Minister for War 1912 and 1914–15. President of the Republic 1920–4.

[2]Grand Duke Nicholas (1856–1929). Grandson of Nicholas I, Tsar of Russia. Appointed Supreme Commander of the Russian armies 1st August 1914, and held that post until 21st August 1915 when, most unwisely, the Tsar himself took over command. The Tsar's last official action was to reappoint him supreme commander in March 1917, but the order was immediately cancelled by the Provisional Government. In March 1919 he was evacuated from the Crimea in a British warship.

[3]Joseph Joffre (1852–1931). French soldier. C-in-C, French armies of north and north-east 1914 and of all French armies in west from Dec. 1915–Dec. 1916, when he was replaced by General Nivelle. Marshal of France 1916.

I wish you could see the pitiable condition of Rheims. You would then realise how impossible it is for this war to go through another winter. . . .

Yours ever

Hankey at once sent the letter on to Asquith with a minute stating that as Kitchener had "advocated so strenuously" a conference on the lines proposed by Esher, he "might like to quote this letter at the Council this morning".[1]

In the middle of March Esher wrote again to Hankey, giving the impressions he had gained during a visit to British General Head-quarters, and his views on strategy. General Sir William Robertson, who had recently succeeded Sir Archibald Murray[2] as Chief of Staff to the C-in-C, British Expeditionary Force, had impressed him very favourably. But he entertained serious doubts regarding Field-Marshal French's capacity to co-operate properly with his French allies. The truth was, he said, that "there is a complete failure of . . . frank collaboration in planning, and sincere co-operation in executing operations between the Allied armies"; and he had observed unpleasant parallels with the muddles in the high command during the Crimean war. As to strategy, Esher wrote that "the finest stroke in this war, so far, is at the Dardanelles . . . You cannot destroy the German armies by frontal attack. Experience of seven months proves it. Therefore you must go round their flanks, at all hazards".[3] He asked Hankey to show his letter to Kitchener; but it evidently had no effect on the War Minister's strategic outlook.

Hankey to Esher. 2 Whitehall Gardens. 15th March 1915
I have sent your most interesting letter on to Lord Kitchener to read. I agree with every word of it. I quite agree with what you say about the Dardanelles. Although on general principles this operation is brilliantly conceived, and quite correct, I am not at all satisfied that it is being carried out in the best possible manner. Troops ought to have been there, or at any rate within a day or two's reach, when the bombardment began. There ought to have been no blatant press announcement at the outset, and the bombardment ought to have been announced merely as a demonstration. While the bombardment was commencing the transports ought to have appeared at some entirely different point on the Turkish coast, such as Alexandretta or Haifa . . . Then

[1]Hankey to Asquith 26th Feb. 1915.
[2]1860–1945. Deputy and then Chief of Imperial General Staff 1915. G.O.C. Egypt 1916–17.
[3]Esher to Hankey ? March 1915. The actual date is punched out of the letter.

the troops ought to have come in as a bolt from the blue, and closely supported by the fleet [and ought?] to have captured the plateau overlooking the forts of the Narrows by a *coup-de-main*. I urged this at the outset, but my suggestion fell on deaf ears. Now we have given the Turks time to assemble a vast force, to pour in field guns and howitzers, to entrench every landing place, and the operation has become a most formidable one. Please burn this.

Both as a statement of the principles which should govern a combined operation—careful planning, deception, surprise, inter-service co-operation and so on—and as a prophecy of what would happen when the troops finally arrived at Gallipoli it would be hard to beat Hankey's few lines to Esher. Plainly by mid-March he sensed that a tragedy was in the making.

Diary 19th March 1915
War Council this morning. All rather upset by Churchill reading telegrams . . . announcing the loss of 2 French and 2 British battleships and *Inflexible* damaged.[1] Lord F. and I in the rather unenviable position of being able to say "I told you so". Personally on the first day proposal [to attack the Dardanelles] was made I warned the P.M., Lord K's Chief of Staff, Lloyd George and Balfour that Fleet could not effect passage without troops, and that all naval officers thought so. I also begged Churchill to have troops to co-operate, but he wouldn't listen, insisting that [the] Navy could do it alone. In my belief Churchill wanted to bring off coup by Navy alone to rehabilitate his reputation, which was damaged (unjustly) by [the] Antwerp affair.
Long discussion on partition of Turkey—premature I think. Haldane made impassioned appeal [that] in interest of permanent peace Germany should not be left out. Lunched with Ll. George *tête-à-tête*. Ll.G. wants to chuck Greece over and bribe Bulgaria in by promise of Kavalla.

At the end of that month General Robertson wrote to Hankey with the approval of the C-in-C inviting him to come over to France for a visit.[2] Robertson's purpose was to provide the War Council with first-hand impressions of conditions at the front.[3] Though Hankey was deeply involved in the arguments over the attack on the Dardanelles he felt he ought to go, and Asquith approved his doing so. Accordingly he left London early on 2nd April (Good Friday)—equipped with an armoury of life-saving devices thoughtfully provided by his wife for

---

[1]Actually only three battleships were sunk—the *Ocean* and *Irresistible* (British) and the *Bouvet* (French).
[2]Robertson to Hankey, 28th March 1915.   [3]*Supreme Command*, I, p. 296 ff.

the Channel crossing. That evening he reached British Headquarters at St. Omer, where everything was "very peaceful" he told Adeline.

Hankey evidently appreciated the unwisdom of appearing in the guise of a Staff Officer when he visited the western and other fronts, and he therefore always eschewed the red tabs and cap band which came to be so despised and detested by the front line troops. A distinguished officer of his regiment has recently written that "Sensibly realising that the trappings of a Staff Officer . . . arouse the worst suspicions of knavery and deceit in the minds of beholders, he habitually wore the khaki service dress of the R.M.A. which appears in a hundred memories and pictures".[1]

To Mrs. Hankey. General Headquarters, British Expeditionary Force. 3rd April 1915
. . . I have been out all day with Gorton seeing things. Very interesting, but exactly what I expected. It is very strange how one passes from a peaceful countryside into the war zone. Of the enemy one can see absolutely nothing, and if you drove your car on there would be nothing to prevent you driving straight into the enemy's line. Things are very quiet, and there is only a very occasional shell aimed at a cross roads. I heard no musketry fire at all . . . We went to Vielle Chapelle and lunched with Longridge[2] who is quartered near there, but we didn't go to Neuve Chapelle as it is rather dangerous, and Gorton and I agreed to take no foolish risks . . . I had a very long talk with Sir Douglas Haig,[3] who commands the First Army. He is a most charming personality, and a great man I think . . .

In fact Hankey just missed the battle of Neuve Chapelle, which had opened on 10th March. After a very promising start, in which complete surprise was achieved, Sir John French allowed the enemy a pause in which he was able to bring up reinforcements and so restore the situation. The final gains were insignificant. Hankey's visit to France was not, however, as free from danger as he made out to Adeline. He visited Ypres and the front line trenches near Ploegsteert (the "Plug

---

[1]From an article by Major-General H. S. Wood, R.M.A., privately circulated 1965, and reproduced in condensed form by G. W. M. Grover in *The Naval Review*, Vol. LV, No. 3 (July 1967).

[2]Major J. A. Longridge, formerly of the C.I.D. Secretariat.

[3]1861–1928. 1st Earl Haig 1919. Commanded 1st Army 1914–15. Succeeded Sir John French as C-in-C, British Expeditionary Force in France and Flanders Dec. 1915 and served in that capacity until 1919 despite Lloyd George's mistrust of his strategy and attempts to have him replaced. Field-Marshal 1917.

Street" of the Tommies), and on what he described in his diary as "a rum Easter Sunday" he received his "baptism of fire".

Perhaps the most valuable result of the visit was that Hankey was able to collect the views and opinions of the leading soldiers on current political and strategic problems. Thus Robertson was at first taciturn —"a jolly sulky host" was Hankey's later description[1]—because he believed that Hankey had been "responsible for the naval bombardment of the Dardanelles". But after Hankey had "speedily disillusioned" the General on that score he thawed and became confidentially intimate about his own troubles. He enlarged on the bad relations between French and Joffre, and ascribed them mainly to Churchill's recent visit to the front. Henry Wilson who was in command of IV Corps, "abused Churchill and the Dardanelles expedition"; but, as we saw earlier, Wilson was always one of the most convinced, and plausible of "westerners". One may sense in those conversations the incipient clash between "the frocks and the brass hats", as Wilson later dubbed the politicians and the military hierarchy.

Shortly after his encounter with the soldiers on the western front Hankey turned his attention once more to maritime affairs. He evidently sent a copy of the following letter to Asquith.

Hankey to Fisher. 2 Whitehall Gardens, 22nd April 1915[2]
MOST SECRET
Dear Lord Fisher,
On a general review of the whole situation I think that the German fleet will come out in real earnest in a few days' time. You have often pointed out that the German fleet is merely a wing of the German army, and it is military interests mainly, though not only, that Germany will seek to serve by this desperate step. Here are some of the objects she will seek to obtain by the possible, if remote chance of success:—

1 Germany almost certainly knows that the first "New Army" is practically ready. She may hope by an actual success, or by exciting the supposed nervous apprehensions of the British public . . . to detain this army at home—a prodigious military advantage.

2 Germany probably knows that the Dardanelles attack is imminent. She might hope by the destruction of some of our ships to get the attack deferred . . .

[1]Hankey to Swinton on 5th May 1932, a long letter criticising the draft of Swinton's book *Eyewitness*. Swinton Papers, King's College, London, Military Archive Centre.
[2]Copy in Asquith Papers, Vol. 27, folios 90–2.

3   Germany must be intensely apprehensive of the possibility of early
    Italian and Roumanian intervention. The only certain way of preventing
    this would be a success against the British fleet, and the resulting loss of
    British prestige . . .

4   There is reason to believe that Germany is about to be faced with a real
    shortage of food . . . Public opinion and naval opinion may force Germany
    to make a supreme effort against the British fleet to which she owes so
    many difficulties.

5   Germany is no doubt well aware that great supplies of ammunition are
    now due for delivery from the United States, and these can only be
    prevented by a German success at sea.

6   In a short time the whole of the *Queen Elizabeth* class will be in the line.[1]

    I suggest that the recent manœuvres of the German Fleet all point in this
direction . . .

    Recently, however, there seems to have been a cessation of activity on the
part of the German submarines on the west coast . . . My own strong suspicion is that they have been withdrawn in order to co-operate with the German
fleet in some great plan to be executed by the new C-in-C of the High Sea
Fleet.[2] . . .

    My own belief is that the object of the recent publicly announced excur-
sions of the German High Sea Fleet . . . was mainly to try and discover what
movements our Fleet makes in reply. The German chess player risks his
pawns to discover our opening moves and to try and penetrate our plan.

    On the basis of this reconnaissance the enemy will formulate his plan. It is
nearly certain to depend on the placing of minefields in one part of the North
Sea, and the massing of the highly efficient and practised German submarines
in another . . . The High Sea Fleet will be used as a bait.

    Perhaps this is all nonsense. My feeling though is that the present moment
is one for very great naval vigilance, particularly if the submarine blockade
does not get more active. Its quiescence is, to my mind, like suppressed gout
—alarming in its possibilities.

    Meanwhile rumbles of discontent over the manner in which the large
War Council conducted its business were becoming vocal—in political

[1]These were the five new fast battleships, each armed with eight 15-inch guns—by
far the heaviest armament so far fitted in the capital ships of either side.

[2]The unsatisfactory outcome of the Battle of Dogger Bank (24th Jan. 1915) from
the German point of view led to the supersession on 2nd Feb. of Admiral von
Ingenohl by Admiral Hugo von Pohl (1855–1916) as C-in-C, High Seas Fleet. See
Marder, *Scapa Flow*, II, pp. 165–6.

as well as service circles. In March Edwin Montagu,[1] the Chancellor of the Duchy of Lancaster with a seat in the Cabinet, wrote to Hankey regarding what he regarded as the true function of the War Council and its proper relations with the Cabinet. "You do not get discussions in the War Council", he complained, "differing materially from those in the Cabinet; you have the same protagonists in both, and all you do is to substitute a different set of spectators. The War Council should be used by its political members to get a frank opinion of the military experts, but . . . this is not done and will not be done unless the Council is re-constituted, or unless the president lays down this as its specific duty . . .".[2] There was indeed a great deal in Montagu's criticisms, and by the spring of 1915 it was becoming plain that in the actual conduct of the war the War Council had proved little, if at all superior to the old Cabinet system which it had replaced in the previous November. The cure lay, however, not in revising or re-defining the duties of the War Council but in reducing the size of the Cabinet itself; and that was not to be achieved in Asquith's time as Prime Minister.

The months of April and May 1915 were full of troubles for the British—in the political as well as the military sphere. In the early hours of 25th April the long deferred assault on the Gallipoli peninsula took place. British forces landed at five beaches stretching around the tip of Cape Helles, the Australians and New Zealanders assaulted at Ari Burnu about 11 miles up the west coast of the peninsula,[3] with the intention of seizing the commanding heights, so cutting off the defenders to the south, while French troops made a brief diversion on the Asiatic side and then crossed the straits to take over the eastern section of the Helles front. The plan as a whole was, in the words of the latest historian of the campaign, "bold, intelligent and ambitious"[4]; but that was not enough to bring the quick success hoped for. At most of the Cape Helles beaches resistance was fierce, and heavy losses were suffered before even a secure foothold on shore was gained. At Anzac the splendid troops from the two Dominions got ashore with relatively

[1]Edwin Samuel Montagu (1879–1924). Politician (Lib.). Financial Secretary to Treasury 1914–16; Chancellor of Duchy of Lancaster 1915; Minister of Munitions 1916, resigning in December. Secretary of State for India 1917–22. Co-author of the Montagu-Chelmsford report of 1918 on Indian constitutional reform.
[2]Montagu to Hankey 22nd March 1915.
[3]This point was about a mile north of the small indentation soon to be named Anzac Cove, where the landing was planned to take place.
[4]*James*, p. 89.

light losses—but at the wrong place. They too were soon engaged in a fierce, hand-to-hand struggle to hold what little ground they had won. After a pause the battle was resumed on 6th May, but progress was slight. All General Hamilton's forces were now committed, and a state of deadlock had come to pass—exactly as on the western front. The chief cause of this tragically unsatisfactory outcome was without doubt the loss of surprise.

On 14th May the War Council met to discuss the crisis which had arisen over the Dardanelles undertaking—in an atmosphere which Churchill has described, no doubt correctly, as "sulphurous". Hankey merely recorded in his diary "Lord K. very gloomy . . ." He now found himself in the unenviable position of acting as intermediary between Churchill and Fisher, both of whom he admired and counted among his friends, but whose relations had reached breaking point over the despatch of more warships to the Dardanelles. Hankey exerted all the influence he could to prevent Fisher resigning, and it must have been at this time that Fisher sent him the following undated note.

Fisher to Hankey. c. 12th May 1915. Holograph.
Secret and Private
My beloved Hankey,
I will sacrifice my judgement to yours and wait. If I could show you letters from Jellicoe received during last week you would see I have an impregnable position. I think if I went he [Jellicoe] might do something. The Prime Minister don't realize the bitter feeling afloat, nor do you I fancy. You have no idea how I have been approached, but I have restrained myself. This is for your private eye, but I don't mean to explode my bomb without dead certainty it will act.
Yours F.

Fisher to Hankey. Admiralty, 14th May 1915. Holograph.
Burn
My beloved Hankey,
Again last evening Winston sent off another telegram to de Robeck when Bartolomé[1] had told him I objected! So I had to go to him at 5.30 P.M. and say it was a "casus belli" and then he cancelled the telegram and sent the one I had given to Bartolomé—and then once again at 7 P.M. he re-asserted his conviction that after all in six weeks' time the fleet would have to do it alone!

[1]Later Admiral Sir Charles M. de Bartolomé (1871–1941). Naval Secretary to Churchill and Balfour as First Lord 1914–16. 3rd Sea Lord and Controller of the Navy 1918–19. Retired 1919.

"And would I remain on anyhow quiet for this six weeks"!!! *That is to say I am to aid and abet for 6 weeks!*

What is one to do with such a determined mad gambler? Ask McKenna! secretly—and the Prime Minister says to me "Rely on me. I will never fail you", but Winston ignores the lot and sends the telegrams from *himself*. "Surely I can send a private letter to a friend without showing it to you"!!! That's his argument! "A private telegram of friendship, cordiality and encouragement" (as he terms it) . . .

Unfortunately all Hankey's endeavours to heal the breach proved unavailing.

As Hankey has himself printed the greater part of his diary entries relating to the Fisher-Churchill clash they will not be reproduced here[1]; but a few interesting points which he omitted may be given. The first is that on 15th May he was sent for by the King "at short notice" and spent an hour with him. He recorded that "The King evidently knew nothing of the Fisher incident". As Fisher's first attempt at resignation had been made three days earlier, but was withdrawn when Asquith played the peace-maker, and his actual letter of resignation was dated 15th, it is surely surprising that Asquith should not have told the King what was in the wind, or that the King should not have heard of it from other sources. On the other hand it is possible that the King did know of it and had sent for Hankey to draw him out on the subject, but tactfully refrained from bringing it up himself. Hankey noted that his hour with the King was spent "chatting", and it seems unlikely that as shrewd a man as George V would have deliberately engaged a very busy person in small talk, at a time when a serious political crisis was brewing.[2] Secondly on 19th Hankey wrote in his diary that Fisher was "intriguing horribly with Northcliffe, the Unionist Party *et hoc genus omne*". Lastly on 21st May he wrote that after lunch at 10 Downing Street "Mrs. Asquith got everyone out of the room except Masterton Smith,[3] Bonham Carter,[4] Prime Minister and self, and we gave him

[1] *Supreme Command*, I, pp. 314–18.
[2] From Sir Harold Nicolson's *King George V* (Constable, 1952, p. 263) it appears that Asquith only told the King about Fisher's resignation when he showed him the Admiral's "ultimatum", which was dated 19th May. George V's diary for 15th May merely states "Saw Col. Hankey in the afternoon". Royal Archives.
[3] Later Sir James E. Masterton Smith (1878–1938). Private Secretary successively to McKenna, Churchill, Balfour, Carson and Geddes as First Lords 1910–17. Permanent Under-Secretary of State for Colonies 1921–4.
[4] Later Sir Maurice Bonham Carter (1880–1960) Private Secretary to Asquith

[Asquith] our views as to [the] most suitable arrangements at Admiralty *viz*. Balfour to be First Lord, and either Sir Arthur Wilson or Sir Henry Jackson as First Sea Lord[1]—in former event Sir Henry Jackson to have a seat on the Board as additional Naval Lord, and to take the detailed work. I feel sure this advice will be taken. I find that Masterton Smith still hankers after Churchill as First Lord, owing to his great driving power and capacity for work". In the event Admiral Wilson refused to serve under any First Lord but Churchill—an unsolicited tribute which touched the latter—and Jackson became First Sea Lord.

That same evening Hankey was again at Downing Street, to dine with the Asquiths and a number of their most intimate friends and supporters. After the ladies had withdrawn a discussion on the formation of a Coalition government and on Fisher's recent conduct took place. According to Hankey's diary Spender[2] remarked that "he really believed Fisher was a bit 'off his nut [amended, probably later, to "balance"]' ". "McKenna agreed, and I could not really deny it" Hankey noted. The general trend of Hankey's day by day entries about the Churchill-Fisher crisis leave one in little doubt that the old Admiral, now 74, had suffered a serious nervous breakdown—possibly brought on by the relentless pressure to which Churchill had subjected him. But Churchill's final judgement that "hysteria rather than conspiracy" provided the correct explanation of Fisher's conduct is probably too generous.[3] For Hankey evidently had plenty of evidence of intrigue on Fisher's part, and his "astounding ultimatum" of 19th May to Asquith setting out the "terms" on which he would resume office makes it plain that he was out to gain for himself supreme power in naval affairs.[4] Asquith himself told the King that the letter "showed signs of mental aberration".[5]

After it was all over Fisher wrote to Hankey in chastened mood,

---

1910–16 and married (1915) his eldest daughter Violet, later Baroness Asquith of Yarnbury.

[1]Later Admiral Sir Henry B. Jackson (1855–1929). Controller of Navy 1905–8. Head of R.N. War College 1911–13. Chief of War Staff 1912–14. First Sea Lord 1915–16. President, R.N. College, Greenwich 1916–19. Admiral of the Fleet 1919.
[2]J. A. Spender (1862–1942). Journalist and strong supporter of Asquith, whose biographer he was. Editor, *The Westminster Gazette*, 1896–1922.
[3]*Great Contemporaries* (Thornton Butterworth, 1939), p. 342.
[4]Printed in Marder, *Fisher*, Vol. II, p. 241. [5]Nicolson, *George V*, p. 263.

evidently realising that his "ultimatum" to Asquith had been a disastrous mistake.

Fisher to Hankey. Dungavel, Strathaven, Lanarkshire. 29th May 1915. Holograph.
Private and Personal
My beloved Hankey,
So many thanks for your letter—also for your good advice to keep silence!
But it's difficult to do so! I think I've rather been "engineered" out of it! (as the Daily Mail puts it "Lord Fisher has been routed!") and yet the victory was mine so completely on Monday night (May 29th[1]) when the P.M. wrote to me of re-constituting the government and begging me to hold on in consequence as Winston was out of the Cabinet!

I agree with you the mistake was to have given that paper [i.e. his ultimatum of 19th May] to Bonham Carter! But it's no use whining.
The King will take firm care I don't get back!
Send me a line to this address if anything transpires!
　　　　　　　　　Burn this
　　　　　　　　　　　　Yours　Fisher

Meanwhile the deadlock at Gallipoli, the crisis in the Admiralty, the rising dissatisfaction over the shortage of munitions in France and the costly failure of the last British attacks at Aubers Ridge and Festubert had convinced Asquith that, as he told the King on 17th May, "the Govt. must be reconstructed on a broad and non-party basis".[2] The price exacted by the Conservative Party was the removal of Churchill from the Admiralty and the total exclusion of Haldane.[3] Asquith's acceptance of the latter demand was perhaps the least creditable act of his career, and Hankey felt deeply the loss of a well-tried friend and staunch supporter of the C.I.D.

Hankey to Haldane. 2 Whitehall Gardens, 28th May 1915.[4] Holograph
Dear Lord Haldane,
I cannot let the occasion of your retirement pass without writing to express my sense of deep appreciation for all you have done for us as a nation, for the Committee of Imperial Defence, and for the patient and unfailing help and counsel that you have rendered to me personally.

I suppose that there is no one alive who knows as I do what the country

[1] This must be an error of dating. Possibly 29th April, but that was a Friday, not a Monday. Probably Fisher meant Monday 17th May. See *Murder, Fisher, III,* p. 250.
[2] Roy Jenkins, *Asquith* (Collins, 1964), pp. 360–1. Henceforth cited as *Jenkins.*
[3] *ibid.,* pp. 361–2.
[4] Haldane Papers, National Library of Scotland, Hankey section, folios 181–2.

owes to you, for I have been on the inner side of official life during the whole period of the Renaissance for which you were so largely responsible. It is in my opinion no exaggeration to say that it is to your foresight and patient organic reconstruction of our whole defence system, that we owe it that the allied cause, and with it the British Empire, did not collapse last August. I shall always regard it as a great priviledge [sic] that in certain directions I have been able to carry on the work that you initiated . . .

I suppose that you will now feel justified in taking a rest, but I hope that we may often meet in days to come at this Committee.

Yours very sincerely

It was not in Hankey's nature to sever a friendship such as had developed between him and Haldane over many years because the statesman had been cast into the wilderness, and he continued to seek his advice and even to send him confidential papers on war policy. We do not know whether he had Asquith's approval for doing so, or whether he acted entirely on his own responsibility; but the result was that the association between Hankey and Haldane remained so close that when the latter again achieved high office in 1924 they immediately picked up the threads which had been so abruptly, not to say brutally, severed in 1915. They then once again worked together in intimate cordiality—especially in the comparatively novel field of the application of scientific research to industrial development.[1]

Haldane to Hankey. 28 Queen Anne's Gate, Westminster. 29th June 1915. Holograph

My dear Hankey,

I have received and read your very confidential paper.[2]

I not only agree with its conclusions but I am thankful that the principles they embody have been laid down with General Staff precision.

I only hope they will be impressed on the C-in-C when he comes over. Some of his subordinate Commanders are badly in want of them, and I think he should issue confidential instructions based on these principles, for their enlightenment.

I hope to have a chance of talking with you before long. An evening would be usefully spent so . . .

Yours sincerely

---

[1] See Roy Macleod and E. Kay Andrews *The Committee on Civil Research: Scientific Advice for Economic Development* 1925–1930 (*Minerva*, VII, 4, pp. 680–705).

[2] This was probably Hankey's paper entitled "The Future Policy of the War" dated 24th June 1915. See p. 183.

Under the new régime calm descended on the Admiralty—which was at first welcome. But it soon became evident that it was the calm of uninspired leadership, of conventionality, and of resistance to change— for which a heavy price was to be exacted later. Hankey was of course consulted over the reconstruction of the Board of Admiralty.

Diary 26th May
Mr. Balfour, who had discussed the subject with Masterton Smith and me two days ago, went to Edinburgh to meet Admiral Jellicoe and discuss with him the composition of the new Board of Admiralty. Had a long discussion with Chief of War Staff [Oliver] on subject of Dardanelles and found him anxious to continue and hopeful. Met Churchill on leaving Adty. He thanked me for my "charming letter" and told me he would stay in the Cabinet until the conclusion of the Dardanelles operation.[1] He had received a cheerful private telegram from Sir Ian Hamilton and Admiral de Robeck saying they would see the Dardanelles business through. . . .

On 23rd May Italy, with whom secret negotiations to enter the conflict on the Allied side had been in progress for many weeks, declared war on Austria. At the time this was believed to have brought substantial advantages to the Allies; but it is doubtful whether the enemy forces drawn off by the Italians counter-balanced the support which had to be provided by Britain and France. Four days later the Coalition Cabinet met for the first time; and a deep cleavage of attitude and opinion towards the Gallipoli undertaking soon became apparent.

[1]Despite a bombardment of letters addressed to Asquith stressing his claims to high office Churchill had to be content with the office of Chancellor of the Duchy of Lancaster.

Chapter 7

Under the First Coalition: May—August 1915

AFTER the earthquake produced by the Fisher-Churchill clash had
subsided Hankey and Asquith were probably glad to get away from
London. Hankey spent Sunday 30th May at the Asquiths' Berkshire
house near Sutton Courtenay, where he received a good deal of flattery
from Mrs. Asquith.[1] In the evening he left for France with the Prime
Minister and Bonham Carter, his private secretary. Hankey has printed
most of the diary entries describing the discussions between the
military leaders—French, Haig and Robertson on the British side, and
Joffre, Foch and M. Millerand (Minister of War) on the French side.[2]
For some reason he omitted part of the entry for 2nd June which reads
"I am sorry to say they [the Allied leaders] definitely decided not to
carry out my scheme for devastating Germany's crops, as the French
were afraid of retaliation. In my opinion this prolongs the war for
another year".

To Mrs. Hankey. G.H.Q. North France. Undated. c. 2nd June 1915.
... We had splendid weather and motored out to the same place as I got such
a good view from last time. Unfortunately the whole front was extraordinarily
quiet, and, with the exception of a little shelling of Ypres, which was on fire,
we could see but little. We were only once in a likely shelling zone all day,
and no shell came near it, thank goodness. Poor Ypres is visibly "flatter"
than when I was last here. Swinton took me round in his car, but we went
with the P.M. One brigade, a magnificent set of men, was reviewed for us;
they had been 5 months in the trenches. The P.M. gave them a short but very
stirring address, and they gave him three most splendid cheers ...

After a delayed Channel crossing, on account of fog, the party
reached London in the early hours of 4th June. Hankey was allowed
no rest. He at once had to see Balfour about the recent unfavourable
American reactions to the tightening of the blockade, and Kitchener
about the conferences held in France and the possibility of smoothing

[1]*Supreme Command*, I, p. 338. [2]*ibid.*, pp. 338–9.

the bad relations which had developed between him and French. The review of blockade measures resulted in Hankey writing a new paper on the subject of "Freedom of the Seas", in which he recapitulated all his earlier arguments in support of the stringent application of "Belligerent Rights". A short time later he wrote to Asquith suggesting that "the whole of our policy in dealing with the Americans should be reviewed", and that "it would be wiser to speak very frankly" to them rather than continue to represent that our policy was "directed solely to depriving the [enemy] fighting forces of their armaments". He stressed that our sea power gave us the ability to strangle and starve out the enemy, and he wanted to put it to the Americans that it would be to their own advantage not to try and restrict its effectiveness.[1] However the government preferred to move cautiously in such a delicate matter, and further Orders in Council tightening the blockade were only issued gradually.

Turning to the submarine menace, on the last day of March Hankey had written to Fisher stressing the need to design an efficient mine and produce it on a very large scale, with the object of laying a vast minefield right across the North Sea to bottle up the U-boats inside the Heligoland Bight.[2] Shortly after Churchill and Fisher had left the Admiralty he took the matter up with Balfour, the new First Lord. He told Balfour that Churchill had circulated to the Cabinet a memorandum on anti-submarine measures, but "did not mention whether the Admiralty have as yet formulated any definite and specific policy" for using the "mass of material", such as nets, mines and small vessels, which were being produced. Blocking the U-boats in their bases was, he considered, the ideal measure; but the German fleet was too powerful for it to be practicable. The alternative was a mine barrier, and after investigating various possible sites for it he recommended that it should be laid between Flamborough Head on the Yorkshire coast and Horns Reef off the west coast of Denmark—a distance of 275 miles. Three million mines would be needed to complete the barrier, whose strategic purpose he likened to the Great Wall of China.[3] Though Hankey had been absolutely right to stress the need for an efficient mine, his proposal that it should be used in the manner suggested was not sound. The effort would be enormous and its effectiveness highly dubious—as the

[1] Hankey to Asquith, 20th July 1915. Asquith papers, Box 117, folios 120/3.
[2] Hankey to Fisher, 31st March 1915. Copy in Cab. 21/8.
[3] Hankey to Balfour, 11th June 1915. Cab. 21/8.

North Sea barrier laid with American help in 1917–18 was to demonstrate conclusively. It is surprising that Hankey's strong sense of history did not lead him, even at this comparatively early stage, to the conclusion that the convoy-and-escort strategy was the only really effective countermeasure to the submarine, as it had proved to be against surface raiders in all our earlier wars. But the Admiralty was, perhaps with less excuse, equally blind; and a discussion which Hankey had at this time with Vice-Admiral H. F. Oliver,[1] the Chief of the War Staff, reveals very clearly their conviction that "hunting" was the proper antidote to the new commerce destroyers and not convoy.[2]

One of the first actions by the Coalition government was to replace the War Council by a Cabinet Sub-Committee known as the Dardanelles Committee, which met for the first time on 7th June. Though originally formed to review the problems which had arisen in connection with the Gallipoli undertaking, it soon extended its deliberations to other strategic and operational problems. Like the War Council, but unlike the Cabinet itself, a secretary—who was of course Hankey—was admitted to the meetings of the Dardanelles Committee, and its Minutes and Conclusions are thus admirably preserved. At first it consisted of nine members, all of them Ministers,[3] but three more were soon added[4]; and before it came to an end in October 1915 the 1st Sea Lord and C.I.G.S. regularly attended its meetings.

On his return to London Hankey found, among the "mass of correspondence" which had accumulated during his brief absence, a letter from Churchill asking for copies of the papers which Hankey had circulated on the subject of the forcing of the Dardanelles.

Hankey to Churchill. 2 Whitehall Gardens, June 4th 1915
SECRET
... I enclose two Memoranda which I wrote on the subject of the Dardanelles, and I am not quite sure which is the one you have in mind.

The first was written originally for the Prime Minister's sole use, but by

[1]Later Admiral Sir Henry F. Oliver (1865–1966), Director of Intelligence, Admiralty War Staff 1913–14. Chief of War Staff 1914–17. Deputy Chief of Naval Staff 1917–18. Commanded Home Fleet 1919 and Reserve Fleet 1919–20. Second Sea Lord 1920–24. C-in-C, Atlantic Fleet 1924–27. Admiral of the Fleet 1928.
[2]Diary 4th May 1915.
[3]These were Asquith, Balfour (1st Lord), Kitchener (War), Grey (Foreign Secretary), Selborne (Agriculture), Curzon (Privy Seal), Bonar Law (Colonies), Churchill (Duchy of Lancaster) and Lansdowne (Minister without Portfolio).
[4]Lloyd George (Munitions), Crewe (Lord President) and Carson (Attorney General).

his direction I sent copies to you, Lord Kitchener and to Sir Edward Grey. The second Memorandum was written later and circulated to the War Council and deals rather with the question what we should do in the event of the Dardanelles being forced.

Personally, I have not the smallest desire to shirk any measure of responsibility which can fairly be attributed to me for the Dardanelles operation. Strategically it has always appeared, and still appears, to me to be the right thing to do. I daresay you noticed in the paper Lord Kitchener circulated, and to which you so kindly referred in your letter, that I showed how great an influence the Dardanelles operation had been in bringing Italy into the war. This alone was adequate justification, but I consider the results to be achieved will ultimately be still greater. Never has my conviction on this point been stronger than on my return from France, for I am convinced that unless the Germans can be weakened by diversions elsewhere, such as by the intervention of Italy and Roumania, we can no more force the German lines in front of us than Wellington could force Masséna's lines before Torres Vedras . . .

Nevertheless, I personally never believed in the naval attack, and would have preferred to wait until troops were available. I fully understand your reasons for the naval attack and should probably have done the same if I had been in your position, but from a purely professional point of view I was opposed to it.

This, however, does not in the least affect my sharing your conviction that this thing has got to be pushed through with great vigour, and that we can all have only one thought, namely, to beat the enemy.

The foregoing letter suggests that Churchill was already girding himself for the fight over the continuation of the Gallipoli campaign; or perhaps he foresaw that he would soon be called on to defend himself as its chief instigator. On 18th June Hankey wrote in his diary "Churchill called at 5 o'clock to ask for my assistance and support in his Dardanelles campaign . . . Dined at Montagu's to meet Bonham Carter, Drummond,[1] Masterton Smith and Lt Col. [O. A. G.] Fitzgerald[2] (the 'shadow Cabinet' as the Asquiths call it) to discuss the situation". Next day he and Bonham Carter "told the P.M. the gist of the 'shadow cabinet's' deliberations and urged preparations—financial and military

[1]Sir Eric Drummond, 16th Earl of Perth 1937 (1876–1951). Diplomat. A private secretary to Asquith 1912–15; Secretary-General to League of Nations 1919–33. Ambassador to Italy 1933–9.

[2]Personal Military Secretary to Lord Kitchener as Secretary of State for War 1914–16,

for a campaign in 1916". The last sentence reveals that this quite
informal body had a hand in the preparation of the long paper entitled
"The Future Policy of the War" which Hankey circulated on 24th, and
which he has described as "in a sense a continuation of the Memorandum of 28th December 1914".[1] The main points he stressed were,
firstly, the need to co-ordinate Allied war policy as a *whole* by discussion
around a conference table; secondly that an immediate investigation
should be made into ways and means of financing a long war; thirdly
that the size of the British military establishment should be fixed, at any
rate provisionally; fourthly that the restrictions placed on merchant
ship building should immediately be reconsidered; and, lastly, that
British policy towards the Balkan states should be re-examined. Every
one of the measures he recommended was in fact to prove vitally
important in the very near future.[2] Hankey sent copies of his paper to
Haldane and to the King. Lord Stamfordham wrote in reply that "the
King was so much interested that he trusts you will let him retain a
copy. It will be treated as secret and placed in our War Archives".[3]

In his review of war policy Hankey made only a passing reference to
the mobilisation of manpower and the burning question of whether
conscription should be introduced. We saw earlier how in the pre-war
discussions he had come out strongly against any such measure; but his
views were then conditioned by the hope that British strategy would be
predominantly maritime, and that no large army would be sent to the
Continent. By mid-1915 such hopes were plainly obsolete. None the
less the Liberal members of the First Coalition, and Hankey with them,
still hoped to avoid a measure which was bound to be extremely unpopular in the country. The "Kitchener scheme" for a volunteer army,
launched immediately on the outbreak of war, had by the beginning
of 1915 produced over a million men; and up to that time it was the
shortage of munitions and equipment that had dictated the size of the
new armies. But by the middle of the year the situation was clearly
changing, and on 21st June the government took the essential first
step towards compulsory service by introducing a National Registra-
tion Bill. It became law in the following month.

At this time the need for Hankey to receive additional help was
discussed—and, rather oddly, Lord Selborne, President of the Board of

[1]See pp. 147–9. In *Supreme Command*, I, pp. 346–7 Hankey misdates his 1915 paper
as 26th June.
[2]Cab. 37/130/26.   [3]Stamfordham to Hankey, 5th July 1915.

Agriculture and Fisheries, seems to have been the prime mover in the matter.

Selborne to Hankey. Board of Agriculture and Fisheries, 21st June 1915. Holograph

Yes, there should be someone to co-ordinate the work of the naval and military committees, [and] to link them up. Can you do it yourself? Or do you think Lord Sydenham would do for that? Make it [a] definite, temporary war job and link the converging lines of work in them.

If not why not try Baden-Powell?[1] Or Admiral Bacon[2] or Scott?[3] You know how strongly I feel about this matter, but when and while you are getting it done I will not put in an oar, except to help your efforts and second them in very possible way. So never hesitate to come and see me.

Yours sincerely

P.S. I should regard you as ideal for the job both because you are yourself and because you are a Marine.

None of the four persons suggested by Selborne was likely to have any appeal to Hankey, since all were much senior to him in years and in rank. Ten days later Selborne wrote again, this time suggesting that Hankey might like "to recruit for the war work of your department one of the most brilliant civilians living? I mean Philip Kerr"[4] But even the eulogistic terms in which Selborne spoke of Kerr's abilities failed to move Hankey who, right to the end of his career was very sensitive to any indication that a replacement for himself had appeared on the horizon.

In June the old issue of the Freedom of the Seas came up again when Grey circulated a paper stating that Lord Crewe (Lord President of the Council) had written to him that he considered a Cabinet decision was required "as to whether we should lose anything materially by ceasing to prohibit the import of all foodstuffs into Germany through neutral ports, and by falling back, as far as foodstuffs are concerned, upon the

---

[1]General Sir Robert Baden-Powell. 1st Baron Baden-Powell 1929 (1857–1941). Held Mafeking during Boer War. Retired 1910 to devote his energies to the Boy Scout Movement.

[2]See p. 53.   [3]See p. 40.

[4]1882–1940. 11th Marquess of Lothian 1930. Member of Milner's "Kindergarten" in South Africa after the Boer War. Co-founder of *The Round Table*. A private secretary to Lloyd George 1916–21. Influential in the cause of "appeasement" with the dictator states in the 1930s. Ambassador to U.S.A. 1939–40.

ordinary rules that apply to conditional contraband". Spring Rice,[1] the ambassador at Washington, had reported that the British blockade of foodstuffs was having a bad effect on American opinion, and Crewe was disposed to make concessions.[2] His proposals, which in effect amounted to accepting the views put forward by Colonel House five months earlier,[3] at once set Hankey into action, and a few days later he circulated a counter-blast.[4] The reader will by now be familiar with the arguments he deployed. Evidently he was well satisfied with the result.

Diary 25th June 1915
. . . My reply to Lord Crewe's paper, in which he advocated abandonment of our stoppage of German foodstuffs in return for cessation of sinking of merchant ships by submarines, much appreciated by P.M. and Mr. Balfour. It was really a crushing reply. Had tea with Mrs. Asquith who horrified me by alluding to my scheme for devastating the German crops in the presence of two callers. Bonham Carter took her to task about it, and she wrote to impress on them the importance of secrecy. Indiscreet woman. The P.M. ought not to have spoken to her of it.

In the middle of 1915 the future organisation of the Air Services became a burning issue. Even before the outbreak of war the Admiralty had begun to show signs of separatism with regard to the Naval Wing of the R.F.C.;[5] but Churchill set his face firmly against such a step, declaring that "he had always looked on the Naval and Military Wings as branches of one great service".[6] As long as he remained First Lord unity was therefore preserved. Moreover under his visionary and dynamic leadership good progress was made in the application of the new arm to naval purposes—despite the conservatism of most senior naval officers. But very soon after Churchill had been dismissed from the Admiralty the Board issued a unilateral declaration of independence for the Naval Air Service, which they proclaimed, without consulting the Cabinet, to be "an integral part of the Royal Navy".[7] They

[1] Sir Cecil A. Spring Rice (1859–1918). Diplomat. Minister to Sweden 1908–12. Ambassador to U.S.A. 1912–18. Died shortly after handing over to Lord Reading Feb. 1918.
[2] Dated 18th June 1915. Cab. 37/130/15.
[3] See pp. 157–8. [4] Dated 23rd June 1915. Cab. 37/130/15.
[5] Adm. Circular Letter CW. 13964/14 of 1st July 1914. Adm. 1/8378.
[6] C.I.D. SAS.2 of 25th June 1914. Adm. 1/8621.
Admiralty Weekly Order 1204/15 of 29th July 1915. Adm. 1/808.

thereby initiated many years of acrimonious inter-service controversy.

Hankey always held that if the pre-war arrangements regarding aviation were properly worked by the two departments concerned the rivalry and competition for production, and the disputes over the respective responsibilities of the Navy and Army with regard to aerial operations, would be resolved.[1] But the trouble was that the Air Committee of 1912 never met after the outbreak of war, and the inter-departmental antagonisms and jealousies, having no safety valve to provide an escape for dangerously high pressures, steadily worsened. In June 1915 Churchill sent Asquith a memorandum proposing a wholesale reorganisation of the Air Services by removing them from the Admiralty and War Office and placing them under a new department.[2] Bonham Carter sent the paper on to Hankey with a minute that "It looks to me like a scheme for providing Winston with something to do, and though I would gladly see his energies suitably employed, at first sight I cannot say I like it".[3] Hankey agreed, and sent Bonham Carter a copy of the paper he had just written for the Prime Minister suggesting that revival of the Air Committee was the best way to deal with the problems which had arisen. But in truth this was nothing like a radical enough solution to remedy the overlapping and competition between the Admiralty and War Office. The controversy was to simmer and boil for another 18 months before the government took the step first urged on it in June 1915.

Meanwhile Lord Esher was becoming increasingly anxious about the poor quality of both British and French senior officers, and the lack of co-ordination between the western Allies. It seems likely that Esher's letters inspired the first item in Hankey's memorandum on "The Future Policy of the War" referred to earlier; also that a letter from Walter Runciman (President of the Board of Trade) setting out his proposals to expedite the completion of merchant ships under construction accounts for Hankey's emphasis on the importance of that aspect of the

[1] Memo. of 12th June 1915. Asquith papers, Vol. 27, folios 259–62.
[2] Unsigned memorandum of 10th June 1915. Asquith papers, Vol. 27, folios 255–7. The existence of the original in the Admiralty's records (Adm. 1/8621) proves beyond doubt that it was produced by Captain Murray F. Sueter, the Director of the Air Department in the Admiralty. (See p. 146.) His campaign in favour of an Air Ministry led to his being "exiled" (his expression) from the Admiralty to the Adriatic in 1917.
[3] Bonham Carter to Hankey 6th June 1915. *ibid.*

war effort.[1] Hankey, as the recipient of ideas and suggestions from many sources, was uniquely placed to bring all such suggestions together and place them before the War Council.

Esher to Hankey. Intelligence Anglaise, 20th June 1915. Holograph
I have seen all the fighting on our right. The French are doing moderately.[2] *We* cannot get on at all. Nor shall we. It is not a question of high explosives but of *anno domini*. You have two nations governed and two armies led by old men. No resilience—no adaptivity. Against you the concentrated, unified, organized capacities—scientific, military, philosophical etc. etc. of one of the highest developed nations ever known. On interior lines these people will break us. Make no mistake. The grey beards are not up to the mark and cannot cope with such a situation. *Valete*
Yours ever
Lloyd George's visit to Boulogne is the talk of the army and the country here . . . You can show him this letter, if you like, and tell him to invent asphyxiating gases for the antiquities of both nations.

There was in fact good ground for Esher's pessimism in the early summer of 1915. The Germans had used gas for the first time at Ypres on 22nd April, but had totally failed to exploit the surprise thereby achieved. None the less Sir John French persisted in holding as much of the diminished salient as possible, and the 2nd Battle of Ypres ended in May with a loss to the British army of 60,000 men. The French offensives further south had been equally barren of result, and no less costly. Then, shortly after Italy had joined the Allies on 24th May, their first offensive on the Isonzo lapsed into a stalemate which reproduced conditions on the western front.

Diary 3rd July 1915[3]
The King sent yesterday for a copy of my Memo. on General Policy. The Cabinet, after seeing Sir John French decided approximately as follows:—
(1) We must keep our hands free for eventualities; (2) Subject to this that the western theatre of war was the principal one for our efforts; (3) That we would endeavour to let the French know what forces were coming; (4) That pending the development of our munitions we must act mainly on the defensive . . . (5) That we should take over a large section of the French

---

[1] Runciman to Hankey, 21st June 1915.
[2] Presumably Esher was referring to the French offensives in Champagne and Artois in the spring and early summer of 1915. They were in fact costly failures.
[3] This diary entry accurately summarises the results of the Cabinet meetings on 2nd and 3rd July. Cab. 37/131/3 and 41/36/31.

line . . . I completed my Memo. on Home Defence. Very unsatisfactory, both naval and military, but I don't believe the Germans could invade all the same. Bonham Carter engaged to Violet Asquith . . .

Hankey's proposal that the British and French political and military leaders should meet around a conference table with the object of co-ordinating their war policy was at least acted on quickly. On the evening of 5th July he crossed to Calais with Asquith, Balfour, Kitchener, Crewe and a number of departmental representatives. The conference next day was, at any rate by Hankey's standards, very badly organised. No agenda had been prepared, and as he was not admitted to the high-level discussions, no conclusions were recorded. He entered in his diary what he believed to have been the "unformulated conclusions". The most important of them were that the British would take over more of the western front, where "local offensives on a considerable scale" would be made but "no great offensive . . . which if unsuccessful would paralyse us" was to be launched. The Dardanelles operation was to continue.[1] Despite its obvious failings the First Calais Conference was something of a land mark, in that it was an attempt to arrive at an agreed strategy and war policy.

Meanwhile the future of the Gallipoli undertaking had become a burning question in the Dardanelles Committee and the Cabinet, in both of which bodies a division of opinion was becoming increasingly apparent. On 16th June Hankey sent Asquith a paper in which he discussed a new proposal which was being canvassed—namely the possibility of breaking the stalemate by making a fresh landing on the Bulair isthmus at the northern end of the Gallipoli peninsula. His conclusions were that such an operation was altogether too difficult and hazardous.[2] Churchill was of course very active at this time on behalf of his favourite project, and when the Cabinet decided that they must have first-hand information from the scene of the fighting evidently pressed to go out himself. On 19th July Asquith, very unusually, issued a six line directive "I have decided that Lieut-Col. M.P.A. Hankey shall accompany Mr. Churchill on his visit to the Dardanelles. Colonel Hankey will be independent of Mr. Churchill, and will have full discretion as to his movements, and will be at liberty to communicate with me direct if he thinks necessary. H.H.A."[3] Plainly the Prime

[1] *Supreme Command*, I, pp. 348–9.
[2] G. 18 of 16th June 1915. Cab. 42/3/3.   [3] Original in Hankey papers.

Minister was unenthusiastic about Churchill's participation in the mission. The lack of properly recorded minutes deprives us of knowledge of what passed in Cabinet during the next two days, but the entries made by Adeline in her husband's diary, evidently in part to his dictation, leave one in little doubt that Churchill withdrew under pressure from his colleagues.

19th July 1915
Maurice went up [to London] early to get his kit together and had an interview with K. in the morning and Balfour and the P.M. in the afternoon and evening. K. gave him his own cypher and took him entirely into his confidence. One rather odd thing he said was that he did not intend to let the army go through to Constantinople if they got through the Dardanelles! Maurice is to be quite independent of Winston Churchill and [is] to communicate privately with the Govt. if Winston C. gets out of hand. A very difficult position for M., and one he does not relish. He is armed also with a paper signed by the P.M. to the effect that he is quite independent of W.C. and may return when he pleases.[1] In spite of this M. does not appear very happy about the expedition . . .

At 11.30 P.M. a note marked "confidential" was delivered at our bedroom door. It was from Bonham Carter to say that Curzon and Selborne disapproved of the expedition and that it was postponed. Terrible anti-climax as M. [was] ready to the last button to start early next morning.

Tuesday 20th July
M. went to see Borden off to France by 10 a.m. from Charing Cross. They were to have travelled together. Borden's confidential man said to Maurice that he had heard that M. was *the* man who was running the war!

M. went off to the office and I called for him before lunch to find that he was to go to the Dardanelles *alone* starting early next morning. We went on to lunch with the Asquiths . . . Mrs. Asquith took possession of M. at lunch and a very confidential leave-taking of him afterwards. Maurice was very glad of the short respite and was very busy till late that evening . . . He had interviews with Mr. Balfour etc too. Mr. Balfour offered him a special train though he was going alone, but M. refused. Late in the evening a mountain of packages arrived at the hotel from 10 Downing Street—presents for Arthur Asquith[2] and his friends—which M. regarded with dismay.

[1]Presumably Asquith handed to Hankey the directive quoted above at the interview on the evening of 19th. Hankey obviously told his wife the gist of its contents.
[2]1883–1939. 3rd son of H. H. Asquith by his first marriage. Generally known as "Oc. Asquith". Served in Naval Division at Antwerp 1914 and Gallipoli 1915. Wounded on Gallipoli and later again in France. Retired as Hon. Brigadier-General 1918.

Hankey's misgivings over his mission to the Dardanelles can readily be understood. By the middle of 1915 he can have had no illusions regarding the type of problem, and the clash of personalities, which arose in a democracy at war. He had seen the genius of Fisher flawed by the violence of his hatreds, and that of Churchill ruined—at least temporarily—by his impatience and impetuosity. He had witnessed with disapproval the petty jealousy of French towards Kitchener, and the narrow-mindedness of Conservative politicians, not excluding his beloved Balfour, in refusing to come to War Council meetings lest they should thereby sacrifice party advantage. He had experienced the stubborn conservatism of most senior officers of both services towards the development and employment of new weapons and tactics; while the vacillations of a weakly-led government over strategic issues had long been in the forefront of his thoughts. He had also very recently witnessed the difficulties that arise between Allies; and the French were also involved in the Gallipoli operation. Finally he knew that opinion in the Cabinet, the Admiralty and the War Office was deeply divided over that undertaking, and that a powerful faction of politicians led by Bonar Law, and of soldiers headed by Henry Wilson desired to liquidate the entire venture as soon as possible. Now he was required to report on a situation in which the local commanders were bound to be on the defensive—because of the ill success that had so far attended their endeavours; and he was certain to be regarded as a "government spy" sent out to judge, assess and criticise their past actions. Whatever he wrote would, it seemed certain, antagonise some influential persons; and although he knew that he had so far enjoyed universal confidence it must have seemed to him all too likely that it would not survive the task which had been thrust on him.

The journey across Europe at least provided him with an interlude of rest during which he could sort out his thoughts and plan his line of action. He dropped off the train letters to Adeline and postcards to the children at every possible stop; and the sight of Mont Blanc recalled nostalgic memories "of you and holidays, and boating, and scrambles in the Alps . . . How different to the scene of blood and desolation to which . . . I am now proceeding!" He swore to Adeline that "some day you and I shall come to yonder mountains enjoying them the more for what we are both enduring". In Italy he claimed, probably correctly, to have uncovered a German spy system organised to watch all trains passing through and find out the names, units and destinations of officers. He at once "cabled all over the place and set the machinery going to put the hat on the whole thing". In the same letter (24th July) he wrote "I have also thought out my whole plan of operation at Gallipoli. At first I could not see what I could do, but now I plainly see that I have *a great opportunity*, and I see how to rise to it to the full, if de Robeck and Ian Hamilton give me half a chance". But he warned Adeline that "it may take me rather longer than I first thought".

In Rome Hankey and his travelling companion were hurried by "Cook's man" into a train which was about to leave for Brindisi, and which would get them there 24 hours earlier than the planned connection. They arrived on the evening of the 23rd and at once went on board the light cruiser *Chatham* (Captain S. R. Drury-Lowe[1]) which was waiting for them. Five days later Kitchener's private secretary wrote to Adeline "your husband appears to have arrived safely . . . and to have reached the Australian positions as he has telegraphed to that effect." He offered to send on Adeline's letters and "to keep you posted as to Colonel Hankey's movements."[2] On the same day Admiral de Robeck wrote to Balfour that "Sir Douglas Gamble[3] and Colonel Hankey [have] both arrived and the former has now left for home . . . Colonel Hankey is remaining for the present. I was very glad to see both of these officers and was very surprised to hear from them how little was known in England, at the War Office and Admiralty, as to the real condition of affairs here".[4]

Hankey's misgivings regarding his mission having more or less evaporated during the long train journey he was able to enjoy to the full the prospect of finding himself at sea once again, and in the company of service men dedicated to the task of carrying out to the best of their ability the operations entrusted to them. Moreover the return to his beloved Greece, even though the circumstances were widely different from his pre-war visits, stimulated all his Phil-Hellenism. For once Hankey abandoned his custom of writing to his wife daily. Instead he jotted down descriptions of each day's events and sent them to Adeline about once a week. Those letters were obviously intended to be preserved in substitution for the diary entries he could not make. An

---

[1]Later Vice-Admiral Sidney R. Drury-Lowe (1871–1945).
[2]H. J. (later Sir Herbert) Creedy (1878–   ) to Mrs. Hankey, 28th July 1915.
[3]See p. 104. Admiral Gamble's brief visit to Gallipoli was presumably connected with his earlier experience of the Turkish navy.
[4]de Robeck to Balfour 28th July 1915. Lloyd George papers D/23/4/6.

interesting point is that Hankey's return to the Aegean islands brought
about a recovery of the literary style which had distinguished his earlier
letters—with long, vivid descriptions of places and people, interspersed
with apt quotations from Homer and Byron which had remained in the
penumbra of his mind. There is no doubt that his natural style had by
1915 been greatly vitiated by the daily labour of writing endless
appreciations for Ministers, minutes of meetings, and letters to important people dealing with current events. But his Gallipoli letters of 1915
show that his descriptive gifts, though long suppressed, had merely
been dormant. It was of course natural that he should play down in his
letters to Adeline both the dangers to which he was exposed and the
horrors of the fighting in the cramped, blood-soaked arena of the
peninsula. But his official letters and reports show how deeply aware he
was of all that the troops had come through—and were still to face.

To Mrs. Hankey H.M.S. Chatham Sunday 25th July 1915
. . . I went to early service, and after breakfast I spent two or three hours
studying and making copious extracts from the orders issued to the ships by
Admiral de Robeck, of which Captain Drury-Lowe had a copy. This puts me
pretty well *au fait* with the whole naval situation out here and will simplify
my task considerably.
26.vii.15
. . . We arrived Lemnos this morning, and I was at once transferred to a
destroyer which took me to "a certain island" [Imbros][1] which is the headquarters both of the Admiralissimo and Generalissimo. I lunched with the
Admiral in a yacht he uses as flagship and, after a long talk, went on to tea
ashore with Sir Ian Hamilton. Both received me most cordially and kindly.
Both expressed gratification that I was not accompanied by a certain personage [i.e. Churchill]; and both have offered me every possible assistance . . .

It may help the reader to follow Hankey's mission to Gallipoli if a
brief digression is made here to describe the geography of the peninsula.
The southern end is absolutely dominated by the modest hill known to
the British (incorrectly) as Achi Baba. This was the unattained first
objective of the assault forces landed at Cape Helles. It was only just
over 700 feet high, but its capture was vital to the safety of the landing
beaches, and an essential preliminary to further progress up the peninsula. About ten miles north-east of Achi Baba rises the much higher
Sari Bair ridge, whose three summits (Koja Chemen Tepe, Besim

[1] The omissions here and elsewhere in Hankey's letter to his wife were, of course,
made on security grounds. They have been inserted by the author.

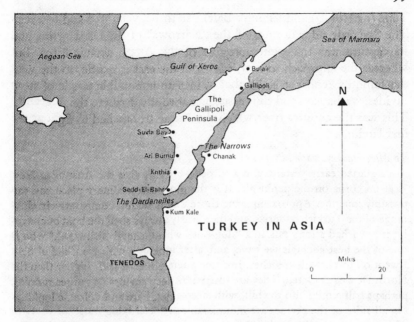

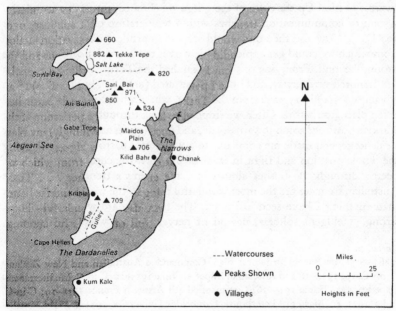

1   The Gallipoli Peninsula and the Dardanelles

Tepe (or Hill Q) and Chunuk Bair) rise to between 850 and 970 feet. The Sari Bair ridge dominated the "Narrows" of the Dardanelles, and its capture was the main objective of the Anzac assault force. But whereas the approach to Sari Bair from the east is gentle, to the west the summits "collapse suddenly . . . into an impossible tangle of steep ravines, washaways and cliffs cascading abruptly down to the Aegean".[1] This was the country over which the Anzac troops had to fight at the first landings.

To Mrs. Hankey. 28th July 1915

. . . I started early yesterday in a torpedo-boat to visit the Australian-New Zealand corps on the peninsula. It is the most extraordinary place you can possibly imagine. Approaching the shore one is within comparatively close range of the Turkish batteries, and they nearly always shell the boat but never hit it . . . I had a long talk in a "dug-out" with General Birdwood,[2] who is one of the best generals we have, and, after lunching with his Chief of Staff I went off to visit the trenches. Imagine a semicircle of cliffs higher than the North Downs at Oxted. They are scarred by deep ravines or gorges running perhaps half a mile into the hill, with steep sides, bare and volcanic looking. On all sides of the ravines are innumerable artificial "dug outs" or caves in which the Australians and New Zealanders live, together with teeming swarms of flies! Up the sides of the gorge we climbed, through a wonderful system of communication trenches with a temperature of, I suppose, over 100°F . . . Now and then one would stop at an artillery observation station from which we could get a splendid view over the Turkish positions and the ground beyond. From one of them I watched the Turks shelling a tunnel a few hundred yards away, and once I penetrated (unwillingly I confess) to an advanced sap only 15 *yards* from the Turks, where a hand grenade battle had taken place just before. Often we stopped to look through a periscope at the Turkish positions some 50 yards away, and once (again unwillingly) my New Zealand general made me come out to a wonderful narrow zig-zag flanking the whole position and right in front of our own trenches, from which we peered through the bushes almost into the enemy's trenches . . . These Australian trenches are the most wonderful thing in the world and far better than anything I have seen in France. The men also are wonderful—huge, strong, intelligent soldiers, devoid of nerves, full of wonderful cunning,

[1] *James*, p. 3.
[2] 1865–1951. 1st Baron Birdwood 1938. Commanded Australian and New Zealand Army Corps 1914–18 and Australian Imperial Force 1915–20. C-in-C, Mediterranean Expeditionary Force 1915–16; Commanded 4th Army in France 1918–19; C-in-C, India, 1925–30. Master of Peterhouse, Cambridge University, 1931–8. Field-Marshal 1925.

every man thinking of nothing but how to beat the enemy. I don't believe we
have anything to touch them. . . . In the trenches one is absolutely safe, but
the beaches are dangerous to the last degree, for sudden death stalks abroad
there . . . In the afternoon [of 28th] I called on Gen. Braithwaite,[1] Sir Ian
Hamilton's Chief of Staff, and had a long talk . . . To-morrow I propose to
visit the Cape Helles end and stay a night if all is quiet . . . After that I am
going ashore to live in a tent at G.H.Q. in peace and quiet, and the rest of
my work will be in rear of the fighting line, examining the extraordinarily
interesting services of supply etc. and writing my big Report . . .

30th July 1915
Years seem to have elapsed since I last wrote, yet in reality it is only two days.
If I remember right I was about to visit Cape Helles. This I did, crossing over
in the trawler which plies daily between General Headquarters and the
mainland. On board was a very nice Frenchman, Captain Berthier, liaison
officer between the British and French armies. He kindly invited me to
lunch at the French headquarters, and on arrival at the beach he took me in
a launch to the French beach. We saw over the old fort of Sedd-ul-Bahr,
which was knocked to pieces by our naval guns. Then they took me to see
the French C-in-C, an old chap of 68, named Bailloud, who only got the
command through the wounds or sickness of his superiors.[2] He is a notorious
pessimist, not only about the Dardanelles, but about the whole war, and
more than hinted that the English are not trying. I had a fearful wrangle and
went for him tooth and nail in fluent but faulty French, to the great amusement of two French staff officers who were present. You know exactly the
arguments I used, and he referred to me as *"un officier tant intelligent que vous
monsieur!!!"*. We parted quite good friends, and I felt that he had not had the
better of me . . . Then we were joined by the Major of the General Staff who
was showing me round . . . and we got horses—mine was lent by the French
—and rode across to the British lines. On the way we spotted Arthur Asquith
of the Naval Div[n] and I had a long talk with him.[3] . . . Next day we called on

[1]Later General Sir Walter P. Braithwaite (1865–1945). Chief of General Staff,
Mediterranean Expeditionary Force 1915. Commanded 62nd Division 1915–18 and
IX Army Corps 1918–19. C-in-C, Scottish Command, 1923–6 and Eastern Com-
mand 1926–7. Adjutant-General to the Forces 1927–31.

[2]In his letter to Asquith of 5th August Hankey described General Bailloud as "the
most confirmed pessimist I have met since the war began . . . He is a stupid old man
and ought to be superseded".

[3]In his letter of 5th August to the Prime Minister Hankey wrote of Arthur Asquith
that he "looked well, tremendously sunburnt and in good spirits"; but judging
from the reactions of the Prime Minister and Mrs. Asquith to his letters (see pp.
228 and 229) the "good spirits" were by no means always present while he was at
Gallipoli.

General Paris[1] who commands the Naval Div^n. He was in good spirits considering what a "doing" the Naval Div^n has had. Then we went on to another distinguished general who commands a distinguished unit—as I am my own censor I will err on the side of secrecy[2]—, who lives on rather a pretty beach from which diverges a wonderful deep ravine known out here as "the Gully". This remarkable feature, which is about 50–70 ft. deep, very winding, with steep rocky sides (just like a nullah I once took you to at Malta) forms a natural communication trench for the British forces near Krithia. Up it we rode for perhaps a couple of miles or more, when we had to dismount. Then there was the usual walk through the usual trenches, and we went right up to the trenches recently captured by the Ghurkas on the extreme left flank. . . . It was nearly 2 hours' ride, which will give you some idea of how big our advance has been here . . .

We did not get back until after 9 p.m. and found the general and his staff just finishing dinner in a cool, dark, tent. I was very tired and thirsty, and glad to get to bed. Considering I was on the bare ground except for the valise, I slept very well, but was woken at 5 a.m. by the loathsome flies which pollute all parts of the Gallipoli peninsula . . .

The previous evening I had received a wire from de Robeck inviting me to go with him for the week-end to a certain port [Mitylene, Lesbos], which is the headquarters of the Smyrna blockade, and, as this was part of my intended programme I gladly accepted. This necessitated my leaving Cape Helles at 11 a.m., I was told, instead of at 4 p.m. Accordingly I bade farewell to the general and marched down to the landing place—one of the famous landing scenes of the original disembarkation . . . Hardly had I settled down in the heat, dust, stench, flies, and general discomfort of this beach than the Turks began to shell it . . . I got under cover of the cliff, and found it very interesting after the first feeling of alarm had passed. They were aiming at some trawlers, but, though they must have fired some 90 rounds in an hour and a half, and had most hair-breadth shaves, it was all wasted ammunition, for they hit no one and nothing . . .

They fired some half dozen rounds of 4 inch shell at my picket boat, which was towing a huge launch, but never got near us . . .

Still, I was glad to turn my back on Cape Helles, which is a disagreeable spot just now, with the flies and shells, both of which swarm everywhere.

[1] Later Major-General Sir A. Paris, R.M.A. (1861–1937). Commanded R.N. Division at Antwerp 1914, Gallipoli 1915 and in France 1916. Retired in consequence of wounds 1917.
[2] This must have been General H. de B. de Lisle who had taken command of 19th Division on the left of the British front at Helles on 4th June.

H.M.S. Arrogant [Aragon][1] *1st August 1915*
Before leaving Helles the Admiral had given me an invitation to accompany
him to Port Icro in the island of Mitylene, where certain operations are
conducted, and, as this was one of the places I particularly wished to visit I
gladly accepted. We embarked in the *Chatham* and went there on the night
of the 30th, returning the night of the 31st. A greater contrast between Helles
and Icro I really cannot conceive. The former a mass of dirt, flies, and shells,
the latter a land-locked, still harbour with clear water surrounded by olive
clad mountains from the slopes of which beautiful fountains gush out and
run in cool streams through the pleasant glades . . .

The next three days Hankey spent on board the *Aragon* recovering
from a touch of the all-prevailing dysentery, and then at General
Hamilton's headquarters, where he settled down to write his report in
rather difficult conditions. There is a gap in his diary letters from 5th to
12th August, and that was perhaps the most tragic week of a campaign
which was full of tragedy. Only very rarely do the gods of war allow
the side which has missed one highly favourable opportunity a second
chance; yet that is what happened at Gallipoli in August 1915.

General Hamilton's plan was to launch on 6th–7th August a holding
attack on the Helles front, while the Anzac forces drove hard for the
Sari Bair ridge. Two recently arrived British "New Army" divisions
(10th and 11th) were to make a new landing at Suvla Bay, some four
miles north of Anzac Cove, and advance inland to gain the commanding
heights, and link up with the Anzac forces. Suvla Bay was then to be
secured and developed as a winter base for the expeditionary force. If
the triple attack succeeded the Turkish forces on the Helles front
would be cut off, and have to beat a hasty retreat, command of the
"Narrows" of the Dardanelles would at last pass to the Allies, and the
fleet could steam into the sea of Marmara virtually unmolested. And,
despite all that went wrong, the plan very nearly did succeed. After
astonishing feats of endurance and gallantry, at dawn on 9th August a
small band of British troops and Ghurkas under Major C. J. L.
Allanson actually stormed the key position of Chunuk Bair, and looked
triumphantly down on the Narrows, and beyond to the Asiatic shore.
Then they came under heavy shell fire—Allanson alleged from British
warships, but the greater probability is that gunners in the old Anzac

[1]Hankey meant the Royal Mail liner *Aragon*. The luxury in which the staff lived on
board her aroused the fury of the fighting men. Thus Hankey's slip of the pen was
not inappropriate. See *James*, pp. 225 and 338.

area, on seeing men on the summit ridge, assumed them to be Turks. At all events the position was lost.

The Suvla landing achieved complete surprise and the troops got ashore with slight loss, though not without difficulties. But the Commander of IX Corps, General Sir Frederick Stopford[1]—an officer who had retired from the Army six years earlier—entirely failed to exploit the opportunity which lay within his grasp, and Hamilton did not impose his authority until too late. Turkish reinforcements were rushed to the scene, and by 10th, despite the heavy losses incurred, stalemate had once more descended on all three fronts.[2] Hankey attributed this lamentable result to what he called "this wretched IX Corps at Suvla".[3] Though some of Churchill's criticisms and conclusions on the Gallipoli undertaking are certainly ill-founded or unjustified one must surely accept his view that "the long and varied annals of the British Army contain no more heart-breaking episode than Suvla Bay".[4]

Telegram. Vice-Admiral, Eastern Mediterranean to Admiralty. August 14th 1915. 8.15 P.M.[5]

991. The following from Lt. Colonel Hankey for Prime Minister and Lord Kitchener. *Secret and personal.* Regret to report that surprise attack has definitely failed, and position is only to be won by hard fighting. Es [sic. Possibly E.F.—Expeditionary Force] can be trusted to hold but cannot achieve big success. Birdwood at Anzac carried his share of operations on August 6th with entire success and only lost Sari Bair ridge subsequently owing to bad luck and lack of support by 9th Corps. He may regain it eventually. From top of ridge whole country up to and across Dardanelles was visible. At Anzac in spite of heavy casualties troops are full of fight though in need of reorganisation. Troops lately sent from England unfortunately failed almost completely, owing partly to water difficulty, but mainly to bad staff work and want of dash and drive. Small enemy force has completely held up nearly four divisions, and inflicted very heavy casualties. Necessary re-organisation may require one week before another attack. This allows Turks time to bring up strong forces and entrench. Already enemy is entrenching within 3,000 yards of Suvla Bay, and hold important Anafarta

[1] 1854–1929. Director of Military Training 1904–6. G.O.C., London District 1906–9.
[2] See *James*, Part IV, Ch. 11 for an admirable account of the fight for the Sari Bair ridge, 6th–10th August 1915.
[3] Hankey to Asquith 12th August 1915.   [4] Churchill, II, p. 432.
[5] Asquith papers, Vol. 28, folios 74/5.

ridge. Field guns on this ridge bombard Suvla Bay and have driven ships to outer edge of bay where there is danger from ledges and anchorage is less sheltered. When enemy mount heavy guns on ridge Suvla Bay will be almost intolerable, as there is little cover on landing beaches. To recover lost opportunity will be difficult and costly, but not impossible with good arrangements as enemy must also be uncomfortable. Stopford and his staff will never do it. Birdwood has a first rate staff and is only General here who has gained big success and impressed his personality on troops. Best chance in my opinion would be to put Birdwood in charge of whole northern area and give him free hand necessary rank being granted. I fear Hamilton will never do this on his own initiative, as Braithwaite underrates Birdwood, and rather dominates Hamilton.

I do not want to embarrass local command, but believe suggestion or order from you to place Birdwood in charge of northern area, in view of his proved competence, might make difference between success and failure.

Important to keep my name out of this.

In any case we have now to face probable winter campaign.

On 28th July and 5th August Hankey sent the Prime Minister long letters describing the operations up to those dates, the local conditions, and the characters, accomplishments and failings of the principal participants on the Allied side. He followed up those letters with a third, dated 12th August, in which he described the recent offensive. All three letters were printed in London, and presumably circulated to the Dardanelles Committee and the Cabinet.[1] They constitute a remarkable record of what he had observed, experienced and concluded; but as he himself published the greatest part of all three letters they will not be discussed in detail here.[2] The last of them ended thus: "I have assumed that I am intended to report fully and frankly, and I have done so. It will be for you to decide how far you will show this to your colleagues, and I suggest you should consult Lord Kitchener, as I have criticised some of the military arrangements rather severely. But I have not exaggerated a bit, and I think any member of the staff here at G.H.Q. would say that I have understated the contrast between the Anzac Corps and the British troops, and between Generals Birdwood and Stopford their respective commanders."

On 15th and 16th Hankey wrote long letters to Balfour describing

[1]The originals are in Asquith papers, Box 117, folios 171–210. Printed copies are in *ibid.*, Vol. 28, folios 60–65.

[2]*Supreme Command*, I, pp. 378–88 and 390–402.

naval problems and deficiencies, and also the qualities and failings of the senior naval officers on the spot.[1] The copy of the second letter in Hankey's papers is inscribed, partly in his hand "The following letter was never sent owing to recall. Contents were communicated in official reports and verbally". The most interesting points in it are, firstly, that he developed a higher opinion of Admiral Wemyss,[2] the second-in-command, than of de Robeck; and, secondly, that although he considered that naval staff work was usually "greatly inferior to military staff work", in the August offensive the opposite had been the case.

To Mrs. Hankey. G.H.Q. British Med,. Expeditionary Force. 12th August 1915
    As I have just spent 6 hours in writing a description of the great battle to the P.M. I cannot attempt a technical account of it here. Besides the situation is too uncertain to permit of it, as the battle still continues. I will only mention some incidents that I saw. From the shores of this island on an extraordinarily clear day I watched the initial bombardment of Achi Baba by a colossal force of ships and land guns. It looked annihilating, but at the end the old Turk rolled out of his dugout and gave our people quite a hot time. He really is a wonderful fighter, and one cannot but admire him! . . . Another day I went over to a certain bay [Suvla], where we had just landed and climbed a hill ending in a knife-edge ridge with a cliff dropping below me sharp to the sea. Down in the plain a regular battle was going on, not more than a mile or two away. In the bay ships and monitors were firing like mad, some British and Turkish field batteries were in action, spattering the beautiful white bursts of shrapnel all over the plain, and there was a great rattle of rifle and machine gun fire, though one could see but little of the infantry . . . One way and another I have seen a lot of fighting, but I am very cautious and don't go too near, and shall not do so unless I have to . . . I doubt, though, if I shall be under fire again, as the interesting point is the new landing place I referred to, and I hope we shall soon get the enemy cleared right out of the surrounding country . . .
    And now you would like to know something of my everyday life here. The camp [on Imbros] is situated on a sandy hill overlooking, and only a few hundred yards from a bright blue bay full of ships . . . Across the bright blue bay the island rises in a series of fascinating hills

[1] Asquith papers, Vol. 28, folios 66–8.

[2] Later Admiral Sir Rosslyn Wemyss. 1st Baron Wester Wemyss 1919 (1864–1933). Was in charge of landings at Cape Helles 25th April 1915. C-in-C, East Indies and Egypt station 1916–17. Deputy First Sea Lord 1917. First Sea Lord 1917–19. Admiral of the Fleet 1919.

"with rocks that as the hours run
show all their jewels one by one
for pastime of the summer sun"[1]

It is always beautiful, but specially so at sunrise, when I see it through my tent door, and at sunset . . . When I arrived here last week I was down with a bad go of diarrhoea and was nervous of dysentery. I found, however, a real friend in need, in Maxwell, formerly the Daily Mail War Correspondent, who is Press Censor here. He is a wonderful campaigner and seems to have with him everything one can possibly require. Anyhow he took me in hand, fed me on Horlick's malted milk, with eggs beaten up, bread and sometimes a little brandy, and made me rest for a whole day, when I was to my intense relief quite cured . . .

Sir Ian is kindness and courtesy itself, and is always willing to see me at any time . . . The Staff were at first rather inclined to regard me as a "spy" and to treat me with bare ceremony, but now I have established good relations everywhere. I live in the Chief of the General Staff's Mess with the Intelligence and Operation Divisions—about 20 all told. Anyhow there I have found several old friends and made some new ones. Among the former is Graves[2] who was Consul General at Salonika when I went there in 1907 . . . Then there is Major Dawnay,[3] who was in the historical section of the C.I.D., but whom I now find disagreeable and too big for his boots. Also Lt. Col Aspinall, who was at Rugby with me.[4] There he was an ass, but he has grown into a very pleasant and capable fellow. . . .

Domestically I suppose I am abominably uncomfortable though those things don't worry if one is fit . . . The sand blows eternally through the tent

[1]From a poem entitled "Greece" by Sir Rennell Rodd, 1st Baron Rennell, 1933 (1858–1941). Ambassador to Italy 1908–19 and author of many works, especially on ancient and modern Greece, in verse as well as in prose. By a curious coincidence in 1942 Lord Rennell's son gave a copy of the poem to Miss Joanna Wright, who was then serving in the W.R.N.S. in the Middle East. In 1962 Robin Hankey, whose first wife had died five years earlier, married Miss Wright, and when Lord Hankey learnt of their intention to spend their honeymoon in Greece he gave them a copy of the same poem—which the present Lady Hankey has preserved.

[2]Philip P. Graves (1876–1953). Journalist and Consular Service Officer. Correspondent of The Times at Constantinople 1908–14. Served with Middle East Force 1915–19 then returned to The Times until 1946. Hankey first met Graves at Salonika in 1907 when they worked together in the Intelligence Field. (See p. 84.)

[3]Later Major-General Guy P. Dawnay (1878–1952). Soldier and business man. Served as Chief Operational Planner in General Allenby's H.Q.s 1917–18 with outstanding success, and then on Haig's staff. Retired after World War I and became Chairman of Dawnay, Day, Ltd., Gordon Hotels, Ltd.; also Vice-Chairman of The Financial Times and Financial News.

[4]Later Brigadier-General C. F. Aspinall-Oglander (1878–1959). Author of Military Operations, Gallipoli (Official History, 2 Vols.) and other works.

and the pestilential flies begin at dawn and badger until sunset . . . I suspect they could do more for me now, but Churchill's brother is the "Camp Commandant"[1] and I suspect that he thinks I pushed his brother out in some way, so will not bother himself . . .

A few days ago I came across from Anzac with 500 prisoners on board a destroyer. They only brought a tiny escort and were sitting on the deck all round us. Some were quite old. They were an extraordinarily docile crowd, and it is difficult to imagine how ever they put up such a good fight. I talked to a number of them through an interpreter. They profess a great hatred of their officers. . . .

I do an enormous amount of writing, as I always seem to have notes to make about something or another . . . It is an odd position here, and requires great tact, but I think I have established good relations all round, and with the P.M. notoriously behind me I have great strength if I choose to use it. I prefer to regard it as reserve power for going up the hills! . . .

H.M.S. Hussar. Sunday 15th August 1915

. . . My last letter to you only left on Thursday last, and all that day I was busy at G.H.Q. writing a most tremendous mail. On Friday I remained at G.H.Q. in the morning, going off to the *Hussar* for a short time as I wanted to see the Captain about certain anti-submarine work of which he is in charge. He was good enough to invite me to go for a cruise with him for a few days starting Saturday which I accepted with alacrity, as I was feeling a bit fed up with G.H.Q. . . . On Saturday morning early I went on board the *Hussar*, uncommonly glad to shake (in a literal sense) the dust of Kephalos . . . off my feet. We first went to Suvla Bay on the peninsula, where the Admiral was, as Captain Heneage,[2] with whom I am staying wanted to see him. I also wanted to see him, for I had a very delicate task to carry out, regarding which I cannot speak here. I had a difficult time with the Admiral [presumably de Robeck] but persuaded him to adopt my view. Then we got up anchor and went off to Tenedos . . . And now, alas, after two days of comparative luxury, I am going back to the discomforts, but I like sailors so much better than soldiers and Heneage is a real topper.

Aug. 16 Nevertheless as events turned out, I was not destined to be very much more at G.H.Q. For on Monday the 16th I met my friend Col. Sykes,[3] who has come out here to run the aerial work, and he told me as a great secret that the seaplane ship *Ben-my-Chree* was going down to the Gulf of Xeros opposite to the Bulair Lines, which I immensely wanted to see, and that the seaplanes were going to go up and try and launch torpedoes at some

[1] Major John S. S. Churchill (1880–1947). Younger brother of Winston Churchill.
[2] Probably Captain Algernon W. Heneage, not Henneage as written by Hankey.
[3] Later Major-General Sir Frederick H. Sykes (1877–1954). Chief of Air Staff 1918–19. Entered Parliament (Cons.) 1922. Governor of Bombay 1928–33.

ships in the Dardanelles. I at once asked for a passage, and the Captain of the ship [C.L'E. Malone], who was present at once invited me to come . . . There were a number of keen young aeroplane officers, one Edmonds, who as it turned out, was next day to perform the great and novel feat of torpedoing a 6,000 ton steamer from a seaplane, particularly took my fancy, he was as interested in the C.I.D. as I was in his flying![1] . . . At 3.30 a.m. I was called to see the start. In darkness and dead silence the seaplanes, fully tuned up, were hoisted overboard, and as the first light of dawn appeared over the heights north of Bulair they disappeared from view over the peninsula on their deadly errand while we waited in suspense. Less than an hour had elapsed before they re-appeared, and imagine the joy when it transpired that both had attacked and sunk enemy ships—the first attempt at a feat of a most suggestive kind. This was the crowning point of my trip, for on our way back I received a cypher message ordering me home at once . . .

On the 18th Sir Ian asked me to go with him to Anzac and Suvla, and, as I wanted to have a final look round and particularly wanted to say goodbye to Gen. Birdwood . . . I accepted the invitation. Unfortunately Birdwood could not come off, though I saw his Chief of Staff, Gen. Skeen,[2] for whom I also have a great admiration. I came in for a last dose of shelling . . . but none came near us, so it was rather amusing to watch! Anyhow I am glad I went, as I got a good last impression of the military situation in this vitally important area . . .

The whole of the 19th was spent in going round the various offices of the army obtaining the very latest particulars and plans on every conceivable subject, and the day passed like a flash. After dining with Sir Ian Hamilton I went off at 10 o'clock in a gale to the ship *Imogene*, the yacht of the British ambassador in Constantinople in peace time, which now carries the King's Messenger bag as far as Athens . . .

That same day Ian Hamilton wrote in his diary "For myself I am glad to think that, amidst the flood of news pouring out by this very mail . . .

[1]Hankey was correct in describing the attacks by the *Ben-my-Chree's* seaplanes as the first air torpedo attack in history; but in the account that follows he confused the first attack, made by Squadron Commander C. H. K. Edmonds on 12th August, with the second attacks, by Edmonds and Flight Lieutenant G. B. Dacre, on 17th. In the first attack Edmonds destroyed a 5,000 ton supply ship—which had in fact already been torpedoed and driven ashore by one of our submarines. In the second attacks Edmonds torpedoed the middle one of three steamers and Dacre, whose engine was giving trouble, managed to torpedo a tug while taxiing on the sea surface. See H. A. Jones, *The War in the Air*, Vol. II (O.U.P., 1928), pp. 64–5.

[2]Later General Sir Andrew Skeen, not Skene as written by Hankey (1873–1935). Chief Staff Officer to General Birdwood at Gallipoli 1915. G.O.C.-in-C., Southern Command, India 1923–24. C.I.G.S., Indian Army 1924–28.

we have, sticking up out of it, even one little rock (or perhaps I should say 'brick') in the shape of an eyewitness"—that is to say Hankey.[1] Nor was Hamilton alone among the senior officers at Gallipoli in paying tribute to what Compton Mackenzie has aptly described as "the bald bulging benevolent head" of the visitor who had carried out such a difficult task with such consummate tact.[2]

Hankey reached Phaleron[3] early on 21st and went straight to Athens with the intention of leaving at once for London with the King's Messenger. But the Italian ship which should have carried him on the first stage of the journey had been seized by the British contraband control service; and although Hankey telegraphed to Malta and to Rome neither the British nor the Italian navy could provide a destroyer. It looked as though he was "in for a long stay in Athens". But Hankey was not the man to repine over being delayed in one of the cities he had always loved best. Business came first, and he had long talks with the British Minister, with Sir Valentine Chirol,[4] the noted Middle East expert, and with J. D. Gregory the secretary to the Holy See,[5] both of whom happened to be in Athens. Though he spent much time working at the Legation he managed to fit in a visit to Daphne to see the "fascinating mosaics" in its Byzantine church, and also climbed up to the Acropolis in company with Chirol and Gregory to view once again "its glorious and imcomparable ruins". After two enjoyable days Admiral Mark Kerr,[6] an old friend of Hankey's who had been lent to command the Greek Navy, managed to fix up a passage to Reggio in a Greek destroyer. The crossing was very rough, and Hankey suffered agonies from seasickness. After disembarking thankfully on Italian soil, he went on to Rome, where he enjoyed once again the company of Sir Rennell Rodd the ambassador,[7] and of course visited St. Peter's.

[1] Sir Ian Hamilton, *Gallipoli Diary* (Arnold, 1920), Vol. II, p. 123.

[2] *Gallipoli Memories* (Cassell, 1929), pp. 358–65. Mackenzie gives a delightful portrait of "that sagacious, sómewhat grubby, clear-eyed, bald, big-headed little man", and was obviously deeply impressed by "the slowness of his gait, the gravity of his expression, the quiet earnest modulation of his voice".

[3] Phaleron (or Phalerum) Bay, the roadstead off Piraeus, the port of Athens.

[4] 1852–1929. Traveller in Middle East, journalist and author.

[5] 1878–1951. Diplomat and author. Assistant Under-Secretary, Foreign Office 1925–28.

[6] Admiral Mark E. F. Kerr (1864–1944). A pioneer of naval aviation. C-in-C, Greek Navy, 1913–15 and commanded Adriatic Squadron 1916–17. Deputy Chief of Air Staff 1918.

[7] See p. 201.

Hankey reached London on 28th August, with his final and comprehensive report on the situation at Gallipoli completed. He was met by Adeline, Swinton and Longhurst, and was probably disconcerted to find that Swinton had just circulated a somewhat pessimistic memorandum on the failure of the recent Suvla-Anzac offensive.[1] In Swinton's view we could either not send reinforcements and abandon the attempt to force the Straits, or send reinforcements and try again. Both alternatives had disadvantages.[2] The debate on those issues was to occupy much of Hankey's time during the next four months.

[1]Swinton acted as Hankey's *locum tenens* during his absence. Reports in the Press that he was to succeed Hankey as Secretary were promptly contradicted from Downing Street. See *The Times*, 20th and 21st August 1915.
[2]Memo. of 18th August 1915. Asquith papers, box 117, pp. 211–15.

Chapter 8

Frustration and Disaster,
August—December 1915

W E have already seen how Hankey completed his report on his mission to Gallipoli, and made all arrangements to have it printed, before he reached London. The report is actually dated 30th August, only two days after his return.[1] It was divided into four parts, but because Part IV ("Remarks on Future Policy") was extremely secret only a few copies were made, and they were circulated in typescript. Part I was entitled "The Tactical Problem", and in it Hankey surveyed the prevailing situation and future prospects in the Cape Helles, Anzac and Suvla areas. His conclusions were that "we shall be able to hold on to our position in the southern [i.e. Cape Helles] area without achieving a substantial advance"; that at Anzac "we have a really good prospect of gaining a footing on the Sari Bair ridges, from which we shall be able almost immediately to harass the enemy's communications, and before long organise a further advance"; and finally, that at Suvla "we are unlikely to achieve any considerable success, and may find ourselves obliged to hold on in a position of some difficulty". Though he warned that "it seems unlikely that an early and complete success can be looked for", he considered that if adequate reinforcements were sent out, and proper preparations were made to meet the deterioration of the weather which was bound to occur with the approach of autumn, the stalemate could still be broken. He then went on to discuss in detail "The means necessary for a continuance of the campaign". He rejected any suggestion that the forces provided for the recent (August) offensive had been inadequate. It was, he said, "quality and not quantity" that was lacking —doubtless with the poor performance of IX Corps at Suvla in mind. "Given drafts [to replace casualties], ammunition and the reinforcements for which Sir Ian Hamilton asks", he continued, "there is no doubt that we have a reasonable prospect of achieving success". But this would, he emphasised, predicate the most careful preparations for

[1] G.19. Cab. 42/3.

a winter campaign; and he went on to specify in great detail everything that was necessary to meet such a prospect. His list was formidable enough to arouse serious misgivings among the departments who would have to find and provide the men and equipment, and among the Ministers who would have to authorise their collection and despatch. But Hankey evidently was determined not to play down the magnitude of the task ahead.

In the third part of his report he surveyed "The Condition of the Rival Armies". He poured gentle ridicule on the view of the Intelligent Department [sic] that "the *morale* of the Turkish troops should be very low". On the contrary it was an "incontestable fact that the Turkish troops are not in the least demoralised, and in the recent actions have fought as they never fought before". After praising the "splendid morale" of the Australians and New Zealanders he went on to point out that the performance of the British divisions had been very uneven. In Hankey's view everything depended on the efficiency and experience of the senior officers. "A policy of ruthless weeding-out of inefficient commanding officers" would, he considered, "probably be fully justified"; and his private letters to Asquith can have left Ministers in little doubt as to where the "weeding-out" should begin.

Finally in the fourth and "Very Secret" part of his report he wrote that "The Government may well ask themselves whether they are justified in continuing a campaign which makes so tremendous a toll on the country in human life and material resources". To assist the Cabinet in making the crucial decision he put forward three possible courses of action, additional to preparing for the winter campaign. The first was "to resume the naval attack on the Narrows"; the second "to find some pretext for withdrawal from the campaign"; and the third "To arrive at an arrangement with the Turks after obtaining the consent of Russia".

As to renewal of the naval attack he recognised that a group of "responsible naval officers" (by whom he must principally have meant Commodore Roger Keyes[1]) had "worked out the operation in detail and believes that with proper preparation and a surprise their object

[1]1872–1945. 1st Baron Keyes 1943. Chief of Staff, E. Mediterranean Squadron 1915. Commanded Dover Patrol 1918, and led attacks on Zeebrugge and Ostend. Deputy Chief of Naval Staff 1921–25. C-in-C, Mediterranean 1925–28 and Portsmouth 1929–31. Director of Combined Operations 1940–41. Admiral of the Fleet 1930.

could be achieved". But the Vice-Admiral (de Robeck), who "is not lacking in dash or courage", and "the overwhelming majority of naval officers" were "utterly opposed" to such a plan. Thus in Hankey's view "it would . . . be a mistake for the Government to *order* an attack of this kind except in the last resort". Turning to withdrawal, Hankey first asked whether it was either tactically or politically possible "having regard to the place that prestige occupies in our system of Imperial Defence". "Tactically", he continued, "it would be a matter of the utmost difficulty"; but emergency plans had been prepared. Nor could he find any practical way of "saving our face in the event of withdrawal." As to coming to an arrangement with Turkey, prolonged negotiations with France and Russia would be inevitable; and, if the Russians assented, means would have to be found "to open a negotiation with Turkey through some very informal channel." He was prepared to offer suggestions on this score if required. Probably he had Admiral Hall's earlier scheme to bribe Turkey out of the war in mind.[1] But even if the government decided to embark on these intricate negotiations he urged that "unceasing preparations for a winter campaign should continue". Obviously Hankey was highly dubious of any of his three alternatives proving either practical or successful; and so in the final issue he was brought back to what he had always considered the only correct solution.

Judged by any standard this report was a remarkable document. In it Hankey placed the issues squarely and firmly before the Ministers who would have to take the crucial decision; nor was there in it anything to which de Robeck and Hamilton could take exception. He had steered a very skilful course between the Scylla of criticising the local commanders and the Charybdis of giving the Cabinet only an equivocal, non-committal gloss on the realities of the situation they had to face. And he at once took steps to inform de Robeck and Hamilton regarding what he had done.

Hankey to de Robeck. 2 Whitehall Gardens. August 31st 1915.[2]
SECRET AND STRICTLY PERSONAL.
Dear Admiral de Robeck,
When I said goodbye to you on August 19th I told you that I anticipated great difficulty in giving a correct picture of the situation at the Dardanelles to my Chiefs. Among responsible people here there are some who are rather

[1] See p. 159.   [2] de Robeck papers. 3/43.

inclined to take a very gloomy view of affairs there, while there are others who will jump at any straw to form an over-sanguine picture.

As soon as I left the Dardanelles, therefore, I set to work to try and compose a report which would picture the situation as it presents itself to me, and at my request Mr. Balfour is sending you a copy privately.

Of course, I cannot expect that you will agree with the report on every point. I felt bound to express my own impressions perfectly fearlessly and independently. Nevertheless, after the conversations I had with you I shall be disappointed if I have overstated the prospects or understated the difficulties in any way. One difficulty I had was that I did not feel justified in any printed report in going into tactical details about the future, or even giving any detailed account of my reasons for believing that the capture of the Sari Bair Ridges is a feasible operation, for fear that anything should leak out on the subject.

In addition to the printed report which has been sent to you I prepared a very secret report which was typewritten, in which I discussed such matters as the possibility of a naval attack, on which you had favoured me with your views; the possibility of the abandonment of the enterprise, on which I endeavoured to reproduce the general views which you and the General had given me; and one other very secret question which I had discussed with you and the General. The general conclusion which I came to, however, was that unless at any time you or the G.O.C-in-C advised to the contrary, "the operations must be pressed ahead", that you must be supported in all your demands . . .

One great difficulty about this is the lack of shipping. There simply is no more shipping to be had, and beyond a certain point, therefore, they cannot reinforce within fixed limits of time. On my way home I had a long talk with the British Ambassador in Rome, and implored him to try and obtain the use of the German and Austrian shipping locked up in Italian ports, and made some practical suggestions on the subject. He seemed to think this might be done, and this might help matters a little.

Since I have come back I have been asked by the Prime Minister, Lord Kitchener and Mr. Balfour, to become a sort of adviser to the Admiralty and the War Office to assist them on any points in connection with the Dardanelles operation which they cannot understand for want of local knowledge . . . Of course, I have promised to give all the assistance I can, but I have begun by making it perfectly clear that all the local measures required to carry out any particular policy which the Government may decide on (e.g. a winter campaign if it becomes necessary) must be worked out locally, and that nothing could be more disastrous than to try and run the business from here in any way. You may be sure, however, that I shall do my utmost to assist the operation in any manner within my power. If I learn of anything which might be likely to help you or the General (e.g. I have just heard of a new way of warming trenches and dug-outs which might be useful, and which I am following up) I will see that you are consulted as to whether you would like it. In fact, with such local knowledge as I have been able to pick up, I will keep my eyes very wide open to try and help either the naval or the military operations in any way.

In conclusion, I wish to express my great gratitude for all the assistance that you have given me while I was at the Dardanelles, which I shall do my utmost to repay by working for you at this end.

I have sent a practically identical letter to the G.O.C-in-C.

Hankey's diary entries and his letters to his wife provide an admirable summary of the discussions which took place during the days following his return home; but as his letters to Adeline usually recapitulate what he wrote in his diary only the latter is generally reproduced here.

Diary 29th August
Sent for by King to Windsor Castle . . . and immediately after lunch spent 1½ hours with the King, who apologised for summoning me so soon after my arrival and explained that he was anxious to hear all about the Dardanelles[1] . . . He seemed relieved on the whole at my account of the situation, though I did not underrate its gravity. In the evening I dined with Lord K. and had a long "heart-to-heart" talk with him. One result of these two interviews was that General Birdwood was promoted to the substantive rank of Lieutenant-General over the heads of any number of Major-Generals, while Egerton[2] was recalled. I feel no misgivings about this, as Birdwood is one of our best Generals and Egerton one of our worst . . .

31st August
Was pilloried all the morning before the Cabinet Ctee. on the Dardanelles.[3] My Report had made a great sensation. Lord Curzon, whom I have always regarded as anti-C.I.D., anti-Dardanelles and anti-me, congratulated and

---

[1]George V's diary for 29th August states "After luncheon saw Col. Hankey who has just returned from the Dardanelles. He told me a lot of interesting things. We shall, I fear, have great difficulty in defeating the Turks". (Royal Archives.)
[2]Later Major-General G. G. A. Egerton (1859–1951). Commanded 52nd Division in Gallipoli 1915. Inspector of Infantry 1916. In fairness to Egerton it should be recorded that Sir Basil Liddell Hart commented "I had a good impression of Egerton when he was Inspector of Infantry . . . I found him very receptive to the new tactical and training ideas that I was putting forward". (Letter to the author 5th Nov. 1968.)
[3]"Secretary's Notes" in Cab. 42/3/20. The discussion was resumed on 3rd Sept. *ibid*. The notes correspond exactly to Hankey's description of the points raised by various Ministers.

thanked me for it in the same breath. I was heckled a good deal by Winston about the possibilities of a naval attack, and badgered a bit by Curzon and Selborne, but all very nicely and I gave my answers very promptly . . . Lord K. gave me the signal not to talk about future operations[1] . . . All rather amusing.

1st September
Adeline's birthday, but she is at Eastbourne. Dull. My Dardanelles Report sent to Cabinet. General Wolfe Murray, the C.I.G.S., sent over on the telephone to say it was the most interesting thing he had read since the beginning of the war. Copies sent to Army Council and Board of Admiralty. The thing that bothers me rather is that some people have jumped from a ridiculous pessimism to an optimism altogether unjustified by my report, which paints rather a grey picture with Birdwood's Corps in rather a high light . . .[2]

The success of Hankey's Dardanelles mission undoubtedly enhanced his standing with Ministers, with the result that Asquith decided to extend and widen his duties. On 2nd September his position was re-defined in a memorandum stating that "The Prime Minister has expressed a wish that the secretary of the Committee of Imperial Defence shall free himself as far as possible from detailed work in order to give his attention more closely to the higher policy of the war". Furthermore Kitchener and Balfour had asked him "to devote a con-siderable amount of his time to advising the War Office and Admiralty respectively on the operations at the Dardanelles". One consequence of this change in Hankey's duties was that Swinton stayed on at Whitehall Gardens "as the under-study to the Secretary"—from which it will be noted that Hankey evidently still wished to avoid any suggestion of a Deputy. Swinton was also to carry special responsibility for the handling of all business connected with production, inventions and research. Lieut-Colonel Dally Jones was to deal with "naval, military and political questions" and "to keep special touch with negotiations with the Balkan States"; while Cyril Longhurst, who had joined the C.I.D. secretariat in 1914 and was to remain with it until 1942, was made responsible for the general organisation of the office and "for dealing with commercial and shipping questions".[3] In a memorandum

---

[1]This was typical of Kitchener's obsessive secrecy, which contributed so much to the Cabinet's loss of confidence in him.

[2]The diary entry for this day is continued in *Supreme Command*, I, p. 401.

[3]Memo. of 2nd Sept. 1915. Asquith papers, Box 119, folios 13–15.

Hankey sent to Asquith a few days later he set out the steps he had
taken to ensure that the War Office and Admiralty made available to
him all the information, semi-official as well as official, which he needed
to discharge his new responsibilities.[1] Thus did he circumvent Kitchener's obsession over secrecy—though he was too tactful to say so.

Diary 3rd September

Another meeting of the Dardanelles Ctee. Carson has become a member. He
is a veritable "Dismal Jimmy". Can't imagine how he ran the Ulster business.
As K. remarked to me. "If any of his men [i.e. the Ulster Volunteers of 1914]
had hurt the tip of his finger he would have chucked up the sponge."
Appallingly bad meeting. Lunched alone with Mr. Balfour at Senior. Made
him communicate news of French expedition to de Robeck in order to ask
about small craft and capacity of harbours.[2] I should have mentioned that on
previous evening I had long and confidential talk with McKenna about
national service and found him as strongly opposed as ever. His argument
briefly is this—that if we take many more men we cannot hope to supply our
Allies, to whom we are committed to the tune of about £1 million a day—
not in money but in goods or credit. His plan is to limit our army, but to give
our doles gratis as a gift not as a loan. Balfour is in general agreement. Saw
Lord Fisher and Churchill, who is at present in rather bad odour and lacking
in influence . . .

To Mrs. Hankey. United Service Club. 7th Sept. 1915.

. . . I find that the P.M. talks as though I was in actual charge of the
Dardanelles operation, which is very embarrassing, as I have no real responsibility whatsoever, and it is very difficult without responsibility to ascertain
exactly what is being done. I am trying to establish good relations with all the
departmental officers concerned, with some success; but it takes a tremendous
lot of time running round and calling on them all. Moreover I cannot make
the Admiralty see the need of more small craft, which I consider to be the
most important thing, because de Robeck always insists he has enough.[3] I
cannot take any responsibility unless I am given power and I cannot very
well get that. Still, I have got a great number of important minor points
looked into and put right, which is something to be thankful for.

[1] Memo. of 10th Sept. 1915. *ibid.* Vol. 28, folio 81A.

[2] The "French expedition" refers to their decision to send two Army Corps to the
Dardanelles. (*Supreme Command*, I, p. 410.) Hankey had stressed very strongly in his
Dardanelles report the need for many more small craft for multifarious duties.

[3] Cf. diary entry for 8th Sept. 1915. ". . . Long discussion [with Balfour] re small
craft for Dardanelles. Have great difficulty in getting Admiralty to send enough . . ."

To the same. 2 Whitehall Gardens. 8th Sept. 1915

. . . I am still plugging away at securing my position in regard to the Dardanelles business. I lunched with Austen Chamberlain at the Club and he astonished me by saying that K. had given the Cabinet the impression that I was in charge of all arrangements for a winter campaign at the Dardanelles. I mean to have my position defined very clearly on paper. At the present moment I am regarded as "holding the baby", and if it comes to a smash (as is quite possible) they may and will turn and rend me. I am a bit too slim to be caught that way though, and to take on other people's responsibilities when things are looking nasty. I am doing my best to help things along, though, and as soon as I find my requirements are not being met shall bleat very loud! . . .

On the same day that Hankey confided his apprehensions regarding the possible effects of his new responsibilities to his wife he sent General Hamilton a long "Secret and Personal" letter. After modestly admitting his inadequacies as a critic of military doctrine, he managed with consummate tact to convey his views on why so many things had gone wrong at Gallipoli. He accepted that some mistakes had been made at home, and then went on to claim that Hamilton's own telegraphed despatches had fully admitted "the mistakes made locally". The chief point of his letter was at the end, where he analysed "the mistakes inherent in our military system"; and those he believed to be "the most serious of all". At Suvla Bay, where he had talked to "the younger regimental and staff officers", he had found that "the regimental officers and the rank and file never knew enough of what is expected of them, and what they have before them". In other words Hankey suggested, quite rightly, that there had been a total lack of communication. He claimed that the same state of affairs prevailed in the New Army units in France, and to drive home his point he sent Hamilton an extract from a letter he had recently received from his brother Donald setting out his recent experiences at the front. "The fault", continued Hankey, "is of course one of system, and until it is reformed radically I realise that it is very difficult for the higher command to insist and ensure that full knowledge gets down to the individual private and [is] ingrained into him". Though he appreciated the need for secrecy about forthcoming operations, he felt "sure that we nearly always err on the side of excessive secrecy".[1] One feels that in this letter Hankey put his finger on one of the greatest weaknesses

[1] Hankey to Hamilton 8th September 1915. Hamilton papers.

in the British military system in World War I—namely the vast gulf between the staff which planned operations and the men who had to carry them out.

When Hankey wrote the foregoing letter he must have realised that General Hamilton's position was, to say the least, precarious; and that his own reports, despite their tactful wording, were not likely to enhance the C-in-C's standing in the eyes of Ministers. But it none the less seems clear that at the time when Hankey sent the letter no hint of Hamilton's supersession had reached him. Rather did he expect that it would be Hamilton who would conduct the next offensive, and also prepare for the winter campaign. He was therefore briefing him with suggestions regarding how a repetition of the August failure could be avoided. Nor does Hamilton seem to have realised that the storm clouds which had been gathering about his head were about to break. On 16th September he wrote to Hankey to acknowledge, among other communications, a copy of the famous "memorandum on the situation".[1] "All I will say now", wrote the General, "is that I believe I shall be able to endorse, and with enthusiasm, every single word of your memorandum. At this moment it seems to me accurate and extra-ordinarily comprehensive. My best congratulations to you on having achieved a double-barrelled success—right barrel, a thorough grip of the situation; left barrel a transubstantiation of what you had gripped into clear and precise English. This is all the greater joy to me because I have never consciously tried to influence you in any way . . . Indeed it is more than a joy, for it considerably strengthens my confidence in my own judgement".[2] Yet the General was in fact living in a state of illusion, and within a month his replacement had been decided on.[3]

Diary 10th September 1915

Spent most of morning with Major Shaw of Meteorological Office. Found he could probably prophecy weather at Dardanelles with some success, provided an expert was sent out to interpret telegrams . . . sent minute to Lord K and Mr. Balfour suggesting that meteorologist be sent out to give advice as to weather prospects . . . Saw Prime Minister who told me that Winston Churchill had asked to be made a *Major-General* and to have command of an

[1] Cab. G. 19 of 30th August 1915. See pp. 206–8.
[2] Hamilton papers.
[3] At the Dardanelles Committee meeting on 14th Oct. 1915. Cab. 42/4 and 22/2. See *James*, pp. 313–17 regarding the discussions and intrigues which preceded that event.

Army Corps. P.M. much embarrassed and told him he would consult Lord K., who told me next day he found the request a most embarrassing one, as he would like to get rid of Churchill, but could not offend the Army. P.M. said Churchill much down on his luck. I read the reports of the Cabinet Ctee. on War Policy, as Lord K. had asked me to do so. It was largely an attack on Lord K. for deficiencies in ammunition, and the "Supplementary Report" contained a strong plea for conscription signed by Churchill, Selborne, Curzon and Chamberlain.[1] It also contained a bad mis-statement Lord K. was alleged to have made at the C.I.D. First he never made it at all, and second the statement he did make, which the Ctee. had perverted, was made not at the C.I.D., but at a conference called to consider a different question altogether.[2] I apprised Lord K. of these facts, as well as the P.M. . . .[3]

Hankey's session with the Meteorological Office had important results; but it seems astonishing that the weather reports, which had been provided to the Admiral in command at the Dardanelles at the beginning of the campaign, had been discontinued in June at his request "when the weather became set". Hankey was familiar with the vagaries of the Aegean weather from first-hand acquaintance, both as a young man and very recently; and he knew that, whether more reinforcements were sent or withdrawal was decided on, the weather was bound to play a vitally important part. He now took action, through the Prime Minister, to get the weather reporting organisation restarted immediately, informing Kitchener and Balfour of what he had done.[4] At about the same time he sent George V his meteorological report on the Dardanelles. "I think the King may be interested to know that we are sending out an expert Meteorologist", he wrote to Lord Stamfordham. That expert should "be able to give notice of the changes in the weather. If he can do so this may be of extraordinary value, enabling the lighters and tugs to be towed into safe harbours before the storms arise, and giving time to make things snug on the

[1]Cab. 37/134/7 of Sept. 1915 is the "Supplementary Report" referred to here.
[2]In his "Note" of 15th Sept. Kitchener used the material provided by Hankey to correct the "mis-statements" in the War Policy Committee's report. They concerned the release of skilled munition workers from the Army and the production of rifles. Cab. 37/134/23.
[3]The concluding part of the Diary entry for 10th Sept., omitted here, is printed in *Supreme Command*, I, p. 411.
[4]Two memoranda, Hankey to Asquith of 10th Sept. 1915, the first of which is endorsed in Asquith's hand "Yes—also report on weather. H.H.A." Asquith papers, Vol. 28, folios 81A and 81C–F.

beaches and piers." He added that he was writing a report on preparing
for a winter campaign and would send a copy to the King; and by way
of keeping the Monarch informed of all that was going on he also
enclosed his "Secret Report on Blockade and Contraband in the
Levant."[1] Stamfordham acknowledged all these documents with
gratitude on the same day.[2]

Hardly had Hankey got his Dardanelles report circulated and his own
position and duties re-defined when he had to cross the Channel to
attend the second Anglo-French military conference, which opened at
Calais on 11th September. This time he and two French officers acted
as joint secretaries. The chief subject discussed was the despatch of four
French divisions to the Dardanelles—a proposal which had aroused
Joffre's violent opposition. The decision was that they should not be
sent until after his forthcoming offensive, and "not at all if the offensive
succeeded". Hankey noted in his diary that the outlook for these
reinforcements was "not good". That afternoon he had "a long yarn"
with Kitchener, the account of which is revealing as to the reasons for
his notorious secrecy.

Diary 11th September[3]
... K. also gave me his estimate of the Ministry, which is a very low one. He
says that Asquith and Balfour are the only honest and capable ones, and
considers even Grey to be stupid. The reason he told them so little was that
they were so "leaky", and now they insist on coming to the War Office to see
the telegrams he has had to warn Sir Ian Hamilton not to tell him his plans.
"If they will only divorce their wives", he said, "I will tell them everything" ...

As Balfour was a bachelor one wonders whether Kitchener, in
talking about Ministers' wives, had in mind not only the fact that
Asquith talked very freely with Margot, who was notoriously indiscreet, but also confided his problems, troubles and cares to Venetia
Stanley (later Mrs. Edwin Montagu) with whom he developed a very
intimate relationship at this time.[4]

[1]Hankey to Stamfordham 17th September 1915. RA. GV. E813/1. The report on
Blockade and Contraband is G.20 dated 7th September 1915. Cab. 24/1. The report
on preparations for the winter campaign (G.22 of 22nd September) was sent to
Stamfordham on 23rd. RA. GV. E813/4.
[2]Stamfordham to Hankey 17th September 1915. RA. GV. E813/2.
[3]See *Supreme Command*, I, pp. 411–12, where the passages reproduced here are not
printed.
[4]See *Jenkins*, pp. 257–9 and *passim*.

Meanwhile the debate on conscription was gathering momentum. On 14th September Hankey wrote a paper "contraverting the report of the Cabinet Committee on War Policy", which had come down in favour of such a measure, and the Prime Minister wanted to circulate it to the Cabinet.

Diary 15th September
. . . Explain [to Asquith] that I don't mind, if we are really at the parting of the ways on this question, but felt bound to explain that, if circulated in my name, it would bring me into terribly bad odour, with the conscriptionist gang, and that, if they came in, they would probably fire me out. On reconsideration he therefore decided not to circulate it under my name but to use it in some other way . . .

McKenna to Hankey. Treasury Chambers. 14th Sept. 1915. Holograph
My dear Hankey,
Your paper is a marvel! It disposes of the whole conscription case.
My own effort is so inferior that I hesitate to send it.
Yours ever

Diary 16th September
. . . Saw Lord K. who asked me to join a new War Office General Staff Committee considering [the] question of future action at the Dardanelles. Churchill also a member. At 5 p.m. Churchill called and told me that the Prime Minister and he both regarded me as responsible for [the] success of arrangements for winter at Dardanelles. This I vigorously repudiated as one cannot have responsibility without authority . . . Churchill then pestered me to take up and press forward provision of a new trench mortar called the Stokes gun . . . This I undertook to do and put Swinton on to it.

17th September
Hurst (F.O. Legal Adviser[1]) called to induce me to take over Lord Crewe's new Trade Co-ordinating Ctee. as part of C.I.D. Very heavy day writing paper on arrangements for winter campaign [at Dardanelles] and stirring up people at Adty. and W.O. on all sorts of details.

18th September
Lunched at 10 Downing St. P.M. has definitely made up his mind in favour of voluntary service and not compulsory service, and has written to Balfour asking him to stand by him on the question. Completed paper on winter arrangements at Dardanelles.

[1]Later Sir Cecil Hurst (1870–1963), Legal Adviser to Foreign Office 1918–29. Judge of Permanent Court of International Justice 1929–46; President 1934–6. Chairman, United Nations War Crimes Commission 1943–4.

20th September

Mr. Balfour called just before lunch to say that he had just had a long conference with the P.M. on national service. He gave me a copy of a fairly long Memo. on the subject which he had circulated to the Cabinet. The great feature of it was the importance of national unity, which he described as one of our greatest assets, and this was bound to be lost if national service was adopted, as the Irish party and Labour party were violently opposed to it. . . .

Asquith's stand against conscription led to the introduction of the "Derby scheme" for recruiting; but although Hankey has described this compromise as "an ingenious device",[1] and the number of recruits accepted did in fact rise substantially in October and November,[2] it did not prevent the "conscriptionists" returning to the charge almost immediately. Hankey regarded this action, taken at a time of crisis, as "hardly playing the game"; and it does seem clear that the predominantly Conservative conscriptionist lobby was not above exploiting the difficulties of the period in order to embarrass the government.[3]

The two papers referred to by Hankey on 18th September dealt with the most critical issues then before the Dardanelles Committee and Cabinet—namely whether Bulgaria and Greece could be enticed into the war on the Allied side, and on the continuation of the Gallipoli undertaking. On 14th the Allies had made a firm offer of territorial aggrandisement to Bulgaria if she would attack Turkey. Hankey's diary shows that the first suggestion regarding the despatch of an expedition to the Balkans reached him from the Foreign Office next day. In the paper he produced and circulated "by direction of the Prime Minister" on 21st he reviewed the action which should be taken if Bulgaria accepted the Allies' proposals, and if the Central Powers riposted by offering a higher price. In the latter event, which Hankey regarded as the more likely development, we could either "make a renewed effort at Gallipoli in the hope of obtaining command of the Straits before the arrival of the Central Powers", or we could "endeavour to rally the whole of the Balkan states to our side by the promise of military support in that region."[4] As to the first alternative, disappointments had been so frequent at Gallipoli that he considered "no confidence can be felt that

---

[1] *Supreme Command*, I, p. 427.
[2] From 71,000 in September to 113,285 in October and 121,793 in November.
[3] In the Cabinet the chief "conscriptionists" were Churchill, Curzon and Selborne.
[4] G. 23 of 21st Sept. 1915. Cab. 42/3/26. Reproduced in *Supreme Command*, I, pp. 414–17.

such an effort would succeed". This left only the second alternative, and a fortnight of feverish proposals and counter-proposals between the Allied nations and the Balkan states, of crises, frustrations and muddles followed.[1]

The other paper which Hankey completed on 18th September dealt in great detail with every aspect of the winter campaign at the Dardanelles, which had been in the forefront of his thoughts ever since his return from that theatre at the end of August.[2] In fact it was almost immediately overtaken by events, since the decision of the Dardanelles Committee, taken on 14th October, to recall Sir Ian Hamilton greatly strengthened the hands of the "evacuationists".[3]

We may review the events of these hectic weeks through the entries in Hankey's diary, very few of which were reproduced in his memoirs.

22nd September
Bulgaria has ordered mobilisation and it looks as if our Balkan policy has failed . . . Saw the P.M. who decided at once to hold a War Council—or rather Dardanelles Ctee. P.M. told me that Cabinet had decided to create a new War Council and asked for my views. I pressed strongly that it should consist only of the P.M., Balfour and Lord K., with perhaps Grey, and that Winston Churchill should on no account be included as Lord K. will never work properly with him. After leaving P.M. went to see Balfour, who is strongly opposed to the new War Council, and has written to the P.M. to say so.

23rd September
Very important meeting of Dardanelles Ctee.[4] Venizelos has asked for 150,000 men from Allies to enable Greek army to go to assistance of Serbia, if Bulgaria attacks. He says the King and General Staff won't mobilise unless we can give it. Dardanelles Ctee. inclined to funk it owing to heavy commitments at Dardanelles. In afternoon Grey sent telegram to Venizelos intended to gain time. Spent whole afternoon with Lord K., helping him and General Staff to investigate the question. Much amused at this illustration of K.'s method of working the General Staff. He sits at the head of the table and talks a lot, and bludgeons everyone into agreeing with him. I was the only one who put up any opposition, the Chief of Staff (Wolfe Murray—or "Sheep" Murray as Winston calls him) merely mumbling assent, and Callwell just agreeing. Then K. proceeds to dictate, and it is dished up next day as a Memo. by the General Staff. K. insists that it is no use going to the assistance of

[1] *Supreme Command*, I, Chs. XXXIX and XL gives a full account.
[2] G. 22 of 22nd Sept. 1915. Cab. 42/3/27. [3] Cab. 42/4. [4] See Cab. 22/2.

Greece unless we can give 300,000 men. This looks like dishing the whole thing . . .

24th September

Another Dardanelles Ctee. meeting in morning.[1] An entire change has come over the Balkan situation. The French Cabinet, with a quicker perception than we, has replied to Greece promising her share of the 150,000 men, and has asked us to do ditto. Greece has mobilised. Result is that the Committee do a *volte-face*; Lord K.'s 300,000 bogie [sic] no longer appeals—in fact he himself is converted; we decide to stand with the French . . .

Two days later Hankey had a long talk with Lloyd George during which he pressed for the supply of munitions, and especially rifles, to the Russians "even at the expense of our own armies", since they possessed "a framework for 3 million men". He recorded that he was "careful not to mention the fact that it would defeat the National Service campaign . . . or at least postpone it *sine die*". But Lloyd George was too astute to be taken in and "had discovered it by next morning".[2]

29th September

Meeting of Dardanelles Ctee.[3] Towards the end of the meeting Ll. George brought out my plan about the rifles [for the Russians]. It was amusing to watch the faces of the conscriptionists fall—Churchill, Curzon, Selborne. The idea was of course combated vigorously, but without logic or argument . . . I lunched with Mr. Balfour to meet a horrible scab called [Keith] Murdoch, an Australian journalist, who had written a poisonous letter to [Andrew] Fisher, the Commonwealth Premier, re the Dardanelles.[4]

30th September

Dardanelles Ctee. met again, Lord K. being absent; but Sir Archibald Murray,[5] the Chief of the Imperial Staff designate, who is now a member of the Dardanelles Ctee., being present. The subject of discussion was the position in the Balkans. The situation was extraordinarily complex, being somewhat as follows:—The Bulgarian King[6] and Govt. have practically decided to go over to the side of the Germans. The only reply they have given

[1]*ibid.*   [2]Diary 26th Sept. 1916.   [3]Cab. 22/2.

[4]See *James*, pp. 312–15 regarding what he calls the "extraordinary episode" of the Murdoch letter. It constituted a violent attack on General Hamilton and almost everyone else at Gallipoli—excluding the Anzacs. Yet it was printed and circulated to the Dardanelles Committee. Cab. G.25 of 28th Sept. 1915.

[5]See p. 167.

[6]Ferdinand, King of Bulgaria (1861–1948). Youngest son of Prince Augustus of Saxe-Coburg and Gotha. Proclaimed King 1908, abdicated 4th Oct. 1918.

to our offer[1] ... has been to mobilise and to introduce German and Austrian officers into their army (so at least our Military Attaché reports). Nevertheless the Bulgarian [parliamentary] opposition, which counts only 14 less members in the Sobranje than the Govt., and has actually a *Bulgarian* majority (since 16 Mahomedans vote with the Govt.) is still favourable to the cause of the Allies ... There is consequently still a bare chance that Bulgaria may hesitate to take the final plunge, particularly as the mobilisation is reported to be highly unpopular, and more especially if the Allies get a success in the West, where a great offensive is in progress and events hang in the balance.[2] From Serbia's point of view, however, the moment is opportune to strike. She is mobilised; Bulgaria is not. If she waits she may be attacked by Bulgaria in the east and the Austro-Germans in the west simultaneously.[3] If she strikes now she might use her central position to crush the Bulgarians and then come back [westwards] to fight the Austro-Germans. Though this is strategically desirable it would be politically deplorable, as Ferdinand would say to the world "You see I was right. They meant mischief all the time ..." Moreover in all probability the Serbians would get so mauled by the Bulgarians that the Austro-Germans would get a walk-over. This we wish to avoid at any cost, for then the Germans would have a through-route to Turkey; we should be shelled out of the Dardanelles; and Turkey would be to a great extent reorganised [? resuscitated]. Meanwhile the situation in Greece is very peculiar. Venizelos is intensely pro-Ally, but the King,[4] who is just as popular as Venizelos, though not actively pro-German is at least a doubtful factor. In order to induce the King to mobilise when Bulgaria mobilised Venizelos had asked the Allies to promise a support of 150,000 men ... We

[1]This was the offer of 14th Sept. (see p. 218). It gave Bulgaria the immediate occupation of territory in Turkish Thrace up to the line from Enos on the Aegean to Midia on the Black Sea agreed by the treaty of London, which had ended the first Balkan War in 1913. Bulgaria lost that territory in the Second Balkan War. The offer also guaranteed possession after the war of the part of Macedonia promised to Bulgaria by the Serbo-Bulgar secret treaty signed before the outbreak of the first Balkan War. Serbia was to receive "equitable compensation" at the expense of Austria-Hungary.

[2]This refers to the British offensive at Loos which had opened on 21st September and to the coincident French offensive in the Champagne. Both were costly failures.

[3]This is precisely what happened, and led to the destruction of Serbia in October 1915.

[4]Constantine I (1868–1923). In March 1915 Venizelos resigned but was re-elected in the following June. From October the rupture between him and the King was complete. Constantine left Greece on 12th June 1917, leaving his son Alexander on the throne; but in November 1920 Constantine resumed his throne. He finally abdicated in Sept. 1922 in favour of his son George after the disastrous failure of the Greek campaign in Asia Minor.

and the French had replied "Done with you" and Greece then mobilised—
at our expense needless to say. Then followed a complicated series of
telegrams as to when our troops were to come. First Venizelos wanted them
at once . . . Then a formal communication came from Greece to say "Thank
you, but we don't want the troops just yet"; but this was followed by a
private telegram saying that Venizelos did want them early . . . We had
therefore said we couldn't send troops so long as there was on record a
formal expression of opinion by the Greek Govt. that they were not wanted
. . . Just before the meeting [of the Dardanelles Committee] we heard that the
French had actually ordered a division to leave the Dardanelles [for Salonika]
—so eventually it was decided that our division [the 10th] should conform
its movements to the French. The Russians were in favour of telling Bulgaria
that we should break off relations unless they either demobilised or joined the
Allies. The Dardanelles Ctee., however, preferred a milder course and
decided . . . merely to warn Bulgaria that, if Serbia were forced by her action
to attack in defence of her vital interests, Bulgaria would find herself at war
with the Quadruple Alliance. As a matter of fact, however, Russia declined
to agree to this.

30th September
Coming out of the War Office just before lunch I met Lord Kitchener, who
button-holed me on the stairs and took me back to his room. For $\frac{3}{4}$ hour he
rampaged against the Cabinet, whence he had just returned, declaiming
particularly against the irresponsible members—Churchill in particular, also
Lord Curzon, Lord Selborne and Lloyd George. Also against the Dardanelles
Ctee. He said that so much time was wasted in arguing with these people that
he simply couldn't get time to do his work at the War Office. He was almost
in a hysterical condition; he even talked seriously of resigning. Drummond[1]
told me afterwards that Sir Edward Grey was almost in the same condition
after a whole week of incessant Cabinet and Dardanelles Ctee. meetings . . .

1st October
Saw Lord K. again. He was still in a very queer state, and I am afraid he may
break down. Went in the evening to The Wharf to spend the week-end with
the Asquiths. Bored at having to go without Adeline, but enjoyed it all the
same.

3rd October
War Committee (as the Dardanelles Committee is now called) in the morning.[2]
Balkan question again. At 2.30 had to see the King . . . Found him with a cold

[1] Sir Eric Drummond. See p. 182.
[2] Actually the Dardanelles Committee met no less than nine times in October and
the first meeting of the War Committee as its successor did not take place until 3rd
November. Cab. 42/4 and 42/5 (22/3/1).

2 The Balkan Peninsula 1915

and rather depressed. Tried to cheer him up, but the defection of Bulgaria to the side of the enemy is very depressing.[1]

7th October
War Committee again in morning. Balkan question again. Ctee. adjourned for the General Staff and [Admiralty] War Staff to prepare a memorandum on the situation and to make suggestions for meeting the imminent probability that the Central Powers may establish through-communication with Turkey and shell us out of the Gallipoli peninsula . . .[2]

8th October
. . . Very interesting private letter from General Birdwood who commands at Anzac.[3]

9th October
Birdwood's letter set me thinking and on arriving at office went straight to Lloyd George at the Ministry of munitions to ask if they could supply apparatus to pump sea water into the Turkish trenches at Anzac and flood them out. He thought it was feasible and asked me to go and see some experiments in Scotland . . . Wrote long letter to Birdwood suggesting this and other methods for getting the Turks out of their trenches . . .[4] Wrote letter to Commodore Keyes, de Robeck's Chief of Staff, suggesting that submarines should carry barrels of my "Greek fire" lashed on, and let it go to burn up lighters etc. in the Dardanelles . . .

11th October
War Committee in afternoon to discuss Balkan imbroglio. Sir William Robertson present. General Staff Memo. discussed. Decision to send a substantial force . . . to Alexandretta as soon as they can be extricated from the line in France—i.e. after the offensive due to commence [at Loos] on 13th. Also either Lord K. or General Sir Douglas Haig to go to Dardanelles to report on situation. Saw Lord Stamfordham at Buckingham Palace immediately after meeting, as the King was making enquiries as to decision.

[1] The first Serbo-Bulgar clash did not actually occur until 11th October, and Britain and France did not declare war on her until 15th and 16th October respectively. But her intentions were abundantly clear at the beginning of that month.
[2] The remainder of the entry for this day is printed in *Supreme Command*, I, p. 428.
[3] Extracts from this letter, which was optimistic about the prospects of holding on at Gallipoli despite the changed situation in the Balkans, were printed and circulated to the Cabinet. Lloyd George papers D/23/5/2.
[4] For the next part of the entry for this day see *Supreme Command*, I, p. 428. Hankey discussed Kitchener's future with Asquith, including the possibility of making Kitchener C-in-C of the British Army. In that event Asquith considered he might take over the War Office himself.

12th October

Sir William Robertson and Lord Stamfordham lunched with me at U.S. Club. Robertson very confident of success in France and most strenuously opposed to Balkan expedition. He also favours abandonment of Gallipoli, and wants the two Indian divisions to be sent away from France. In evening was sent for by Prime Minister at House of Commons and had long talk about situation. Told him I had most reluctantly been forced to conclusion that we ought to get out of Gallipoli and save our face by capture of Bagdad and an attack at Alexandretta or Haifa. He was not so strongly opposed to this as I expected . . . Dined with Montagu and rest of so-called "Shadow Cabinet" . . . Learnt that National Service question had again become acute. Very odd position. Churchill, Curzon, Selborne and the other conscriptionists, who have for a long time been attacking Lord K., are now basing a tremendous National Service push in the Cabinet on a Memo. of Lord K.'s.
. . .

13th October

On arrival at office I dictated a short Memo. on the subject of National Service. The burden of it was that as the difference between the numbers to be maintained [? obtained] by compulsory and voluntary service was only a beggarly 10 divisions of troops necessarily inferior, owing to lack of trained staffs and officers, it was ridiculous to split the country, more especially as they would only be armed at the expense of the Russians who have 500,000 trained men with adequate staffs waiting for rifles which could only be obtained from England or America. Sent [Memo.] to P.M. and McKenna.[1]
. . . When I saw the P.M. the previous evening the Balkan position was that, if Greece came in, we were committed (with France) to send 150,000 troops to assist her in fulfilling her treaty obligations with Serbia. We were therefore sending a force to Egypt to be utilised in the Balkans or elsewhere in the Mediterranean as necessary. After my visit to the P.M., Churchill and Lloyd George, who had already seen Lord K., saw the P.M. Imagine my astonishment at finding a telegram in the morning offering Greece and Roumania that we would send 200,000 men on condition that they entered the war—this in the face of the warning in the recent General Staff appreciation on Serbia regarding the difficulty of operations there! Presumably Churchill and Lloyd George had bounced everyone into this. They are a danger in the Cabinet and I deeply regret and dread the consequences of a campaign in the Balkans. My own policy would be to give 500,000 rifles to Russia at once plus half our future output; to cut our losses at Gallipoli; to take Bagdad and to attack Alexandretta . . .

[1]Memo. of 6th October 1915. Cab. 22/2.

The total failure of the diplomatic effort of the Allies, and especially of Britain, in the Balkans in the early autumn of 1915 justifies a brief digression to investigate its basic causes, and Hankey's contemporary appreciation of them; for there is no doubt that at the time of the launching of the Gallipoli operation Bulgaria did seriously consider joining the Allies, and had she done so the whole course of events in the Near East would have been different. Apart from the age-old hatred between Serbia and Bulgaria and the Russian desire to dominate the affairs of the Balkan States, which greatly complicated all negotiations, there is no doubt that the lack of interest in, and even ignorance of strategy and war operations in the Foreign Office under Sir Edward Grey and his Under-Secretary of State Sir Arthur Nicolson[1] contributed greatly to the failure.[2] The activities of the Foreign Office were carried out in isolation from military planning, and took little or no account of the forces available to make the diplomatic approach credible to their recipients. Thus the decision to send troops to Salonika was inspired by diplomatic motives, yet took little or no account of whether the forces available were adequate, or whether they could successfully support the diplomacy. Hankey's whole evidence before the Dardanelles Commission of 1916, which we will examine in some detail later,[3] makes it plain that he was probably the only person near to the seat of power who understood and foresaw the consequences of the divorce between diplomacy and strategy. To quote only one example, when he was being pressed by one of the Commissioners on the issue whether it would not have been better "to wait a few weeks till the troops were ready to make the combined attack" he replied that "The circumstances were very, very pressing indeed; we were giving no display of any sort of interest in the Near East; *our whole diplomacy was going to pieces from the fact that there was no display of force*" (italics supplied).[4] The fact that this statement was a strong indictment of Grey and the Foreign Office seems to have escaped the Commissioners' notice. One of the most recent students of these events has concluded that "Hankey's logical mind was, as subsequent events demonstrated, capable of thinking about war and diplomacy. He did not, however, possess sufficient weight to

---

[1]See p. 108.
[2]P. Cosgrave in an unpublished doctoral thesis *Sir Edward Grey and British Foreign Policy in Bulgaria 1914–15* (Cambridge, 1968) remarks on "the detachment, even lack of interest of the Foreign Office in Eastern operations" (p. 186, typescript).
[3]See pp. 296 and 299. [4]Cab. 19/33. Question 455.

dominate the War Office, and he received no support from Grey"—a conclusion with which this biographer entirely agrees.[1]

Diary 14th October
War Committee in evening at 5.30. Sir E. Carson not there.[2] Decided *inter alia* not to go on to Bagdad until General Staff have examined the question a bit further. This is in my opinion a great mistake, and after [the] meeting I went back to Admiralty with Mr. Balfour and convinced him of this. Unquestionably we ought to follow up success red hot.[3] It was also decided to recall Sir Ian Hamilton from Dardanelles as he is generally reported to have lost the confidence of his troops. Gen. Monro[4] to succeed him and report as to best disposition of troops to be sent to Levant. Bonar Law lost his temper rather and is very anxious to withdraw from Dardanelles.

15th October
. . . Spent most of day on a revised Report re arrangements for a winter campaign at Dardanelles[5] . . . This evening, apparently at an informal meeting, it was decided to offer Cyprus to Greece as a bribe to her to enter the war.

16th October
Lunched with Prime Minister and had a very long talk of an hour's duration afterwards with him and Bonham Carter. It appears that Ll. George is out to break the Govt. on conscription if he can . . .

18th October
Lunched again at 10 Downing Street. P.M. seemed all right, but in afternoon at the Cabinet at House of Commons he was taken ill and had to adjourn, thereby postponing discussion of conscription question . . . Serbians have given the Germans a knock, but those swine of Bulgarians are coming in on their communications. French troops have gone up to neighbourhood of Strumnitza, but our 10th Division is still sitting at Salonika without orders . . .

[1]Cosgrave, *op. cit.*, p. 300 (typescript).
[2]Cab. 22/2. Carson had in fact resigned, but his resignation had not yet been announced.
[3]This refers to General Townshend's recent success near Kut, after which his cavalry pursued the Turks half way to Baghdad.
[4]General Sir Charles Monro (1860–1929). C-in-C, Dardanelles Oct. 1915 and Mediterranean Expeditionary Force 1915. Commander, First Army in France 1916. C-in-C, India 1916–20. Governor and C-in-C, Gibraltar, 1923–8.
[5]G.29 of 23rd Oct. 1915. Cab. 24/1. Hankey's reluctant conversion to the necessity of cutting our losses and withdrawing from Gallipoli had obviously caused him to revise his earlier paper (G.22 of 22nd Sept. See p. 219). Now he proposed to hold on for two months at the least, and preferably until April 1916 when fine weather would be reasonably assured.

Hankey added to the diary entry for this day a note, dated 7th October 1920, that "Mr. Bonar Law told me that at this time the Govt. was on the point of breaking, and that he believed Asquith's indisposition to be due partly to worry and partly to his desire to avoid the conscription issue". Though the historical value of Mrs. Asquith's letters is somewhat vitiated by the emotional style in which she always wrote, and she certainly sometimes committed her views to paper without her husband's knowledge or approval, the following missive does support Hankey's view that a ministerial crisis was imminent.

Mrs. Asquith to Hankey. 10 Downing Street. 15th October 1915 6 a.m. Holograph
Dearest Colonel Hankey,

Does Arthur Balfour realise what is happening? It is clear as day that Ll.G., Curzon and Winston are going to try and wreck the Gov.

If any weakness or wobbling takes place to-day in the Cabinet over conscription I consider a <u>vital</u> mistake will have been made and my husband *done for*.

Will Arthur [Balfour] play fair? And will K. play fair? Who are the wreckers? <u>Inside</u> we know Ll. G., Winston and Curzon—outside the same lot led by Northcliffe who broke our Lib[eral] Gov. Are they to break the Coalition?

Do be brave and go and see Balfour directly you get this, and just say to him "You've read Ll. G's and Winston's and K.'s memorandums [sic], it must be clear to you that things are rocky—if you don't support the P.M. and stand close to Grey, Crewe and the P.M. you play into the hands of Ll. G. and Co."

You are the only person who can do this—you sd. also see K. or his Fitzgerald on this subject.

I have written <u>very</u> clearly to K. and told him his memorandum was a mistake, giving an impression of disloyalty to Henry wh. I'm sure he never meant.

You want men of action in a crisis.

<u>You are the man.</u> I've written Crewe and K. but not Arthur. Ian Hamilton sd. be <u>immediately</u> recalled to report. His life would be safer if he by chance went among the men in Gallipoli. Believe me this is not gossip. Our boy [Arthur, see p. 189] has written telling he [Hamilton] doesn't even write. The demoralisation out there is complete and Hamilton useless. For God's sake get someone to show a little action soon.

Yours affec.

M.A.

Mrs. Asquith obviously did not know that the decision had just been taken to recall Hamilton; but her reference to Arthur Asquith's letters from Gallipoli is interesting, since there is some evidence that the Prime Minister, and possibly some of his colleagues, were influenced by his pessimism. Later in the year Asquith sent one such letter on to Hankey with a covering note in his own hand reading "I got the enclosed this morning from Oc. It is very melancholy reading, and increases one's desire to clear out of Helles."[1] There is also an unsigned and undated extract from a letter which may have come from Arthur Asquith in the Lloyd George papers. It reads "You will think I am a grouser, but this Ian Hamilton is the limit, and it is so obvious to all out here what a terrible mess and massacre he has made of the expedition from the start. I don't believe he has ever been in any of the front trenches, and I can honestly say that I have never seen any of his staff officers there".[2] The reader will recollect that in his private telegram to Asquith and Kitchener of 14th August Hankey had shown a lack of confidence in Hamilton.[3] This, and the letters referred to above, probably contributed to the decision to replace him, and also strengthened the hands of the "evacuationists". By mid-October Bonar Law was the acknowledged leader of that group in the War Committee and Cabinet.

Diary 19th October
Saw the King at 10.30 to tell him exactly how matters stand. Found him very much opposed to the Balkan campaign and disgusted at the muddle we are in . . . M. Millerand conferred with Cabinet, who eventually agreed to some formula apparently indicating that we were sending an expedition to Serbia, but leaving *us* free to send *our* troops to Egypt or Dardanelles . . . Had long talk with Mr. Balfour re possibility of forcing Dardanelles by Navy, as Commodore Keyes, Adl. de Robeck's Chief of Staff, is being sent home, I suspect in order to get permission to try. Rather tempted to gamble on it, though I doubt its success . . . P.M. still in bed but better.

20th October
. . . In morning had long talk with Gen Monro, just appointed to succeed Sir Ian Hamilton at Dardanelles . . . Then I had to go and see Bonar Law, who quite frankly said he felt very ignorant of military affairs, especially in the east, and asked me to help him. We had a long talk and he asked if he might come to the C.I.D. [? office] and discuss things.[4] Carson, who has just

[1]Asquith to Hankey 24th Dec. 1915.
[2]Lloyd George papers D/23/4/18. [3]See pp. 198–9.
[4]Hankey remarked later (*Supreme Command*, I, p. 432) that "he never came!".

resigned from the Cabinet, was there when I arrived. I didn't know what to say, as I disapproved his resignation, so said nothing . . . V.G. paper by Esher and Selborne suggesting (1) establishment of central [? war] direction for allies in Paris (2) a small War Committee at home. I quite agree these are urgently needed reforms . . .

21st October

Cabinet War Ctee. in morning to consider advance on Bagdad. Lord Crewe in chair. Kitchener and Curzon apparently opposed to advance—in fact the usual shilly-shallying, no grip, no courage. Eventually decided to refer to Viceroy [of India], although nearly 3 weeks have elapsed since our victory at Kut-el-Amara, which ought to have been followed up red hot. Lunched alone with Sir Edward Grey at Churchill's house, which he is renting. Urged strongly that we should push on to Bagdad without delay, and on arrival issue a proclamation that we had occupied the city temporarily and for military reasons only, and that we were favourably disposed towards the formation of an Arab Empire independent of Ottoman rule, to which Bagdad might be handed over. Grey agreed and my views found echo in the telegram sent to the Viceroy. I also explained to Grey my whole ideas on policy in the east viz. to rearm Russia, even at the expense of our own armies, to have a final push at Gallipoli with the intention of retiring if we failed, and to push on to Bagdad. He seemed to agree . . .

At about this time Adeline came to London, presumably because Hankey found it impossible to get down to Highstead regularly, and they took lodgings at 52 Oxford Terrace. The enjoyment of a home near to his work must have helped to mitigate the strains and anxieties of a very difficult period. The future of Winston Churchill, Kitchener and French were among the pressing personal problems of the time. Hankey suggested to Asquith that Churchill might be sent to north Russia to stimulate the importation and transport of munitions; but Churchill evidently had other ideas. Balfour was vastly amused by the suggestion he had put forward to Asquith that he should be made "Governor General and Military Commander-in-Chief in British East Africa". As to Kitchener, the Cabinet was becoming increasingly restive over his obsessive secrecy, and his extraordinary method of conducting his department's business. On 1st November Hankey recorded that Asquith had told him that the Cabinet "were unanimous that Lord K. ought to leave the War Office"; but the Prime Minister finally compromised by sending him out to Gallipoli to report on the situation.[1] Kitchener promptly asked that Hankey should accompany him, and he

[1] *James*, pp. 328–32.

and Asquith thereupon "wrangled over my body". In the end Hankey did not go. The supersession of Sir John French was also in the air, and Hankey wrote in his diary (27th October) that Asquith was "obviously disposed towards getting rid of him. I hope he will". On 29th Hankey went to General Hamilton's home at 1 Hyde Park Gardens—evidently with some apprehension. "An embarrassing but not unpleasant inter- view" followed, and the satisfactory outcome evidently owed a lot to "Sir Ian's great charm of manner". Hankey finally gave the General copies of his letters to Asquith from Gallipoli, and of his official report on the situation there. Understandably he did not disclose his more critical telegrams to Asquith.

General Sir Ian Hamilton to Hankey. 1 Hyde Park Gardens, 30th October 1915
Holograph
My dear Hankey,

My first impression was instantly to return you these papers unread, so utterly alien to me was the idea that you could have wrought me any injury. My second, and happier impulse was born of sheer, vulgar curiosity. To this I have succumbed, and certainly I am very glad I did for I have thoroughly enjoyed the perusal. Your last letter especially,[1] a model as it is of lucidity and of insight, is of real value to me if only from the despatch writing aspect of the thing. But the whole file, in my humble opinion, will one day possess priceless historical value, and I heartily congratulate you on having been its author.

Always yours very sincerely

Meanwhile the "evacuationists" were steadily gaining ground. On 2nd November Asquith candidly admitted in the House of Commons, in a statement which Hankey had helped to prepare, that the operation had failed.[2] Bonar Law was threatening resignation unless evacuation was carried out, and Hankey worked hard both to dissuade him from so drastic a step and to support his own desire to make one more bid for success. However neither a personal meeting nor an eloquent written appeal caused Law to yield an inch, and on 10th November he wrote somewhat curtly to Hankey to say so. In fact two days earlier Asquith had averted Law's resignation by promising his support for evacuation; and thus was the die cast.

One need feel no surprise that such a display of disunity and of lack of strong leadership in the highest quarters at a time of crisis should

[1] This must refer to Hankey's letter of 12th August to Asquith. See p. 199.
[2] Parl. Deb., Commons, Vol. LXXV, Cols. 509–15.

have caused heart-searchings regarding the existing organisation for the direction of the war. On 4th November, the day Asquith vetoed Hankey's departure with Kitchener, he wrote in his diary that "In the evening the P.M. sent for me to say that . . . he wanted me to help him to reorganize the system (or lack of system!) for running the war. He wanted me to have a room in the War Office, of which he intended to take charge". In fact Asquith's purpose was to achieve a drastic reorganisation of the military hierarchy during Kitchener's absence—in which he was successful.[1]

The first meeting of what Hankey called "the revised War Council" took place on 5th November. Those present were Asquith, Balfour, Grey and Lloyd George, with the First Sea Lord and C.I.G.S. in attendance.[2] When however on 11th Asquith informed the House of the composition of the War Committee, as it was to be called, he gave the membership as himself, Balfour (First Lord), Lloyd George (Munitions), McKenna (Exchequer) and Bonar Law (Colonies). However Grey (Foreign Office) always attended, as did Kitchener after his return from Gallipoli. Thus with the First Sea Lord and C.I.G.S. also present the real membership was nine; and later on other Ministers, notably Curzon (Shipping Control Board) and Austen Chamberlain (India) also joined. Hankey wrote in his diary that he was "bitterly disappointed when the Cabinet decided on so large a number, as I have been working for a small one and during the last week, working with only four, it has been so easy and business like". A later entry (7th and 9th October 1920) provides an interesting comment on how the composition of the War Committee was actually decided. "I recall", he then wrote, "that Bonar Law also told me how when Asquith was forming his War Committee he [Law] overheard him [Asquith] telling McKenna on the front Government bench of the House of its composition, and his own name was not included. Meanwhile the Unionist whips had got hold of it and were making a row with the Liberal whips, with the result that later in the afternoon Bonar received a message from Asquith asking him [Law] to see him [Asquith]. When he arrived Asquith said

[1] See *Jenkins*, pp. 382–4.
[2] The Public Record Office's *List of Cabinet Papers 1915–1916* (H.M.S.O. 1966) shows the first meeting of the War Committee as taking place on 3rd November 1915, and a number of Ministers undoubtedly did meet that day to consider Kitchener's visit to the Middle East. But Hankey's diary makes it plain that the first properly constituted meeting of the War Committee took place on 5th. Cab. 42/5/2 and 3.

he had sent for him to ask him to join the War Committee! Bonar then told him what he had heard on the bench". But whether Bonar Law was only included as an afterthought or not, the one certain fact is that the two leading opponents to the evacuation of Gallipoli—Churchill and Curzon—were excluded.[1]

Many years later Hankey was asked to remark on a Cabinet Office paper giving the history of the establishment of the secretariat, and wrote an *aide mémoire* for an interview on the subject with Sir Norman Brook,[2] then Secretary of the Cabinet. It appears that after World War II consideration was being given to reverting to something like the pre-1916 organisation and procedure. As Hankey's paper throws interesting light on the formation of the Cabinet Committees of 1915–16 it is relevant to reproduce parts of it here.

Extracts from Aide Mémoire by Lord Hankey for conversation with Sir Norman Brook, 23rd November 1948
. . . In September 1915, on return from my mission to the Dardanelles campaign, I found that a Cabinet Committee had been set up on War Policy, which had recommended compulsory service and was overlapping the Dardanelles Committee; but Mr. Asquith scotched it by reorganising the ill-conceived Dardanelles Committee into a better balanced War Committee. Lord Crewe, the Chairman of the War Policy Committee, which had no Secretary, sent for me and . . . turned over to me all the papers.

The Dardanelles Committee, . . . was itself in theory a Cabinet Committee, and held its first meeting without a Secretary. But Asquith, Balfour, Kitchener and Lloyd George insisted on a Secretary, and I was brought in and succeeded in gradually infiltrating it with the Chiefs of Staff and all the procedure of the C.I.D. . . . In February 1916 a Cabinet Committee was set up on man power . . . and I was its Secretary from the first.

The above examples . . . which could probably be multiplied by further search, illustrate how the C.I.D. system was influencing the Cabinet system throughout the first sixteen years of the century.

So sloppy were the methods—or rather lack of methods—of the old régime that I never had any doubt myself that in time the Cabinet would be compelled to adopt the C.I.D. system, and even before 1912, when I became Secretary of the C.I.D., I used to discuss it with my colleagues. From the

[1] Churchill declined to remain in "well-paid inactivity" as Chancellor of the Duchy of Lancaster and left to command a battalion on the western front. *Churchill*, II, pp. 497–9.
[2] 1902–67. First Baron Normanbrook 1963. Deputy Secretary (Civil) to War Cabinet 1943. Additional Secretary to the Cabinet 1947–62.

first Lord Haldane, and later Mr. Balfour and Lloyd George, favoured the idea; but Mr. Asquith, who was slightly Gladstonian in his attitude, while admitting that something had to be done, never quite accepted the Cabinet system *en bloc* . . . It would be interesting to know whether the King received Cabinet Memoranda before the establishment of the Secretariat. After its establishment he received everything. King George V told me several times that until he received Cabinet Minutes and papers (which he used to read assiduously) he had never been fully informed of what was going on. The Cabinet letters, of course, often gave a very meagre report.[1] A Prime Minister, after a long meeting, with important guests awaiting him at luncheon upstairs, with questions to answer in Parliament and sometimes a speech to make, often could not find time for an adequate letter, which had to be written in his own hand . . .

While the new War Committee was settling down to its difficult task Kitchener sent home an extraordinary series of telegrams about future operations in the Middle East. Hankey has printed most of the diary entries for 13th and 14th November describing how General Monro had been sent to the Dardanelles "as a sort of Pope whose word was to be final. When he recommended evacuation they refused to accept his opinion and sent Lord K. as a sort of Super-Pope . . .".[2] Kitchener now appeared to recommend evacuation, but advised a new landing at Alexandretta. Hankey at once appreciated the political and military perils of such a proposal, and after visiting the War Office and consulting Balfour he obtained agreement to the immediate holding of a staff conference with the French to try and arrive at an agreed policy with regard to the Gallipoli and Salonika undertakings. During a hectic Sunday (14th November) he made all the necessary arrangements, and on the Monday evening left for Paris in company with Asquith, Grey, Balfour, Lloyd George and the naval and military chiefs.

The principal results of the Paris conference in the military field were to negative the Alexandretta proposal, to decide to send two more British divisions to Salonika, and to await Kitchener's report on the Gallipoli situation. In the administrative field the two governments agreed to set up a Joint Standing Committee to co-ordinate policy, and it was Hankey who drafted its terms of reference.[3] But as it was to be merely an advisory body it suffered from exactly the same weaknesses as the C.I.D.; and moreover the French refused to agree to a permanent secretariat being created for it. The nomination of Hankey and a

[1]See p. 139.   [2]*Supreme Command*, II, pp. 449–50.
[3]G.40 of 20th Nov. 1915. Cab. 37/137. Another copy in Robertson Papers 1/9/31.

French officer as "Secretary-Liaison Officers" was, in the opinion of the former, an inadequate substitute. Though one may see in the Committee of November 1915 the first move towards the creation of an executive Inter-Allied authority, another two years were to elapse before that very desirable step was actually taken; and the first tentative and cautious move in that direction actually accomplished little. Hankey's diary entries make it plain that his experience of the pre-war C.I.D., and his preference for an advisory body, were influential in limiting the functions of the new committee.

On 18th November Hankey was back in London, and was at once involved in a whole series of War Committee meetings at which the evacuation of Gallipoli was the chief issue. Four days later the Committee recommended evacuation—which made Hankey feel "desperately depressed"; but the final decision was reserved to the Cabinet, and that body hesitated to take the plunge. Curzon was still working against such a decision and on 26th he produced what Hankey described as "one of the most able papers I have ever read" in favour of holding on. Next day he and Hankey met to discuss the matter.

Curzon to Asquith. 1 Carlton House Terrace. 27th November 1915. Holograph
My dear Henry,

Before the Cabinet decide on Tuesday [30th] we ought surely to have all available evidence of an authoritative character.

You sent out Hankey in the autumn to report and advise. He did so in a very excellent paper.[1] He is capable of looking at things from a detached and all round point of view and was cited yesterday by Bonar Law. Would it be possible and even desirable to ask him to write a paper on the present situation for circul[n]. to Cabinet before Tuesday? I think there is real value in this suggestion.

Yours sincerely

Asquith sent the above letter straight on to Hankey, noting on it "I think it is a good suggestion". Two days later Hankey circulated a paper entitled "The Future Military Policy at the Dardanelles".[2] He began by remarking that this paper was "a departure from the usual practice of the Secretary of the Committee of Imperial Defence, who makes it a point not to obtrude his personal conclusions on controversial questions". To do so, he continued, would be "contrary to his constitutional position, which compels him to keep an open mind". This was perhaps too modest an assessment of his own functions and

[1]See pp. 206–8. [2]G.43 of 29th Nov. 1915. Cab. 42/5/25.

influence; but he obviously had to take account of the fact that his paper was addressed to a War Committee and Cabinet which were still deeply divided within themselves. After reviewing enemy and Allied strategy and also "the Tactical Position" at Gallipoli he pointed out that "we are already long past the time when the continuance of fair weather can be counted on", and that a sudden storm while evacuation was actually in progress was "one of the most dreaded eventualities". By holding on until April "good weather could be almost relied on", and many dangers would be reduced or eliminated. "To hold on even for two months would diminish the risk of an attack on Egypt", which might well be endangered if Turkish forces were immediately released from Gallipoli. Furthermore Admiral Wemyss, who had taken command of the naval forces during de Robeck's visit to England, had recently telegraphed that "it is already too late in the season to carry out the desperately difficult operation of evacuation without a strong probability of tactical disaster". "If this is the case", asked Hankey, "would it not be better to go down fighting, if we must go down, or better still to stick it through?" Finally, in summarising all the issues involved, he wrote that "As it is too late to meet the plan in Serbia, and the Alexandretta project has been ruled out, the arguments in favour of holding up the plan in the Gallipoli peninsula [i.e. to evacuate] appear overwhelming . . .".

This document was certainly the most direct and uncompromising expression of what Hankey believed to be the correct policy on a major issue which he had so far put forward; and as he must have known that the "evacuationists" were in a majority in the War Committee and Cabinet it showed considerable moral courage. Next day Sir Archibald Murray wrote from the War Office "I think your memorandum is excellent and I am very glad it has been added to those already before the Cabinet. I wonder what view Lord Kitchener will now take."[1] So did a good many others; but when Kitchener reached London on 1st December Hankey wrote in his diary that at the War Committee he had been "rather woolly". Next day the Cabinet heard de Robeck's views, which certainly did not strengthen the hands of those who wished to hold on; but Hankey was still hopeful, since outside the Cabinet room Lord Buckmaster,[2] the Lord Chancellor, told him that

[1]Murray to Hankey, 30th Nov. 1915.
[2]Stanley O. Buckmaster (1861–1934). 1st Viscount 1915. Solicitor-General 1913. Lord Chancellor 1915–16.

his paper "had decided the Cabinet", while Sir F. E. Smith[1] (Attorney General) "said it was a perfectly splendid paper".

On 4th December Hankey again crossed the Channel for another Anglo-French conference at Calais. The decision to withdraw from Salonika was taken; but within a couple of days the French rescinded their agreement. Thus the two biggest issues of the period—Gallipoli and Salonika—still remained undecided after more than a month's discussion. That same day Bonar Law circulated a paper which was not only strongly "evacuationist" in outlook but in which he attacked the whole conduct of the war.[2]

Diary 7th December
Cabinet met in morning and decided to evacuate Suvla and Anzac, retaining Helles for the present. No decision as regards Salonika . . . This delay in decision is absolutely fatal . . . The Government are really dreadfully to blame. They put off decisions, squabble [and] have no plan of action or operation, and allowed themselves to be dragged into this miserable Salonika affair at the tail of French domestic politics. I see only one solution—to suspend the constitution and appoint a dictator.

8th December
. . . In the afternoon the P.M. sent for me and showed me a letter from General Robertson to Lord K. Apparently K. had asked R. to become C.I.G.S. (why do they want to get rid of Murray?). Robertson had replied by formulating conditions—the War Ctee. to be the supreme authority, but no military operations to be discussed by it without going first through the General Staff . . . He had said bluntly that a professional man as S. of S. was impossible under his scheme. Curiously enough, said the P.M., Lord K. had told him he fully agreed and had proposed to resign as S. of S. and become a sort of wandering Commander-in-Chief of the British Army . . . The P.M. is very anxious to get rid of Lord K. who, he says, darkens counsel and is a really bad administrator, and he evidently wants to find some way of fitting K. into his scheme so that the Govt. can still use his great name and authority as a popular idol . . . Personally I can see no way of fitting him in without making him a cipher in every sense . . .

In the event a considerable reorganisation of the military high command did take place in December 1915. Haig replaced French as

---

[1]Sir Frederick E. Smith (1872–1930). 1st Earl of Birkenhead 1922. Solicitor-General 1915. Attorney-General 1915–19. Lord Chancellor 1919–22. Secretary of State for India 1924–8.
[2]Memo. of 4th Dec. 1915. Asquith papers, Box 122, folios 44–6.

C-in-C in France, and Robertson became C.I.G.S. in place of Murray, who was given the chief command in Egypt. Hankey remarked in his diary (16th Dec.) that "General Henry Wilson (arch intriguer) is sick at not getting one of the plums in the redistribution of offices"; but he had never liked, or trusted, Wilson since their pre-war encounters in the C.I.D.[1] Hankey was also "a good deal disturbed" by Haig's choice of General L. E. Kiggell as Chief of Staff,[2] and immediately tackled Robertson about him—though without success. Events were to prove that, over both Wilson and Kiggell, Hankey's judgement of character was very near the mark.

Probably the most far-reaching consequence of the changes in the military hierarchy was that for the next two years the western front was, in the eyes of the War Office, the only theatre of war that mattered. All possibility of exploiting our sea power in "warfare on the littoral", to reproduce the term coined by Hankey more than 20 years earlier, disappeared with the accession of so pronounced a "westerner" as Robertson to the post of C.I.G.S.

Diary 14th December
Busy day. First thing in morning had to see Lord K., Austen Chamberlain and P.M. in rapid succession about some minor detail of the Mesopotamian affair . . . Then I had to see the King, who kept me over an hour. This is the first time I have seen him since his accident.[3] He looked much better and was very talkative but very lame. He told me all about the forthcoming changes [in the War Office and B.E.F.] . . . and rather hinted that he had done the whole thing. He was cheerful on the whole about the war and very keen that Lord K. should remain as Secretary of State . . . In the afternoon I saw Mr. Balfour and urged on him the difficulty of holding Cape Helles if Anzac and Suvla are abandoned. He was very full of some news received from an absolutely reliable source that the Greek General Staff were in communication with the Austro-Germans to learn when their attack on Salonika was to be made in order that they might time the withdrawal of Greek troops accordingly . . . We concocted a telegram to Salonika and to the French—

[1]See pp. 101 and 102–3.
[2]Lieut.-General Sir Launcelot E. Kiggell (1862–1954). Chief of General Staff, British Armies in France, 1915–18.
[3]On 28th October 1915 King George V was seriously injured in France. His horse reared when the men of the R.F.C. whom he was inspecting cheered, and fell on the slippery ground with the King partially trapped beneath it. The King's pelvis was fractured in two places and he suffered severe shock. Those close to him considered that he was never again quite the man he had been before this accident. See Sir Harold Nicolson, *George V. His Life and Reign* (Constable, 1952), pp. 267–8.

rather difficult because the source of the information must be concealed. Then I went off to tell the P.M. The latter told me a secret known only to McKenna and himself, viz. that they have sent off a trustworthy Greek [Sir Basil Zaharoff[1]], a very large shareholder in Vickers who lives in Paris, with £1,400,000 in his pocket to buy the whole Greek administration and Government. Apparently McKenna knew the man to be reliable and had insisted on the P.M.'s acceptance of his offer . . .[2]

In accordance with the Cabinet decision of 7th December preparations to evacuate Suvla and Anzac were now being pressed ahead by General Monro. The thoroughness and care with which those plans were prepared contrasts so strongly with the mistakes and muddles which had sullied every earlier stage of the Gallipoli operation that it is difficult not to judge Hamilton's period of command harshly. For the final night (19th–20th December) 20,000 men remained to be taken off, and when dawn broke not one of them had been left behind. The sole entry in Hankey's diary for that day reads "Anzac and Suvla successfully evacuated with no loss. A great relief". A week later the Cabinet decided on the evacuation of Cape Helles as well, and the withdrawal of men and equipment began. On 7th January a violent Turkish attack, intended to drive the defenders into the sea, was beaten off with heavy loss to the enemy; and on the very next night, in a rising sea and rapidly deteriorating weather, the last of the expeditionary force were safely removed. However severely one may judge the planning and execution of the Dardanelles undertaking, the evacuations, carried out at the worst possible time of year, were an astonishing achievement.[3]

After he had made his final effort to postpone withdrawal at the end of November Hankey took no further initiative with regard to the Dardanelles. He probably realised that the weight of political and

---

[1] 1850–1936. Banker and financier with very wide industrial interests, especially in the British and French armament industries.

[2] In his diary for 2nd June 1916 Hankey wrote that Asquith had told him, in McKenna's presence, that "the old Greek [i.e. Zaharoff] . . . had now a more ambitious scheme to buy up for 4 million pounds the whole of the Young Turk Party, who would hand over Constantinople and the Dardanelles to the Allies and bolt to America. It seemed far-fetched and unlikely to come off, but as there was to be no pay until the goods were delivered there seemed no objection to letting him try." The original proposal to suborn the Greek Government, if made, was unsuccessful. As the scheme to bribe the Young Turk Party also never came off it seems unlikely that any of the money promised to Zaharoff was actually paid over.

[3] For a graphic account of the evacuations see *James*, pp. 339–47.

military opinion in favour of evacuation had become overwhelming. When it was all over Birdwood sent him a long account of the final weeks, which may well have made Hankey feel that his efforts to dissuade the government from taking the irrevocable decision had been fully justified.[1]

While the last days of the Gallipoli operation were approaching Hankey became deeply involved in the political crisis which had blown up over the decision to introduce a measure of conscription,[2] and had to devote much time and energy to dissuading McKenna and Runciman from resigning on that issue. In the final event only Sir John Simon, the Home Secretary, left the government. A letter written by Mrs. Asquith on the last day of the year confirms, despite her customary hyperbole, the impression given by Hankey's day by day diary entries —that he played a significant part in preventing the First Coalition breaking up at this time.

Mrs. Asquith to Hankey. 10 Downing Street. 31st December 1915. Holograph
PRIVATE
Dearest Col. Hankey,

Henry said to me last night "I think the worst is over. I don't think Grey will go now—Simon has gone. I think Pringle's[3] remark to him or of him that he always resigned and then withdrew his resignation makes it more difficult for him to return again". He paused and then said in his most moved and earnest way "There are 3 men who have worked day and night and of whom no praise can ever be too high—Rufus,[4] Hankey and Montagu."

He was walking up and down my room just after midnight, I was in bed. I said you were all the salt of the earth, with glorious natures, power of love and devotion that is the greatest of God's gifts. He was deeply moved, and I must add he has said the same thing to me yesterday morning and Wed. night.

---

[1]Birdwood to Hankey 11th Jan. 1916.

[2]This was the Military Service Bill, introduced on 5th Jan. 1916. It received Royal assent on 27th Jan.

[3]William M. R. Pringle (1874–1928). Politician (Lib.). A staunch "Asquithian".

[4]Sir Rufus D. Isaacs (1860–1935). 1st Marquess of Reading 1926. Solicitor-General 1910; Attorney-General 1910–13. Lord Chief Justice 1913–21. Special Ambassador to U.S.A. 1918. Viceroy of India 1921–6. Foreign Secretary 1931. The subject of Kipling's famous "hate poem" *Gehazi*, inspired by Isaacs's appointment as Lord Chief Justice shortly after his involvement in the notorious "Marconi Scandal" of 1912. Perhaps it was Asquith's loyalty to him at that time that caused Isaacs to "work day and night" to prevent the government breaking up in December 1915.

I thought you would like to hear it. I think you know Henry and I are very devoted to you and deeply grateful . . . This has been a terrible year for us all . . . It has brought with its sorrows certain shocks in my estimates of my fellow creatures. Some men like Ll.G with infinite charm and genius make me shudder. Popular heroes without courage or resolution or reliability like K. make me smile—grand creatures like Grey letting self come in and destroy as it always does all that is great in one, and an infinite variety of vanity and self-centredness have I seen in colleagues and countrymen. But I have seen what is better than all this in the personal devotion and enormous sympathy and steadfastness of friends like you, Edwin Montagu and Rufus. You will ever be dear to me, and if there is anything good in me you can count on it always.

Yours

Interesting confirmation of Mrs. Asquith's assessment of Hankey's part in resolving the crisis is also provided by Montagu's biographer. "The miracle of reaching a compromise", he states, "was achieved largely by the skill of Lord [sic] Hankey who, on 30th December persuaded McKenna to accept in principle an offer from Sir William Robertson, and arranged a meeting between them that day. This enabled Grey, who had also resigned, both to withdraw his resignation and to persuade McKenna and Runciman to do likewise. The next day Asquith told his private secretary (Vaughan Nash) that Hankey had done very well, and told his wife that no praise could be too high for Reading, Montagu and Hankey".[1]

So ended a year which had brought nothing but disaster to the Allies. Their Balkan diplomacy had collapsed when Bulgaria joined the Central Powers and the Venizelos government fell in Greece; and that led to the conquest of another small and gallant nation, Serbia. The Gallipoli operation totally failed of its purpose, proved very costly and ended in withdrawal. On the western front General French's offensive at Loos, undertaken against the advice of Haig, the commander of the 1st Army who was to carry it out, and of Robertson, Chief of Staff to French, cost 60,000 casualties for a gain of some 8,000 yards. The autumn offensives in Champagne and Artois were equally barren, and added some 250,000 men to the heavy toll already taken of the British and French armies. In the east Falkenhayn's break-through at Gorlice resulted in a loss to the Russians of two million men and vast quantities of irreplaceable munitions. In Italy Cadorna's offensive on the Isonzo

[1] S. David Waley, *Edwin Montagu, a Memoir* (Asia Publishing House, 1964), p. 82.

front was finally broken off in December—again after enormous losses had been suffered. Finally in Mesopotamia, from which the British government had hoped to extract some crumbs of comfort, General Townshend's advance on Baghdad had ended with his army invested in Kut-el-Amara with no prospect of early relief. It was true that on the oceans British sea power was supreme, and German trade had been almost completely strangled except in the Baltic; but even on that element the new challenge of submarine warfare on merchant shipping was already producing shortages, and causing anxiety to those responsible for feeding the British people and producing the munitions of war on which all the Allied nations were, to a greater or lesser extent, dependent. But perhaps the most depressing feature had been the signs of faltering leadership, faulty judgement and lack of unanimity in the highest circles on virtually every issue—strategic, tactical and political. Hankey, though he had a great personal admiration for Asquith, and also for many of his colleagues, was deeply aware of these failings, and had worked hard, within the severe limitations imposed by his lack of executive authority, to create not only a small, compact body to direct the war effort but also to achieve the necessary inter-Allied co-ordination. So far, however, his endeavours had not been crowned with any significant degree of success.

Chapter 9

The Crumbling of the Coalition; January—May 1916

ON New Year's Day 1916 Hankey was summoned at short notice to 10 Downing Street to take secretarial notes for the new Committee (known as the Committee on Co-ordination of Military and Financial Effort) which consisted of Asquith, McKenna and Austen Chamberlain. In spite of the passage of the Military Service Bill[1] the issue that lay at the heart of its deliberations was the old one whether Britain should supply more men, or more munitions and money for the prosecution of the war. This body was to occupy a great deal of Hankey's time and effort during the next three months.[2]

Diary 8th January
Spent whole week in almost daily meetings of the P.M.'s Military and Finance Ctee. Masses of evidence from the Chief of the Imperial General Staff, Adjutant-General,[3] Sir George Barnes[4] of Board of Trade, Lloyd George etc. Spent intervals in seeing members of Ctee. and witnesses and in writing a huge report, which I actually succeeded in circulating by Saturday afternoon [7th Jan.]. The whole affair a tremendous strain . . .

10th January
Spent a good deal of day trying to find a basis of agreement . . . but found opinion had hardened everywhere. The P.M. ought to have rushed the position on Saturday with the conclusions I had drafted. Now we are, so to speak, up against trench warfare. Saw Robertson who was civil and friendly but rather unyielding, and Lord K. who was like a child, petulant and silly and altogether unreasonable . . . I have a plan up my sleeve if only I can get a concession from Runciman.

[1] It received Royal Assent on 27th January 1916.
[2] The papers of the Committee are in Cab. 37/141/38 (Jan. 1916) and Cab. 37/145/20 (April 1916). The Asquith papers, boxes 123 (folios 126–36 and 208–221), 124 (folios 60–71) and 126 (folio 152) contain drafts of the proceedings and of the two reports, dated 4th Feb. and 13th April 1916, sent by Hankey to Asquith.
[3] Lieut.-General Sir Henry C. Sclater (1855–1923).
[4] Sir George S. Barnes (1858–1946). Joint Permanent Secretary, Board of Trade 1915. Member of the Council of the Viceroy of India 1916–21.

The schism in the Cabinet revolved around the number of men required for munitions work. The Board of Trade and Ministry of Munitions assessed the figure at 220,000—which Hankey believed to be greatly excessive. His plan was, by personal negotiation, to get Runciman "to give a few more men from trade to the army", thereby going some way towards meeting the War Office's demands. On 14th "the Board of Trade withdrew the whole of their figures for revision"; and Hankey was confident that "this revision must be in a direction favourable for the War Office". "This", he recorded in his diary, "is a tremendous triumph for me, as I have stuck to this point like a leech! My mind is greatly relieved, as it looks as if we might tide over this crisis, in which case the Coalition Govt. will probably stick together and win the war. I have greatly dreaded the simultaneous resignation of McKenna and Runciman . . .". Three days later he added "the Board of Trade, to everyone's astonishment, suddenly produced figures which gave the War Office all they required"; but Hankey saw "that McKenna didn't half like it, as it spoiled his case and I at once began to fear mischief". He therefore persuaded Asquith to allow him to send the Board of Trade's proposals to the War Office "as a mere provisional scheme, not approved by the Treasury or the Committee, [and] put forward [merely] as a basis for negotiation". This was an extremely clever gambit, as it frustrated the temperamental Chancellor's apparent readiness to split the government on the issue that financial considerations should outweigh the demands of the military. None the less all was not yet plain sailing, and the Committee continued its deliberations until the beginning of February, when Hankey saw in proposals put forward by Austen Chamberlain the chance to reach an agreement. He "whispered the suggestion to the P.M." that Chamberlain should be asked to draft the long-awaited conclusions of the Committee, and Asquith at once did so. Next day (2nd February) Hankey was able to write "Conclusions reached, thank God! Mutual exchange of compliments between P.M., Chamberlain and McKenna. Not a word of thanks to me, though I had done all the work and sweated blood over it for weeks and weeks, saving a complete breakdown time after time by sheer and incessant hard work, lobbying and negotiation". Study of the documents and statistics first put forward by the Board of Trade, which Hankey was instrumental in getting withdrawn, certainly lends support to his claim.[1]

[1]Cab. 37/142/11 is the first report of the Committee, dated 4th Feb. 1916. This

The crisis of January–February 1916 enhanced the respect and affection which Hankey felt towards Asquith; and he certainly shared the tempered irritation which the Prime Minister developed towards McKenna and Runciman. After another week-end at The Wharf Hankey commented in his diary on his host's "simple, honest and fearless character devoid of any trace of 'swank' and 'side'." "It is", he continued, "a great privilege and satisfaction to me that he always confides in me, and asks my advice in difficult times such as the crisis through which we are now passing".

On 18th January Hankey dined with St. Loe Strachey,[1] editor of *The Spectator*, to meet "Colonel" E. M. House,[2] President Wilson's personal emissary to Europe. Hankey had not met House when he first visited London in February 1915, but had then stood out strongly against the American's proposals for "Freedom of the Seas" and relaxing the British blockade.[3] At their first meeting, nearly a year later, Hankey's initial impressions of House were distinctly unfavourable; but the fact that nearly all those present at Strachey's dinner party affected teetotalism as a measure for helping the war effort seems to have prejudiced him against the guest of honour.[4] In fact House had come over this time to fly what Hankey described as "Peace Kites".

Diary 22nd January
. . . Lunched alone with Mr. and Mrs. McKenna . . . McKenna thinks we should probably get a better peace now than later when Germany is wholly on the defensive, and I am inclined to agree. He admitted to me that he had discussed the matter with Colonel House. His [? House's] scheme is that France should have Metz and the French part of Alsace-Lorraine; Belgium should be wholly evacuated; Poland should become autonomous under Russian suzerainty; Italy should get the Trentino; Bulgaria the contested and

---

document, of 30 printed pages full of complicated statistics, was revised no less than four times in Jan.–Feb. 1916—a good example of the strain placed on the C.I.D. secretariat by the Committee's deliberations, and frequent changes of opinion. Asquith papers, boxes 123 and 124. For a succinct account of Asquith's handling of the issue see *Jenkins*, pp. 387–91.

[1] J. St. Loe Strachey (1860–1927). Journalist and author. Editor and proprietor of *The Spectator* until 1925.
[2] See p. 157. [3] See pp. 157–8.
[4] The greater part of the diary entry for 18th Jan. 1916 is printed in *Supreme Command*, II, pp. 378–9. In contrast to Hankey's critical remarks on Strachey's party House described it as "a quiet and pleasant dinner". See C. Seymour (Ed.) *The Intimate Papers of Colonel House*, Vol. II (Benn, 1926), p. 126. Henceforth cited as *"House"*.

uncontested zones [of Macedonia]; the Turks should keep Constantinople; Germany should have some of her colonies back, and should recoup herself in Turkey for what she has lost elsewhere. I know that Grey and Balfour together, and McKenna and Lloyd George secretly and separately have discussed peace possibilities with Col. House.[1] Curious how they all confide in me! . . .

To-day we are deeply aware both of the terrible toll of destruction and suffering which the years of 1916–18 were to exact, and of the failure of the 1919 peace settlement. Thus with benefit of hindsight it is tempting to argue that the proposals put forward by House for the cessation of hostilities and an attempt to achieve a compromise peace would have been of vast benefit to mankind. Unhappily the truth is that there was not the slightest possibility that the Central Powers, who had so far been consistently successful on land, would accept terms such as President Wilson's emissary had in mind.[2]

Hankey was very soon to receive irrefutable proof regarding the true purpose of House's mission. It came to him through his close association with Captain W. R. Hall, which owed a good deal to Hankey's earlier work in Naval Intelligence. Hall had been a guest of Strachey's at the dinner party referred to above, and it is entertaining to speculate on the cynical amusement with which the brilliant if none too scrupulous D.N.I. must have listened to the ideas put forward by President Wilson's emissary when he knew precisely what House was reporting back to Washington.

Diary 25th January
Montagu called on me to explain a scheme of his for placing forged German bank notes in circulation, in which I promised to try and help. It appears that the Governor of the Bank of England,[3] with the knowledge of the Chancellor of the Exchequer and Prime Minister, has produced some marvellous forgeries. It seems rather a dirty business, but the Germans deserve it and Napoleon used to do it. There is some reason to suspect that the Huns have already played this game on us . . .

[1] Though the wording of Hankey's diary does not make it clear whether the peace proposals were House's or McKenna's they do in fact correspond closely with those put forward by the former. See *House*, II, pp. 121, 135 and 170 fn. 1.
[2] House's proposal was that President Wilson should call a conference of the belligerents, backed by the threat that, if Germany refused to attend, the U.S.A. would enter the war on the side of the Allies. Grey and Balfour gave a good deal of encouragement to this idea; but Wilson was not prepared to *guarantee* a declaration of war. *ibid.*, p. 171.
[3] Walter Cunliffe, 1st Baron Cunliffe 1914 (1855–1919).

27th January

. . . I called on Captain Hall, the Director of Intelligence at the Admiralty, and asked him to help in the banknote scheme. I had a very interesting conversation with Hall re Col. House. Hall has succeeded in discovering his private cipher to President Wilson and has deciphered his telegrams. It is quite clear that all my suspicions were correct, and that House is over here on a peace "stunt". I saw telegrams describing conversations with Grey and Balfour, of which the latter had given me some account. But what really horrified me was that Grey seems to have given House the impression that he would bargain the "Freedom of the Seas" against German militarism—a most ridiculous idea when one remembers that we keep treaties and the Hun don't. House added his doubts as to whether Grey would ever get his colleagues to agree. I can imagine no greater folly, when one remembers the experience of this war on the subject . . .

1st February

Saw Captain Hall again first thing in the morning. He showed me more of Col. House's telegrams, sent from Berlin. Their trend was to indicate, firstly, that the Germans will not agree to the proposals of the U.S.A. for settlement of the *Lusitania* episode: secondly that the reason for this is that the German Adty. have built big submarines, and seriously believe that they can blockade England (this may be bluff, but I fear they have some reason); thirdly that this may force America to break off negotiations and produce war with the U.S.A. I found that Hall had not shown the telegrams to the First Lord. This information is of course priceless. It is clear that we must prepare for a bitter and relentless submarine campaign, and take measures to meet it. It may also be worth while to make great concessions to the U.S.A. in order to try and draw them into the war. We must also educate Col. House that America's rôle, if she becomes involved in the war, will be one of finance and supplier to the Allies; not military . . .

Hankey's foresight regarding the need to prepare for intensified submarine warfare was to be abundantly justified; but his anticipation that the rôle of the U.S.A. in the war would not be military was wide of the mark. It is however fair to remark that in the early months of 1916 Britain and France had not yet been bled white by the slaughter on the western front. Thus the need for the U.S.A. to replace their lost military man power had not yet arisen.

The discussions on House's proposals continued into March when Hankey got approval to put the issue before the C.I.G.S. and First Sea Lord in order to ascertain their views on whether an Allied victory was likely that summer. He expected that the peak of the Allies' military effort would be reached at about that time, after which it would decline. If the service chiefs were sanguine about an early victory he considered the government "would be justified in going ahead" with the plans for a great offensive. Otherwise he considered that "they ought to test House's suggestion in order either to discuss peace before we have passed our zenith or to get the U.S.A. behind us, in which case we could go on for ever".[1]

Diary 15th March
To-day I was shown the Colonel House papers. Colonel H. when in England on his return from Berlin had a conference with Sir E. Grey of which a record was made. The purport of it was that, if the Allies would state their peace terms to President Wilson the latter would invite Germany to a conference to discuss them. If Germany stuck out for impossible terms the U.S.A. would *probably* then join the Allies. The papers included a telegram from Col. House to Sir E. Grey stating President Wilson's concurrence in the record, so far as he was in a position to speak for the U.S.A., but insisting on the word "probably" [being inserted in the sentence threatening that the U.S.A. would declare war if Germany refused to attend the proposed conference.[2]]

Next day Hankey discussed the American proposal with Grey and Asquith. He wrote in his diary that the latter "affects to regard the whole thing as humbug and a mere manoeuvre of American politics"; and, with a Presidential election in the offing, there may well have been a measure of truth in Asquith's somewhat harsh judgement. But Grey felt deeply the responsibility which rested on him. If he ignored House's approach "and the war went wrong", wrote Hankey, "he would have missed a great opportunity either to get a decent peace or to bring in America". But even Grey felt that "if we were likely to be completely victorious it would be better to ignore it".[3] Grey therefore brought the matter before the War Committee; but that body decided not to follow up the American approach. Instead they decided, with little regard for logic, to set up a Reconstruction Committee to review the

[1] Diary 11th and 14th March 1916.
[2] Diary entry for 16th March 1916. *Supreme Command*, II, p. 480. Hankey's summary of House's proposals is absolutely correct, except that he does not make it clear that it was President Wilson who toned down the threat of the U.S.A. entering the war by adding the word "probably" to the memorandum agreed between Grey and House on 22nd Feb. See *House*, II, p. 199.
[3] Diary 16th March 1916.

measures needed to restore the nation to a peace basis—when the time came.

On 24th January Hankey received the first recognition of his efforts during the war. Surprisingly this came from the French government, and not from that which he had served so faithfully. Captain Doumayrou, the French Liaison officer at the War Office, brought round to 10 Downing Street a message from M. Briand,[1] the French Premier and Foreign Minister, asking Asquith to decorate Hankey with the Légion d'Honneur. The Prime Minister did so with a little speech in which he said that "he knew no one who deserved it better". It seems possible that this informal investiture made Asquith aware of the fact that his own government had not been exactly forward in giving tangible recognition to the Secretary's efforts. Be that as it may, little over a week later the Prime Minister made amends.

Asquith to Hankey. 10 Downing Street, 3rd February 1916. Holograph
Private
My dear Hankey,

The King is going to give you at my instance the K.C.B., which is a distinction that no one in my judgement, since the war began has so well earned.

I cannot adequately express my appreciation of and gratitude for your unstinted and invaluable service, rendered in so many different ways, but always with the same willingness and efficiency.

My own debt of personal obligation to you throughout these trying and testing times is more than I measure.

Yours always sincerely

Hankey to Asquith. 2 Whitehall Gardens, 4th February 1916. Holograph
My dear Prime Minister,

Very many thanks for your kind and appreciative letter acquainting me that the King at your instance is giving me the K.C.B.

When you appointed me, though inexperienced and unknown, to succeed my distinguished predecessors, I remember writing to say that I would not disappoint you, and I can have no greater satisfaction than to know from your letter and from the distinction to be conferred on me that I have kept my promise. I should like to add, though, that I owe this to the loyal co-operation and untiring devotion to duty during these strenuous times of

[1]Aristide Briand (1862–1932). Ten times Premier of France. Combined Foreign Ministry with that of Premier Oct. 1915 to March 1917 and Jan. 1921 to Jan. 1922. Played a large part in the Locarno Agreement of Oct. 1925.

my colleagues in this Office, more especially Col. Swinton, Col. Jones, and Mr. Longhurst. You may rely on all of us to spare no effort to be worthy of your confidence in the future.

Yours very sincerely.

The award was announced on 5th and Hankey spent the next day answering "the prodigious number of letters and telegrams of congratulation". Among those which he probably appreciated most were the letters from Esher, Haldane, Selborne, Reading, Beresford, Robertson and Ian Hamilton. Even Lloyd George, who never put pen to paper if he could avoid doing so, sent a postcard inscribed "Heartiest congratulations"; while Montagu wrote to Asquith "To-day's honour to Sir Maurice is very gratifying to all his admirers and friends. He is undoubtedly the discovery of the War. I do not think I have ever met a man with the same coolness and impartiality of judgement".[1]

Diary 8th February
Invested with the K.C.B. privately at Buckingham Palace at 11.30 a.m. After Knighting me by striking my shoulders with a sword the King shook hands and made me a little speech. He said that the Prime Minister on the previous evening had told him that I had been absolutely indispensable, and that he could never have run the war and kept his government together without me. He also said that Lord Kitchener had expressed great pleasure at hearing that I was to have the K.C.B., had spoken most highly of my work, and had emphasised that in very difficult circumstances, when I might have sided with Ministers against him, I had always been perfectly straight. The King then said, rather significantly, "You have got on because you have been absolutely straight". We then talked familiarly for nearly an hour on various subjects connected with the war. In the afternoon Colonel Swinton, by my arrangment, took the King out to see the "Caterpillar" [i.e. the trial model Tank]. I was glad to give Swinton this chance.

The C.I.D. Secretariat produced an invitation to a dinner at the Army and Navy Club in Hankey's honour in highly original form. Printed on the pale green paper always used by the C.I.D., and in exactly the proper format, "Memorandum K.C.B.1" was headed "To Celebrate the Occasion of Honourable Recognition of the Secretary's Work and Ability". Swinton proposed the guest's health in what Hankey described as "a most amusing speech", and he and all the staff signed the menu of the eight course dinner—which Adeline carefully

[1]Quoted S. David Waley, *Edwin Montagu, a Memoir*, p. 89.

preserved in her scrap book. For Hankey it must have been a heart-warming occasion, and a most welcome interlude at a time of severe strain.

At the very moment when Hankey was being honoured the Army-Navy dispute over the control of aviation and the provision of aeronautical material flared up again. General Sir David Henderson[1] circulated a challenging paper in which he proposed that the War Committee should define the duties of the R.N. Air Service and R.F.C. and should settle the order of importance of those duties; also that the available material should be allocated according to the priorities established.[2] The War Committee considered this paper on 10th and 15th February, and a deep schism between the Army and Navy representatives at once became apparent.[3] Hankey's solution was the same as he had put up when the dispute had been aired nearly a year earlier—namely that the pre-war Air Committee should be revived, but in more compact form with a Cabinet Minister as chairman and representatives of the War Office and Admiralty as members. He regarded "the creation of a new Ministry of the Air", which "had been put forward from a good many quarters" as "open to many objections".[4] The Cabinet, no doubt influenced by Hankey, set up on 25th February a Joint War Air Committee, of which Lord Derby[5] was chairman and Lord Montagu of Beaulieu,[6] an ardent advocate of an Air Ministry and separate Air Service, as an "independent member". But that body soon found itself quite unable to reconcile the fundamental cleavage between the two service departments. This derived from competition for the available material, and from the refusal of the Admiralty to surrender as part of its functions what came later to be called "Strategic Bombing". The dispute continued throughout March, with Balfour, the First Lord, holding to the Navy's claims in the War Committee, while

[1]1862–1921. Director-General of Military Aeronautics 1913–17 and a member of the Army Council from 22nd Feb. 1916. Vice-President of Air Council Jan.–April 1918.

[2]C.I.D. G.55 "Duties of the Royal Naval Air Service and the Royal Flying Corps", dated 28th Jan. 1916.

[3]69th and 71st Meetings. W.C. 23 and 25.

[4]Hankey to Asquith 9th Feb. 1916. Cab. 42/8/5.

[5]17th Earl of Derby (1865–1948). Secretary of State for War 1916–18 and 1922–4. Ambassador in Paris 1918–20.

[6]2nd Baron Montagu of Beaulieu (1866–1929). A pioneer of motoring and of aviation.

Curzon, the Lord Privy Seal, came out strongly against the Admiralty.[1]

If the first months of 1916 brought Hankey still closer into Asquith's confidence, the same period produced for him a whole succession of difficulties with Lloyd George—both as Minister of Munitions and after he became Secretary of State for War in July. To quote only a few examples, in January Lloyd George vented on Hankey his annoyance over the conclusions of the War Committee with regard to the transfer of responsibility for design from the War Office to his own Ministry. "I have never read a more grotesque travesty of any decision", he wrote, and asked for that matter to be discussed again at the next meeting.[2] Hankey replied patiently that he was "getting out a short Note giving the grounds for the Conclusion"; but he had been through the Proceedings and "did not see what other Conclusion could have been drawn".[3] However he would arrange for the subject to be placed on the agenda for the next meeting. Lloyd George's next protest concerned a Conclusion of the War Committee recording their concurrence with the C.I.G.S.'s view that a big offensive in the Balkans was ruled out by shortage of shipping, and that a small offensive offered no "military advantage". This time Asquith inserted some qualifying words, which apparently mollified his difficult colleague's strongly held mistrust of the "westerners' " strategy.[4] March produced no less than three objections by Lloyd George to War Committee Conclusions. On 2nd he wrote to Hankey that "if these Minutes are passed by the Prime Minister I am afraid I must ask you to be good enough to insert a note intimating that I cannot assent to them until I first of all have Lord Fisher's statement."[5] Little more than a week later he came at the Secretary again, to disagree with a Conclusion that the carriage of grain "should be considered a first charge on our merchant shipping"[6]

[1] Memos. by Balfour of 3rd April (Cab. 37/145), and by Curzon of 14th Feb. and 16th April 1916 (Cab. 37/142 and 37/146 respectively).
[2] Lloyd George to Hankey 28th Jan. 1916. Lloyd George papers D/17/3/12. The conclusion to which Lloyd George objected was in the minutes of meeting held on 26th Jan. Cab. 42/7.
[3] Hankey to Lloyd George *ibid*. D/17/3/13. See Cab. 42/8 for minutes of meetings on 1st and 3rd Feb. 1916.
[4] *ibid*. D/17/3/19. The minute he objected to is in Cab. 42/9 under 22nd Feb. 1916.
[5] Lloyd George to Hankey 2nd March 1916. *ibid*. D/17/3/21. The minutes referred to concerned the meeting held on 1st, at which the naval situation was discussed. They covered 69 pages of print.
[6] Lloyd George to Hankey 11th March 1916. *ibid*. D/17/3/23. The conclusion he objected to was in minutes of meeting held on 10th March. Cab. 42/10.

—though it is hard to see precisely why the Minister of Munitions should have considered such a subject within his province. Next he wrote that he had "altered the Minutes [of the meeting held on 21st March] to represent what I would consider to be the true decision of the Committee" about the supply of machine guns to Allied armies.[1] All this pin-pricking must have been intensely irritating to Hankey and his hard-pressed staff; but he never showed it.

To return to naval affairs, it was not only over the aviation dispute that the Admiralty got itself into increasingly bad odour with Ministers at this time. There was also widespread dissatisfaction with the lack of drive and imagination of the Balfour-Jackson régime; and the consequential unrest was spreading to the public and the Press. We saw earlier how, largely as a result of American protests, the Germans called off their first unrestricted submarine campaign in August 1915.[2] Early in the following year they tried again, and sinkings rose sharply—to 191,667 tons in April. It appeared that, despite the warnings received, the Admiralty had done little towards safeguarding Allied shipping— let alone mastering the submarine. The rising uneasiness with regard to the conduct of the naval war was reflected in Hankey's diary. In February he sent Asquith a memorandum "on naval inefficiency", and "talked to him at great length about the defects of the Admiralty". He pointed out that not a single member of the Board had any war experience at sea, that although the Admiralty had assumed operational control of naval forces outside the Grand Fleet "none of the Board ever went near the fleet or inspected anything". Lastly he protested that the Chief of War Staff (Oliver) was not only trying to conduct operations personally but "was also charged with the distribution of the fleet as a whole, [for] arrangements with our Allies and [for] the main naval policy of the war". This was far too great a burden for one man to carry, and Hankey urged that "drastic changes" were necessary.[3] This was strong stuff, especially as Hankey was normally very sympathetic towards naval men and their point of view. Yet the criticisms were to a very large extent justified.[4] One person who was very well aware of the rising dissatisfaction with the Admiralty was old "Jacky" Fisher, who had been watching the trend of events from the sidelines ever since his

[1]Same to same 22nd March 1916. *ibid.* D/17/3/24.
[2]See p. 180. [3]Diary 28th February 1916.
[4]For a balanced criticism of the Balfour-Jackson régime of 1915–16 at the Admiralty see Marder, *Scapa Flow*. II, Parts II and III. Ch. IX.

resignation in May 1915, and never ceased to work and intrigue for his return to office.

To Lady Hankey. 2 Whitehall Gardens, 7th March 1916
I went down to the "Talking Shop" this afternoon to hear A.J.B. introduce the Navy Estimates. He made a rather rambling and woolly speech. Then Winston got up and "strafed" the Admiralty for lack of ginger. It was intensely dramatic, especially at the end when Winston delivered an impassioned appeal for Fisher's return as First Sea Lord! He buried the hatchet and let "bygones be bygones". Jacky was sitting just in front of me over the clock with a face like an Indian god . . . One significant fact—when A.J.B. spoke in terms of commendation of his naval colleagues on the Board of Admiralty there was a profound and ominous silence. When Winston said the Board lacked driving power there were unmistakable and loud murmurs of assent, though his suggestion to bring back Fisher was received only moderately enthusiastically.[1]

I wonder how it will all end. Winston said all the things I am feeling, and there was no mistaking the sympathy in the House with his views. It is an awkward situation for the Government . . .

Next day Fisher was called to give his views to the War Committee; but he made no very good impression. His earlier association with Hankey made it perfectly natural that he should use him as the channel through which to propagate his ideas and further his aims, and in the early months of 1916 many letters passed between them. The following are typical examples of Fisher's style and methods.

Fisher to Hankey. 36 Berkeley Gardens. 12th February 1916. Holograph
Secret and Private
My beloved Hankey,
I am going to await the action that follows Jellicoe's attendance on the War Council [War Committee] before taking the drastic step I have in view for replacing Philosophic Doubt [i.e. Balfour] by Ruthless Energy [himself]! I have prepared my "Form of Words" and I sincerely think them to be the best of my life! Short, sharp and decisive! The newspaper agitation by a cunning stroke has been diverted from the very grave causes of anxiety for our hitherto assured Naval Supremacy due to an effete Naval administration (so beautifully expressed yesterday by an Admiralty messenger "Lor' Sir, we are ever so much quieter now than we was in Peace, Sir!") I say the Public anxiety has been craftily side-tracked into an investigation as to how old *I* am! My age, my Personality and my now keeping a chemist's shop in

[1]See Parl Deb., Commons, Vol. LXXX, Cols. 1401–20 for Balfour's speech and Cols. 1420–30 for Churchill's.

Cockspur Street[1] has nothing whatsoever to do with a possible vital Naval disaster due to three old women governing the Navy.

Yours

I think you will admit this letter is totally unfit for publication!

Same to same. 11th March 1916. Holograph
Private and Secret

My beloved Hankey,

Your very nice letter much delighted me!

I met an influential person yesterday who told me it was being "spread about" that I utterly "fizzled out" at the War Council [War Committee] and Balfour "wiped the floor with me". Such is Life! But this makes it the more incumbent on me to ensure a right record of what passed being circulated to the War Council. Crease[2] tells me that Balfour is utterly at fault in his statements of the monitors delaying Battleships, as only the "Spare guns and spare mountings" were taken, and so if new orders to replace them had been hustled up probably no default at all, or possibly the last ship a bit delayed; but a Minister with a Department at his beck and call can always knock over any outside opponent.

I think the Government will be turned out in about 3 weeks' time. There *is* Seething Discontent throughout the masses.

Yours for evermore

Hankey always answered Fisher's letters promptly, and included in them a few tit-bits of information which he knew his old friend and supporter would appreciate. For example on 9th March he wrote "I fear that Winston, whose conduct is in striking contrast to yours, did not do you much good. He gave A.J.B. a chance he was not likely to miss".[3] Hankey must also have been aware that a section of the Press strongly favoured Fisher's recall. C. P. Scott, for instance, the influential and distinguished editor of the *Manchester Guardian*, wrote to Lloyd George that "an immediate change is needed at the Admiralty. Fisher must come back . . . the one man of real resource and energy . . .".[4] But Hankey, though much in sympathy with Fisher's strictures on the Balfour-Jackson régime, also knew that to both Asquith and George V

[1] An oblique reference to his chairmanship of the Board of Invention and Research. Its offices were at Victory House, Cockspur Street.
[2] Captain T. E. Crease (1875–1942). Naval Assistant to Fisher as First Sea Lord 1914–15. Secretary of Board of Invention and Research 1915–16. Private Secretary to Sir Eric Geddes as First Lord and Secretary of Allied Naval Council 1917–19.
[3] Hankey to Fisher 9th March 1916. Lennoxlove papers.
[4] Scott to Lloyd George 29th Feb. 1916. Lloyd George papers D/18/15/9.

the return of the old Admiral was unthinkable; and he therefore never held out to him the slightest hope.

A happier episode than the quarrels in the Joint War Air Committee and the exposure of the incompetence of the Admiralty was the successful trial of the "Caterpillar Machine Gun Destroyer" (i.e. the prototype Tank) held at Hatfield early in February. Hankey called this event "a great triumph to Swinton and me as we have had to climb a mountain of apathy and passive resistance to reach this stage".[1] Alas, he could not have known that he and the other supporters of this revolutionary development had not by any means reached the summit of the mountain in question. Indeed the real peak did not come in sight until the first tanks reached France in the following summer. None the less he was greatly encouraged by the War Committee approving an order for 100 to be built.

In the middle of February Hankey managed to get away for a week's holiday with Adeline at Eastbourne. He confided to his diary that he was "tired and wanted freshening up after my incessant labours".[2] But he returned to London once during his holiday, to attend a War Committee meeting on naval affairs at which Admiral Jellicoe, the C-in-C, Grand Fleet, was present. "My uneasiness about the Navy not at all relieved" was his comment. On 21st he was back in the saddle again, and immersed in all the problems which had been on the War Committee's agenda before he went away.

Meanwhile the Germans had launched, on 15th February, their great offensive against Verdun, which was to last almost until the end of the year. Not only did this grim and costly struggle produce France's "supreme sacrifice and her supreme triumph",[3] but it impaired the whole Allied plan of campaign for 1916 by frustrating French participation in the projected offensive on the Somme, and by making it urgently necessary for the British army to take some of the weight off their Ally.

Diary 14th March
. . . On arrival at office I found that the King had been telephoning to see me, so I went off to Buckingham Palace, where I spent an hour chatting with the King. He looked very well and talked very confidentially, even asking my opinion as to Mr. Asquith's suitability as Prime Minister. On my saying that he was the only man who could handle his team, even if he shared the whip

[1]Diary 2nd February 1916.   [2]Diary 13th February 1916.
[3]*Liddell Hart*, p. 287.

rather too much, the King fully agreed, and said he could not see any other possible Prime Minister. He talked of Selborne in terms of disparagement, but spoke highly of Lord Curzon. From the King I went to Sir William Robertson to warn him that the Col. House question [presumably the proposed peace conference] was coming up, and that the decision would largely depend on what he and Sir Henry Jackson thought about the prospects of the war. Robertson thanked me for coming but appeared upset about something. I learnt from Lucas, his A.D.C.[1] that he had had a bad morning with the Australian Prime Minister Hughes,[2] who had insisted that Gen. Birdwood should command the Australian Corps coming to France, instead of Godley,[3] whom the English generals wanted, as they say that the latter keeps better discipline. This is really preposterously absurd to anyone who has been at Anzac. Birdwood could make his men do anything, whereas Godley was regarded as second-rate . . . It is this meticulous clinging to our obsolete, undemocratic standard of what they are pleased to call discipline— saluting etc.—that has made the English Army so rotten that it has never achieved one successful offensive in the whole course of the war. In fact its history is largely a history of retreats—Mons, Gallipoli, Salonica and Bagdad. The Australians under Birdwood have a looser but better discipline, which makes men dig without grumbling and die readily for their commander . . .

Hankey was of course completely justified both in his preference for Birdwood over Godley and in his assessment of the nature and quality of Anzac discipline; but there were in 1916 hardly any senior British army officers who would have agreed with him. In fact at the very time when he penned his angry remarks about the War Office and the soldiers a long letter was on the way to him from Birdwood, who was still in Egypt, telling him of the recent reorganisation and strengthening of the Anzacs to a total of 78 battalions, 90 batteries and 50 squadrons of cavalry. He was understandably keen to command this splendid force himself, and hoped that it would be allowed to maintain its entity on reaching France and not be broken up between various British armies. "I am seeing each battalion in turn as it goes off", he wrote, "and speaking to them all very straightly—impressing on them how

[1]Major C. C. Lucas, R.A. Actually Personal Secretary to Sir W. Robertson as C.I.G.S.
[2]W. M. ("Billy") Hughes (1864–1952). Australian politician (Lab.). Prime Minister 1915–23, and held many Ministerial offices 1908–41. Member of Imperial War Cabinet 1917–19 and delegate to Paris Peace Conference 1919.
[3]General Sir Alexander J. Godley (1867–1957). Commanded New Zealand Expeditionary Force 1914–18. C-in-C, British Army of Rhine 1922–4. G.O.C. Southern Command 1924–8. Governor and C-in-C, Gibraltar, 1928–33.

much I rely on each individual to uphold the honour of Australia when in France, and I feel quite confident that this will be done". Then he added as a postscript "I have just heard I accompany 1st Corps to France. I do hope that 2nd Corps may follow it in due course and that we may then form an Army—indeed I imagine this is sure to come."[1] In the selection of the Anzacs' commander "Billy" Hughes had his way; but unfortunately the goodwill won by Birdwood from his men on Gallipoli was to a great extent dissipated when they were flung into the holocaust on the Somme in the following summer and lost 23,000 men for a tiny territorial gain.[2]

Towards the end of March Hankey was much occupied with preparations for an Inter-Allied Conference in Paris, which was to be the first such meeting at which Italy would be represented, and with the arrangements for Asquith to go on to Rome for further discussions with the Italian political and military leaders. Until almost the last moment there were doubts whether Hankey should accompany the British delegation. The reason was that, to quote from his diary, "there is a rumour in the wind of a political plot to be got up in his [Asquith's] absence by Lloyd George, Carson and Churchill, and Montagu and Bonham Carter think I ought to stay—though what I can do I don't know". It was perhaps for this reason that Asquith, to whom Hankey had "exposed the whole plot beforehand", insisted on Lloyd George accompanying himself, Grey and Kitchener to Paris. Hankey noted that "this will keep Ll. G. out of mischief for a day or two, if it be true that he is on mischief bent".[3]

The party, which finally did include Hankey, left London on 26th March, and reached Paris safely that afternoon. The conferences started next morning.

To Lady Hankey. Hotel Crillon, Paris. 27th March 1916
. . . Our journey here was quite uneventful—no submarines, no mines and not even sea-sickness! I find myself quite a "Swell" here since I got my K.C.B. I get invitations to the Quai d'Orsay [French Foreign Ministry] and the Elysée [President's palace], which I never had before, and various distinguished persons leave their cards (which by the way I cannot return as I didn't bring any!) . . .
To-day was a perfectly desperate day, during which I attended no less than

[1]Birdwood to Hankey from Ismailia, 16th March 1916. 5 pp. typescript, the post-script in holograph.
[2]*Liddell Hart*, p. 326.   [3]Diary 25th March 1916.

four conferences and an official *déjeuner* where I sat between a Cabinet
Minister and a distinguished Senator.[1] Rather tiring, but very good for one's
French and very interesting . . . I feel I am getting to know the French very
well. It has all been extremely interesting meeting Briand, Pasitch (the Serb),
Sonnino, Salandra, Broqueville (the Belgian) and many others[2] . . . It looks
as though I should go on to Rome, but it is quite undecided . . .

As always Hankey made the most of his opportunities to study and
observe the characters of the chief participants in an international
conference. The comments he jotted down in his diary on this occasion
show a shrewd and developing judgement in his assessment of men and
of the motives which inspired them. The conference held its final
session on the afternoon of 28th. Its achievements were in truth slender
—"much froth and little business" was Hankey's comment—and the
chief decision was the negative one of the British delegates yielding to
French objections to the withdrawal of troops from Salonika. That
evening, on returning from a performance at the Folies Bergères,
Asquith showed Hankey a telegram from Montagu "to the effect that
the conscriptionists were on the war path and I ought to come home
instead of going on to Rome with the P.M.". In the end Hankey was
told to send Montagu a summary of the results of the conference,
which had indicated that the French were desirous of maintaining "the
rôle of the principal Allied military power", and that "if we don't have
a costly offensive this spring we don't need our men so fast, and [the
views of] all parties can be met".[3] The long term effects of the German
offensive at Verdun had obviously not yet been appreciated by either
country's leaders.

To Lady Hankey. Hotel Crillon, Paris. 28th March 1916
. . . The P.M. has now decided to take me to Italy. It is only intended as a

---

[1]According to Hankey's diary these were M. Sembat, a Deputy and Minister of
Public Works, and M. Cruppi, a former Minister for Foreign Affairs.
[2]See p. 249 re Briand. Nikola Pasitch (more correctly Pašíc) (1845–1926) was Chief
Minister of Servia 1905 and 1910–18 and Prime Minister under the new constitution
of Yugo-Slavia 1921–26. Baron Giorgio S. Sonnino (1847–1922) was Italian Foreign
Minister 1914–19. Signed Secret Treaty of London on behalf of Italy with Allies
April 1915. Senator 1920. Antonio Salandra (1853–1931) was Italian Prime Minister
1911–12, 1912–18 and twice between 1932 and 1934. Count de Broqueville (1860–
1940) was Belgian Prime Minister 1911–12, 1912–18 and twice between 1932 and
1934. Hankey here misspelt his name Brockeville.
[3]Diary (loose leaf) 28th March 1916. The greatest part of the diary entries for the
visits to Paris and Rome are printed in *Supreme Command*, II, pp. 482–6.

"hurrah" party and should be quite a holiday. In order to give the Italian Ministers who are at present in Paris time to return and arrange the P.M.'s reception we are not to start from here until Thursday [30th] so we shall have a clear day to-morrow.

We had a long session of the conference this morning, followed by a colossal luncheon with the President[1] at the Elysée in a most beautiful room. I sat between two Ministers—Albert Thomas,[2] the Minister of Munitions and Cruppi who I fancy is without portfolio.[3] The former, who is a socialist and man of the people and very ambitious was the more interesting . . .

I have been rather torn in my mind between returning to you and going to Italy, but it is not every day one has the chance of a state visit to Rome with a Prime Minister, including probably visits to the King and Pope, so I think it would be wrong to miss it . . .

Hankey and Asquith spent the brief interlude between the Paris conference and the journey to Rome visiting the battlefields of the Marne and Ourcq, where, as Hankey told Adeline "the German tide was stemmed and rolled back to the Aisne [5th–11th September 1914]". But the price paid for that success plainly shook him. "The shocking casualties", he wrote, "are shown by the masses of graves stretching away across the country for miles and miles, all carefully tended by women and children."

To Lady Hankey. In the train near Mont Cenis. 30th March 1916
. . . We got off at about 11 a.m. and were seen off by a crowd of Cabinet Ministers etc., the P.M. in his particularly shabby pepper and salt travelling suit . . . We have the President's train for the trip—a most luxurious affair consisting of three coaches, one containing a beautifully decorated saloon full of ordinary arm chairs, where I am sitting writing, also a number of fair sized "sleepers", a very up-to-date restaurant car . . . It is all extraordinarily luxurious, and will quite spoil one for ordinary travelling. Up to date the journey has been entirely uneventful, but we are a very congenial party,[4] the

[1]Raymond Poincaré (1860–1934). President of France 1913–20. Prime Minister and Foreign Minister 1922–24, being then responsible for the occupation of Ruhr 1923, and again 1926–29.

[2]1878–1932. French politician (Soc.). Minister of Munitions 1916–17.

[3]M. Cruppi actually held no ministerial office in 1916.

[4]In addition to Hankey only Maurice Bonham Carter, Asquith's private secretary, and Hugh J. O'Beirne (1866–1916), a Minister Plenipotentiary in the Diplomatic Service, then serving in the Foreign Office, accompanied the Prime Minister to Rome. O'Beirne was lost with Lord Kitchener when H.M.S. *Hampshire* was sunk on her way to Russia on 6th June 1916. See pp. 280–1.

Prime Minister is delightfully informal and is taking a thorough rest I am glad to say . . . What a lark it would be if you and I could travel like this together one day! Perhaps we shall! Who knows? Someone has to represent the country both for functions and business. Why not us? After all I am practically second string to the Prime Minister on this stunt! . . .

On their way from Rome station to the British embassy Asquith and his party were, according to Hankey, given "a great popular demonstration". Hankey was accommodated at the Grand Hotel in "a magnificent suite of apartments on the first floor", as the guest of the Italian government. But as the party had to set out almost immediately on a long round of official visits he was not allowed much time to revel in his new-found luxury. While in Rome Asquith was always accompanied by Sir Rennell Rodd, the British ambassador, for whom Hankey had developed a great admiration ever since their first meeting in Greece 18 years earlier.[1] He now described him in his diary as "artist, archaeologist, student and a veritable mine of information on all things Italian . . . I felt he was a worthy companion to the P.M., whose vast store of knowledge on all classical and historical matters fills me with amazement and envy."[2]

To Lady Hankey. British Embassy, Rome. 1st April 1916.
I am spending my [39th] birthday amid the most delightful surroundings . . . The functions only occupy a short time, and there is lots of time in between for sight-seeing . . . Yesterday we had a more or less official reception at the station and after an interval I accompanied the Prime Minister to visit the Queen, the Duke of Genoa (the Regent, as the King is at the front) and the Queen Mother. The Queen, who is the daughter of the King of Montenegro, is a most charming and simple person, who has converted all the state rooms of the palace into hospital wards which she appears to supervise a good deal herself . . . The Duke of Genoa was not particularly interesting, but the Queen Mother was a splendid old lady, who spoke English fluently and seems to take an interest in everything.[3] For example she wanted to know

[1]See p. 201. [2]Diary 2nd April 1916.
[3]Victor Emmanuel III, King of Italy (1869–1947) succeeded to the throne in 1900 on the assassination of his father. Abdicated 1946. Married Princess Elena, daughter of the first and last King of Montenegro. The Queen Mother was Margherita (b. 1851), the only daughter of Prince Ferdinand of Savoy and a cousin of the future King Umberto I whom she married in 1868. As she has been described as "the only uncontestably regal character in modern Italian History" (Ency. Brit., 1967 Ed., Vol. 11, p. 831) Hankey's assessment of her qualities has authoritative support. Tomaso, Duke of Genoa, the Regent of 1916, was an uncle of the King.

about the R.M.A., which is always hard to explain to a foreigner. In the evening we had a dinner at the Consulta [Ministry of Foreign Affairs] . . . My Italian came in useful, and I talked with astonishing volubility (!) in Italian and French—and towards the end of the dinner (after drinking at least 10 different sorts of wine) in both at once! . . .

. . . This morning we paid an official visit to the Pantheon, theoretically to lay wreaths on the tombs of the royalty there, though in fact . . . no one so much as touched the wreaths, which were there before we arrived! After that Bongie [Bonham Carter] and I went off sight seeing. The P.M. went to visit the Pope,[1] but owing to the susceptibilities of the Italian Govt. it was done in rather "back door" manner, and it was thought better that he should not be accompanied by an officer in uniform . . . I understand that the Pope made some remote and more or less academic allusion to the question of peace, but the P.M. pursed up his mouth and said "*Nous continuerons jusqu'au bout*", or words to that effect . . .

Hankey plainly revelled in the opportunities afforded by the Rome visit, and recaptured much of his earlier enthusiasm for sight seeing. But the serious background to the mission was none the less never out of his mind, and his final views on the attitude of the Italians to the war are interesting. "Personally", he confided to his diary, "I did not feel that the Ministerial and upper circles whom we met had any real enthusiasm for the war; they are in it up to the neck and know they have to go through with it, but they have no great courage or confidence in themselves, and lean to an extraordinary extent upon us, and will continue to do so more and more. They have an unbounded belief in our strength and greatness . . . but we shall continually have to support them more and more both in material and moral sense".[2] Which was a very accurate prophecy of what the following year was to bring.

From Rome Asquith and Hankey went on to the Italian General Headquarters at Udine, where they met the King, who lived in conditions of the greatest simplicity close up to the front line. Hankey was plainly impressed by his military knowledge, and by the serious way he took his responsibilities. He accompanied Victor Emmanuel and Asquith on visits to the mountain front in the north-east and to the Isonzo front, all the time making mental notes or jotting down points

[1]Benedict XV (1854–1922). Elected 1914; formerly Archbishop of Genoa. He made many efforts, culminating in his message of 1st Aug. 1917 to the heads of the belligerent states, to persuade them to stop the process of mutual self-destruction.
[2]Diary 2nd April 1916.

which might prove useful at home such as "Why don't our people concrete their trenches?" and "Why not hire Italian labour on short engagements to work in our docks, railways and mines?" Indeed his keen eyes and agile mind never missed anything which might prove useful to his country; and his remarkable memory ensured that whatever he had noted could be recalled instantly should the need arise.[1]

On 5th April the party started homewards and reached London in the early hours of the following morning. Hankey was especially delighted by the personal success achieved by Asquith in Italy, and was glad that in the end no other British Ministers had been present to share in the acclaim with which he was greeted everywhere. As to the front line experiences, Hankey was considerably impressed by much that he saw, and especially by the ingenuity and skill shown by the Italians in driving new roads through very mountainous country for the supply of the front line troops, and by their construction of defences in depth. The actual fighting soldiers also made a good impression; but Hankey failed to appreciate that their successes and high morale arose from the fact that so far they had only fought against the long-hated Austrians, and for territory which they regarded as "*Italia irridenta*". He did not foresee that German intervention was to expose most cruelly the fundamental weaknesses of the Italian military machine.

The return of Asquith and Hankey to London was immediately followed by renewal of the dispute in the Military-Finance Committee over conscription, with all the undertones of political discord it implied; and other serious troubles had descended on the government before April 1916 ended. On 13th the Committee met again, and Hankey believed they had reached the stage of instructing him to draft a report on agreed lines. Indeed he had already started to draft such a document. Then Austen Chamberlain suddenly, and without any warning, produced a memorandum of his own, which, so he told Hankey, "he had the inspiration to write after an extra glass of port at lunch, taken to keep neuralgia at bay". Without any discussion the Committee adopted the Chamberlain memorandum as the basis of their report, and Hankey was "directed to edit it and circulate it to the Cabinet the same evening"; when he studied the document he "did not half like it". He considered some of the figures given were inaccurate, and did not believe that the anti-conscriptionists would accept statements such as

[1]Cab. G.68 of 6th April 1916 contains the recommendations which arose from Hankey's visit to Italy. Asquith papers, box 126, folio 97.

that "it might still be necessary to call up all men 'capable of bearing arms' ". None the less late that night the edited version was ready for next day's Cabinet.[1] Immediately it was over Montagu told Hankey what had transpired.

Diary 14th April

. . . It appears that Ll. George, who has been sulking for ten days or so and has not attended the War Ctee. on the plea of illness, came to the Cabinet in a most furious rage, the real reason being that he had been left out of the Co-ordination [i.e. Military-Finance] Ctee. Anyhow he refused to agree to the Report unless it was accepted by the Army Council; Bonar Law backed him up, and it was decided that the Co-ordination Ctee. should meet the Army Council to discuss it to-morrow. This, of course, is an absurdity. The Committee did not recommend compulsory service, whereas every soldier has demanded this for years, and the Army Council were bound to "plonk" for it. The whole object of the Co-ordinating Ctee. was to co-ordinate conflicting interests, and here it was proposed to set up one of the interests as judge over the other. It appeared to me . . . that the P.M. in agreeing to this had given away the fact (?) of voluntary service . . .

Hankey was kept late in the office again that night, preparing the necessary documents for the Army Council. Adeline having returned from their temporary winter London lodgings to Highstead for the summer he was now staying with his sister Hilda whenever he was detained late in London.

Diary 15th April

At 11.30 I went to see Mrs. Asquith, who was of course very worried over the political crisis, and she made me see the P.M. who had been seeing Grey and Lord Reading. He was quite cheery about it. I advised him that if the Army Council proved difficult, to postpone a decision on some excuse or other, and afterwards to see K. and Robertson and explain that it probably meant his own resignation. This was practically the course he adopted, except that he gave them a hint of the political difficulties involved during the meeting instead of afterwards. Austen Chamberlain at the close of the meeting made an extraordinarily eloquent appeal to the soldiers, setting forth most ably all the wider considerations . . . In the afternoon the woolly-headed soldiers met in solemn conclave—and of course "plonked" again for general conscription. It was 8 o'clock before I got their report, which had to be sent off to the P.M., who had gone to Sutton Courtney for the week-end. Consequently it was 10.30 before I got home to Limpsfield—dog tired after my strenuous week . . .

[1]Diary 13th April 1916.

The next day (Sunday) Hankey spent at home "mainly sleeping". But on his return to London he found that the crisis was still unresolved. During the following week he was constantly at 10 Downing Street for conferences or committees, and generally stayed on for lunch or dinner with the Asquiths. On 20th he heard that the Cabinet had reached agreement on the basis of a compromise proposed by Henderson,[1] the only member of the Labour Party in the First Coalition government. The essence of this scheme was that "unattested" married men were to be given a further opportunity to come forward voluntarily; but unless 50,000 of them did so by 27th May and 15,000 a week thereafter, general conscription was to be introduced. It was to be put before both Houses of Parliament by Asquith and Crewe in secret session a few days later.

The lull in the long debate at least enabled Hankey to spend a quiet Easter Sunday (23rd April) in his garden. On the Monday he returned to prepare notes for Asquith's speech, and drove down to The Wharf with them that same afternoon. His reception was, as usual, very warm. After some discussion, in which Hankey's knowledge of Asquith's habits played a part, it was agreed that they should go back to London that evening; for Hankey, who likened himself to the trainer of a "Bantam", was determined that he should "go into the ring in the pink of condition". He recorded that Asquith "was very chatty and jolly and I thoroughly enjoyed the ride". They reached Downing Street at 12.30 a.m. to find the first news of the Easter rebellion in Ireland awaiting them. Asquith merely said "Well, that's really something" and went off to bed.[2]

Parliament met in secret session on 25th and 26th, and it was on the first day that Asquith spoke on the man-power issue. Hankey met him immediately afterwards, and noted that he was "very flushed" and "a trifle hesitating" about the effects of his speech. In truth it had been badly received, and on 27th Hankey noted that "To-day Parliament forced the Govt. to withdraw the military service bill which embodied the compromise". Asquith then accepted that no alternative remained other than the introduction immediately of legislation for compulsory

[1]Arthur Henderson (1863–1935). Politician (Lab.), Chairman of Parliamentary Labour Party 1908–10 and 1914–17. President of Board of Education 1915–16. Labour Adviser to the government 1916. Minister without Portfolio in War Cabinet 1917. Home Secretary 1924; Foreign Secretary 1929–31.
[2]Diary 24th April 1916.

service.[1] We may here carry the story on to the end. On 2nd May Asquith himself introduced the Military Service (General Compulsion) Bill, and by 25th it had passed through all stages and received Royal Assent. Thus was the conscription issue at last decided; nor did it produce any resignations, as Hankey had always feared would be the case. But the manner in which it was forced on the government certainly did not enhance its credit or public standing; and Hankey shared in the defeat of those who had stood out so long for the voluntary principle. Furthermore by an ironical chance the final report of the Military-Finance Committee, to which Hankey had devoted an enormous amount of time and effort, was at last ready for circulation at the very moment when Parliament rendered all its deliberations obsolete.[2] Small wonder that Hankey's diary entries at this time are unusually bitter.

Diary 2nd May 1916
Spent morning preparing notes for P.M.'s speech to introduce compulsion for married men. P.M. was very "short" when I saw him and obviously hated the job. I dropped into the House after lunching at the Club and heard the speech. It was not a very good one—not so good as the one I gave him. The House was astonishingly cold.[3] The fact was that the people who want compulsory service don't want Asquith, while those who want Asquith don't want compulsory service; so he fell between two stools! It is really an astonishing situation. The only real military case for the Bill is the great offensive. For an ordinary campaign there are heaps of men. That is to say we could fight the whole summer and lose men on the same scale as we lost them last year, which included Gallipoli, Neuve Chapelle, Loos and Festubert, and still have 50,000 men up our sleeve at the end of the year. But the Army want a regular orgy of slaughter this summer, and it is for this that they demand the extra men. Thus the Cabinet have yielded to a demand based solely on carrying out the plan for a great offensive, a plan which no member of the Cabinet and none of the regimental soldiers who will have to carry it out believe in, a plan conceived in the heads of the red-hatted, brass-bound brigade behind, who know little of the conditions at the actual front and are out of touch with real regimental opinion. It is alleged that we must do this thing to save the Russians—yet the French did it all last summer, with

[1] *Jenkins*, pp. 393–4.
[2] The final report, dated 13th April 1916 is in Cab. 37/145/35 and 36. The Cabinet discussed it next day, further revisions were made and it was not finally circulated until 27th April. (C.I.D. 432.) Asquith papers, box 126, folio 152.
[3] Parl. Deb., Commons, Vol. LXXXI, Cols. 2611–15. The debate was on an Adjournment motion.

the result that they are now bled white and have no reserves left . . . Yet we are asked by the "scientific" soldier to repeat the process, notwithstanding that it may jeopardise the financial stability of this country on which the whole future of the Allies rests! Strongly though I feel on this matter I find it extraordinarily difficult to take any action, because I am not the constitutional military adviser of the government. Yet I have my own plan, which I have communicated to Robertson and Robertson to Haig, and which I am certain must succeed . . . Came home much depressed.

Hankey's cri de cœur was to be echoed by the fighting soldiers up and down the western front before the Battle of the Somme died away in the following autumn; and one cannot but regret that he was not the "constitutional military adviser of the government". Only a few weeks later Asquith described Hankey as "the most useful man in Europe—he has never been wrong".[1] But by that time much of the "orgy of slaughter" which he had foretold, and which destroyed the flower of British manhood, had taken place. If Asquith felt such confidence in Hankey's military judgement why did he not stand out firmly against the "great offensive" as conceived at British G.H.Q.? The answer must surely lie in the fact that, as Hankey told the King, he had a difficult team to drive, and if he forced a showdown with the soldiers he knew that the team would fall to pieces. That Asquith possessed many of the qualities of greatness is beyond dispute; and Hankey repeatedly emphasised his admiration for the Prime Minister's sturdy imperturbability, as well as for his intellectual brilliance. Indeed it was at this very time that Curzon, who was certainly not politically sympathetic with Asquith, commented to Hankey on the Prime Minister's "astonishing physique and equanimity, which he considered to be his greatest asset and an indispensable one".[2] But for all his qualities Asquith's character was surely flawed by lack of the moral courage to adopt the course in military affairs in which he believed, because of the likely political consequences. And in the end that weakness destroyed both him and the Liberal Party.

Hankey, of course, was not the man to repine or lose heart even over a major decision which he was convinced to be wrong. Indeed even before the debate of 2nd May he had taken steps to get his alternative plan adopted, and to mitigate the slaughter which he foresaw would arise from the orthodox offensive.

[1]About August 1916. *Jenkins,* p. 412. [2]Diary 28th April 1916.

Diary 27th April

. . . Lunched with General Seely.[1] He spoke in most disparaging terms of our generals. Not one in a thousand, he said, had the brain power of the worst Cabinet Minister. I rather agree. He also saw that with proper arrangements and a more intelligent use of machine guns we could probably hold our bit of the line in France with about 250,000 men instead of the 1,200,000 who now hold it. He considered that the proposed offensive had no earthly chance of success in which I agree. He admitted, though, that it is just possible that Swinton's "Caterpillars" might make the difference. He laughed to scorn the Corps to which he is attached which is termed "the army of pursuit". I told him of a letter I had recently written to Sir William Robertson urging the following plan:—postponement of the offensive until August, when the "Caterpillars" are ready; meanwhile compel the Germans to keep their reserves in the west, instead of going east to smash the Russians, by making every preparation for a great offensive up to and including artillery preparation. After we had done this once or twice the Bosches would say "These fellows are not for it" and would go east. Then we would make our real attack with the "Caterpillars".

Next day Hankey recorded that Robertson had sent his letter on to Haig. At about the same time he wrote to General Henderson "suggesting the formation out of surplus aeroplanes suitable only for instructional purposes a corps of 'grasshoppers' to work with Swinton's 'Caterpillars' and attack heavy guns with bombs, flying at low altitudes and armoured".[2] The reader will recall that this use of the new element of air power had formed part of Hankey's original tactical scheme for breaking the deadlock on the western front.[3]

Here we may take temporary leave of the preparations for the Somme offensive in order to review other events. In April reports from Russia indicated that the munitions supply situation was becoming desperate, and on 28th Asquith discussed the matter with Lloyd George in Hankey's presence prior to a meeting of the War Committee. Calling Hankey over to join him Asquith said that he "had come to the conclusion that Lloyd George ought to go to Russia" rather than the French Minister of Munitions Albert Thomas, who was in London with a similar intention. According to Hankey Lloyd George then said "he wanted some officer thoroughly well up in the military situation to accompany him", and "looked meaningly" at him. He, however, had no desire to be involved in such a mission, so put on an air of obtuse

[1]See p. 116.   [2]Diary 29th April 1916.   [3] See p. 148.

innocence. Later that day Hankey heard from the War Office that Kitchener wanted to go to Russia. He at once told Asquith, who was "much amused"—probably because he remembered his earlier efforts to get Kitchener out of the War Office.[1] A few days later the War Committee discussed the matter. Hankey considered that Kitchener's proposal should be accepted, and did a little quiet lobbying to that effect. Accordingly when McKenna put the suggestion forward formally it was accepted. "K. likely to accept and will probably ask me [to accompany him]—but I shan't go" wrote Hankey in his diary.[2] Thus was initiated the mission which was to result in Kitchener's death; and Hankey's firm resolve not to be involved in it undoubtedly saved his life.

At the end of the War Committee meeting on 29th April Asquith told Hankey that Kut-el-Amara, in which General Townshend's army had been besieged since the previous December, had fallen—a tragedy which Hankey had in fact long foreseen to be inevitable. This disaster, coming so soon after the victory of the conscriptionists renewed his anger and depression over the incompetent conduct of our military affairs. "When will the people discover", he asked his diary rhetorically, "that we are not a military nation, that our only victories have been naval, economic and financial, and that on these we ought to concentrate our strength?"

After dinner at Downing Street next day Asquith began to talk about the vacant Chief Secretaryship for Ireland, since the replacement of Augustine Birrell,[3] who had resigned as a result of the Easter rebellion, had become an urgent matter. "After considering all candidates", wrote Hankey, who was present, "he offered it to Montagu. M. was obviously taken by surprise and disconcerted. He pointed out all the objections; his own Jewish race, his lack of physical courage and interest in the Irish race. He said he would only take it out of personal loyalty to the P.M. and if he absolutely insisted. He at once asked for Drummond or me as Under-Secretary; but the P.M. at once said he could not have me!"[4] In the end Asquith took on the job himself as a temporary measure. Though this certainly showed that he did not lack physical

[1]See p. 230.
[2]Diary 4th May 1916. Cab. 42/13, Minutes of War Committee meeting of same date.
[3]1850–1933. Politician (Lib.) and author. Chief Secretary to the Lord Lieutenant of Ireland 1907–16.
[4]Diary 1st May 1916.

courage, one may doubt whether it was wise for the Prime Minister to add to his heavy burdens, and in a task which took him away from London, at a very difficult time.[1] To underline the political dangers, it was at this very time that Hankey learnt about a new plot against Asquith. His close friend and future colleague Sir Mark Sykes[2] warned him that Leo Amery,[3] who was serving in the Intelligence Department of the War Office, was in constant touch with Milner, Carson and Geoffrey Robinson[4] editor of *The Times*; and that Amery was "the very soul of the Unionist War Committee—or rather of all its horrible intrigues against the government". Hankey "went straight to the Prime Minister and told him the whole thing, and suggested that he should ask Robertson to send Amery to Salonica or somewhere equally salubrious!"[5] Asquith would probably have been wise to heed this warning; but he was always reluctant to believe in, let alone act on rumours of political intrigues against himself.

On 9th May Hankey had a long and confidential talk with Lloyd George, and won his support over not starting the offensive in France before August, when the "Caterpillars" would be available. Lloyd George then told him that he was seriously thinking of leaving the government, because he felt he could do more good outside. "Parliament", he remarked, "is the only thing the government are afraid of",

[1] *Jenkins*, pp. 395–402 gives a full account of Asquith's efforts as Chief Secretary to settle the Irish question. Not until late July was H. E. Duke, a Unionist lawyer, appointed to take over the appointment.

[2] Soldier, traveller and politician (1879–1919). Served on missions to Balkan states, Russia and Mesopotamia in World War I. Advocate of Arab independence and signatory on behalf of Britain of the Sykes-Picot agreement of May 1916 regarding Russian, British and French spheres of influence on the break-up of the Ottoman Empire. As Assistant Secretary in the War Cabinet Secretariat 1916–19 Sykes won Hankey's affection as the caricaturist of the Secretariat. One of his drawings shows the four of them with downcast, modest eyes and demurely folded hands sitting in the secretary's gallery of the House of Commons behind the Speaker's chair and hearing themselves described as "a more self-sacrificing, honest, open-minded and noble body of men have not been seen in this or in any other age". Another shows Hankey himself equipped with symbols of all his varied accomplishments as Marine, Sailor and Soldier, initiator of the Tank, Supremo of the C.I.D. Secretariat etc. Adeline preserved all Sykes's caricatures in her scrap book.

[3] See p. 95.

[4] 1874–1944. Changed name to Dawson 1917. Editor of *The Times* 1912–19 and 1923–41.

[5] Diary 5th May 1916.

and decisions would always be quickly taken if Parliament insisted.[1] It is difficult, however, not to feel that Lloyd George's acute political perception told him that the First Coalition would not last much longer, and that his hour might come more quickly and more certainly if he worked from within the government rather than through Parliament. Hankey duly passed Lloyd George's ruminations on to Asquith that same evening.

Another matter that caused Hankey much work at this time concerned the constitution and functions of the Air Board under Curzon, which was about to take over the duties of the defunct Joint War Air Committee under Lord Derby.[2] On 4th May Hankey circulated to the War Committee a "Note" on the Terms of Reference for the new body[3]; but the Admiralty, which has been accused, not unreasonably, of having wrecked the Derby Committee, at once began to show similar tendencies towards the Curzon Board. They evidently did not appreciate that, although, like its predecessor, it was only an advisory body and lacked any executive authority, Curzon was a far more redoubtable antagonist than Derby. Next day Hankey saw Balfour, the First Lord, to try and persuade his department to co-operate effectively with the Air Board; but the only result was that "we wrangled a long time about the co-ordination of the Air Services, in regard to which the Admiralty are being very sticky".[4] None the less the Air Board was formed on 11th—and at once ran into the very troubles which Hankey had tried to forestall.[5] By no means the smallest of them arose from the character and methods of its chairman.

Diary 12th May 1916
... I have had much trouble with Lord Curzon to-day about this Air business, and he rings me up on the telephone half a dozen times a day. He has asked me to attend the first few meetings of the new Air Board to get them going. Thank goodness I shall not have much to do with it.[6] Curzon is an intolerable

[1]Diary 9th May 1916. The greater part of this entry is printed in *Supreme Command*, II, p. 555.
[2]See p. 251. [3]Cab. 42/13 of 4th May 1916. [4]Diary 5th May 1916.
[5]Cab. 37/147 of 11th May 1916. Apart from the President the Board was to consist of a naval and a military representative, who were to be members of the Board of Admiralty and Army Council respectively, one additional representative from each service, "a member of independent administrative experience" and a Parliamentary representative.
[6]This hope was entirely unfulfilled. Hankey became deeply involved, and finally had to take a big hand in drafting the War Committee's conclusions on the first report of

person to do business with—pompous, dictatorial and outrageously conceited. I have several times had to dig my toes in and refuse to draft things in a sense to which I knew the Admiralty could not agree. Curzon much amused me yesterday by saying . . . "But in official life we often have to work with people we don't like. Here am I sitting in the Cabinet with Lord Kitchener, with whom I had the biggest row a man ever had, and which I have neither forgotten nor forgiven". Really he is an intolerable person, pig-headed, pompous and vindictive too! Yet an able, strong man with it all . . .

Thus was initiated one of the most celebrated and protracted duels of all time, aptly described by Hankey as "the rapier [Balfour] versus the bludgeon [Curzon]".[1] It continued right to the fall of the First Coalition in the following December, and although the dialectics of the principal antagonists make extremely amusing reading we here are concerned only with Hankey's repeated but unsuccessful attempts to mediate between them and to find an acceptable compromise.[2] The debate revolved mainly around the placing of contracts for air frames and engines, of which the Admiralty had acquired more than what the War Office regarded as its fair share, and the participation by the Navy in what later came to be known as "strategic bombing" from shore airfields. Although, as we have often remarked, Hankey's outlook and standpoint were generally more sympathetic towards the navy than the army, in the great dispute over the future of the air services he took the wider view that what really mattered was the most effective use to which the new element of air power could be put. He regarded with strong distaste the Admiralty's selfish accumulation of equipment from which they could not extract the greatest possible value, and their insistent adherence to a function which plainly did not lie within their proper province.[3]

The Air Board had only been in existence a few days when Hankey wrote to tell Asquith, who was in Ireland, that it "would break down".[4] The Prime Minister replied, calmly as always, that he feared the Board

---

the Air Board, which he completed shortly before the fall of the First Coalition. See pp. 346–7.

[1] *Supreme Command*, II, p. 551.
[2] Cab. 37/142 of 14th Feb., 37/146 of 16th and 29th April and 37/147 of 6th May 1916 are the chief items in this dialectical contest.
[3] See *Supreme Command*, II, pp. 550–1.   [4] Diary, 15th May 1916.

"is a rickety infant which will have some difficulty in surviving the troubles of teething".[1]

Though Hankey could exert little direct influence on the War Office and G.H.Q. over the launching of the Somme offensive, and in his dealings with the War Committee he always had to move with extreme circumspection, he could at least make certain that the latter body received all the information from the departments to which it was plainly entitled, and so base its decisions on complete and accurate knowledge. Accordingly on 22nd May he had a long talk with Lloyd George, to whom he pointed out that the War Committee was being denied information which it was plainly entitled to receive.[2] Evidently Hankey convinced Lloyd George that the situation was thoroughly unsatisfactory, since next day he sent Asquith a memorandum telling him that, as the Minister of Munitions had asked to have "the supply of information to the War Committee" placed on the agenda for the meeting on 23rd, he had "anticipated" Asquith's approval for doing so. He then went on to state the constitutional position and authority of the War Committee. It was, he said, "the Commander-in-Chief in commission of all the forces and resources of the British Empire". Thus the Committee "and not the General Staff are responsible to Parliament, the country and the Empire for the conduct of the war". He submitted "that the information they [the War Committee] receive, both from the Admiralty and the War Office, is utterly inadequate for the proper discharge of their great responsibilities". This almost overt attack on the conduct of the Service Departments, and especially on the General Staff, was certainly strong stuff; but with typical thoroughness and insight into the implications of what he was putting on paper Hankey went on to substantiate his allegations regarding the with-holding of vital information by giving numerous examples. Thus reports from British military missions overseas and military attachés were not being sent to the War Committee; nor were "the vast number of Secret Intelligence reports". Equally information regarding the reinforcement of the B.E.F. in France and of the movement of troops to that front from Egypt was not being provided. "I believe", he wrote "that several Divisions are at present in process of being shipped over [to France], but no communication of the fact has been made to

[1]Asquith to Hankey from the Viceregal Lodge, Dublin, 16th May 1916. Holograph.
[2]Diary 22nd May 1916.

the War Committee". Much the same state of affairs prevailed in the Admiralty with regard to the result of recent operations, the sinking of enemy submarines and many other matters. Nor did the Ministry of Munitions escape censure, despite its Minister having raised the whole issue—at Hankey's instigation of course. Though it was, Hankey added, "important not to overwhelm the War Committee with too much information", the departments' "very large staffs ought to be able to produce an intelligent summary" of all the subjects he had outlined. He proposed that these should be presented "either weekly or monthly, whichever is considered the more convenient".[1] It is difficult not to conclude that what Hankey was really attacking in this paper was the enormous build-up of the army in France in preparation for the "great offensive", and that he still hoped to prevent the "orgy of slaughter" which he had foretold as its outcome.

While the launching of the offensive on the Somme hung in the balance Colonel House's efforts to bring the belligerents to the conference table took a new turn, and underlined yet again the divisions in the Cabinet.

Diary 24th May 1916
War Ctee. . . . in morning. Frightful row about a minute by the Army Council threatening to resign if the War Committee insisted on an inquiry into the peace question. At the beginning of the meeting all except the Cabinet members were turned out of the room for nearly an hour while the Cabinet members discussed Colonel House, who seems to have sent a communication to the effect that the time has come to avail ourselves of the offer by President Wilson referred to earlier[2] . . . McKenna, with whom I walked home to lunch, told me that they had not reached a decision, but that he, the P.M., Grey and Balfour had been in favour of accepting President Wilson's good offices, owing to the black financial outlook, while Bonar Law and Ll. George were averse . . . He [McKenna] thought there was every prospect of the proposal being accepted. Apparently Grey had submitted one draft telegram, but another was being prepared on lines proposed by Balfour.

That same day, probably as a result of the Wilson-House proposals Hankey discussed with Balfour the question of "Compulsory International Arbitration" in the post-war world; and next day he followed

[1]C.I.D. 501A. Cab. 42/14/12.
[2]This must refer to House's telegram to Grey of 19th May, which he followed up with his letter of 23rd May 1916. See *House*, II, pp. 286–88.

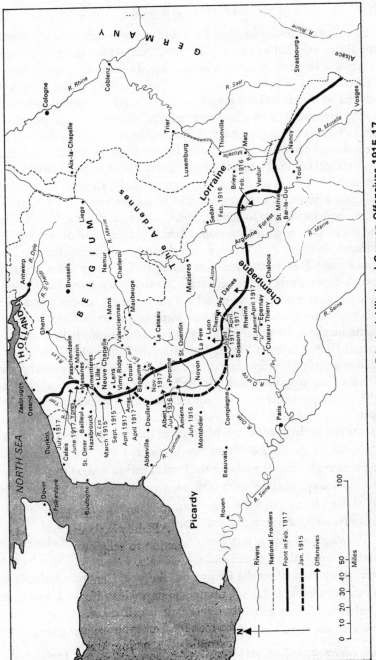

3 The Western Front showing Principal Allied and German Offensives 1915-17

up the conversation by sending Balfour a survey of the whole subject. Compulsory arbitration was, in his view, "dangerous to us, because it will create a sense of security which is wholly fictitious"; and he cited the Declarations of Paris and of London as examples of the difficulties produced by "international conventions". He felt no confidence at all in such agreements, because in time of war "the enemy will not abide by them". Hankey prophesied that the conflict then in progress would, for economic reasons, be followed by 25 years of peace, and that "international conventions will persuade the nation to go to sleep so far as its military preparations go". If, as was likely, another crisis arose "the United States as likely as not will be on the eve of a Presidential election and unwilling to lend a hand". Nor could the U.S.A. "be relied on to take part in European affairs". At the time of writing, he continued, Britain was "very strong"; and we should be able "to maintain ourselves at any requisite strength for many years without excessive expenditure on armaments". Assuredly we should and would reduce our armaments "if we could get adequate guarantees"; and such a policy was, he considered, "a more virile and more practical course" than the idealistic proposal for compulsory arbitration. Balfour merely endorsed Hankey's letter "bring this up at the office when I have time to dictate a reply".[1] A few days later Hankey recorded in his diary that he "had a long argument with Mr. Balfour about international arbitration"[2]; which probably accounts for Balfour never answering his letter.

Such were Hankey's initial reactions to the first proposals for an international body to enforce arbitration in the case of a threat to peace. His forecast of the failure of that whole concept was as accurate as his prophecies regarding its effect on the British nation and on the duration of peace—except that he over-estimated the latter by five years. He never shifted from that view regarding international organisations for the maintenance of peace. Indeed shortly after the outbreak of World War II, when he was a member of Chamberlain's War Cabinet, he reminded Lord Halifax, then Lord President of the Council, how he had "never believed in either the League or Collective Security. Indeed my criticism goes back as far as June 1916, in a commentary I wrote on Colonel House's first proposals for a League of Nations".[3]

At about the same time Hankey took the offensive over a speech by

[1] Balfour papers. B.M. Add. MSS. 49704, pp. 3–8. [2] Diary 27th May 1916.
[3] Hankey to Halifax 22nd Jan. 1940.

President Wilson advocating "Freedom of the Seas". He sent what he called "a very stiff minute" to Asquith on the subject, and a copy to Balfour pointing out that "if this was a condition of American intervention the American peace would be more dangerous to the British Empire than the German War". He also "primed" Archibald Hurd[1] of the *Daily Telegraph* "to take the line 'hands off our sea power' in respect of the President's speech". But his anxieties were soon somewhat eased by a telegram from Spring Rice, the British ambassador in Washington,[2] stating that Wilson's speech was "mere electioneering", and should not be treated as a serious statement of U.S. policy. In that assessment the ambassador's judgement proved faulty, since Freedom of the Seas became a cardinal point in Wilson's plans for the post-war settlement, and indeed figured prominently in his famous "Fourteen Points" of January 1918.

On the last day of May 1916 the Battle of Jutland took place in the North Sea. At 6.15 p.m. Hankey got a telephone call from the Admiralty that great events were in progress and at once went across there. He was shown into the First Lord's room, where he found Balfour, most unusually, "in a state of very great excitement". He then carried such news as had come in to Asquith, who was listening to a debate in the House of Commons. Hankey was "most impressed with the way he took it. He showed no sign or trace of anxiety or nervousness, but only delight at having brought them [the German fleet] to action".[3] But as more telegrams arrived giving the tale of British losses, and actually presenting too depressing a picture, Hankey's spirits plummeted. He called "the first trial of strength between the two fleets . . . the most bitter disappointment of this disappointing war". Not until 3rd June was he able to form a fairer picture of the outcome; and his final summary corresponded closely with the conclusion reached by the latest historian to study the battle—namely that although it was tactically inconclusive, "from the strategical point of view . . . the Grand Fleet was, beyond a shadow of doubt, the winner".[4] None the less the tactical indecisiveness of an encounter which the British public

[1]Later Sir Archibald Hurd (1869–1959). Journalist and naval historian. Served on editorial staff of *Daily Telegraph* 1899–1928. Joint editor of Brassey's Annual 1922–28. Author of official history of Merchant Navy in World War I and of many other books on 20th century naval affairs.
[2]See p. 185.
[3]Diary 31st May 1916.
[4]Diary 1st–3rd June 1916. See Marder, *Scapa Flow*, III, p. 205.

and the Royal Navy had confidently expected to produce another Trafalgar did nothing to restore the declining prestige of the First Coalition; and as the summer solstice of 1916 approached it was becoming increasingly doubtful whether Asquith could hold together his fissiparous team much longer, or whether public opinion would not soon force a change.

Chapter 10

The Dardanelles Commission.
The First Coalition under Pressure.
June-October 1916

THE fall of Kut-el-Amara resulted in heavy pressure to lay papers dealing with the disaster before Parliament; and when the government yielded to that pressure the House of Commons seized the opportunity to widen the issue by demanding that papers dealing with the Dardanelles campaign should also be laid. On 1st June Bonar Law, who was acting as Leader of the House, rashly conceded in principle the new demand. This was done without, as far as can be ascertained, any proper discussion of the matter in the War Committee or Cabinet. Certainly the Service Departments and Foreign Office were not consulted. The government's promise at once aroused Hankey's gravest misgivings, since publication of the Dardanelles papers was bound to reveal British policy, plans and intentions. On 3rd he discussed the matter with Balfour, who agreed that Hankey should urge the Prime Minister to retract. Two days later he accordingly sent Asquith a long memorandum setting out the likely consequences of the government's decision being allowed to stand.[1]

Diary 6th June 1916
When I arrived at the office I found Winston Churchill there again to read the War Committee proceedings on the Dardanelles. Shortly after, while he was still in the room, Masterton Smith rang me up to communicate the dreadful tragedy that the *Hampshire* had been mined or torpedoed and sunk with all hands including Lord Kitchener and his staff. I managed to control myself and gave Winston no hint—for all I knew the news might be secret and it might be wished to keep it quiet for a few hours . . . After the meeting [of the War Committee at 11.30] General Robertson had drawn me aside to speak

[1]Diary 3rd and 5th June 1916. Most of those days' entries are printed in *Supreme Command*, II, p. 518.

of K.'s successor . . . He was very anxious not to have Lloyd George, and rather inclined to Austen Chamberlain. I said he had better speak his mind to the P.M. and promised to try and secure an opportunity. Later in the afternoon I spoke to the P.M. about this and found that Robertson had already mentioned it to him. The P.M. said that there was much to commend Austen Chamberlain . . . In the evening I discussed with the P.M. the fact that Lord Montagu [of Beaulieu] had communicated to a parliamentary enquiry on the Air an extract from a C.I.D. report that ought not to have been in his possession, and obtained his instructions to write to Lord M.[1] He also returned my Memo. re publication of the Dardanelles papers, saying that he agreed with it, but that Parliamentary pressure was so great that he would have to publish something . . .

The foregoing diary entry is important for several reasons. In the first place Churchill's chance presence in Hankey's room when the news of the loss of the *Hampshire* was telephoned to him may have had unhappy long-term repercussions. According to Lawrence Burgis, who later became Hankey's Private Secretary, Churchill at once asked what the call had been about—probably because he saw that it had shaken Hankey. He replied "Oh, it was only a routine call". But Churchill of course quickly found out the truth; and, according to Burgis, the origins of the later troubles between Hankey and Churchill may be traced to the annoyance of the latter over the extreme discretion on this occasion shown by the former.[2] In defence of Hankey's reticence it should, however, be mentioned that Churchill was out of office at the time, and so was not entitled to receive secret information. Secondly Asquith's refusal to rescind Law's promise about publishing the Dardanelles papers shows how accurate was Lloyd George's view that only parliamentary pressure would force action on the government.[3] It is difficult not to feel that on this issue Asquith showed the same infirmity of purpose as became apparent in the long conscription debate.[4]

Coming so soon after the loss of many old friends in the battle of Jutland, including his former Commander of *Ramillies* days Horace

[1] This must have been either one of the papers of the Joint War Air Committee, of which Lord Montagu was an Independent Member, or one of the papers of the recently formed Air Board under Lord Curzon. See pp. 251 and 271. The J.W.A.C. papers are in Cab. 27/52. Another set is preserved in Lord Montagu's papers in the Military Archive Centre, King's College, London University, but Hankey's letter of reprimand has not survived in the latter collection.

[2] Burgis to the author 20th Sept. 1967.

[3] See p. 270. [4] See pp. 240–1 and 263–5.

Hood,[1] the death of Kitchener and of a number of more recent, and highly valued friends (such as O'Beirne, who had been with Hankey during the brief but enjoyable days in Italy just two months earlier) brought the effects of war very sharply home to him.

Hankey was at this time very occupied with preparing the agenda for another meeting with representatives of the French government, which was to take place in London. His spirits, and also those of all the politicians and service men around him, had recovered quickly from the depths of discouragement produced by Jutland and by Kitchener's death, since on 5th June the Russians under Brusilov launched a great offensive in Galicia and soon achieved astounding success. The Germans were forced to rush reinforcements eastwards, so relieving pressure on Verdun—as indeed the western Allies had hoped; the German plan for a counter-blow to the forthcoming British offensive on the Somme was upset; and Roumania was persuaded to enter the war on the Allied side—to her own rapid undoing.[2] Hankey was delighted that his policy of giving the Russians priority for the supply of munitions, though never carried out in full, appeared to have justified itself. But neither he nor anyone else realised how illusory their success would prove; or that the enormous losses finally suffered (a million men) undermined still further the shaky Russian government and military machine. The Brusilov offensive was to prove their last really effective effort, and its failure contributed greatly to the *débâcle* of 1917.[3]

In the early summer Hankey was again at cross purposes with Lloyd George—this time over the supply of munitions to Roumania. "If they [the French] are right to do so", he wrote, "we are surely wrong to refuse supplies . . . there is a great need for co-operation between the Allies on this matter".[4] That the proposal held little appeal to the Minister of Munitions suggests that he felt little confidence in the prospects of the latest Ally. Yet Lloyd George was still in favour of an Anglo-French offensive on the Salonika front, and on 8th June he protested that at the previous day's War Committee he "certainly never

[1]See p. 49.
[2]Roumania actually declared war on Germany and Austria on 27th August. She was quickly overwhelmed by General von Falkenhayn's lightning campaign, and Bucharest fell on 6th Dec. 1916.
[3]See *Liddell Hart*, pp. 298–301.
[4]Hankey to Lloyd George 1st May 1916. Lloyd George papers D/17/3/28.

understood we were committing ourselves to the view that we had 'a strong objection to any offensive operations from Salonika' . . . I could not therefore agree to the Minute in its present form".[1] In fact the offending minute represented the oft-repeated view of Robertson and the General Staff; and Hankey was obviously trying to preserve a fair balance between the War Office "westerners" and Lloyd George and his "easterners".

Diary 9th June 1916
Spent the whole day at the conference with the French. It was most interesting and dramatic. In the morning we only, so to speak, skirmished. In the afternoon Balfour, Curzon, Ll. G. and the P.M. all delivered speeches of considerable length and admirable logic. Ll. G.'s intervention was the most dramatic event of the day. Bonar Law told me that he had on the previous day expressed his intention of not taking part, and as a matter of fact he arrived more than an hour late. But when he spoke, he spoke as a convinced "Balkanist", but as strongly against an offensive [in France] at present. This was a crushing blow to Briand . . . The French were completely outpointed in argument but would not yield . . . Eventually it was arranged that we should give the French Ministers a summary of our views to take back with them. I remained behind with the P.M. and Grey to help draft it . . .

Yet the truth was that, neither Lloyd George's eloquence nor what Stamfordham called the British ministers' "firm front", had made the slightest impression on the War Office and the "Westerners", whose preparations for the "great offensive" were in fact already far advanced. And Hankey's carefully prepared memorandum setting out the British point of view was scrapped by Asquith because he felt that, as M. Briand and his colleagues had not been convinced by verbal argument, there was no hope of converting them by correspondence.[2] According to the account which Hankey sent to Esher, Joffre and Briand were satisfied with the outcome. "It was a very cordial meeting", he wrote, "though our people had to take a tough line. The gist of the conclusion was 'No offensive at present, but we are willing to reconsider this when the Salonica force is properly equipped' "—which Hankey expected "to coincide with the Greek Kalends".[3]

Stamfordham to Hankey. Buckingham Palace 10th June 1916. Holograph
Dear Hankey,
    The King greatly appreciated your promptness in letting him know the

[1]Lloyd George to Hankey 8th June 1916. Lloyd George papers D/17/3/37.
[2]Diary 10th June 1916. [3]Hankey to Esher 13th June 1916. Esher papers.

result of yesterday's conference, for he knows how very busy you are. H.M. is much pleased with the firm front which we presented to our friends across the Channel. H.M. will expect you at 5.45 to-day . . .

Yours very truly

Diary 10th June 1916
. . . I had to see the King to tell him about the Conference. He talked a good deal about Lord Kitchener, said he [Kitchener] had always tried to keep him [the King] posted with information, and asked me to try and fill his place to some extent in this respect. He said that Lord K. had often talked about the desire some of his colleagues in the Cabinet had that he should resign, but that he had told the King he would never do so unless the King wanted [it] (which he didn't). He also talked to me very fully about Lord K.'s successor and asked my views. I said Chamberlain first and Ll. George second. The King said Chamberlain was his own first string, but went into a most violent diatribe against Ll. George, as I thought he would. I kept trying to stand up for Ll. George and reminded the King of all he had done and how useful he is on the War Ctee., and of the dangerous political consequences if he "ratted"; but the King would hardly listen. We then gossiped about the recent naval battle and Haig's plans and the war generally, and it was 7.15 before I got away. . . .

Despite Hankey's preference for Chamberlain and the King's strong antipathy to Lloyd George on 24th Hankey heard from Bonham Carter that Lloyd George was to have the War Office; and on 5th July he learnt that Montagu was to take Lloyd George's place as Minister of Munitions.[1] Three days later Hankey wrote in his diary that the first visitors to seek Lloyd George out in his new department had been Northcliffe and Churchill—the latter "with a big box of papers". Hankey had long entertained serious misgivings about Lloyd George's close association with Northcliffe, whom he knew to be hostile to Asquith and the coalition government. Churchill, he considered, was acting only "to clear his own character" over the Dardanelles undertaking.[2] In both cases his interpretation of their motives was soon to be fully substantiated.

There now followed for Hankey a brief interlude in Scotland with Asquith, who wished to make a speech in his constituency of East Fife, and combine that purpose with a visit to warships which had been damaged at Jutland and were being repaired in Rosyth dockyard. They

[1]Diary 24th June and 5th July 1916. [2]Diary 8th July 1916.

stayed at Kilmaron Castle as guests of Sir James Low,[1] whom Hankey described as "a fine specimen of a self-made Scot". Hankey obviously enjoyed the brief return to naval society, including meeting his former captain R. G. Lowry; but it turned his ever-active mind to the need to extract the greatest possible value from the many lessons learnt at Jutland. On returning to London he at once stressed that point in conversation with Balfour,[2] who showed him "a rather pessimistic letter from Jellicoe about the excellence of German gunnery, German night fighting arrangements and searchlights, in all of which they seem to have been slightly superior to us". "Rather discouraging", commented Hankey, "but Jellicoe is always rather a pessimist".[3] It is thus plain that Hankey was one of the first to recognise the marked strain of pessimism in Jellicoe's character—though it is only fair to remark that his health was not at all good at that time.[4] Later on Lloyd George, Beaverbrook and Dr. Thomas Jones, who joined the Cabinet Office secretariat in December 1916,[5] all expressed opinions identical to Hankey's on this matter[6]; yet Jellicoe was appointed First Sea Lord in succession to Admiral Jackson in the following December.

On 24th June the great preliminary bombardments started on the Somme front, and Hankey, who was full of anxiety over what would happen when the infantry attacks followed, listened apprehensively to the thunder of the guns, which could be clearly heard at Highstead. That day he lunched with the Asquiths, and although he described the meal as taking place "en famille" they were soon comparing notes on Jellicoe's Jutland despatch, which was to be published. Asquith called it "the worst despatch I have ever read" and "everything a despatch ought not to be". Finally Hankey was commissioned to go across to the Admiralty and get the offending document amended. He saw Balfour, who sent for Admirals Jackson and Jellicoe, who happened to be in the building. As soon as Hankey saw that his criticisms had been accepted he took himself off to report the results to Asquith—"who

[1] 1849–1923. Managing Director of Lindsay Low Ltd. of Dundee.
[2] Diary 17th June 1916.   [3] *ibid.* 22nd June.
[4] See A. Temple Patterson (Ed.) *The Jellicoe Papers*, Vol. I (Navy Records Society, 1966), pp. 2–3 and *passim*.
[5] 1870–1955 Assistant and later Deputy Secretary to the War Cabinet and Cabinet 1916–30. Secretary of Pilgrim Trust 1930–45, then a Trustee and from 1952 Chairman.
[6] See *Supreme Command*, II, pp. 553–4; Lord Beaverbrook, *Men and Power* (Collins, 1956), pp. 155–6 and Thomas Jones, *Lloyd George* (O.U.P., 1951), p. 118.

was much amused". On his way out of the Admiralty Hankey called in to see Hall, the D.N.I., who, he recorded "agreed with me in every detail" about the despatch. "These extraordinary people at the Admiralty", he wrote, had never consulted Hall, though he "was the one person who could criticise it from the point of view of the enemy's Intelligence Department". Thus did Hankey's waning confidence in the Balfour-Jackson régime suffer a further decline.

Towards the end of June the Cabinet devoted almost its whole attention to Asquith's endeavours to resolve the Irish question—so much so that on 30th the War Committee did not get through its agenda; and when Hankey asked for a further meeting to be held as soon as possible Asquith refused. Yet all his efforts to achieve an Irish settlement were destroyed by the revolt of the "old Conservatives", and especially by Lord Lansdowne's speech of 11th July insisting that the exclusion of Ulster from a united Ireland must be permanent. Then the bitterness aroused in Ireland by the execution of fifteen leaders of the Easter rebellion after summary trials by courts martial was exacerbated by the Cabinet decision—taken with a rare unanimity—that Sir Roger Casement should be hanged.[1] Thus were sown the seeds of the long and murderous civil strife of the early 1920s.

On 1st July the successive waves of British infantry went "over the top" on the Somme, to be met by withering crossfire from the machine guns which had survived the prolonged bombardments. Because of the great strain which the German offensive at Verdun had thrown on the French army, the Somme battle finally became very largely a British responsibility. It very soon proved "both the glory and the grave of Kitchener's Army"[2]; and neither the Asquith nor the Hankey family escaped the loss of sons or brothers in the holocaust. On 2nd July, almost simultaneously with the opening of the battle, Adeline gave birth to a daughter; but the duty of telling her that it had been born dead, strangled apparently by its umbilical cord, fell to her husband. Though the blow hit them both hard Adeline made a good recovery; and Hankey returned to the office to bury his sorrow in his work.

Diary 3rd July 1916
War Ctee., for Cabinet members only, on finance question. Very strained relations between Ll. George and McKenna, but we reached an agreement.

[1] *Jenkins*, pp. 395–404 gives an admirable account of how Asquith's proposals for the settlement of the Irish question were frustrated.
[2] *Liddell Hart*, p. 303.

After the meeting I had some talk with Balfour and Ll. George about this offensive which, as I fully anticipated, appears to have almost completely failed, with very heavy losses. We had 23 Divisions and the Germans only 6 or 7[1]; we had about 750 big guns and an equal number of field guns. It always seemed to me to be utter folly. I cannot see a trace of any strategical conception in it. To deliver a frontal attack on an entrenched force provided with every possible defensive organisation violates every military principle ... Ll. George reminded me of my Memo. of Dec. 1914 where I pointed out that no increase in men would enable us to break the front in the west, and urged that victory was only to be obtained in the eastern theatre of operations.[2]

Three weeks later hard evidence enabled Hankey to assess the results of the Somme battle more accurately. Esher had written that he thought it "the beginning of the end"—which Hankey considered highly optimistic. In truth, he confided to his diary, the 120,000 casualties already suffered in three weeks exceeded the losses in the whole Dardanelles campaign of eight months. The offensive seemed to Hankey "to involve the maximum of effort and the minimum of result"; but he admitted that more had been accomplished than he had expected, and that if the "Caterpillars" were a success the yield might be even greater.[3] A few days later his view received strong support from a somewhat unexpected quarter. Churchill circulated a strongly worded memorandum about the futility of the huge sacrifice of life on the Somme. "We could have held the Germans on our front", he wrote, "just as well by threatening an offensive as by making one ... So long as an army possesses a strong offensive power it rivets its adversaries' attention. But when the kick is out of it ... the enemy's anxiety is relieved and he recovers his freedom of movement". But the comments on Asquith's copy of the paper show that it was very ill received in government circles.[4]

---

[1]Hankey's figure of 23 Divisions cannot have applied to Rawlinson's Fourth Army only, which was charged with the main attack between Maricourt and Serre, as it comprised only 18 Divisions. He must have included three Divisions of General Gough's Fifth Army, which were in the reserve, and two from Allenby's Third Army. Rawlinson's army was in fact faced by only six German Divisions. The British artillery concentrated on the Fourth Army front was, as Hankey stated, about 1,500 guns. See *Liddell Hart*, p. 249.
[2]This must refer to Hankey's "Boxing Day Memo.". See pp. 147–50.
[3]Diary 22nd July 1916.
[4]Churchill's memorandum was forwarded by Asquith by "F.S.", which may have

In early July Hankey devoted much time to the preparation of a reasoned statement against publication of papers relating to the Mesopotamia and Dardanelles campaigns. Though the principles involved were in general the same in both cases, we may here ignore the Mesopotamian enquiry, since Hankey had not been personally involved in that campaign—as he certainly was in the case of the Dardanelles undertaking. On 8th he circulated his views and recommendations in a long and at times strongly worded memorandum.[1] After recapitulating, as was his wont, the historical background to the demands which were being pressed on the government, and reporting that he had told all the departments concerned to prepare their own collections of papers, he went on to set out the objections to publication. The first, and greatest, was that the Foreign Office had notified him "that all diplomatic documents must be excluded", because they concerned Britain's allies and many neutral nations as well. Thus the whole "diplomatic background" to the campaign would be withheld from the enquiry. As to the Admiralty's papers, the secretariat had "recovered from Colonel Churchill a set of the papers he considers ought to be published"; but these included many private telegrams sent by him as First Lord. Churchill had also urged that the "Secretary's Notes" of the relevant War Council and Dardanelles Committee meetings should be published—a proposal which Hankey viewed with the strongest disfavour. He then went on to outline the sort of personal problems which were bound to arise if the papers were published, and reproduced a letter from Lord Fisher to Asquith[2] in which the former First Sea Lord claimed that incidents which had occurred but were not recorded in the Secretary's Notes or anywhere else—such as his protests at Dardanelles Committee meetings—should be included in the documents to be published. This would obviously breach still more widely the principle of secrecy which had long governed the proceedings of what were in effect Cabinet Committees. Other points were that our Intelligence sources in the Middle East were bound to be compromised to some extent, and that much valuable information would be presented to the enemy without his making the slightest effort to collect it. To the

stood for "Financial Secretary". This was T. McKinnon Wood (1855–1927), who was also Chancellor of the Duchy of Lancaster in the First Coalition. The memorandum is heavily sidelined with question marks and ejaculations such as "Rubbish" —probably in Bonham Carter's hand. Asquith papers, box 129, folios 15–17.
[1]Cab. 42/16/4 of 8th July 1916.   [2]Dated 2nd June 1916.

foregoing masterly summary of all the objections to publication Hankey appended a minute by Robertson, the C.I.G.S., which fully supported his own views.

Three days later Hankey believed he had won, and expressed his profound relief in his diary. On 12th July he therefore briefed Asquith with a statement declining the appointment of Select Committees to investigate the two campaigns—in case such a demand was put forward as an alternative to the "laying of papers" before the House.[1] But Hankey's relief was soon severely shaken by the realisation that Asquith was again wavering; for two days later the Prime Minister "tried to suggest there was no harm in publishing"—a view which Hankey "vigorously opposed".[2]

Among those most concerned over publication of the Gallipoli papers was, of course, General Sir Ian Hamilton. On 13th he wrote to Hankey that "Callwell has sent me back my documents and writes to tell me it has been decided to publish no Gallipoli papers at present. So be it! . . . If I am neither to be proved guilty nor to be cleared then I should not in the mean time be punished". He therefore solicited the help of Hankey, whom he regarded "personally as a friend" to whom he could "open his heart", in obtaining a new appointment. Hankey sent the letter on to Asquith saying that he personally thought Hamilton "has been rather hardly used, and that some job should be found for him if possible"[3]; but his appeal bore no fruit, and Hamilton was never employed again.

On 18th Asquith, perhaps fortified by Hankey's strong objections, told the House that the Dardanelles papers would not be published.[4] This resulted in his being "sniped [at] a good deal from all sides of the House", which produced an outburst in Hankey's diary about the "miserable crew . . . all out for some personal end, to whitewash themselves (like Churchill), to get some general's head on a charger (like Aubrey Herbert[5] . . .) or to blackmail the Govt. I see no sign of a

---

[1] Asquith papers, box 128, folio 85.   [2] Diary 14th July 1916.

[3] Hamilton to Hankey 13th July and Hankey to Asquith 14th July 1916. Asquith papers, Vol. 17, No. 25.

[4] Parl. Deb., Commons, Vol. LXXXIV, Cols. 850–60.

[5] Aubrey N. H. M. Herbert (1880–1923). Politician (U.), diplomat and traveller in Near and Middle East. Served in Gallipoli, Mesopotamia, France and Italy in World War I. According to Hankey Aubrey Herbert "wanted Sir Beauchamp Duff's head" at this time. General Duff (1855–1918) was C-in-C, India, 1913–16

sincere desire to help the war . . .".[1] Next day Asquith was declaring that he would also resist the proposal for Select Committees, and he instructed Hankey to collect precedents in support of such action—a demand which Hankey had foreseen, and had already delegated to the staff of the C.I.D.'s Historical Section. He soon had "a very fine case full of apt quotations from speeches by Lord Porchester (1810), Gladstone and Palmerston", and from the published works of authorities on parliamentary procedure. Then, on 20th, he heard that the enquiries were, after all, to be granted—a decision which he stigmatised as "sheer cowardice" and attributed mainly to Bonar Law.[2] It is not surprising that this *volte face* should have shaken very seriously Hankey's faith in Asquith. Indeed in the calmness of retrospect he recalled that the effect "in the great departments of State was staggering", and "that the Coalition never recovered from its decision".[3]

Despite Hankey's intense preoccupation with the issue whether the two enquiries should take place he found time to write a letter of sympathy to Haldane over the renewal of "mischievous and ungenerous" attacks in the Press on his former friend and supporter. He assured Haldane that if after the war an opportunity arose "to show a little of what the country owes to you" he would be the first to come forward to do so.[4] Loyalty to old friends who had fallen on hard times was always one of the most constant and attractive traits in Hankey's character.

At about the same time he sent Esher his views on the correct strategy to adopt, in the light of the small results achieved by the offensive in the west and the optimism aroused by the Russian success in the east—soon to be proved transitory.

Hankey to Esher. 2 Whitehall Gardens, 17th July 1916. Holograph[5]
Secret and Personal
. . . Our military authorities say that the only way to win the war is to beat the Germans in the west, when all the outlyers—Colonies, Turks, Austrians etc. will collapse. I agree in principle. But supposing you can't beat the

---

and Herbert's animus towards him almost certainly arose out of his experiences in the Mesopotamia campaign.
[1]Diary 18th July 1916.
[2]Parts of the diary entries for 11th, 18th, 19th and 20th July 1916 are printed in *Supreme Command*, II, pp. 520–2.
[3]*ibid.*, pp. 518–25.
[4]Hankey to Haldane, 13th July 1916. Haldane papers. [5] Esher papers.

Germans, what then? Surely in this latter event, instead of breaking your strength in these frightful frontal attacks, which violate every military principle, it is better to beat the enemy piece-meal, eating up first his present colonies (as we have done), then his future colony (Turkey), then his Allies (Bulgaria and Austria), until at last we have to deal with Germany only . . .

These remarks of course have no reference to this year's campaign. We are absolutely committed to the western offensive, and I should be the last person to wish to diminish our effort. It is Robertson's policy, and Robertson is the best man we have got. Consequently I have backed him for all I am worth—not because I thought his strategy the best possible, but because I would sooner see an inferior plan carried out thoroughly, as he will carry it out, than a better plan bungled, as for example the Dardanelles plan was bungled.

But as regards the future my remarks have some bearing. Supposing the summer's fighting shows (as it may show) that the policy of offensives in the west is costly out of all proportion to its success, then I think we should adopt some such policy as the following:—

1. Sufficient strength in the west to ensure safety, and to enable us to keep up an intense artillery activity; gradual advances on the "Verdun principle.[1] Personally I think these advances should be in the Belgian coast sector.
2. Our main efforts to be concentrated on the thorough and complete equipment of the Russian army . . .
3. The Russians to be encouraged to complete the process of knocking out Austria . . .
4. An effort to be made to wipe out Turkey. This must be accomplished mainly by the Russians, but we must . . . adopt an offensive policy in Syria from Egypt.

Of course it may not come to this. The western offensive may succeed completely this year . . . so as to justify its resumption on the same lines next summer, in which case I would throw to the winds the views I have tentatively expressed. But this is the time for looking all round the future—and as you know my work has always been concerned more with the future than with past or present . . .

Esher, who had always favoured the offensive in the west, apparently replied in very optimistic vein about its outcome; since in his next letter Hankey accused him of being "mercurial", and suggested that he had been too much influenced by his "French friends". However he agreed with Esher "that Haig and Robertson have been quite splendid".[2]

[1] By this Hankey meant the small counter-offensives by which General Mangin had recently regained most of the ground won at such high cost by the Germans at Verdun. See p. 307.
[2] Hankey to Esher 20th July 1916. Esher papers.

The explanation for Hankey's expression of that surprising opinion, which he was very soon to modify drastically, probably lies in the fact that he knew that Esher was on intimate and cordial terms with Haig, and was not prepared to risk criticism of the military hierarchy reaching the General's ears.

To Lady Hankey. United Service Club. 20th July 1916.
. . . The damned fools have decided in their weakness to grant two inquiries —one into the Dardanelles and the other into the Mesopotamian campaigns. "Whom the gods wish to destroy they first make mad".[1] It fills me with horror! I shall probably be tortured in the witness box for weeks; How am I to avoid slaughtering the reputations of the P.M., K., Winston, Jackie and others who have been my friends I can't conceive. Neither can I see how I am to find the time, if I am to devote my energies to the war. . . . Winston mentioned me by name in the House to-day. This is the beginning!

Before Hankey had to divert his energies chiefly to preparing the papers for the Dardanelles Commission, which he has described as "one of the most dreary tasks that has ever fallen to my lot",[2] he was at least able to enjoy a brief but pleasant interlude at Thetford in Norfolk where 27 of Swinton's "Caterpillars" showed their paces before a very distinguished company. The success of their "attack" on a "prepared battlefield" seemed to augur well for their first appearance on a real one. But, unfortunately, the two circumstances were very different; and many of the requirements specified by Swinton and others were disregarded by the Generals in France. None the less a few days after the Thetford trials Hankey's hopes were raised by Robertson telling him that Haig had agreed not to use the Caterpillars "until a large number were available, except in case of great need".[3] This was a point Hankey had repeatedly stressed—that the great benefits of tactical surprise should not be thrown away by premature use of small numbers of tanks.

On returning from Thetford Hankey was alarmed by a suggestion from Lloyd George that he should "speak for the War Council" at the Dardanelles enquiry. Having no wish to shoulder such an embarrassing responsibility he reminded Lloyd George of the part he had played in

---

[1] Hankey here slightly misquotes the Latin version of a Greek maxim, based probably on a Euripides fragment though Plutarch has preserved the adage as a fragment of Aeschylus. "*Quem deus vult perdere, prius dementat*"—"Whom God would destroy, he first makes mad".
[2] *Supreme Command*, II, p. 523. [3] Diary, 1st August 1916.

the undertaking, and asked him "how he would like me to say it all at the Committee". The mere possibility of this involvement gave Hankey a sleepless night, but by morning he had thought of a possible solution —that he might "limit himself to handing in the Minutes . . . and make the Committee call each Minister to defend his own action". Though this would have been a reasonable, and self-protective compromise Hankey soon discarded it in favour of offering to present the Government's case himself—an offer which Asquith accepted with alacrity.[1] It is difficult not to feel that Hankey's action was inspired chiefly by his deep affection for and sense of loyalty towards Asquith—which had already survived so many blows.

Day after day, from late July to late September, when Hankey actually appeared before the Dardanelles Commission to act, in effect, as defending Counsel for the government, he spent a large part of his time working on the mass of papers received from the departments, as well as on those accumulated in his own office about the Gallipoli operation. He jotted down in his diary each day how long he had spent in this way, and by mid-October he had achieved a cumulative total of 178 hours. After mid-October the record he kept is less regular; but it is plain that the enquiry cost him some 200 hours of labour—the equivalent of nearly three weeks' work at 10 hours a day! Small wonder that he regarded the whole inquisition with extreme repugnance—the more so since he knew very early on that the Australian government, which might have regarded itself as deeply involved, fully shared his view and had telegraphed to their High Commissioner in London, Andrew Fisher,[2] that he was only to appear before the enquiry "as a private individual", and was not to "sit as Commonwealth representative".[3] This information was, according to Hankey, suppressed by the "Imperialist papers" and only appeared in the "radical" Press; but the Australian government soon changed its mind, since Fisher, and also his New Zealand colleague Sir Thomas Mackenzie,[4] became full members of the Dardanelles Commission.

---

[1] *ibid.* 24th and 26th July 1916. See *Supreme Command*, II, pp. 522–3.

[2] 1862–1928. Australian politician (Lab.). Prime Minister of Australia 1908–9, 1910–13 and 1914–15. High Commissioner in England 1916–21.

[3] Diary 29th July 1916. See *Supreme Command*, II, pp. 524–5.

[4] 1854–1930. New Zealand politician (Lib.) Prime Minister 1912. High Commissioner in England 1912–20. Represented New Zealand at Paris Peace Conference 1919.

Nor was the distaste with which Hankey regarded the enquiries peculiar to himself. On 3rd August Esher wrote from Paris "I have just got back, after a week at the Front. I am shocked to hear that your time is going to be absorbed by the Gallipoli Committee—if so, it is a perfect scandal that your attention should be taken off vital things at the very crisis of the war, merely for the purpose of satisfying the curiosity and vanity of Members of the House of Commons . . ."[1]

Next day an interview Hankey had with Grey revealed that he too was "very disgusted at the weakness of the Govt. in granting the inquiry . . .", and agreed "that the Govt. ought to have resigned rather than give in to it". That same day Hankey "ghosted" a letter for his old chief Sir Charles Ottley to send to *The Times* in protest at the waste of time and effort[2]; but that august journal, after keeping the letter for about a fortnight, refused to publish it unless it was toned down considerably.[3]

Meanwhile the weakening of Asquith's personal position was becoming more pronounced—exactly as Hankey had foretold. In the early hours of 2nd August he received a "frantic letter" from Margot Asquith on the subject—to which he replied very firmly that "the Govt. couldn't go on as at present, that they ought to demand a vote of confidence and, if defeated, go to the country and say they couldn't fight the Germans if they had to spend all their energy in fighting their critics." Though well aware that Margot would not like it he added that "as the P.M. had made Lloyd George Secretary of State for War, he must be consistent in his policy, flatter Ll. G. and play on his vanity; and above all send for and consult him on everything".[4] Next day Hankey received at second hand a report that at a dinner at which Lloyd George and Churchill had been present the former had declared "we must get rid of the old man". Hankey's only comment was the expletive "Blackguard!" None the less Lloyd George's remark was a straw which showed which way the political wind was blowing.

Nor was the actual composition of the Dardanelles Commission easily decided. On 25th July Bonar Law wrote on Asquith's behalf to Milner inviting him "to be Chairman of the Committee appointed to examine the Dardanelles operations". The other members were, he

[1]Esher, *Journals*, IV, pp. 43–4. Original, in holograph, in Hankey papers.
[2]Diary 4th August 1916.
[3]*ibid.* 13th Sept. 1916. The letter in question was never published.
[4]Diary 2nd August 1916.

said, to be the Australian and New Zealand High Commissioners in
London (Andrew Fisher and Sir Thomas Mackenzie) and members of
Parliament drawn from each party.[1] But Milner declined the somewhat
dubious honour, and the chairmanship finally fell to Lord Cromer.[2]
The two enquiries were set up by the "Special Commissions (Dardanelles and Mesopotamia) Act of 1916", which gave the commissioners
powers to compel the production of documents and to take evidence
on oath in public or in private.[3]

As soon as the government's decision became known Hankey was
flooded with letters from or visits by the principal witnesses seeking his
advice on those aspects which particularly concerned themselves. Thus
on 9th August Lord Fisher took up most of his day and "rehearsed to
me the whole of the evidence he proposes to give"; and he was soon
followed by Churchill, Grey, Balfour, Haldane and others.[4] On 11th
Grimwood Mears, the commission's secretary, called to deliver the
unwelcome news that Lord Cromer wanted to call Hankey as the first
witness—and in six days' time. This caused Hankey to give Mears "a
bit of my mind", since the piecing together of his evidence and the
collection of the necessary documents could not possibly be completed
in so short a period.[5] That same day Hankey sent to Asquith, Grey,
Lloyd George and Balfour, the only members of the War Committee
who had also been members of the War Council of 1914–15, a set of the
"Secretary's Notes" of the Council's meetings up to mid-May 1915,
various memoranda and papers connected with the first phase of the
Dardanelles operation, and the proof of a paper he had written "setting
forth the reasons for which the various decisions in regard to the naval

[1]Bonar Law to Milner 25th July 1916. Milner papers, Vol. 142.

[2]The other members of the Dardanelles Commission were: Field-Marshal Lord
Nicholson (1845–1918), who had been C.I.G.S. 1908–12, and Admiral of the Fleet
Sir William May (1849–1930), C-in-C, Home Fleet 1909–11, representing the
fighting services. Andrew Fisher and Sir Thomas Mackenzie (see p. 292) represent-
ing Australia and New Zealand respectively. Sir William Pickford (1848–1923), 1st
Baron Pickford 1918. Sir Frederick Cawley (1850–1937), M.P. (Lib.). 1st Baron
Cawley 1918. Captain Stephen L. Gwynn, M.P. (Irish Nationalist) (1864–1950).
James A. Clyde, M.P. (U.) (1863–1944), later Lord Clyde. Walter F. Roch,
M.P. (Lib.) (1880–1965). The Secretary was E. Grimwood Mears, Kt. 1917 (1869–
1963).

[3]6 and 7 Geo. 5. c.34. The Act received Royal Assent on 17th Aug. 1916. See also
Cab. 19/33.

[4]Diary 9th and 14th August 1916. [5]ibid. 11th August 1916.

attack were taken". He also asked the Ministers a number of very cogent questions which required immediate answers now that "the Bill has passed all stages short of Royal Assent". The most important of these was whether "a general case for the Government and War Council of 1914–15" was "to be presented to the Commission"; and if so by whom? Though Hankey could not keep out of this admirable exegesis a note of complaint about "the great strain" which the demands of the enquiry had placed on his small office he left the Ministers in no doubt at all that he would see the matter—and themselves—through.[1] Four days later he attended a meeting of the same four Ministers at which it was decided that he was "to give a complete exposition of the Government's case", and that he could offer the Commission "any Memoranda prepared for the War Council"; but he was not to produce the minutes of that body's meetings unless asked to do so.[2] This was at least a clear, if by no means a simple brief for the government's defending counsel.

While the preparation of the documents and evidence for the Commission was in progress Asquith insisted on Hankey accompanying him and other Ministers to Calais for another conference with the French leaders. The agenda was entirely concerned with the financing of the war, and after a good deal of haggling "like a lot of old Jews in the Smyrna bazaars" a credit of £25 millions a month was promised to the French until mid-March 1917 in return for £50 millions in gold.[3] The British party was back in London again in the early hours of 25th August.

That day Hankey learnt from Balfour that the telegraphic channel by which the Wilhelmstrasse communicated with the German embassy in Washington was through the Swedish Foreign Office, which forwarded the cables sometimes through Russia and sometimes through England. As Admiral Hall's famous Room 40 had already broken the German diplomatic cipher, this enabled the British government to keep itself completely informed with regard to German policy vis à vis the U.S.A. Thus we knew that Bernstorff,[4] the German ambassador in Washington, had been given the plainest warning that unless unrestricted submarine warfare, which had been renewed on 1st April 1916, was stopped the U.S.A. would inevitably be drawn into the war; also that Bernstorff had

[1]Memo. of 11th August 1916. Asquith papers, box 129, folios 58–61; also box 30, folio 192 A–D.
[2]Diary 15th August 1916. [3]ibid. 24th August 1916. [4]See p. 157.

been instructed to cultivate friendly relations with President Wilson in case his intervention on Germany's behalf was needed.[1] Balfour also told Hankey that Colonel House was coming over again in October, presumably to renew his overtures for a compromise peace; but in fact that visit did not take place—because House could not leave the U.S.A. at the time of the Presidential campaign which ended with Wilson's re-election, though only by a very narrow majority.

By the beginning of September Hankey had completed his "Notes for Evidence" to be given before the Dardanelles Commission. These twenty pages of print were a masterly summary of the whole story of the origins and execution of the purely naval attack, and of the despatch of the expeditionary force[2]; but as we have already followed those events in some detail there is no need to recapitulate them here. Among all the Ministers and service men whom Hankey had consulted in compiling this document Lloyd George was the only one to express dissatisfaction.

Diary 4th September 1916
Saw Ll. G. at 11 a.m. He was in a great fuss about my Dardanelles evidence —in a regular stew indeed—as he thought I had not done justice to him. The fact is he is funking the inquiry and trying to wriggle out of his responsibility. As a matter of fact I had put his point of view, but had not associated it with his name, as I thought his attitude was not a very nice one. He had allowed the troops to be sent to Lemnos, hoping always to dish the whole thing and get them for Salonika. Still, after hearing his point of view, I added a few deft touches, which satisfied him, so we parted good friends . . . After lunch I saw the P.M. who was positively enthusiastic about the Dardanelles paper, and said it had made him a violent Dardanellian . . .

The whole immense dossier which Hankey had so laboriously compiled was actually sent to Mears on 6th September. The enclosures included many documents we have already encountered, such as the pre-war deliberations of the C.I.D. on the prospects for an attack on the Gallipoli peninsula, through Hankey's famous "Boxing Day Memorandum" of 1914 on possible ways of breaking the deadlock in the west, to

[1] Diary 25th August 1916. The German government again stopped unrestricted submarine warfare on 24th April, after the sinking of the French passenger steamer *Sussex* had aroused vigorous American protests.
[2] Cab. 19/29. Asquith Papers, Vol. 30, contains drafts of Hankey's evidence and other papers relating to the Dardanelles Commission.

the reports of his visit to the Dardanelles in August 1915 and the recommendations that arose out of that visit.[1]

There now followed an interlude, during which no doubt Lord Cromer and his colleagues were digesting the substantial meal placed before them. On 5th September Asquith, accompanied only by Hankey and Bonham Carter, set off to visit G.H.Q. in France and make a short tour of the Somme battlefields. As always when Asquith got away from the cares of office Hankey found him "very cheery and informal". Hankey seized the opportunity to press on senior army officers his view that the much cut up Somme battlefield was not the right place to spring the surprise of the "Caterpillars"[2]; but he found Generals Kiggell and Butler "not very receptive to his ideas".[3] "Before the tanks were used on the Somme", he wrote many years later, "I visited Haig's G.H.Q. with Asquith. He did his best with Haig and Murray and I with Butler . . . to stop them from putting in the tanks in the pot-holes and debris of the Somme battlefield, and to open up a new front. We made an impression, but failed to persuade them to alter their plans."[4]

On this occasion, as on his earlier visits to the fighting fronts, Hankey made notes regarding the principal characters he encountered. Thus Allenby,[5] commander of the Third Army, he described as "rather a stupid man" and Plumer of the Second Army as "not very impressive"[6]—both of which judgements he later amended substantially. On the other hand he was "immensely impressed" by the "broad grasp, energy, fitness and capacity" of his old friend Birdwood,

[1]The covering letter is C.I.D. 623 of 6th Sept. 1916 and the enclosures included Cabinet Papers G2, G5, G6, G7, G9, G10, G19, G22 and G29, most of which have been encountered earlier (see Chapters V to VII). The student who wishes to study the evidence offered to the Dardanelles Commission in detail will find all the documents in Cab. 19/29.
[2]*Supreme Command*, II, pp. 512–13.
[3]See p. 238 regarding General Kiggell. Lieut.-General Sir Richard Butler (1870–1935) was Deputy Chief of General Staff, Western Front 1916–18.
[4]Hankey to Liddell Hart, 3rd April 1948. Holograph. Liddell Hart papers.
[5]1861–1936. 1st Viscount Allenby 1919. Commanded Third Army, B.E.F. 1915–17. As C-in-C, Egyptian Expeditionary Force 1917–19 conducted final campaign against Turkey. High Commissioner for Egypt 1919–25. Field-Marshal 1919.
[6]1857–1932. 1st Viscount Plumer 1929. Commanded Second Army B.E.F. 1915–17 and 1918. G.O.C. Italian Expeditionary Force 1917–18 and Army of Rhine 1918–19. Field-Marshal 1919. Governor and C-in-C, Malta 1919–24. High Commissioner for Palestine 1925–28.

whom he regarded as "the most fit and competent man out here", and his Anzac Corps as "the finest in the world". But he admitted that "Haig and most of the generals out here crab him"—which he regarded as "sheer jealousy", aroused by the fact that Birdwood was not a member of "the Aldershot ring". On the way home Asquith got hold of Hankey's "trashy novel", and after jeering at such a choice of reading matter, became so absorbed in it that he "put it in his bag to finish it". Hankey therefore passed the time setting down his impressions of the Somme battle.

Diary 9th September 1916
. . . On the whole I think our people have an exaggerated opinion of our superiority over the enemy. The Germans are undoubtedly still very strong. They dig better than our men . . . and consequently their losses are probably far less. The prisoners, of whom I saw hundreds on the roads, are fine, well set-up, intelligent looking men . . . The German artillery fire on the Somme is very heavy, though probably not as heavy as ours, and our losses are considerable. I believe that Haig's tactics are quite wrong. It is no good hammering away at the Somme, where the enemy has accumulated vast numbers of men and guns to resist us. No war was ever won by such methods. He ought to open up a new front as a surprise, and I understand that he has alternative attacking positions both in [? for] the Third and Second armies, but does not intend to use them. The "Caterpillars" would provide the means for such a surprise . . . I do not think we shall see a decisive British success in the west this autumn. The "Caterpillars" are the only chance, and they are being mishandled . . .

In fact the first use of the tanks took place on 15th—exactly a week after Hankey was on the Somme. Only 60 were available, and more than half of them never reached the starting point. Furthermore their crews had not been fully trained. In "the shell-mangled chaos" of the Somme they were thrown away for the price of a minor tactical success —the capture of the village of Flers.[1] Small wonder that Hankey and Swinton were bitter about the folly and conservatism which had in a few hours undone all the farsighted thinking and technical inventiveness devoted to the new development over nearly two years. Perhaps it was fortunate for Hankey's peace of mind that he did not appreciate the full extent of the tragedy until Swinton was sent home in the following month; and he may have derived some comfort when, at a War Committee meeting, Grey said that Hankey's name ought

[1] See *Liddell Hart*, pp. 328–30 and 336–40.

to be mentioned when the first employment of the tanks was announced.

Hankey appeared twice to give evidence before the Dardanelles Commission—at the second and fourth sessions on 19th and 27th September. Though it would be tedious here to try and summarise his evidence, on the first occasion he was asked no less than 500 questions and on the second 164; and many of them were so long and complicated that no simple answer was possible. The transcript of the two days' proceedings covers 35 pages of closely printed double-column foolscap size pages.[1] Hankey showed considerable forensic skill in dealing with leading questions, some of which showed definite hostility towards the actions of the government and of individual Ministers such as Churchill and Kitchener. To protect them, or at least leave those who were still alive to conduct their own defence without the tribunal having been previously prejudiced, Hankey was always very cautious in his answers —especially in dealing with Lord Nicholson who, as Hankey well knew from his pre-war association with him as C.I.G.S.,[2] had always been strongly opposed to "warfare on the littoral".

Diary 19th September 1916
Spent whole day under examination by the Dardanelles Commission . . . Most searching cross-examination. I think I acquitted myself well, but they unbared all the weak points! By instructions from the Prime Minister I had to refuse the Secretary's Notes of War Council meetings. They talked big about their powers, and were apparently discussing whether in the event of continued refusal, they should send someone to the Tower—though whether it was to be the Prime Minister, the War Ctee, the Cabinet or me I don't know![3]

Hankey's satisfaction about his first appearance before the Commission received quick confirmation through a letter from Mears telling him that the question of making the Secretary's Notes available "can stand over for a day or two", and that Cromer had asked him to tell Hankey "how admirably you gave your evidence. There is no division of opinion among the Commissioners on that point".[4]

On 20th Hankey wrote privately to Asquith, who had not been present at that day's War Committee meeting, that after an hour's

[1]Cab. 19/33. [2]See pp. 102-3.
[3]These remarks obviously refer to Questions 164-171 asked by Lord Cromer and Sir William Pickford about the "Secretary's Notes". Cab. 19/33.
[4]Mears to Hankey 21st Sept. 1916.

discussion the Committee had failed to reach a decision on the vexed question of whether the Secretary's Notes should be sent to the Dardanelles Commission.[1] He recapitulated what he had said on the subject to the Commission, and told Asquith that Bonar Law and Lord Robert Cecil,[2] "considered that a very difficult Parliamentary situation would arise if they [i.e. the Notes] were refused". Lloyd George had, to some extent, gone along with those two Ministers. On the other hand Curzon and the rest of the War Committee held "that it would be absolutely wrong to give these notes", and "contrary to the whole system of collective Cabinet responsibility". Hankey went on to say that he had therefore suggested a *via media*, namely that two members of the Commission should be allowed to inspect the notes; but that had not satisfied Law and Cecil, and the conclusion had been that the matter could not be settled in Asquith's absence. About his own recently given evidence he ruefully admitted that he was "unaccustomed to cross-examination", and that he was therefore "anxious lest I may have said anything compromising".[3] On 25th the War Committee again discussed the question of the notes, this time with Asquith present. Agreement was finally reached that they should be shown to the Chairman of the Commission only, a compromise which Lord Cromer accepted.[4]

In between his two appearances before the Commission Hankey had to go through Churchill's evidence with him, coach Grey on the same subject, and correct the proofs of the transcript of his own first day's evidence; and, to make matters worse he was laid up in bed one day "with a terrific cold". "First day I have been laid up since the beginning of the war" was his resentful comment.[5]

At this time more evidence came to Hankey about the trouble which was brewing between Robertson and Lloyd George. The C.I.G.S. told him "that Lloyd George had made the worst possible impression on his recent visit to France". According to Robertson he had spent most of his time with the French, and had "asked General Foch's opinion of

[1] Secretary's Notes of 115th Meeting of War Committee. Cab. 42/20/6.

[2] 1864–1958. Viscount Cecil of Chelwood 1923. Minister of Blockade 1916–18; Lord Privy Seal 1923–4 and Chancellor of Duchy of Lancaster with special responsibility for League of Nations affairs 1924–27.

[3] Hankey to Asquith 20th Sept. 1916. Asquith papers, Vol. 30, folios 202 A–D.

[4] Secretary's Notes of 116th Meeting of War Committee. Cab. 42/20/8.

[5] Diary 22nd Sept. 1916.

the English Generals, whom he himself criticised severely". Foch had "promptly telephoned the whole thing to Haig and to Joffre", with the result that when Lloyd George had asked to see Joffre the latter refused a meeting unless Haig was present.[1] Obviously at this stage Lloyd George's devious methods caused the British and French military leaders to close their ranks. The existence of the intrigue against Robertson was confirmed next day when Asquith showed Hankey a letter from Lloyd George proposing that Robertson should be sent to Russia. Hankey's reply was "that this was merely a ruse of Ll. G.'s to get Robertson out of the way and push his Salonika idea".[2]

Hankey's second appearance before the Dardanelles Commission went better than the first one—perhaps because he had in the interval obtained approval for the Secretary's Notes to be released to the Chairman. "They treated me well", he commented in his diary; "Lord Cromer came to me and thanked me for the way I had given my evidence, and said that he personally was much impressed by it."[3]

Curzon to Hankey. 1 Carlton House Terrace. 28th September 1916. Holograph
Dear Sir Maurice,
I have read through Parts I, II [and] III of your evidence laid before the Dardanelles Committee,[4] prepared as it seems to me with great ability and excellent judgment. I hope that in due course you will let me see the later parts—*quorum pars magna fui.*[5]
Yours sincerely

No sooner were Hankey's own appearances before the Commission over than he felt obliged to help Lord Fisher prepare himself for a similar ordeal.

Hankey to Fisher. 2 Whitehall Gardens. 28th September 1916
Private and Personal
My dear Lord Fisher,
I have now finished my evidence in regard to the origin and inception of both the naval attack and the joint naval and military attack on the Dardan-

---

[1]Diary 26th Sept. 1916. See V. Bonham Carter, *Soldier True* (Muller, 1963), p. 188 regarding this incident.
[2]Diary 27th Sept. 1916. [3]*ibid.*
[4]Curzon must have been referring here to Hankey's written "Notes for Evidence" (Cab. 19/29) and not to the transcript of his verbal evidence (Cab. 19/33).
[5]"A matter in which I played a large part". From Virgil, Aeneid, Book II. Aeneas is speaking about his part in the Trojan war.

elles. I spent two days with the Commission, and was cross-examined very searchingly on the subject. I do not think that I have done anything to injure you in any way. Nevertheless, I think that before you give evidence it would be just as well that you should ask the Commission to see both my original memorandum of evidence and copies of my cross-examination. The only point on which I have the smallest misgiving is that Lord Nicholson asked me whether it was not the custom for one representative of a Department, either the ministerial or the professional head, to speak at the Committee of Imperial Defence for the Department, to which I answered in the affirmative. He then asked me whether, if no other member of that Department spoke, silence was not assumed to imply consent, and I replied that this was usually the case. Nevertheless, I had repeatedly pointed out that you had implied disagreement when you said the Prime Minister knew your views, even if you had not definitely explained what your disagreement was. Another point which I want you to know of is that yesterday one of the members suggested that there was a certain inconsistency between your remark on May 14th, that you had never been a party to the Dardanelles operations, and your failure to make an active protest at the War Council. They pressed me to offer any explanation. My recollection is that I said that it might seem a reasonable assumption that you had disliked the thing but had not carried your dislike to the point of an active protest, but that they had much better ask you your opinion on this. I rather regret this answer, and think that I should have declined to answer at all, but it is rather difficult, with a lot of people cross-examining you, to weigh your words entirely beforehand.

At any rate, I saw no sign of personal hostility towards you on the Commission, and my own view is that if you take the line I have already suggested all will be well.

I am very tired, as this Dardanelles work has imposed a very great additional strain on me, and I am off for ten days to Cornwall, and my one wish is to get away from it all for a short time. After that I suppose I shall be mixed up in the later stages of the Dardanelles Inquiry.

Do not omit to tell them the story of the "bloody lobster" and the landing at Malta.[1]

Yours ever

In the event, however, the old Admiral showed himself fully capable of presenting his own defence. When Hankey read the transcript of his evidence it made him "laugh until tears rolled down my face". For Fisher had told the Commissioners that Balfour " 'had the

[1]Lennoxlove papers. I have failed to trace the original of the story referred to in Hankey's final sentence.

brains of Moses and the voice of Aaron' and 'would charm a bird off a tree' "; and he had also produced for the Commissioners' benefit one of his favourite dog-Latinisms "totus porcus"—to signify going the "whole hog".[1]

As the Commission's prolonged investigations drew to a close, and they settled down to compose their report, it became clear to Hankey that, despite the enormous care he had taken in preparing the government's case, and the consummate tact he had shown under severe cross-examination, the Commissioners were far from convinced by what they had read and heard from the government's side. For in their reports they came down heavily against the whole conception of the Dardanelles enterprise.[2] However Hankey lived long enough to draw consolation from the fact that the conclusions of the Commission have by no means found full support in the works of historians who have been able to re-survey the campaign in the calm retrospect of forty or fifty years on.[3] Looking back to-day at the questions asked by the Commissioners and the broad tone of their reports it is indeed difficult not to feel that their findings reflect the anti-government, and still more the anti-Churchill bias of some of their number, rather than present a judicial attitude towards the whole controversial affair. In all the Commission asked 31,253 questions, and the transcript of evidence covers 1,687 closely printed pages.[4] Even a cursory glance through its proceedings leaves one flabbergasted that so much time and effort could be wasted on what was after all merely a prolonged *post mortem*— and at a time of serious crisis for the Allies on every front on which their forces were engaged. Furthermore, as Hankey had always realised, there was real danger that his own position and standing might be jeopardised by the part he had felt obliged to play as principal

[1] Diary 14th Oct. 1916. The "Summary of Lord Fisher's Evidence" is in Cab. 19/29; but to catch the full flavour of his inimitable style one must go to the transcript of the Commission's proceedings. (Cab. 19/33.)

[2] Cmd. 8490 (First Report) and 8502 (Supplement to First Report). *James*, pp. 350–1 aptly sums up the Commission's grotesquely biassed conclusions as having been "that the operations had been ill-conceived and ineptly executed, with the vain expenditure of thousands of valuable lives". Of those who took part only General Monro received any expression of approval—for recommending evacuation.

[3] *James*, pp. 351–3 and Marder, *Scapa Flow*, II, pp. 325–9 sum up and discuss the findings of less partial and more recent writers on the campaign.

[4] Cab. 19/33.

witness for the government. And the chief threat to him, as to Asquith, lay of course in the power wielded, entirely without scruple, by the Northcliffe Press.

Diary 28th September 1916

. . . War Ctee at 11.30. Lunched with Harold Baker[1] who told me he had had some conversation with Colonel Repington, the Military Correspondent of *The Times*.[2] Col. R. had criticised the C.I.D., but on Baker's saying that it had been absolutely essential to our well-being in the war, Repington admitted that something of the kind was necessary, but complained that I was too much in the position of military adviser to the Prime Minister, especially at the beginning of the war. "Hankey is a very nice fellow, and a very able fellow", he said, "but the thing is wrong in principle, and we shall have to clear it up at the end of the war". I have noticed lately that *The Times* has been pushing my name into the paper nearly every day in connection with the Dardanelles inquiry, saying either that I had given evidence, or am about to give evidence, or cannot give evidence. They have planned this inquiry against Asquith, and they probably want to bring me down with him. If, as is alleged, Lloyd George is really trying to push the Prime Minister out this makes me uncomfortable in view of Lloyd George's close association with Northcliffe and *The Times*. I never thought I was important enough to have a conspiracy against me, but I have always played straight and so don't care.

After Hankey's part in the tragi-comedy had been played out to the end he was allowed nearly a fortnight's holiday—his first break of more than three days since the beginning of the war. He and Adeline spent it alone at Newquay and Fowey, leaving the children at Highstead.

On 12th October Hankey was back in the saddle, and the first problem to face him concerned the future of Swinton, whose enterprise and originality over the design, production and proper employment of the tanks had made him highly unpopular with the military hierarchy—especially after the failure to follow his recommendations had resulted in the first batch being "pawned for a song" on the Somme. The result, typical of the period, was that Swinton was first removed from command of the tank unit in England, and then sent back from France in

[1]Harold T. Baker (1877–1960). Politician (Lib.). Member of Army Council 1914; Inspector of Quartermaster-General Services 1916. Warden of Winchester College 1936–46.
[2]See p. 95.

something not far removed from disgrace. Fortunately for Swinton, and indeed for the country, Hankey was in the position immediately to take him on again in the C.I.D. secretariat; but one may doubt whether, even in that capacity, his great gifts were exploited to anything like their full extent.[1]

Diary 12th October 1916
... War Ctee at 11.30 I was most cordially and almost affectionately greeted by the members on my return from leave, and the Prime Minister to my surprise made a little speech of welcome ... Afterwards he gave me a full and most amusing account of a frightful row between Ll. George and Robertson, reading passages from an acrimonious correspondence between them.[2] Apparently they have settled their differences for the moment. He also showed me letters proving that both Lord Northcliffe and Gwynne[3] of the *Morning Post* will back Robertson against Ll. George. All this, together with his speech yesterday,[4] have enormously strengthened the P.M.'s position.

Unfortunately Hankey's belief that Asquith and the first coalition had survived the consequences of their ill-judged agreement to an inquest on

[1]Diary 12th and 16th Oct. 1916. In 1932 Swinton submitted the typescript of his book published that year as *Eyewitness* (Hodder and Stoughton) to Hankey for official scrutiny. He replied that he would ask for no changes on the grounds of "public interest", but made a number of criticisms and suggestions, nearly all of which Swinton accepted. In the typescript Swinton evidently quoted Hankey as saying that the treatment accorded to him in 1916 had been "a damned shame"; and Hankey wrote that he had "not the least objection" to the remark being reproduced. However, someone must have objected since in the book (p. 302) Swinton merely states that Hankey's "indignation was great". Perhaps the change was made by the publisher. In 1932 it was not generally acceptable that even "six letter words" should appear in print. Hankey to Swinton 5th May 1932. Swinton papers, King's College, London.
[2]This is obviously the correspondence of 11th October described in V. Bonham Carter *op. cit.*, pp. 188–9. In his autobiography *Soldiers and Statesmen 1914–18* (2 Vols., Cassell, 1926) Robertson drew a discreet veil over this fracas with Lloyd George.
[3]H. A. Gwynne (1865–1950). Journalist and War Correspondent in Balkan, S. Africa and China wars for Reuter's 1893–1903. Editor of *The Standard* 1904–11 and of the *Morning Post* 1911–37.
[4]This must refer to Asquith's speech in the House of Commons on 11th Oct. 1916 when he moved that a further Supplementary Vote of Credit of up to £300 millions should be granted for the prosecution of the war. His speech was well received and the resolution agreed to Parl. Deb., Commons, S.5, Vol. LXXXVI, Cols. 95–161.

their own conduct of the war was soon to be proved highly optimistic. Furthermore Asquith himself had been terribly shaken by the death in action on the Somme on 15th September of his eldest son Raymond, "the most generally gifted" of his children. Those closest to the Prime Minister, including Hankey, felt that he never recovered from this blow.[1]

[1]See *Jenkins*, pp. 413–15 for an account of how the news of Raymond Asquith's death was received by his family. John Roskill, father of the author of this biography, and H. H. Asquith shared chambers for many years at 1 Paper Buildings, Temple, and Raymond Asquith was taken into the same chambers when he was called to the Bar in 1904 after coming down from Oxford with a triple first. Thus the author can well remember the shock of Raymond's death. The three names H. H. Asquith, J. H. Roskill and R. Asquith were kept up at the chambers almost to John Roskill's death in 1940.

Chapter 11

The Fall of the First Coalition.
October-December 1916

As the summer of 1916 drew into autumn the offensive on the Somme continued to produce heavy losses for small gains until in mid-November, the onset of the winter rains brought it to an end. By that time the men were utterly exhausted, and their transport was bogged down in the all-pervading and glutinous mud of the devastated battle field. The only compensation, and it was certainly not a negligible one, was that the heavy British sacrifices contributed to saving Verdun, where German pressure declined in July. In the last two months of the year the French, by a welcome change of tactics, regained most of the lost ground at surprisingly small cost. Hankey, as we saw earlier, had never believed in the Somme offensive, though he held some hope that if the tanks were used skilfully and effectively they might bring a substantial success. His old friend Colonel Seely, formerly Secretary of State for War,[1] who returned on leave from France at this time, held exactly the same view, and described the Somme offensive as "a ghastly and tragic blunder" in which we had "lost men out of all proportion to the results". He described British tactics as "antiquated" and "our general staff wooden and unreceptive to modern ideas". "There is much truth in this", commented Hankey, "but as I pointed out the Red-Hatted Staff are in complete control and, until you can convince them, there is nothing to be done. A big expedition to Salonika would fail, as the Dardanelles failed, and for precisely the same reason, namely that the 'western front' school would wreck it".[2] This amounted to acceptance of defeat for all that he had argued for in the preceding years; and it seems true to say that after the summer of 1916 Hankey himself became a reluctant "westerner", on the grounds that "it is better to have a second best plan, which the army have their hearts in, and to conform all your policy and strategy thereto, than a more perfect plan which those who have to carry it out don't believe

[1] See p. 116. [2] Diary 18th Oct. 1916.

in".[1] The weakness of this argument lay of course in the fact that it ignored the promise shown that the tanks, though still only an embryo concept, did open the prospect of "a more perfect plan", and created the possibility of a break-through in the west which had not existed before.

On 16th October the dreadful losses on the Somme were brought home personally to Hankey by the news that his brother Donald, the "Student in Arms",[2] had been killed while leading his platoon of the 1st Royal Warwickshire Regiment in an attack. According to his diary he received the news in a letter from his sister Hilda; but Lawrence Burgis recalls that Hankey was dictating in his office at Whitehall Gardens when the telephone rang and he answered it. On putting the receiver back he merely remarked "Donald's gone". Then, to the stenographer, after a brief pause, "where was I Owen?".[3] This seemingly heartless reaction shocked those who heard it. Yet the explanation is simple. Either Hankey had already heard the sad news from Hilda, and the telephone call was merely confirmatory; or, if the telephone call was the first intimation of Donald's death, he controlled his emotion by a great effort of will power, and carried on with his work. Both alternatives are possible; and the second certainly accords with Hankey's character and upbringing. What is unacceptable is the suggestion that, even at a time when hardly any British family escaped loss, Hankey was impervious to such ill-tidings; for the evidence of the deep bonds of affection that existed between him and Donald is abundant and convincing.

Two days later Hankey crossed the Channel again with Asquith, who was supported by Grey, Balfour, Lloyd George, Robertson and a number of lesser lights, to take part in another Anglo-French conference, this time at Boulogne. The destruction of Roumania was now looming on the horizon; since a mainly Bulgarian force under General von Mackensen had swept north-east into the Roumanian province of Dobruja, and by early October von Falkenhayn's offensive from Transylvania in the north was developing most dangerously. The unhappy Roumanians were in fact caught between the two arms of a gigantic pincer movement, and the chief item on the agenda at the

[1]ibid.
[2]The pseudonym under which Donald Hankey's famous essays were first published in The Spectator. (Collected edition A. Melrose, 1918).
[3]F. W. Owen was Hankey's "second private stenographer".

Boulogne conference was whether more men and munitions should be sent to Salonika in an endeavour to avert disaster.

Hankey was considerably amused by the tortuous manœuvres employed by Lloyd George to gain French support for the reinforcement of the Salonika front. He first pressed for Edwin Montagu to join the British delegation—despite the fact that the agenda did not really concern the Ministry of Munitions. When Montagu declined to do more than send a subordinate Lloyd George said to Hankey "You must really telegraph to Paris that a high official of the Munitions Dept. is coming", thus ensuring that his French ally Albert Thomas, who also held responsibility for munitions supply, would attend; and Thomas he well knew would support the despatch of reinforcements to Salonika. "Absurd and transparent subterfuge" was Hankey's comment[1]; but it undoubtedly embarrassed Asquith, who had accepted Robertson's view that it was too late in the year to do much at Salonika, and that continuation of the Somme offensive was the best way of helping the Roumanians. In the end it was decided to send out two more British and a like number of French divisions, and the eastern Allies were informed accordingly—"a communication which would have been more reassuring if it had been made some months earlier" was Hankey's reasonable if acidulous conclusion.[2] The truth was that the vacillations in Allied strategy had once again resulted in "too little too late" being sent.

It was at this time that the Greek political entanglement, which had started at the time of the Dardanelles campaign, moved a stage nearer solution in the Allied favour. In June the intransigence of King Constantine and his pro-German government had led to a "pacific blockade" of Greece, but in October the Venizelist revolt spread and its leader set up a provisional government in Salonika. At the Boulogne conference the question of the western Allies' attitude towards both Greek governments was discussed; but whereas the British wished to deal drastically with Constantine, whose duplicity was by this time thoroughly exposed, the French government, which had earlier advocated taking a tough line with him, now urged moderation. The result was an ineffective compromise; and although the Venizelist

[1] Diary 19th and 20th Oct. 1916.
[2] *Supreme Command*, II, pp. 536–7. Papers relating to the Boulogne Conference are in Cab. 42/21 and 42/22. The conclusions of the conference are attached to the minutes of the War Committee meeting of 24th Oct. (Cab. 22/59 in volume 42/22).

government declared war on Germany and Bulgaria on 23rd November, the final solution was not achieved until Constantine was forced to abdicate in favour of his son Alexander in June 1917, and Venizelos once again became Prime Minister of a more or less united Greece.

Meanwhile, as a further embarrassment to the Asquith government, the conflict between Curzon and Balfour showed signs of coming to a head when, on 23rd October, the former circulated his First Report as President of the Air Board.[1] Balfour replied to that document, which he described as being "of formidable proportions, eloquently written, consisting of thirty folio pages, mostly filled with attacks on the Admiralty", with great dialectical skill[2]; but to Hankey, who had always held that the inter-departmental squabble over the control of aircraft and the allocation of aeronautical material could and should be resolved by negotiation around a table, such paper polemics were both tedious and distasteful. However even his tactful work as intermediary proved of no avail on this issue.

Hankey spent the last two days of October preparing a "General Review of the War" for the benefit of the War Committee. This was the sort of work at which he excelled. He drew on memoranda prepared by the various departments, added a number of touches of his own, and presented all the essentials within the remarkably short compass of six and a half printed pages. He began with a summary of "The Objects of the Allies and of the Enemy", and then went on to consider in greater detail both "The Naval Plan" and "The Military Plan" by which the Allies were attempting to achieve their purposes. The "offensive" side of the naval plan was the blockade of the Central European Powers; but although the blockade had been steadily tightened, and was putting great economic pressure on the enemy, opinion was "almost unanimous that the objects of the Allies cannot be achieved by economic means alone, and that military success is essential". On the other hand the "defensive" side of the naval plan, by which Hankey meant the security of the British Isles and the far-flung territories of the Empire, had "succeeded completely". He went on to review "The Defence of Trade" and admitted that the decline of British shipping by some 600,000 tons, and fairly heavy Allied and neutral losses, were "a cause of anxiety".

Turning to "The Military Plan" he recalled that on 28th December 1915 the War Committee had decided that "France and Flanders are

[1] Cab. 22/75.
[2] "A Reply to the First Report of the Air Board" dated 6th Nov. 1916. Air 1/2311.

the main theatre of operations". Because the strategy of the war was, he said, "a matter for the Chief of the Imperial General Staff", he did not propose to discuss it; but one does wonder why Hankey should have denied the War Committee or the Cabinet responsibility for strategy. He also claimed, somewhat optimistically, that on the whole "the offensive in the West may be said to have come up to the expectations of the General Staff", and that it had not "involved losses in excess of anticipations". He then went on to review how the additional number of men now called for by the War Office could be obtained; and his chief conclusion was that a reduction of the Home Defence forces was both justifiable and advantageous.[1]

To us the greatest interest in the foregoing memorandum lies in the divergence it reveals between Hankey's diary entries about the Somme offensive and the western front strategy, and the view of these matters which he was prepared to place before the War Committee. One must assume that he was not prepared at this stage either to challenge General Robertson and the "westerners" himself (which is entirely understandable), or to provide Ministers with ammunition with which they might challenge the military hierarchy. Indeed the diary entries for the very days when Hankey was writing his "General Review" reveal a widely different attitude from that contained in the memorandum. The truth surely was that Robertson's views enjoyed such complete ascendancy in the military hierarchy that Hankey knew that it would be hopeless for someone like himself, who lacked any executive authority, to attempt to combat them.[2]

Diary 28th October 1916
Had a long talk with the P.M. before lunch about the war generally. Ll. George had just been to him very depressed about the war, very disappointed with the lack of imagination of the General Staff, and very disgusted at the heavy losses involved in the offensive on the Somme as contrasted with the

[1] Cab. G. 92 of 31st Oct. 1916. A printed proof copy with the number G.85 of the same date is in Asquith papers, Box 131, folios 61–4. Except for the addition of one footnote it is identical to G.92. For once the admirable "List of Cabinet Papers 1915 and 1916" prepared by the P.R.O. appears to be in error, since G.85 appears there (p. 100) as by General Robertson and dated 15th Oct. 1916.
[2] See Sir William Robertson *From Private to Field Marshal* (Constable, 1921), p. 281 "the Somme battle marked a definite stage on the road to victory. The final overthrow of the enemy was henceforward no longer in doubt, provided the Allies resolutely kept up the pressure at the decisive point *and resisted the temptation to embark on side issues*" (italics supplied).

relatively small success achieved. I could not offer much comfort. To a great extent I agree with Lloyd George, but the General Staff are so intolerably complacent and self-satisfied that they won't listen to any outside view. Meanwhile they are bleeding us to death, as I warned the Prime Minister they would do on the very day of the announcement of the formation of the new armies. Stayed to lunch at 10 Downing Street. Arthur Asquith,[1] invalided from the front with broken ear drums after being buried by a Minenwerfer [minethrower], absolutely scorns the idea of breaking the German lines, as a few machine guns with barbed wire can stop anything but the Tanks.[2]

1st November
I lunched alone with Ll. George at Sir Arthur Lee's house[3] . . . Ll. G. considered that the Somme offensive had been a bloody and disastrous failure; he was not willing to remain in office if it was to be repeated next year . . . I warned him that he was not dealing now with munitions workers . . . but with armies led by the most conservative class in the world, forming the most powerful trades union in the world. That I had never been a western front man myself, but that I had acquiesced in and supported Robertson to the best of my ability because he was the best soldier in the Staff "ring" . . . He said that Lord Fisher and I were the only service men with a spark of imagination, and that he had asked me to lunch to get ideas for a talk on the general situation which he had arranged for that evening, having invited the Prime Minister, Grey and Balfour to dinner. Later I wrote a minute to the Prime Minister about the great danger from submarines, urging that the naval desire for 1,000 guns to be mounted in merchant ships should take precedence over every other claim . . .[4]

In between the composition and circulation of Hankey's "General Review" he accompanied Asquith to the Dardanelles Commission's hearing at which the Prime Minister was to give evidence. Though Hankey was himself "recalled and further examined", on this occasion he generally only confirmed, amplified, and very occasionally corrected the Prime Minister's statements about the working of the War Council and Cabinet.[5] The manner in which Asquith acquitted himself revived

[1]See p. 189.
[2]This day's entry down to "I could not offer much comfort" is printed in *Supreme Command*, II, p. 556.
[3]Viscount Lee of Fareham 1922 (1868–1947). Director-General of Food Production 1917–18. President of Board of Agriculture 1919–21. First Lord of Admiralty 1921–2. A great patron of the Arts. Donor of the Chequers estate to the nation for use by its Prime Ministers.
[4]Parts of the diary entry for this day are printed in *Supreme Command*, II, p. 556.
[5]Cab. 19/33. 18th Session of Dardanelles Commission, 31st Oct. 1916.

all Hankey's affection for and admiration of him, which had been so badly shaken by the decision to permit the enquiry. "He was simply splendid", he remarked in his diary. "Answered all questions with extraordinary promptitude . . . great dignity and confidence, and perfect urbanity and good humour. My impression was that my original Memo. had not been shaken in the slightest degree, and that the Commission could hardly report unfavourably so far as the War Council was concerned. P.M. very pleased with himself as we walked home . . .".[1] Though the Commission continued in session until September 1917, and in all met on no less than 89 days, in so far as Hankey was concerned the long ordeal was now over. But his apprehensions regarding the damage the government would suffer through accepting the enquiry were to prove all too well founded; and he was to be proved over-optimistic about the Commissioners' findings.

A long memorandum which Hankey sent to Asquith on 6th November lends further support to the view that he had felt inhibited from stating his full and candid opinion in the "General Review" which he had circulated a week earlier. He first admitted that at the beginning of that document he had been "groping towards" expression of the need for the Allied statesmen to "lay down the policy which they desire to achieve". He went on to discuss whether "the complete and decisive defeat of the Central Powers", which had been the object expressed by Robertson in November 1915, still remained the broad purpose of the Allies; for he believed that in the intervening year "the enemy has given up all idea of an unlimited result". Hence arose the need for "the statesmen who direct the cause of the Allies" to "consider whether we are still justified in continuing warfare with an unlimited object". If the answer to that question was in the affirmative "nothing remains to be done but to prepare for the campaign as planned"; but if on the other hand military advice was "that unlimited objects can no longer be hoped for, the statesmen should set to work to define the limited objects which we should seek to attain". In the latter event he put forward "three sets of principles" namely those "relating to actual operations", "the minimum objects to be sought for at the end of the war", and "the individual aspirations" which the Allied nations "will do their best to promote". Under each of those headings he set out what he regarded as the principal requirements for a change on the part of the Allies from unlimited to limited objects.[2] Though these requirements were in fact

[1] Diary 31st Oct. 1916. [2] Asquith papers, box 131, folios 77–80.

cast so wide that no German government could conceivably have accepted all of them in 1916, Hankey's evident desire to get away from the concept of "the complete and decisive defeat of the Central Powers", and to substitute more limited aims, is interesting. In the first place he thereby anticipated by a few days a memorandum in which Lord Lansdowne[1] urged the need "to take stock of the situation, military, naval, financial and economic . . . of our Allies as well as ourselves", and that "we ought at any rate not to discourage any movement . . . in favour of an interchange of views as to the possibility of a settlement".[2] This was, of course, a forerunner to Lansdowne's famous "Peace Letter" of 29th November 1917.[3] Secondly it seems possible that Hankey was coming round, though very cautiously and tentatively, to the concept of a negotiated peace such as Colonel House had put forward earlier in the year.[4] Be that as it may, Hankey's paper makes it clear that as 1916 drew to a close he was no longer committed to the doctrine of total victory, and even entertained doubts whether such an object was attainable. Asquith, however, seems to have given his paper scant attention, except to side-line a few points with question marks. Certainly it was never circulated to the War Committee or the Cabinet.

The first weeks of November also found Hankey deeply involved in the rising threat of the submarine campaign, which as we have seen, occupied a prominent place in his "General Review". Jellicoe, who must have known that his position as C-in-C, Grand Fleet, had not been strengthened by the indecisive outcome of the battle of Jutland, had offered to come to the Admiralty, even without a seat on the Board, "to undertake anti-submarine work".[5] Though Balfour was apparently agreeable, and when Asquith consulted Hankey he advised that the offer

[1] 5th Marquess of Lansdowne (1845–1927). Governor General of Canada 1883–8; Viceroy of India 1888–94; Foreign Secretary 1900–5. Minister without Portfolio 1915–16.

[2] Memo. of 13th Nov. 1916. This was strongly attacked by Robertson in a memorandum dated 24th Nov. Asquith papers, box 131, folio 141. See *Jenkins*, I, pp. 417–19 and Lloyd George, *War Memoirs*, I, pp. 514–20. This source is henceforth cited as *Lloyd George*.

[3] See article by Harold Kurtz in *History Today*, Vol. XVIII, No. 2 (Feb. 1968) for a full discussion of the "Lansdowne letter".

[4] See pp. 245–6.

[5] Diary 2nd Nov. 1916. On that day Jellicoe attended a meeting of the War Committee at which the submarine menace was discussed. See A. Temple Patterson (Ed.), *The Jellicoe Papers*, Vol. II (Navy Records Society, 1968), p. 89.

"should be accepted provided Beatty should have the command [of the Grand Fleet]", in fact such an appointment would obviously have cut right across the proper chain of command. On 8th Hankey noted in his diary that Balfour had told him Jellicoe's offer had been declined. His own man for the job was Admiral R. H. Bacon,[1] then in command of the Dover Patrol, and on the last day of October he wrote to Balfour urging him "to pick Admiral Bacon's brains on the subject of measures against submarines". His "extraordinary ingenuity, technical ability and driving power" would, in Hankey's view justify making him responsible for "the general question of anti-submarine warfare".[2] This was a considerable over-estimate of the abilities of Bacon, who was in fact superseded at Dover in 1918 because the Admiralty was dissatisfied over anti-submarine measures in the Channel.

In truth the Admiralty's attitude towards the submarine campaign was at this time thoroughly defeatist. On 20th November Admirals Jackson (First Sea Lord) and Oliver (Chief of War Staff) circulated a paper which amounted to an admission that they had no solution. "It may definitely be stated", it ran, "that naval resources are practically exhausted as far as small craft for hunting submarines are concerned . . . It is therefore suggested . . . that the question be considered whether it is not worth while shaping military strategy as far as can now be done to assist in the reduction of the submarine menace through the destruction of as many of their home bases as is practicable".[3] Such a request for the Army (and the R.F.C.) to solve the Navy's problems was not likely to appeal to Hankey, whose mind was in fact fertile with ideas on how the threat should be countered. Furthermore at almost the same time Balfour sent Asquith a memorandum on the same subject, apparently unaware that his chief executives had already gone into action.[4] To a man of Hankey's logical mind and well-ordered methods such lack of co-ordination was not likely to enhance his confidence in the Admiralty. But the idea that the capture of the Flanders U-boat bases was the solution to the threat to Allied shipping none the less took firm hold in the Admiralty.[5]

If Jellicoe's position as C-in-C, Grand Fleet, and Jackson's as First

[1]See p. 53. [2]Balfour papers. B.M. Add. MSS. 49704.
[3]G.97 of 16th Nov. 1916. Cab. 42/4/9. A copy in Asquith papers, box 131, folio 120 is dated 20th Nov.
[4]Asquith papers, box 131, folio 129. Memo. dated 19th Nov. 1916.
[5]See pp. 387 and 404–5.

Sea Lord were by this time shaky, so was Robertson's as C.I.G.S.; and the project, initiated by Lloyd George, was once more afoot to send him on a mission to Russia—which, as Hankey remarked, had come to serve as the "Stellenbosch" of World War I.[1] Hankey now evidently felt it incumbent on him to send Robertson a statement on "the general attitude of the War Committee about future strategy and operations"; and he combined it with a somewhat circumlocutory warning. Having first assured Robertson that his own and Haig's positions were "as strong as ever", he went on to say that as "the ultimate responsibility" rested with the War Committee they had to feel "absolutely sure before approving any particular policy". In other words it would be wrong, and dangerous, for the C.I.G.S. to press his views too hard, let alone claim a prerogative over strategic issues. Hankey then went on to explain why the War Committee desired to examine all possible alternatives to the continuation of the offensive in the West. He did not believe that there was any support for Lloyd George's idea of rein-forcing the Salonika front with the object of striking at the Bulgarians —because the physical and logistic difficulties were too great. An advance on Sofia he stigmatised as "a chimera". On the other hand there was "a strong inclination" to send sufficient supplies and equip-ment to the Russians to enable them to launch a really effective offen-sive. We have already seen that this was Hankey's favourite plan. For this reason the great majority of the War Committee wanted "someone with real and great authority" to go to Russia and explain to General Alexeïev[2] why an offensive from Salonika was impracticable and what the western allies hoped the Russians would do instead. He ended by flattering the C.I.G.S. with the assurance that "the visit of a great General will have far more effect than that of any politician".[3]

Robertson was, however, too obtuse to read between the lines of Hankey's letter; and he regarded the proposed visit to Russia merely as a device to rusticate him from London in order to eliminate his in-fluence on strategic issues—particularly with regard to the continuation

[1]Stellenbosch was the base to which *dégommés* Generals were consigned during the South African War. "To Stellenbosch" someone became a commonly used verb during that conflict.

[2]General Mikhail V. Alexeïev (1857–1918). C-in-C, western Russian front April 1915 and Chief of General Staff 1915–c. October 1917. Then joined White Russian forces operating under General Denikin against the Bolsheviks.

[3]Hankey to Robertson. Secret and Personal. 9th November 1916.

of the offensive in the west. That same evening he wrote to Hankey "that he would not go to Russia and . . . was out for a row without kid gloves on".[1] None the less Hankey did not give up. On 10th he sent the obstinate soldier another "Secret and Personal" letter telling him that he had consulted Lloyd George, who had vigorously denied that the mission to Russia was a repetition of "the Lord K[itchener] dodge". Indeed Lloyd George had "spoken most warmly" of Robertson. Hankey then tried to close the plainly widening gulf between the rising politician and the soldier. He wrote that he "would give almost any-thing" to see the two of them "closer together", and that a complete breach would be "an almost irremediable calamity". He went on to sing Lloyd George's praises for what he had done in the field of munitions production, and lauded him as "the only man who is likely to bring about the re-awakening of national enthusiasm and effort".[2]

Hankey's efforts to damp down this dangerous antagonism were partially successful, since on 15th the War Committee accepted that Robertson would not go to Russia; but Lloyd George continued to threaten resignation unless there was a fundamental change in Allied strategy.[3] And while these dangerous fissions in the government's ranks continued to widen the business of the War Committee fell increasingly into arrears.

Diary 10th November 1916
. . . At 11.30 yet another War Ctee. These have been really dreadful [meetings] . . . Yesterday the P.M. was writing answers to Parliamentary questions all the time, with the result that the discussion was never kept to the point. . . . Today Ll. G. came up with an undigested and stupid proposal for a "Shipping Dictator" which wasted the whole meeting.[4] Yet the subjects for discussion are absolutely vital, involving no less than our economic power to continue the war next year . . . I have always foreseen that we should be strangled by our armies, and it is actually happening. Supplies short, prices high and no shipping to be got. There are only two solutions—either to reduce the size of the army or to introduce foreign labour, and the Govt. won't adopt either . . . Thus and thus is the British Empire governed at a critical stage of the war. I have done all I can to get meetings; to crystallize woolly discussions

[1]Diary 9th Nov. 1916.
[2]Hankey to Robertson. Secret and Personal. 10th November 1916.
[3]Diary 11th Nov. 1916.
[4]Hankey's dislike of this proposal was unjustified, and very soon after the formation of the Second Coalition in the following December Sir Joseph Maclay was appointed Minister of Shipping. In that capacity he did remarkable work.

into clear-cut decisions, and to promote concord—but the task is a Herculean one! . . .[1]

Meanwhile an Inter-Allied political conference had been arranged in Paris, and on 12th (a Sunday) Hankey motored down to Walton Heath with Adeline and Lloyd George's family to go over the papers with Lloyd George. Then he went on to The Wharf to go through the same process with Asquith, who flatly declined to include the greater part of what Hankey called Lloyd George's "most lugubrious and pessimistic document" in his own statement to the conference. Finally Hankey came back to London to tell Lloyd George "how the land lay"; and in consequence the latter decided to hand the paper in to the conference himself.[2] Two days later the large party of ministers and military men and their advisers crossed to Paris. Hankey was at once enmeshed in the toils of getting Asquith's speech into its final shape and translated into French—which he described as "a desperately complicated business" because the Ministers went on altering it until almost the last moment.

The conference opened on the morning of 15th November with a "heart to heart talk" between Asquith and Lloyd George on the British side and Briand and Admiral Lacaze[3] on the French side. Hankey was not admitted, but Asquith told him afterwards that "they spent most of their time abusing the narrow-mindedness of the British and French Generals"—an attitude "in which", he remarked, "I fully concur". In the afternoon he attended the formal conference, which was enlarged by the presence of Italian and Russian representatives. "The most important resolution", he noted, "was that the Govts. must not allow themselves to be run by their General Staffs, but having the responsibility, must undertake the direction of operations on the technical basis prepared by their Staffs".[4] This no doubt sounded very strong and resolute around a conference table; but, as Hankey had long since pointed out to Lloyd George, if operations in which they did not believe were forced on the soldiers, failure was certain.[5]

---

[1] Two short extracts from this day's entry are printed in *Supreme Command*, II, pp. 557–8.
[2] Diary 11th Nov. 1916.
[3] Marie J. L. Lacaze, French admiral (1860–1955). Minister of Marine, not of War as stated in Hankey's diary, 1915–17. Commander, Toulon naval district, and then Vice-President French Navy Board until 1922.
[4] Diary 15th Nov. 1916.   [5] See pp. 307–8.

Next day the British delegation enjoyed a respite, and Hankey spent the first part of it on "a stroll with Lloyd George who was full of schemes . . . We discussed at great length who should accompany him to Russia. Very early on 17th Lloyd George sent for Hankey again, and they breakfasted with Albert Thomas who, as we have seen, had become a close associate and political ally of Lloyd George's.[1] He was now convinced "that Roumania is going to collapse", and Thomas had assured him that this would bring about the fall of the French government. Lloyd George was therefore now determined not to go to Russia "as he would be required at home". Surely he must have foreseen that another fiasco in the Balkans might well bring about the fall of his own government, and so bring him the chance for which he had long been working. Observing that Lloyd George had, in Hankey's words "quarrelled with Robertson in his endeavour to make him go to Russia", and "had released him in order that he might go himself", Hankey's annoyance at Lloyd George's change of front is understandable. But, as he philosophically remarked, "The P.M. always said this would happen".[2] That evening the whole party returned to London.

It was probably Hankey's strong awareness of the need for security, combined with his knowledge of how careless Ministers could be over the custody of secret papers, that made him always clear up the table at which the delegates to any conference had sat—a practice which he continued right to the end of his career. It had one amusing by-product in the "doodles" left behind by the famous, which he collected and gave to Adeline to paste in her scrap book. Thus the Paris conference of November 1916 brought him a coloured sketch, probably by Curzon, of General Joffre's leg and "Jemima boots"[3]; while the Anglo-French conference of the following month yielded a rather charming landscape drawn in blue pencil by Arthur Balfour. One feels that the collection of doodles assembled over the years by Adeline might provide a rewarding field for study by a psychologist!

While the Paris conference was in session the Somme offensive at last came to an end in the mud and slush of the autumn rains; but the sterility of Allied strategy is nicely illustrated by the decision that the campaign for 1917 "is to consist again of pressure all round, and a big

[1]See p. 309. [2]Diary 17th Nov. 1916.
[3]The doodle is inscribed in Hankey's hand "How G.C. (? George Curzon) contributes to the conference. General Joffre's leg and Jemima boots". Presumably the French military boot was known by that nickname in British circles.

effort in the Balkans".[1] Once back in his office Hankey put the proceedings of the conference on paper for record purposes, and gave
Stamfordham a verbal summary for the information of the King.[2] He
also quickly learnt that discontent with the Admiralty was rapidly
coming to a head; for Balfour and Curzon were still locked in strife in
the Air Board, and the Prime Minister was urging Balfour to replace
Sir Henry Jackson, on whom a good deal of the odium for the department's obstructive attitude over aviation issues had, not unreasonably,
fallen. Balfour was evidently at first averse to Jellicoe handing over the
Grand Fleet to Beatty and taking the First Sea Lord's chair; but he
yielded to Asquith's insistence that a change should be made.[3]

Trouble was also still brewing between Lloyd George and Robertson,
and at the War Committee meeting on 21st November the former
"hinted that he had lost any influence over the C.I.G.S. owing to the
fact that someone had poisoned the latter's mind with the idea that
the desire to send him to Russia was what Robertson called "the
K[itchener] dodge". Several people, including McKenna, asked Ll. G.
whom he suspected. Ll. G. then looked pointedly at McKenna and said
"Well, you ought to know". Hankey's comment was "they do hate one
another those two!"[4]

At this time Lloyd George's determination to achieve the formation
of what Hankey called "a new inner War Committee" consisting of no
more than four members took clearer shape. On 21st over lunch he told
Hankey that its members should be Carson, Bonar Law, Arthur
Henderson "to conciliate Labour", and himself. This appears to be the
first mention of the body which finally became the War Cabinet.[5]
Hankey told Lloyd George that he "liked his proposal in principle but
not his personnel"—by which he obviously meant the inclusion of

[1] Diary 16th Nov. 1916.
[2] The conclusions of the Paris conference are in the Cab. 28 series, Allied (War)
Conferences. See also War Committee Minutes of 21st Nov. 1916. Cab. 22/72.
[3] The telegram calling Jellicoe to the Admiralty is dated 27th November 1916, and
he was "read in" as First Sea Lord on 4th December. See A. Temple Patterson
(Ed.), *The Jellicoe Papers,* Vol. II (Navy Records Society, 1968), pp. 102 and 111–12.
See also Balfour to Geddes, 8th March 1918, quoted S. W. Roskill *The Dismissal of
Admiral Jellicoe,* Journal of Contemporary History, Vol. I, No. 4 (Oct. 1966).
[4] Diary 21st Nov. 1916.
[5] *ibid.* 22nd Nov. 1916. See also *Supreme Command,* II, p. 564, where part of this day's
entry is reproduced. *Jenkins,* p. 421, states, no doubt correctly, that Lloyd George
had formulated this plan before leaving London, and had "commissioned Sir Max
Aitken to enlist the support of Bonar Law."

The Prime Minister's visit to Rapallo
Left to right: Hankey, J. T. Davies and Frances Stephenson (L.G.'s
Private Secretaries), General Smuts, General Wilson standing behind

Lloyd George, Painlevé and Foch on a visit to France

British supply convoy and artillery resting during the German offensive, March 1918

The Imperial War Cabinet, March 1917
Left to right (front): Mr. Walter Long, Sir Robert Borden (Canada), General Smuts (South Africa), Mr. Lloyd George, Sir J. Weston, Mr. W. F. Massey (New Zealand), Mr. R. Rogers, Sir George Perley (Canada), Mr. Balfour, Mr. A. Henderson and Sir Maurice Hankey; *(back)*: Mr. Bonar Law, Mr. D. Hazen (Canada), Sir Joseph Ward (New Zealand), Mr. Austen Chamberlain (India), Sir E. Carson, Sir Satyendra P. Sinha, the Maharajah of Bikanir (India), and Lord Curzon

Carson and Henderson, and especially the former.[1] He told Lloyd George, who had evidently proposed "to present a pistol at the P.M.'s head" on this matter, that the result would be "to put absolute power into his [Ll. G.'s] hands", and declined to dine that evening with him, Carson and Bonar Law to discuss the matter. Such is the beginning of the intrigue which culminated in the fall of the First Coalition.

That week the War Committee met no less than five times, and the drafting of the minutes and conclusions strained even Hankey's stamina so greatly that he described himself to Lloyd George as "a squeezed lemon".[2] But the following week, when the crisis came to a real head, proved far worse. It began for Hankey with a long interview with the King, during which he stressed the need to stiffen Jellicoe's resolution when he took over as First Sea Lord, especially with regard to providing the necessary defensive armaments for merchant ships—for which Hankey had been agitating for some time. Then he saw Archibald Hurd, naval correspondent of *The Daily Telegraph* "and did my best to induce him not to attack Mr. Balfour personally". It is difficult to say whether Hankey, who had for a long time been very dissatisfied with the Balfour-Jackson régime at the Admiralty, believed that the replacement of Jackson by Jellicoe would cure all the prevailing troubles, or whether he was merely defending his old friend and supporter Balfour; but if the former is the case he was soon to be proved wide of the mark. Then followed a long War Committee "on the ridiculous Air Board", when Curzon and Balfour continued their polemical tourney. To Hankey's disgust Asquith agreed "to continue the futile discussion tomorrow", thereby dislocating his carefully planned agenda. "This rotten Air Board question is purely academic", he wrote, "since the Air Services are already in good hands. It is a miserable waste of time, when we have so many really urgent matters to consider...". But in truth the dispute over the future of the air services ran far deeper than Hankey at this stage realised; and it could not have been resolved through his favourite ploy of setting up an inter-departmental committee under an impartial and judicial chairman. In fact the dispute had not been resolved at the time of the fall of the First Coalition, and Hankey's very carefully worded conclusions were held over for consideration by the new government nearly a month later. Small wonder that the whole squabble, which really arose out of the

[1]Diary 23rd Nov. 1916.
[2]*ibid.* 25th Nov. 1916. Cab. 42/25 for Minutes of the five meetings.

obstinate, jealous conservatism of the Admiralty clashing with the offensive verbosity of Curzon, caused him profound disgust.[1]

The last days of November brought the long gestating crisis in the government to a head. On 28th Asquith asked Milner to come and see him "about serious matters", and apparently invited him to join the Government—an offer which Milner declined.[2] Next day Hankey, prodded by Mrs. Asquith to "shake Henry up" about what was brewing, had a long discussion with him about the reform of the War Committee. On 30th there took place what he called "an epoch making meeting" of that body at which "several of us combined to make the P.M. take hold of the Committee and get decisions taken promptly". But the very next meeting made it plain that the new-found resolution had come too late.

Walter Runciman to Hankey. Board of Trade, Whitehall Gardens, S.W. Holograph
Sir M. Hankey,

I would be glad if you would record the fact that I was not present when the decision on industrial conscription or compulsory service was discussed. Nor has the opinion of the Board of Trade, the Industrial Commission or the Board's Labour Advisers been asked for by the War Committee, and I am not aware that the War Committee were in possession of information from these quarters or from the representatives of organised Labour before the decision was reached. As at present advised I am unable to concur in the adoption of industrial conscription for all men up to the age of 60.

W.R. 30th Nov. 1916.

On 1st June 1917 Hankey endorsed the above extraordinarily stiff missive: "Note. It was alleged by some people in a good position to judge, though denied by Mr. Asquith, that this letter precipitated the crisis which ended in the fall of the Asquith Government. This is my view, as the letter exasperated Lloyd George into taking action". Though there may be some substance in Hankey's suggestion that it was Runciman who actually applied a match to the powder train, the truth surely was that a whole concatenation of circumstances were combining to produce a chain reaction.

[1] Diary 27th Nov. 1916. For the prolonged discussions at the War Committee meetings on 27th and 28th Nov. see Cab. 42/25 and 42/26. The reader who wishes to follow the story of the dispute over naval aviation in detail may be referred to the present author's *Documents Relating to the Naval Air Service 1908–1918* (Navy Records Society, 1969).
[2] Asquith to Milner 28th Nov. 1916, and endorsement in Lady Milner's hand about the offer of office and her husband's refusal of it. Milner papers, Vol. 143.

Diary 1st December 1916
War Ctee. at 12.45. I noticed that the P.M. was rather piano and I learned afterwards that Ll. George had delivered his ultimatum, practically threatening to resign unless the War Ctee. was reconstituted with himself as Chairman, and demanding that Carson should have a place in the Govt. and Balfour leave the Admiralty. It is all an intolerable nuisance and is precipitated by the tragedy of Roumania's collapse.[1]

That same day Asquith replied to Lloyd George accepting the principle of the small War Committee but "insisting on his own chairmanship".[2] The only other serious difference between them was that whereas Asquith wanted Balfour to stay at the Admiralty Lloyd George wanted him to be replaced by Carson; but that comparatively minor issue was to assume surprisingly large proportions during the next few days. Hankey himself has reproduced the greater part of his diary entries for 2nd–4th December,[3] but as he omitted certain significant passages (italicised below) it has appeared justifiable to print the whole of them here. For the inside story of Sir Max Aitken's part in the "palace revolution" and of the extraordinary conduct of the Conservative Ministers, especially Bonar Law and Curzon, the reader must be referred to Aitken's own account and to the far more impartial study made by Asquith's most recent biographer.[4]

Diary 2nd December 1916
During the day the political crisis became very serious. *The morning papers contained a deal of information obviously inspired by Ll. George.* I suggested a solution to the P.M., but it was not well received. I lunched at 10 Downing St., but very shortly after lunch the P.M. left by motor for Walmer Castle. It was very typical of him that in the middle of this tremendous crisis he should go away for the week-end. Typical both of his qualities and of his defects; of his extraordinary composure and of his easy going habits. After lunch, at Mrs. Asquith's request, I saw Bonar Law, and learned from him that he had called a party meeting of Unionist Cabinet members for the following day, and that he would probably "send a letter" (viz. of resignation) after it. He explained that he must do this in order not to appear in the

[1] *Supreme Command*, II, p. 565 and *Jenkins*, p. 428 reproduce all except the last sentence of this day's entry. The latter (p. 429) also quotes Lloyd George's "ultimatum", which, according to Jenkins, was "the first definite proposal for his own exclusion [from the reorganized War Committee] which was put to Asquith".
[2] *Jenkins*, pp. 429–30.
[3] *Supreme Command*, II, p. 565.
[4] Lord Beaverbrook, *Politicians and the War* (Oldbourne, 1960), Chs. XVI–XXIV. *Jenkins*, Ch. XXVI.

eyes of his party to be dragged at the heels of Ll. George (*which is the case*). *Each is watching the other for fear he should get his resignation in first and so, I imagine, be supposed to be the leader.* Bonar Law told me he might put off his party meeting if he was sure that Ll. George would not resign first—and so give the unfortunate Prime Minister time to think it out. So I went to Lord Reading, who had been commissioned by the P.M. to use his personal influence with Ll. G. in this direction. Reading, however, had only been able to persuade Ll. G. to postpone action until to-morrow (Sunday). I went back to Bonar Law, but this was not good enough for him and he decided to go on with his party meeting. So back to Downing St. where we arranged that Bonham Carter should follow the P.M. to Walmer and bring him back to-morrow morning. I walked home with Lord Reading. We both agreed that the whole crisis is intolerable. There is really very little between them. Everyone agrees that the methods of the War Ctee. call for reform. Everyone agrees that the P.M. possesses the best judgement. The only thing is that Ll. George and Bonar Law insist that the former and not the P.M. must be the man to win the war. The P.M. however quite properly says that if he is not fit to run the War Ctee. he is not fit to be Prime Minister. The obvious compromise is for the P.M. to retain the Presidency of the War Ctee. with Ll. George as chairman, and to give Ll. G. a fairly free run for his money. This is my solution. *The irony of it all is that if there is a split, as seems almost inevitable, Ll. G. will stump the country with hysterical speeches, and give away an enormous lot to the enemy, encouraging him beyond measure, and every sort of national unity will be broken. There will probably be a general election, and who, meanwhile, is to put the drive into the conduct of the war which is absolutely essential at this moment to a decent issue? It is Ll. G's publicity and press methods that are so intolerable. Meanwhile the P.M., as usual in the moment of crisis, is cheery and imperturbable.*

3rd December 1916
After tea I went down to 10 Downing St. to find out if I could help in any way in the political crisis, having heard that the P.M. had come back to town. Lloyd George was closeted with the P.M. In Bonham Carter's room I found assembled Montagu, Bonham Carter, Masterton Smith, Davies,[1] and Marsh.[2]

---

[1]Hankey spelt the name Davis in *Supreme Command*, II, p. 565 as well as in his diary. But it is probable that the person in question was either J. T., later Sir John Davies (1881–1938), Private Secretary to Lloyd George 1915–22, or David D. Davies, later 1st Baron Davies of Llandinam (1880–1944), Parliamentary Private Secretary to Lloyd George 1906–29. Sir John Davies became a British government director of the Suez Canal Co. in 1922, and was succeeded in that appointment by Hankey in 1938. No Davis is mentioned in Lloyd George, *War Memoirs*.

[2]Later Sir Edward Marsh (1872–1953). Assistant Private Secretary to Mr. Asquith 1915–16; Private Secretary to Mr. Churchill 1917–22, and later to other politicians. A distinguished patron of the Arts.

At the Unionist Ministers' meeting in the morning a resolution had been passed demanding the resignation of the P.M., which Bonar Law had transmitted, but no-one seemed to regard it as more than a bluff to force the P.M. to give Lloyd George the chairmanship of the War Ctee. Shortly after I arrived Ll. G. came out, and after a short palaver with Montagu, asked to see me, as he was awaiting the arrival of B.L. who had been sent for. Ll. George then told me that the Unionists had insisted that he should become Prime Minister, but he had flatly declined, and had insisted that he would only serve under Asquith.[1] Apparently the P.M. had agreed that Ll. G. should have a free hand with the War Ctee, but there was a difficulty about personnel. Ll. G. insisted on Balfour's leaving the Adty. He himself intended to remain S. of S. for War, and he saw that the First Lord in this event must also be a member, but he would not agree to Balfour. *The only reason he gave for this was "too much wool", but in my opinion he wants to be virtually "Dictator" and Balfour is too strong and dialectically too skilful to allow this.* The P.M. however is in a difficult position in getting rid of Balfour, because, when he forced him a week or two ago to substitute Jellicoe for Jackson as First Sea Lord, he added his strong wish that Balfour should remain in office. Lloyd George wishes the War Ctee. to consist of Bonar Law, Carson, and Henderson the Labour man, and apparently the P.M. will put up with this but boggles only over Balfour, who cannot be left out if he remains at the Adty. *While Ll. G. was with the P.M. we had foreseen this and Montagu had sent in a note to suggest that Balfour would probably be willing to offer his resignation, if he knew how much depended on it.* Then Bonar Law arrived and he and Lloyd George were closeted with the Prime Minister for half an hour or so. Eventually they agreed, that the Cabinet should resign and the Prime Minister should reconstruct on the basis of the Lloyd George plan. *This expedient enables the P.M. to get rid of Balfour decently by an exchange of offices. How the Unionist members will take it, and how McKenna and Runciman will take it remains to be seen. The new War Ctee. is really ridiculous. Bonar Law is by common consent the poorest figure on the present War Ctee. Carson, on the old Dardanelles Ctee. was positively pitiful and worse than Bonar Law. Henderson is an untried man, and it is scarcely possible that his education can have fitted him for the job. Really it all depends upon Lloyd George, who is brilliant but often unsound. The others are merely representatives of the noisiest groups in the House of Commons to prop him up, and there is no member of the House of Lords. No one would say that these four were the wisest heads to win the war—two are really feather heads. It is a mere political expedient of*

---

[1]Jenkins comments on this passage (*op. cit.*, p. 441). "Thus is history quickly confused by even the most intimate participants—or misreported by even the most reliable witnesses". The reader must be left to decide for himself whether Lloyd George "confused history" at this point or whether Hankey misreported him. To this historian the first alternative seems much the more likely.

the most transparent kind to tide over a difficult crisis. My own position, if I retain the Secretaryship of the War Ctee., will be very difficult. If they do foolish things I shall be bound to go to the P.M. about it and Ll. G. will always be suspicious of me and probably shunt me. Then there will be interminable rows with the General Staff, and Ll. G. is nearly certain to shunt Robertson and quite possibly may try and saddle me with the responsibility of giving military advice, a responsibility that in the first place does not pertain to my constitutional position, and in the second place will bring me into serious trouble with the General Staff and its Press myrmidons. Altogether a most difficult position, and one which I look forward to with the utmost apprehension, though not unmixed with amusement. If only I was financially independent, I should not mind a bit, and as it is, it has a spice of adventure that is attractive.

4th December

Early this morning I received a long letter from Mrs. Asquith, very friendly but rather reproachful and full of abuse of Ll. George. I spent my first hour at the office in a reply setting out the whole situation and explaining how dangerous it was at the moment for reasons of wider statesmanship for the P.M. to quarrel with Lloyd George, and giving the arguments in favour of the Ll. G. compromise. Then I had a message from Ll. G. asking me to see him at the War Office. I found the entrance to the W.O. surrounded by a mob of journalists, mostly with cameras, but passed unnoticed. I found Ll. G.'s ante-room crowded with a mob of rather dim looking people who looked like Welsh M.Ps. and journalists, but I was at once ushered into "the Presence". I found "The Presence" lying back in an armchair by the fire side, looking very tired. He and I were then both under the impression that his scheme was accepted. He asked me to draft some "rules for the new War Ctee.", which should be enunciated to members of the new Cabinet before they took office, and after hearing his views I agreed to do so on the understanding that I should first talk them over with Montagu, as they were to include a statement on "industrial compulsion" on which Montagu's Ctee. is working day and night. *Then we had some talk about the new Ctee. and I told Ll.G. that I would work with him loyally and wholeheartedly. Then he suggested that I ought to strengthen my staff. I agreed to take in a naval officer, but refused to change my military staff without further consideration. I felt profoundly suspicious of this proposal, because I feel sure Ll. G. will quarrel with the General Staff and will try and set me up as an independent "expert" to counter them and my constitutional position is one of "machinery" and not "advice". I should not have the responsibility for carrying out my advice and in war it is impossible to divorce responsibility from advice, as Robertson has always insisted. Then I went to Montagu who came out from his Ctee. but said he had just seen the P.M., who was beginning to back out of his agreement with Ll.G., mainly owing to an intolerable, one-sided, and obviously inspired "leader" in The Times (N.B. Northcliffe was in the W.O. with Ll. G. last night). For Ll. G. to fire in this new ultimatum would, Montagu said, settle the P.M. to resign. Montagu added that he had persuaded the P.M., instead of resigning, to send a letter to Ll. G. protesting against his intolerable publicity methods, which rendered govt. decisions so difficult. I then looked in at 10 Downing St. to verify Montagu's statement, and found the P.M. had gone to see the King and was inclining to resignation. And so back to Ll. G., after preparing a draft on his lines, though I intended to dissuade him from sending it. At the War Office I found such a mob of people in Ll. G.'s ante-room, trying to see him— Lord Derby, Arthur Lee, and any number of others, that I merely left a message with his Secretary, though the latter offered to push me in. Then I went on to see Robertson, and told him of Ll. G.'s idea of strengthening my Staff and assured him that I would never allow myself to trespass on his functions or to overstep my constitutional functions. Then to 10 Downing St. to lunch. The P.M. was outwardly cheerful but I noticed his hand trembled a bit, and no wonder. He read a letter from Ll. G. disclaiming* The Times *article.*[1] *Masterton Smith was there and we talked Admiralty a good deal. The P.M. talked in half jest about where he would go for his "holiday" on Wednesday, if he was out of office. Mrs. Asquith was a bit sobered by my letter and in saying goodbye said in her impetuous way "You are an angel. I love you!" (N.B. Adeline says she is not a bit jealous!). Then back to the office. Very soon Lord Stamfordham, the King's Private Secretary arrived. "You have a cool head" he said "and I should like to hear your views on the situation generally." We talked out the situation very fully, I favouring the Lloyd George compromise, and he inclining to the P.M.'s resignation, the idea being that Bonar Law would be asked to form a Govt. and would fail; then Ll. G. would try and would fail; so that the P.M. would come back stronger than ever, and Ll. G. would be discredited. Apparently he and the King are intensely indignant with Ll. G., whom they regard [as] a blackmailer, whom it is better to tackle and have done with. I think he must have been sent by the King, for he asked my advice as to what the King ought to do in different circumstances. Among [other] things he asked if I thought the King would [?should] perhaps take a more active share in the Govt. of the*

---

[1]See *Jenkins*, pp. 447–8 for Asquith's protest and Lloyd George's disclaimer about *The Times* leader of 4th Dec. Jenkins correctly remarks of the latter "Disingenuous or not, this reply was clearly conciliatory". In his diary for 15th December 1920 (see *Supreme Command*, II, pp. 567–8) Hankey tells how at a dinner at Lord Reading's house that day Lloyd George recounted that during the previous week-end at Cliveden Geoffrey Dawson, editor of *The Times*, had told him that "he wrote the article himself at Cliveden . . . without prompting from anyone, and without communication of any sort or kind with Northcliffe, and because he disliked the arrangement agreed between Asquith and Lloyd George. The particulars of the proposed arrangement had been given him by Carson". Hankey at once accepted this version as "the true history of this episode", and it must again be left to the reader to decide for himself whether, four years after the event, Lloyd George, who was at the time still in power, reported Dawson accurately, and whether the latter told the whole truth. It is perhaps significant that, as Hankey noted in his diary, Northcliffe was with Lloyd George on the evening of 3rd December—the day before *The Times* leader was published.

country. I replied at once that the War outlook was so doubtful from a financial and economic point of view that I was sure that the King ought on no account to take a hand, though I added that I wished he could, because, though he talks too much, he has admirable common sense. On leaving he asked me to let him know if I had any suggestion to make at any time. Then I saw Robertson by appointment, as he was bothered at having been let in for breakfasting with Carson at Lord Derby's house, but I reassured him, and promised to make it all right with the P.M. Later I saw the P.M. as Grey wants the War Ctee. to meet about Greece notwithstanding the difficulties of the sitn., and arranged to have an informal meeting of the Depts. concerned. The P.M., after seeing Grey, Runciman and McKenna had decided either to resign himself or to call for Lloyd George's resignation. He seems to think that Lloyd George and Carson have compounded with the Irish, and that if Ll. G. cannot get his way about the War Ctee., he will form an odd hotch-potch Govt. of Carsonite Unionists, Ll. G. liberals, [Irish] Nationalists, and Labour, who will be bribed by several seats in the Cabinet. I recall that Sir Mark Sykes has been used as an intermediary between Carson and the Nationalists, and told me that an agreement was in sight. How intolerable are these muddy politics in the midst of a great war! I shall wash my hands of them as far as possible.

10th December

Owing to the great pressure of work it became impossible to keep my diary going and I can only briefly summarise events from Dec. 5th (Tuesday) until to-day. On the evening of the 5th Ll. George had resigned and Asquith, unable to obtain the support of the Unionists, had also resigned. I dined with Montagu. Before dinner I conceived the idea and during dinner, after consultation with Montagu, Drummond, and Masterton Smith, I decided to have a last try at mediation. So in the middle of dinner I went off to Buckingham Palace running all the way, to see Lord Stamfordham and try to get the King to intermediate. While I was with Stamfordham Bonar Law came down from the King, who had already invited him to form a Govt. This was embarrassing and I bolted, but Stamfordham told him of my plan and he assented to it. Then, after a fresh consultation with Montagu and Co. I went to see Lloyd George in his flat at St. James's Court. I had to wait for him until midnight, but, as I had anticipated, I found him still anxious to be reconciled. He agreed that the breakdown was due to The Times article. I promised to breakfast with him next morning and discuss the detailed procedure. I got to bed at 1.30. On the 6th Montagu, Masterton Smith, and I breakfasted with Lloyd George, and it was arranged that Ll. G. should advise the King to see him and Asquith together with a view to mediation. In the meanwhile Bonar Law had invited Asquith to join him in a Govt. but Asquith had declined. At 11 a.m. I had an embarrassing interview with Mrs. Asquith, who had learned that I breakfasted with Ll. G. and was inclined to think it was "trading with the enemy". However I was able to reassure her that I was only working in the P.M.'s interests. At noon I was called to

*see Ll. G. and found that they had dropped my plan, and that it had been decided,
apparently at Balfour's suggestion (we had agreed at breakfast that Masterton Smith
should induce Mr. B. to offer the King his good offices) that the King should see Asquith,
Ll. George, Bonar Law, and Balfour with a view to the formation of a Coalition Govt.
Then I dropped out for a bit. The negotiations of the King failed and Lloyd George
was asked to form a Govt.* On the night of the 7th (Thursday) I was summoned
by Mr. Lloyd George to the War Office at about 10 p.m. He informed me
that he was now Prime Minister, though he didn't much like it, and we had
a long talk about the personnel of the new Govt., the procedure of the new
War Ctee., and the future of the war. He and Bonar Law who was there part
of the time, consulted me on many points, and I almost thought they were
going to offer me a place! Ll. G. asked me to write a Memo. giving my views
on the war. *I spent a great part of the 8th in dictating this Memo to my two shorthand
writers alternately, amid many interruptions up to 8 p.m. I also wrote farewell letters
to Asquith and Mrs. A. I felt very much affected at parting with both officially, seeing
the desperate times we have lived through together. In many respects he was the greatest
man I have ever met, or ever hope to meet, and Mrs. Asquith's kindness and hospitality
to me, treating me in every respect as one of her own family, are such that I can never
forget or repay. I lunched with the Asquiths on the 8th and 9th and with Montagu
every other day this week.* By the 9th it was "off with the old love and on with
the new" and I spent the whole day with the new "War Cabinet", the
completion of the Minutes keeping me at the office until 9 p.m. I now find
myself Secretary, not of the War Ctee. but of the Cabinet, which consists of
Lloyd George, Lord Curzon, Mr. Henderson, Lord Milner, and Bonar Law.
An odd turn of the wheel indeed to take place within 7 days! On the 10th
(Sunday) to-day I stayed in bed until 11.30, being much exhausted, and then
motored down to lunch with Lloyd George at Walton Heath. He had a bad
cold. After lunch we smoked a cigar together and he rehearsed to me the
great speech he intends to make in the House next Thursday, and I gave him
many suggestions. We also discussed future plans for the war, and he was
delighted with my Memo. He is awfully down on Robertson and I more than
fear lest he should out Robertson and put me in his place—a job for which
I have no desire at all! Then Bonar Law turned up and I left and *while I was
there Lloyd George had a long talk on the telephone with Lord Northcliffe, whom he
seems to funk. My travelling companion in the car was an odious fellow called Sutherland,*[1] *some sort of political parasite of Ll. G.'s.* Then on return to town I had to
see Lord Milner by appointment and spent two hours with him. I have always
hated his politics but found the man very attractive and possessed of personality and got on like a house on fire. I had the mission of asking him to go to

[1]Later Sir William Sutherland (1880–1949). Politician (Lib.). Private Secretary or
Parliamentary Private Secretary to Lloyd George in all his Ministerial capacities
1915–20. A Lord of Treasury 1920–22.

the conference in Russia and he consented. I left him the Memo. I had written for Lloyd George.

To amplify Hankey's diary entries about these hectic days, on 4th December Asquith wrote to Lloyd George to the effect that "if he was to remain Prime Minister he was going to reconstruct the Government as he wished, and not as Lloyd George wished".[1] Next day Lloyd George replied making it clear that he intended to fight. Also that day the Liberal and Unionist Ministers met separately, and the replies which the latter gave to Asquith's questions were such that he was left with no alternative but to resign; for he plainly lacked the support necessary to carry on. The King first asked Law to form a government, in accordance with his constitutional duty. Asquith demurred at Law's suggestion that he might serve under him. On 6th a conference of both parties took place at Buckingham Palace, after which there were further consultations between Asquith and the Liberal Ministers, which produced agreement that no attempt should be made to form a government without Lloyd George and the Unionists, and a majority agreement that Asquith should not offer to serve in a subordinate post. The decisions were conveyed to Law, who in consequence declined the King's commission to form a government. The commission was therefore passed at once to Lloyd George, as had been decided at the Buckingham Palace conference, and within 24 hours he had succeeded in discharging it. The new government was principally, though not exclusively, Unionist, and no Liberal member of the late government (except Lloyd George himself) joined it. Carson became First Lord and Balfour, "whose shift of allegiance had been crucial", moved "with speed but dignity from the Admiralty to the Foreign Office".[2] Asquith did not accept his fall from power philosophically, and entertained bitter feelings about the Press campaign which had been conducted against him with such malevolence; and one can hardly blame him for that.

A few comments on Hankey's part in the crisis, and his outlook towards the principal participants, may not be out of place. Many years later he summed up his position, as follows:—

My own concern as Secretary of the War Committee was the avoidance of a big split which would dislocate the machinery for running the war. My plan was that Mr. Asquith should relinquish the day to day running of the War

[1] *Jenkins*, p. 451.   [2] *ibid.*, p. 459.

Committee to Mr. Lloyd George, as a Deputy, retaining the running of the Cabinet and of Parliament, with, of course, an overall right to oversee and keep in close touch with the War Committee as, of course, of all Cabinet Committees. This plan received much support, and was on the point of acceptance, when the false rumour about the origin of a leading article in *The Times* of Monday December 4th, reopened the rift. From that time onward, until the end of the crisis on December 7th, Montagu and I,— sometimes in consultation with other members of the original "Shadow-Cabinet", worked arduously for a reconciliation. Every day we lunched together,—or dined together, either alone or at No. 10. But it is a long and very complicated story, which would take us to august circles on [? into] which, even to-day, it is inadvisable to penetrate. It is sufficient to say that our joint effort for conciliation was finally rejected at the highest constitutional level.[1]

The foregoing extract however plainly requires amplification. In the first place, as we saw earlier, Hankey had for a long time suffered from serious frustration and felt grave discontent over the large War Committee's method of conducting business. He fully supported Lloyd George in his desire to replace it with a much smaller body, armed with executive authority. Secondly his desire that Asquith should continue as Prime Minister, though delegating much authority to the new body, was no doubt to a great extent the product of the admiration and affection he felt towards the chief he had so long served. Thirdly he was as much aware of Lloyd George's qualities of energy, vision and administrative ability as of his defects. He believed that it would be to the nation's advantage if Lloyd George's exuberance were tempered by Asquith's wisdom and experience, and his deviousness checked by Asquith's more solid qualities. Furthermore he profoundly mistrusted Lloyd George's association with Northcliffe; and he

---

[1]From a letter to Sir David Waley of 2nd Feb. (? month unclear) 1957. Waley was at the time collecting material for his biography of Edwin Montagu. (Asia Publishing House, 1964). The reader will note that Hankey here completely accepts Geoffrey Dawson's 1920 account of the origins of *The Times* article of 4th Dec. 1916 (see above, p. 327). Also in 1957 Hankey wrote to Milner's biographer "I too was up to the neck in it, working for a settlement, which at one moment was accepted by both Asquith and Lloyd George, but shattered next day by Geoffrey's *Times* article. I contended with the Asquithians that Lloyd George's repudiation to me of previous knowledge of it was true. Asquith believed me, but Margot and the other Ministers did not. It was years later that Geoffrey told me that he wrote it at Cliveden". Quoted Sir Evelyn Wrench, *Alfred Lord Milner 1905–1925* (Eyre & Spottiswoode, 1958), p. 315.

anticipated, correctly, that it would be difficult to avoid a head-on collision between Lloyd George and General Robertson. His admiration of Balfour had not blinded him to the deficiencies of the Admiralty under his guidance, but he believed that the replacement of Admiral Jackson by Jellicoe would produce the desired improvement without a change of First Lord. In this respect his judgement was to prove over-optimistic. Nor did Hankey exhibit the surprise and distaste one might have expected from him when he became aware that Balfour had, with fastidious nonchalance, changed over from the "gentlemen's team to that of the players' "—as Roy Jenkins has ironically described them.[1] Hankey thoroughly mistrusted Carson, and did not want to see him in the new War Committee or in high office—in which respect his judgement was soon proved much sounder than Lloyd George's. As regards Curzon, although Hankey did not fully appreciate his falseness and duplicity, he was all too well aware of his overweening pride and ambition. Bonar Law he despised, and believed to lack the qualities of leadership required at a time of crisis; but he was of course unaware both of Law's highly equivocal conduct in not actually showing Asquith the Unionist Ministers' resolution which had been agreed at Law's house on 3rd December,[2] and of Aitkens's busy manœuvres behind the scenes. Hankey's anxiety with regard to his own position if Lloyd George and the Unionist caucus got their way is surely understandable. For he relished his position at the centre of the spider's web in which so many power-seeking politicians were manœuvring, and he wished to maintain the trust he had so assiduously cultivated with, and won from, virtually all of them. Moreover he believed, rightly, that his ability and experience could continue to contribute much to the nation's cause. Therein may probably be found the motive behind his long and arduous, though ultimately unsuccessful, attempts to act as mediator in alliance with Montagu. In terms of history Hankey at least comes out of the crisis with his reputation untarnished. Bearing in mind the extraordinary complexity of the political manœuvres of November-December 1916 this was a remarkable accomplishment.

Hankey to Asquith. 2 Whitehall Gardens. 7th December 1916. Holograph[3]
Dear Mr. Asquith,

I cannot let the present occasion pass without writing to give some expression to the overwhelming regret and deep emotion with which I am

---

[1]*Jenkins*, pp. 460–1.   [2]*ibid.*, pp. 434–5 and 438–9.
[3]Asquith papers, box 17, folios 198–9.

filled by the prospect of the severance, temporary though I hope and believe it to be, of the official ties which have bound me to you for nearly nine years, during close on 5 of which I have been in direct and personal association with you as Secretary of this Committee.

The one slight alleviation is that the personal and individual, as apart from the official, ties, which have grown up under the stress and strain of war, are too strong to be broken. The fact that you have given me so generously your friendship and confidence has been a continual source of pride and happiness to me, and I can say from the bottom of my heart has made the heaviest tasks light.

. . . The country at present has only a slight conception of what it owes to your courage, nerve, tact, unswerving straightness, incredible patience, and indomitable perseverance. History however will record it, and when the appropriate time comes I shall not fail to give my own testimony . . . If in this last and most hateful crisis I have offered advice or taken any step, which you think was mistaken, I have at least never been animated by any other sentiment than personal devotion to you, which to me has been synonymous with devotion to the true interests of the country.

I only hope that the day may not long be postponed when I may once more be privileged to serve you again in an official capacity, and in the meantime, if ever opportunity occurs for me to serve you and yours, you may rely on my personal devotion and affection.

Yours as ever

Asquith to Hankey. 10 Downing Street, 8th December 1916. Holograph
Private
My dear Hankey,

You wrote me a most kind and generous letter which I shall always treasure. There is no one so well qualified as you to appraise the work which I have striven to do. Like you, I greatly regret our severance, for no Prime Minister has ever been so loyally and efficiently served as I have been by you.

Yours always,

Chapter 12

The War Cabinet in Action.
December 1916-March 1917

THE War Cabinet met for the first time at 11.30 a.m. on Saturday 9th December 1916, with Lloyd George in the chair and Bonar Law, Milner, Curzon and Arthur Henderson[1] present. Carson, Hardinge, Jellicoe and Robertson were "in attendance". Hankey and Colonel Dally Jones acted as secretaries, and the first Minutes recorded that the Cabinet Office was to be accommodated temporarily in Montagu House at the south end of Whitehall Gardens—until the houses on either side of No. 2, which were requisitioned at this time and converted into additional accommodation for the secretariat, were ready. The War Cabinet also discussed the desirability of strengthening the secretariat; but that was "deferred for further consideration".[2]

Here may be introduced the retrospective view which a very distinguished diplomat has recorded about Hankey in his new capacity. "A secretary was admitted to the arcana [i.e. the War Cabinet]", writes Lord Vansittart, "and it was Maurice Hankey, who progressively became secretary of everything that mattered . . . He grew into a repository of secrets, a Chief Inspector of Mines of information. He had an incredible memory . . . [of] an official brand which could reproduce on call the date, file, substance of every paper that ever flew into a pigeon-hole. If St. Peter is as well served there will be no errors on Judgement Day".[3]

Lloyd George showed no consideration at all for the strain to which Hankey had been subjected during the recent political crisis, and as soon as he assumed office he increased the pressure in every direction. But Hankey rose magnificently to the occasion, and at once prepared a long memorandum covering every aspect of the war. This was another of the broad surveys which, as we saw earlier, he had started in Asquith's

[1]See p. 265. [2]Cab. 23/1 of 9th Dec. 1916.
[3]*The Mist Procession* (Hutchinson, 1958), p. 164.

time, and gradually developed into his own special contribution to the prosecution of the war. For clarity of thought and of expression they could scarcely have been improved; and no reader of them could have been left in the slightest doubt regarding the chief issues to be faced. Moreover on the present occasion Hankey managed to complete his memorandum on the day *before* the War Cabinet met for the first time. He forwarded it to Lloyd George under cover of the letter reproduced below. In the prevailing circumstances the note of slight protest in the opening sentences can readily be forgiven.

Hankey to Lloyd George. 2 Whitehall Gardens. 8th December 1916.[1]

I enclose the Memorandum that I promised. It is the best that I can produce in the time, and, owing to the pressure under which it has been completed, is not a very finished literary production. I have tackled the question entirely from the point of view of the War Committee [Cabinet] and the order in which I think it should attack the problems confronting it. I am, however, not fully acquainted with the conditions you have made with the Labour Party, and these would, no doubt, affect it.

So far as my personal views go, I should be inclined to adopt some such principles as the following:—

1 The maintenance of sea-power is the first consideration, and the restoration of our complete maritime supremacy against submarines should be a first charge on all our resources . . .

2 We must be absolutely secure for Home Defence, but the present margin of military force is unnecessarily large . . .

3 The Western Front must continue to absorb the larger part of our forces, as it is essential not only to make it absolutely secure but to be capable of taking a very powerful offensive there to counter or anticipate another Verdun. In fact, I think an offensive is absolutely unavoidable, although I have still the gravest doubt whether we can smash the German Army by means of it.

4 Subject to the Russian Conference, I should drop the project of overwhelming Bulgaria, and adopt a defensive rôle at Salonika . . .

5 Subject to its practicability and to the consent of the Italians, I should carry out the scheme of transferring guns to Italy with a view to a great attack on the Carso, the objective being Pola.

6 I should prepare for an intensification of the operations from Egypt by transferring Divisions from Salonika, and possibly one from Mesopotamia.

7 I should stimulate to the utmost production of every kind in this country, with a view to a gradual diminution of our dependence on oversea

[1]Cab. 42/19/2.

resources. . . . In order to do this I would not hesitate to adopt Industrial Compulsion in whatever form Labour will consent [to], nor to the introduction of foreign labour for our munition factories, ports, mines and agriculture . . .

8 I should adopt an entirely conciliatory policy towards Ireland.

In any public pronouncement I should adopt the attitude that victory is only to be achieved by a tremendous national effort, but that if this effort is made there is little doubt that a satisfactory and lasting peace can be secured.

All this, as arranged between us, is for the private use of yourself and any of your colleagues to whom you may like to show it, and it is subject to the remarks on my relations to the General Staff contained in the beginning of the Memorandum.

In the 30 page memorandum which Hankey attached to the above letter he developed his argument about the strategic purposes of the Allies under four headings. These were, firstly, "Naval and Shipping Policy", in which he discussed the submarine menace and possible counter-measures at length. He was particularly concerned about the recent steep rise in losses of Allied and neutral shipping, and reverted to his earlier proposal for "a complete barrage of mines and nets right across the North Sea" as one possible remedy.[1] But he considered the arming of all merchant ships the best deterrent, because it would restrict the U-boats' mobility by forcing them to make submerged attacks with torpedoes rather than gun attacks while on the surface. We may note that at this stage Hankey made no suggestion that convoy should be adopted. Turning to "The Military Policy of the Allies" he enlarged on the points made in his covering letter about adopting the defensive at Salonika and preparing for offensives from Egypt against the Turks and on the Italian front. But in addition to this peripheral strategy he wanted "to prepare for a great offensive in the West next year", thereby revealing his acceptance, albeit reluctantly, of the view of the "westerners". Under "Economic Policy" he discussed man-power, finance, economic pressure on the enemy, our own supplies of food and raw materials, and measures to increase agricultural production. The financing of purchases from U.S.A. gave grounds for concern, and he recommended that all Allied gold stocks should be pooled for such purposes. The blockade of the Central Powers was, he considered, being well handled, though the collapse of Roumania had obviously weakened it by providing the enemy with new sources of

[1]See pp. 180–1.

supply for wheat and oil. These would "probably tide him over 1917". Lastly under "Political Considerations" he urged the need for "a settlement of the Irish question", because it would release a large number of troops for service in the war theatres. If a permanent settlement was impracticable he advocated the conciliation of Irish opinion by measures "such as the release of prisoners under proper safeguards", and other steps which would help "to keep the country quiet and stimulate military recruiting". The "maintenance of good relations with the United States" was, in Hankey's view, likely to prove especially important in the immediate future; but as this had long been a guiding feature of British policy no change was involved. Thus did Hankey block out the broad questions which demanded early consideration by the War Cabinet. Though his paper was never circulated as an official document subsequent events were to show that in almost all respects his judgement was well founded.

Meanwhile Hankey had turned his attention to the procedural rules which should govern the conduct of the War Cabinet's business, and the reorganisation of the Secretariat to meet its demands. Lloyd George evidently delegated to Milner the task of handling the Secretariat's problems on behalf of the War Cabinet, and on 10th December Milner wrote to Hankey that he was convinced that he needed "a great deal more assistance". Milner wanted to divide the Secretariat into Military and Civil sides, and find a suitable "colleague" for Hankey to deal with the latter, as well as "several good subordinates".[1] He invited Hankey to discuss these matters; but Hankey does not appear to have taken up the offer—probably because he had already developed his own ideas and wanted to deal directly with the Prime Minister. His first step was to circulate a draft of the "Rules of Procedure for the War Cabinet", and his wording was obviously designed to leave the Government Departments in no doubt regarding the power and authority of the new body. For example he stated that its conclusions "would become operative decisions to be carried out by the responsible Departments" as soon as they had been initialled by the Prime Minister. He went on to lay down how issues should be raised to the War Cabinet by its own members or by any department; the manner in which departments would be consulted on matters which concerned them, and how they would be informed of the decisions arrived at. He made proposals regarding when the War Cabinet would meet ("as a rule at least once on

[1] Milner to Hankey 10th Dec. 1916.

every weekday, and more often when required"); what "experts" would be called to attend meetings; and the responsibility of the departments for keeping the Cabinet properly informed (a matter about which he had complained in Asquith's time[1]). Finally he proposed that the Secretary should be given "direction . . . to communicate to Heads of Departments and others concerned information received by the War Cabinet from various sources".[2] Obviously Hankey was determined to eliminate at one stroke all the failings of the old War Council and War Committee. Equally obviously his own position would be strengthened, and his influence increased.

In working out the changes in the Cabinet system Hankey was probably heartened by the knowledge that he enjoyed the support of his old friend Esher. "The War Council was a farce", Esher wrote. "I am heartily glad it is dead, and I hope it will not be revived in another form. The old C.I.D. was buried beneath that amorphous excrescence. It was a sad pity.[3] Now you have a chance of setting it to work. It should be revived—and it should do what long, long ago I suggested to you, that is to say prepare the details and ground work of the discussions that must take place in the *Cabinet*. Day by day the C.I.D., composed of men who will *work out detail* should sit. They should form a body of living Reference for Carson, Curzon and Ll. G. They should read what those people will not read, digest what they will not digest, and be prepared to reply to all questions, and to help with every sort of information . . ."[4] Although the C.I.D. was not revived in name, its system was in effect put at the service of the War Cabinet; and Hankey and his assistants did jointly provide the "living Reference" which Esher had in mind. But at the beginning things did not go at all smoothly for them, and even Hankey showed impatience at the suddenness with which long and complicated memoranda were demanded—often to be ignored after they had been produced at the cost of much time and effort. Perhaps this was inevitable while the new machinery was being run in; but the long-suffering Secretariat certainly had some cause for complaint.

[1] See pp. 273–4.
[2] Milner papers, box 123, folio 129.
[3] This is the opposite to the view Esher expressed shortly before the outbreak of war, when he held that the C.I.D.'s "doors should be closed: yes, at the first shot". See p. 140.
[4] Esher to Hankey. Holograph, from G.H.Q., France, 10th Dec. 1916.

Diary 11th December 1916
. . . I lunched alone with Ll. G., who discoursed mainly on his plans for a big military coup in Syria. I did not feel very happy with the new War Cabinet, who do not know much of administration and seem to think that the only thing to be done is to build up a gigantic office of satellites and clerks. I am getting hold of them one by one and trying to educate them . . .

12th December
I breakfasted alone with Lloyd George. He is very anxious to foist on me a Welshman called Thomas Jones, whom I interviewed after breakfast. Before I saw him I received a message from J.T. Davies, Lloyd George's private secty. and a good fellow, that Thomas Jones is a peace-monger and a syndical-ist.[1] Still I rather liked the man, despite rather a sly face like Ll. G.'s and I think I could use him on the industrial side. Anyhow he had ideas, and as a result of our interview I caught on to a scheme of organisation of the office into two groups—machinery and ideas . . .

Thus began, with a somewhat equivocal attitude on Hankey's part, a relationship between him and "T.J." which was to last for 14 years. Though each appreciated the other's ability and qualities they never became intimate friends. The letters that passed between them rarely show warmth on either side, Jones's usually beginning "My dear Chief" and Hankey's "Dear T.J.". In truth they stood far apart on political, economic and religious issues. Jones's radicalism contrasted with Hankey's conservatism (or perhaps right wing liberalism); Jones's burning interest in social welfare and education with Hankey's dominant concern with defence; and Jones's Non-conformism with Hankey's orthodox Protestantism. And, finally, in the 1930s when Hankey was pressing for rearmament, Jones was moving in the "Cliveden set" and was very much in favour of the policy described as "appeasement". Although Jones paid a warm tribute to Hankey in his memoirs, as "the prince of secretaries . . . He was endowed with immense vitality, a prodigious memory, high organising capacity and a gift for distilling circumambient conversations into well-ordered memoranda", he qualifies that praise by adding that "He conserved nervous energy by political objectivity and indifference to measures other than those bearing on national defence . . ."[2] And other published

[1] Syndicalism "a movement among industrial workers having as its object the transfer of the means of production and distribution from their present owners to unions of workers, the method generally favoured for the accomplishment of this being the general strike". (Concise O.E.D.)
[2] *A Diary with Letters 1931–1950* (O.U.P.), Ch. XVIII.

letters and remarks by Jones reveal that he indulged in no uncritical adulation for his "Chief".[1]

One of the first matters Hankey had to get settled was how to keep the King informed under the new arrangements, since the establishment of the Cabinet Secretariat could be said to eliminate the need for the Prime Minister to send a personal letter about each Cabinet meeting as in former times. Hankey obviously realised that this matter needed careful handling.

Hankey to Stamfordham. 2 Whitehall Gardens, 10th December 1916. Holograph[2]
Dear Lord Stamfordham,

I saw the Prime Minister at his house at Walton Heath this afternoon and asked his instructions about sending the War Cabinet Minutes to the King, as I thought he might want to send something in his own handwriting.

Mr. Lloyd George, who had rather a bad cold, said that as the business was entirely what in former days would have been treated as War Committee business, and in no sense corresponded to Cabinet business, he thought His Majesty would probably prefer to receive the full Secretary's Minutes rather than a personal summary of his own.

I accordingly have sent by Mr. Lloyd George's directions a copy of the draft which I have sent round to members [of the War Cabinet] for their remarks, and I trust that this course will meet with the King's approval.

Stamfordham replied the same day "Yes! I think that so long as the Cabinet business is confined to what is purely War Committee affairs the Secretary's full Minutes is [sic] sufficient for the King. I assume that the Prime Minister will adhere to the time-honoured custom of reporting in his own hand the conduct of actual *Cabinet* business, as such reports are the sole record of the proceedings of a Cabinet meeting".[3] Evidently Stamfordham had not grasped that the C.I.D.'s procedure was now to be applied to Cabinet meetings; and to ask a Prime Minister who detested putting pen to paper as much as Lloyd George to continue the "time-honoured custom" of personal letters to

---

[1]For example his recording of Lloyd George's disapproval, which Jones obviously shared, of Hankey having given evidence before the Royal Commission on the Private Manufacture of Arms (Cmd. 5292, 1936)—"So unlike Hankey to have done this". Also his letter to Lady Grigg of 18th March 1937 alleging Hankey's jealousy when Cabinet Minutes which Jones had taken were accepted by Austen Chamberlain "without a comma changed". *op. cit.*, p. 325.

[2]RA. GV. K1037/1.

[3]Stamfordham to Hankey 10th Dec. 1916. Holograph. Lloyd George papers F/23/1/1.

the Monarch about each Cabinet was to ask altogether too much. Hankey sent the reply on to Lloyd George saying that he proposed to forward a copy of the Minutes of each meeting "with the usual formula 'The Prime Minister presents his humble duty etc.'." "Personally", he added, "I hate time-honoured customs that waste time".[1] So did Lloyd George, and in fact the personal letters stopped at once; but Stamford-ham continued suspicious of the new organisation and, as we shall see, moved quickly to the attack if he considered that the King was not being kept properly informed.

At this very busy time Hankey received what must have been an embarrassing request from Asquith—for copies of the same "Secretary's Notes" of War Committee meetings which had caused so much trouble at the beginning of the Dardanelles Commission's investigations.[2] He wrote very frankly to Asquith, meeting his request but telling him that he had felt bound first to consult Lloyd George—which had led to "speculative discussion as to why you want them". Hankey had thereupon suggested that the former Prime Minister "wanted to be forearmed against any statement he [Lloyd George] might make" in Parliament; to which Lloyd George had replied that "he did not mean to include in his own speech anything of the past, or any sort of reflection on your Government, nor anything in the way of recrimination". He "only meant to deal with his policy for winning the war", and readily gave Hankey permission to inform Asquith accordingly. To Asquith Hankey went on to say "My own position is singularly detestable. Necessarily from my position and knowledge I am the linch-pin, more or less, of the new government. They have to turn to me on every occasion and on every kind of subject. I do not altogether like this after serving you so long, but as a patriotic Englishman I am bound to, and intend to strain every move to make the new machine a success, and indeed to like and respect my new chiefs, so far as in me lies. But my loyalty to a new Prime Minister is a loyalty to the country, and does not abate by one jot my personal loyalty to you".[3] Thus did Hankey strive to mollify the natural antagonism felt by the former Prime Minister, now Leader of the Opposition in Parliament, towards the man who had displaced him—in order that the prosecution of the war might not suffer; and at the same time he plainly hoped to salvage

[1]*ibid.* [2]See pp. 287 and 299–300.
[3]Hankey to Asquith 12th Dec. 1916. Holograph. Asquith papers, box 17, folios 247–8.

from the wreckage of the outgoing government his own warm friendship with, and admiration for Asquith.

To Lady Hankey. 3 Radnor Place. 13th December 1916
It would be cruelty to animals to expect a serious letter to-night. I breakfasted with Ll. G. at 9.15, had 3 meetings—morning, afternoon and evening—and dictated Minutes as I eat[1] my lunch and tea (in the office by the way!) and have come home for dinner dog tired . . . The fact is there has been an almost unexampled rush of urgent questions to decide. Ll. G. has crocked up again after this morning's meeting, and has been ordered to see no-one at all for 24 hours. Awkward. I am beginning to think that the plan of altering the whole system of Govt. and having this terrific upset in the middle of a great war has definitely failed—but we may pull it through . . .

To the same. 3 Radnor Place. 14th December 1916
Once more I am home to dinner and am writing before the meal. I knew that Ll. G. was making the pace too hot and that either he or I would crack up. And after all "the dog it was that died", for Ll. G. has crocked to-day and is confined to his bed and not allowed to see a soul. Meanwhile I slept 10 hours solid, was quite fresh this morning and have had a relatively light day, so I feel quite cheery again . . . I am still fighting about my staff, and am in great jeopardy of having Steel-Maitland[2] foisted on me as equal, simply because no-one else will have him; but I have made a move to turn their flank. Otherwise I feel I have made some progress towards winning the confidence of my new team . . .

As Hankey himself has published nearly the whole of the diary entries for these hectic days they will not be reproduced here.[3] On 13th December he circulated a "Note on the Composition of the Secretariat of the War Cabinet", which followed closely on the lines of what he called the "brain wave" which had come to him in the early hours a few mornings previously.[4] The functions of the Secretariat, he wrote, "may be divided into two categories classed roughly as:—(a) Machinery (b) Ideas." The former category would include keeping the records of all meetings, and "the preparation of Agenda papers, the collection and distribution of all information required for the War Cabinet's delibera-

---

[1]Among the oddities of Hankey's letters and diary is that he commonly wrote "eat" for "ate", and also mis-spelt intrigue "intreague".
[2]Later Sir Arthur H. D. R. Steel-Maitland, Bart. (1876–1935). Politician (Cons.). Parliamentary Under-Secretary for Colonies 1915–17 and (joint) for Foreign Office 1917–19. Minister of Labour 1924–9.
[3]*Supreme Command*, II, pp. 594–6.
[4]Memo. dated 13th Dec. 1916. Milner papers, box 123, folios 124–8.

tions, and the dissemination of the decisions" of that body. "The skeleton of the machinery", he pointed out, already existed in the Secretariat of the War Committee; but the inclusion of what had until now been the responsibility of the civil departments and Cabinet business would necessitate a considerable increase of staff. It was, however, on the "ideas" side that the greatest change and expansion was required; and Hankey started off by outlining what he regarded as the constitutional responsibility of members of the War Cabinet and of the departmental heads. What the former would need was "an expert staff . . . to collect from the departments, or elsewhere, the data which the War Cabinet require for the development of the ideas and the formulation of the wider schemes" which he had already reviewed. He therefore proposed that as a start each Minister in the War Cabinet should nominate an Assistant-Secretary, and the Prime Minister the civilian Secretary; and he outlined the duties which would fall to each of them. He wanted the Military Assistant Secretaries (Colonel E. D. Swinton, Colonel Dally Jones and Major L. Storr) to continue as before, and wrote most warmly of their special qualifications and qualities. But he proposed to ask the Admiralty to nominate a Naval Assistant Secretary.[1] The Historical Section under Julian Corbett was also to remain unchanged.[2] Next day he particularised on his scheme in a letter to Lloyd George, in which he took action to forestall the appointment of Steel-Maitland, the nominee of Milner, to the civil side of the Secretariat. He first urged that Lloyd George should "absolutely reserve this appointment to yourself", since it was essential that "the civil, like the military secretary must be thoroughly congenial to, and in sympathy with . . . yourself". If Steel-Maitland was the Prime Minister's choice he would do his utmost "to help him and to work cordially and loyally with him"; but he none the less considered the appointment would be a mistake—chiefly because he doubted whether Steel-Maitland possessed "sufficient tact". He supported that criticism by stating that, to the best of his belief, Steel-Maitland had not been a success in the Colonial

[1]This was approved. The first holder was Fleet Paymaster (later Paymaster Rear-Admiral) Philip J. H. L. Row (1870–1932). Hankey misspelt his name Rowe in *Supreme Command*, and usually in his diary too; but the Navy Lists of the period and the Cabinet Office records agree that Row is correct.

[2]The other members of the Historical Section of the C.I.D. were at this time Mr. (later Sir John) Fortescue (1859–1933), Captain C. T. Atkinson (1874–1964). military and naval historian and Fellow of Exeter College, Oxford, with Major E. Y. Daniel, R.M. as "the very experienced Secretary".

Office or the Conservative Chief Whip's office; nor was he "liked in the House of Commons", which he regarded as "a very fair barometer". His own choice was Edwin Montagu, whom he considered "the ideal man for the post"; but he realised that the War Cabinet was considering him for the new post of Director of National Service.[1] Failing Montagu he pressed the claims of Sir Mark Sykes,[2] whose many-sided qualities, "breadth of vision" and "unique position in the Irish question as practically a Conservative Home-Ruler" made him particularly well qualified to handle the multitude of complex problems which were bound to arise in the future. For the subordinate posts Hankey proposed Thomas Jones, G. M. Young[3] and Captain Clement Jones[4]— "another Welshman!"; and, "as Lord Milner insists", he would accept Leo Amery—though he suspected him "of being anti-Russian, and would much sooner see him elsewhere".[5]

As Hankey foresaw, Milner did write pressing for Steel-Maitland's appointment to the Civil Secretaryship "as an equal colleague of Hankey", and also proposed G. M. Young and Amery for two of the subordinate posts.[6] But the idea of having "an equal colleague" held as little appeal to Hankey as did Steel-Maitland for filling it. Though we have no documentary confirmation the probability is that he followed up his letter of 14th December by discussing the matter with both Lloyd George and Milner. At any rate on 20th he sent an "Immediate" letter to The Secretary, Welsh Insurance Commission, stating that at their meeting two days earlier the War Cabinet had decided to appoint Mr. Thomas Jones "to be one of its *Assistant Secretaries*" (italics supplied) and requesting his very early release for that purpose.[7] Probably Hankey realised that Jones would in fact soon become the Civil Secretary, though under himself; and he wanted to get him into

[1]This recommendation was not implemented. Montagu remained out of office until August 1917, when he became Secretary of State for India. Sir Auckland Geddes became Minister for National Service on the same date.
[2]See p. 270.   [3]George M. Young. Historian (1882–1959).
[4]Later Sir Clement Jones (1880–1963). Secretary, Shipping Control Committee 1915. Assistant Secretary, War Cabinet 1916–20. Secretary, British Empire Delegation to Paris Peace Conference 1919. Chairman, Commonwealth Shipping Committee 1947.
[5]Hankey to Lloyd George 14th Dec. 1916. Lloyd George papers F/23/1/2.
[6]Milner to Lloyd George 14th Dec. 1916. Lloyd George papers F/38/2/1.
[7]K. Middlemas (Ed.), *Dr. Thomas Jones, Diary*, Vol. I, 1916–25 (Oxford U.P., 1969), pp. 16–17.

the office quickly in order to eliminate Steel-Maitland's claims. At any rate it is clear that, apart from having reluctantly to accept Amery, he got everything that he wanted.

To Lady Hankey. 3 Radnor Place, S.W. 16th December 1916
I had no time to write yesterday. Things are straightening up a bit in the office. I have actually engaged two of my new civilian assistants—Young, Mr. Arthur Henderson's Secretary, and Captain Clement Jones, late Secty. of the Shipping Control etc, two altogether admirable persons, with whom I feel sure I can work. I have also, I think, defeated the Steel-Maitland intreague [sic]. In addition I have entirely reorganised my office, and to-day I looked over my new premises. All this on top of at least one meeting of the War Cabinet every day and sometimes more . . . I am aiming at remaining the *sole* Secretary, in which case I shall divide my office into three sections:—

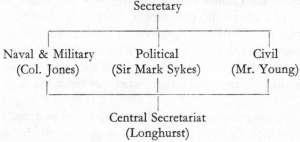

Secretary

Naval & Military	Political	Civil
(Col. Jones)	(Sir Mark Sykes)	(Mr. Young)

Central Secretariat
(Longhurst)

. . . I intend to have a private secretary to look after my personal needs.[1] There is a good deal of detail still to be worked out, but I shall have it all completed next week . . .

Ll. George is still ill and I only saw him in bed for a minute or two to-day. I think he will be all right for his great speech on Tuesday.

I am dining again with Montagu, as Bongie[2] has the flue [sic]. The Prime Minister and the War Cabinet have charged me with the mission of trying to get him [presumably Montagu] to accept a very important job.[3] I am getting

---

[1]A. J. Sylvester took over as Hankey's private secretary from Cyril Longhurst at this time, Longhurst becoming responsible for the administration of the War Cabinet office. Sylvester served Hankey until 1921, when Lloyd George "carried him off as his own private secretary" (*Supreme Command*, II, p. 591). In 1918 Lawrence Burgis joined the War Cabinet secretariat, and he replaced Sylvester three years later to remain Hankey's private secretary until 1937.

[2]Sir Maurice Bonham Carter, Asquith's private secretary. See p. 174.

[3]This probably refers to the Ministry of Reconstruction, which Montagu was offered but refused in July 1917. In that month Austen Chamberlain's resignation over the government's handling of the Mesopotamia Commission's report (see pp. 407-9 and 412-3) left the India Office vacant, and Montagu accepted it.

on very well with my new chiefs and am making great friends with Henderson, the Labour man . . .

In the calmness of retrospect Lloyd George wrote about Hankey's
work as Secretary of the Cabinet that "he discharged his very delicate
and difficult function with such care, tact and fairness that I cannot
recall any dispute ever arising as to the accuracy of his Minutes or his
reports on the action taken".[1] Though the broad impression Hankey
left on Lloyd George's mind was certainly correct he had evidently
forgotten how often he himself had challenged the minutes recording
the War Committee's deliberations in 1916, and that Robertson was not
alone in taking exception to minutes of the War Cabinet in the following
year.[2] Furthermore, as will be told later, Hankey's records of the
proceedings of the Council of Four at the Paris Peace Conference of
1919 produced a serious disagreement with the Americans.[3] Difficulties
of this nature do not of course reflect on the care and integrity with
which Hankey compiled the minutes. What they do show is that, by
denying that any dispute ever arose out of them, Lloyd George gave a
false impression of the troubles that sometimes beset the hard-worked
secretary.

One of the unfinished pieces of business, inherited from the War
Committee, which Hankey was anxious to get out of the way, was
approval of the Cabinet Conclusions on the first report of the Curzon
Air Board which, as we saw earlier, were still in a state of suspense at the
fall of the First Coalition.[4] On 22nd December he brought the matter
before the War Cabinet, which wisely decided that as so much time had
been expended on the subject by their predecessors, they could do
no better than approve the draft which Hankey had put forward
nearly a month earlier.[5] Thus was born the second Air Board under
Lord Cowdray.[6] Its importance lies in the fact that, as it was set up
under the "New Ministries and Secretaries Act" of 1916,[7] it was in fact,

[1]*Lloyd George*, II, p. 1081.   [2]See pp. 252–3 and 426.
[3]About the Japanese mandate over the island of Yap in the Pacific, recorded in the
minutes of the Council of Four meeting on 9th May 1919.
[4]See pp. 271–2.
[5]Cab. 37/162. Also Adm. 1/8475 and 1/8478. See also *Documents Relating to the Naval
Air Service*, Vol. I, Ed. S. W. Roskill (Navy Records Society, 1969), No. 151.
[6]Weetman D. Pearson, 1st Viscount Cowdray 1916 (1856–1927). Head of S. Pearson
& Co., Contractors, and Politician (Lib.). President of Air Board 1917. Resigned
Nov. 1917.
[7]6 & 7 Geo. 5 c.68.

though not yet in name, a Ministry of the Air endowed with the executive authority which had been denied to the Derby Air Committee and the Curzon Air Board.

It was natural that the War Cabinet's first efforts to instil drive and vigour into the conduct of its business should have produced some disgruntlement in Hankey's mind—though he only gave vent to it in his diary and in his letters to his wife. On Christmas Eve he wrote in the diary a description of what his days had recently been like, starting by breakfasting with Lloyd George, then to the office to deal with papers, then at least two War Cabinets, one before lunch and one in the afternoon or evening; and while he was trying not to allow the Conclusions of those meetings to fall into arrears, he was constantly being pestered by Ministers or heads of departments on a multitude of subjects.

Diary 24th December 1916[1]
. . . The new War Cabinet are very tiresome and exacting. They are making the mistake of "bustle for business'. For example on Thursday [21st], in connection with the American "peace note"[2] they suddenly demanded a complete Memorandum on the effect on the Allies and on America, of an "Act of non-intercourse" by the U.S.A. and insisted it must be ready the same evening, though subsequently they extended this to Friday. I at once put on Young, the best man I had free, and by a tremendous effort he produced a very good paper, which . . . was reproduced and circulated. Although on Thursday morning they had insisted that this was essential to their discussion, when they tackled the question on Saturday, they seemed to have forgotten all about it . . . Yet this work had tremendously upset half the Departments in the Govt. and placed an almost intolerable strain on my office! Again, this afternoon in another access, they ordered the British Ambassador in Rome to return at the shortest possible notice, involving his departure on Xmas day, in order to take their instructions on a scheme for lending heavy guns to

---

[1] See *Supreme Command*, II, p. 595 for the first part of this day's entry, summarised above.

[2] This must refer to President Wilson's Note of 20th Dec., sent in reply to Bethman Hollweg's peace feeler of 12th. Wilson acted without informing Colonel House; and, as the latter well understood, the inclusion in his Note of a typical Wilsonian phrase stating that Allied and German war aims were "virtually the same" made its rejection by the British and French governments certain. See *House*, II, pp. 400–9; and *Lloyd George*, I, pp. 659–60. On Germany's real war aims see Fritz Fischer's recent full study *Germany's Aims in the First World War* (Eng. Trans. London and N.Y., 1968).

Italy, in exchange for 3½ Italian divisions to be sent to Salonika, although neither project has been examined by the General Staff, and both are suspected of being impracticable . . . All this has been very exhausting to the War Cabinet and its secretariat, and it was a terrible blow when we received a telegram to-night that three French Ministers had started from Paris to join us in a series of conferences lasting over Xmas!

26th December 1916

The Frenchmen did not come for Xmas after all so I got a short holiday. . . . To-day was very busy. At 11.30 the War Cabinet; lunch with Lloyd George and Mantoux[1] the French interpreter; conference with the French from 3 to 6.30; then I had to see Robertson about a conference he was to have the same evening with some French officers; then back to my office to check the conclusions of the morning's meeting . . . and to dictate for the King a summary of the conference. I found Robertson in a very disgruntled state threatening to resign. The new War Cabinet are really up against it, as they don't believe in Robertson's "Western Front" policy, but they will never find a soldier to carry out their "Salonika" policy. Moreover the complete breakdown of shipping renders the latter policy impracticable, and they won't recognise it. I am inclined to think they will come a cropper before long. Lloyd George told me that Milner had made a very bad impression on him . . . The new Govt. amused me much by their telegram to the Dominion Govts. inviting the Prime Ministers to attend meetings of the War Cabinet to discuss "questions of great urgency". As a matter of fact they have not a notion what they are to discuss, and as Bonar Law said "When they are here, you will wish to goodness you could get rid of them".

1st January 1917

The old year had gone out without my having time to write up my diary, as last week was busier than ever. The Anglo-French Conferences took a long time, lasting three whole days.[2] On Wednesday [27th Dec.] we had two War Cabinet meetings and two busy conferences. At the end of the day when I was absolutely dead beat, at about 7.45 Lloyd George turned round to me and said "I should like to have some conclusions ready by to-morrow morning." So George Clerk,[3] who was helping me with the secretarial arrangements, and I went off to dine, drank a bottle of champagne, and drafted the most admirable conclusions, which were agreed to by all concerned, in a state of semi-

[1]Paul Mantoux (1871–1956). French historian. Professor of French History and Institutions, London University 1913. Acted as interpreter at Inter-Allied conferences 1915–18 and at Paris Peace Conference 1919.
[2]Minutes in Cab. 28. IC.13.
[3]Sir George R. Clerk. Diplomat (1874–1951). Ambassador to Turkey 1926–33, to Belgium 1933–4 and to France 1934–7.

intoxication. . . . The French are playing a very crooked game over Greece. At the conference they agreed that General Sarrail,[1] should take no action against Greece without the approval of the two Governments, and two days later they were asking us to give him a free hand to attack the Greeks. The fact is that politically they are in a hole, and the Radicals who are the descendants of the revolution, want to have a republic in Greece, and Briand is too weak to resist them. My office is developing satisfactorily. Amery, who has been foisted on me by Milner let me in for a row with the Colonial Office by his tactlessness, and I only just averted serious trouble by seeing Walter Long,[2] the Colonial Secretary . . . To-morrow we leave for Italy for a conference with the Italians. Balfour has commissioned me to bring Baron Sonnino, the Italian Foreign Minister, back with us.

On 2nd January, after "a short meeting of the War Cabinet", Hankey set off for Paris and Rome with Lloyd George, Milner, Robertson, Sir Rennell Rodd, Sir George Clerk, W. T. Layton[3] (Munitions Department) and Thomas Royden[4] (a member of the Admiralty's Shipping Committee). They put up as usual at the Hotel Crillon, and next morning Hankey accompanied Lloyd George on visits to Briand and General Lyautey, the new War Minister.[5] The purpose was to achieve Anglo-French agreement on the agenda for the Rome Conference. That evening the party, now joined by Briand, Albert Thomas and Lyautey, entrained for Rome. The journey proved very trying for Hankey, with constant conferences in the swaying and overheated saloons. He slept badly—and, incidentally, formed a very poor opinion of the much-advertised Lyautey, which was quickly to be substantiated.

[1] Maurice Sarrail (1856–1929). French soldier. C-in-C, Salonika Army 1915–18. High Commissioner, Syria 1924 but recalled after the Druse revolt.

[2] Walter H. Long, 1st Viscount Long 1921 (1854–1924). Politician (Cons.). President, Board of Agriculture 1895–1900 and of Local Government Board 1900–5 and 1915–16. Chief Secretary for Ireland 1905. Colonial Secretary 1916–18; First Lord of Admiralty 1919–21.

[3] 1st Baron Layton 1947 (1884–1966). Economist, journalist and politician (Lib.). Served in Ministry of Munitions 1917. British delegate to World Economic Conference 1927. Editor of The Economist 1922–38. Director-General of Programmes, then Chairman of Executive Committee, Ministry of Supply 1940–2. Head of Joint War Production Staff 1942–3.

[4] 1st Baron Royden 1944 (1871–1950). Shipowner and business man. Chairman, Liverpool Steamship Owners' Association. President Chamber of Shipping of the United Kingdom.

[5] Louis H. G. Lyautey (1854–1934). French soldier. High Commissioner and C-in-C in Morocco 1912–16. Minister of War for 5 months under Briand 1916–17. Marshal of France 1921.

The British and French delegations to Rome were in fact deeply divided, both within themselves and towards each other. Lloyd George's purposes were to avoid a repetition of the costly and fruitless offensive of 1916 on the western front, and instead to encourage the Italians by the loan of artillery to take the offensive against the Austrians on the Carso; but such ideas were, of course, anathema to Robertson, who displayed considerable cunning, not to say disloyalty, in forestalling and frustrating his Prime Minister. The French were much keener to reinforce the Salonika front, and in order to further their Balkan strategy wanted to give General Sarrail full powers to coerce the Greek government. Nor were the Italian politicians and soldiers any less disunited than those of their British and French allies. Hankey was left in no doubt regarding the true form from the very beginning; since within a few hours of his arrival in Rome Lloyd George asked him to seek out General Cadorna,[1] the Italian C-in-C, and sound him about the artillery proposal. He then found that Robertson had got in before him, and had successfully cooled any enthusiasm Cadorna might have felt for such an idea. Obviously Hankey was in danger of either falling into the Charybdis of Lloyd George's displeasure or of wrecking himself on the Scylla of Robertson's obstinacy; but he successfully extricated himself from both dangers.

That evening Lloyd George displayed no less cunning than Robertson in preparing the ground for his strategy. On first sighting the Italian Cabinet Hankey singled out Bissolati,[2] the socialist, as having the strongest personality; and it was he whom Lloyd George now enlisted in his cause.

Diary 5th January 1917
... Before I had been there [at the British Embassy] many minutes I received a mysterious message by an Italian servant that Ll. George wanted me in the Ambassador's study. When I got there I found Lloyd George in confabulation with Bissolati ... [who] had been smuggled in in this clandestine manner because, not being a member of the Italian inner Cabinet, he had no excuse for official relations with Lloyd George; besides which he is the *enfant terrible* of the Italian Cabinet. I was most favourably impressed by Bissolati, who seemed greatly superior in intelligence and breadth of view to any other

[1]General Count Luigi Cadorna (1850–1928). Italian C-in-C 1915. Replaced by General Diaz after the disaster at Caporetto in 1917. Marshal 1924.
[2]Leonida Bissolati. Italian politician (Soc.). Commissioner for War Services 1916 and then Minister without Portfolio in the Boselli government.

member of the Italian Cabinet. He was a tremendous partisan of Lloyd George's scheme for a concentration on the Italian front, and eventually went off promising to see Cadorna and try to induce him to press [for] the scheme . . . It was midnight when I left the Embassy in company with Bissolati. There were several people outside on the other side of the street, and they must have included "watchers" from the French Embassy, for [Albert] Thomas next day knew all about Bissolati's visit.

Late that evening Hankey, who always liked to keep at least one step ahead of his masters, dictated a series of Resolutions for Lloyd George to put to the conference. Early next morning he took them to Milner, who "would scarcely look at them, as he said my drafts were always all he could wish". But Lloyd George, probably sensing that the conference would come out strongly against his own strategic ideas, proved "irritable and in a thoroughly bad temper".[1] The first session began at 10 a.m. on 6th at the Consulta (Ministry of Foreign Affairs), and it produced little except wrangles about Greece. It was continued in the afternoon and evening, when Briand made an eloquent appeal for the reinforcement of the Salonika front. Lloyd George then "propounded his project for Italian co-operation, which was respectfully but rather coldly received", the Italians making little comment and the French being very suspicious that it would withdraw forces from the western front. Cadorna who was called in, gave it "rather lukewarm support". Early next morning Lloyd George summoned Hankey to the British Embassy, where Sarrail soon turned up and argued fervently that "the British and French governments should shut their eyes and turn their backs for a fortnight", during which he would of course have resolved the Greek dilemma by force. According to Hankey Lloyd George let him "run on in this wild manner for some time", and then "took him in hand", explaining firmly that such a proposal would outrage neutral opinion—especially in America. It was better, said the Prime Minister, to accept a risk in Greece than in the U.S.A.; and Sarrail finally cooled off and promised to do nothing without the approval of the British government. "Then", wrote Hankey, "they shook hands dramatically".[2]

That afternoon the draft Resolutions Hankey had sketched out were accepted by the conference "practically without amendment". They were in fact very amorphous except with regard to Greece, which was to be given an ultimatum to withdraw all her forces into the Peloponnese within a fortnight—and which achieved its purpose. Otherwise

[1]Diary 6th Jan. 1917. [2]Diary 7th Jan. 1917.

the conference did no more than express the need for closer co-operation and for more frequent conferences, stressed the importance of
material assistance to Russia (the need for which must have been
obvious to all), and approved the development of a new line of communications by road from the Adriatic coast to Salonika, which would
reduce the amount of shipping required to supply the forces on that
front. Lloyd George's scheme was "remitted for examination by the
Staffs"—which of course doomed it.[1] Indeed the one clear outcome of
the Rome conference was that the "westerners" had again prevailed.

On 10th January Hankey was back in his office again—to find "a
terrible congestion" because the new accommodation was not yet
ready for his greatly increased staff, who were therefore falling over
each other in the old rooms at 2 Whitehall Gardens. He was also
annoyed by the way the Press had handled the announcement of the
appointment of the new Assistant Secretaries.

Diary 10th January 1917
. . . The infernal Press have been active and have been putting misleading
paragraphs in about my secretariat, which is very annoying—particularly
certain statements that Sir Mark Sykes and Amery are to be joint secretaries
with me. I wished at once to make a formal announcement about the
secretariat, but Lloyd George would not sanction it. Lloyd George also
refused to sanction Montagu's appointment as joint secretary and all this
makes me suspect that something is amiss . . . Walter Long the Colonial
Secretary lunched with me. He was full of complaints of Amery, who, he
said, was quite untrustworthy and ought not to be present at meetings,
particularly owing to his intimate association with *The Times*. . . . In the
afternoon I saw Amery, who asked to have two Assistants to *him* appointed.
When I asked what he wanted them to do he said that he himself proposed
to keep up a regular correspondence with the Dominion Prime Ministers and
that he proposed that one of these fellows, namely Howard d'Egville,[2] the
Secretary of the Dominions' Inter-parliamentary Association, should send
variants of his letters to various parliamentary "bottle-washers" in the
Dominions. This fairly took my breath away, but I reserved judgement.
Later I had a long interview with Henderson, the Labour member of the
Cabinet, who is discontented with his position, and had to devise with
Young a scheme of organisation to keep him amused . . .

[1] Cab. 28. I.C.15.
[2] Later Sir Howard d'Egville. Traveller and writer on Imperial Defence. Hon. Sec.
United Kingdom Branch of Empire Parliamentary Association and General Editor
of its publications. Editor, Journal of Parliaments of Empire 1919. Served in
Cabinet Secretariat 1918–19.

Memento of Anglo-French Conference Dec. 27, 1916. – by Mr. Arthur Balfour M.P.

Balfour and Briand's doodles. Captions in Hankey's hand

Calais Conference
26. Feb? 1917.
Drawn by M. Briand

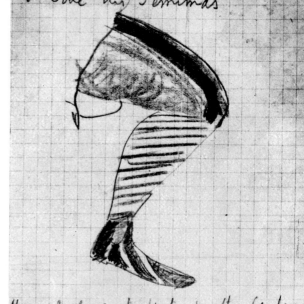

Clemenceau's drawing of Joffre's Jemima Boots. Caption in Hankey's hand

How G.C. contributes to the Conference
General Joffre's Leg & Jemima Boots; Allied Conference at P.
November 16, 1916.

Balfour, L. G., Painlevé, Foch and Hankey and General Smuts at Chequers, October 1917

12th January 1917
Saw Amery first thing and told him I could not possibly have his scheme of
a subterranean line of communication with the Dominions, . . . and he
frankly admitted that his ultimate idea was to displace the Colonial Office,
and substitute my office as the means of communication between the
Dominions and the Prime Minister. I don't mind his principle so much,
though I doubt its desirability, but anyhow I won't have his methods and told
him so flat. He is a scheming little devil and his connection with *The Times*
would make it possible for him to oust me, so the position is delicate.[1] Then
I got a message from the Foreign Office that Sonnino had telegraphed for my
notes of the Rome Conference with a view to a *procès verbale*, and I had to
"sport my oak"[2] and dictate for four hours on end . . . Providentially the
War Cabinet did not meet until 5 p.m. At the end of the meeting Ll. George
suddenly postponed to-morrow's meeting, which had been most carefully
organised for 11.30, until the afternoon, which involved putting off a dozen
or so of experts summoned for the different items. . . . These horribly
unbusinesslike methods of Lloyd George's render organisation almost
impossible.

At the time when Hankey was expanding the Cabinet Secretariat
Lloyd George set up his own group of Private Secretaries who, because
they worked in temporary buildings erected in the garden of 10
Downing Street, were always known as the "Garden Suburb". Among
them were such distinguished persons as Philip Kerr (later Marquess
of Lothian)[3] and Professor George Adams.[4] Hankey's view of the
Garden Suburb is best taken from a letter he wrote much later to
Lothian's biographer.

Hankey to Sir James Butler.[5] *Highstead, Limpsfield. 10th November 1955.*
Holograph
. . . The Garden Suburb were never officially linked with the War Cabinet

[1]Hankey somewhat revised his view of Amery later. See Diary for 18th March 1917
(p. 371).
[2]That is shut his outer door. A university colloquialism indicating that no-one is to
disturb the occupier of a room.
[3]See p. 184. In 1916 Hankey offered Kerr, on Milner's recommendation, a post on
the War Committee Secretariat; but Kerr declined it on the grounds that he did not
at that time wish to become a civilian official.
[4]1874–1966. Economist and social scientist. Founder and Editor of *The Political
Quarterly* 1914–16; a secretary to the Prime Minister 1916–19. Member of the Royal
Commission on Oxford and Cambridge Universities 1921–22. Chairman, National
Council of Social Services 1920–49. Warden of All Souls College, Oxford, 1933–45.
[5]See also Sir James Butler, *Lord Lothian* (Macmillan, 1960), pp. 64–5.

Secretariat. Like the Foreign Office and the Departments we regarded them at first with some suspicion, which proved not unfounded because they had contacts with the Press, which we did not. Moreover Parliament and Press very naturally confused them with the War Cabinet Office, and occasionally I was attacked for the Garden Suburb's activities—it eventually became almost a joke between Philip and myself that I was his "whipping boy"; but it was a wry joke for me because the War Cabinet Office was an object of suspicion . . .

Other evidence suggests, however, that there was more friction between the Garden Suburb and the War Cabinet Secretariat than Hankey recalled nearly 40 years on.[1]

It was at this time, to be precise on 18th January, that Hankey started the famous "A" series of "specially secret" Cabinet papers, the records of which he usually kept only in manuscript. He circulated them around the Ministers concerned with the subject discussed, and after they had all initialled the paper it was returned to him. Sometimes only a part of a Cabinet Minute was included in the "A" series, but those papers have proved a veritable gold mine for historians—not least because Hankey expressed himself much more freely in papers "withheld from circulation" than in those which were printed and given a wide distribution. Thus it is in them that the historian feels really closely in touch with events, and with the men controlling them.[2]

Diary 18th January 1917
Usual War Cabinet at 11.30. They began by a discussion among themselves on the War Cabinet Office and I was asked to withdraw, so I suppose they were discussing me. In two or three minutes, however, I was recalled and as they were particularly friendly I suppose they were satisfied . . .

With sinkings of merchant vessels by U-boats continuing at an uncomfortably high figure of over 300,000 tons per month, and the likelihood that losses would go still higher as the number of boats available to the Germans increased, Hankey now began to give much attention to that aspect of the struggle. On 22nd January he lunched with Lloyd George and Jellicoe, and the latter declared that the

[1]Lawrence Burgis, when interviewed by the author (April 1967) recalled that "the bright lads of the Garden Suburb produced many difficulties for the War Cabinet Secretariat."
[2]The "A Series" in Cab. 23/13 starts on 18th Jan. 1917 and ends on 25th Nov. 1918 in Cab. 23/17.

Admiralty only possessed 1,100 mines, which were of a type distinctly inferior to the German mines. This astonished and horrified Hankey, who had, as he put it, "written Memo. after Memo. to one First Lord after another urging that the best talent in the Navy should be put on to mining".[1] Though Jellicoe was at this time chronically pessimistic what he had stated about mines was no more than the bare truth.

By the end of January the German militarist clique (or "Hawks" as they would be described in modern parlance) had gained the ascendancy over the political "Doves", and Unrestricted Submarine Warfare on all ships approaching or leaving the British Isles was declared on 1st February. Their belief was that if monthly sinkings of 600,000 tons could be maintained for five months Britain would be forced to her knees. Nor were they far wrong in their calculations. The United States broke off diplomatic relations a few days later; but that brought little comfort or easement to the Allies. At Hankey's suggestion all neutral ships in ports of the British Empire (some 600 totalling about 900,000 tons) were "temporarily" detained—lest they should be recalled to their own countries for fear of the U-boat blockade. But sinkings at sea rose rapidly—to 540,006 tons in February—and it was at once plain that the Allies were facing a crisis of the first magnitude. On 8th Hankey wrote in his diary "The submarine warfare has become frantic. We seem to be sinking a good many submarines, but they are sinking a terrible lot of ships. Carson is a fearful pessimist—but he always was. Jellicoe almost as bad—but he always was . . . My prophecy seems to be coming true, that our military effort would so far exhaust us that we cannot maintain our sea power and our economic position".[2] Nor was it the case that we were "sinking a good many submarines". The Admiralty's claims were far too optimistic, and in fact only two were sunk in January and five in February. Furthermore the strength of the U-boat fleet, which had numbered 133 on 1st January, was rising rapidly.

Diary 11th February 1917 (Sunday)
Had a brain wave on the subject of anti-submarine warfare, so ran down to Walton Heath in the afternoon to formulate my ideas to Ll. George, who was very interested. I sat up late completing a long Memo. on the subject. My Memo. was an argument for convoys, but contained a great number of suggestions.

[1]Diary 22nd January 1917.
[2]See pp. 244, 247 and 355.

13th February 1917

Breakfast with Ll. George, Carson, Jellicoe and Duff,[1] the Admiral in charge of anti-submarine warfare to discuss my theories as regards the adoption of convoys. They [surely meaning the Admiralty representatives, not including Lloyd George] resisted a good deal but I think the discussion did good. They admitted that they were convoying transports, and agreed to enquire about the results of a big convoy of transports coming in from Australia. . . .

Hankey's "brain waves" usually seem to have come to him on a Sunday—probably because that was the only day when he was not working under constant pressure, and could therefore allow his ever-active mind to roam over the whole field of current problems. We do not know whether his brain wave about convoys was entirely original, or whether any outside agency had filtered the idea through to him. His strong interest in history makes the former contingency perfectly feasible, since in every earlier war in which Britain had been engaged merchant ships had been convoyed, at least through the most dangerous part of their voyages. On the other hand we know that Hankey was the constant recipient of ideas and confidences from a very wide variety of sources, and that he often passed them on to those in authority. Also there is at least a possibility that the convoy proposal came to him in the first place from a quite junior officer on the Admiralty's War Staff—Commander R. G. H. Henderson.[2] What is certain is that early in 1917 Royal Navy and Merchant Navy opinion were virtually united in believing that in modern conditions convoy was impracticable or dangerous—or both.[3]

Fortunately for Britain there was a small body of opinion which was not prepared to accept the arguments against convoy—at least until it had been given a fair trial. Henderson belonged to that body, and so did Norman Leslie,[4] who was serving in the Ministry of Shipping

[1] Later Admiral Sir Alexander L. Duff (1862–1933). Director, Mobilisation Division Admiralty War Staff 1911–14 and of Anti-Submarine Division 1917. C-in-C, China 1919–22.

[2] Later Admiral Sir Reginald Henderson (1881–1939). Rear-Admiral, Aircraft Carriers 1931–3; Third Sea Lord and Controller of Navy 1934–9.

[3] See A. Temple Patterson (Ed.), *The Jellicoe Papers*, II (Navy Records Society, 1968), pp. 144–51.

[4] Later Sir Norman A. Leslie (1870–1945). Shipping executive. Served in Transport Department, Admiralty 1915–16; Ministry of Shipping 1916–18. Author of *The System of Convoys for Merchant Shipping*, 1917.

which Lloyd George had established under Sir Joseph Maclay[1] in December 1916; and as Leslie was the liaison officer between the Ministry of Shipping and the Admiralty he was uniquely placed to understand the problems of both parties, and their attitudes towards possible solutions. Leslie was unquestionably a strong advocate of convoy, knew Henderson well and had no confidence in Admiral Duff. And it was Henderson who discovered that the statistics which the Admiralty was presenting to the War Cabinet every month setting out "safe arrivals" and "losses" presented a totally false picture, because in the former category was included every arrival at every port in the country, including coasting vessels which called at a great many ports. What is more likely than that Henderson himself, perhaps in conjunction with Leslie, should have communicated the true state of affairs to Hankey in order that it might reach the War Cabinet?[2] Hankey could not possibly put on paper anything about such action by a junior officer, because he was acting without the knowledge and behind the backs of his superiors, and contrary to their policy. Such "disloyalty", if discovered, would have ruined his career; and only those who served in the Royal Navy in that period, or for a long time afterwards, can understand how heinously "disloyalty" was regarded by senior officers —even though the "disloyal" person might be absolutely right.[3] Perhaps the strongest piece of evidence that Henderson did, at some stage, approach Hankey on the subject of convoys is contained in a letter from Churchill written in 1937. ". . . I well remember", wrote Churchill to Hankey, "how you played an essential part in saving the country over the convoy system, and *how when young officers came to you and told you the truth, against service rules, you saw that the seed did not fall on stony ground . . .*" (italics supplied).[4] To whom could Churchill have been referring if not to Henderson? Hankey himself handles the whole matter with extreme discretion in his memoirs, making no mention of

[1] 1857–1951. 1st Baron Maclay 1922. Shipowner of Glasgow. Minister of Shipping 1916–21.
[2] This paragraph is based chiefly on study of Sir Norman Leslie's papers and on discussions with his daughter Miss Cecil Mary Leslie in 1967. See also Leslie's lecture at the Royal United Service Institution, published in R.U.S.I. Journal, August 1929.
[3] Lady Duff's letters to the author of 21st Nov. and 1st Dec. 1968 recall her husband's resentment of Henderson's action in passing on his discovery of the fallacy in the Admiralty's statistics without Admiral Duff's knowledge. But Henderson obviously did so because he knew it would be futile to act through the "proper channels".
[4] Churchill to Hankey, 16th Oct. 1937.

Henderson[1]; but Churchill has written that "A junior officer, Commander R. G. Henderson, working in the anti-submarine department *and in close contact with the Ministry of Shipping* (italics supplied) broke up this monstrous and tamely accepted obstacle" (i.e. the Admiralty's objections to convoy).[2] And he does full justice to Hankey's part in that accomplishment. Unfortunately, since nothing was recorded in writing, we have no means of knowing whether Henderson's approach to Hankey took place before or after the latter wrote his famous memorandum of 12th February; but for what it is worth this historian feels that the balance of probability is that it took place before that date, since Hankey was not the man to open what was obviously going to be a difficult battle without his magazines being well stocked with ammunition.

As Hankey himself has printed the greater part of the memorandum, modestly entitled "Some Suggestions for Anti-Submarine Warfare", and it is also reproduced in the official history,[3] we will here merely note that he urged the need for "an entire reorganization of the Admiralty's present scheme of anti-submarine warfare . . . It involves the substitution of a system of scientifically organised convoys, and the concentration on this service of the whole of the anti-submarine craft allotted to the protection of trade routes . . . It further involves the concentration on to the convoy system of every means of anti-submarine warfare . . .". Rarely, if ever, did Hankey argue a case more forcibly; yet nothing was done at once, and in March shipping losses rose to 593,841 tons. The explanation for this surprising inactivity may well be found in the fact that Lloyd George did not yet feel strong enough to force a show-down with Carson and the Admiralty; for he had at this time plenty of troubles on the military side, and to quarrel simultaneously with both fighting services might well have proved fatal to his government. We will return later to the crisis of the U-boat war in April, and its solution.

On 15th February Hankey took home with him as leisure reading a copy of the long-gestating report of the Dardanelles Commission. He thought it "a very unfair document and much too hard on Asquith,

---

[1]*Supreme Command,* II, pp. 641–7.   [2]*Thoughts and Adventures* (1932), p. 97.
[3]*Supreme Command,* II, pp. 646–7; Sir Henry Newbolt, *Naval Operations,* Vol. V (Longmans, Green, 1931), pp. 10–14. In 1933 Hankey sent Lloyd George a copy of this memorandum, for use in writing his memoirs. Lloyd George papers G/8/18/19.

dwelling insufficiently on the difficulties of the times and the tiresome personalities whom Asquith had to handle".[1]

Diary 16th February 1917

Three War Cabinets. At the first I expressed the view that the publication of the Dardanelles Report would lead to an immediate demand by the persons involved for the production of the evidence. But the War Cabinet, obviously delighted because it hits Asquith hard, decided to publish immediately . . . They were most vindictive and unpleasant, especially Lloyd George and Curzon, in their observations about Asquith—who is a bigger man than any of them—and though they themselves are guilty of many of the lapses for which Asquith is blamed . . . The Dardanelles Commission specially thank me for my evidence—but it is quite possible, I foresee, that the papers may try and treat me as mixed up in the defects of the Asquith War Council. If so I have my defence, having both orally and in writing warned Asquith of the trouble he was laying up for himself by his rather easy and slipshod, or perhaps I should say unsystematic methods. I lunched with Ll. George and told him about Walter Long,[2] but he replied that he didn't give a d——n if Walter Long resigned or not, and would rather welcome a row in the House and a General Election. I had a short talk with Winston about the Dardanelles Report. He said he was satisfied, but the tone of his voice indicated disappointment.

Next day, Saturday, brought to a close what Hankey described as "a terrific week", with eleven War Cabinets; but "huge questions" such as "nationalisation of shipping, import restrictions, and a far-reaching agricultural policy" had been "hammered out".[3] Sunday he enjoyed a quiet day, and in the afternoon went to "the dear Temple Church, where they did Mendelssohn's unfinished Oratorio 'Christus' most exquisitely". Obviously music brought him solace, and relief from the

[1]Diary 15th Feb. 1917. See *Supreme Command*, II, pp. 525–6.
[2]On 15th Feb. Hankey recorded that he had "found him [Long] in a very disgruntled state, complaining much of the War Cabinet system, which he says is unworkable, and about its Irish and agricultural policy . . . He hinted at resignation". Next day Long wrote to Hankey that he was "really shocked by the agricultural proposals [which were part of the government's plans to stimulate home production]; the guarantee of prices for 6 years is wasteful and uncalled for, while the proposed control of landlords and farmers will be bitterly resented". Long himself was a big landowner.
[3]Diary 17th Feb. Hankey did not mean "nationalisation" of shipping in the modern sense of state ownership; he meant the assumption by the government of complete control for the duration of the war.

strains of his work. "Uncommonly glad of a rest", he ended the day's entry, "but the education of this Cabinet work is tremendous". Could he have meant that it was educating him for political office? Such an idea was not, as we shall see shortly, entirely absent from his mind in 1917.

The following week saw the War Cabinet engaged chiefly on what Hankey called "a tremendously drastic curtailment of imports and the elaboration of a great agricultural policy"[1]—both of them measures forced on the government by the submarine campaign. On 23rd Lloyd George spoke eloquently in the House about the necessity for these, and other measures.[2] Hankey wrote in his diary "I met the P.M. in the corridor just after [his speech] and he called me up to speak to him, putting his hand on my shoulder as he did so. He was literally trembling in every limb with the excitement of his peroration. It was a very fine effort". If Lloyd George worked himself up to a state of high emotion by his own rhetoric Hankey was evidently not entirely immune from its influence.

Here we must explain what Hankey aptly described as "the rocket-like rise and fall" of the French General Nivelle,[3] who had replaced Joffre in command of the French armies on 13th December 1916. This arose out of disillusion with Joffre's attrition strategy, and the striking success achieved by General Mangin under Nivelle at Verdun in the previous October. When the British delegates were on their way back from Rome Lloyd George received a message that Nivelle would like to meet him; but as it was plainly injudicious to consult with the French C-in-C in Haig's absence Lloyd George invited them both to come to London for a War Cabinet meeting. On learning about this Robertson was typically antagonistic, but cautious. He wrote to Hankey "I certainly think that Sir Douglas Haig should attend [the War Cabinet], as he is almost bound to be wanted to reply to some of the points put forward by General Nivelle, and also it is only right that he should hear what General Nivelle states to the Cabinet",[4] But neither

[1] *ibid.* 22nd Feb. 1917.
[2] On a motion for the adjournment. Parl. Deb., Commons, Vol. XC, Cols. 1591–1614.
[3] Robert G. Nivelle (1856–1924). Commanded French Third Corps 1915–16, and for counter-offensive at Verdun April 1916. Commanded Second French Army May 1916, and replaced Joffre as C-in-C 13th December. Dismissed in favour of General Pétain 15th May.
[4] Robertson to Hankey, 13th January 1917.

Robertson's wariness, nor Haig's scepticism proved of any avail against Nivelle's persuasive eloquence; and even Hankey's normally sound judgement on people deserted him on this occasion.

Diary 15th January 1917
Conferences and Cabinet all day with General Nivelle, the new French C-in-C, who made a very favourable impression on the War Cabinet and on me.[1] Sir Douglas Haig was there. Robertson gave a dinner in the evening which I attended.
16th January
Breakfasted with Ll. George and Milner. Continuation of the conferences with Nivelle. It was decided to give him all he asked for, Haig and Robertson being over-ruled i.e. we take over an additional section of the line in France, and we agree to an earlier offensive than had previously been intended . . .
17th January
. . . Saw P.M. in the evening, who told me he had received confidential information that General Nivelle is very disturbed about Sir Douglas Haig, whom he finds rigid, inelastic and unaccommodating. Ll. G. would like to get rid of Haig but cannot find an excuse. He is always trying to get me to say Haig is no use, but I refuse to do so.

Lloyd George and the War Cabinet having been carried away by Nivelle's self-confidence, the stage was set for one of the greatest tragedies of the war.

Almost exactly a month later (15th February) Lloyd George interrupted a conversation between Hankey and Bertier de Sauvigny,[2] the French liaison officer at the War Office; and Bertier's report confirms what Hankey wrote in his diary about Nivelle having completely won Lloyd George's confidence, and about his intention to place the British Army under the French General for his forthcoming offensive—even if it meant getting rid of Haig.[3] Hankey, who in this context has recently been described as "a much wiser and better informed man than Lloyd George",[4] at once appreciated the full implications of his master's scheme. But he does not seem to have taken any immediate action to

---

[1]Minutes in Cab. 23. War Cabinet (34) and (35).
[2]Hankey and Sir Edward Spears both spelt Bertier's first name "Bertier"; but Esher used the form "Berthier", which is incorrect.
[3]Berthier's report is reproduced by Sir Edward Spears in *Prelude to Victory* (Cape, 1939), Appendix IX. See also John Terraine, *Douglas Haig* (Hutchinson, 1963), pp. 265–6.
[4]Terraine, *op. cit.* p. 270.

warn Lloyd George of the dangers to the Allied cause which were implicit in his intention.

The extension of the British line delayed Nivelle's offensive by a month; and before it opened the plan was totally disrupted by the German withdrawal to the Hindenburg Line, which began on 25th February and was skilfully carried out. They shortened their front considerably and economised about 12 Divisions, leaving the evacuated zone devastated.[1] Yet Nivelle obstinately refused to recognise the changed circumstances.[2]

As soon as the House of Commons debate of 23rd February was over Hankey had to turn his attention to preparing for the Anglo-French Conference, which was to open at Calais three days later. With regard to the preliminary discussions on Haig and Nivelle's "merits and demerits" in the War Cabinet he recorded that the "general conclusion was that Haig is the best man we have, but that is not saying much, and that as between Haig and Nivelle, Ll. G. should support the latter".[3] This discussion confirmed Bertier de Sauvigny's warning about the extraordinary proposal which Lloyd George intended to put forward at Calais. The events of the two hectic days of conference are best described in Hankey's words.[4]

Diary 26th February 1917
To Calais with Ll. George and Robertson . . . Dull conference on railway matters to start with. This was followed at 5 p.m. by a conference that was by no means dull.—Ll. George, Briand, Robertson, Gen. Lyautey, Haig, Nivelle and myself alone being present. The French had been invited to bring a secretary also, but paid me the delicate compliment of leaving the secretarial arrangements entirely to me. Nivelle and Haig explained their plans for the forthcoming push in detail. Ll. G. then asked Nivelle if he was satisfied, and if not to explain quite frankly what he wanted. Nivelle got red in the face; talked generalities; and beat about the bush, Briand and Lyautey failing to help him out at all. So Ll. G. broke up the conference and asked the French to put down in writing what they wanted. Ll. G. and I then went for a walk through Calais.

Soon after our return I was sent for to Ll. G.'s room where I found Ll. G., Briand, Lyautey, and Nivelle. Ll. G. handed me the document and said "What do you think of it?"—It fairly took my breath away, as it practically demanded the placing of the British army under Nivelle; the appointment of

[1] *Liddell Hart*, p. 391.   [2] *ibid.* pp. 409–10.   [3] Diary 24th Feb. 1917.
[4] In *Supreme Command*, II, pp. 615–17 a considerable amount of the following diary entries is omitted.

a British "Chief of Staff" to Nivelle; who had powers practically eliminating Haig and his C.G.S., the scheme reducing Haig to a cipher. I showed no emotion and said I wanted time to consider it. After dinner I was sent for by Ll. G., who had dined alone in his room. He was in an extraordinary frame of mind and really seemed rather to like the French scheme. I warned him that it was quite impossible, but felt I must handle him very carefully. Then Robertson and Haig came in. They of course were aghast and urged every possible objection. Ll. George was extraordinarily brutal to Haig. When Haig objected that the "Tommies" wouldn't stand being under a Frenchman Ll. G. said "Well, Field-Marshal, I know the private soldier very well. He speaks very freely to me, and there are people he criticises a good deal more strongly than Gen. Nivelle!" He more than hinted that Haig would have to resign, if he didn't come to heel, and treated him with a good deal of contumely. It was uncomfortable for me as both Haig and Robertson had the air of regarding me as with Ll.G. against them. They wouldn't see me afterwards so I went to bed, but before retiring drafted a formula which I thought might suit all parties.

27th February
I had my formula typed by my secretary, Sylvester, first thing and saw Robertson at 8 a.m. He was in a terrible state and ramped up and down the room, talking about the horrible idea of putting "the wonderful army" under a Frenchman, swearing he would never serve under one, nor his son either, and that no-one could order him to. He had not slept, for the first time in the war, he said. I could do nothing with him, so left him.

I then went to Ll. G., who had also slept badly. I tried to frighten him by the probable results of Robertson's and Haig's impending resignations, and he was affected, though he swore he was not going to be beaten over this. Then I warned him he could not fight on the basis of the outrageous French document and he agreed and asked me to draft something on which he could fight. This was the psychological moment to pull my formula out of my pocket. He read it, accepted it, sent for Robertson who accepted it with intense relief and took it to Haig, who accepted it after palaver. Ll. G. then showed it to Briand, Lyautey and Nivelle, who accepted it. All therefore was well. Robertson and Haig, who had taken no notice of Ll. G.'s invitation to them to breakfast with him and me were satisfied—and all had been effected by my little scrap of paper.[1] Moreover all recognised my efforts and thanked me for it. In fact it was a great personal triumph . . .

Hankey's self-satisfaction over the acceptance of his "formula" was fully justified; for he succeeded in reducing, at least temporarily, the

[1] The agreement signed at Calais on 27th Feb. is in Cab. 23. I.C. 17. Hankey reproduced it in full in his memorandum of 1st Sept. 1917. G.T. 1925. Cab. 24/25.

blood pressure of the British Generals, which Lloyd George's ill-considered scheme had raised to a dangerously high level. "But for Hankey", John Terraine has commented, "it is hard to see how a crisis of the most serious nature could have been avoided".[1] But the compromise did not entirely save the British armies from involvement in Nivelle's ill-starred plan. Not only did they have to take over a sector of the French front, but they were required to launch an offensive further north in order to draw off German reserves from the Champagne, where Nivelle's optimistically conceived blow was to fall. Back in London the Calais agreement produced as little enthusiasm in political circles as it had among the soldiers. Bonar Law told Hankey "that he didn't much like them [the Calais arrangements] himself, but he regarded Ll. George as dictator, and meant to give him his chance"[2]; which spoke more for Law's loyalty than for his political or moral courage.

When an account of the proceedings at Calais reached the Palace the King evidently showed strong interest not only in what had transpired but in how his Generals had been treated. On 2nd March Hankey saw Stamfordham and "had to explain to him for the King exactly what had happened at Calais re Haig".[3] But this statement evidently did not satisfy the Monarch, since two days later Hankey received from Stamfordham an unusually peremptory demand for further enlightenment. Had he, Stamfordham asked, informed Robertson of the War Cabinet decision of 24th February "that General Nivelle should be in command of the French and British armies during the coming operations"? Robertson, he continued, knew nothing about it until told of it by the Prime Minister at Calais. Then in an equally peremptory postscript Stamfordham asked "Did you communicate to Robertson the Minutes of the meeting of the War Cabinet of 24th February as in the terms published in the printed Minute of War Cabinet 79 . . .?"[4] Hankey's reply was typically firm both in defence of himself and in loyal justification of the procedure adopted by Lloyd George—though he was careful to avoid giving any opinion regarding the proposals which the latter had originally put forward, and drew a discreet veil over Robertson's violent reaction to them.[5]

Esher, of course, relished involvement in the manœuvring which

---

[1] *Douglas Haig*, p. 272.   [2] Diary 2nd March 1917.   [3] *ibid.*
[4] Stamfordham to Hankey 4th March 1917. RA. GV Q1079/16.
[5] RA. GV Q1079/17.

had preceded the Calais Conference; but he got the story wrong in part. He first wrote to Haig giving him the version of the discussion in London on 15th February, which Bertier de Sauvigny had passed to Nivelle. On 9th March Esher followed up his letter with a cypher telegram saying that the original proposal put forward by Lloyd George was "evidently [the work] of George and Hankey and others in London."[1] Far from that being the case Hankey knew no details about it until Lloyd George showed his proposal to him on the evening of 26th February at Calais; and he then recorded that it "fairly took my breath away". What is interesting in Esher's record is the statement that the "French Generals [i.e. Nivelle and Lyautey]" knew nothing about Lloyd George's intentions until they arrived at Calais; and that they then "heard to their stupefaction that neither Robertson nor D. H. [Haig] had been told" about it.[2] That was certainly not true in the case of Nivelle, who had been forewarned by Berthier. According to Esher, Lyautey "knew of Berthier's talk with Ll. G. and Hankey in London, but he maintains that the meeting was accidental"; and that, as we saw earlier, was very near the truth. In sum although Lyautey may reasonably be acquitted of any marked degree of complicity with Lloyd George the same cannot be said of Nivelle; and that probably explains his "getting red in the face" and "beating about the bush" at the meeting on 26th February—as the alert Hankey did not fail to notice.

While the aftermath to the Calais conference was still reverberating around Whitehall Hankey had to cope with the delicate problems produced by the impending arrival in London of the representatives of the Dominions, whom Lloyd George had, somewhat impetuously, invited to attend War Cabinet meetings.[3] Mr. W. F. Massey,[4] Prime Minister of New Zealand, had insisted that Sir Joseph Ward,[5] his colleague in a rather uneasy coalition government, should always be present; whereupon Sir Robert Borden[6] of Canada insisted that his country should also have two representatives. Hankey expected the

[1] Esher to Haig 9th March 1917. Esher papers. [2] loc. cit. [3] See p. 348.
[4] 1856–1925. New Zealand politician. Leader of Opposition 1903–12. Prime Minister as Leader of "Reform Party" 1912–25. Formed National Government 1915.
[5] 1856–1930. New Zealand politician (Lab.). Prime Minister 1906–12. Took office in National Government formed by Massey 1915–19. Again Prime Minister 1928–30.
[6] See p. 120.

other Dominions to put forward similar claims, which would "raise the number to an unwieldy extent". Lloyd George therefore decided that "the whole caboodle must be asked". Hankey considered that the affair had been "badly stage managed" and was thankful he had no share in it[1]; for whereas by 1st March Massey, Borden and Sir Edward Morris[2] (Prime Minister of Newfoundland) had arrived, W. M. Hughes[3] (Australia) and General J. C. Smuts[4] (South Africa) were not expected for some time. None the less a start was made at the War Cabinet on 2nd, which was attended by Borden, Massey, Ward and Morris. According to Hankey the two New Zealanders then expressed their "marked disapproval of the decision to publish the Dardanelles report"; and to detract still further from the spirit of unity and resolution which this meeting was intended to stimulate Jellicoe presented "a very pessimistic statement about the submarine campaign", with regard to which he could produce "no glimmer of light or shade of hope."[5] "It cannot be too strongly impressed upon all concerned", wrote Jellicoe, "that the losses in February are bound to be exceeded in the succeeding months".[6] Small wonder that Lloyd George's confidence in the Admiralty's drive and capacity should have plummeted at this time. Nor was the Cabinet of 2nd March a very happy augury for what was to become the Imperial War Cabinet.

Hankey's letters to his wife, together with his diary entries for the early days of March 1917, show how deeply involved he was in the delicate negotiations which followed the Calais Conference. For Nivelle

[1] Diary 1st March 1917. But see Lloyd George, *War Memoirs*, pp. 1032–36 for his very reasonable explanation of the need to bring the Dominions into high-level policy discussions.

[2] 1859–1935. 1st Baron Morris 1918. Newfoundland politician. Held ministerial offices as a Liberal 1898–1907. Leader of Peoples' Party 1908. Prime Minister 1909–18.

[3] See p. 257. In the event political considerations in Australia prevented Hughes attending the first session of the Imperial War Cabinet.

[4] 1870–1950. South African soldier and statesman. Fought against Britain in Boer War. Took office under Botha 1907–10. Minister of Defence 1910–19. Commanded Imperial Forces in E. Africa 1916. Prime Minister 1919–24 and Deputy Prime Minister to Hertzog 1933–9. Again Prime Minister 1939–48, bringing South Africa into World War II. Field-Marshal 1941.

[5] Diary 2nd March 1917.

[6] Jellicoe's statement was almost certainly based on the memorandum of the same date preserved in the Carson papers (Public Record Office of Northern Ireland) D.1507/2/14.

at once sent Haig a letter "couched in peremptory terms". The British C-in-C very reasonably replied that the German withdrawal to the Hindenburg line threatened to make Nivelle's plan obsolete, whereupon the French government accused Haig of trying "to upset the Calais agreement".[1] This correspondence surely provides the clue to what Hankey described to Adeline as a "most delicate and difficult matter" on which he had to advise Lloyd George, and also the "very difficult despatch" from the Prime Minister to Briand which he helped to draft.[2] One result of the fracas at Calais was that it heightened Lloyd George's regard for Hankey—probably because he realised that it was his "formula" which had extricated him from an impossible situation. At any rate Hankey wrote in his diary at this time "As a matter of fact he [Lloyd George] does like me, for he told me that he had more than once said I was the only person that the war had brought to the front".[3]

Diary 10th March 1917[4]
... This point [the temporary nature of Haig's subordination to Nivelle and the "unprecedented concession" made by Haig in accepting it] was insisted on strongly at the War Cabinet on Friday [9th] and I incorporated it in the Cabinet Minutes—though I expect Lloyd George (who is away for the week-end) will be annoyed when he sees it. Balfour sent an admirable letter on the subject to the French ambassador, after consulting me. The net result was that the French are coming over on Monday [12th] to discuss the question. [Albert] Thomas, that stormy petrel, is coming with them. I suspect him to be at the bottom of the intreague [sic] to upset Haig; Nivelle being a puppet who plays (unwillingly perhaps) when Thomas and his ramp pull the strings ... But of all this I have no evidence. Altogether it has been a hard week for me—Haig and Nivelle at loggerheads; Nivelle trying to get rid of Haig ... Derby and Robertson threatening to resign if Haig goes; the whole lot of them sending for me at all times of the day and night to discuss it; no Assistant Secretary allowed to attend the daily War Cabinet meetings with me, so that all the spade work falls on me; much other work; on top of it all the publication of the Report of the Dardanelles Commission, which drives me mad at the way my evidence had been treated to damage people's reputations, the explanation not being put in many cases ...

[1]Diary 10th March 1917.
[2]To Lady Hankey 8th and 9th March 1917.
[3]Diary 10th March 1917.
[4]This is the part excluded in *Supreme Command*, II, p. 618.

18th March 1917[1]

... The French conference was resumed on Tuesday [13th] and an agreement was reached exactly regulating the relation between Haig and Nivelle. Lloyd George seems, for the present at any rate, to have got over his aversion and contempt for Haig. I am glad to say that he did his best to give the impression that Haig had the full confidence of the War Cabinet—as indeed he always has had, except so far as Ll. George himself is concerned. The French Minister agreed that Nivelle's letters to Haig had been brusque and unfortunate in tone—those indeed of a superior to an inferior (say) a Divisional General, and not those of one equal to another who has temporarily and for a specific purpose and at considerable sacrifice of *amour propre* been placed under his orders—but they alleged that subordinates were responsible. I thought that the French Ministers appeared quite pleased at the results of the conference, but Nivelle did not look very happy, and the group of staff officers sitting behind had very sour looks . . .

On 2nd March Bonar Law commissioned Hankey to undertake "the rather delicate mission" of explaining to Asquith the government's reasons for censoring certain passages in the Dardanelles Commission's report before publication. It would go beyond the scope of this biography to probe the extent of the excisions made, and the reasons for making them[2]; but Asquith apparently raised no serious objections. The first report of the Dardanelles Commission, published by H.M.S.O. (at the very moderate price of 6d) was issued on 8th March, and on 21st Asquith, on a motion for the adjournment of the House, made an admirably balanced and moderate defence of those whom the Commissioners had criticised—and especially Kitchener.[3] His speech was well received, and the House was obviously disposed to let sleeping dogs lie and get on with the war, rather than engage in a witch hunt. But to re-read the report at this distance of time leaves a strong impression of prejudice, and it certainly caused deep hurt and resentment to not a few persons whose position made it impossible for them to answer the criticisms contained in it.

The only ray of light to pierce the gloom which pervaded London in the early spring of 1917 came from the Mesopotamian front, where on

[1] Two short extracts from this day's entry are printed in *Supreme Command*, II, pp. 526 and 659–60.
[2] For the benefit of the student who wishes to investigate this matter the most profitable sources are likely to be in Cab. 17 and Cab. 19.
[3] Parl. Deb., Commons, Vol. XCI, Cols. 1753–1831.

11th March Baghdad fell to General Sir Stanley Maude's army.[1] This success on the most remote flank of the Central Powers was important not only as a stimulant to Allied morale at an anxious time; it also showed that there still was a viable alternative to the slaughter in the west. Furthermore it is not without interest that Maude's success was achieved in the face of Robertson's strong dislike of the whole Mesopotamian venture, and of Jellicoe's warning that the Admiralty could not find the shipping to sustain it.[2] Thus did Jellicoe act, deliberately or not, as the catspaw of the extreme "westerners"—with results which were, before the end of the year, to produce perhaps the greatest agony endured by the British Army in the never-to-be-forgotten horror of Passchendaele.[3]

Though the fall of Baghdad shed some much needed light on a depressing scene, in far distant Russia there took place almost simultaneously an event which was fraught with far greater consequences for the world. On 13th March the widespread resentment against Tsarist misrule and military mismanagement produced open disorder in Petrograd. The abdication of the Tsar followed, and the Provisional Government set up in place of the Romanov autocracy declared its intention of continuing the war against Germany. But the truth was that the succession of heavy defeats, and the appalling losses suffered since 1914, had broken the will of the Russian people to continue; and the "March Revolution" in fact marked the beginning of the end of the war for them. On the very day that the disorders broke out, Milner, who had recently visited Russia on a munitions supply mission,[4] wrote that "There is a great deal of exaggeration in the talk about revolution" —an unhappy prophecy which Hankey preserved, and produced much later as an example of "the difficulties of predicting peace".[5]

Meanwhile Hankey was very much occupied with preparing for the

[1] 1864–1917. A successful Divisional Commander in Gallipoli campaign 1915. Commanded Mesopotamian army 1916. Died of cholera at Baghdad shortly after its capture.
[2] See *Liddell Hart*, pp. 351–6 and Jellicoe's memo. to Carson of 2nd March 1917. Carson papers D. 1507/2/14.
[3] See pp. 404–5.
[4] From 20th January to 2nd March 1917. See J. E. Wrench, *Alfred, Lord Milner* (Eyre & Spottiswoode, 1958), pp. 322–6.
[5] G.131 of 13th March 1917. Cab. 24/3. Hankey kept a catalogue of examples where such predictions had quickly been falsified, and produced it in 1931 when the notorious "Ten Year Rule" was under review. C.I.D. 1055B of 23rd June 1931.

Anglo-French conference which was to set the final seal on the Calais agreement,[1] and for the first Imperial War Cabinet. On 13th March he wrote to Smuts, who had arrived in England the previous day, to tell him the arrangements he had made for the Dominion Prime Ministers to see official telegrams and reports and the drafts of War Cabinet minutes in a room specially set aside for that purpose at Whitehall Gardens. He added a postscript "I should like to add personally that I will do everything in my power to render you any assistance in connection with the forthcoming Cabinet meetings. If I or my Assistant Secretaries can be of any use to you I hope you will not hesitate to utilise our services".[2] Four days later he circulated a "Note" outlining the purposes of the meetings. The Imperial War Cabinet would sit at 10 Downing Street under Lloyd George's chairmanship to deal with day-to-day administrative problems, decide on war policy and examine the reports of the two committees which had been considering peace terms. Less urgent problems were to be delegated to an Imperial War Conference presided over by Walter Long at the Colonial Office, which would generally meet on days when the Imperial War Cabinet was not in session.[3] Experience was to show that the War Conferences were redundant and time-wasting[4]; but that was not Hankey's fault, and he made all the preparations for both series of meetings with all his usual care and thoroughness.

Diary 18th March 1917 (Cont.)

. . . On Wednesday evening (14th) I dined with Lord Milner to meet General Smuts, Mr. Massey, Sir Joseph Ward, Lord Hythe[5] and Amery. I sat next to Smuts whom I got on with first rate. After dinner they discussed closer imperial co-operation; Massey and Ward all for it, though quite deficient in ideas; Smuts most reluctant to discuss it at all, and, I thought, very suspicious of Milner.[6] Rather an interesting evening. The War Cabinet has met every

[1] Minutes in Cab. 23. I.C.18.
[2] Hankey to Smuts 19/a/7 of 13th March 1917. Smuts Archive, Capetown University, folio 163. Postscript Holograph.
[3] GT.193 of 17th March 1917. Cab. 24/7.
[4] Smuts certainly found them so. See W. K. Hancock, *Smuts*, Vol. II (Cambridge U.P. 1968), pp. 427–31.
[5] Viscount Hythe, son of 1st Earl Brassey.
[6] Hankey's perceptiveness about Smuts's feelings was well founded. Sir Keith Hancock remarks about the meetings of the Imperial War Cabinet that Smuts "disliked the look of the new British government, which included . . . his old antagonist Milner". *Smuts,* Vol. II, *The Fields of Force 1870–1919* (Cambridge U.P., 1968), p. 424.

day this week, but is not working satisfactorily. They never discuss their Agenda paper at all—in fact they have not done so properly for a fortnight ... Consequently all the work is dreadfully congested—far worse than it ever was under the so-called "Wait and See" Government.[1] Another difficulty is that Lloyd George will not initial the conclusions (without which they do not become operative), and will not give me a reasonably free hand to act without them, so that all the business of the War Cabinet gets in arrears, and the Departments, tired of waiting for their decisions, get discontented ... On top of all this we have these infernal "Imperial War Cabinets" with the Dominion Premiers, and the preparation of these has given me more work last week, and difficulties connected with Walter Long's dislike of Amery, who devils for me admirably in this matter ...

19th March
War Cabinet 4.30–7.30 p.m. Ll. George sent for me in the morning with intent to upset the whole of the Agenda and arrangements for the Imperial War Cabinets, which had been so carefully worked out by Lord Milner, Lord Curzon, Austen Chamberlain, Walter Long, Amery and myself. I resisted strenuously, after consulting Lord Milner on the telephone, and was eventually fairly successful ...

20th March[2]
The first of the Imperial War Cabinets was held to-day. It began with a fiasco as Major Storr, my Assistant Secretary, whom I had specially warned to be there early arrived late with the cards showing people where to sit, ... Next Lloyd George, when all were arranged, turned round to me and said "Where are the Staff and the First Sea Lord?" I then reminded him that by a decision of the previous day they were not to be invited. None the less he insisted on their being brought over and crammed into my already closely packed table. He really is appallingly unbusinesslike. The meeting was not stimulating and hardly worthy of the occasion ... There was a debate this afternoon in Parliament on the Dardanelles Commission's Interim Report, and Longhurst tells me that my name was received with loud applause in the House of Commons, when Asquith mentioned me.[3] I was too busy to go down to the house myself.

[1]A phrase first used by Asquith on 3rd March 1910 ("We had better wait and see"). Thereafter produced quite frequently by him to stall persistent Parliamentary questions. See J. A. Spender and Cyril Asquith, *The Life of Lord Oxford and Asquith*, Vol. I, p. 275.
[2]The greater part of this day's entry is printed in *Supreme Command*, II, pp. 526–7 and 611.
[3]Parl. Deb., Commons, Vol. XCI, Col. 1755. Asquith spoke of Hankey as "that most able and efficient public servant ... who acted throughout, and I believe still acts, as Secretary of the Committee [i.e. the War Council or War Cabinet]."

The first session of the Imperial War Cabinet lasted from 20th March to 2nd May 1917, during which period fourteen meetings took place.[1] Hankey acted as secretary at all of them, and the preparation of papers and agenda, together with the taking of minutes, added greatly to his burdens; for the ordinary War Cabinet continued to meet at least once and not seldom twice or even three times daily as well. Hankey constantly acted as go-between for the Imperial War Cabinet and War Conference, briefing Long about the former's discussions and Lloyd George about matters of importance raised at the latter; but he did not involve himself directly in the deliberations of the Conference. Although he never became fully reconciled to the cumbrous mechanism set up by Lloyd George, whereby two different bodies met separately to discuss matters which were closely related, he did take advantage of the occasion to get to know the Dominion statesmen, and his long-lasting friendship with and admiration for General Smuts dates from the meetings of March–May 1917. One may also reasonably deduce that it further stimulated his interest in all aspects of Imperial Defence, thus sowing the seeds which bore fruit in between the two World Wars, when he strove hard to bring the Dominions fully into the home country's C.I.D. system. But schemes for "Imperial Federation", though discussed informally at this time, made no progress at all, because of the growing sense of "nationhood", and of the need to show complete political independence, among most of the Dominion statesmen—especially those from Canada and South Africa.

Diary 23rd March 1917
War Cabinet in morning and Imperial War Cabinet in afternoon, where a very interesting discussion took place. Gen. Smuts, the S. African, made a long, courageous, and interesting speech on the lines adopted by Massingham[2] in the National Review, advocating the idea that it is impossible to crush Germany and that we adopt a more modest programme and conform our policy and strategy thereto. A very logical and interesting case, I thought, but the others downed him, and were all for jingoism. . . .

While the Imperial War Cabinet was in session shipping losses continued to rise and the peril of the country from the unrestricted submarine campaign grew steadily more threatening. One obvious and

[1]Minutes in I.W.C. series. Cab. 23.
[2]Henry W. Massingham (1860–1924). Journalist. On staff of *Daily Chronicle* 1892–5 and Editor 1895–9. Editor of *The Nation* 1907–23. Joined Labour Party and transferred to *New Statesman* 1923.

urgent need was to increase merchant ship building; and that could only be done by some sacrifice of naval construction. Early in February Hankey had, at Lloyd George's insistence, brought together Carson, the First Lord, and Sir Joseph Maclay, the Shipping Controller, in order to try and achieve a "concordat" regarding where their respective responsibilities lay, and where the cuts in naval building should fall.[1] But he found Carson very "sticky" and difficult over any reduction of his department's responsibilities; and that, taken with Jellicoe's chronic pessimism, further reduced his confidence in the Admiralty's ability to surmount the crisis while under their leadership. At the end of March he addressed the following sombre memorandum to Lloyd George on the subject.[2]

Prime Minister.

Unless we are to lose this war I submit that the following measures should be taken in regard to the food and shipping problems:—

a *Immediate Measures.*

The Minister of Munitions whose output can be reduced owing to the German withdrawal and the consequent reduced expenditure of ammunition, to release a large amount of shipping to bring wheat from Canada and the United States.

I have been in communication with Sir Joseph Maclay and the Minister of Munitions about this. Dr. Addison[3] is quite agreeable, but says he cannot do it without Lord Derby's permission. He has written to Lord Derby and I have also written to Lord Derby to try and induce him to give a prompt decision.

b To organise the ports for night as well as day work. This would greatly increase the rate at which ships are turned round and set free tonnage. This will mean an increase in Transport Workers' Battalions.

c *Measures to increase output of shipbuilding.*

To comb out from the Ministry of Munitions great numbers of men who can be used in shipbuilding yards: it is far more important that they should go to shipbuilding than to the Army.

[1]Hankey to Carson 2nd and 3rd Feb. 1917. Carson papers D/1507/4/103 and 101.
[2]Hankey to Lloyd George 29th March 1917. Cab. 21/95.
[3]Dr. Christopher Addison, 1st Viscount Addison 1945 (1869–1951). Physiologist and politician (Lib., then Lab.). Minister of Reconstruction 1917. First Minister of Health 1919–21. Minister of Agriculture 1929–30. Secretary of State for Commonwealth Relations 1945–7; Paymaster-General 1948–9; Lord Privy Seal 1949–51. Leader of House of Lords 1945–51.

d To put at the disposal of the Shipping Controller some of the "square-headed men" who helped you to organise munitions. These experts should insist that much of the detailed work of engine making and shipbuilding is farmed out to other firms, just as you arranged for particular firms to concentrate on parts, shells, fuses, &c. In fact, the Controller of Shipping should work in the very closest touch with the Ministry of Munitions, who would very likely organise this for him. If the Admiralty care to join in the scheme so much the better.

I submit that the shipping peril is so great that we run a great risk of losing the war unless most drastic measures of this kind are adopted, and that nothing should be allowed to stand in the way.

At about the same time he urged on General Maurice,[1] the Director of Military Operations, "the vital importance from a naval point of view of an operation destined to deprive the enemy of the use of the Belgian ports". Next day he told Lloyd George about this idea while walking around St. James's park.[2] Thus the plan to block Ostend and Zeebrugge by a raid from the sea was, almost certainly, yet another original product of Hankey's fertile brain. We do not know what Maurice's reaction to the idea was; but as another year and more was to elapse before it was carried out the D.M.O. can hardly have been enthusiastic.

At the end of March Hankey confided his growing anxiety about the submarine campaign to his diary.

Diary 30th March 1917
. . . Personally I am much worried about the shipping outlook owing to submarines and the inability of the Adty. to deal with it, and their general ineptitude as indicated by their stickiness towards every new proposal. I have many ideas on the matter, but cannot get at Ll. George in regard to it, as he is so full of politics. I am oppressed by the fear I have always had that, while moderately successful on land, we may yet be beaten at sea. Something like a million tons of shipping have been lost in the last 2 months—and that takes a lot of replacing.[3]

He passed a gloomy 40th birthday with his family at Radnor Place, and on 3rd April Adeline and the children moved back to Highstead,

[1]Major-General Sir Frederick B. Maurice (1871–1951). Director of Military Operations 1915–18. Dismissed in consequence of his letter to the Press of 7th May 1918 (see pp. 528–31 and 539–52). Professor of Military Studies, London University 1927. Principal, Queen Mary College 1933–4.
[2]Diary 26th and 27th March 1917.
[3]This figure was actually too low. Total losses were 540,006 tons in February and 593,841 tons in March 1917.

while Hankey again joined his sister Hilda for the summer months at
11 Launceston Place. That day President Wilson announced "America's
intention to wage war on Germany". Hankey's spirits at once rocketed,
and at the Imperial War Cabinet he "produced a draft telegram to
U.S.A. placing in order our needs, putting shipping first. Ll. George
read this out and it had the desired effect".[1]

[1]Diary 3rd April 1917.

Chapter 13

The Darkening Scene. April–June 1917

THE entry of the United States into the war, though as heartening to the Allies in April 1917 as it was to be to hard-pressed Britain in that fateful December 24 years later, brought no immediate relief; for America was as little prepared for war on the earlier occasion as she was to prove on the later one. In London the Imperial War Cabinet and War Cabinet continued in virtually continuous session right up to the Easter week-end (7th–8th April) during which Hankey was allowed a brief respite at Highstead.

The first War Cabinet after Easter found Lloyd George in one of his most difficult moods. According to Hankey he "refused to look at, much less initial three lots of War Cabinet minutes, thereby holding up all the business of the office most effectively",[1] and instead "slipped off to Walton Heath". No doubt Hankey's irritation derived from the wide gulf between his own highly systematic methods and his master's somewhat idiosyncratic ways. The only decision of importance taken at the meeting in question was that Balfour agreed to go at once to America to press the Allies' most urgent needs, and institute the necessary political and military co-ordination. Hankey described this as "a very sporting effort for a man of 70 who loathes sea voyages beyond everything",[2] and had a hand in briefing him before his departure. Only when Bonar Law took the chair at Cabinet meetings, in Lloyd George's absence, was business conducted as Hankey considered it ought to be done.

On 9th April Allenby's Third Army attacked at Arras in accordance with the plans agreed with the French. Though the Canadians captured the dominating Vimy Ridge the hoped for break-through just to the north of the Hindenburg Line was not achieved. A week later Nivelle launched his much publicised offensive, to which Allenby's attack had been the prelude; and all the optimistic predictions of the French

[1]Diary 9th April 1917. [2]*ibid.* 10th April.

General were quickly and entirely shattered. Immense losses were incurred for trivial gains, and the great mutinies in the French army soon followed.

Diary 18th April 1917
Crossed to France with Lloyd George in a destroyer. Bad passage. Was nearly seasick. Arrived Paris 6 p.m. General Macdonogh[1] and I dined alone at the Crillon. I interpreted for an interview between Lloyd George and M. Painlevé, the new Minister of War.[2] Painlevé was very downhearted about the failure of Nivelle's offensive, and his whole conversation was a repetition of the fact that he had warned Nivelle that his attack must fail. The fact is that Nivelle had talked so big about breaking through that he had encouraged absurdly high hopes. Moreover all Paris had known where and when the attack was to take place, and the enemy had got wind of it. Painlevé also much disappointed about the failure of the Tanks . . .[3] Ll. George also had a mysterious interview with a mysterious person and laid great stress on Painlevé's not knowing it, so I had to keep guard and arrange they should not meet. Later on he told me, as a very great secret, that it was the brother of the Austrian Empress, who had an autograph letter from the Austrian Emperor making peace overtures.[4] Only M. Ribot knew of it in France, and both he and Ll. George were sworn not to reveal it to the Italians or to their colleagues. Ll. G. told me, as he felt that in case of an accident [to himself] an Englishman ought to share the secret. That night Ll. George, General Macdonogh, [J.T.] Davies and I left with Ribot[5] in a special train for St. Jean de Maurienne.[6]

The letter from the Austrian Emperor referred to by Hankey was dated 24th March 1917 and was brought to Paris six days later by the Empress's brother Prince Sixte of Bourbon, who was serving in the

[1]Later Lieutenant-General Sir George M. W. Macdonogh (1865–1942). Director of Military Intelligence 1916–18. Adjutant-General to the Forces 1918–22.
[2]Paul Painlevé (1863–1933). French mathematician, politician and pioneer of aviation. Minister for War 1917 and 1925–9. Prime Minister 1924–5. Minister for Air 1930–1 and 1932–3.
[3]This must refer to the failure of the French tanks used for the first time in the offensive on the Aisne on 16th April 1917. See *Liddell Hart*, pp. 391 and 415.
[4]The Austrian Emperor was Charles (or Karl) I (1887–1922). Succeeded to throne of Austria 21st Nov. 1916 on death of Francis Joseph his great-uncle. Married Princess Zita of Bourbon-Parma 1911. Abdicated Nov. 1918 and after an unsuccessful attempt to regain throne 1921 was transported to Madeira.
[5]Alexandre Ribot (1842–1923). French politician (Repub.). Five times Prime Minister. Minister of Finance 1914–17.
[6]In Savoie near to the Italian frontier.

Belgian army. Ribot had shown it to Lloyd George at Folkestone on 30th, and on the day that Lloyd George took Hankey into his confidence he met Sixte in Paris. On 19th April the Anglo-French delegates met Boselli, Sonnino and Count Aldrovandi, Chef de Cabinet to the latter, in the snowy setting of the Savoy mountains. Though the question of a separate peace with Austria was discussed the existence of Karl's letter was not revealed to the Italians.[1]

Diary 19th April
... We attended the conference for many hours, discussing Italian aspirations in Asia Minor and the position in Greece. It was a very tiresome conference and Sonnino was as obstinate as ever. The fact, however, that Sonnino was no longer so hostile to the French attitude towards Greece, and that Ribot made no opposition to the Italian demand for Smyrna, Adalia and Konia as the Italian "cut off the joint of Turkey" made it clear that there had been some sort of understanding between them.[2] Ll. G. told me that Sonnino at the morning meeting had been strongly opposed to the idea of a separate peace between Austria and the Allies—which I much regretted. It was a pity they could not tell him of the Emperor's offer . . . During the conference Ll. G. spoke very straight to Sonnino about Italy's inadequate efforts in the war compared with her inordinate demands. . . .

Thus did the chickens hatched in the secret treaty of London of April 1915 come home to roost.

On 23rd the British delegates were back in Paris. According to Hankey Lloyd George there "obtained an undertaking that Nivelle should continue his offensive to draw reserves off Haig, who is doing well [at Arras], and also laid the foundations for a bargain that, if we would help the French to clear up the situation in Greece, they would agree to a reduction of force from Salonika.[3] Lloyd George was certainly now piping a very different tune from that sung at the Calais conference in relation to the British and French offensives; and he had also trimmed his sails to the French demand for stronger action in Greece, which, as we saw earlier, he had opposed at the Rome con-

---

[1] The text of Karl's letter is printed in *Lloyd George*, IV, pp. 1997–8.
[2] Smyrna (now Izmir) on the Aegean coast of Turkey. Adalia a seaport on the south coast. Konia an important town and railway centre far inland in Asia Minor and capital of the province of the same name.
[3] Diary 22nd April 1917. It was certainly not correct of Hankey to write here that the British army "is doing well" at Arras. After the initial success on 9th April strong resistance was encountered for small gains. See *Liddell Hart* pp. 407–16.

ference.[1] It was these sudden, unpredictable shifts of allegiance and changes of purpose or opinion which made him such a difficult master for the Generals and Admirals to serve.

From Paris Hankey motored with Lloyd George to Abbeville, and as he found the Prime Minister in a receptive frame of mind he seized the opportunity to reopen the subject of the submarine campaign. "He had evidently carefully studied the paper I wrote last Saturday and Sunday [21st and 22nd April], and at last seemed to have grasped the danger . . .", wrote Hankey in his diary, "though earlier in the trip he had said 'Oh well, I have never regarded that matter as seriously as you have' "—a truly astonishing lapse of judgement by Lloyd George in view of all the facts about the shipping situation which Hankey had many times placed before him.[2] On the evening of 22nd they were safely back in London, and the earlier routine of War Cabinets and Imperial War Cabinets was at once resumed.

Next day *The Times* reported that the Imperial War Conference had proposed that in future India should be represented on an equal footing with the Dominions. Hankey at once wrote to Lloyd George "I think this is a point you might refer to on Friday [27th April in a speech in the House of Commons]. It is an event of very great importance and a reference to it might help India".[3] Two days later he wrote to Smuts that the War Cabinet had instructed him to ask the General if he "would be so good as to furnish them with a Memorandum of your views on the general strategical and military situation, as well as with the impressions you gained from your visit to the Western front".[4] This was the first time the War Cabinet had straightforwardly asked for the guidance of the South African soldier-statesman; but other similar requests were soon to follow. Even more significant was the approval given by the War Cabinet at the same meeting to the Conclusion that Lloyd George himself should "investigate all the means at present used in anti-submarine warfare, on the ground that recent inquiries had made it clear that there was not sufficient co-ordination in the present efforts to deal with the campaign". Churchill has remarked of this mildly worded Minute that "the menace [to the Admiralty] in this procedure was unmistakable".[5] Though that may have been the im-

---

[1]See p. 351. [2]Diary 22nd April 1917.
[3]Hankey to Lloyd George 23rd April 1917. Lloyd George papers F/23/1/6.
[4]Hankey to Smuts 25th April 1917. Smuts Archive, folio 164.
[5]See W. S. Churchill, *Thoughts and Adventures* (Odhams Press, 1932), p. 98.

pression made on his mind in April 1917, there were in fact no grounds for threats—for reasons to be explained shortly.

Diary 29th April 1917[1]

In one way this has been one of the most dreadful weeks of the war, owing to appalling mercantile losses from submarines. These have depressed me very much, but at last, when it is almost too late, the Govt. are taking action. I spent the whole morning dictating a long Memo. to help Ll. G., who has undertaken to investigate the whole question at the Admiralty on Monday. I also had a talk on the telephone with Lord Stamfordham, who says the King is very angry with the Press attacks on the Admiralty, though in my opinion these attacks are largely justified. For example a few weeks ago they scouted the idea of convoy. *Now they are undertaking it on their own initiative* [italics supplied], but apparently want weeks to organise it—though this at any rate might have been done earlier. They don't look ahead. As Lord Fisher has lately written to me the problem is "Can the Army win the war before the Navy loses it?" My horrible prophecy when Lord K.'s army was first conceived, that we should lose at sea without winning on land, threatens to come true . . ."

Fisher evidently saw in the current crisis an opportunity to achieve his recall to power, and once again used Hankey as his intermediary. He asked the busy secretary to dig out the correspondence in which he had made a number of remarkable prophecies before the war, in order that he might show the government how often his foresight had proved correct. Hankey tactfully replied that Fisher's letter was "the truest thing I have ever read". His own conscience was, he said, clear, because when the first Kitchener armies had been formed he had given Asquith "a solemn warning" that "We may win on land, but lose at sea".[2] But although Hankey was perfectly prepared to give Fisher full credit for his far-sightedness he was obviously determined not to make any move on his behalf with the War Cabinet.

Hankey closed the first volume of his diary on the sombre note of the entry for 29th April. It was a singularly appropriate moment for the curtain to be rung down on the first Act in the drama of the submarine campaign, because, behind the scenes, the stage was being set for the opening scene of the next Act—in which Lloyd George at last took action on the lines Hankey had recommended nearly three months earlier.

[1] Most of this day's entry is in *Supreme Command*, II, pp. 649–50.
[2] Hankey to Fisher 23rd April 1917. Lennoxlove papers. Printed in Marder, *Fisher*, III, p. 455.

All published accounts of Lloyd George's foray across the Horse
Guards' Parade to the Admiralty on 30th April have leant heavily on
his own *War Memoirs*, on Churchill's *World Crisis* and *Thoughts and
Adventures*, and especially on Beaverbrook's *Men and Power*.[1] Although
there is no disputing the events that led to the meeting it actually
proved something of an anti-climax, and all three writers have considerably over-dramatised it. For example for Beaverbrook to write that
in the late winter of 1917 "Lloyd George at once became the ardent
exponent of the convoy principle" is a gross exaggeration; so is his
statement that "on 30th April . . . the Prime Minister descended upon
the Admiralty and seated himself in the First Lord's chair". Hankey's
account is surely far more reliable, since he was actually present—as
Churchill and Beaverbrook were not; and the memorandum which he
wrote immediately after the encounter for the War Cabinet fully
supports the diary entry.

For the truth is that three days before Lloyd George, supported by
Hankey, crossed from Downing Street to the Admiralty the Board had,
albeit belatedly, changed their mind, and had decided to run an
experimental convoy from Gibraltar home. On 26th Admiral Duff
"submitted a detailed minute in favour of the adoption of convoy to
Jellicoe, who approved it next day".[2] Study of that minute lends
support to the view that "not only does its length and the importance
of the subject virtually preclude the possibility of its having been
thrown together in a few hours after the Cabinet's decision of 25th, but
Admiral Duff's later correspondence with Jellicoe contains an explicit
and emphatic statement (born out by Jellicoe's own recollections) that
it was based on a change of mind about convoy . . . and that he was not
even aware that Lloyd George's visit had any connection with the
convoy question".[3] On the other hand according to Hankey's almost
invariable practice, the minutes of the Cabinet meeting of 25th would
have reached the Admiralty that same day; and they would surely have
been seen at once by Duff and Jellicoe. In that event the change of mind

[1] See respectively *Lloyd George*, III, pp. 1160–70; Churchill, IV, Ch. XV and *Thoughts
and Adventures*, pp. 129–30, and Beaverbrook, *Men and Power* (Collins Ed.), pp. 152
and 155.
[2] A. Temple Patterson (Ed.) *The Jellicoe Papers*, Vol. II (Navy Records Society,
1968), pp. 114–15. Duff's minute is printed in full on pp. 157–60. See also the
italicised sentence in Hankey's diary entry for 29th April.
[3] *ibid.*

could have been prompted by what Churchill regarded as the minatory wording of the minute in question. And surely the Admirals, on reading the minute, must have been aware, from what had gone before, that convoy was at the very least on the agenda for 30th?

In sum, although one can reasonably criticise the Admiralty for their slowness and reluctance to introduce the traditional strategy, it is also reasonable to ask why Lloyd George should escape all the blame for the delay in starting convoy and be accorded so much of the merit for the change, when Hankey's original memorandum on the subject had been in his hands since 1st February. If the Admiralty was slow to adopt convoy, the Prime Minister and his colleagues in the War Cabinet showed no very marked alacrity in picking up the ball which Hankey had placed at their feet. Thus in terms of history it is surely unfair that Carson and Jellicoe should so often be represented as the villains of the piece, and Lloyd George as the saviour of the country from their ineptitude and conservatism. After all, as late as 22nd April, Lloyd George had told Hankey that the shipping situation was not as serious as he made out.[1] Indeed if any one person deserves the credit for having grasped, and represented, the real needs at an early stage it is surely Hankey—possibly briefed by Henderson and Leslie; and he certainly never put forward any such a claim.

On 30th April, the day of Lloyd George's visit to the Admiralty, Hankey began the second volume of his diary.

Diary 30th April 1917
My second diary opens in a period of very great stress and activity. The Imperial War Cabinet, still in session though nearing an end of its labours, is still imposing on me a heavy burden of work. The offensive in the west is in full blast, but the French have failed to realise the absurdly high expectations encouraged by Gen. Nivelle, who will probably be *dégommé* . . . The submarine campaign has become a most serious menace to us and will probably ultimately compel us to withdraw our forces from Egypt. The Russians are obviously weakening, and to-day a procession of workmen, officers, soldiers, German and Austrian prisoners marched through Petrograd. The U.S.A., totally unprepared for war, can render us but little assistance. Peace rumours are rife everywhere, and I think the nations will very soon force it. At last Lloyd George has set himself to tackle the submarine problem seriously— when it is almost too late. Yesterday afternoon he sent for me to come to Walton Heath to discuss the mode of conducting an inquiry into the

Admiralty . . . Lloyd George then carried me off to town. I supped with him at 10 Downing St. and worked up into the form of questions a number of Memoranda by Milner, Curzon, Gen. Robertson, and a long one by myself . . . This morning Ll. G. and I went to the Admiralty and spent the whole day there very pleasantly lunching with Adl. Jellicoe and his wife and four little girls—Ll. G. having a great flirtation with a little girl of three. I spent the whole evening up to 8.30 dictating a long and epoch-making report, embodying a large reconstruction of the Admiralty and more especially of the Adty. War Staff . . .

That same day Lloyd George circulated to the War Cabinet the "Note" on the meeting in the Admiralty drafted by Hankey. It was a forthright, and a critical document—especially as regards the over-centralisation of work in the hands of Jellicoe and of Admiral Oliver, the Chief of the War Staff. The subjects investigated are reproduced below; and at the end of the Note Hankey set out in a "Summary of Recommendations" sweeping proposals for improving the internal organisation of the staff side and for dealing effectively with the sub-marine menace.[1]

Subjects Investigated

A The organisation of the Admiralty and more particularly of the War Staff, in connection with Anti-Submarine warfare:
B The scientific statistical basis of the Admiralty's arrangements:
C The relations between the Admiralty and the Shipping Controller:
D The arrangements for the control over the movements of merchant ships in those areas where the submarines operate:
E The arrangements for controlling the ports of destinations of merchant ships:
F The question of convoys which the Admiralty are now working out:
G The distribution of destroyers and the possibility of obtaining more assistance in this respect from the United States of America and Japan:
H The effect on Anti-Submarine warfare of reducing our military commitments in the Balkans:
I Minesweeping, including paravanes:
J The supply of submarines mines and minelayers:
K The various weapons used to combat the submarine:
L Mammoth ships.

As an appendix to Hankey's contemporary record of how the introduction of convoy was achieved we may here introduce the retrospective

[1]GT. 604 of 30th April 1917. Cab. 24/12.

view which he expressed on two subsequent occasions. The first occurred in July 1919 when Lloyd George, his intimate friend Sir George Riddell[1] and Hankey were discussing the turning points of the war. According to Riddell Hankey remarked that his own "most important contribution had been what he did in relation to the submarine campaign"; and Lloyd George replied "You performed a great service in the matter. You were always urging adoption of the convoy system".[2] The second recollection was put down fifteen years later, when Lloyd George asked Hankey to read and criticise the chapter of his *War Memoirs* dealing with 1917. "The Submarine Chapter is wonderful", wrote Hankey in reply; and he recalled that "We had horrid rows with Jellicoe at the time and I had to intervene myself".[3] Though he did not make clear exactly how and when he had "intervened" his remark does suggest that, prior to the meeting of 30th April, he was engaged in more strenuous arguments with Jellicoe and the Admiralty than either his diary entries or his memoranda for the Cabinet indicate.

One other point of historical interest merits mention before we leave the subject of convoy. There is at the very least a strong likelihood that Leslie got Smuts on his side, and that the latter strengthened Lloyd George's determination to force a show down. For Leslie's daughter clearly recalls an appointment for her father being made with Smuts at this time, though the documentary proof of it is now lost.[4] If Smuts was briefed in this manner by Leslie it seems almost certain that he would have consulted Hankey before going to Lloyd George; and Hankey was of course very much an ally of Leslie's on the convoy issue.

The report on the conference in the Admiralty was approved by the War Cabinet without amendment at its next meeting on 2nd May. Though no change in the office of First Lord was made until July it obviously rang the death knell for Carson in that capacity. "The thoroughly capable business man" whom Lloyd George sought to take over responsibility for the ship-building side of the Admiralty's

[1]1st Baron Riddell 1920 (1865–1934). Newspaper proprietor and author. Chairman, News of the World Ltd. Represented British Press at Peace Conferences 1919–21 and at Washington Conference 1921–22.
[2]*Lord Riddell's Intimate Diary of the Peace Conference and After* (Gollancz, 1933), p. 104.
[3]Hankey to Lloyd George 2nd April 1934. Lloyd George papers G/8/18/22.
[4]Conversations and correspondence with Miss Cecil Leslie and Miss Gertrude Thompson 1964–7.

responsibilities had been met by the appointment of Sir Eric Geddes as Controller of the Navy[1]; and it was he who replaced Carson as head of the department three months later.

Diary 1st May 1917
. . . Terrible day:—War Cabinet 11.30. At 12.30 I was left single handed, [as] the subject was very secret—our military policy . . . At 3.15 I went through my report on the Adty. with Ll. George. He was delighted with it, and warmly commended it. At 3.45 the War Cabinet reassembled to continue the morning's discussion. At 5 p.m. Imperial War Cabinet, followed by a meeting of the War Cabinet to consider the perpetuation of the Imperial War Cabinet—making 4 meetings in a day . . . My head reels when I think that in 24 hours I have dealt exhaustively with—the constitution of the Admiralty; the whole military policy of the Allies; military policy in the Balkans and Foreign policy in Greece; the future constitution of the British Empire; peace desiderata, territorial and otherwise, to say nothing of a number of minor questions . . .

The "very secret subject" discussed by the War Cabinet on 1st May in fact concerned "the attitude to be adopted by the British representatives at a forthcoming Inter-Ally Conference at Paris".[2] The decisions taken were, firstly, to "press the French to continue the offensive"; and, secondly, that if the British representatives "were not satisfied that the French offensive would prove effective they [the British representatives] should insist on our entire freedom of action and on the French Army re-occupying the trenches recently taken over by the British forces". It is difficult not to feel that the War Cabinet showed considerable lack of realism with regard to the consequences of Nivelle's catastrophic failure; but they were probably influenced by General Smuts's view that the Germans should not be allowed "time to recover their spirits", and that "if we could not break the enemy's front we might break his heart".[3] Though Lloyd George disliked the whole concept of the projected Flanders offensive he did not at this stage offer resolute opposition to it.

May 2nd was a red letter day for Hankey, since not only did the War Cabinet then accept his comprehensive solution to the shipping crisis

[1]1875–1937. Rail transport expert and politician (Cons.). Inspector-General, Transportation for all war theatres 1916–17. Controller of Navy 1917; First Lord of Admiralty 1917–18. Minister of Transport 1919–21.
[2]War Cabinet 128A of 1st May 1917 Minute 1. Cab. 23/13.
[3]*ibid.* p. 15.

but the Imperial War Cabinet held its last meeting—which provoked an expression of heartfelt thanks in his diary.[1] Next day he was off to Paris again with Lloyd George, Lord Robert Cecil and Sir Eric Geddes for conferences with the French on what should be done in face of the disastrous failure of Nivelle's offensive.

Diary 4th May 1917
Ll. G.'s methods much amuse me. Scarcely had he set foot in Paris than his scouts were out to try and pick up all the political gossip, particularly in regard to the status of the principal ministers, their personal prospects as well as those of the Ministry, the various parliamentary groups, the position of the leading generals such as Pétain and Nivelle etc. etc. His scouts included Col. David Davies,[2] Mantoux the interpreter, Lord Esher and others . . . At 10 a.m. he and Lord Robert Cecil and I were at the Quai d'Orsay, conferring, and were joined later by Robertson, Haig, Jellicoe, Maurice, Pétain, Nivelle, and French admirals. The main object of this visit was to ginger up the French to renew their efforts on the western front, and to give the enemy no respite. The French were very down on their luck about their heavy losses and depleted reserves—only 35,000 men remaining in the depots—but Ll. G. was in great form and we brought them to our point of view viz. to continue the policy of remorseless hammering. All day we conferred with an interval for the usual gargantuan déjeuner at the Quai d'Orsay. At the latter I sat next to General Pétain. I asked him how he liked the change to Paris from commanding a field army. He replied "During this war I have only applied for 48 hours' leave. At the end of 24 hours I was tired of Paris and went back. That is the measure by which you can judge my liking for my new position." He struck me as a very reserved and soldierly man. He wore no decorations. In speaking of military matters he talked in low tones close to my ear, as though he didn't want the civilians on either side of us to know what he was saying. The general atmosphere of Paris struck me as very bad—a weak Government, a tiresome Chamber, intreague [sic] everywhere, and a troubled and rather dejected people. In the afternoon we discussed Salonika and Greece; it was rather a bad wrangle, M. Léon Bourgeous[3] being suspicious and rather obstructive, and the task was none the easier that [? because] our people themselves had not decided quite what they wanted. As soon as the

[1]Minutes in Cab. 23.
[2]Once more Hankey misspelt the name. This was almost certainly David D. Davies, later 1st Baron Davies of Llandinam (1880–1944), Parliamentary Private Secretary to Lloyd George 1916–22.
[3]French politician (1851–1925). Nine times a Minister; Prime Minister 1895–96. Foreign Minister at time of Hague Conferences 1895, 1899 and 1907. President of Senate 1920–23.

conference was over, I sat down and drafted a series of Resolutions, which I believed represented the maximum concessions we could make to the French. They announced definitely our intentions of withdrawing immediately part of our forces from Salonika and included rather an ingenious idea which Lord Robert Cecil and I had planned for purchasing the Thessaly harvest; placating the Greeks by raising the blockade; and enabling Gen. Sarrail to obtain virtual occupation of Thessaly by establishing control posts to prevent the illicit removal of the harvest . . .

Ll. G. had a parliamentary delegation to breakfast, so I could not get him and Cecil and Robertson together to consider the Greece-Salonika question . . . The result was that we went off to the conference again quite at sixes and sevens among ourselves and the morning session was unproductive. After lunch however I got them all together and we hashed up a new protocol based on my original draft. This was handed to the French in the afternoon and eventually accepted *ad referendum* to the French Cabinet. They made a frightful outcry about the reduction of the Salonika force, and the point was only conceded after the Prime Minister had warned them that Jellicoe would resign if it was not done (which no British Government could stand) and after Jellicoe himself had stated that, if the forces were not withdrawn from Salonika, they would starve—in which he was supported by Admiral Lacaze[1] the French Minister of Marine, Admiral de Bon[2] the Chief of the Staff, General Robertson, and General Pétain. The French politicians were furious with their soldiers and sailors but had to yield . . .

On 6th May most of the British delegation returned home, but Lloyd George, Cecil and Hankey set off by car for the British G.H.Q. near Arras, stopping on the way to visit the cathedrals of Beauvais and Amiens. At the latter a service was in progress, which apparently fascinated Lloyd George. They spent the night with the thunder of guns in their ears, and a near miss from a bomb further disturbed their slumbers.

Diary 7th May 1917
G.H.Q. made the usual impression on me of unbounded and quite unjustified optimism, which is never to be found either among the men in the trenches, on whom falls the burden of the fighting, nor among those at home who have the responsibility for the wider policy, but only among the persons who have the control of the larger units of our armies. I believe that this is true of every army in the field, our own, our allies, and our enemies . . .

[1]See p. 318.
[2]Ferdinand de Bon (1861–1923). French admiral. Chief of naval staff 1916–19. Commanded French naval forces in Mediterranean 1919. Head of French naval mission to Washington Conference 1921–22.

General Charteris, Haig's Chief of Intelligence Staff, made an interesting comment about Hankey in his diary for the same day. "Hankey", he wrote, "who is said to know more about everything than anyone else in the Empire, preserved an almost unbroken silence all through dinner. Probably that is how he acquires his knowledge".[1] Though there may have been some truth in the General's last sentence it seems more probable that on the occasion in question Hankey was pondering on the lack of realism—of which Charteris himself was certainly a principal propagator—which he always found at G.H.Q.

Once back in the saddle Hankey renewed his efforts in the field of shipping and anti-submarine warfare. He first drew the attention of the War Cabinet to the need to give a high priority to the allocation of steel for shipbuilding.[2] Next he obtained approval for the powers given to Geddes as Controller of the Navy to be widened to include responsibility for ship construction for the merchant navy and army. Evidently there was great difficulty over defining the relative responsibilities of Geddes and Sir Joseph Maclay.[3] On 11th the War Cabinet placed the whole responsibility on the former; but this nearly led to Maclay resigning, and Hankey had to spend most of the day acting as go-between for him and Geddes. He finally managed to produce a draft which, although it actually gave Geddes the centralised authority and extended powers which Lloyd George supported, managed to smooth the ruffled feathers of the Shipping Controller. "Dined with Geddes to celebrate the birth of the new department", wrote Hankey in his diary, "Not the first by a long way at whose arrival I have assisted".[4] Lloyd George was meanwhile pressing Smuts to take command of the army in Palestine—which the South African declined on the grounds that the War Office was certain to treat that campaign as a side show and starve it of forces,[5] and rumours were afoot that Montagu and Churchill were both to join the War Cabinet.[6]

Anxiety over the recent disaster in France and the submarine campaign was increased by the realisation that Russia might soon be

[1]Brigadier-General John Charteris, *At G.H.Q.*, Vol. II, p. 224 (Cassell, 1931).
[2]GT. 666 of 8th May 1917. Cab. 24/12.   [3]GT. 685 of 10th May 1917. *ibid*.
[4]Diary 11th May 1917.
[5]See W. K. Hancock, *Smuts*, Vol. I, *The Sanguine Years*, pp. 433–5.
[6]Montagu was at this time Vice-Chairman of the War Cabinet's Reconstruction Committee, of which Lloyd George was chairman. He did not regain ministerial rank until he took over the India Office in July 1917, the same month that Churchill returned to the government as Minister of Munitions.

eliminated as an ally, thus releasing enormous German forces to the western front; for confidence in Kerensky's Provisional Government was waning rapidly. On 12th Curzon, Cecil, Amery and Hankey met informally at the Foreign Office to discuss the military implications; but their deliberations produced no comfort at all.[1] Had the British War Cabinet known of the extent of the mutinies which had broken out in the French Army on 3rd May, and which spread so rapidly that very few divisions could be relied on, their anxieties would have been enormously increased. Fortunately the French managed to conceal the full truth not only from their allies but, more miraculously, from the enemy as well; for had it been known in Germany a great effort would surely have been made to force a decision in the west during May or June 1917.[2] On 12th Hankey learnt that Nivelle had been asked to resign but had refused. Three days later he was replaced by Pétain.

At this juncture even Hankey's stamina showed signs of giving way, and Lloyd George told him to take a few days' rest. But his great efforts over the submarine campaign were in fact already beginning to bear fruit. The experimental convoy from Gibraltar sailed on 10th May and arrived safely at Plymouth ten days later. The Admiralty now appointed an Atlantic Convoy Committee, and its report, dated 6th June, provided a comprehensive scheme for the introduction of convoy on all the most important shipping routes.[3] The effects became apparent quickly. In May shipping losses fell from the catastrophic April total of 881,027 tons to 596,629. Although in June they rose again to the menacing figure of 687,507 tons that rise proved a transient phenomenon, and as the convoy strategy became more and more widely applied losses fell to 511,730 tons in August, and thereafter never again exceeded half a million tons in a month. Furthermore sinkings of enemy submarines increased from the very modest total of 10 in each of the first two quarters of the year to 22 in the third quarter—which was about inversely proportional to the decrease in losses of merchant ships.[4] If Hankey had done nothing else for his country in the First World War

---

[1] Diary 12th May 1917.
[2] See Richard M. Watt, *Dare call it Treason* (Chatto & Windus, 1963) for a vivid account of the mutinies; also *Liddell Hart,* p. 392.
[3] Copy in papers of Sir Norman Leslie.
[4] For full statistics of merchant ship losses and U-boat sinkings in World War I see respectively C. E. Fayle, *Seaborne Trade,* Vol. III (Murray, 1924), Appendix C, and Robert M. Grant, *U-boats Destroyed* (Putnam, 1964), Appendix B.

his contribution to surmounting the crisis of the submarine campaign merits the everlasting gratitude of its people.

After three days' "pleasant holiday" with his family at Highstead Hankey was back at his office on 21st May to find of course a huge accumulation of work. However the news that his salary was to be raised to £2,000 per annum, a very high figure in the Civil Service of those days, strengthened his unflagging perseverance and indomitable resolution. Settlement of the much-debated "Irish Question" (that is to say Conscription, possibly combined with a measure of Home Rule) once again stood high on the Cabinet's agenda; but Carson's obstinate intransigence over any compromise involving union between Ulster and the rest of the country once more proved an insuperable obstacle.[1] Carson's attitude on the Irish question, combined with dissatisfaction with his administration at the Admiralty, must have strengthened Lloyd George's desire to get rid of him; but the need not to offend his Tory colleagues forced him to tread warily.

Meanwhile the Austrian Emperor had sent a second letter about peace talks by hand of Prince Sixte, who arrived in London with it on 22nd May. Unfortunately Count Czernin, the Austrian Foreign Minister,[2] had shown himself to be strongly opposed to making any concessions to Italy; and on the French side influential persons, such as the brothers Paul and Jules Cambon,[3] would not countenance a separate Austro-Italian peace. Thus no progress at all was made in a direction which Hankey had always regarded as hopeful, and in which Lloyd George himself seems to have been prepared to move.

Diary 24th May 1917
Interesting discussion at morning War Cabinet on subject of the articles on the submarine question in The Times and Daily Mail, and all the Northcliffe press, which supply most valuable propaganda to the enemy, who makes full

[1]See for example Carson to Hankey 20th April 1917. "I desire to make it clear that I did not agree to the proposal of the 6 counties voting out [of a united Ireland] by a 55 per cent majority. I definitely stated that I must not be taken as accepting this proposal." Carson papers D1507/1/1917/44.
[2]Count Czernin von und zu Chudenitz (1872–1932). Austrian statesman and diplomat. Foreign Minister 1916–18.
[3]Jules Cambon (1845–1935). French diplomat and colonial administrator. Ambassador at Washington 1897, at Madrid 1902 and at Berlin 1907–14. Secretary-General, Foreign Ministry, 1915–19. Paul Cambon (1843–1924). French diplomat and colonial administrator. Ambassador at Madrid 1886, at Constantinople 1890 and at London 1898–1920.

use of it. Ll. G. very angry about it, which amuses me, as, before he became Prime Minister he could talk of nothing except "telling the people the truth". He is now trying to persuade the War Cabinet to send Northcliffe to America to co-ordinate the purchases, transport arrangements etc. of the various Depts. This, of course, is really a dodge to get rid of Northcliffe, of whom he is afraid. I am certain N. will not accept it, even if he is asked.[1] . . .

A few days after Lloyd George had brought up the question of Northcliffe going to America a telegram reached Hankey from Drummond, who had gone out with Balfour in April, saying that he considered such a proposal would prove "quite disastrous". The war was, he continued, unpopular in the U.S.A., and Britain must rely on the President and the Administration "to arouse the country". Anything tending to show that the American government was "acting under the advice of Great Britain, or that we wished to hustle them unduly" might, in Drummond's view, "have deplorable consequences".[2] It is interesting to find a Foreign Office official using Hankey, instead of his own department as the channel for the communication of opinions obviously intended for the War Cabinet. In spite of Drummond's misgivings Northcliffe did go to U.S.A., where he received a predictably chilly reception from the British Embassy.[3]

On 25th Hankey, careful as ever to lay solid foundations for any proposal he intended to put forward, had a long talk with Milner about the arrears in the War Cabinet's business and how such troubles could best be overcome. They agreed that a measure of decentralisation, to clear up minor issues before the beginning of each plenary session, was the best solution.[4] Then he had to turn his attention to the agenda for the Anglo-French conference which was to assemble shortly in London, and at which another attempt was to be made to resolve once and for all the tiresome problem of King Constantine of Greece.

The French wished to seize Athens by force and compel Constantine to abdicate; but the War Cabinet preferred the plan which Lord Robert Cecil had hatched to achieve the same purpose by seizing the Thessaly harvest and facing the Athens government with the threat of starvation. Hankey mistrusted General Sarrail, and believed he would seize

[1] This prediction by Hankey proved wrong. In his memoirs (*Supreme Command*, II, pp. 665–6) he praises Lloyd George's decision to send out Northcliffe as "a masterstroke" designed "to harness this restless and turbulent spirit".
[2] Drummond to Hankey 27th May 1917. Balfour papers, Add. MSS. 49704, p. 14.
[3] *Lloyd George*, III, pp. 1688–96. [4] Diary 25th May 1917.

any chance to land troops and solve the dilemma by force—as indeed he had proposed at the Rome Conference in January.[1] Hankey anticipated that such action would land the Allies in "a horrid imbroglio" with a Greek army in the Morea "threatening our maritime communications", and the Salonika army too weak to resist an attack by the Central Powers.[2] After two days of strenuous argument Cecil's plan was finally accepted, and Hankey at once drafted the necessary agreement. Yet when it came to the point the French did land troops in Athens, to the great indignation of Cecil and Hankey. Constantine abdicated in favour of his son Alexander, and early in June Venizelos was back in power. A prolonged controversy had been resolved—though by methods which Hankey regarded as unscrupulous and unjustified.

While the Anglo-French conference was actually in session Hankey circulated his memorandum on how the War Cabinet should improve the conduct of its business and avoid the accumulation of arrears. He pointed out that since 6th May the number of items on the "Immediate List" had risen from 14 to 25, and that many minor issues had been awaiting decision for weeks. He always did his best to get such issues settled outside the Cabinet room, but could not entirely overcome the tendency of departments "to throw decisions on the War Cabinet" which could have been settled by inter-departmental discussion. After considering various ways in which the prevailing difficulties could be reduced by more decentralisation he put forward his own solution. This was that "in future statements by the Naval, Military and Foreign Political Advisers should not take place at the beginning of the meeting but an hour or so later . . .", thus enabling the War Cabinet to start dealing with the real agenda as soon as it had assembled.[3] Three days later Lord Robert Cecil put forward a proposal that pressure on the War Cabinet could best be reduced by establishing three Standing Committees—"for external affairs, internal affairs and Labour questions".[4] In a rather different form this was finally done by, for example, the creation of the War Policy Committee, to be referred to again shortly. But the plain truth was that the unquestionable advantages of having a small War Cabinet, as compared with its much larger predecessor the War Committee, made overloading inevitable; and not even Hankey's administrative ingenuity and hard work could entirely eliminate that

1See p. 351.   2Diary 29th May 1917.
3GT. 857 of 28th May 1917. Cab. 24/14.
4GT. 926 of 1st June 1917. Cab. 24/15.

handicap. None the less his airing of the whole subject did produce results.

Diary 30th May 1917
On Monday I had found time to write a Memo. pointing out the heavy congestion of War Cabinet business. They discussed this at the War Cabinet this morning and were seriously alarmed. So they set to work with a will and with the determination to clear up all arrears in two days with a view to a Friday to Monday holiday. They are all rather done up and I felt very cruel. They sat all the morning, and from 3.30 to 6.30 in the afternoon. In the morning Lord Curzon's private secretary had come to me to say that Lord C. *must* have a holiday and was on the verge of a breakdown. I repeated this to Ll. George, who said his information was that Lord C. was so done that he had been known to burst into tears . . .

31st May
We plugged on all day again at War Cabinet business from 11.30 until 6 p.m. I lunched with Ll. George and Lord Northcliffe(!) The latter is off to America as head of the British Naval, Military, Shipping, and Munitions Missions. I drafted his instructions! He was very quiet and restrained, and much pleasanter than I found him before . . . He little knows that one of Ll. G's principal motives in sending him out is to get rid of him. I had some talk with Ll. G. in the evening about the fact that he won't initial my Minutes, and I told him that I had been obliged to issue the Minutes without his initials and he only said "Well, I can repudiate them and they will hang you instead of me!" . . .

Hankey to Lloyd George. 2 Whitehall Gardens, 31st May 1917. Holograph[1]
My dear Prime Minister,
I write to thank you for my re-appointment with increased salary. Also for the handsome way in which the services of my staff have been acknowledged in the forthcoming honours list—though nothing could be too good for them.
I should like you to know that I feel these incidents very deeply as an expression of confidence on the part of the War Cabinet and particularly of yourself in me and my office, and I can assure you that we shall all do our utmost to deserve this confidence,
Yours sincerely,

We saw earlier how, towards the end of the First Coalition, Lloyd George frequently queried Hankey's War Committee Minutes, and in general showed lack of consideration for, and perhaps some lack of

[1]Lloyd George papers F/23/1/9.

confidence in the hard-worked secretary.[1] However he certainly changed his tune soon after he achieved the highest office in the land, and by the middle of 1917 their correspondence, taken with Hankey's diary entries, shows that a strong bond of intimacy and of confidence had grown up between them. This probably arose chiefly from Hankey's realisation that Lloyd George was the only politician capable of holding the Allies together and leading them to victory, or at any rate to a satisfactory compromise peace. But at the same time he was always very much aware of the mercurial Prime Minister's deviousness, and of his lack of scruple in furthering his own political ends. To give only one example of the closer intimacy between them on 1st June Hankey wrote to Lloyd George that "Although the Colonial Secretary [Walter Long] is fussing rather about Smuts, and is specially anxious that he should not formally join the War Cabinet until a reply is received from Lord Buxton,[2] I have invited Smuts to the War Cabinet on Monday".[3] Thus did the South African statesman become a member of the supreme authority directing the war effort of the whole British Commonwealth and Empire; but his consequential involvement in European affairs was, in the long view, to contribute greatly to the decline of his authority in his own country.[4]

The first days of June brought Hankey a brief but welcome break, part of which he spent with Adeline on the river at Maidenhead ("a delightful day"), and part at Highstead with Tom Jones as their guest; but he devoted the whole of his last day's holiday to studying the report of the Mesopotamia Commission, which had been appointed by Asquith to investigate the events leading to General Townshend's surrender at Kut-el-Amara.[5] This body, like its twin brother the Dardanelles Commission, found much to criticise in the conduct of the operations under scrutiny—especially on the part of the Government of India and the Indian Army. And once again the victims of criticism, being given no chance to defend themselves, felt most unjustly treated.

[1] See pp. 252–3.
[2] 1st Viscount Buxton 1914 and Earl Buxton 1920 (1853–1934). Politician (Lib.) and author. Postmaster-General 1905–10. Governor-General, Union of South Africa 1914–20.
[3] Lloyd George papers F/23/1/10.
[4] See Sir Keith Hancock, *Smuts*, Vol. II, *The Fields of Force* (Cambridge U.P., 1968).
[5] See pp. 269 and 279. The report is Cd. 8610 dated 17th May 1917. The Chairman was Lord George Hamilton. Commander J. Wedgwood, M.P., submitted a minority report, which was even more critical of the Government of India.

Hankey never budged from his original opinion that it was both politically and militarily unwise to hold such inquests in time of war; and that to publish the reports was to aggravate the original mistake and increase the sense of grievance among the victims.

One of the first memoranda which Hankey circulated on returning to his office after his brief holiday concerned the need to prepare for "The Eventual Peace Conference" in good time, since it was his view that the occasion might arise "with great suddenness". He therefore suggested that "the more mechanical arrangements", such as "the composition and organisation of the British delegation" should be thought out well in advance, and that he himself should be instructed to prepare "a list of representatives and organise . . . the secretarial and office arrangements, maps, library and accommodation likely to be required."[1] Although such far-sightedness may seem premature, at any rate at a time when the Allies seemed quite likely to lose the war before American participation became effective, it was in the end to pay very handsome dividends in the superb secretarial arrangements at the Paris Peace Conference of 1919.

While Hankey was turning his mind to the preparations for a peace conference no progress at all had been made over the approaches for a separate peace which the Austrian Emperor had initiated in March and again in May.[2] On 6th June his emissary Prince Sixte returned from London to France, and although what Lloyd George has called the "final, negative answer of France" was not pronounced until Ribot delivered it in a speech in the Chamber on 12th October it was plain long before that date that the forces in France which were antagonistic to Karl's appeal were too strong. Lloyd George has blamed what now seems a tragic lost opportunity entirely on the French; yet it is hard not to feel that in the early summer of 1917 he himself could have done more to press them in a direction which might have brought untold benefits to mankind—as indeed he evidently realised long after the event.[3]

On the day after the departure of Prince Sixte a squall suddenly blew up out of the clear sky which had recently warmed Hankey's relations with the Prime Minister.

Diary 7th June 1917
Two War Cabinets. Lunched with Ll. George. After lunch he took me aside

[1]GT. 938 of 5th June 1917. Cab. 24/15.   [2]See pp. 377 and 390.
[3]*Lloyd George*, IV, pp. 2028–32.

and told me that Lady Cunard[1] and Mrs. Asquith had got knowledge of the fact that Mr. Balfour had telegraphed advising against Northcliffe's appointment. He was very agitated at this having leaked out, and suggested that it must have got out through my minutes, which he had some idea went to Montagu. I felt instinctively that he suspected *me* of having given it away. I tried to reassure him but he wouldn't trust a word I said. So I went back to the office and discovered that the minutes contained no hint of the *gist* of Balfour's telegram (I am always very discreet about such matters). So I sent him a copy, together with a distribution list of the minutes, and accompanied it with a private letter saying that, in case any possible suspicion might have entered his mind, I could [give] him my word of honour that I had not given it away, and I showed that in fact, owing to the holiday, I could have seen none of the Asquith crowd. At the evening Cabinet meeting the psychological atmosphere was very sultry, and I still felt that he distrusted me. Moreover he made me withdraw with my Asst. Sectys. when the War Cabinet discussed something very secret. So I felt distinctly uncomfortable and was very bored at having to attend Col. Norton-Griffiths'[2] monthly-dinner to discuss Imperial development.[3] However I made a very successful extempore speech advocating the development of a thinking dept. side by side with the War Cabinet staff, to include representatives of the Dominions and to form with the War Cabinet Secretariat the Office of the Imperial War Cabinet. (Lord Sydenham fully agreed.) . . .

Hankey to Lloyd George. 2 Whitehall Gardens. 7th June 1917. Holograph[4]
My dear Prime Minister,

Lest any possible suspicion could have entered your mind, owing to my former intimate association with the Asquiths, that I myself let slip any hint of Mr. Balfour's telegram to anyone in the Asquith entourage, I feel bound to give you my solemn word of honour that this has not been the case.

I put aside altogether the fact that I set before myself a very high standard

---

[1] Maud (renamed herself Emerald) Cunard (1872–1948). Wife of Sir Bache Cunard and a well-known London society hostess of those days. See Daphne Fielding, *Emerald and Nancy* (Eyre & Spottiswoode, 1968).
[2] Later Sir John Norton-Griffiths (1871–1930). Contractor and politician (Cons.). Served on staff of Engineer-in-Chief, B.E.F. during World War I.
[3] This probably refers to the current discussions on "Imperial Federation"—a doctrine strongly favoured by the Round Table Group organised by Lionel Curtis, of which Philip Kerr (see p. 184) was a member. It was chiefly Smuts who, by the resolution which he drafted and which was approved by the Imperial War Conference on 16th March 1917, ensured that the doctrine of "Colonial Nationalism" should prevail over that of Imperial Federation. See W. K. Hancock, *Smuts*, Vol. I *The Sanguine Years* (Cambridge U.P., 1962), pp. 429–32.
[4] Lloyd George papers F/23/1/11.

in the matter of reticence—never more so than on those rare occasions (twice only since you came into office) when I run across the Asquiths.

As a matter of fact I have seen no member of the Asquith family since Mr. Balfour's telegram was received, which was in Whitsun week. I believe that they were at The Wharf all that week, and I was at my home at Limpsfield from Saturday to Monday inclusive, and at Richboro' on Friday—the War Cabinet meeting having been held on Wednesday. I was with *you* all day Thursday, including lunch.

The only friends of the Asquiths whom I have seen are Bonham Carter, who lunched with me yesterday, and Montagu with whom I lunched the day before yesterday, but [? in] neither case was the subject even alluded to.

Montagu never sees our Minutes—and, as a matter of fact the War Cabinet Minute contained no allusion to the gist of Mr. Balfour's telegram.

It is an intensely irritating case of leakage, and I should much like to nail it, as I am very jealous of the honour of my office, and the War Cabinet.

I do not think it was necessary for me to write this letter, because I believe you know that I am absolutely loyal and devoted to you and your Government, but I wanted you to feel quite sure that I had not been indiscreet.

Yours sincerely

The same day that Hankey tried to convince Lloyd George that he had no hand in the "leak" of Balfour's telegram—and one may well feel that with a less suspicious master it should not have been necessary for him to clear his name in writing after having done so verbally—Carson sent Jellicoe a letter in which he tried to rebut recent criticism of the Admiralty, particularly about the lack of "offensive" naval operations. He wanted a special section of the War Staff instituted to plan such operations.[1] Jellicoe minuted on this letter that he had "been informed that the Prime Minister sent for Captain [H. W.] Richmond (I presume in connection with this proposition), and I presume that this was done at the instigation of Colonel Hankey. I do not make any comment on this interference with Admiralty administration by Colonel Hankey if I am correct in my assumption, but if Captain Richmond is likely to be suitable in other respects, I think he would probably be useful at the Admiralty . . .". Though the First Sea Lord's assumption that Hankey had inspired Lloyd George's meeting with his old friend and shipmate of *Ramillies* days[2] was probably correct, his prickly minute shows how resentful Jellicoe was of Hankey's influence. This almost certainly derived from the part he had played in the recent convoy controversy.

[1]Carson to Jellicoe 7th June 1917. Adm. 1/8489. [2]See p. 42.

Diary 8th June 1917

Saw Lord Milner before War Cabinet . . . and outlined my whole scheme of Imperial Development; explained how I had wanted to get in W. L. Grant[1] as an Assistant Secretary . . . as the nucleus of a Dominions' Staff. He was very sympathetic . . . War Cabinet at 11.30. The psychological thunderstorm had cleared and Ll. George was most cordial. I lunched with him and Gen. Smuts, and he told me the latter was to be a member of the War Cabinet. Smuts came back with me to the office and I spent 2 hours coaching him on the latest developments of the military and political situation. He is a delightful and attractive creature. Although I am glad that his fresh and active brain is to be at the disposal of the War Cabinet it increases my own difficulties. Even to-day I had to draft a minute with great cunning and adroitness in order not to offend a representative of a Dominion. Before I went home . . . I had to see Lord Milner again . . . We also had a long talk about a new Committee on War Policy, (P.M., Curzon, Milner, Smuts, and self as secretary), which it was decided this morning to set up. The new feature in the sitn. to-day is that Gen. Sir H. Wilson, our liaison officer with Pétain, came to the War Cabinet this morning to warn us that the French would not stick it much longer, and that Pétain had to fail in his promise to carry out an offensive on the 10th in support of Haig's attack on the Messines ridge. This report is confirmed more or less by Lord Esher, and has made us all very anxious. Mention of the Messines battle reminds me that the plan of concentrating mines and preparing for an offensive months ahead was suggested by me and pressed on the soldiers both personally (to General Fowke[2] the C.R.E. in France) and through Swinton by letter in the first 6 months of 1915. I believe the first idea was mine but Norton-Griffiths carried it out.

The ill tidings brought over by Henry Wilson seem to have been the War Cabinet's first intimation that something was seriously wrong with the discipline of the French Army. In a Specially Secret Cabinet Minute written that same day, which covered seven foolscap pages in Hankey's own hand, he enlarged on the matter at length. "The War Cabinet felt", he recorded, "that the very grave information communicated by General Wilson strongly reinforced the arguments given by Lord Milner . . . in favour of a fresh stocktaking of the whole war situation". Lloyd George, however, took a more sanguine view than Wilson, and after making some harsh remarks about the "large number of instances

[1]William L. Grant (1872–1935). Canadian educationist and author. Professor of Colonial History, Queen's University, Kingston, Ontario 1910–15. Served with Canadians in B.E.F. 1915–17.

[2]Later Lieutenant-General Sir George H. Fowke (1864–1936). Engineer-in-Chief, B.E.F. 1914–16. Adjutant-General in France 1916–19.

all through the war [in which] the advice of the experts had proved wrong" he went on to emphasise his belief that "we could achieve both a military and a diplomatic success". Once again he had his eyes on the Middle East, where he hoped that, if we could "get Syria into our hands", both Turkey and Bulgaria might sue for peace. Moreover Italy's intransigence over the Austrian peace overtures, which derived from Baron Sonnino's territorial greed, was probably now lessened by the shakiness of the Italian government. Hence, although Lord Robert Cecil, who was acting as Foreign Secretary during Balfour's absence in U.S.A., thought that "no further step could be taken in the Austrian negotiations without discussion with Italy", Lloyd George insisted that "Austria was at least entitled to a reply". Here was Lloyd George at his best—facing bad news with courage, yet resolved on probing every possibility of peace. The final decisions were, firstly that Cecil should telegraph to Rome asking for Sonnino to meet British and French representatives; and, secondly, that the Committee on War Policy, referred to earlier, should be set up.[1] The latter proposal had been put forward by Milner, who had urged that "four or five people, having the time and the necessary qualifications should concentrate their minds upon *the military and political situation in the Balkans as a whole*"; also that "any fresh and well-equipped mind, entirely free from prepossessions [should be] brought in to help them". "We happen to have such a mind available, and quite unburdened at the present moment", concluded Milner, "in General Smuts".[2] His proposal was accepted, and from that date Smuts played an important part in Imperial defence and always maintained his close association with Hankey.

Hankey recorded the Cabinet's discussion of 8th June in his own hand, and it was given only a very limited circulation. The gist of it was that Lloyd George now proposed to abandon the British offensive in Flanders, and try to isolate Germany by making a separate peace with Austria—despite the certainty that Italy would object.[3] We will return shortly to the reaction of Haig and Robertson to those proposals.

Diary 9th June 1917
Spent morning writing in my own fist the Minutes of yesterday's War Cabinet meeting, which were very secret, dealing with Henry Wilson's

[1] War Cabinet 159A of 8th June 1917. Cab. 23/16.
[2] Memo. of 7th June, circulated as Appendix to War Cabinet 159A.
[3] War Cabinet 159A of 8th June 1917. Cab. 23/16.

French news and the possibility of a separate peace with Austria. At 3 o'clock I met Mr. Balfour and delivered to him the War Cabinet's letter of thanks and congratulations. At 4.30 he dropped in to tea and spent 2 hours, during which I rehearsed to him all that had happened during his absence in the U.S.A., and he gave me some account of his visit. It is only in the last two days, during the long recitation I have given to Gen. Smuts and Mr. Balfour that I have realised what a vast and encyclopaedic knowledge I have of the events of this cataclysmic war . . .

The British offensive in Flanders opened in the early hours of 7th June with the surprise explosion of nineteen huge mines—an idea for which, as we saw earlier, Hankey claimed a share of the credit. The purpose was to straighten out the notorious Ypres salient, and the capture of the dominating Messines ridge was a heartening, though limited success. As soon as the Germans had recovered from the initial shock the battle resumed a static form—though with Plumer's Second Army better placed through possession of the geographically insignificant but tactically vital high ground, and the German "bulge" south of Ypres eliminated.[1] Nothing further was attempted in this sector until the start of the Third Battle of Ypres at the end of July.

While the Messines offensive was in progress Hankey's assistant G. M. Young sent him a long and perceptive account of conditions in Russia. Writing from Petrograd he began by qualifying his views with a *caveat* that "in Russia you never know what will happen next"; but he none the less prophesied "that the offensive will be tried and will be abortive". His confidence that it would fail was based on his knowledge that "even if a miracle restores the moral[e] of the Army" the transport system would prove completely inadequate. The only way that Young could suggest to counter the catastrophic consequences which another failure would bring in its train was "to induce Austria to make a separate peace". He pressed the view that nearly all the problems to which both Russia and Austria were parties (Transylvania, Bosnia, Galicia, Trieste and Trentino) were "of a kind to which the method of plebiscite might be applied". An offer to submit the ownership of such territories to plebiscite would, he believed, appeal to the Russian people and might restore the credit of the Provisional Government. He therefore considered that "the only question to be put to Austria is—'Will you submit the future of Galicia etc. to plebiscite on lines to be approved by the Allies?' " Hankey sent Young's letter on to Lloyd George

[1] *Liddell Hart*, pp. 417–22.

without comment; but the Prime Minister does not seem to have given
it any serious thought. It remains in the Lloyd George papers to this
day as an example of the seed of a constructive proposal which fell on
"stony ground"—despite the fact that Austria herself had very recently,
as we have seen, put out peace feelers.[1]

The new War Policy Committee met for the first time on 11th June
with Hankey as secretary, and thereafter met almost daily. The Cabinet
was meanwhile wasting a lot of breath and effort discussing the Mesopotamia Commission's report.

Diary 14th June 1917
War Cabinet 11.30. After terrific discussions decided to grant amnesty to
Irish prisoners in order to create a favourable atmosphere for Irish conscription. Drummond lunched with me very late. He is anxious to go ahead
with the Austrian peace offer. He tells me that a fresh line of communication
is open with Austria through Gregory,[2] a curious continental sort of man in
the Foreign Office, whom I saw a good deal of in Athens on my way home
from the Dardanelles, and who is a Roman Catholic like Drummond. It
appears that Gregory is a friend of the Empress's brother. Drummond says
the Emperor wants us to send an emissary to Austria, and suggests Gregory
as a *persona grata* there. Lord Derby called in afternoon and ramped up
and down in my office like a bull in fury about some remarks the P.M. had
made about cursing(?) the Army. I gave him "soothing syrup" and went off
to Milner to ask him to give him more. Mr. Balfour sent for me at the Foreign
Office in the afternoon. He was very sniffy about the Prime Minister's essays
in diplomacy, which he considers very dangerous, particularly his angling
with the Austrians. I rather stood up for Ll. G. and pointed out that he would
be very much blamed if it turned out eventually that he had missed a chance
of a separate peace with Austria, to which our soldiers and sailors both
attach great importance . . .

15th June 1917
War Policy Ctee. 11. a.m. . . . After a long discussion as to whether one of
them should go to Paris on the subject[3] they reached a vague sort of decision
that I was to put pressure on the French and Italian Govt. to do whatever
was necessary and to send Sir Guy Granet[4] to France. War Cabinet at 12.30
mainly to discuss Italy and Asia Minor. I lunched with Ll. George, who is

[1]See pp. 377 and 390. [2]See p. 204.
[3]Presumably restoring the military capacity of France.
[4]1867–1943. Business man and railway expert. Director-General of Movements and
Railways and member of Army Council 1917. Representative of Ministry of Food
in America 1918. Chairman L.M.S. Railway Co. 1924–7.

still very tired, and Philip Kerr of the "Garden Suburb". The latter very eloquent and convincing on the subject of Germany's inevitable decline and ultimate collapse from economic causes, if the allies only stick it . . .

16th June 1917
. . . Drummond called to say that he had seen Ll. G. who is going to write a letter to President Wilson and wants some material. I therefore had to drop everything else and draft a "heart to heart" for Ll. G. to send to Wilson, describing the difficult position of the French in regard to drafts, the danger of a French collapse and possibility of chaos and revolution before the U.S.A. can pull their weight, and hinting that Wilson should encourage recruiting in the U.S.A. for the French army. Rather a delicate business.

Hankey sent the draft of this "delicate" letter to Lloyd George that same day[1]; but the Prime Minister does not appear to have sent any such letter to President Wilson. Possibly he decided that the suggestions it contained would, as Hankey evidently feared, be construed as unwarrantable interference in American affairs.

The 17th June was a Sunday, and Hankey spent most of the day "in our delightful cool wood at home" bringing his diary up to date, and summarising the vast amount of business that had passed through his hands recently. He also recalled some events about which we have not yet learnt his views, and ruminated on the character of the principal Ministers with whom he was working.

Diary 17th June 1917
. . . In this diary I can only touch on a small proportion of these [subjects] . . .
For example I have not even mentioned the forcible deposition of King Constantine; the horrid breach of faith, which in my opinion it involves . . . the callous breach by the French of the promise at the recent London conference not to land troops in Athens; Lord Robert Cecil's furious indignation with the French; and Lloyd George's delight at the whole thing, and utter disregard of the allied breach of faith with the Greeks and the French breach of faith with us. With him "nothing succeeds like success" and honesty and good faith don't matter. Success is the only criterion. These are his faults, which are I think essentially Welsh faults, but of course he has very great compensating gifts—personal attraction, astuteness, eloquence, imagination, the gift of picking people's brains, and above all "flair". I have also said but little of the Mesopotamia Report; the strong objection of Balfour and Smuts for publication on the ground that it would damage our prestige at a moment when we were trying to induce the U.S.A. to take our advice, and more

especially in India; the vindictiveness of Lord Curzon, who wants to punish everyone. The tremendous discussions on the Irish amnesty have also only been barely mentioned. Still, this is the best I can do . . .

The continuation of the Flanders offensive now came once more before the War Policy Committee. On 19th Haig was called home to hear their views and express his own—which followed the expected pattern. He reinforced his arguments for continuing the offensive with two memoranda, in which he urged that the pressure should be kept up. If we failed to do so "waning hope in Germany would", he wrote, "be revived, and time would be gained to replenish food, ammunition, and other requirements. In fact many of the advantages already gained by us would be lost, and this would . . . have a depressing effect on our armies in the field".[1] Next day Hankey sent Robertson his notes of the meeting, and Robertson passed them on to Haig with the remark "Will you please read and correct as necessary and then return to me?" The file copy is in fact heavily amended in Hankey's hand—presumably as a result of the Generals' scrutiny. The matter is important only because a few months later Robertson complained that he had not been properly consulted by the War Policy Committee on these issues—an accusation which, as we shall see, aroused Hankey's wrath.

For the last ten days of June Hankey was too busy to write up his diary, but on 30th he made a long entry summarising the events which had kept him so "desperately busy".[2] Apart from coping with the usual War Cabinet meetings and with those of the War Policy Committee, Haig had come over for prolonged conferences on future strategy. This led to what Hankey called "a regular battle royal" between Lloyd George and the Generals. Haig and Robertson were determined to launch their "great attack on the Belgian front"; but the Prime Minister held that it had "no decent chance of success" and must incur losses out of all proportion to the likely gains. He therefore wanted "to mass heavy guns on the Italian frontier" and deal Austria such a blow that she would sue for peace. This plan held no appeal at all to the Generals, but after a week of strenuous argument in the War Policy Committee Lloyd George gave way because "he felt he could not press his amateur opinions and overrule them". Haig was therefore authorised

[1] Memo. of 12th June 1917. The second memo. is dated 17th June. Both in Cab. 27/7.
[2] Parts of the entry for 30th June 1917 are in *Supreme Command*, II, pp. 654–5 and 682–3.

to continue his preparations, though the final decision was not to be taken until a conference had been held with the French, to persuade them to make a simultaneous attack further south.

Jellicoe attended one of the meetings with Haig and, in Hankey's words, showed "unconcealed pessimism" by declaring that "after this year we should not be able to continue the war for lack of shipping." To Haig and others present "this was a bombshell"[1]; and the Admiral's pessimism also "caused great irritation" to General Pershing[2] and the Americans. Haig insisted that "the question could not remain where it was." Geddes, who was now Controller in the Admiralty, was therefore brought in, and discussions took place firstly between him, Milner and Lloyd George and then with Curzon and Smuts. Geddes "under seal of strict privacy spoke out very frankly", and revealed "a very unsatisfactory state of affairs in his department". Unfortunately his opinions reached the ears of Robertson and Maurice, with the result that Geddes came to Hankey "in a perfect fury" because what he had said was now bound to get known in the Admiralty where his position would be made "intolerable". "I have rarely known a man in such a state" commented Hankey; but he at once set to work to soothe the outraged Geddes and deter him from resigning. To try and get at the truth regarding the Admiralty he visited the Shipping Controller (Sir Joseph Maclay), and received "startling allegations about Admiralty maladministration, particularly in regard to the control of shipping". He reported the gist of his investigations to Lloyd George, who had meanwhile escaped to Walton Heath, and found that he had decided to get rid of Carson "by the simple expedient of 'booting' him up to the War Cabinet." He was inclined to appoint Geddes First Lord in Carson's place, but had not yet made up his mind. Hankey then "asked if he had ever thought of me in this connection", and Lloyd George jumped at the idea. But Hankey quickly had second thoughts about the danger of entering "a rather rocky ministry" and having to "incur the odium of sacking a lot of Admirals." Moreover he was quite inexperienced in handling Parliamentary matters. So he finally told Lloyd George that he would only take on the job "under pressure of a very high sense of national duty, and under persuasion from the whole

[1] John Terraine, *Passchendaele and Amiens*, I, R.U.S.I. Journal, Vol. CIV, No. 614 (May 1959).
[2] John J. Pershing (1860–1948). C-in-C, American Expeditionary Force 1917–19. Chief of Staff, U.S. Army 1921.

Cabinet". On their return to London Lloyd George discussed the proposal with Milner, who was apparently "unresponsive"; and so it was dropped. One wonders why Hankey ever put it forward. The probability is that he was profoundly worried about the state of affairs in the Admiralty, and the effects it was having on the war. He may, with some reason, have felt that he could put things right, and made the suggestion without having fully thought out the consequences. At any rate he evidently realised that he had been unwise, for he admitted that the whole incident left him "in a somewhat unsettled frame of mind".

Though there is, very understandably, no contemporary evidence that Haig and Jellicoe acted in collusion to further the strategy favoured by the former, Hankey did much later express the opinion that the Admiralty's statement about the outlook for the submarine campaign was "rigged", and that "Jellicoe's air of sincerity prevented the Cabinet demurring".[1] Be that as it may, the First Sea Lord's pessimism and his insistence on the need to capture the Flanders U-boat bases did strengthen the case for persisting with the Ypres offensive; and its disastrous prolongation into the autumn of 1917 must therefore be attributed, at any rate in part, to the Admiralty's mishandling of the submarine menace.[2]

[1] Note of "Talk with Sir Maurice Hankey at U.S. Club" 8th Nov. 1932. Liddell Hart papers.
[2] See S. W. Roskill, *The U-Boat Campaign and Third Ypres*, R.U.S.I. Journal, Vol. CIV, No. 616 (Nov. 1959).

Chapter 14

Britain the Cornerstone. July-September 1917

THE summer solstice of 1917 found the War Cabinet absorbed chiefly with the unrest in Ireland, the aftermath to the Mesopotamia Commission's report, the need to improve the Admiralty's administration, the effects of the increasingly probable collapse of Russia, and the question whether a major British offensive should be launched in Flanders—for which, as we saw earlier, Haig had been given authority to prepare. Hankey enjoyed a few quiet days at home at the beginning of July, but was thereafter deeply involved in all these issues.

Diary 3rd July 1917
As I anticipated Ll. G. sent for me immediately on his return to tell me of his conversations with Adl. Beatty. He also told me of his talk with Milner about the question of First Lord. Milner had said exactly what I told Ll. George he would say, namely that I was practically irreplaceable at the War Cabinet; that I should no doubt be quite an effective First Lord; but that the public would not understand the appointment. Ll. G. had evidently cooled on the idea and was for Geddes. But he was hot for getting rid of Jellicoe. . . .
4th July
War Policy Ctee. all the morning and a terrific War Cabinet all the afternoon from 3.15 to 7.30, without a break and without even a cup of tea. The first subject was Ireland. Lord Midleton,[1] the Lord Lieutenant, General Mahon,[2] and the head of the Irish Constabulary and Dublin Police gave evidence regarding the disturbed state of Ireland and the disaffection among Sinn Feiners, though the general trend of the evidence, though serious, did not cause great anxiety. This part of the meeting was remarkable for a terrific outburst by Duke, the Irish Secretary,[3] who tried to make out that the whole

[1]St. John Brodrick, 9th Viscount Midleton. 1st Earl 1920 (1856–1942). Politician (Cons.). Secretary of State for War 1900–3 and for India 1903–5. Served on Irish Convention 1917–18.
[2]General Sir Bryan T. Mahon (1862–1930). Commanded Salonika army 1915–16; C-in-C, Ireland 1916–18. Senator, Irish Free State 1922.
[3]See p. 270.

affair, starting from General Mahon's letter, was a "ramp" against him. He spoke like a man overworked and overwrought and on the verge of a breakdown. More notable however was the discussion on the question of disciplinary action against the officers impugned by the Mesopotamia Commission, which filled me with deep disgust. The attitude of the War Cabinet as a whole was bad enough, but that of certain individuals was contemptible. At an early stage the Cabinet had appointed a Committee under Lord Curzon which had only recommended serious disciplinary action against one officer —Col. Hathaway.[1] The others were merely to be shelved. Now however, owing to the irresponsible clamour of our gutter press and of a few of the lower class and more disreputable members of the present contemptible House of Commons, the Cabinet are out for blood and to find some miserable scapegoat! They want to courtmartial most of the officers named in the Report, and though they did not go so far as to insist on Lord Hardinge's[2] retirement, they wanted to give him a hint that they would find his resignation convenient.[3] Bonar Law reached the lowest depths by saying that in his opinion anyone who was publicly attacked and unpopular, whether a Minister or a public servant, ought in the public interest to retire in war time. Whereat Balfour flippantly commented "Oh! Vive Lord Northcliffe!" My disgust was beyond expression—to think that Ministers should go so far as to refuse to defend unoffending public servants! Both Balfour and Chamberlain threatened resignation if Hardinge was not defended, and eventually it was decided to defend him, but a strong desire was evinced that someone should give him a hint to retire. Personally I do not intend to give him the hint, though I daresay it is expected of me. I feel that if scapegoats are to be sought for no-one is safe now-a-days. Lloyd George himself might become a scapegoat for adopting General Nivelle's rotten plan and putting Haig under Nivelle against all his military advisers, thereby sacrificing tens of

[1]Though Hankey spelt the name "Hatherway" he must have been referring to Surgeon-General H. G. Hathaway, who had become Principal Medical Officer in Mesopotamia in April 1915. He was severely criticised in the Commission's report for the "lamentable breakdown of the medical services". Cd. 8610 (1917), pp. 64–81 and 93.

[2]1858–1944. 1st Baron Hardinge of Penshurst 1910. Diplomat. Permanent Under-Secretary of State for Foreign Affairs 1906–10 and 1916–20. Ambassador at Petrograd 1904–6; Viceroy of India 1910–16; Ambassador at Paris 1920–23.

[3]The majority report of the Mesopotamia Commission (Cd. 8610) was critical of Hardinge's administration, e.g. "The Government, rather than the governed, were the laggards" in providing financial support for the expedition (Part XI, para. 41). Commander J. Wedgwood's Minority Report contained much more astringent criticisms, e.g. "I find that, throughout the tenure of office of Lord Hardinge, the Government of India showed little desire to help and some desire to obstruct the successful prosecution of the war." (P. 131, para. 47.)

thousands of men in a wholly futile operation at Arras. Carson and Jellicoe would certainly be scapegoats for the loss of merchant ships owing to their neglect of the advice of the Shipping Controller's Ctee. Ll. George and the War Cabinet should be scapegoats for permitting, not to say encouraging the recent offensive in the Balkans, where 6,000 British troops were sacrificed in an operation which never had the smallest chance of success. Many examples could be given, and I have no doubt that I could be made a scapegoat for a good deal myself (though I don't exactly know what) if we are to go scapegoat hunting. Yet Parliament itself should be the first scapegoat. No-one outside knows the astounding extent to which it interferes with the Higher Command by its useless debates, and innumerable frivolous or deliberately mischievous questions. Day after day the War Cabinet has to turn from its proper business to some outrageous yet tricky and difficult question or debate on the adjournment etc.—to say nothing of its preposterous Dardanelles and Mesopotamia Commissions, which do no good, but infinite harm by wasting the time of the executive, drawing energy off the war and exposing the blackest spots in the blackest chapters of the war, unrelieved by the many bright and creditable incidents, thereby weakening confidence at home, and among our allies, encouraging the enemy, and giving him priceless material for propaganda. Perhaps the greatest advantage the enemy has over us in fighting the war is the absence of parliamentary control—though I admit that in a wider sense democratic Govt. is far the better. The trouble is that the present parliament is ignorant, irresponsible and tiresome. It is a drag instead of a ballast, as it should be. I yield to no-one in my admiration of the democratic system, nor in my contempt for the present parliament, a contempt which is shared by almost every leading man I know . . .

Hankey's anger over the Mesopotamia Commission's report, and especially the criticisms it contained of Lord Hardinge, who had recently returned from the Viceroy's palace in Delhi to take over as Permanent Under-Secretary in the Foreign Office, was so great that he evidently sent him a letter of sympathy.

Hardinge to Hankey. 24 Gloucester Place, 14th July 1917. Holograph
PRIVATE
My dear Hankey,
   Many thanks for your very kind letter of sympathy. I cannot help feeling thoroughly disgusted at the attacks made upon me and other officers and officials almost as though we were criminals, and at the fact that had it not been for Mr. Balfour's chivalrous courage I should have been thrown to the wolves. It is perfectly monstrous that [the] Govt. do not recognise their duty

to protect their servants from unfair attack, but in these days honourable service and loyalty to duty seem to be at a discount.

If there is another Court of Inquiry of a judicial character I shall welcome it, as I long to get my knife into the Commission's Report which I regard as a travesty of fact and of justice.

Thank you again so much for your kind letter.

Yrs sincerely.

Diary 6th July 1917

War Policy Ctee. followed by War Cabinet in morning. Mr. Barnes,[1] the Labour Minister acting for Henderson, lunched with me. It has been decided that Sir Eric Geddes is to be First Lord. Ll. George has offered it to him and he told me on the telephone he had accepted. Ll. G.'s difficulty is to "boot up" Sir Edward Carson to the War Cabinet without his realising that he is really "*dégommé*."[2]

The change at the Admiralty was to a great extent the result of a campaign which Haig had launched towards the end of June with the object of getting rid of Jellicoe as well as Carson. His motives are obscure, but genuine dissatisfaction with the pessimism of the Admiral was probably among them. It was Milner who solved Lloyd George's dilemma by suggesting the simple expedient of kicking Carson upstairs into the War Cabinet. Jellicoe, though his position was obviously weakened by Carson's removal, remained on—for a time.

On the same day that the Cabinet approved the change of First Lord Hankey had once again to cope with an attack on the Admiralty from the Ministry of Shipping. He received from Sir Norman Hill[3] a letter stating that "by forcing us to concentrate [merchant ships] in areas which are admittedly inadequately protected, the lives of our men, our ships and the essential supplies of the country have been, *and are being* thrown away"—a charge which, Hill declared, he was "ready to maintain at any time and anywhere".[4] This was in effect an attack on the Admiralty's system of bringing in merchantmen through "patrolled lanes", which they had introduced about a year earlier. The submarines

[1]George N. Barnes (1859–1940). Politician (Lab.). Minister of Pensions 1916–18. Member of War Cabinet 1917. Minister without Portfolio and Minister Plenipotentiary at Paris Peace Conference 1919.

[2]The last sentence of this day's entry is omitted from *Supreme Command*, II, p. 655.

[3]Solicitor and notary (1863–1944). Secretary and Treasurer Liverpool Steamship Owners' Association 1893–1923. Chairman, Board of Trade Advisory Committee on Merchant Shipping 1907–37 and of Ports and Transit Executive Committee 1915–19. Vice-President, Chamber of Shipping 1924.

[4]Letter of 6th July 1917 from Ministry of Shipping. GT. 1308. Cab. 24/19.

merely concentrated in the easily discovered lanes, which thus became death traps. Though Hill's protest had in fact been overtaken by the introduction of convoy, the full effects of that change of strategy had not yet become apparent, and Hankey therefore minuted that "the charge is so grave that I cannot take the responsibility of not sending it [Hill's letter] at once to the War Cabinet".[1]

Next day Hankey witnessed the first big daylight air raid on London, which he described as "rather alarming". His anxiety was increased by the fact that he had parted from Adeline only a few minutes before it took place; but she wisely took shelter in the Westminster Hospital. The Cabinet met in the afternoon to discuss this new peril, after which Hankey drove round London with Lloyd George, Milner, Smuts and Barnes to see the damage.[2] On Lloyd George, who lacked physical courage, and thereafter always tried to keep out of London when an air raid was likely, the effects were profound[3]; for the bombing of London, and the resultant outcry in the Press, influenced his whole attitude towards aviation policy—of which more shortly. Parliament met in Secret Session on 9th to discuss this new development in warfare, and Hankey listened to the debate—without deriving any comfort from it.

At this juncture Hankey found himself once again at cross purposes with the Admiralty. About ten days earlier he had written to Graham Greene, the Permanent Secretary, asking tactfully what progress had been made in developing the Statistical Department, as recommended in his memorandum of 30th April, to provide the Cabinet with reliable information on the merchant shipping situation—about which they had been so seriously misled in earlier months.[4] On 7th July Hankey received two letters from Greene. The first was a "hedging" answer to the straightforward question of when the first products of the new department would be available. This was pretty unsatisfactory, but Greene's second letter really got Hankey's blood up; for he wrote that "the suggestion that a representative of the Shipping Controller should be associated with the Trade Division in connexion with the movement of merchant ships has not been found very practicable"; and, worse still, that "As regards the alteration and deviation of routes through the submarine danger zones, this is entirely a naval matter, and it is not

[1]*ibid*. [2]Diary 7th July 1917.
[3]See A. J. P. Taylor, *English History 1914–1945* (O.U.P., 1965), p. 72.
[4]See p. 357.

seen in what manner the Shipping Controller could give useful advice".[1]
With Sir Norman Hill's vigorous protest on that very score fresh in his
mind Hankey at once went into action.

Hankey to Lloyd George. 9th July 1917[2]
THE PRIME MINISTER

I feel that I must bring the accompanying letters particularly to your
notice.

They are in connection with the decisions arrived at after your visit to the
Admiralty on 30th April last and in reply to letters from me asking what
progress had been made in carrying out your recommendations and the War
Cabinet decisions.

As regards the development of the Statistical Department I pointed out to
Sir Graham Greene that no reports had yet reached the War Cabinet showing
the work of this Department, and you will see from his reply that although
over two months have elapsed the Department is not yet completely
organised.

The other letter refers to the appointment of an Official from the Ministry
of Shipping to act as liaison officer between that Department and the Trade
Division of the Admiralty.

In this connection you will see that no action at all has been taken on the
War Cabinet decision mainly on the grounds that as the information is of a
highly confidential nature it is not thought desirable that this information
should always be communicated to the representative of the Ministry of
Shipping.

Sir Graham Greene seems to have overlooked the fact that it is of vital
interest to the Shipping Controller to know when a ship is diverted to a
route which changes her pre-arranged destination for discharge, quite apart
from the fact that the Admiralty have failed to carry out the orders of the War
Cabinet.

My personal view is that the disregard of your recommendations is a
positive impertinence and shows great stupidity.

In view of the foregoing onslaught one can feel no surprise that early
in August Graham Greene was replaced by Sir Oswyn Murray[3] who in
Lord Chatfield's words, thus became "for over twenty years [actually
nineteen years] the wise and trusted counsellor to many successive

---

[1]Graham Greene to Hankey, two letters of 7th July 1917. Lloyd George papers
F/23/1/17.
[2]*ibid.* The last paragraph is holograph.
[3]1873–1936. Permanent Secretary of the Admiralty 1917–36.

Boards of Admiralty".[1] This was the first of the many changes made
by Geddes, who had been assured by Lloyd George of his support for
such measures when he took over as First Lord.

Diary 11th July 1917[2]

Once more the whole morning was taken up by the War Cabinet with the
attitude to be adopted in regard to disciplinary action in connection with the
Mesopotamia Report. If once you decide on head hunting the problem is
really perplexing. The soldiers can very easily be dealt with by Courts Martial
—but, as the Mesopotamia and Dardanelles Commissions Act provided for
complete indemnity to witnesses, and much of the evidence was given by the
persons impugned, the Report and its evidence cannot be used as evidence in
a court of law. Consequently the whole of the evidence must be taken afresh,
if disciplinary action is to be taken, and as the statute of limitations expires
in Nov. and the summary of evidence, which by law must precede a Court
Martial, will itself take several months to prepare, as the witnesses are
scattered all over the world, the whole thing will perhaps be null and void
before the Court could assemble. Nor is this the only difficulty, for the scalp
hunters demand that civilians shall also be indicted. But a civilian cannot be
tried by Court Martial; and in fact the lawyers advise that no charge can be
laid against any civilian. If the Govt. had any "guts" they would flatly
decline to take proceedings, and merely put the officers concerned on the
retired list, where necessary, and take no action against Lord Hardinge, who
they all agree deserves no great blame. But the wretched cowards are in such
a blue funk of the House of Commons. Balfour in the Cabinet made a superb,
noble and complete defence of Hardinge. Nevertheless the Govt. decided
after a very long discussion, to endeavour to proceed by Court of Enquiry
under the "Barret Act", whereby a military Court, with judges on it, but
appointed by the Army Council, would try civilians.[3] Obviously it was a
miserable expedient, that would not hold water, but having promised a
statement in the afternoon, they rushed into any decision, however bad,
rather than take a courageous course. To my disgust I was asked to prepare
a statement for Bonar Law and Curzon to make in both Houses. I turned on
Swinton and Row to prepare one draft and I set to work on another. It was
a fearful rush, as I only had ¾ hour to set out a most complicated question.
My draft was preferred, as I expected it would be (though scrawled out on
foolscap paper). Bonar Law made it in the House of Commons, and I had to
get it from him directly it was read and take it to Lord Curzon in the House

[1]Lady Murray, *The Making of a Civil Servant* (Methuen, 1940), p. 204.
[2]Parts of this day's entry are printed in *Supreme Command*, II, pp. 527–8.
[3]This must refer to the Army (Courts of Inquiry) Act, 1916 (6 & 7 Geo. 5, c.33)
which amended the Army Act on the lines stated by Hankey.

of Lords. On entering the Lobby of the Upper House I met several of my acquaintances who said "Oh you can't see Lord Curzon, he has to make an important statement in a few minutes" to which I replied, pointing to a bundle of untidy papers in my hand "But, here is the statement!", which evoked much laughter. . . . Of course both houses shouted at the proposed new court, and the Cabinet had to meet again from 6.30 to past 8.30.[1] Balfour again made an impassioned appeal for Lord Hardinge, and Chamberlain wanted to resign, but was persuaded to postpone his decision. I walked afterwards with Balfour to Dean's Yard where he was dining. He was in a great state of righteous indignation at the whole proceeding, threatening to resign . . .

To Hankey's disgust the debate on the Mesopotamia Commission's report dragged on for another two days, thereby dislocating his carefully planned programme of business for the War Cabinet. The chief result was the resignation of Austen Chamberlain from the government, and one may well sympathise with the outburst on the subject which Hankey confided to his diary.

Diary 13th July 1917[2]
Once more the fatal Mesopotamia report dogs the work of the War Cabinet. To-day being Friday the House met at noon and, as the debate was continuing, the War Cabinet had to break up early—though yesterday and to-day we made a little progress with the question of the control of merchant shipping. Not much, though, for everyone's mind was on the Mesopotamia debate. Among the questions which are held up are:—the decision as to the next offensive; the control of merchant ships (the Shipping Controller and the ship owners maintaining that the Admiralty's methods are a mere death trap), future policy in the Balkans, Egypt and Mesopotamia; policy in Ireland, where there is dangerous unrest; price of bread and meat; the appointment of Sir Eric Geddes as First Lord; Indian reforms—which for a month or more the Indian Govt. have maintained is critically in need of a decision; policy towards Norway; the working out of the merchant shipping programme; the gun programme for 1918. These questions, all of first rate importance and great and immediate urgency have been held up owing to this miserable parliamentary and press outcry for hunting down a few wretched people, who have been impugned by a non-judicial and none too efficient Commission of rather second-rate people in connection with the

[1]See Parl. Deb., Commons, Vol. XCV, Cols. 1917–22 and Lords, Vol. XXV, Cols. 878–887 for Bonar Law's and Curzon's statements on the proposed Court of Inquiry on 11th July 1917.
[2]Parts of this day's entry are printed in *Supreme Command*, II, pp. 528–9.

suffering and loss of a relative handful of men in a secondary theatre two years ago. Deplorable though their sufferings may have been, to jeopardise the very future of the war, to take up all the time of the War Cabinet—the supreme command indeed—to unsettle the whole of the people, to throw a searchlight on to these obscure events, to belittle ourselves in the eyes of the world, our enemies, and our allies at the very moment when the war seems to be taking a turn in our favour—surely all this reveals an incredible loss of perspective on the part of Parliament and Press.

15th July (Sunday)
While at church in the morning I received a note that Ll. George urgently wanted Adeline and me to lunch at Walton Heath—so I walked out, like the proverbial doctor trying to build up a practice. We lunched at Walton Heath, and Ll. George and I had a very long and full discussion about the offensive. He is still hankering after a great attack on Austria on the Italian front. I agree with him in principle, but am convinced that he must first allow Haig to have his attack. I urged him to get Cadorna to make preparations to receive a great accession of heavy guns, and to pile up ammunition and make all plans. If Haig is successful then the combined attack on Austria will not come off and Cadorna will have to do the best he can without our assistance. But if Haig fails to get on, we can switch all the artillery we can spare, after providing for the defensive, to Italy. The attack will then be made in the autumn when fighting is still possible on the Carso but not in Flanders, and when the approach of winter in the mountains renders an attack from the dangerous Trentino salient impossible. Ll. G. told me he proposed to make Montagu S. of S. for India. He is very delighted at Bethmann-Hollweg's disappearance, which he ascribes to his Glasgow speech.[1]

Next day the decision was taken at a dinner at 10 Downing Street, at which Hankey was present, "to allow Haig to begin his offensive, but not to allow it to degenerate into a drawn out battle of the Somme type".[2] The qualifying clause was, of course, little more than an expression of hope, since all experience had shown that, once a major offensive had been launched, nothing except the exhaustion of the troops would force the Generals to halt it. The War Cabinet, in endorsing the foregoing recommendation of the War Policy Committee, added a further rider—to the effect that in case the offensive in the west

---

[1] Theobald Bethmann-Hollweg (1856–1921). German politician. Minister of Interior of Prussia 1905 and of German Empire 1907. Chancellor 1909–17. In 1916 opposed resumption of unrestricted submarine warfare and favoured a compromise peace. Dismissed 12th July 1917.
[2] Diary 16th July. *Supreme Command*, II, p. 683.

was called off, preparations should be made "for a great offensive against Austria" supported by British and French artillery. But that instruction to Haig was also somewhat unrealistic, since it was not very likely that he could or would effect "a gradual accumulation of reserves of ammunition . . . and [carry out] all other measures that can be taken in advance to facilitate the execution of the [Italian offensive] plan" at the time when he was preparing for his great attack in Flanders.[1]

Two days after the Cabinet had confirmed the War Policy Committee's recommendations Hankey was asked to produce a full report on the war situation. By dropping all other work he managed to complete that task by the evening of 19th.[2] Once again his report earned him warm praise from Ministers, and even from Robertson, who could not understand how such a prodigious task could have been completed in little over 24 hours. Hankey confided to his diary that he had in fact "been working at it in odds and ends of time for weeks"—ever since the institution of the War Policy Committee.[3] Then he had to turn his full attention to preparing for another Inter-Allied Conference in Paris.

Diary 22nd July 1917 [Sunday]
Quiet day at home in garden until the evening when Winston Churchill, who has just become Minister of Munitions, rang up from his house near Lingfield and asked Adeline and self to come over to tea, him sending a car for us.[4] We went right enough and I had an interesting walk and talk with him, rambling round his wild and beautiful property. Lloyd George had given him my War Policy report, and he was already well up in [the] whole situation and knew exactly what our military plans were, which I thought quite wrong. He had breakfasted with Ll. George that morning. On the whole he was in a chastened mood. He admitted to me that he had been "a bit above himself" at the Admiralty, and surprised me by saying that he had had no idea of the depth of public opinion against his return to public life, until his appointment was made. He was hot for an expedition to Alexandretta, but I put all the objections and difficulties to him.

[1] These conclusions of the War Cabinet were reproduced by Hankey in his recapitulation of the events leading up to the third battle of Ypres. GT.1925 dated 1st Sept. 1917. Cab. 24/25, p. 199.
[2] Diary 18th and 19th July. *Supreme Command*, II, p. 683.
[3] Diary 20th July 1917.
[4] The Churchills were at this time living at Lullenden near East Grinstead. They bought Chartwell in September 1922, but did not move in until about the middle of 1924.

Hankey crossed the Channel once again on 23rd, in company with Lloyd George, Balfour and Smuts, and on reaching Paris the Prime Minister at once set about gaining the support of his old ally Albert Thomas for his Italian offensive. "He did it with great skill", Hankey recorded, "first arousing all Thomas's contempt of the French generals and disbelief in their ability to gain a victory, and ending by springing his alternative plan".[1] That evening Lloyd George told Hankey to draft some resolutions which he could produce at the conference, which was to begin next day at the Quai d'Orsay. Hankey was excluded from the Ministers' discussions, and spent a thoroughly boring day in the ante-room "with its red chairs, gilt mirrors and bawdey [sic] tapestries".[2] Next day G. M. Young turned up with hot but depressing news from Russia.

Diary 25th July 1917
I breakfasted with Lloyd George and General Pershing, the American C-in-C., and Major Bacon,[3] who used to be U.S.A. Ambassador in Paris, and Major Waldorf Astor M.P.,[4] who is acting as Ll. G.'s secretary during the illness of J.T. Davies. Before breakfast Young turned up from Petrograd, where he had been with Henderson. The gist of his news was that Henderson's head had been turned a bit by the fact of hearing 180 millions of Russians chanting in chorus *"Mir bez anneksii i kontributsii"*[5] (peace without annexations or indemnities); that he had it in his mind to "rat" and head a great British labour-socialist peace movement; but that he was drawn in the opposite direction by the sweets and emoluments of office. Young appeared to be working on him to lead the socialists without leaving office, and without necessarily abandoning our war aims. I communicated all this to the P.M. The big conference was at 10 a.m. It was the most appalling waste of time that I have ever known. The whole morning was spent in discussing and wrangling over a ridiculous question of moving one division from Salonika

[1]Diary 23rd July 1917. [2]*ibid.* 24th July 1917.
[3]Robert Bacon (1860–1919), American banker and diplomat. Secretary of State 1909. Ambassador to France 1909–12. Served on staff of General Pershing with A.E.F. 1917.
[4]2nd Viscount Astor 1919 (1879–1952). Inspector of Quartermaster-General Services 1914–17. Parliamentary Secretary to Prime Minister and to Minister of Food 1918, and to Minister of Health 1919–21. Owner of Cliveden near Maidenhead, the meeting place of the so-called "appeasers" of the 1930s.
[5]Hankey (or G. M. Young) got this slogan, which was a saying of Lenin himself, wrong, the former quoting it in his diary as *"bir mez annexi y indemnitzi"*. But the meaning is clear, as in Hankey's translation.

to Egypt, all the representatives of the assembled nations . . . making long and eloquent speeches on the subject. I am bound to say that our people (Mr. Lloyd George and Mr. Balfour) stood out head and shoulders above all the rest for the clearness of their speech no less than in the loftiness and breadth of their views . . . After the afternoon conference I had a long talk with Ll. G. and Captain Aubrey Herbert M.P.,[1] who is on his way home from Switzerland, where Turkish agents have made some sort of a peace overture, on behalf, or purporting to be on behalf of Talaat,[2] the Grand Vizier . . . On my warning the P.M. that this might be a dodge to separate the allies, he told me that at one of the conversations he had told Ribot and Sonnino that some such approaches had been made, and had secured their assent to sending someone to Switzerland to find out what they were up to. Mr. Balfour confirmed this, but both he and the P.M. said it had been discussed, as it were, in an aside, and that no importance had been attached to it. In the evening the P.M. contracted a slight sore throat, which he made the excuse to get out of Ribot's dinner, and he, Astor, Young, and self dined quietly on his balcony, and Young gave us an account of his Russian experiences. I dosed the P.M. with aspirin and he was all right next morning.

26th July 1917
[Written in the train 27th July]
More "conversations" and more waiting in the red room, but about half way through the morning I was called in to take notes. All very futile and mainly concerned with the movement of the wretched one Divn. from Salonika to Egypt. This was continued after lunch, when the P.M. put the whole discussion on wider lines by introducing the report of the military conference on the effect of Russia's withdrawal, and brought in the question of an attack in Italy.[3] He was not well supported . . . After this the "Duma" assembled with representatives of all the allies (Montenegro, Portugal, Serbia etc.) the speeches being formal and no business done. I asked the Prince de

[1]See p. 288.
[2]Talaat Pasha (1872–1921). Turkish politician. Member of "Young Turk" party. Minister of Interior 1913 under Enver Pasha. Grand Vizier 1917–18. Assassinated by an Armenian in Germany 1921.
[3]As an example of the accuracy of Hankey's diary the official record of this day's discussion may be quoted. "In the course of a conversation between the representatives of the British, French and Italian Governments at the Paris Conference on July 25th–26th the Prime Minister, during a discussion on the possibility of Russia being forced out of the war, raised the question of an attempt being made to anticipate this contingency by forcing Austria out. Diplomacy, however, he pointed out, could not achieve this unless preceded by a military success, and on these grounds he urged the study of a combined Allied attack on the Italian front". Cab. 28, I.C. 24(a) and Cab. 24/25 GT. 1925, p. 200.

Béarn, the Secretary of the conference, in jest if Siam was to be present. He looked horrified and replied "*Non. Mon Dieu, nous les avons oubliés*", and rushed off to the telephone! Afterwards I went on a motor drive in the Bois with Ll. G., who was very depressed with the futility of it all, and with his failure to get his plans adopted, and was talking wildly of resigning and "telling the country the truth". The news from Russia, where several hundred guns have been lost has depressed him a good deal . . . I find more and more a tendency among the foreigners at these conferences to try and get at Ll. G. through me.

Hankey was struck by Lloyd George's evident popularity in Paris. "Everywhere", he recorded, "he was cheered and greeted with 'Vive Lloyd George! God bless you' and with smiles and salutes as he walked about the streets." The two of them motored back to Boulogne together "very pleasant, no war talk as we were both rather tired" was Hankey's description of the ride. The Prime Minister had, understandably, refused Haig's invitation to him to witness the start of an offensive in which the former felt no confidence,[1] and on 28th they were back in London. The next trouble to beset the War Cabinet was an internal crisis.

Diary 30th July 1917[2]
War Cabinets at 11.30 and 5.30. The great subject at the moment is Henderson's visit to Paris with Ramsay MacDonald. A member of the War Cabinet and a pacifist! Great scandal! There would be more of a scandal if it was realised how far Henderson's head was turned by his Russian trip . . .

31st July
War Cabinet 11.30. Lunched with Lloyd George, Carson and Milner. All rather upset by the bad Russian news . . . I tried to test whether there was any inclination towards peace, by inquiring whether in the last resort they would be willing to hand back the German colonies in exchange for a German evacuation of Belgium. Not much response. In fact the talk was still of a war *à outrance*, and of getting President Wilson to come over and swear to support us. The news from U.S.A. however is all rather in the direction of Wilson's idea of "peace without victories". Afterwards Winston Churchill came in and talked in the same vein. Personally I don't feel sure we couldn't get a fairly satisfactory peace *now*.

The great artillery bombardment on the Flanders front had opened on 22nd July, when Hankey's quiet day at home was interrupted by

[1] Diary 27th July 1917.
[2] The part of this day's entry printed in *Supreme Command*, II, p. 691 is misdated 3rd July.

Churchill's summons to Lullenden. On the last day of the month, when his thoughts had turned to the possibility of a compromise peace, the infantry of General Gough's Fifth Army, strengthened by one Corps of Plumer's Second Army and a French Corps, advanced on a fifteen-mile front—in torrential rain which continued for days without a break. By destroying the intricate drainage system the bombardment turned the whole area into a swamp—as indeed Tank Corps H.Q.s had warned G.H.Q. would be the case. Thus was a bad plan in the strategic sense turned into a tactical impossibility. The first phase ended after some progress had been made on the left (or northern) flank, but in the more vital central sector on the Menin road there was complete failure. The one redeeming feature was that time had been gained to allow the French army to recover its morale under Pétain's careful nursing.

On 1st August Hankey noted in his diary that the War Cabinet held its 200th meeting—excluding Imperial War Cabinets and "specially secret" meetings. This was an average of nearly one meeting a day throughout the eight months of the War Cabinet's existence. At that time, while the unfortunate soldiers were floundering and dying in the Flanders mud, the War Cabinet's time was chiefly taken up by what Hankey described as the "*affaire* Henderson". After Arthur Henderson returned from his mission to Russia he went to Paris with Ramsay MacDonald, then one of the leading British pacifists, in order to discuss the invitation of Russian socialists to meet them and representatives of other socialist parties, including those from enemy countries, in Stockholm. Though the Labour Party Conference rejected representation at Stockholm by a large majority Henderson did not use his influence against the resolution in accordance with the War Cabinet's wish.[1] The result was that he was forced to resign from the government, his place being taken by George Barnes.[2] Though Hankey regretted Henderson's departure the mood of the country as a whole was at the time undoubtedly opposed to a compromise peace.

An interesting point about what G. M. Young called "the Henderson embroglio [sic]" is that early in August Young sent Hankey a long letter on the subject. He regarded the widespread belief that Henderson was "a man of sterling honesty" as "one of the most inexplicable of

[1]Meeting of 1st Aug. 1917. Cab. 23/13 (A. Series).
[2]The letter from Lloyd George forcing Henderson's resignation was approved at the afternoon meeting of the War Cabinet on 10th August but was not sent until next day, by which time Henderson had resigned. Diary 10th and 11th Aug. 1917.

popular delusions", and considered that such delusions could and should be destroyed. He went on to build up a damning indictment of Henderson's equivocal actions and statements ever since his return from Russia; and as he and Young had signed a joint report on their mission to that country, and "the views there expressed" were "totally at variance with his [Henderson's] subsequent actions" publication of the report and of certain supporting documents would shatter the popular myth about the Labour Minister.[1] Hankey evidently sent Young's letter straight on to the Prime Minister; but Lloyd George found it more judicious to speak in conciliatory and regretful terms when the matter was debated in Parliament, probably because he wished to avoid antagonising other members of Henderson's party at a time when there was much unrest in the labour movement and in the factories.[2] However in his memoirs Lloyd George wrote a good deal more strongly about the affair, and as his argument closely follows the lines proposed by Young in 1917 it seems that his paper must have been resurrected and used when the time came for Lloyd George to write his autobiography.[3]

Diary 3rd August 1917
. . . War Cabinet at 3.30. Mr. Balfour raised question of a separate peace with Bulgaria, overtures of some sort having been made by that country through a spy. It was decided to reply in the sense that we should be prepared to listen to any reasonable proposals. This is the only record of this transaction . . .

That evening Hankey went off to join Adeline and the children for "three very happy days at Eastbourne", which he spent bathing, playing on the sands and going for long walks with Robin, now twelve years old and apparently able to emulate his father's tremendous energy. On 7th he returned to London for an Inter-Allied Conference. As so often before he then found his knowledge of French and Italian invaluable; but the task of interpreting from two foreign languages simultaneously, combined with making a record of the very secret discussions single-handed, left him "frightfully tired". Lloyd George

[1]Young to Hankey. Undated, but obviously written early in August 1917. Holograph. Lloyd George papers F/83/1/20.
[2]Parl. Deb., Commons, Vol. XCVII, Cols. 109–934. The debate was on a motion for the adjournment.
[3]*Lloyd George*, IV, pp. 1898–1924.

once more tried to gain support for "his theories for action on the Italian front", but failed. "I agree with him", wrote Hankey, "that rain has spoiled Haig's Flanders plan and that we ought to do something else".[1] The tragedy was that the War Cabinet did not insist thus early on stopping the Flanders offensive—as they had in fact decided to do in the event of it getting bogged down.[2] Nor was there any agreement among the Allied governments regarding an alternative strategy.

Diary 14th August 1917
War Cabinet 11.30. At 1 p.m. both the Asst. Sects. were cleared out and the P.M. informed the War Cabinet that he had received private information of certain very secret peace negotiations in Switzerland between a French agent under M. Painlevé's direction, and Austria, which promised favourably for a real break between Austria and Germany. There was also a preliminary discussion on the Pope's peace proposals, which, it was agreed, must have been connived at by Austria.[3] No minutes were kept, and this is the only record . . .

That same day Hankey sent Curzon a hastener about the report of the War Policy Committee, which the Lord President was evidently holding up. Curzon replied "I returned it unaltered to-day and thought it a most admirable document which no one but you could have compiled".[4]

At this time Hankey circulated a memorandum drawing attention to the need to establish clear rules regarding the return of Cabinet documents by resigning Ministers—notably Austen Chamberlain and Arthur Henderson. His proposal was that they should be passed to the successor of the Minister in question, as had been done in the case of C.I.D. papers.[5] However he evidently changed his mind a short time later, since instructions were given that all such papers were to be

---

[1] Diary 8th Aug. 1917.
[2] Lloyd George later reproached himself on this score. "Could I have stopped Passchendaele?" he asked of Liddell Hart. "He [Lloyd George] thought of giving the order—and Haig would have obeyed it; he would not have resigned. But they would have said I had spoilt the chance of a decisive success, and of saving us from danger from the submarines. Haig was sure he could reach Roulers, and so free Ostend". Note of "Talk with Lloyd George at Criccieth 24th Sept. 1932". Liddell Hart papers.
[3] See p. 262 regarding the Peace Message of 1st Aug. 1917 from Pope Benedict XV.
[4] Hankey to Curzon 14th Aug. 1917, endorsed by latter.
[5] GT. 1710 of 14th Aug. 1917. Cab. 24/13.

recovered by the Cabinet Secretariat. None the less this matter proved a constant thorn in Hankey's flesh almost to the end of his career; and some Ministers, notably Lloyd George and Churchill, managed to hold on to most of their Cabinet papers.

Diary 15th August 1917[1]

War Cabinet 11.30 at War Office, where we adjourned to the balcony to watch a procession of U.S.A. troops marching through London . . . In the afternoon the War Cabinet met again for a couple of hours. After this I had a short talk with the Prime Minister and Lord Robert Cecil. I impressed strongly on the former that he ought to investigate the question of the Flanders offensive, which seems to be rather hung up, with a view to the possible adoption of the alternative Italian plan before General Cadorna had started. I found him unresponsive, though he sent for Robertson in order to instruct him to report on Haig's next objective. In this connection it must be noted that Robertson is going to France to-morrow. The P.M. is obviously puzzled, as his predecessor was, as to how far the Government is justified in interfering with a military operation. In the evening I dined with Lady Cunard; Mr. Balfour, Montagu and Young were present and a lot of rather mischievous gossiping women, mostly American by birth . . . Lady Ancaster,[2] who sat next to me knew far too much about our military affairs, and even knew the secret that at a certain stage in the operations a landing behind the enemy's lines is contemplated—a fact that I have never written down even in the Cabinet Minutes, or in this locked and carefully guarded diary! The real danger of secrets leaking out lies in these high society gatherings. The English ladies learn from their husbands and menfolk—especially young men home from the front who are most indiscreet; they tell their American lady friends, who repeat them to other Americans, who in turn repeat them in neutral countries, where they leak to the enemy. This is how we get much of our information of the enemy, and without doubt it leaks out in the same way.

Having for once a few minutes to spare, I will jot down a few remarks about some of the political congeries which I have encountered in London during this war, and which exercise a varying amount of influence on affairs. Among the most influential at the present moment I would place the Round Table group. They dine every Monday usually either at the house of Major Waldorf Astor M.P., Sir Edward Carson, or Oliver.[3] Milner is the real leader

---

[1] A small part of this day's entry is in *Supreme Command*, II, p. 693.
[2] Eloise Breese, the American-born wife of 2nd Earl of Ancaster (1867–1951).
[3] Frederick S. Oliver (1864–1934). Barrister, historian and businessman. Director of Debenhams Ltd.

of this group, which includes Amery, Philip Kerr, and the editor of *The Times* Geoffrey Robinson (who has just changed his name), as well as the various young men associated with the Round Table. Ll. George sometimes attends their gatherings. Another group—far less influential at the moment —is the set of young M.P.s with whom I dined last Monday—Sykes, Lord Hugh Cecil,[1] Ormsby-Gore,[2] Bridgeman,[3] and one or two others, who dine in a small room just off the terrace at the House of Commons, also on Mondays. There is another group which I associate with Tom Jones, which also meets more or less weekly. It comprises, besides Tom Jones, Professor Adams, Vaughan Nash,[4] Philip Kerr and Astor intermittently, and I suspect is in rather close touch with H.A.L. Fisher, the Minister of Education.[5] It is rather socialist in character. This group probably exercises a good deal more influence than one would expect from its composition. Then there is a small group of ultra-Imperials, of which Norton-Griffiths M.P.,[6] a clever man in a technical sense but stupid, unpractical and visionary in his ideas, appears to be the centre. This group includes Hannon the secretary of the Navy League,[7] General Cockerill,[8] Worthington Evans M.P.,[9] Amery and a number of minor M.P.s. Nearly all of this group are insufferable bores. Their aim is Imperial Federation, but their ideas are woolly to the last degree. They dine and wine at intervals. I do not think that they exercise any serious influence. Balfour, Bob Cecil, and Drummond form a little group of

---

[1] 1869–1956. 5th son of 3rd Marquis of Salisbury. 1st Baron Quickswood 1941. Politician (Cons.).

[2] William G. A. Ormsby-Gore, 4th Baron Harlech (1885–1964). Politician (Cons.), educationist and businessman. Parliamentary secretary to Lord Milner and Assistant Secretary, War Cabinet 1917–18. Under-Secretary for Colonies 1922–24 and 1924–29. Postmaster-General 1931. Secretary of State for Colonies 1936–38.

[3] William C. Bridgeman, 1st Viscount Bridgeman 1929 (1864–1935). Politician (Cons.). Home Secretary 1922–24. First Lord of Admiralty 1924–9.

[4] 1861–1932. Private Secretary to Campbell-Bannerman 1905–8 and to Asquith 1908–12, both as Prime Minister. Secretary, Minister of Reconstruction 1917–19.

[5] Herbert A. L. Fisher (1865–1940). Politician (Nat. Lib.), Educationist and author. President, Board of Education 1916–22. President, British Academy 1928–32. Warden of New College, Oxford 1925–40.

[6] See p. 396.

[7] Sir Patrick J. H. Hannon (1874–1963). Businessman and politician (Cons.). A strong supporter of Navy League and of all British naval interests.

[8] Brigadier-General Sir George K. Cockerill (1867–1957). Soldier and politician (Cons.). Deputy Director of Military Operations and Military Intelligence, and of Special Intelligence 1915–19.

[9] Sir Laming Worthington-Evans (1868–1931). Politician (Cons.). Parliamentary Secretary to Ministry of Munitions 1916–18. Minister of Blockade 1918, of Pensions 1919–20 and Without Portfolio 1920–21. Secretary of State for War 1924–29.

their own, in which I have perhaps a place, which without the fixed meetings or any formal bond whatsoever, is very influential, particularly in foreign affairs. These are the principal influences behind the scenes at the present time, so far as I see them. There are no doubt many others, particularly in the labour world which I have not yet come into contact with. It is notable that women play no active part in any of these groups. All those that I have mentioned have made approaches to me, but (excepting my personal admiration and friendship for Balfour, and the privilege I feel it to be in his confidence) I have hitherto thought it advisable to keep clear of the groups . . .

16th August 1917

No War Cabinet this morning, as the P.M. is preparing his speech on the motion for the adjournment. Sir Mark Sykes came in to tell me that he had guaranteed to the Seamen and Firemen's Union £600, in order to make up a fund of £1,000 required for their Inter-Ally conference on the Stockholm Conference—their attitude being that they will not carry the Western Allies to Stockholm. Sykes, by some freakish political incident, is a member of the Union, but of course it is vital that it should not be known that he gives this guarantee—which he will only be called on to carry out if some co-trustee of the Union's funds declines to sanction the use of these funds for the purpose. Sykes has drawn no pay and makes the guarantee out of the fund which has accumulated at the bank from this reserve. An odd position for a Tory M.P.!

17th August 1917

Short War Cabinet at 11 a.m., the House of Commons meeting at noon. There was a second War Cabinet in the afternoon. I was anxious to get away early and spend the week-end at Eastbourne, but to my disgust I was rung up by Sir Eric Geddes, who was on the point of resigning the post of First Lord. It all came out of a quite innocent suggestion of Churchill's that some of the naval guns might be taken out of the old ships, which could be laid up now that the U.S.A. have joined us, and adapted for military use. The suggestion had been made at a meeting on the afternoon of the 15th, in the absence of any Adty. representation, the question having cropped up suddenly. Unfortunately I had allowed the draft Cabinet Minute on the subject to be worded in such a way that it appeared as though an inquiry was to be conducted into whether the Adty. could spare the guns, instead of what should be done with the guns they could spare. I at once went to see Geddes and wrestled with him for over an hour, missing my train to Eastbourne. He was shockingly obstinate and narrow, and I had to play up to his vanity by saying that he would smash the Govt. if he resigned, and that this might lose us the war! At last I induced him not to send the letter of resignation he was writing before Monday! What had caused this crisis was that earlier in the afternoon he had written a long letter to the P.M., based on the Cabinet draft Minute, but ending in a long complaint about Churchill. I had been with the P.M. when he received it; he had been very angry and wanted to write an irate reply, but I dissuaded him and suggested he should see Geddes later in the afternoon and talk it over quietly. When I saw Geddes he had just come back from this interview. The P.M. had told him he was suffering from "swelled head" and had been very rough with him. *Hinc illae lacrimae* [Hence these tears]. Eventually I pacified Geddes, as I have said, and I undertook to get the draft Minute amended. And so, off to the P.M. to get his concurrence to this, whom I found in his bedroom, changing his clothes and talking to Churchill. So I talked very plainly to them both, and told them they must "let the clutch in gently" with Geddes, if they wanted to keep him. I think they were rather annoyed. After this storm in a teacup I went back to the office. Who should turn up there but Lord Derby, who had just come from Geddes, and I will be jugged if he wasn't talking of resigning too! All because Churchill, during a discussion at the War Cabinet on the supply of guns to Russia had dared to say that Haig was better off than had been calculated for as regard 6″ howitzers, owing to the longer life of these weapons, and that a few guns could be spared! "What right has he to express an opinion? He is only an ironmonger". Here was a pretty kettle of fish! However, I soothed him down too—by telling him I was tired and wanted a rest at Eastbourne, begging him to keep Geddes from resigning before Monday etc. Like setting a naughty little girl to mind the baby . . .

The trouble between Geddes and Churchill produced the following letter.

Hankey to Smuts. Offices of the War Cabinet. 17th August 1917. Holograph[1]
Private and Confidential.
My dear General,

I write to warn you that there is a very delicate situation in regard to the Committee at which you were asked to take the Chair on the subject of adapting naval guns to military purposes.

The whole question is raised by the suspicions which the Admiralty seem to entertain of Churchill. They very strongly resent his intrusion into this question. I had a very trying hour with Sir Eric Geddes this evening.

The final result was that I offered to submit a redraft of the terms of reference to your Committee in the following terms:—"A Committee composed &c &c should investigate whether any *heavy* guns and ammunition, *which the Admiralty could release*, could be adapted for military use, and report the result of their inquiries to the War Cabinet." (Amended passages underlined.)

[1] Smuts Archive, University of Capetown, folio 167.

The Prime Minister accepts this re-draft, as does Sir Eric Geddes. I hope that you will also accept it.

The question is a very delicate one, for the reason I have stated, and I think it would be desirable to defer action in the matter until Monday, to gain time for the temperature to cool.

I should rather like a few words with you about it on Monday.

I am off to Eastbourne for Saturday and Sunday, though I expect I may be recalled, if this affair does not quiet down in the meantime,—though I hope this will be the case . . .

That same day Hankey also had a brush with Robertson on the subject of a Cabinet minute about the supply of guns to Russia. The C.I.G.S. claimed that he had made an interpolation to the effect that he and Haig had stressed "the necessity of concentrating all our resources" —on the western front of course; and that "if they were not so concentrated it was necessary for the War Cabinet to realise that the operations were not being supported in the way recommended". Hankey, who had himself taken the notes of the meeting, consulted his Assistant Secretaries and Milner, none of whom had any recollection of such an interpolation. He therefore showed it to Lloyd George, who "instructed me to omit it"; but the C.I.G.S.'s complaint obviously put him to a lot of trouble.[1] He must indeed have been glad to get away and rejoin his family at Eastbourne for a short week-end; but when he got back to his office on 20th he found a surly letter from the C.I.G.S. protesting about his remarks "not [being] fully taken down". "As the Minutes in question have now been printed", he grumbled, "there is I presume no more to be done"; but he asked for his letter to be kept "for record".[2] So it has been.

The 17th August was in fact an important day in British history for weightier reasons than the Geddes-Churchill fracas or Robertson's surliness. For on that day the committee which Lloyd George had set up under Smuts on 11th July to study and recommend on the future organisation of the air forces rendered its report.[3] They recommended that "a real Air Ministry responsible for all air organisation and operations should be set up", and that "a unified air service" should absorb

[1] Hankey to Robertson 17th Aug. 1917 and enclosure with minute by Robertson in holograph. Robertson papers. I/21/38/1.
[2] Robertson to Hankey 20th Aug. 1917. ibid. I/21/39.
[3] GT. 1658 of 17th Aug. 1917. Cab. 24/22. This was the Smuts Committee's second report. Its first report had dealt only with the defence of London against air raids.

and replace the Royal Flying Corps and Royal Naval Air Service. The Cabinet approved the report on 24th August, overruling the objections and reservations of the Admiralty and War Office. Thus was a term put to the long controversy over aviation; but in the long view the amputation of the R.N.A.S. was to have very unhappy results for the Royal Navy.[1]

On 20th the Cabinet discussed the Pope's Peace Note, and Hankey had to take the minutes himself. The decision was "to reply in the sense that we could give no detailed answer until the Central Powers [had answered], as, when we formulated our terms in reply to President Wilson's peace note, they had not responded".[2] This negative attitude obviously inhibited any move towards a compromise peace; but it is only fair to recall that Germany had shown no willingness at all to accept even such fundamental requirements for peace as the evacuation of Belgium. Indeed the collapse of Russia and the prospect of success in the west had greatly strengthened the hands of the military extremists in Germany.

Diary 21st August 1917
War Cabinet in morning. Ll. George had yesterday announced his intention of going off on leave. I decided to do ditto and spent most of my day arranging and winding up my affairs. In the evening I had a most delicate interview with Mr. Arthur Henderson at the Labour Party's Headquarters, in order to recover his secret papers. He is in a very prickly state owing to what he regards as his bad treatment by Ll. George. However I treated it in a "permanent official" spirit and talked of my responsibility as custodian of these secret documents etc. and all went well, in fact the interview was most cordial and he ended by reciting all his grievances at great length . . . The awkwardness of the secret paper business was that under the old Cabinet system, documents remained the personal property of Ministers on retiring. Now that there are Cabinet Minutes, and far more papers, the War Cabinet having absorbed the C.I.D., a new system had to be designed by me—and Henderson, a labour man retiring in a pique—was the first person to whom it had to be applied! The whole business has given me a lot of trouble. Austen Chamberlain is also a similar case, though not a member of the War Cabinet . . .

---

[1]For the original papers on the Smuts Committee see S. W. Roskill (Ed.), *Documents Relating to the Naval Air Service 1908–1918* (Navy Records Society, 1969), and for the subsequent controversy the same author's *Naval Policy between the Wars*, Vol. I (Collins, 1968). The latter is henceforth cited as "Roskill, *Naval Policy*".
[2]Diary 20th Aug. 1917. See p. 347 re Wilson's note.

Hankey took care to lay firm foundations for his spell of leave—and believed he had been successful. Bonar Law sent him a line saying "go by all means. You need a holiday as much as anyone"[1]; and an even rarer scrawl from Lloyd George read "Quite right. Take a day or two off. You have had a racking time and you will be all the better for a couple of days complete rest".[2] In fact Lloyd George's forecast of "a couple of days" proved nearer the mark than Hankey's hope for a longer break, and on 26th August (a Sunday) he was called over to Danny Park near Hurstpierpoint in Sussex,[3] where the Prime Minister was staying with Sir George Riddell. The reason was that news of Cadorna's success on the Carso had just arrived, and Lloyd George was "in a ferment of excitement" about it, wanting at once to reinforce the Italians with artillery and send Robertson out to exploit the opportunity—which in fact the C.I.G.S. was quite certain not to do. Hankey himself was engulfed in the wave of optimism, and believed that the Italian success might offset Haig's failure in Flanders.[4]

The result of the excitement was that Hankey stayed on at Danny Park, which became a temporary office of the War Cabinet. Thus Lloyd George got his holiday, but Hankey's was destroyed. Among the guests was Lord Reading, the Lord Chief Justice,[5] who was shortly leaving on a special mission to U.S.A., and wanted "some knowledgeable official" to accompany him. Lloyd George suggested Hankey, and then quickly withdrew the suggestion. Strategy was much discussed, to Hankey's concern since Lord Burnham,[6] owner of the *Daily Telegraph*, was another guest and Lloyd George "talked much too freely considering that Burnham and Riddell are both great newspaper proprietors". The strategic discussions were, according to Hankey, "mainly 'crabbing' the western front policy"; but any chance of exploiting the opportunity in Italy disappeared when Philip Kerr returned with the news that Robertson was away and that General Maurice, the

[1] Bonar Law to Hankey, 21st Aug. 1917. Holograph.
[2] Lloyd George to Hankey. Undated but probably 21st Aug. 1917.
[3] In his diary, and also in his memoirs, Hankey generally described Danny Park as being near Lindfield, but it is actually much closer to Hurstpierpoint—see diary for 13th July 1918.
[4] Diary 26th Aug. 1917. Printed in full in *Supreme Command*, II, pp. 693–4.
[5] See p. 240.
[6] 1st Viscount Burnham 1919 (1862–1933). Newspaper proprietor (*Daily Telegraph*) and politician (Cons.). President Empire Press Union 1916–28.

Director of Military Operations "had strongly opposed the Italian plan".[1]

The next day found Lloyd George "in a peevish, changeable mood" —probably because he realised that his Italian plan was again to be frustrated. However he decided to call Robertson down to Danny Park. Milner had also joined the party, and so Hankey, "still without any kit", had to stay on. Conducting the war from a country house was made more difficult by storms having cut all telephone communication.[2]

On 29th, Robertson and Maurice arrived and the long debate was resumed—with no result except to send a telegram to Rome telling the ambassador "that we could only assist [the Italians] at the expense of an abandonment of the Flanders offensive"; but that "we would even consider facing this if we were assured that a really great victory could be won without our aid on the Italian front". Robertson was, of course, far too shrewd not to realise that such an assurance would certainly not be forthcoming. Maurice told Hankey that Haig "still believed we could clear the Flanders coast". "I am bound to say", remarked Hankey in his diary, "that I could not share this optimism".[3] That evening the party returned to London.

Diary 30th August 1917[4]
. . . I spent the evening re-drafting Ll. G.'s letter to President Wilson as Kerr's draft, inspired by the P.M., appalled me. Ll. G. had insisted on putting in all his complaints against the military management of the war; his protests against western front policy; his desire to knock out Austria and Turkey; and a new, and not very well thought out scheme for an allied Council and General Staff in Paris to direct the war. I had pointed out without much immediate effect that this letter would be bound to leak out; that his colleagues did not share his views, that he would become embroiled with them and with the military pundits; and that he would be accused of intreaguing [sic] behind the backs of his colleagues with the head of a foreign state. Eventually I converted Kerr to my views and I hope the eventual letter will be no more than an attempt to enlist President Wilson in the Councils of the Allies . . .

---

[1]Diary 27th Aug. 1917. Extracts from this day's entry are printed in *Supreme Command*, II, p. 694.
[2]Diary 28th Aug. 1917. The whole entry is in *Supreme Command*, II, p. 694.
[3]Diary 29th Aug. 1917. The whole entry is in *ibid.* pp. 694-5.
[4]Part of this day's entry is in *ibid.* p. 695.

31st August 1917

No War Cabinet. Spent morning reading up various papers that came in while I was away and on other office business. Although Ll. G. had entirely spoiled my leave in bringing me up to town I could not get at him until the evening, when at Bonar Law's request, I showed him some rather violent remarks that Robertson had added to the draft minutes of the Italian discussion last Tuesday [28th]. He allowed the remarks to stand, but decided to answer them and instructed me to prepare his brief. This involved the very heavy job of making a précis of all the circumstances bearing on the preparation of our war plans for 1917. I set to work at once. . . .

Robertson's intransigent attitude at the Cabinet meeting on 28th August with regard to supporting Italy evidently came near to bringing the long-smouldering quarrel between him and Lloyd George to a head[1]; and of course Hankey could not escape involvement once the Prime Minister had instructed him "to prepare his brief".

Hankey to Lloyd George. Offices of the War Cabinet. 1st September 1917[2]
Secret and Personal
My dear Prime Minister,

I have been at work all day as well as part of last night in connection with the statement you propose to make on the subject of Sir William Robertson's remarks at the War Cabinet last Tuesday.

When I really got to grips with the matter, I found that the preparation of a complete summary of all the circumstances in which the decisions in regard to the main operations of 1917 were taken, involved a very detailed and rather complicated enquiry into the Minutes of the War Cabinet, and of innumerable Inter-Ally Conferences. I found, indeed, that the result would be much too long for you to include in any personal statement you could make at the Cabinet. I, therefore, came to the conclusion that the best plan would be for you to instruct me, as Secretary, to prepare a completely impartial statement of the circumstances, in the form of a Memorandum by the Secretary, and that your statement should merely take the form of a commentary on my Memorandum and General Robertson's statement to the War Cabinet.

I, therefore, enclose the following documents:—

1. A preliminary rough draft of your statement to the War Cabinet.
2. My own Secretary's Memorandum.
3. The Minutes of the Meeting at which General Robertson made his statement.

Neither of the two former documents are quite complete. I had no copy

[1]War Cabinet 225A.   [2]Cab. 21/89.

of General Cadorna's plan; Miss Stevenson,[1] who has a copy, was away; and consequently I shall probably have to rewrite the paragraph dealing with this. Moreover, I have not been able to compare my draft of your statement with my own Memoranda, as the latter is still being typed, and I have had to prepare it from memory. Nevertheless as it is now late, and I am anxious for you to receive the whole dossier this evening I thought it advisable to send it in its present form.

I shall be at Limpsfield to-morrow in case you require me. I rather hope you won't, as I have arranged for Lord Milner and Amery to come over in the afternoon, but of course, I can put them off.

Attached to the above letter was a strongly worded "Draft statement by the Prime Minister" in which Hankey challenged Robertson's remarks. He wrote that the C.I.G.S.'s statement that "the General Staff . . . had no hand in not adopting the Italian plan. It was ruled out by the War Cabinet" conveyed "an entirely false impression"—as indeed any student of the history of World War I must surely agree. He also advised Lloyd George to "demur to the implication of the C.I.G.S. that he was not fully consulted by the Cabinet Committee on War Policy", and to "demur strongly" to Robertson's suggestion "that the War Cabinet have no real confidence in the plan they adopted after long and careful consideration" (i.e. the Flanders offensive). Rather had it always been agreed that the plan "should be re-examined from time to time"; and because bad weather had resulted in the offensive "not making anything like the progress . . . hoped for" the War Cabinet would "be failing in their duty if they had not instituted enquiries . . . as to the desirability of adopting an alternative plan".[2] The second document sent to Lloyd George by Hankey was a factual but damning contradiction of Robertson's claim that he had not been properly consulted about the alternative plan to the Flanders offensive. Hankey pointed out that Robertson had been present at nine of the War Policy Committee's sixteen meetings when the matter was considered, and had been accompanied by Haig at five of them. The discussions at the other meetings had not been relevant. Observing that Hankey had so often stood by Robertson on earlier occasions when he had been at cross purposes with Lloyd George this indictment is the more surprising. Obviously Hankey was nettled not only by the C.I.G.S.'s inaccurate

[1]Frances Stevenson (1888–   ). Private Secretary to Lloyd George 1913–43, when by his second marriage she became Countess Lloyd George.
[2]Cab. 21/89.

and tendentious statements, but by his implied criticism of the secretariat's system. Yet Lloyd George, though provided with ample
ammunition, forbore to dismiss Robertson. Hankey's diary entries for
the succeeding days, taken with the fact that his "Secretary's Memorandum" of 1st September was never circulated officially to the War
Cabinet probably provide the explanation for the Prime Minister's
forbearance.

Diary 3rd September 1917[1]
War Cabinet at 11.30. Ll. George did not come up from Walton Heath to the
meeting. We received at the morning meeting a telegram from our liaison
officer in Paris,[2] actually addressed to the Director of Military Operations,
stating that the French Govt. wanted to send 100 guns to Italy; that Gen.
Foch and Pétain wanted to take them from the first French army in Flanders
attached to Haig's command; that Foch was coming at once to London to see
Robertson; and that if Robertson could not agree to his proposals the French
Govt. hoped the British Govt. would over-rule the C.I.G.S.! Fancy addressing such a communication to D.M.O.! Robertson was at once recalled; Haig
was brought to England; and Ll. G. telephoned up that he would hold a
Cabinet after dinner . . . At 9.15 p.m. the War Cabinet met—all rather
sulky at being hauled out. Practically no business was done, as Foch had not
arrived, and there was no fresh news. Ll. G. appeared to be funking the row
with Robertson, which had seemed inevitable. I had with great difficulty
persuaded Ll. G. that he ought to read his letter to President Wilson which
Lord Reading, starting next morning, was to take. He did this, and his
colleagues approved, so a serious danger to Ll. G. was averted . . . The
letter was a curious medley of all the drafts that Philip Kerr and I had
prepared at Lindfield [i.e. Danny Park], but did not make a bad whole—
though too long. In the main it was a carefully worded plea to President
Wilson to take part in the allied councils. After Ll. G. had read this there was
some rather important talk about the importance of an attack on Turkey, of
which I had a full note prepared . . .

4th September 1917[3]
No War Cabinet in morning, but in the afternoon there was a War Cabinet
first, followed by a meeting with Foch. The net result was that a conference

[1]Short extracts from this day's entry are printed in *Supreme Command*, II, p. 696.
[2]This was Colonel (later Major-General Sir Edward) Spears, originally spelt Spiers
(1886–   ). Soldier, politician (Nat. Lib. then Cons. from 1931) and author. Head
of Military Mission, Paris 1917–20. Personal representative of Churchill as Prime
Minister with French Prime Minister 1940. The first British Minister to Republics
of Syria and Lebanon 1942–44.
[3]Part of this day's entry is printed in *Supreme Command*, II, p. 696.

was arranged between Haig, Robertson, Foch and Pétain with a view to scraping up 100 French heavy guns for Italy on the basis that Haig should release 50 from the French First Army . . . attached to his command on condition that 50 more were got together from other parts of the French front, thus making a really important contribution to Cadorna's artillery . . . I have no doubt that M. Thomas, who had at Lindfield the previous week shown great enthusiasm for the Italian idea, had inspired the French message. Then Ll. G. had been very truculent about the idea of overruling the soldiers, but when he came to the point, he funked it. In fact, after the meeting with Foch, he said to me "I think this is the best we can do, don't you? I do not think this is the moment for a row with the soldiers". Haig again showed himself very confident, though I could discover no good reason for his confidence. One thing that impressed me was his great desire to capture a ridge from which he could interrupt the Roulers-Thierout[1] railway, which runs parallel to and a few miles behind the enemy's front in Flanders. I asked him why he could not interrupt it with aircraft. He replied that they were no use for this. His opinion strongly supports my own views that the offensive value of aircraft is greatly exaggerated . . .

That same day Hankey sent a long letter to Curzon, who was ill, to bring him up to date about all that had happened since the meetings held at Danny Park ten days earlier, including Robertson's opposition to supporting the Italians and the more recent proposal to send them 100 guns.[2] Though Hankey never liked Curzon, or trusted his judgement, he was evidently determined to keep so influential a Minister fully *au courant* with the important events then taking place. Curzon had also taken up with Hankey the omission of his remarks from earlier Cabinet minutes, to which Hankey replied at length explaining how "from the very first day that the War Cabinet was inaugurated" the system of recording its discussions had been "a matter of great difficulty". The broad principle arrived at had been that, because Cabinet decisions "had to be regarded as the collective decision of its members" it was "undesirable to bring out the individual views of members". The interpretation of that principle had been "left more or less to my [Hankey's] discretion"; and he went on to explain how he had applied the authority delegated to him. He reminded Curzon that in the days of the War Committee it had been his practice to produce "full Secretary's Notes of what everyone said"; but that system had been "criticised a good deal on constitutional grounds"—which were even more relevant

[1]Now Roeselare-Torhout. [2]Hankey to Curzon 4th Sept. 1917. Cab. 21/89.

in the case of the War Cabinet's deliberations. Furthermore the frequency with which War Cabinet meetings were taking place, as compared with the War Committee, would mean that the "Notes", if reverted to, would be so voluminous that he himself might well "lose the grip on the form and style of the Minutes". Finally, he pointed out how under the prevailing system he was able to send decisions to the departments which would have to carry them out in the authoritative form of the relevant Cabinet minute. Obviously Curzon's desire to have a more or less verbatim record of discussions would weaken, indeed probably terminate, this simple and practical way of translating Cabinet decisions into executive action. In other words Hankey put Curzon gently in his place, and showed that he had good reasons to continue exactly as he was doing.[1]

Quite apart from the difficulties with Curzon, Hankey's relations with Lloyd George were going through one of their periodical bouts of strain at this time. It was probably brought on by the Prime Minister's frustration over the conduct of the war in general, and the intransigence of the top soldiers in particular. On 5th September Milner sent Bonar Law a letter on the subject of control of military commanders. As it echoed Hankey's views so very closely it is likely that it derived from the talks they had together at Danny Park. If, as is probable, Lloyd George saw the letter it must have influenced his decision to avoid an open breach with Robertson.". . . In the first place", wrote Milner "it seems very important not to try to make naval or military commanders carry out operations of which they really disapprove . . . That was the fundamental error in the Dardanelles proceedings. It is not that the idea of the Dardanelles expedition was wrong. On the contrary it was probably right. But in the face of the real disapproval of Lord Kitchener and Lord French it was bound to lead to disaster".[2] And, of course, the same argument could be applied in the summer of 1917 to the attitude of Robertson and Haig to the Italian front and to the Salonika and Palestine campaigns.

Diary 5th September 1917
War Cabinet at 11.15. Mainly confined to discussion of the previous night's aeroplane raid over London. A great deal of foolish exaggeration over the matter. In the afternoon Ll. G. went off to N. Wales and Birkenhead. I was very glad to see him go. He has been restless and neurotic, unstable and

[1]Hankey to Curzon 4th Sept. 1917. Kedleston papers.
[2]Milner to Bonar Law 5th Sept. 1917 (misdated 10th Sept.), Milner papers, Vol. 144.

rather infirm in purpose, neuralgic and irritable, exacting and difficult to please. He spoiled my leave last week, and, though I am off for a few days, I fear I shall not be able to catch the holiday spirit again, particularly as we have left Eastbourne.

Hankey now made another effort to get a real break, but after a few days at Highstead Lloyd George called him over to Criccieth—just when he was about to take the family to Littlehampton. Truly Lloyd George could prove himself a selfish, as well as an exacting taskmaster; and at such times Hankey must have looked back nostalgically to the days when he could enjoy the mellow, cultured tranquillity of the Asquith régime. Meanwhile the news from Flanders was very discouraging—as Hankey learnt when Lord Burnham gave him the reports of Philip Gibbs[1]—"the admirable correspondent of the Telegraph and Chronicle".[2]

On reaching Criccieth Hankey found Lloyd George "quite seriously ill", "rather despondent at the failure of the year's campaigning" and "disgusted at the narrowness of the General Staff and the inability of his colleagues to see eye to eye with him". He was also very much aware of the Staff's capacity to "twist their facts and estimates to suit their arguments"[3]—which reads ironically in the light of Lloyd George's capacity for using facts and figures to his own advantage when it suited his book to do so.

However, the Welsh air and mountain scenery soon dispersed Hankey's disgruntlement, and he enjoyed sightseeing and visiting the scenes of Lloyd George's childhood in company with Philip Kerr, George Riddell and Lloyd George's daughter Olwen (now Mrs. Carey Evans). On 16th, a Sunday, Lloyd George was well enough for Hankey to tackle him about the urgent need to revive the War Policy Committee, which he wanted to use as the instrument for destroying the claim of the General Staff to dictate war policy—which he regarded as "unjustifiable and arrogant". By such means he hoped "to bring Robertson to heel without a row"; but he was careful not to be explicit on that point in the paper on the subject he wrote for Lloyd George's benefit.[4]

---

[1]Later Sir Philip Gibbs (1877–1962). Journalist and author. War correspondent with French and Belgian armies 1914, and British armies in France 1915–18.
[2]Diary 13th Sept. 1917.
[3]*ibid.* 14th Sept. 1917. Nearly the whole entry is in *Supreme Command*, II, p. 697.
[4]Diary 16th Sept. 1917. See *Supreme Command*, II, p. 697.

Next day Milner joined the party, and after long discussions "it was agreed that our proper course . . . was to concentrate on Turkey, as there was little hope of achieving definite success on the western front". The difficulty of convincing the soldiers on such a matter, regarding which Milner had recently expressed himself so cogently, appears to have been ignored.[1] On 18th Hankey took a long walk with Milner, who had "come completely round to Ll. G.'s view . . . that it is necessary to devote our main efforts against Turkey", and that "success in the Turkish theatre can only be achieved if the soldiers were in it whole-heartedly". Neither Milner nor Hankey seems to have grasped that, as long as Robertson was C.I.G.S., the two requirements were totally incompatible. However Hankey gained Milner's support "to prevent Ll. G. from delivering a frontal attack on Robertson"—an intention to which the Prime Minister had constantly recurred in their recent talks, and from which Hankey had "been trying to dissuade him". "Now I have an ally" Hankey recorded in his diary.[2] Yet it is surely the case that it was Lloyd George who saw the truth—that a peripheral strategy could not be successfully carried out unless changes were made in the military hierarchy; and it is reasonable to conclude that his depression and irritation at this time stemmed from the knowledge that he could not expect much support for such purposes in the War Cabinet. One feels that in this case Hankey overplayed his customary rôle as peacemaker—to the detriment of strategic considerations. None the less he sent Robertson a series of letters "asking for information on the Palestine campaign [and] Mesopotamia . . . and for a complete estimate of relative forces in western and all other theatres, of enemy and allies".[3] Then he settled down to revise his great memorandum on the proposed offensive against Turkey. Incidentally while at Criccieth Hankey got Riddell to promise "a good journalist post" for his old mentor of Greenwich days General Sir George Aston,[4] who was about to retire from the R.M.A. Riddell also gave Hankey "useful tips about using standardised abbreviations in taking notes", which he intended to adopt in his office. Hankey never lost an opportunity to exploit outside brains for the improvement of the efficiency of his own department, or to gain the influence of powerful persons for the benefit of old friends.

[1]Diary 17th Sept. 1917. Nearly the whole entry is in *op. cit.* p. 697.
[2]*ibid.* 18th Sept. 1917. Part reproduced in *op. cit.*, pp. 697–8.
[3]*ibid.* 20th Sept. 1917. A part is in *op. cit.,* p. 698.   [4]See p. 33.

Diary 22nd September 1917[1]

... We have news from our Ambassador at Madrid that the Germans want to open peace negotiations with us, and we have accordingly invited Painlevé the new French P.M. to come to London, or alternatively we may have to meet him at Boulogne next week. I had a walk before lunch with Lloyd George. He and I agreed that the first step is to obtain some outline of Germany's proposals. If favourable to us and to those of our allies who have pulled their weight in the war it might [be] necessary to present an ultimatum to Russia and to say that either they must pull themselves together and fight properly, or else we should have to agree to a peace at their expense. We also received the answer of the C.I.G.S. to the request for information *re* prospects in Mesopotamia, and I had to write to the C.I.G.S. asking whether it would not be advisable to assist Gen. Maude by sending the British heavy artillery now in Italy to Egypt, either to enable Gen. Allenby to make a diversion or to be transferred, in case of necessity, rapidly to Mesopotamia. Cadorna has announced his intention of making no further offensive, but of awaiting an Austrian attack, and then counter-attacking. This is very difficult to account for, unless there is truth in rumours of insurrection in Italy, as the French guns were sent for the specific purpose of enabling Cadorna to attack.

On Sunday 23rd September the informal War Cabinet at Criccieth broke up, and the whole party returned to London. The ten days Hankey spent there ended better than they had begun, Lloyd George having shaken off both his neuralgia and his depression. Indeed towards the end some of the evenings appear to have been quite hilarious, with Lloyd George leading informal concerts with his favourite Welsh hymns, and the rest of the party joining in with other songs. One would especially like to have heard Hankey and Lloyd George singing "The Bay of Biscay" as a duet.[2]

Diary 24th September 1917[3]

War Cabinet in morning. The last hour was devoted to a discussion of the German proposals, when Mr. Balfour told us that a definite offer had been made to France through von Lancken,[4] First Secretary at the German Embassy in Paris before the war, and M. Briand through the intermediary of some lady friend of Briand (quite respectable). Germany is alleged to be willing to give up Belgium, Alsace Lorraine, Serbia, concessions to Italy, and

---

[1]Part of this day's entry is in *op. cit.*, p. 698. [2]Diary 22nd Sept. 1917.
[3]Part reproduced in *Supreme Command*, II, pp. 698–9.
[4]Baron von der Lancken was at this time First Secretary of the German Legation in Madrid.

colonial concessions to us; but no word of Russia, Roumania or Turkey from which it is deduced that Germany wants to recoup herself at Russia's expense.[1] This rather fits in with Ll. G.'s idea; and no-one turned it down, though Milner considered it would leave Germany too strong and lead to another war in 10 years' time. The discussion turned largely on the question of whether we should tell our allies that we had received this proposal before or after we received details . . . Balfour was in favour of assembling the Ambassadors of U.S.A., France, Italy, Russia, and Japan and telling them at once that our intention was to act as a post-office, on the ground that otherwise Germany would say we were engaging in negotiations behind their backs. The rest of the War Cabinet was in favour of seeing the proposals and deciding whether the Germans meant business or not before informing them. Eventually decided that the P.M. should see Painlevé at once and tell him.[2] I lunched with Mr. Balfour and Sir Eric Drummond, his private secretary. They showed me absolutely reliable secret service information to show that the German peace offer is genuine and that the Germans are very exhausted. In the afternoon the War Policy Ctee. met and discussed operations against Turkey. At 8 p.m. we started for Dover . . .

The British delegates, led by Lloyd George, crossed the Channel in the early hours of 25th September and met Painlevé and his advisers at Boulogne.[3] The conferences that followed were unprofitable, as the French Premier was occupied chiefly with his own political problems, and his government was, according to Hankey, obviously "rocky". The French showed no enthusiasm for sending an expedition to Alexandretta, and by twice postponing their offensive on the Chemin des Dames they had ensured that the main German effort remained concentrated against the British in the Ypres salient. After the conference the British delegates motored to G.H.Q. to meet Haig. Hankey found that he objected "to the proposed Ministry of the Air . . . as much as I do"; but that die had, as we saw earlier, been cast at the War

---

[1]*Lloyd George*, IV, pp. 2082–2101 gives a full account of the German peace feelers put out by von Kühlmann, the Foreign Minister, through Madrid and Brussels in September 1917. Ribot and Painlevé were against entering into any negotiation; Briand was in favour of doing so. Lloyd George's visit to the French and British G.H.Q.s (see below) had as one object the ascertainment of the views of Foch and Haig on the military prospects, now that Russia was out of the war. He found Haig obsessed with the Flanders offensive.

[2]See Hankey to Balfour 27th Sept. 1917, with endorsements by them both. Cab. 23/16.

[3]The whole of this day's diary entry is in *Supreme Command*, II, p. 699.

Cabinet meeting of 24th August.[1] The following day was spent in conference with the soldiers, and in watching on the map the progress of the current attack in the Ypres salient. Then the party motored around the area in rear of the fighting, stopping to meet some of the leaders of the Fifth and Second Armies, observing all the vast paraphernalia collected for the offensive, and taking a glimpse of captured prisoners—whose excellent discipline evidently impressed Hankey. Thence they went back to Boulogne and so to England.[2] In all, at Criccieth and in France, Hankey had been away from his office nearly a fortnight—an unprecedented absence. Inevitably this meant that he was faced with a huge accumulation of arrears; and the air raids, which made Lloyd George "very fidgety", probably made it still harder for him to catch up.

On 20th September, when Hankey was at Criccieth with Lloyd George, the offensive on the Ypres salient had been renewed by the Second Army in the area where the initial offensive had failed—on either side of the Menin Road. Fairly good progress was made at first, and all counter-attacks were repulsed. Six days later another push took place—the one whose progress Hankey and Lloyd George had watched from G.H.Q. Then on 4th October the attacks were renewed, and despite torrents of rain the main ridge to the east of Ypres was won. But the battle field was now a deeper and fouler morass than ever; and despite a satisfactory haul of prisoners and some restoration of prestige, the truth was that the continuation of the offensive had absorbed the reserves which, had they been available, might have turned the tactical success obtained further south on the comparatively dry ground near Cambrai in November into a major victory. But that runs ahead of the stage now reached in our story.

[1]See p. 427.
[2]The whole of the diary entry for 26th Sept. 1917 is in *Supreme Command*, II, pp. 699–700.

Chapter 15

Stalemate in Flanders: Disaster in Italy. October–December 1917

THE last quarter of 1917 opened quietly except for air raids on London, during which the Cabinet and its secretariat took shelter in the Foreign Office basement. At the beginning of the month the Cabinet decided to institute reprisals for these raids, and so the process nowadays described as "escalation" moved a step further in the direction of total war.[1] Hankey was laid up with a bad cold and feverish attack for a few days early in October, and on returning to London found the old conflict of politics and personalities had also escalated.

Diary 6th October 1917
. . . No War Cabinet, being Saturday. Saw Lord Milner in the morning, who told me that on the previous day they had a highly unsatisfactory meeting of the War Policy Ctee; Robertson had apparently strongly opposed the despatch of two divisions to Egypt as a reserve for Palestine or Mesopotamia, and the Prime Minister had handled him very badly with much recrimination and reminders of the past deficiencies of military advice. I lunched with Balfour, who told me that the British Ambassador at Petrograd had advised letting the Russians know of the German peace overtures through Madrid, and that consequently he had that morning seen the Ambassadors of France, U.S.A., Japan, Russia, and Italy, and told them that this approach had been made and that we had replied that we were prepared to receive them and discuss them with our allies.[2] . . .

9th October 1917[3]
. . . The usual War Cabinet at 11.30, a great deal of business being accomplished. The main subject was the Economic Offensive and development of *post-bellum* threats, which was eventually remitted to a Committee under Sir Edward Carson . . . In the afternoon the War Policy Ctee. assembled again, and once more discussed the Turkish question without much result. Ll. G. still refuses to recognise any merit in Sir Douglas Haig's offensive. A letter

---

[1]Diary 1st and 2nd Oct. 1917. [2]See *Lloyd George*, IV, p. 2104.
[3]Part of this day's entry is in *Supreme Command*, II, pp. 749 and 768.

from the Prime Minister to M. Painlevé was approved, urging decisive operations this winter against Turkey. Gen. Smuts strongly favours a landing operation at Haifa. He told me after the meeting that he would be willing to assume the command. Personally I am opposed to heroic measures of this kind at this stage of the war, as I believe that if we pursue even a western front policy steadily we shall exhaust the Central Powers . . . M. Painlevé and General Foch are arriving unheralded to-day. No-one knows the reason for their visit. I read to-day an article by Spenser Wilkinson[1] in the *Nineteenth Century* on the Dardanelles operations which contains some rather spiteful remarks on myself.[2] However, he has always attacked the Committee of Imperial Defence and both my predecessors, and is, I think, rather an extinct volcano.

On 10th October Painlevé arrived in London with proposals that the British should take over another 60 miles of the western front, and for an amphibious assault on the coast of Syria. The latter expectedly aroused Robertson's antagonism, the more so because the Cabinet decided to discuss it at a "Council of War"—which he professed to regard as a "vote of no confidence" in himself. Hankey once more tried to act as peacemaker, but in the evening Derby told him Robertson had offered his resignation, and Curzon was foretelling that, if it took effect, most of the Conservative ministers, "probably" including himself (a typical piece of Curzonian fence-sitting), would leave the government.[3] Two days later Hankey managed to enlist Geddes's support to deter Robertson from resigning "merely because the War Cabinet wanted to hear someone else's views".[4] In this purpose he was successful—for a time.

Diary 11th October 1917
Before the War Cabinet I walked round St. James's Park with Ll. George and Philip Kerr. I repeated Curzon's warning in very straight terms and he

[1]H. Spenser Wilkinson (1853–1937). Military historian and journalist. Chichele Professor of Military History, Oxford University 1909–23.
[2]Wilkinson's article "Common Sense in War" (*Nineteenth Century*, Vol. 82 (Sept. 1917), pp. 454–69) was in part an attack on the Gallipoli operation, which the author alleged to have been "attributed by Lord Fisher to Sir Maurice Hankey", and in part an attack on the principles involved in the appointment of a secretary to the C.I.D. or other policy-making body in war. "The Secretary", wrote Wilkinson, "will either be a mere clerk, or he will dominate both the services". Though he did not say so the obvious implication was that Hankey came in the second category.
[3]Nearly the whole of this day's entry is in *Supreme Command*, II, pp. 712–13 and 749.
[4]Diary 12th October 1917. Part reproduced in *Supreme Command*, II, p. 713.

took the hint very quickly. The result was that at the War Cabinet, which was the first "War Council",[1] French and Wilson being present, he was quite at his best, handling Robertson (who was as sulky as a bear with a sore head) quite admirably, and explaining the whole situation, including the western front and Palestine alternative plans, quite impartially and judicially. I told Curzon what I had done and he said I had rendered a very considerable public service . . . I did another public service on my walk round St. James's park by persuading Ll. G. to sanction telling the Prime Ministers of the Dominions of the German peace overtures . . .

Meanwhile discontent was rising over the fact that, despite the Cabinet having approved the Smuts Committee's report on the reorganisation of the Air Services nearly two months ago, nothing had been done about appointing the new Minister. Lord Hugh Cecil, writing from the Air Board, informed Milner that Lord Cowdray, his chief, "is evidently not the man".[2] Assuming that Smuts was not available Milner's first choice was Sir William Weir[3]; but he did not press Weir's candidature at this stage, merely circulating a paper urging that the appointment of an Air Minister should be made without further delay.[4] Lloyd George, however, had his own ideas about the most suitable incumbent; and that, as we shall see shortly, produced an explosion in Whitehall.

More important than the appointment of an Air Minister was the progress at last made with the introduction of convoy, over which the Admiralty had unquestionably been dragging its feet—despite the acceptance by the War Cabinet of all Hankey's recommendations of the previous May and those of the Atlantic Convoy Committee set up in June. Outward convoys from British ports were not started until mid-August; and in the Mediterranean, where losses had been heavy in the late summer, the introduction of the same strategy was delayed until October for outward and November for homeward convoys. However the late autumn did at last see something approaching a

---

[1] This unofficial body must not be confused with the Asquith Cabinet's War Council of November 1914–May 1915. See pp. 146 and 181.
[2] Cecil to Milner 11th Oct. 1917. Milner papers, box 122.
[3] 1st Viscount Weir of Eastwood 1938 (1877–1959). Engineer and businessman. Chairman G. and J. Weir 1912–53. Secretary of State for Air 1918–19. An ardent advocate of air power and unofficial adviser to the government on air rearmament in the 1930s.
[4] GT. 2409 of 26th Oct. 1917. Cab. 24/30. Another copy in Milner papers, box 122.

universal convoy system in use; and that was by far the greatest factor in bringing about the defeat of the U-boats.[1]

On 12th October Hankey motored down to Chequers for what he called the "inaugural week-end" at the lovely house which Sir Arthur Lee[2] had recently presented to the nation for the use of its Prime Ministers.[3] In addition to Lloyd George, Balfour, Smuts and Lee, the French mission consisting of Painlevé, Foch and Franklin-Bouillon,[4] who had recently arrived in London, were included in the party. The first event was that Painlevé decorated Hankey with the Légion d'Honneur, which brought him the congratulations of all those present. On the Sunday a conference took place and Lloyd George "horrified" Hankey "by raising the question of an inter-Allied War Council and *permanent General Staff* (his italics) in Paris". His horror at the proposal must surely have arisen from his understanding of the likely reaction of Robertson and Haig. "Why is he [Lloyd George] so blind sometimes?" he asked in his diary. Yet in retrospect it is plain that Lloyd George's first and cautious move towards the establishment of an integrated command system was as timely as it was necessary.[5]

On Monday the whole party returned to London after an interlude which Hankey obviously enjoyed.

Diary 15th October 1917
Breakfast with Ll. G. Afterwards we had a great argument about war policy. I supported Haig's policy and Ll. G. opposed it. Eventually he committed himself to the view that we could only win in 1919 and that we must conserve our strength for this. This, I pointed out was a new idea, which he had never told his colleagues, and I suggested he ought to lose no time in doing so. He replied that he had made so many speeches in Cabinet to them, that he didn't want to make another, and asked me to see some of them, particularly Balfour and Curzon, and tell them what had passed between us . . . I lunched alone with Balfour and told him the whole story, including a statement by

[1] For a full account of the introduction of convoy see Marder, *Scapa Flow*, IV.
[2] See p. 312.
[3] Hankey muddled the dates in his diary at this time. In *Supreme Command*, II, p. 713 he showed the start of the Chequers week-end as 11th October, which was a Thursday. He also amended the dates, in some cases wrongly, in his diary—notably altering Sunday 14th to read 15th, which was a Monday.
[4] Henri Franklin-Bouillon (1870–1939). French politician (Radical). Minister of Propaganda in Painlevé cabinet 1917.
[5] Parts of the diary entries for 12th–13th October are in *Supreme Command*, II, pp. 713–14, but are misdated (see above).

Ll. G. that, rather than forego his policy he would hand over the reins of office to some other [person] who would carry it through . . .

Hankey expanded the foregoing diary entry into a long memorandum recording his discussion on war policy with Lloyd George; but as he has reproduced it in full it will only be summarised here.[1] The principal points, additional to those mentioned in the diary entry, were Lloyd George's insistence that we should "avoid in 1918 the terrific losses" which would certainly be incurred by Haig's plan of "remorselessly hammering the enemy". Lloyd George's remark that "a man took 21 years to make, and human life was very precious" further confirms the view that by the autumn of 1917 he was determined by one means or another to prevent a repetition of the holocausts produced by the Somme and Third Ypres offensives. Hankey on the other hand had moved some way towards accepting the Generals' view—"that it would be absolutely essential to take some offensive on the Western Front next year"; and he rejected both "Pétain's tactics of striking here and striking there . . . but never carrying it through to a prolonged offensive" and carrying out such a policy "in conjunction with a great offensive elsewhere, for example in Turkey". Neither he nor Lloyd George apparently reverted at this discussion to the offensive on the Italian front, by which the Prime Minister had set such great store earlier in the year.

On 20th October Hankey circulated Henry Wilson's paper entitled "The Present State of the War, the Future Prospects and Future Action".[2] Whatever one may think of Wilson's capacity for intrigue, and discounting the probability that he saw in the current troubles between Robertson and Lloyd George the opportunity for securing his own advancement, this superbly argued case for a small War Cabinet and for integrated "Superior Direction" lends support to Churchill's view that in Wilson "the War Cabinet found for the first time an expert adviser of superior intellect, who could explain lucidly and forcefully the whole situation and give reasons for the adoption or rejection of any course".[3] Hankey, for all his earlier mistrust of Wilson, had come round to a similar view.

As an example of the confidences which continually poured into Hankey from all sorts of sources we may here mention that on 20th

[1] See *Supreme Command*, II, pp. 703–7 and John Terraine, *Douglas Haig*, pp. 373–4.
[2] WP.61 of 20th October 1917.
[3] *Churchill*, IV, p 392.

October Swinton sent him from Washington a telegram to Davidson[1] drafted by Lieut-Colonel Arthur Murray (Assistant Military Attaché) and Maynard Keynes[2] in which they said "We have come to the conclusion separately that Spring-Rice[3] cannot be regarded as mentally responsible. It should be realised on your side that he is in a serious nervous condition and incapable of properly conducting business".[4] It had not been sent, wrote Swinton, because Davidson was away and "it would not have done for it to have fallen into wrong hands". He therefore left the matter in the hands of Hankey, who at once sent the telegram on to the Prime Minister. Probably it contributed to the decision to appoint Lord Reading as ambassador a short time later.

Hankey next became involved in a somewhat petty squabble between the Generals over whether the papers written by Lord French and Henry Wilson on future strategy and the creation of a supreme directing authority should be rendered to the C.I.G.S. or to the War Cabinet. Robertson was in a typically "prickly state" over this issue, and Hankey had to tread warily—because French's report "hit out hard at Robertson and Haig, whose views were challenged in principle and in detail".[5] With some reason he regarded the whole manœuvre as "a clever plot" on the part of Lloyd George, as he had obtained the support of French and Wilson by "playing on their ambition and known jealousy and dislike of Robertson". He had meanwhile allowed Haig to continue his offensive, knowing that the appalling weather would prevent him achieving any substantial success; and thereby further strengthened his own case. Then Lloyd George "guilelessly proposed the 'War Council' knowing perfectly well that the jury is a packed one"—thus fortifying himself "with apparently unbiassed military opinion in the great struggle with Robertson and Haig". Hankey considered Lloyd George's

[1] John C. C. Davidson, 1st Viscount Davidson 1937 (1889-   ). Politician (Cons.). Private Secretary to Bonar Law 1915–20 and Parliamentary Private Secretary to him as Prime Minister 1922–23. Chancellor of Duchy of Lancaster 1923–24 and again 1931–37. Chairman, Conservative and Unionist Party Organisation 1926–30.
[2] John Maynard Keynes, 1st Baron Keynes 1942 (1883–1946). Economist. Joined Treasury 1915. Principal Treasury representative at Paris Peace Conference, resigning on questions of reparations and frontiers. Author of The Economic Consequences of the Peace and of other very influential works. First British Governor of International Monetary Fund and International Bank.
[3] Sir Cecil A. Spring-Rice. See p. 185.   [4] Lloyd George papers F/23/1/25.
[5] Diary 21st Oct. 1917. Part reproduced in Supreme Command, II, pp. 714–15 but there misdated 20th Oct.

methods "unsavoury" but admitted he was "very skilful". One feels
that he read the Prime Minister's mind very accurately. But he saw the
dangers to the government in the schism which was developing; since
the resignation of Haig and Robertson on the grounds that "they
could not be responsible for a policy they did not agree in" would
probably result in the resignation of Derby, Curzon, Cecil and other
Conservative Ministers. He therefore saw Derby to try and find some
common ground between the two military factions, and then discussed
the French-Wilson memoranda with Milner. He held that "Robertson
must see them at once" and agreed "that the government would very
likely come down over it."[1] At the end of it Hankey described that day
as "black Monday", with high shipping losses, a menacing situation in
Ireland, the failure to deal with recent Zeppelin raids and the recent
successful German attack on a Scandinavian convoy.[2]

On 24th Hankey saw French and Wilson with the object of persuading
them "to soften some of the phrases [in their memoranda] to make them
less offensive to Robertson"—a purpose with which Lloyd George had
agreed. But French flatly refused "to praise Haig's tactical handling of
the situation", and declared that "he was always repeating the same
mistake". French frankly admitted that his object was to get rid of
Robertson. "We shall do no good", he said, "until we break down the
Haig-Robertson ring". "There was envy, hatred and malice in the old
boy's heart as he spoke" remarked Hankey perceptively;[3] but he considered his duty was "to try and push the government machine along"
with the object of winning the war, and to avoid being drawn into
political manœuvres and intrigue. His task was not made easier by
Sykes telling him that M. Picot[4] had warned him that Painlevé was well
aware of the "serious differences between the British politicians and
their generals".[5] However he succeeded in getting French to modify

[1]Diary 22nd Oct. 1917.

[2]On 17th Oct two German cruisers sank ten out of the twelve merchant ships and
both the escorting destroyers in a convoy homeward bound from Bergen. See
H. Newbolt, *Naval Operations*, V, p. 149–56.

[3]Diary 24th Oct. 1917. Part reproduced in *Supreme Command*, II, p. 715.

[4]François Georges Picot. French diplomat and co-author with Sykes of the agreement signed in Petrograd in May 1916 for dividing the Ottoman Empire into
British, French, Italian and Russian spheres of influence. Lloyd George, *The Truth
about the Peace Treaties*, II, p. 1023, described the agreement as "this egregious document". For another view see Elie Kedourie, *England and the Middle East* (London,
1956). [5]Diary 25th Oct. 1917.

his critical paper, and on 25th handed Derby the revised version. To make the "Inter-Allied Council" more acceptable to Haig and Robertson Derby proposed that Asquith should be appointed ambassador in Paris and permanent British representative on the new body, with Henry Wilson or Maurice as his military adviser; and Hankey agreed to put the suggestion to Lloyd George. Expectedly the Prime Minister "wouldn't look at it", because he regarded the proposal "as merely a dodge to pack the Council . . . and outwit the whole plan."[1] However he did show less hostility to Robertson and offered various concessions. By 26th Hankey believed that he had succeeded in calming the soldiers. "Derby was much relieved", he commented, "and so was I". Meanwhile trouble had blown up again with the Admiralty.

Diary 26th October 1917
. . . Earlier in the day Balfour had told me that he and Carson (as ex-First Lords) had been summoned to meet the P.M. and Geddes to discuss the question of superseding Admiral Jellicoe. It appears that from the Adty. inquiry it has transpired that the latter had been fully warned by highly secret, but absolutely reliable information,[2] of the probability of the recent attack on the Norwegian convoy, and had neglected to act. Geddes regards this as an example of Jellicoe's lack of energy, if not timidity, and wants to replace him by Adl. Wemyss. We are all worried at the serious Italian reverse . . . On reaching home I telephoned to Ll. George at Walton Heath, what Derby told me about Robertson.

The foregoing diary entry is important because it proves that Lloyd George was right when, early in the following January, he supported Geddes's statement to his naval colleagues that before dismissing Admiral Jellicoe he had consulted the Prime Minister and his two predecessors as First Lord (Balfour and Carson)—which Carson had denied. Geddes, we now know correctly, gave the date of the meeting as 26th October, and Lloyd George wrote to him "I am perfectly clear that such a meeting took place at which the four of us were present— perhaps about two months ago".[3] Lloyd George's veracity has often been called in question, not wholly without reason; but in the matter of the dispute over Jellicoe's dismissal his memory is now confirmed.

[1]Diary 26th Oct. 1917.
[2]This must refer to Intelligence from cryptographic sources.
[3]Lloyd George to Geddes 4th January 1918. Quoted by S. W. Roskill, *The Dismissal of Admiral Jellicoe*, Journal of Contemporary History, Vol. I, No. 4 (Oct. 1966).

On 24th October six German and nine Austrian divisions, assembled in great secrecy, suddenly struck at the eastern tip of the Italian Isonzo front, choosing with skill a spot which was very weakly held. Aided by a drizzle of rain and snow a complete break-through was achieved, and Cadorna had first to order a precipitate retreat to the Tagliamento river, where a short breathing space was gained at the end of the month, before making a further retreat to the Piave. In the disaster of Caporetto 600,000 men were lost, and the Italian Second Army was virtually destroyed. Britain and France, as well as the Italians, were caught by surprise and the reinforcements which Haig and Robertson had refused to send to Italy for offensive purposes earlier in the year had to be rushed out to save the situation.

The news of Caporetto was carried by Hankey to Lloyd George in the singularly-incongruous setting of the golf club house at Walton Heath. There the decision to send "substantial help" was promptly taken, after which the party resumed their game, though playing it "appallingly badly" according to Hankey, who was watching. Both he and Lloyd George recalled with some bitterness how at the Rome conference in the previous January they had urged that at least a defensive, if not an offensive plan for the Italian front should be made. Now the Germans had struck "at the weak link, just as he himself [Lloyd George] wanted to do, [and] on the very same spot—a plan which the General Staff rejected with contempt."[1] One can readily sympathise with the "outburst" this produced from Lloyd George at the next Cabinet.

Diary 27th October 1917
War Cabinet 11.30. Ll. George very upset and snappy about Cadorna's defeat and at having to make a speech to move the vote of thanks to our sailors and soldiers. Owing to the Italian affair he has to re-write his speech and left the Cabinet early for this reason. Before he left he had an outburst, in the course of which he sneered at the General Staff. Lord Derby threw me across a note, announcing his intention of resigning. I threw it back with a note on the back pointing out that Ll. G. was upset, and that this was a moment when the wisest heads must keep cool. He then said he would not resign, but felt inclined to. When he had gone Bonar Law said "Well, I don't think we can do any more business without the Prime Minister". I then spoke

[1]Diary 27th Oct. 1917, reproduced almost in entirety in *Supreme Command*, II, pp. 716–18.

out and said I thought it my duty to warn the War Cabinet that their work was badly in arrears; that many questions were awaiting decision; and that there were at least three questions on the Agenda paper that they could settle without the Prime Minister. This shamed them into continuing. But, by this time, I found that Mr. Balfour, Lord Derby, Sir Eric Geddes, and Adl. Jellicoe, all of whom were concerned in these questions, had slipped out of the room. So I ran out into the passage, where they were putting on their coats, and said "Look here, you must not blame me if your departmental affairs at the Cabinet get in arrears. There are questions on the Agenda which concern you all, and here you are all bolting off." So they all filed back, and we got a good deal of business done. After lunch I saw the P.M. for a moment. He told me that he would not go on unless he obtained control of the war. He meant to take advantage of the present position to achieve this . . . I went to tea with General Maurice, the Director of Military Operations, who is acting for Robertson during the latter's visit to Italy. I told him that in my opinion very serious trouble was brewing for Robertson, unless he could see his way to drop the idea that the only way to win the war was by hammering away at the same spot on the western front. Maurice took a very sensible line, and I promised to try and arrange for Ll. G. to see him with a view to a reconciliation with Robertson.

30th October
War Cabinet at 11.30, most of which I had to take single-handed. The proposal for an inter-allied Council and General Staff practically accepted in principle. Balfour wanted me to lunch, but Ll. George insisted on my staying to meet McCormick,[1] an American Congressman and journalist, who impressed me not at all . . . At 7.15 I called on Ll. George, who had just returned from meeting Painlevé at the station and gossiped with him. He was very gloomy owing to the loss of Udine by the Italians, but pleased at the hope of "dishing" the soldiers by establishing the allied council . . .

Thus was the stage set for the most important of the many Inter-Allied Conferences. The establishment of a Supreme War Council and Inter-Allied General Staff was discussed by the War Cabinet on the last day of the month, and Hankey was instructed to draft a constitution for them in conjunction with Maurice. He considered it a "cunning" move on Lloyd George's part to take advantage of Robertson's absence in

---

[1]This must have been either Vance C. McCormick (1872–1946), American newspaper publisher and member of war mission to Britain and France 1917, or Robert R. McCormick (1880–1955), American editor and lawyer, editor and publisher of the *Chicago Tribune*; served on General Pershing's staff 1917. But neither of above was a Congressman at that time.

P

Italy in this way.[1] Next day he and Helbronner, his French colleague, went a step further by drafting rules for the Secretariat which would be required to serve the new organisation.

Diary 2nd November 1917
Ll. G. met Painlevé, Bouillon, and Gen. Pétain at breakfast. The latter seems to have been gloomy about the Italian prospects, and to have suggested that the only chance is to get the Italian army under allied control. He proposed a scheme for dividing into two the whole line from the Channel to the Adriatic, the northern half under the British, and the southern half, including the Italian army, under French command. It had accordingly been arranged that the P.M. and Painlevé should go to Italy and try and force some such arrangement, or some variant of it, such as British control, on the Italian Government. This was approved more or less by the War Cabinet in the morning, and I spent the rest of my day in making arrangements ... There was another War Cabinet in the evening at 6 p.m., so it was a desperately busy day ... Among other things the War Cabinet to-day approved the scheme for the Inter-allied Supreme Council and General Staff (advisory), and Sir H. Wilson's appointment as British representative on the latter.

On that same day Balfour signed a letter to Lord Rothschild conveying to him "on behalf of His Majesty's Government, the following declaration of sympathy with Jewish Zionist aspirations, which has been submitted to, and approved by, the Cabinet". Then followed the Cabinet minute, thenceforth known as the "Balfour Declaration" stating that "His Majesty's Government view with favour the establishment of a national home for the Jewish people"—in Palestine. Considering that Hankey must have known about this minute, and indeed probably had a hand in drafting it, it is odd that he made no mention of it in his diary; but as it was also ignored in *The Times* it seems plain that very few people in high places realised at the time the momentous implications of this document. A principal advocate of it was Sir Mark Sykes, who was a recent convert to Zionism; and as Hankey had long entertained a profound admiration for Sykes the natural conclusion is that he allowed the new-born enthusiasm of the latter for a Jewish state in Palestine, as part of his far-reaching scheme for the post-war division of the Turkish Empire, to go through without any careful consideration of the long-term consequences. Be that as it may, the Balfour Declaration not only led to British involvement in a bitter civil war in Palestine, but contributed greatly to the alienation of Arab sympathies throughout

[1]Diary 31st Oct. 1917.

the Middle East, and so to the total destruction of British influence in that area after World War II.[1] A likely explanation of the seemingly casual way in which the Declaration was approved and published is that Hankey and all the War Cabinet were at the time deeply involved in preparing for the historic Rapallo conference. On the very next day the British delegation left for Italy.

Diary 3rd November 1917
I saw the P.M. at Downing St. for a few minutes in the morning. He was very indignant with Haig for sending Gen. Kiggell over to tell the P.M. that the proper way to save Italy was by renewing the attack on the western front. At 12.25 Adeline saw us off at Charing Cross. Uneventful journey with the P.M., Smuts, Henry Wilson, Maurice, Gregory of the Foreign Office, whose appearance the P.M. characterised as "jesuitical" (he is in fact an R.C., and a bad choice for this trip, as the P.M. will tell him nothing). I persuaded Gen. Maurice to show the P.M. a despatch brought me by Gen. Kiggell from Haig, notwithstanding that it would add fuel to the flames, but I felt bound to warn Maurice that Ll. G. would otherwise think something was being kept back from him. Maurice himself disagrees with Haig and thinks that the only way to save Italy is by direct assistance.

4th November 1917[2]
Breakfasted [at the Hotel Crillon, Paris] with the Prime Minister, General Pershing (U.S.A.), General Smuts, Wilson and Maurice. The P.M. made a very fair statement on the lack of co-ordination among the allies and the evils attendant thereon, and urged General Pershing to come to the conference in Italy, if only as a spectator with a watching brief. General Pershing agreed in the principle of more unity of control, but evidently felt great hesitation in attending the conference in view of the difficulties made by his Government about attending previous conferences. The P.M. alluded, rather tactlessly I thought, to the rigging of press campaigns by the military against the politicians and I don't think Maurice much liked it. A case of "the pot calling the kettle black", I thought . . . Meanwhile Lord Bertie,[3] our ambassador, called, and gave me the latest Paris political gossip, namely that Clemenceau was likely to come into office for a time. He also, as usual, told me much scandal about the relations between Briand and various ladies . . . Nothing

---

[1]For a full discussion of the subject see Christopher Sykes, *Cross Roads to Israel* (Collins, 1965) and E. Kedourie, *England and the Middle East* (London, 1956).
[2]Part of this entry is in *Supreme Command*, II, p. 719.
[3]Francis L. Bertie, 1st Viscount Bertie 1918 (1844–1919). Diplomat. Ambassador at Rome 1903–4 and at Paris 1905–18.

very eventful happened during the afternoon except that we heard from Rome that General Porro, Cadorna's chief of staff would probably be the military representative on the Inter-Ally General Staff. As his daughter is married to a German, and Porro himself is suspected of pro-Germanism and not trusted by our soldiers or the French, I was instructed to wire to Sir Rennell Rodd to do his best, without giving offence, to keep him out, which I did . . . The P.M. saw Briand and Haig, but I was not present at either interview. Haig seems as cocksure as ever that he is going to bring off a big coup this year. At about 8.45 we left for Italy. The Italians at first chose Nervi for the rendezvous (what a chance for the comic papers in the present state of Italian "nerves"!) but luckily changed it for Rapallo.

5th November 1917
Spent whole day travelling to Rapallo arriving about 6 p.m. I was occupied a good deal in helping Gen. Henry Wilson to organise his section of the inter-allied staff. Arrived Rapallo about 5 p.m. and had a conference that night between the British and French representatives and Foch and Robertson, who had arrived from Rome, at which the general attitude to be taken up towards the Italians was discussed . . . I ought to mention that to-day, on the journey, the Prime Minister showed me the actual text of the letter from Briand to Painlevé, sent some time ago, setting forth the terms of the German peace overtures. They struck me as extraordinarily reasonable, and I cannot understand why the French did not pursue the matter after inviting our permission to do so. The basis included the evacuation of Belgium, an arrangement about Alsace-Lorraine (though definitely excluding the left bank of the Rhine) and evacuation of all conquered territory by the enemy. It seems to me to have been a great responsibility (?) to reject so satisfactory a basis for negotiation, practically without consultation among the allies.

In fact Hankey, like Briand, had been badly misled about the German peace overtures, as had become plain when, early in October, Von Kühlmann made his notorious "No, never" speech—referring to the return of Alsace-Lorraine to France.[1]

On the very day that Hankey set out for Italy he wrote at length to Eric Drummond of the Foreign Office, who was about to leave for U.S.A., setting out what he regarded as the most important functions of his mission. The first priority was to ask the Americans "to send minelayers to assist us"; and he believed the Admiralty had "overlooked this point". Secondly he wanted to organise joint pressure on the South American republics "so as to compel them to put the German [merchant] ships in [Allied] service". Thirdly he urged Drummond "to warn the

[1] *Lloyd George*, IV, pp. 2104–9.

U.S.A. Government very seriously" against repeating Kitchener's mistake "of allowing skilled men in shipbuilding and munition works etc. to be recruited". And, lastly, he wanted to prevent the Americans "wasting their resources on the construction of unsuitable classes of vessels for anti-submarine warfare". He had heard that motorboats, which he considered useless, were being built in large numbers for such purposes, and wanted the Americans to consult the Admiralty, which had "very wide experience . . . before any special craft were built". The reader will remark that all the foregoing matters had recently been discussed by the War Cabinet.[1] Hankey knew their views and was merely briefing Drummond to ensure that the Americans took full advantage of British experience; but the proper channel for such advice was of course from the Foreign Office to the British Embassy in Washington. It seems likely that it was Spring-Rice's ill health and mental instability that caused Hankey to take direct action with Drummond. By sending Balfour a copy of his letter he protected himself against any charge of short-circuiting the Foreign Office.

As the Rapallo Conference has often been described, and Hankey himself published a large part of his diary entries for 6th–12th November[2] we will here only summarise the story of the first step in the creation of a Supreme Allied Command organisation. On arriving at Rapallo, whose "exquisite bay" Hankey had last visited when he was serving in the *Ramillies* in the closing years of the previous century,[3] his first task was to convince Robertson that the War Cabinet was "absolutely committed" to the scheme of a "Central Council of Allies", and that it would be futile, and probably fatal to himself, to maintain his attitude of sullen opposition to it. Then the conferences began, and continued in steady succession for two days with Hankey all the time striving to keep pace with his *procès-verbaux*. On 7th the British and French delegates learnt the full extent of the disaster at Caporetto. The Italian High Command, Hankey noted, had "lost all grip of the situation", and it even seemed doubtful whether the Piave line could be held. If that position was abandoned "Venice and the command of the upper Adriatic will be lost" he remarked. Lloyd George's reaction was typically firm and courageous. The first step was, he insisted, the replacement of Cadorna; but that was made difficult by the Italian desire to "save his prestige". It was Hankey who discreetly produced

[1]Hankey to Drummond 6th Nov. 1917. Balfour papers. B.M. Add. MSS. 49704.
[2]*Supreme Command*, II, pp. 719–26. [3]See pp. 39–53.

the solution of kicking him upstairs to the post of Italian permanent military adviser to the Supreme War Council; but he never dared tell Lloyd George he had done this, because he had "heard him [Lloyd George] say he wanted a better brain than Cadorna" in that body. Having surmounted that hurdle the British and French Prime Ministers promised the Italians "ample help"—to the tune of eight divisions. That day, 7th November, the Supreme War Council was formally set up, with a permanent military staff; and Hankey now saw "great possibilities in this institution"—in the post-war world as "the germ of the real League of Nations" as well as in war time. He acted as senior secretary to the conference, his French and Italian colleagues (Helbronner and Aldrovandi) agreed to accept his versions of the *procès-verbaux* as official; and he himself drafted all the agreements, including those relating to the constitution of the new body.[1]

It was Robertson who struck the only really discordant note at the Rapallo Conference. Despite all Hankey's warnings the C.I.G.S. continued to regard the Supreme War Council merely as a device of Lloyd George's to circumvent, and ultimately get rid of himself. Though such a view certainly contained an element of truth, it is equally certain that it was not the Prime Minister's only, or indeed his main purpose— which was, quite simply, to establish a centralised and co-ordinated system of strategic direction. On 7th Robertson walked ostentatiously out of the conference, asking Hankey to record his action in the Minutes.[2] After such a display of intransigence, not to say public bad manners, it is surprising that Lloyd George did not dismiss Robertson on the spot.

If it was Lloyd George who turned adversity and defeat in the field to advantage by seizing the opportunity to impose a long overdue reorganisation of the command system, it was Hankey who translated his aims into concrete form.

On the evening of 7th the British and French delegates entrained for Peschiera on Lake Garda where they were to meet the King of Italy at his G.H.Q. Hankey described him as "plucky and in good heart, but a pathetic figure with his country tumbling about his ears". Victor Emmanuel accepted the replacement of Cadorna without demur; but there was disagreement about his successor. Foch and Robertson wanted the Duke of Aosta, but he was regarded as unacceptable "for

[1] Diary 7th Nov. 1917. Part reproduced in *Supreme Command*, II, pp. 720–1.
[2] See Victor Bonham Carter, *Soldier True* (Muller, 1963), p. 300.

dynastic reasons".[1] The choice finally fell on Armando Diaz,[2] despite the fact that he had only been a corps commander for about three months.

That evening the French delegates were dropped at Brescia, while the British party went on to Aix-les-Bains, with the double object of enjoying a brief rest and allowing time for Lloyd George to prepare the speech which he was to make on returning to Paris about the creation of the Supreme War Council. The letter reproduced below is a revealing description of Lloyd George's methods of manipulating the Press to gain support for his policy.

To Lady Hankey. Aix-les-Bains. 10th November 1917

As General Smuts is hastening home to-morrow I have another opportunity for a letter. This morning the Prime Minister asked *me* to hurry home as rapidly as possible, in order to show Milner the draft of the very drastic speech that he is to deliver in Paris on Monday. If Milner approved, he was to set about rigging the Press in favour of the speech. This evening the idea developed a good deal. As Milner is not *bien vu* by the Liberal press, I was asked to see Donald of the Chronicle and Scott of the Manchester Guardian and other gentlemen who would influence the provincial Liberal press. After thinking the matter over I decided that it would not do . . . This, of course, I did not say to Ll. G. What I did say was that I would do anything to serve him, but I was not convinced that I could best serve him in the long run in this particular manner. That I occupied rather a unique position, as a public servant of unassailable integrity; outside all political movements; and known to be absolutely set on winning this war. That this position was a really valuable asset to him, but that it might be to some extent undermined by this excursion for the purpose of influencing the Press. The General Staff, though not really attacked in Lloyd George's speech more than politicians, will assume it to be intended as an attack on them. When they get to know—as they probably will—that I have been rigging the Press against them (as they will conceive it) I shall at once lose their confidence. They will let the whole thing leak out, and I shall be attacked in the organs hostile to Lloyd George. Hence in order to achieve an ephemeral advantage he will lose such solid asset as my position and reputation is to him . . . He and Smuts were both very quick to take my point, and decided that the best plan would be for

---

[1]Emmanuel-Philibert, Duke of Aosta (1869–1931). A member of the cadet branch of the House of Savoy. Commanded Italian forces without much success against Austrians in World War I. Awarded Marshal's baton 1926.

[2]1861–1928. Commander-in-Chief, Italian armies at defence of Piave 1917, and battle of Vittorio Veneto 1918; for which he was made "Duke of Victory". Minister for War in Mussolini's first cabinet 1922–4. Marshal 1924.

Smuts to go home and undertake the Press campaign while I should accompany the Prime Minister to the lunch, where he is to make the speech. I was much relieved by this decision . . .

On the morning of 11th the party reached Paris, where Lloyd George at once immersed himself in French politics. Thus he did his best to persuade his old ally Albert Thomas, now out of office, to join Painlevé's government instead of attacking it. Then he went off to see Clemenceau,[1] whom Hankey described as "this curious old character, this bitter-tongued political journalist patriot", with the object of persuading him to support the Supreme War Council in his paper *L'Homme Enchainé*.[2] Next Venizelos, whom Hankey had long admired and now described as "vivacious and clear-headed", appeared on the scene; and over dinner Lloyd George did his best to persuade Painlevé to form a coalition government on the model of his own, with Thomas as Minister of War and Briand playing the part of "the French Bonar Law".[3] However none of these suggestions held any appeal for Painlevé, who clung to office until defeated. Next day, after "a final tuning up" Lloyd George delivered his carefully prepared speech. Hankey described it in his diary, no doubt correctly, as "a wonderful rhetorical performance"; but in his memoirs he also called it "a terrible indictment of the lack of unity in counsel and in action by the Allies".[4] Presumably by the time he wrote those volumes he had forgotten how he himself had originally been "horrified" by Lloyd George's concept of a "Council of Allies".

While in Paris Hankey had "a long walk and talk with Lord Esher", who reported that Robertson was "in a resentful mood" and that the General Staff was likely to ostracise Henry Wilson and the Supreme Council—unless some powerful politician like Milner was on the spot to see Wilson was given fair play.[5] In his journal Esher also made a record of that conversation. "He [Hankey] will have to work hard to keep the new Allied General Staff from perishing of atrophy", he wrote, ". . . Every man's hand is against it . . . Henry Wilson cannot

[1]Georges Clemenceau (1841–1929). French journalist, politician (Radical, then Repub.) and patriot. Prime Minister and Minister of Interior 1906–9. Again Prime Minister 1917–20. With Lloyd George the chief architect of the Allied victory of 1918. Justifiably earned the nickname of "Le Tigre".
[2]When in 1914 the censor suppressed Clemenceau's paper *L'Homme Libre* for its criticism of the government he continued to publish it under this new title.
[3]Diary 11th Nov. 1917.
[4]*Supreme Command*, II, p. 726.   [5]*ibid.*

stand alone. Hankey will back up hard, and although he is not over-hopeful, thinks that Ll. G. is the only possible saviour of the compromised position. He has served under Asquith and is sure that Ll. G. is the better man for the war".[1] But in truth both Hankey and Esher underestimated the cleverness with which Lloyd George had chosen both the time and the setting to play his cards; and events were moving rapidly in favour of his *protégé* Henry Wilson.

Diary 13th November 1917
Arrived Calais about 8 p.m. and travelled to London. On board the boat I had a long talk with M. Venizelos, who was very strong on the point that the Greeks could have carried the Dardanelles by landing a force at the time of the naval bombardment. He also said that the reason for Constantine's pro-Germanism was simply his desire to secure the supremacy of autocratic over democratic Government. Lunched with Ll. George and Milner, during which I arranged an understanding that Milner should go to Paris to inaugurate the new Supreme War Council, remaining some weeks. Cabinet at 4 p.m. at which Ll. G. described our recent visit to France and Italy . . .

14th November[2]
War Cabinet as usual at 11.30. The Army Council had put in an absurd paper suggesting that they alone had the right to issue instructions to the Permanent Mily. Adviser of the Supreme War Council. It was decided that Carson and Smuts should go into the question. We had a meeting on the following afternoon [15th] and they prepared a reply based on a draft that I had put up viz. to the effect that the Army Council undoubtedly possessed the right they claim, but that the instructions they could issue must be based on the instructions of the Govt., and we relied on their co-operation in this important innovation. In the afternoon I heard Ll. G.'s statement in Parliament re the Supreme War Council.[3]

In fact Lloyd George was answering a Private Notice question by Asquith about "the precise functions of the proposed Inter-Allied Council and in particular of its Military Staff", and whether the House would be given an early opportunity to discuss "the proposed arrangements and the statements made in connection therewith in the Prime Minister's Paris speech". The Cabinet evidently considered and approved Lloyd George's reply, which consisted of reading the terms

[1]Esher, *Journals*, Vol. IV, pp. 158–9.
[2]This entry is partly reproduced in bowdlerised form in *Supreme Command*, II, pp. 727–8.
[3]Appendix to W.C.273 of 14th Nov. 1917. Cab. 21/91. Parl. Deb., Commons, Vol. XCIX, Cols. 389–90.

of the actual agreement signed at Rapallo. He offered to set aside a day in the following week if the House desired, and the debate took place on 19th.

On the same day that Lloyd George was answering Asquith's somewhat hostile question in the House the Painlevé government fell; and, as Lloyd George has put it, "France seemed to have exhausted its waiting list of possible and seasoned Premiers . . . There was only one man left, and it is not too much to say that no one wanted him".[1] Very reluctantly President Poincaré summoned the 76-year-old Clemenceau to the Elysée and asked him to form a government.

It seems clear from the next day's diary entry that Asquith was involved in an attempt, instigated by Robertson, to embarrass, if not upset, the government on the issue of the powers of the Supreme War Council; and, typically, Mrs. Asquith at once plunged into the fray in what she conceived to be her husband's interests.

Diary 15th November 1917[2]

War Cabinet at 11.30. I lunched with the Asquiths, having Ll. George's consent. Venizelos was there. Asquith, while talking of the Italian situation, let the cat slip out of the bag, mentioning that he had seen Robertson that morning. I have no doubt that Robertson is intreaguing [sic] like the deuce. Last night Col. House let slip that Robertson was coming to see him this morning. His private secretary, thinking I was on Robertson's staff, came in to say that the American Gen. Bliss[3] particularly wanted Robertson to repeat to House, what he had said to him! Why does Robertson cut the War Cabinet and see Col. House and Mr. Asquith, leader of the opposition. Was it in order to intreague against the Supreme War Council? I suspect . . . In the evening Storr[4] showed me a letter he had received from some friend in the city to the effect that at a lunch where he had been, one of the guests was Robertson's sister-in-law. She had arrived v. late and had explained the reason to be that Mrs. Asquith had rung up to beg her to use her influence with Robertson to induce him and Haig to resign, on the ground that if they did the Govt. would fall on Monday! Carson told me this afternoon that he was very sick with Ll. George's speech and opposed to the Supreme War Council, but meant to stick to him, because he thought he was the only man to win the war. Had a long talk at teatime with St. Loe Strachey of [The]

[1] *Lloyd George*, Vol. V, p. 2675.
[2] Part of this entry only is in *Supreme Command*, II, p. 728.
[3] General Tasker H. Bliss (1853–1930). American soldier. Chief of Staff, U.S. Army and U.S. Military Representative on Supreme War Council 1917. A "Commissioner to Negotiate Peace" 1918–19.
[4] Lieut.-Colonel L. Storr. Assistant Secretary of War Cabinet 1916–20.

Spectator, who has written a violent article against Ll. G. I put Ll. G's point of view, and he said he was glad he had not seen me before, because he would not have written his article.

16th November
Batterbee, Walter Long's rather gloomy private secretary, came to me early with a face like his chief's name to give me a message for the P.M. from Long. This was to the effect that some person in Asquith's entourage had been to Long and told him (a) that Robertson and Haig had intended to resign over the Allied Supreme War Council, but that Asquith had induced him not to and (b) that Ll. G. had asked Asquith to join the Govt. Ll. G. told me that the latter was untrue. War Cabinets at 11.30 and 6 p.m., the latter to consider a reply to the Army Council, which was agreed to and transmitted by me to the secretary of the Army Council after the meeting . . . Lunched with Aston[1] and suggested he should take Amery's place.

It was probably a result of the Rapallo conference, and of the discussions in Paris that followed it, that caused Hankey at this time to come out whole-heartedly in favour of Henry Wilson being appointed to the Supreme Council. The memorandum reproduced below shows how fundamentally Hankey had changed his mind regarding Wilson since the Admiralty-War Office clash over strategy in 1911.[2]

Hankey to Lloyd George. Offices of the War Cabinet. 16th November 1917[3]
CONFIDENTIAL
Prime Minister
Note in regard to General Sir Henry Wilson.
It will be difficult to find any Officer in the British Army more peculiarly suited to the post for which he is designated than General Sir Henry Wilson. He is a profound student of war. *He was one of the officers in whom the late Lord Roberts had the greatest confidence.* Before the War for three years he held the post of Commandant of the Staff College at Camberley, subsequent to which he became Director of Military Operations on the General Staff, a post which he was holding when war broke out. As Director of Military Operations one of the principal duties of General Wilson was to organise the transport of the original Expeditionary Force to, and its concentration in, France. It is largely due to the success of these arrangements that the British Army was enabled to arrive in time to take up its invaluable position on the left of the French

[1]General Aston, Hankey's former mentor in the R.M.A. (see pp. 33 and 113) did join the War Cabinet Secretariat in 1918 on Amery being transferred to Versailles as Hankey's link with the Supreme War Council (see p. 464).
[2]See pp. 101–2.
[3]Cab. 21/91. The original is in Lloyd George papers F/23/1/27 and includes the italicised sentence in holograph.

armies. During the War General Wilson has filled a considerable variety of appointments, including that of Head of the British Mission at the French General Headquarters, the Command of a Corps, and a visit to Russia as the principal Military expert on Lord Milner's Mission. He was present at the Rome Conference of the Allies last January, and within the last few days has been engaged on important duty on the Italian front. Very few British Officers of any rank have the same intimate knowledge of and sympathy with the French Army. Not the least valuable of General Wilson's qualifications for this post is his close personal friendship with General Foch, who has been selected by the French Government as their Permanent Military Representative with the Supreme War Council.

Diary 19th November 1917
War Cabinet 11.30. Attended House of Commons to hear P.M.'s great and remarkable speech in reply to Asquith on subject of Supreme War Council.[1] Had to stay late at House, and dined with Astor at his beautiful house, 4 St. James' Square. The "Round Table" group were there Milner, Carson, Geoffrey Dawson (editor of *The Times*), Philip Kerr, and [F. S.] Oliver. The amusing thing was the intense desire of Geoffrey Dawson that Lord Northcliffe, the proprietor of *The Times*, should return to America.

To return to the question of the formation of an Air Ministry, on 11th November Milner circulated a memorandum saying that he had talked to both Sir William Weir and J. L. Baird[2] who, like himself, "believe wholly in Independent Air Warfare". Hankey, as we have seen, was very lukewarm about the whole idea—which may well account for the slow progress made since the Cabinet had approved the Smuts Committee's report in August. Lloyd George, however, unquestionably sounded Northcliffe about becoming Secretary of State for Air; and when on 16th November Northcliffe published a letter in *The Times* declining the office the fat was in the fire. Lord Cowdray, the President of the Air Board, who had naturally regarded himself as the heir apparent to the new Ministry, at once resigned and the Cabinet was faced with the need to find a substitute.[3] The choice finally fell on Lord

[1] Parl. Deb., Commons, Vol. XCIX, Cols. 893–906.
[2] 1874–1941. 1st Viscount Stonehaven 1938. Politician (Cons.). Parliamentary Member of Air Board 1916–18 and Under-Secretary of State for R.A.F. 1918. Parliamentary Under-Secretary of State, Home Office 1919–22. Minister of Transport 1922–4. Governor General of Australia 1925–30. Chairman, Conservative Party Organisation 1931–6.
[3] See S. W. Roskill *Documents Relating to the Naval Air Service 1908–1918* (Navy Records Society, 1969) for a full account of this fracas.

Rothermere,[1] Northcliffe's younger brother; and that, as we shall see, was not a success.

Diary 20th November 1917
Breakfast with Ll. George, Milner, Smuts, Kerr, Lord Reading and Swinton to consider the P.M.'s speech to the U.S.A. mission. Conference with the Mission at 11.30. Busy afternoon getting out Minutes, in order to show the Yankees (and Northcliffe who was present) how quickly we work. Helped Kerr to get out a press communiqué. Dined with Milner at Brooks's to meet Johnny Baird M.P. and Weir, both of the Air Board, the object being to see whether Weir would do as Air Minister. Milner suggested I should take it, but I said I wouldn't look at it. Personally I don't think Weir has the personality and would prefer Churchill or even Austen Chamberlain.[2]

Here we may take leave of the political jockeying in London which arose out of the formation of the Supreme War Council, and of the prolonged and difficult birth pangs of the new Air Ministry and return to events on the western front. On 20th November 381 tanks "rolled forward in the half light upon the astonished Germans" in the Cambrai sector, and there followed "perhaps the most dramatic of all episodes in the World War".[3] But the original plan for a large scale raid, to set off to some extent the costly stalemate at Ypres, had been changed to a major offensive with far-reaching aims; and virtually no reserves had been assembled to exploit the success achieved by the initial surprise. Despite the three main German defence lines having been quickly overrun, they were allowed time to recover from the shock, and on 30th they counter-attacked so successfully that General Byng's Third Army was for a time endangered. Thus was one of the greatest opportunities of the war sacrificed by misuse of the new weapon and faulty planning. Hankey's initial optimism was shared by the whole country, for on 21st the bells of London rang out in joyous but premature peals of victory; and his disappointment at the final outcome was all the more acute because of the part he himself had played in the development of the tank.

[1] Harold S. Harmsworth, 1st Baron Rothermere 1914 (1866–1940). Director-General, Royal Army Clothing Department 1916–17. Secretary of State for Royal Air Force Jan.–April 1918.
[2] This judgement of Weir was to be falsified by his service as Secretary of State for Air in 1918 and by his efforts to prepare the Royal Air Force for World War II in the 1930s. See W. J. Reader, *Architect of Air Power* (Collins, 1968) for a full assessment of his work—generally behind the scenes.
[3] *Liddell Hart*, pp. 435–48.

Diary 21st November 1917

The great event to-day is the full news of the great tank attack near Cambrai, where 400 tanks have burst right through all the German lines of defence and let through the cavalry. It is in a sense a great personal triumph for me, as I have always from the first day of the tanks advocated an attack on these lines. Also we are within 4 miles of Jerusalem, and have nearly finished the job in East Africa. A great day after all the doleful news from Italy. I attended a lunch given by the P.M. to the American mission, sitting next to Auchincloss, Col. House's private secretary.[1] I gave him my plan for a League of Nations with a great central bureau (like an International War Cabinet) built up among the allies during the war and extended after the war to their present enemies. He was much interested and promised to talk to Col. House about it. Lord Robert Cecil, to whom I had explained it on the previous evening had also been very interested. Afterwards I took him [? Auchincloss] to my office and gave at his request, an exposition of the War Cabinet system, with a view to an adaptation to the needs of the U.S.A.[2] Had a long talk with Carson in the evening about Amery and whether he is to go to the staff of Gen. Wilson on the Supreme War Council.

22nd November

War Cabinet 11.30. Lunched with Ll. George, Gen. Smuts, and Gen. Henry Wilson. Afterwards arranged with Henry Wilson to establish an outlying branch of my office at Versailles, in connection with the Supreme War Council . . .

23rd November

War Cabinet 11.30. The Admiralty having received information which leads them to believe that the Bolsheviks mean to hand the Russian fleet over to Germany, the following action by the Admiralty was approved:—(1) British submarines to be destroyed and the crews brought home; (2) Russian officers faithful to the allies to be encouraged to man the Russian destroyers and make a dash for the entrance to the Baltic; (3) Russian officers to be induced to blow up the four Russian "Dreadnoughts". The v. serious political consequences were not overlooked . . . I drafted the above conclusion, which was to be recorded as a single manuscript copy with a copy to the First Lord. I then went to show the draft to Geddes and afterwards to the Prime Minister. Both told me of a new scheme whereby Geddes is to become director of all Allied Transportation by rail and ship, in order to improve the

[1]Gordon Auchincloss (1886–1943). American lawyer. Married a daughter of Colonel E. M. House 1912. Secretary of U.S. Mission to Britain and France 1917, and to Colonel House during Armistice and Peace negotiations 1918–19.
[2]On 19th Nov. Hankey circulated a "Note" on the subject of the American mission attending next day's War Cabinet. GT. 2671. Cab. 24/32.

arrangements on the Western and Italian fronts, and for bringing over the Americans. The P.M. said he would like me as First Lord in Geddes's place, but that he could not run the War Cabinet without me. He was very flattering. . . . N.B. I find I have omitted two matters of some importance. The first is that Ll. George told me this evening that he had decided to risk his whole political reputation, if necessary, in order to stop these bloody attacks of the Somme-Flanders type. The second is that Sir Grimwood Mears, the Secretary of the Dardanelles Commission, called to say that the Report contained nothing detrimental to the future military career of Sir Ian Hamilton, and that Mr. Justice Pickford, the Chairman of the Commission was prepared to say as much in writing to the P.M. This was important, because Ian Hamilton had been to see me yesterday morning to say that by Dec. 16th he would have been unemployed for 2 years, and would automatically go on the retired list; and that Lord French had applied for his appointment to the Eastern Command. I therefore reported the matter to Lord Derby and the War Cabinet. Eventually it was decided that the Prime Minister should obtain an advance copy of the Report, and that the decision should be taken after he had read it.[1] . . .

24th November
I woke at 6 a.m. with a "brainwave" on the subject of the Future Policy of the War, which is to be discussed by the War Cabinet on the 26th. I lit candles and wrote in bed until 8.30 and sent the manuscript up to town to be typed, and forwarded to Ll. George at Walton Heath . . . The object of my Memo. was to crystallise Ll. G.'s policy, in order to shorten the discussion, rather than to set forth my own views. Personally I think that, if Russia has really decided to make a separate peace, we ought to make [a] plan also at Russia's expense, since, anyhow, Germany will take what she can from Russia and would probably give up gladly what we want, whereas by prolonging the war we shall stiffen her back, and we may not be strong enough to take what we want by force. Thus Germany may be the gainer east and west. If, however, the war is to be prolonged, I am in agreement with Lloyd George's military policy, and not with that of Haig and Robertson.

26th November 1917
War Cabinet at 10.30 a.m. The plan was to have a full dress discussion on military policy conducted from 10.30 to 12.0 by the War Cabinet themselves . . . reassembling with military experts at 12.30, and continuing all day without intermission until a decision was reached. The first part of the programme was realised, and, at the noon adjournment the Cabinet were on the verge of very important decisions with regard to priority of shipbuilding

[1]In fact General Hamilton was not given another appointment.

in general. When, however, they re-assembled, after hearing Bonar Law, who had been urging us not to prejudge the questions to be discussed at the Supreme War Council, suddenly said "Well, George,[1] we have nothing further to discuss have we" and to my astonishment the meeting was broken up! During the morning I showed Gen. Smuts the Memo. I had written on Saturday [24th]. He was very taken with it and asked for a copy, which I gave him. The Prime Minister told me he had come with the intention of using it as his brief, but that Milner and Bonar Law had dislocated his intentions ... I had been told not to record any Minutes, but I did so, because they had been on the verge of such important conclusions ... In the afternoon at 3 p.m. I saw Lord Derby whom I found to be still very hostile to the Supreme War Council. He has not yet made Henry Wilson a full General as desired by the War Cabinet, and flatly declines to make Amery a Lt. Col. and G.S.O.I. on taking up his new appointment at Versailles.

Next day Hankey crossed to France once again, this time with "an enormous crowd" of politicians and military and naval experts from all the Allied nations—some 60 persons in all—for further conferences on the setting up of the Supreme War Council. As Esher had foretold, and Hankey had always feared, the birth-pangs of the new organisation proved difficult.

Diary 27th November 1917
... During the journey Lord Northcliffe was badgering me continually about a telegram he had received from Canada to the effect that Borden is short of funds for his election campaign: that Laurier[2] is amply supplied (Northcliffe thinks from German sources); and that the election, and with it, the principle of compulsory service, necessary for the maintenance of the Canadian divisions, will be lost. I had great difficulty in enlisting Ll. George's interest, but eventually got his permission to send a telegram to Bonar Law to the effect that the Government would have nothing to do with the matter, but that perhaps he privately could pass it on to some private individual who would take the matter up. I did this because I knew that Bonar Law had many Canadian friends. I dined with Frazier of the U.S. embassy,[3] and Auchincloss, Col. House's private secretary, to whom I gave a note prepared by Swinton under my instructions, describing the methods by which we ran the War Cabinet ... Before dinner Helbronner had called and had asked me

[1]Lloyd George loathed being addressed as "George", and Bonar Law seems often to have done so with the object of annoying him.
[2]See p. 107.
[3]Though Hankey sometimes wrote this man's name as Frazer or Frasier it was almost certainly Arthur H. Frazier (1868–?). American diplomat. Second Secretary at Vienna 1911–15 and Secretary at Paris embassy from March 1915.

to dinner on Thursday to meet Painlevé, which I accepted . . . After Helbronner came Col. Spears our Liaison officer who told me—

1   that Clemenceau is out to wreck the scheme of a Supreme War Council.
2   that it was only the previous day that he had consented to the establishment at Versailles of the permanent military representatives.
3   that he was aiming at a single Commander-in-Chief.
4   that he intended that Foch should be Chief of the Staff, as well as the French permanent military adviser to the Supreme War Council, a point which Ll. George had hotly contested and fought against at Rapallo, in order to avoid the domination of the French War Office.

I reported these matters to the Prime Minister before dinner. It was clear that Foch had been at work on the new French Prime Minister, just as Robertson had been at work on Foch in Italy, to wreck the new scheme and substitute the Chiefs of the various General Staffs for the Permanent Military Representatives, as the advisers of the new Supreme War Council. After dinner I had a talk with Lord Reading and Sir William Wiseman,[1] an Englishman in Col. House's confidence who accompanies the U.S.A. mission. They gave me the astounding news that Ll. George was willing to adopt a proposal made by M. Clemenceau to Col. House that the civilian element should be dropped out of the new Supreme War Council. I pointed out that, although this might be very convenient to the Americans, who find it impossible to establish a civilian counterpart to the British, French, and Italian Prime Ministers on the new Council, it would make the machine quite unworkable . . . The machinery for communicating the recommendations of the Council to four separate Governments and for adjusting differences of opinion, would be infinitely cumbersome. Moreover matters which concern the place and approximate dates of military operations and require excessive [sic] secrecy, do not lend themselves to such methods. All that would happen would be to substitute incessant conferences for the Standing Council. I felt absolutely certain that, if the Prime Minister had agreed to anything of the kind, it had only been because he *knew* that this would be the case. During the evening, Count Horodyski, the Pole, buttonholed me and developed a scheme for rallying together the Poles and Cossacks and Czechs, with a nucleus of American troops, in Russia. I don't like the fellow, whom I regard as a self seeker and possible spy, but Eric Drummond, George Clerk and others think well of him.

[1] 10th Baronet (1885–1962). Businessman and Head of British Intelligence in U.S.A. in World War I. Acted as intermediary between British government and Colonel E. M. House, with whom he established a close friendship. Returned to business in U.S.A. between the wars, and in World War II gave much assistance to the British Missions in that country.

28th November 1917

Before breakfast I tackled the P.M., whom I found in bed, on the subject of civilian control in the Supreme War Council, and found, as I had anticipated, that any sacrifice of civilian control that he had possibly appeared to assent to had only been because he knew that *ad hoc* conferences would have to be substituted for a permanent Council. I stiffened him up against any yielding, pointing out that Clemenceau and House were absolutely new and inexperienced in this thing and that he must stick to his guns. I did this, not because I have any special affection for the Supreme War Council, but because I am bound to back my Chief, and I see that he would become ridiculous if it was thrown over and revised now, as it would be by the withdrawal of the Prime Ministers, who constitute the civilian element. After breakfast I accompanied Ll. George to the French Ministry of War, and sat in the ante-room while he saw Clemenceau. The interview was satisfactory, except that Clemenceau told Lloyd George that General Foch would not be the French Permanent Military Adviser to the Supreme War Council. Lloyd George undertook that I would draft his opening statement for the Supreme War Council next Saturday.

Among other things M. Clemenceau told Ll. George that he would make peace with Turkey on any terms; that he did not want Syria for France; pressed on this point, he said that if Ll. George could get him a protectorate over Syria for France he would not refuse it "as it would please some reactionaries", but he attached no importance to it; he agreed that Palestine should not be given back to Turkey. He gave Lloyd George a free hand to negotiate with Turkey and make the best terms he could. This is of some importance because Ll. George saw a Greek named Zaharoff (the same man whom Asquith and McKenna had employed earlier in the war in Greece[1]), who has been in touch with Enver [Pasha] Z. reports that Enver is unwilling to treat. He says, however, that the Turks are in a state of great depression. They are short of food and call vainly on the Germans to help them. They are short of coal, and their railway communications are in consequence utterly disorganised. This has prevented them from any attempt to recover Bagdad, on which they set great store. Ll. George is very indignant with Robertson for not pressing on more strongly in Palestine in these circumstances, and has been bursting out on the subject all day. At 11 a.m. Milner turned up, and he and I discussed a statement to be made by Clemenceau to the Supreme War Council, which Ll. G. has asked me to draft. Then I got to work . . . I find in yesterday's diary I omitted to mention two important peace overtures mentioned by Drummond:—Firstly Waugh,[2] late Consul-General in Constantinople, is to meet some Turks in Mytilene in connection with prisoners,

[1]See p. 239.
[2]Later Sir A. Telford Waugh (1865-1950). Consular Service officer. Organised for

but is authorised to listen to any proposals. Secondly Lord Newton[1], who was travelling with us en route to Switzerland to discuss prisoners of war with a Turkish delegation, has an F.O. [Foreign Office] man with him, who is authorised to listen to proposals. Thirdly Austria has made through Berne a serious proposal for a separate peace. Balfour has replied very stiffly, asking for proposals in writing for us to discuss with our allies, but influences are at work to induce a more pliant attitude on his part . . .

29th November 1917

Spent a very fussy [sic] day with many callers and in long discussions with Lord Milner and Gen. Wilson. In the afternoon I accompanied P.M. to Foreign Office at about 5 p.m., Balfour, who was having conversations there having sent for him urgently. I was not admitted to M. Pichon's[2] room and sat outside with Count Aldrovandi and an American. While we were waiting we received news that the Russians were making an armistice with the enemy. Meanwhile very important discussions were taking place inside. In fact Ll. George had succeeded in extracting permission to hear what the Austrians had to say about a separate peace, in which direction they have made advances at Berne. Balfour is rather annoyed about it, but I am sure it is right . . .

30th November 1917

Breakfast with P.M., Lord Reading, Painlevé, Franklin Bouillon, and Helbronner. Like everyone else they think that Clemenceau will not last long—only long enough to clean up the *"affaire* Bolo" and the *"affaire* Malvy".[3] The conference opened at 10.30 a.m. an absurd affair with about

the British Contraband Department control of Greek trade during World War I. Consul-General at Constantinople 1920–29.

[1]2nd Baron Newton (1857–1942). Diplomat and politician (Cons.). Paymaster-General 1915–16. Controller of Prisoners of War Department 1916–19.

[2]Stephen Pichon (1857–1933). French politician (Radical). Senator 1906–24. Foreign Minister 1906–11, 1913 and 1917–20 during which he was a member of French War Committee.

[3]This refers to Clemenceau's ruthless cleaning up of the Augean stables of corruption and treachery which he found on his accession to power. Paul Marie Bolo (dubbed Bolo Pasha by the Khedive of Egypt in 1914) was an utterly fraudulent purveyor of German (or Egyptian) gold for the subversion of France. He was shot for treason on 17th April 1918. The Minister of Interior at the time had been Louis Malvy (1875–1949), and on Clemenceau's instigation he was brought to trial before the Senate. Clemenceau then set out to break the radical politician Joseph Caillaux (1863–1944), who had played an equivocal, though probably not overtly corrupt or treacherous part in these affairs. He too was tried and sentenced to imprisonment. See Richard M. Watt, *Dare Call it Treason* (Chatto & Windus, 1964).

120 persons present of every imaginable race and colour . . . It was wisely
broken up by Clemenceau at once into Conferences and Sub-Committees . . .
In afternoon the conference at F.O. was renewed. I was present this time.
Subject—the question of a declaration to Russia, and Japanese co-operation
in the war. No business done. Spent evening dictating long *procès-verbal*.
Dined with C.I.G.S. and Curzon, who spent the whole time in abusing the
new Supreme War Council, which was rather depressing, expecially as it had
a personal (?) snap. However I counter-attacked and gave as much as I got,
eventually bombing (?) them out of their position by chaff.

The first meeting of the Supreme War Council took place at the
Hotel Trianon, Versailles, on Saturday 1st December and its success
exceeded Hankey's expectations—thanks largely to the preliminary
talks which had taken place between Lloyd George and Clemenceau.
The opening speech by the latter, which Hankey had drafted on Lloyd
George's instructions, followed closely the memorandum he had
written shortly before leaving London. In it Clemenceau laid great
emphasis on aspects of the war such as the economic "staying power"
of the Allies, the shipping and shipbuilding situation, and the most
efficient employment of man-power, as well as on current and future
military problems. We have already seen how Hankey had for a long
time been stressing to the War Cabinet that civilian problems were just
as important as military ones. Thus the prominence given to them at
the Versailles meeting gave him considerable satisfaction. "The
meeting was a great success", he recorded in his diary; and added, not
very modestly, "the P.M. and I were in the best possible form". The
whole of the secretarial arrangements were carried out by the small
contingent Hankey had brought over from his office. He himself
drafted the eight resolutions which were adopted, and the *procès-verbal*
was "in the hands of every member of the Council the same evening".
The only jarring note was struck by Robertson's continued surliness;
but at least he and Henry Wilson, in an exchange of notes abusing the
Council, appeared to Hankey to be "beginning to get on terms".
Hankey spent the evening of that climactic day "winding up affairs",
and after a very short night's rest started home early on 2nd.[1] One
cannot but admire the skill with which Lloyd George exploited the
opportunity offered by the crushing defeat suffered in Italy to get
an integrated command organisation adopted. He and Hankey

[1] Diary 1st Dec. 1917. Parts of this entry are reproduced and other parts summarised
in *Supreme Command*, II, pp. 732–3.

both allowed themselves a few days' well-earned rest on their return home.

Diary 5th December 1917

War Cabinet at 11.30. Ll. G. is frightfully indignant with Haig for the recent reverse near Cambrai. He suggested to me that I was wrong in advising him to retain Haig last spring, and that our comparative lack of success this year is due to this. He forgets that, if he had upset Haig, he would have been upset himself, and that he had lately said repeatedly what an admiration he has for Haig. Lunched with the Asquiths.

6th December 1917[1]

War Cabinet at 11.30. Decided to appoint a Committee to review the whole question of manpower. The War Office representatives (Derby and Gen. Macready[2]) made a very bad impression by suggesting that if large numbers of men are not recruited and sent out at once Haig's army would not be able to hold the line . . . This is absolutely inconsistent with Haig's continued reports of bad German moral[e], and that the German Divns. have been put through the mill in Flanders and knocked out one by one. Only a week or two ago he was seriously urging a recommencement of the Flanders offensive in February or March even on the assumption that 30 [German] divisions can be brought from the Russian front . . . The fact is, however, that the War Office figures and statements are utterly unreliable, and their facts are twisted to support their arguments. If they want men they make out that they can hardly hold the line (although we and the French have a numerical superiority of nearly half a million rifles over the enemy). If they want to do an offensive they make out that the enemy is exhausted and demoralised, and that they have lots of men . . . Afterwards I saw Bonar Law to discuss with him the personnel of the new Committee, over which the P.M. wants to preside. In the afternoon Philip Kerr called on me and outlined to me my own scheme (which he has arrived at independently) for the development of the Supreme War Council into a League of Nations.

The last month of the year opened with Lloyd George unwell and Hankey afflicted with lumbago. Both were obviously suffering from the great strain of past few weeks. Yet the problem of reviewing and re-allocating Britain's dwindling resources of manpower had to be tackled. Accordingly on 6th December a committee was set up under the Prime Minister's chairmanship "to produce a scheme for co-ordina-

[1]A small part of this entry is in *Supreme Command*, II, p. 739.
[2]Later General Sir C. F. Nevil Macready (1862–1946). Director of Personal Services 1910–14. Adjutant-General, B.E.F. 1914–16 and Member of Army Council 1916. Adjutant-General to the Forces 1916–18. Commissioner of Metropolitan Police 1918–20. G.O. C-in-C, Forces in Ireland 1920–2.

tion of Man-power".[1] This greatly added to Hankey's burdens, and his diary suffered in consequence. For the latter part of the month he only found time for weekly summaries.

Diary 16th December 1917
. . . The whole position is very difficult. Russia practically out of the war; Italy very much under the weather after [her] defeat; France unreliable; the U.S.A. not nearly ready; our own man-power much exhausted by the senseless hammerings of the last three years; and great demands for labour to build ships and for agriculture, timber cutting etc.; labour in a disgruntled state and unwilling to make concessions for combing out even those few men who can be spared. The total deficit for the army is about half a million category "A" men and over 800,000 men of all classes. Ll. G. rightly refused to allow a continuance (?) of strategical methods that are so wasteful in human life and wants to get rid of Haig and Robertson. His mind has constantly been dwelling on this throughout the week. . . . The most promising hope is to get Austria out, and it is now definitely decided that Smuts is to go to Switzerland to meet Count Mensdorff.[2] . . . On Saturday [15th] the Man-Power Ctee. met again. They never even opened my draft report, but talked for 2 hours on all sorts of subjects, many of them having no relation to man-power. Finally the P.M. summed up his own views and asked me to re-draft my report on these lines and to circulate [it] in time for the Cabinet to discuss it on Monday. As the report covers more than 30 pages of foolscap this meant circulating [it] the same evening if anyone was to have time to read it. So, after a snack of lunch, I settled down at about 2.30 and worked incessantly until nearly 10 p.m., when the report was circulated. . . .

Hankey sent the draft "Notes for a Report by the Man Power Committee", referred to in the foregoing diary entry, to Lloyd George from Highstead on 13th. Considering that it was prepared at such very short notice it was an astonishingly complete survey of the enemy's as well as the Allied nations' situation and problems.[3] Although, as we will see shortly, it did not gain acceptance as it stood, it won for Hankey the warm praise of at least one member of the Committee.

Curzon to Hankey. 1 Carlton House Terrace, 21st December 1917. Holograph
My dear Hankey,
    Before we separate permit me to congratulate you on the splendid piece of

[1] Minutes in Cab. 27/14. The report was not finally rendered until 1st March 1918.
[2] Count Albert Mensdorff Pouilly. Austro-Hungarian ambassador in London 1904–14.
[3] Original (slightly incomplete) in Lloyd George papers F/23/1/30.

work you have done in writing and rewriting the Reports of the Man Power Committee.

No one else could have performed the task with anything approaching the same mastery of the facts, marshalling of the evidence and balance of judgements.

Wishing you a happy Xmas I am

Yours ever

At this juncture Hankey was forced to turn his attention to Robertson's attempt to cramp the power of the Supreme War Council and clip the wings of the British Military Representative. On 7th December, only six days after the new body first met, the War Office told Henry Wilson that he was to inform them of any advice he might intend to give the Supreme Council—an instruction to which Wilson took understandable exception.[1] He protested on this score to Hankey who, scenting a plot by the General Staff to strangle the infant organisation at birth, at once asked Lloyd George if he wished the matter to be raised in Cabinet.[2] Lloyd George, however, did not do so—possibly because he had so many other problems on his mind or possibly because he was already planning his next move to unseat Robertson.

Diary 23rd December 1917[3]

. . . It has been an unsatisfactory, unbusinesslike week so far as the War Cabinet are concerned. Two days were spent on discussion of my draft man-power report, but entirely on questions of detail which ought to have been done by the Committee. Much time was wasted later in the week in interminable and unprofitable discussions on Russian policy, Ll. G. having got [it] into his head that we ought to support the Bolsheviks . . . On Tuesday [18th] morning early I had a "brain-wave" for Lloyd George's speech on the adjournment of the House, and went down to see him before breakfast. We walked round the park . . . and I told him he ought to try and get the people back to the old idealistic spirit of the early days of the war; that he should make a speech on "war aims"; that in the forefront he should place the "League of Nations" of which already we have the beginnings; that finally he should show how neither the Turkish, nor Austrian, nor even the German people stands in the way of this ideal, but only the spirit of the Prussian bureaucrat and militarist. He was very interested and, as I was too busy to write it all down, he asked me to switch on Tom Jones to work it up. This I did; but Tom Jones was out of form and did not make much of a fist of it,

[1] War Office letter 121/9134 (C1) of 7th Dec. 1917.
[2] Hankey to Lloyd George 20th Dec. 1917. Lloyd George papers F/23/1/31.
[3] A small part of this day's entry is in *Supreme Command*, II, p. 737.

and next day I lunched alone with Ll. George and C.P. Scott, editor of the Manchester Guardian to try and get my points into Ll. G. I was only partially successful and I did not think the speech he made, (which I heard) was very good . . . On Saturday [22nd] I lunched alone with Lord Haldane and we talked much of *post-bellum* reconstruction. The previous day I had lunched in the next house with Sir Eric Geddes, who is very anxious to get out of the Admiralty, away from the Admirals whom he finds so difficult to work with, and go to take charge of all transportation. On Saturday afternoon while I was with Ll. George, Smuts and Philip Kerr returned from Switzerland, where they had been to meet Count Mensdorff and discuss a separate peace with Austria. Mensdorff made it clear that Austria could not make a separate peace, but tried very hard to discuss a general peace. Beyond removing the idea that we want to extinguish Austria and wipe it out, the trip had no very concrete result.[1] . . .

When Hankey met Geddes over lunch on 21st the First Lord must still have been hesitating over the change of First Sea Lord which, as we saw earlier, he had for some time wished to make. Probably he realised that such action was bound to produce a storm in political as well as naval circles. It seems that Hankey at the very least said nothing at this meeting to deter Geddes from dismissing Jellicoe, and may even have stiffened his resolution; since on the very next day Geddes asked Admiral Sir Rosslyn Wemyss, the Deputy First Sea Lord, whether he would be prepared to step into Jellicoe's shoes.[2] After some slight hesitation Wemyss agreed to do so, and the result was that on the evening of Monday 24th Jellicoe found on his desk a letter of dismissal. Though Geddes tried to soften the blow by the promise of a peerage, and referred (by no means accurately) to the "very cordial relations which have existed between us" the anticipated storm blew up immediately. The Sea Lords, excepting Wemyss, threatened resignation—only to withdraw the threat when Geddes firmly insisted that they were challenging his constitutional right; and Carson and Balfour became involved through Geddes telling the Sea Lords he had consulted them before reaching his decision. A somewhat heated correspondence followed, especially on the part of Carson. But Lloyd George supported Geddes both in his action and in his claim that a change of First Sea Lord had been discussed in the presence of himself,

[1]On the Smuts mission to Switzerland see W. K. Hancock, *Smuts*, Vol. 1, *The Sanguine Years* (Cambridge U.P., 1962), pp. 466–7.
[2]See A. Temple Patterson (Ed.) *The Jellicoe Papers*, Vol. II, (Navy Records Society, 1968), pp. 121 and 240–7.

Carson and Balfour towards the end of October. This statement, as we saw earlier, is fully supported by Hankey's diary.[1]

On the day of Jellicoe's dismissal there was a War Cabinet at which Lloyd George was "in a very pernickety and irritable state of mind", according to Hankey, and "exasperated everyone including me".[2] One wonders whether his irritation derived from the tension produced by knowledge of the bombshell which Geddes was about to explode on the other side of the Horse Guards Parade. But the matter does not appear to have been discussed in Cabinet. Hankey spent all the rest of the day on revising his Man-Power report, and then went home to enjoy a quiet Christmas with his family. He does not seem to have learnt about Jellicoe's fate until he returned to London on 27th. Though he had for a long time been highly critical of the Admiralty in general, and of Jellicoe in particular, he sent the Admiral a short letter of sympathy. In the circumstances the divergence between his description therein of Jellicoe's contribution to the defeat of the U-boat and his earlier attacks on the Admiralty and the First Sea Lord for dragging their feet so protractedly over the convoy issue can be understood.

Hankey to Jellicoe. 2 Whitehall Gardens, 27th December 1917. Holograph[3]
My dear Admiral,
    I was most awfully sorry to read in the newspaper this morning that you were leaving the Admiralty, and I should like to say how much I have admired the way you have tackled the difficult problems with which you were confronted, and literally put a new face on the submarine warfare.
    May I at the same time offer my congratulations on the well-earned peerage?

Yours sincerely,

Jellicoe to Hankey. 28th December 1917. Holograph[4]
My dear Hankey,
    Thank you very much for your letter and when you hear of the manner of my dismissal you will be surprised, if one can ever be surprised at the deeds of those in power nowadays. I am very sorry our association is at an end.

Yours sincerely,

Meanwhile Esher was, as always, keeping Hankey closely informed

[1]See p. 447. The full correspondence is in S. W. Roskill, *The Dismissal of Admiral Jellicoe*, Journal of Contemporary History, Vol. I, No. 4 (Oct. 1966).
[2]Diary 24th Dec. 1917. [3]B.M. Add. MSS. 49036, folios 124–5.
[4]Written on Admiralty paper, though in fact Jellicoe went on leave from the Admiralty on the day following his dismissal.

about developments in France. On 24th December he sent a long letter in which he described Clemenceau's handling of the case against Joseph Caillaux, the former Finance Minister and Prime Minister, whom "the Tiger" was determined to break because he had been tainted by the Bolo and Malvy scandals referred to earlier. Esher considered that Haig's position had been weakened by the creation of the Supreme War Council, and by "the admission that he retained a B.G.I. [Brigadier-General Intelligence] for two years who is judged incompetent and a danger to the Army".[1] The Supreme Council, he considered, "seems to be growing in self confidence", and Henry Wilson's recent visit to Haig had "passed off very well". "If", he concluded, "mischief makers would leave them alone [an obvious reference to Northcliffe's attacks on G.H.Q.] there would be no friction".[2] Finally this letter reveals that it was on Esher's recommendation that Lawrence Burgis, Hankey's future private secretary for 17 years, joined the War Cabinet secretariat a short time later.[3]

Diary 29th December 1917
I awoke at 6 a.m. with a "brainwave" in regard to the reply to be made to the German peace offer to the Bolsheviks. I spent most of the morning dictating it out. Briefly the idea was to be firm but conciliatory; to give the Germans a loophole, if they mean business; if they don't, to show our own people and the enemy that we have made a reasonable offer, and so induce them to continue in the war. Ll. G. sent for me to lunch, and, curiously enough, proceeded to formulate his own views, and ended by asking me to prepare a Memorandum. I was able to reply that I had done it, and so closely did our views coincide that I only found it necessary to alter the draft in one paragraph, and that only involved an inversion in the order of the arguments. My own opinion is that our prospects in the war are extremely rocky with Russia out, all the enemy's forces available for concentration against us, and the blockade broken on the eastern side. I consider that, if we can get anything like a decent peace, we ought to do so. I had rather an uncomfortable instance of Lloyd George's underhand methods. He had had a letter from F.S. Oliver, among other things crabbing Lord Derby. Ll. G., in spite

[1] This must refer to Brigadier-General John Charteris (1877–1946) the head of the Intelligence Section of G.H.Q., who was a strong advocate of the Flanders offensive of 1917. Because the Intelligence on which it was based was in many respects quite erroneous, he must carry a share of the responsibility for its failure. Lloyd George (*War Memoirs*, IV, p. 2102) refers to "the joyous arithmetic of the optimistic Charteris" at that time.
[2] Esher to Hankey 24th Dec. 1917. Holograph.   [3] See p. 345.

of the fact that he is very friendly and intimate with Derby, constantly enjoying his hospitality, practically told me he was determined to get rid of him. It is this that makes one feel that one's personal position is so very insecure and uncertain.

So ended a year which, although it had brought to the Allies the promise of vast American help in men and material, did not see that promise redeemed. On almost all fronts and in most theatres—save only in Mesopotamia and Palestine—it had been a year of defeats. The disaster of the Nivelle offensive had reduced the French army to a condition not far short of impotence, and had forced the British Empire to relieve its ally of much of the strain. Then came the crushing defeat suffered by the Italians at Caporetto. The glimmer of light revealed in the Cambrai tank offensive was rapidly extinguished, and at Ypres the gains were by no stretch of the imagination commensurate with the losses suffered. At sea the unrestricted U-boat offensive had come within measurable distance of success, and the collapse of Russia presaged a vast increase in the enemy's strength on the western front. Hankey's view that, if reasonable peace terms could be secured, it would be folly to reject them certainly appeared to be based on a sound appreciation of future prospects. It was not until after the war that we realised the full extent of the pressure of the British blockade; and how by the end of 1917 the German and Austrian people were suffering very severely from shortages of every kind. Furthermore quite recent research in German documents has provided convincing support for the view expressed in Lloyd George's memoirs—that as long as the Kaiser remained on the throne and the Prussian military clique headed by Hindenburg and Ludendorff exerted the dominant influence in court and political circles there was not in fact any likelihood of peace being achieved on terms which came near to satisfying the fundamental causes for which the Allies were fighting—namely the restoration of an independent Belgium and the return of at any rate the French-speaking parts of Alsace-Lorraine to France.[1]

[1] See *Lloyd George*, IV, pp. 2104–9 and Fritz Fischer, *Germany's Aims in the First World War* (Eng. trans. Norton, N.Y. and London 1968).

Chapter 16

Calm before the Storm.
January-March 1918

ALTHOUGH the New Year opened relatively quietly on the fighting
fronts, for Hankey it was an extraordinarily busy period, since none of
the strategic and administrative problems involved in planning the
campaigns for 1918 had been firmly resolved. True enough shipping
losses had fallen, and there were manifold signs that the convoy
strategy would defeat the submarine offensive. But demands for
shipping were still greatly in excess of the available tonnage; and the
fact that transport of the American Expeditionary Force and all its
multifarious supplies to Europe was bound to fall mainly on the
British Merchant Navy made it plain that the deficiency in shipping was
not going to be eliminated for a long time. The extreme "Westerners"
—including Jellicoe—had wanted to save tonnage by reducing the
Allied military commitments in the Balkans and the Near East; but that
policy held no appeal for Lloyd George—nor indeed for Hankey.
Apart from the shipping shortage—and indeed inseparable from it—
was the great shortage of man power. In his draft report of 13th
December 1917 Hankey calculated that for the armed forces alone this
amounted to between 500,000 and 600,000 men; while "civilian
demands" (mainly for munitions production and shipbuilding) came to
another 100,000 immediately and 400,000 prospectively. Obviously
shortages on such a scale could not be eliminated without some drastic
measures, such as lowering the age for General Service, raising that for
Military Service, or applying conscription to Ireland; and Hankey had
reviewed and rejected each of those measures except "as the very last
resort".

Hankey's principal recommendations to mitigate the man power
shortage were, firstly, that the C.I.G.S. should "impress on the High
Command" in all theatres that they should adopt "systems of strategy
and tactics calculated to reduce casualties to a lower level than has

hitherto been the case"; and, secondly, that the number of battalions in a Division should be reduced. In other words there was to be no repetition of the holocausts of the Somme and Third Ypres. But Robertson would plainly be as unwilling to give such instructions as Haig would be to carry them out.[1] Small wonder that the report of the Man Power Committee remained on the War Cabinet's agenda for three months. On New Year's Day Hankey went over his draft of the report with Lloyd George, who was "very pleased" with it but insisted on a number of alterations—which aggrieved the Secretary because he had already approved that it should be printed and circulated, and he now had to recall all copies and arrange for reprinting.[2]

The labour troubles arising from the demands of munition workers for more money, mentioned in Hankey's diary at this time, were only a part of the increasing unrest in mines and factories. In the same month Ormsby Gore sent him a gloomy prophecy of serious trouble in the very near future; and Hankey forwarded it to Lloyd George with a minute saying that it was "entirely confirmed by Tom Jones, who has just returned from a visit to South Wales".[3] This was the beginning of the wave of industrial strife which swept the country soon after the end of hostilities.

At this point there exists a unique and irreconcilable difference between Hankey's diary and his letters to his wife. On 1st and 2nd January he wrote to Adeline from Criccieth, where he was staying with Lloyd George, whom he described as being "in holiday vein". The envelopes of those letters are postmarked from Caernarvonshire on 2nd and 3rd January, and the first of them makes it plain that he went down there by train via Holyhead on the night of 1st–2nd—and "slept like a top" during the journey. Yet the diary entries make it appear that he was in London throughout the first week of the New Year. As it seems that the letters to Adeline are correctly dated the only possible conclusion is that Hankey was with Lloyd George in Wales on 1st and 2nd, returned to London late on the latter day, and misdated the entries in his diary which he then wrote up.

Diary 2nd January 1918 (misdated for 3rd or 4th)
War Cabinet at 11.30. Afterwards there was some private discussion on the reply to the Central Powers, and it was agreed that Gen. Smuts should go to

[1]Draft report of the Man Power Committee of 13th Dec. 1917. Lloyd George papers F/23/1/30.
[2]Diary 1st Jan. 1918. [3]Lloyd George papers F/23/2/1.

Switzerland again to meet Count Czernin. I might mention here that Ll. George wants to make Smuts Foreign Secretary in Balfour's place and General Macdonogh Permanent Under-Secretary . . . In the afternoon Sir T. Royden, our Shipping representative in U.S.A., called on me. He said that the War Cabinet, and our organisation generally, had made a tremendous impression on Col. House's mission. When they returned to America they told their Govt. "Compared with the English we are just a bunch of Boobs"! He gave a badish impression of American organisation, and shipping especially.

Next day Lord Fisher sent Hankey a violent attack on the Admiralty's conduct of the war in general and the submarine campaign in particular —written at 4 a.m. after "an hour cogitating over your kind and valued advice last evening". Obviously the old Admiral was still hankering for a return to office; and one must admit both that his handwriting was as firm and clear as ever (despite his 76th birthday being only three weeks ahead), and that his pleading for amphibious assaults to be made on the German U-boat bases with "huge hippopotami . . . impervious to gunfire and immune from attack by submarine[s] and drawing so little water as to pass over mines" had sound strategic sense behind it. Indeed his proposal foreshadowed the Tank Landing Craft of World War II. Hankey at once sent the letter on to Lloyd George with a note "The enclosed is worth reading. Lord Fisher called on me yesterday. He was full of energy, but he has been ill and got rather thin. He is frightfully down on the Admiralty; but you will find all that in his letter".[1] Lloyd George, however, having so recently supported Geddes's dismissal of Jellicoe, was very unlikely to countenance a further change at the Admiralty.

Diary 4th January 1918
War Cabinet at 4 o'clock to consider final draft of War Aims statement. Ll. G. had seen Asquith at lunch and had secured his agreement as to the general lines of the statement. I lunched with Ian Malcolm[2] at the Carlton, where I had much too good a lunch for war time. I picked him up at the Foreign Office where I had been to represent to Lord Robert Cecil how

[1]Hankey to Lloyd George 3rd Jan. 1918. Lloyd George papers F/23/2/2. Hankey's diary does not mention a call by Fisher on 2nd, but this letter obviously confirms that he must have been in London on that day.
[2]Later Sir Ian Z. Malcolm (1868–1944). Diplomat and politician (Cons.). Attaché at Berlin, Paris and St. Petersburgh 1891–6. Private Secretary to Mr. Balfour at Versailles Conference 1919. British Government director of Suez Canal Co. 1919–39.

urgent it was not to include in the War Aims statement a general adherence to the principle of self-determination of nations. I pointed out that it would logically lead to the self-determination of Gibraltar to Spain, Malta to the Maltese, Cyprus to the Greeks, Egypt to the Egyptians, Aden to the Arabs or Somalis, India to chaos, Hongkong to the Chinese, South Africa to the Kaffirs, West Indies to the blacks etc. And where would the British Empire be? At best it would lead to a violent propaganda under German instigation. He agreed, and the phrase was altered in the final draft.

5th January

Prime Minister made his great statement on War Aims.[1] In a sense it originated in my Memo. written last Saturday [30th Dec.]; none of the actual text of this, but many of the ideas remained in the final statement, which was based partly on a draft by Gen. Smuts, partly on one by Lord Robert Cecil with several additions by Lloyd George. It was a very fine effort, and has been discussed by the War Cabinet nearly every day this week. I think it should prove a first step towards a general peace, though this depends upon the enemy's response, and may take a long time. Robertson called on me this morning, and after havering about as though he had something on his mind, went off without unburdening himself . . .

It is a fair guess that what Robertson had on his mind was his increasing unwillingness to accept the Supreme War Council as the directing body for the entire Allied war effort, including strategy, and the creation and employment of a General Reserve in the west which would be at the disposal of the Supreme Council.

Diary 9th January

War Cabinet in morning. The subject was to have been Manpower. I found to my disgust that Amery, who is over from Versailles, where he had seen an advance copy of my man-power report, had been butting in and upsetting or trying to upset the figures given by the Adjutant-General, and interviewing all sorts of people without my authority. As it is a most complicated subject, in which I have been saturated for months he naturally made a mess of it, and upset many personal and most delicate factors which were in my own hands. The result was that the Prime Minister was fogged and refused to discuss the matter until this question had once more been discussed.[2] In the afternoon

[1]This refers to Lloyd George's speech to the Trade Unions delivered at the Caxton Hall on 5th Jan. 1918. Its origins are discussed in *Lloyd George*, V, pp. 2484–8 and it is printed in full as Appendix II to Chapter LXX.
[2]Hankey to Derby 10th Jan. 1918 (Copy in Smuts Archive f. 84) informed him that a number of statistical tables were to be prepared giving the estimated casualties for the year on various alternative "bases", e.g. of "hard" or of "light" fighting.

Smuts, Auckland Geddes,[1] the Director of National Service, and I had a conference about it and remitted all the figures to Auckland Geddes. . . . I was very indignant with Amery and issued an office order that no more draft reports are to be sent to Versailles. Lunched with Ll. George to meet Haig, most of the members of the War Cabinet and several Ministers. Many bets about duration of war. Ll. G., Churchill and I thought it would last more than a year more. Haig, Cecil, Barnes, Lord Derby and Lord Reading thought it would be over [this year?]. Churchill bet Derby £50 to £40 against it being over, and Ll. G. bet Derby 100 cigarettes to 100 cigars.

Amery's indiscretion in "interviewing all sorts of people" about Hankey's draft report on the man power problem makes one wonder whether the notorious Colonel Repington, the military correspondent of the *Morning Post*, who constantly travelled between London and Paris at this time and always had his ear very close to the ground over the military-political discussions of the period,[2] may not have been among those to whom Amery talked. Lloyd George, in his virulent attack on Repington, assumes that he got his information from someone on the General Staff, and points an accusing finger at General Sir Frederick Maurice, the Director of Military Operations. But in his *War Memoirs* Lloyd George also wrote that "in connection with the Cabinet inquiries *regarding the man power situation*, Colonel Repington had written articles, published by the *Morning Post*, containing *figures regarding our strength and reserves*" (italics supplied)[3]; and that remark, which is confirmed by Repington's diary, taken with Hankey's anger over Amery's indiscretion, suggests that the Military Correspondent's informant may have been Amery and not Maurice. Hankey at any rate acquitted Derby of any complicity in the intrigue—as indeed does Lloyd George; for on 11th he recorded in his diary that "Derby is most indignant about the Amery episode".

On the same day that Hankey took Amery to task for his indiscretion he wrote to Lord Justice Pickford that the Cabinet had decided that "it is not in the public interest to publish the Second Report of the

---

[1] 1st Baron Geddes 1942 (1879–1954). Physiologist, politician (U.) and diplomat. Professor of Anatomy, Dublin and McGill (Montreal) Universities. Director of Recruiting, War Office 1916–17. Minister of National Service 1917–19. Minister of Reconstruction 1919. President, Board of Trade 1919–20. Ambassador to U.S.A. 1920–24.
[2] See C. à Court Repington, *The First World War*, Vol. II of 2 Vols. (Constable, 1920).
[3] *Lloyd George*, V, p. 2803.

Dardanelles Commission for the present". And even the fact that it was not to be published was "strictly confidential". Hankey wrote that this decision had been based on "urgent representations from the Admiralty and General Staff that a good deal of information [in the Report] . . . might be of value to the enemy".[1] But it is difficult not to conclude that a determination not to repeat the fatal error of the Asquith government in giving publicity to its own failings and errors also played a part. The second and final report of the Commission was not actually published until 1919—when it attracted very little attention.[2]

Diary 12th January
Lunched with Lord Haldane to meet the Sidney Webbs[3] and discuss with them the subject under consideration by Lord Haldane's Ctee. on the future British constitution. She was a woman of great knowledge and considerable charm. He a much less impressive person, rather like his brother Fabian my neighbour Pease.[4] I agreed to give evidence before the Committee.[5] I found them very sound and reasonable until politics were touched on, when they at once revealed a certain obstinacy, and a quite absurd insistence on the rights of labour over all other claims of the community.

It is hardly surprising that Hankey's first encounter with the Sidney Webbs should have produced an unfavourable reaction; but it was generous of him to give evidence before a committee dominated by two leading Fabians—the more so because the Man Power Committee was in almost continuous session at the time.[6]

On 8th January President Wilson announced his famous "Fourteen Points" for peace and reconstruction—without any prior consultation with his country's Allies. At first little attention was paid to them in

[1]GT.3316 of 9th Jan. 1918. Cab. 24/39. [2]Cmd. 371.
[3]Sidney J. Webb, 1st Baron Passfield 1929 (1859–1947). Politician (Lab.), social reformer and historian. Founder of London School of Economics and Political Science 1895. Served on Executive of Labour Party 1915–25. President, Board of Trade 1924. Secretary for Dominions and Colonies 1929–31.
Mrs. Sidney Webb, wife of above (1858–1943). Social reformer and author. Member of many government and private committees on social welfare.
[4]Edward R. Pease (1857–1955). A founder of Fabian Society 1883, its Secretary 1890–1913 and Hon. Secretary 1914–38. Member of Executive of Labour Party 1900–13. Biographer of Beatrice and Sidney Webb.
[5]This refers to the Webbs' committee on "War Aims", established on 28th Dec. 1917. Apart from the Webbs, Arthur Henderson and Ramsay MacDonald were members. Its report was published by the Labour Movement in 1918. See Margaret Cole, *The Webbs and their Work* (Muller, 1949), pp. 172–5.
[6]Diary 14th and 15th Jan. 1918.

London or Paris—for the obvious reason that the war was still far from won. But Hankey had in fact already been thinking about a future world organisation for the maintenance of peace, and he now put on paper his idea that it should be based on the Inter-Allied Council already in existence at Versailles. On 12th he wrote to Lloyd George "I enclose a very rough note which I have made in regard to the League of Nations. I believe the time is fast approaching when if we want to take our proper place in the world, we shall have to launch something of this kind. . . . I sent a copy to Lord Robert Cecil, who is very interested".[1]

Diary 18th January 1918[2]

. . . I lunched with Ll. George, Gen. Smuts, and Lord Reading. The former in great spirits after his brilliantly successful speech in secret session the previous evening and again to the Trades Unionists that morning. The conversation drifted on to the subject of our army leaders and the failure of the War Office to allow any Territorial or New Army officers to reach the higher commands, a deputation of Liberal Ministers having waited on the P.M. that very morning on this subject. Suddenly Ll. George said to Smuts "I wish you would go out to the Western front and go right round in order to find out who are the rising men, and to see the new defences they are making to meet the forthcoming German offensive". Smuts agreed to go at once, and Ll. G., then turned to me and said "I think you had better go too", which I agreed to do. Ll. G. in a subsequent conversation said that if he had his way he would make me Haig's Chief of the General Staff, but Smuts said "No. Hankey has a bigger job as Chief of Staff to the War Cabinet. It needs a wider outlook than C.G.S. of the Expeditionary Force." At 4.30 we had a meeting of the War Cabinet of a very secret character to consider first our naval policy and second the proposed resumption of Smuts's conversations [on peace feelers by Austrians]. The Navy have at last adopted the policy I have urged all the war, viz. to wall in the enemy with mines. There also came out the defective construction of our armour piercing shells, which I have known of for a long time and which is now being put right.[3] In regard to Austria, we have received another communication from Berne stating that Count Czernin would be prepared to meet Ll. George to continue Smuts's conversations. After a long discussion it was decided that Ll. G. could not

[1] Lloyd George papers F/23/2/17.
[2] The first part of this day's entry is in *Supreme Command*, II, pp. 755–6.
[3] At Jutland it was found that the British shells exploded on impact if the angle of striking was far out of the vertical, instead of penetrating right into an enemy ship before exploding. The whole of the outfit of armour-piercing shell had to be replaced. See Marder, *Scapa Flow*, III, pp. 168–71.

possibly go, but that Smuts might with advantage meet Czernin. No-one had any great hope of achieving peace by these means, but it might be possible to drive a wedge into the evident gap which exists between Kühlmann[1] and Czernin on one side and the German militarists on the other . . .

We have already seen how often Hankey was pestered with complaints by Ministers or officials about their not being properly consulted before issues which concerned them came before the War Cabinet, or about not receiving the Minutes of meetings at which such matters had been discussed. These complaints seem generally to have had little foundation—for Hankey took immense trouble to keep the proper people informed about the Cabinet's deliberations; but they always caused him to rise to the defence of the Secretariat. Thus on 18th January he sent Lloyd George his recent correspondence with John Anderson,[2] the secretary of the Ministry of Shipping, in which the latter had protested about alleged lack of consultation. "I think that Mr. John Anderson's criticisms of the War Cabinet are most improper", he wrote, "and I should have told him so in my reply, except that I regard it as my duty to keep the machine working smoothly, and consequently, while putting him right on the constitutional point, I ended on a conciliatory note"[3]; which exactly sums up the principles on which he consistently worked.

Diary 19th January 1918
A very busy day, winding things up before I go to France on Monday [21st] . . . First I had to get out the Minutes of the meeting of the previous evening. They were so secret that I had to write them in manuscript and they were very long. Then I had to see Gen. Smuts to make sure that he agreed. Then Sir Eric Geddes, the First Lord, with whom I lunched. Then I had to get the P.M.'s approval. I caught the P.M. after lunch. He tells me he is expecting Carson to resign, owing to the difficulty over the Irish question. I am not surprised. He will not be missed. The P.M. also talked a good deal about Robertson . . . Ll. G. has almost made up his mind to get rid of him and send him as C-in-C, India. He is particularly incensed at some very gloomy

[1]Richard von Kühlmann (1873–1948). German diplomat. Minister for Foreign Affairs 1917. Negotiated treaties of Brest Litovsk with Bolsheviks March 1918 and of Bucharest with Roumanians May 1918.
[2]1st Viscount Waverley 1952 (1882–1958). Civil Servant and politician (Nat.). Secretary, Ministry of Shipping 1917–19. Chairman, Board of Inland Revenue 1919–22. Permanent Under-Secretary, Home Office 1922–32. Governor of Bengal 1932–37. Home Secretary and Minister of Home Security 1939–40. Lord President of Council 1940–43. Chancellor of Exchequer 1943–5.
[3]Lloyd George papers F/23/2/10.

comments in the General Staff's weekly appreciation on our prospects on the western front . . .

Carson did in fact resign on 21st—the day that Hankey left for France with Smuts. His comment to Adeline was "I cannot honestly say I regret it, though I always found him a kind-hearted, gentle and sentimental creature"—which certainly gives an unexpected view of the character of the intransigent champion of Ulster.

A calm crossing relieved the perennial anxiety with which Hankey always faced salt water, and he reached G.H.Q. in time for dinner, at which he sat between Haig and General Sir Herbert Lawrence,[1] who had recently succeeded Kiggell as Chief of General Staff to Haig. As always on these occasions Hankey did more listening than talking, and he was surprised to hear "a considerable amount of peace talk". "Even the young sprigs of A.D.Cs", he wrote in his diary, "who used to buck so much about victory, were only talking about peace prospects. It was very clear that the army is absolutely 'fed up' with the war".[2] It seems likely, however, that Hankey's taciturnity on this occasion arose at least in part from the embarrassing knowledge that the real purpose of his mission was to meet Lloyd George's urgent desire to find a replacement for Haig—as is frankly admitted in the former's memoirs.[3] And the fact that Smuts and Hankey were unable to suggest any better Commander-in-Chief for the British armies was of course an indirect tribute to Haig which the Prime Minister was bound to find distasteful. Not surprisingly he described their report as "very disappointing".[4] Interesting light is, however, thrown on the Hankey-Smuts visit to France by what Lloyd George told Liddell Hart about it many years later. The purpose of the mission was "to 'vet' all the generals for possible successors to Haig", and Lloyd George remarked of Hankey "that's a good brain, always gave me the greatest possible support". Apparently the only name Hankey and Smuts were able to put forward was that of General Claud Jacob[5]; and they were

[1]1861–1943. Soldier, banker and industrialist. Commander successively of 53rd and 52nd Divisions at Gallipoli. In charge of evacuation of Cape Helles. Chief of General Staff, B.E.F., 1918–19. Chairman, Vickers Ltd., 1926 and of Glyn's Bank 1934–43.
[2]Diary 21st Jan. 1918.
[3]*Lloyd George*, III, pp. 1530–43. See also John Terraine, *Douglas Haig*, pp. 388–9.
[4]*ibid.*
[5]Later Sir Claud W. Jacob (1863–1948). Commanded II Corps 1916–19. C.G.S.,

insufficiently keen on him to regard his selection as "worth risking all the attacks in Parliament etc. that would have followed."[1] No doubt this explains Lloyd George's disappointment.

Hankey reproduced in his memoirs nearly the whole of the following days' diary entries,[2] but the letters he wrote to Lloyd George give more intimate impressions of his visit to the front.

Hankey to Lloyd George. Tuesday 22nd January 1918. Holograph[3]
Personal and Confidential
My dear Prime Minister,

I will not trouble you with a long letter, but you may like to learn my first impressions formed from conversations with a very large number of officers, mainly at G.H.Q.:—

1 No-one now talks of the offensive, nor thinks that anything can be done in that line. The Americans they believe will not be of much use for the offensive before 1920. The army is tired of the war, and there is a general feeling that peace is not very distant, or at least that the diplomatists ought to be feeling the ground in that direction.

2 Most people here feel doubtful whether the Germans will really attack in force, but everyone is preparing to meet the attack if it comes. The design of the defences is good and sound. Very good progress is being made. The defences are already strong, and in six weeks time, if the enemy lets us alone, will be very strong. So hard have they worked, that the supply of barbed wire is for the moment almost exhausted and for a time will be diluted with ordinary wire.

3 I will not commit myself yet to any view of the spirit of the army. I can only say that there is now absolutely no trace of that spirit of irritating over-optimism that used to precede and accompany our offensives. Neither have I encountered pessimism. Optimism is steady but subdued.

4 General Lawrence made a most favourable impression on me, though of course it is difficult to size a man up definitely in so short a time. All the same, I would back him as a good horse.

5 There is a very strong feeling indeed against any extension of the line beyond Barisy [usually Barisis]. Any forced extension would be extremely unpopular here, particularly now that the divisions are being reduced.

India 1920–4. C-in-C, India, 1925. Secretary, Military Department, India Office 1926–30. Field-Marshal 1926.
[1]"Note of conversation with Lloyd George at Criccieth 24th Sept. 1932." Liddell Hart papers.
[2]*Supreme Command*, II, pp. 756–60.   [3]Lloyd George papers F/23/2/11.

6   The reduction from 12 to 9 battalions begins to-morrow (Wednesday) in the first division selected and will take several weeks. It will wipe off the deficit and leave a pool of some 22,000 men, who for the present will be used for digging.

7   I cannot learn of any reduction of cavalry beyond the two Indian divisions. I think you should inquire at the War Cabinet how great a total reduction is contemplated.

No more now,
Yours ever

Hankey's reference in the above letter to "extension of the [British] line beyond Barisis" requires some amplification. At the Boulogne Conference in September 1917 the principle that the British line should be extended was accepted, but the distance to be taken over and the time at which it should be done was left to the two Cs-in-C to arrange. Accordingly Haig and Pétain met at Amiens in mid-October, and although the former was very reluctant to divert strength from the Flanders battle he accepted extension as far as Barisis (between St. Quentin and Soissons, just south of the river Oise). However the heavy German counter-attack at Cambrai at the end of November, together with the need to reinforce the Italians after Caporetto, caused Haig to postpone execution of the agreement. In December Clemenceau, who had been showing understandable impatience, referred the matter to the Permanent Military Representatives at Versailles. He and Pétain now both threatened resignation unless the British line were extended to Berry-au-Bac—on the river Aisne—37 miles more than had been agreed. The British, whilst agreeing that the extension to Barisis must be carried out, refused to accept this proposal. On 17th December Haig met Pétain again and promised to complete the take-over to Barisis by the end of January 1918. His promise was fulfilled. On 10th January the Permanent Military Representatives recommended extension to a point 14 miles beyond Barisis, and when the Supreme War Council met at Versailles on 30th they considered both this proposal and the extension to Berry-au-Bac for which Clemenceau and Pétain were still pressing. Haig first protested against but finally accepted the smaller extension; but in fact it was not carried out, and at the time of the great German offensive of March 1918 the British line had only been extended to Barisis.[1]

[1]For detailed accounts of this involved story see Lloyd George, *War Memoirs*, V, pp. 2760–83; Hankey, *Supreme Command*, II, pp. 752–75 and 770–2; *Military*

Next day, 23rd, Hankey told Adeline that, as he was to meet Lloyd George at Versailles for a Supreme War Council, his trip would be more protracted than he had expected. He also sent her vivid but harrowing descriptions of the scene in the actual battle zones of the First, Fourth and Fifth Armies, all of which he visited with Smuts. The tenacity and courage of the French peasants, who continued to till their fields despite the fighting in progress all around them, and of their families, who managed to make some sort of home in the ruins of their villages, moved him deeply. "Within 30 yards of the [British] guns", he wrote, "an old man and a woman were ploughing. Nearby a family, including girls and children, were living crowded together in the last corner of a half destroyed cottage".[1] But despite his preoccupation with the military problems he had been sent out to investigate he found time to press on Lloyd George the need to hasten approval of the Man Power Committee's report.

Hankey to Lloyd George. G.H.Q. 1st Army 24th January 1918. Holograph[2]
Personal and Confidential
My dear Prime Minister,
   May I most strongly urge that the man-power conclusions be adopted *now*, without waiting for the new figures which the War Office are producing.
   My reason for this suggestion is that the draft conclusions have very nearly all been adopted by the Departments and are being carried out. The few that are not (e.g. ship-yard labour) ought to be.
   These conclusions are based on figures given by the War Office and other Departments, which have been checked and counter-checked by those Departments.
   It ought to be on record that the decisions were based on these figures, and, if any alteration is required in the Report or conclusions it ought to be clear that the responsibility rests with the department who furnished in-complete figures and not with the Committee.
   If the new figures affect the Report materially we can have a new Report or a supplement explaining the whole thing.
   If the War Cabinet do not like to commit themselves to my draft Report in detail, let it stand as a summary of evidence by the Secretary, and let them formally adopt only the conclusions.

Operations, France and Belgium 1918, I, Ch. II and Liddell Hart, *The War in Outline*, pp. 198–202. For the point of view of Haig and Robertson respectively see John Terraine, *Douglas Haig*, pp. 363–4 and Victor Bonham Carter, *Soldier True*, Ch. 11.
[1]To Lady Hankey. From H.Qs 4th Army 24th Jan. 1918.
[2]Lloyd George papers F/23/2/12.

In your own interests and in those of the War Cabinet I earnestly press this.

Yours

P.S. I am not quite ready to write my further impressions here, though they are taking shape. We had a tremendously interesting day east of Ypres yesterday. To-day it is Vimy. etc.

On 26th Hankey reached Boulogne, where he drafted the report which Smuts would place before the War Cabinet.[1] Among other points he "strongly opposed the extension of the British line to the south, as desired by the French". His general opinion was that the Army was "in splendid fettle" and would "hold against any attack"; but that "it would not be right to expose it to another prolonged attack of the Somme-Flanders type". Though Hankey's confidence in the defensive strength of the British line was soon to be proved over-optimistic he was undoubtedly right to throw his weight both against further extension of the British line and against any more attrition battles such as Third Ypres; and Lloyd George no doubt agreed with him whole-heartedly on the latter point. The Official History remarks that "the state of the Army was admirably summed up in a Memorandum prepared for the War Cabinet", but gives no indication of its authorship.[2]

On 27th, a Sunday, Hankey was back in London and at once went down to Walton Heath to report to Lloyd George on his visit to the front. However, the presence of a large number of journalists considerably stultified his purpose, though he did gather that the Prime Minister was "more suspicious of the soldiers than ever".[3] That evening Adeline picked up her husband and took him back to High-stead for the only night he was to spend in his home for some time. Next morning Hankey went to London, whence he at once set off for Versailles in company with Lloyd George and Milner and a large number of "hangers on" whose presence he considered quite unnecessary.

Haig to Hankey. Hotel de Crillon, Paris. 29th January 1918. Holograph

My dear Hankey,

I am sending Col. Cavendish[4] with this. He has just come from Compiègne

---

[1]GT. 3469. Cab. 24/40.
[2]*Military Operations, France and Belgium 1918*, Vol. I (Macmillan, 1935), pp. 40–1, where a long extract from the report is reproduced.
[3]Diary 27th Jan. 1918.
[4]Presumably Brigadier-General Hon. W. E. Cavendish (1862–1931).

and can give the latest information of the views held at the G.Q.G. [*Grand Quartier Général*] on the subject of:—

(1) Extension of front

(2) Reserves

I think the P.M. shd. see him.

Yours v. truly

The formal meetings of the Supreme War Council started on 30th and did not go at all smoothly.

Diary 29th January 1918[1]

Conferences in the morning and afternoon with Sir Douglas Haig and General Pershing ... mainly on the question of the incorporation of American battalions in British brigades. Much misunderstanding, because Pershing wanted the troops attached mainly for training, though willing that they should do their share of the fighting, while Robertson wanted them mainly for fighting, though willing that they should be trained.

To Lady Hankey. Supreme War Council, British Section, Versailles. 29th January 1918

... This is a very delightful place ... and, in spite of two conferences I have found time for two very nice walks ... The P.M. is in rather a difficult frame of mind to manage just at present. He would be so infinitely more useful if he would take an occasional holiday.

To the same. 31st January 1918

... We are in a most frightful muddle—largely due to Ll. George. As usual he insisted on bringing over everyone he could think of. The result was that at yesterday's meeting we had present no less than three sets of military advisers—the Permanent Military Representatives on the Supreme War Council, the Chiefs of Staff, and the Commanders-in-Chief. They all gave different advice, and the meeting got into a worse state of chaos than I have ever known in all my wide experience!

Lloyd George then made matters infinitely worse by demanding that each General Staff[2] (there are 4 of them!) should, by to-day at noon, give a complete estimate of the armies and man-power of the allies and enemy respectively—in fact they should produce in concentrated form the results of a man-power inquiry which would require to be spread over about 4 months to complete! Of course the estimates will be totally irreconcilable. The worst of it is that *I* had to produce the forms on which the information is to be given, and the subject is so full of snags that the thing is impossible.[3]

[1] See *Supreme Command*, II, pp. 764–5.

[2] The Chiefs of General Staff were Robertson, Foch, Bliss and Diaz for Britain, France, U.S.A. and Italy respectively.

[3] IC. 39–44, pp. 7–8. Cab. 25/121.

Ll. G at present is really impossible to work with. He is petulant, irritable, perpetually demanding impossible information which he doesn't need, abusing and quarrelling with the soldiers, suspicious, sly, and dog-tired but refusing to rest.

It will be with great difficulty that I can work with him during the next few months, but will do my best.

Hankey's strictures on the organisation of the Inter-Allied Command at this time require some explanation and qualification. He had, as we saw earlier,[1] expressed misgivings about the appointment of Permanent Military Representatives to the Supreme War Council (now Henry Wilson, Weygand, Bliss and Cadorna for Britain, France, U.S.A. and Italy respectively). Probably he foresaw that the creation of a new set of advisers, additional to the Commanders-in-Chief and the Chiefs of Staff, would cause confusion; and he certainly realised that Lloyd George's real motive in pressing for this scheme was to clip the wings of Robertson and Haig. But in fact it was only the British who spoke with three voices—to their grave disadvantage in the current debates on military policy and strategy. For Weygand had been Foch's Chief of Staff and was his *alter ego*, and similarly Cadorna was merely the mouthpiece of Diaz, the Italian Chief of Staff.[2] Finally the Americans, showing complete logic, had appointed Tasker Bliss, who had just vacated the post of Chief of Staff on reaching the age limit, their representative at Versailles. Henry Wilson's biographer thus truthfully remarks that his position was "the exceptional one".[3] It therefore seems likely that Hankey's strictures arose from the embarrassing experience that it was only his country which failed to show a united front in the military field[4].

Diary 31st January 1918
I had a walk in the morning with Lord Milner and worked in the sun on the balcony for some hours, as there was no meeting. At the afternoon meeting of the S.W.C. no secretaries were present. . . . It is rather dangerous however to have no Secretary. Afterwards Ll. G. and Milner told me all about it. I got

[1]See pp. 453–9.
[2]Diaz was effectively also the Italian C-in-C, but the King held that position nominally.
[3]See C. E. Callwell, *Field Marshal Sir Henry Wilson* (Cassell, 1927), Vol. II, p. 33.
[4]See John Terraine, *The Western Front 1914–1918* (Hutchinson, 1964), pp. 96–113 for the view of Haig's apologist on this subject.

Wright,[1] the interpreter to get out a short *procès-verbal* for purposes of record, but Ll. G. repudiated it, and refused to reckon it as a record of the meeting, so I shall be dragged in to-morrow somehow.

Despite Hankey's complaints about Lloyd George's methods he was soon forced to applaud the skill with which he handled the jealous generals and their abhorrence of the Supreme War Council.

Diary 1st February 1918
. . . The conferences sat all the morning and all the afternoon, so I had a terrifically heavy day, with a long *procès-verbal* to do in the luncheon hour and another in the evening . . . During the conference Clemenceau turned to Ll. George and said "You know you like me. You can't help yourself. You like me!" The old fellow (76) is just like a schoolboy, a great character . . . In the morning it was agreed to adopt the plan of campaign proposed by the Permanent Mily. Representatives, viz. a defensive in the west and an offensive in the Turkish theatre, the latter only being agreed to after a terrific struggle, as the soldiers had got at Clemenceau to oppose it and concentrate everything in the west. It was also provided that the Generals were to send all their plans to Versailles for co-ordination etc. In the afternoon the Chiefs of Staff (Foch and Robertson), who are bitterly opposed to Versailles, when discussing the plan of a big allied General Reserve, tried to upset the whole scheme by putting up a plan by which Foch and Robertson would command the reserve,

[1]There is a mystery about Peter Wright. On 30th March 1918 Hankey recorded in his diary that he had engaged him on Amery's recommendation despite the fact that he "inspired me with instinctive mistrust", and that he had received a warning about him "from the Secret Service people". As, however, there was "nothing in his dossier" except "some indiscretions 18 months or so ago" Hankey kept him on. Then came a peremptory demand from the Secret Service "to recall him at once". "I must handle him carefully," wrote Hankey, "because he is a lawyer by trade and would love to bring a libel action if he dared. The Prime Minister strongly supported my actions". It seems certain that the man in question was the Captain Peter E. Wright whose attack on Gladstone's morals in his book *Portraits and Criticisms* (London, 1925) led to one of the most notorious libel actions of the 1920s; for *The Times* recorded that Wright, a former scholar of Balliol who had been called to the Bar but never practised, had served as an Assistant Secretary to the Supreme War Council in 1917–18. Lord Gladstone, the statesman's son, engineered Wright's expulsion from the Bath Club, of which both were members, and described him as "a liar and a coward". Wright sued the Bath Club for breach of contract and was awarded nominal damages of £125 (*The Times* 14th–16th July 1926). He then accepted Lord Gladstone's challenge to sue him for libel and the case was heard before Mr. Justice Avory and a Special Jury early in 1927. Wright showed up badly under Norman Birkett's penetrating cross-examination, the Judge summed up strongly against him and the Jury returned a verdict for the defendant. (*The Times* 28th Jan.–4th Feb. 1927).

and all plans would be sent to *them*. Ll. G., with consummate skill, so manipulated that Orlando, Sonnino, and Clemenceau turned down this scheme. Thus, he got his way without appearing as a principal, and the meeting adjourned for a new scheme to be drawn up for the command of the reserves.

2nd February [1]

I brought down to breakfast with me a scheme for the reserves, which Ll. G., Milner, Gen. Wilson and I discussed at breakfast. Eventually they decided that the reserve should be under the control of a Ctee., consisting of the British, Italian, and U.S.A. Permanent Mily. Reps. with Gen. Foch in the chair. Having with some difficulty persuaded the Italians to accept it Ll. G. in a speech of great skill announced it to the Council bringing tears to the eyes of Foch, Clemenceau and even Orlando. Foch was so moved that he could make no reply. After that we had no difficulty, as, on all the remaining questions, the French (in their delight at the great position conceded to Gen. Foch, who practically becomes Commander-in-Chief) made concessions including the controversial question of the extension of the British line. Thus Haig and to a less extent Robertson were satisfied. The conference was distinguished for two remarkable outbursts, one on the part of Haig, who made out that his divisions would be reduced from 57 to 37 by the end of the year (which was to some extent refuted by Ll. G.), and one on the part of Robertson, who entered a solemn protest against the Turkish campaign. R. afterwards apologised to Ll. G. for this, explaining that he was afraid of being left in the same position as Fisher was over the Dardanelles affair . . . Ll. G. instructed me *not* to circulate the *procès verbal* of the Versailles Conference, as he did not want the Cabinet to see Robertson's outburst . . .

On Sunday 3rd February Lloyd George and Hankey returned to London, and during the journey the former outlined his plans for reconstructing the government. Balfour was to join the War Cabinet, Lord Robert Cecil, or possibly Lloyd George himself, would take over the Foreign Office, and Milner become Secretary of State for War in place of Derby, whom Lloyd George proposed to console with the Paris embassy. In the event, however, Balfour remained at the Foreign Office, without a seat in the War Cabinet[2]; and Lloyd George hesitated until the middle of April before he finally gave Milner the War Office.

[1] Extracts from this day's entry are in *Supreme Command*, II, pp. 769 and 773.
[2] See Blanche E. C. Dugdale, *Arthur James Balfour*, 2 Vols. (Hutchinson, 1936), Vol. II, Ch. XII and Kenneth Young, *Arthur James Balfour* (Bell, 1963), Ch. 17. Balfour, though not a member of the War Cabinet, always enjoyed ready access to the Prime Minister.

Lloyd George certainly had reason to be satisfied over the final outcome of the Versailles meeting.[1] The importance he attached to the creation of a General Reserve, and to placing it under Foch as chairman of the newly formed Executive Committee, undoubtedly derived from his awareness of the fact that he who controlled the reserve would be able to exercise great influence over strategy; and Lloyd George was determined that there should be no more Passchendaeles. His handling of the whole issue, and his outflanking of Haig and Robertson, was, as Hankey finally recognised, typically astute; and one feels that the irritability which he showed in the early stages, and which aroused the usually patient secretary's animadversions, almost certainly arose from the fact that he knew he was steering for another collision with the Generals. All the signs are that these encounters greatly increased Lloyd George's nervous tension; but Hankey never seems to have appreciated the cause.

Diary 7th February 1918
War Cabinet 11.30 to discuss the question of our relations with the Bolshevists. Lunch with P.M. to meet Sir Edward Carson (who has left the Govt. and has just returned from stumping Ulster) and Gen. Harington,[2] Chief of Staff to Gen. Plumer. Ll. G. had thought of him as a possible successor to Gen. Robertson, but I thought it quite clear that he didn't take a wide enough view . . .

8th February
War Cabinet at noon on the Russian and Roumanian question. Decided to make some advance towards recognition of Bolshevists by allowing Lockhart,[3] whom we sent specially to Petrograd for the purpose, to become a recognised intermediary. Ll. G., who is half a Bolshevist himself, wants to get into closer relations with them, and seems to have forgotten that they have shamefully broken Russia's solemn treaty with us, repudiated the enormous sums we have lent Russia, seized our property, allowed the guns

[1] See *Lloyd George*, V, pp. 2730–59.
[2] Sir Charles ("Tim") Harington (1872–1940). Chief of Staff to General Plumer (Second Army) 1916–18. Deputy C.I.G.S. 1918–20. G.O.C. Army of Black Sea 1920–21. G.O.C. Northern Command 1923–27, Western Command, India, 1927–31 and Aldershot Command 1931–33. Governor of Gibraltar 1933–37.
[3] Sir Robert Bruce Lockhart (1887–1968). Consular Service officer, banker and author. Acting Consul-General, Moscow 1915–17. Head of Special Mission to Soviet government 1918. Editorial Staff, *Evening Standard* 1929–37. Foreign Office, Political Intelligence Department 1939–40. Director-General, Political Warfare Executive, 1941–45.

we supplied to fall into the enemy's hands, and that they are engaged in a war against all civilised institutions. Cecil on the other hand is too much anti-Bolshevist. Balfour, as usual, rather on the hedge between these. The discussion got rather hot at one time, as they were getting to fundamentals, the rights of property owners etc., when I hastily intervened, and brought them back to business. A very amusing meeting.

11th February[1]

During my absence on Saturday Ll. G. had got himself into a regular mess about the Versailles business. After consultation with Lord Derby on Saturday he had offered Robertson the post of Military Adviser at Versailles, while Wilson was [to be] brought home and offered the appointment of C.I.G.S. An extraordinary thing to do. Wilson, who is a good strategist and gets on well with foreigners, and has been a brilliant success at Versailles, but is very much distrusted by the army, is to be C.I.G.S., while Robertson, who is a good administrator and is popular with the army, but cannot get on at all with foreigners is to go to Versailles! I am bound to say that I was appalled when he told me at the War Cabinet in the morning . . . At a second War Cabinet in the evening it was decided to seize The Morning Post in consequence of Repington's disclosure of the Versailles decision.[2]

12th February

At the War Cabinet this morning it transpired that Robertson had refused Versailles. There was a long, but inconclusive discussion as to whether Robertson should be allowed to remain on as C.I.G.S., with his powers reduced in order to confer the necessary authority on Wilson to carry out the scheme for the control of the reserves at Versailles, or whether he should be fired out. The P.M. delivered a tremendous tirade against Robertson, but appeared unable to screw up his courage to the point of firing him out. Milner was all for firing him out. The others about equally divided, that feather brained Lord Derby wanting to keep him. No decision was reached. Meanwhile the decision re Morning Post had been [?] reversed on the previous evening at a late informal conference held after the War Cabinet . . .

As Hankey has himself published the remainder of the above diary entry and also the greater part of the entries for the succeeding days, except for some personal remarks about individuals, we will only here summarise the course of the crisis over Robertson.[3] Neither Lloyd

---

[1]Part of this entry is in *Supreme Command*, II, p. 776.
[2]See *Lloyd George*, V, pp. 2788–2804 regarding the *Morning Post* articles inspired or written by Colonel Repington about the decisions recently taken by the Supreme War Council.
[3]See *Supreme Command*, II, pp. 776–9.

George nor Hankey was at his best at the time, as both of them were suffering from heavy colds.

On the afternoon of 12th February Lloyd George made a poor showing in the House in answering some awkward questions posed by Asquith and his supporters during the debate on the Address.[1] This, together with "the failure to take strong action against The Morning Post, to refuse to be dictated to by Robertson . . . and the failure to answer questions about the General Reserve", remarked Hankey, "have had a very damaging effect on the Government".[2] Next day Esher wrote to Hankey "All this indecision is having a bad effect. I hear that the opposition is crystallizing, and that Mr. A. [Asquith] spends hours at Lansdowne H[ouse]. You can realise what this portends . . . H.W. [Wilson] ought not to be hanging about in London . . . If he goes to the W.O. it will do him no good to have been here. If he does not, it will weaken him at V[ersailles]. I do not like the look of things . . ." Hankey at once sent this letter on to Lloyd George with a note saying "I think you should see this, as similar information has reached me from other quarters".[3]

Lloyd George next told Hankey that he "could not sack Robertson" because the Northcliffe press had been attacking the C.I.G.S. with all its customary virulence, and if he was dismissed "all the world would say it was [done] at Northcliffe's dictation". Lloyd George's close association with newspaper magnates thus proved a two-edged weapon. Meanwhile Derby—"poor wobbly thing" Hankey called him —had veered round to placing Wilson at Versailles "definitely under Robertson"; while Milner was naturally annoyed over Lloyd George's hesitations. Hankey, as so often, acted as go-between for the Prime Minister in negotiating between the three of them.

Next day, the 14th, Hankey recorded that "Robertson seems definitely to have declined the Versailles post or to remain as C.I.G.S. under the new conditions"; but the Cabinet decided that another effort should be made, using Balfour as intermediary, to "invite and persuade him to accept". If Robertson proved stubborn the post of C.I.G.S. was to be offered to Plumer, while Wilson was to stay on at Versailles. Hankey, who doubted whether Balfour had properly understood his mission, went straight off to find him, and deposited him at the War Office to see Derby. None the less Balfour, according to Lucas,

[1] Parl. Deb., Commons, Vol. 103, Cols. 14–91. [2] Diary 12th Feb. 1918.
[3] Esher to Hankey 13th Feb. 1918. Lloyd George papers F/23/2/14.

Robertson's personal secretary, "never properly made the offer". Next Lloyd George told Derby to telegraph to Plumer offering him Robertson's post; but the Prime Minister wisely asked Hankey to see the draft telegram. He found it was "quite calculated to make Plumer refuse", and therefore redrafted it. Derby now told Hankey he "intended to resign"; and the latter "did not discourage him".[1]

Diary 15th February 1918
War Cabinet at 11.30, without Ll. G., who was still upstairs and very seedy. A very difficult question arose owing to Foch having advised that two British Divisions ought to (?) be brought to the Western front from Italy. Robertson supported him. Milner insisted that the question ought to be decided by Versailles . . . It was stubbornly contested, and we had to adjourn upstairs to discuss it with Ll. G. He decided in favour of Robertson, because, as he explained to me afterwards, he could not afford to have another row on his hands. He was convinced it was all a ramp on the part of Derby and Robertson to make trouble for the Govt. and give them better ground than the Versailles question for resigning! . . .[2]

Next Plumer's reply was received—"couched in terms of general support to Robertson". Hankey thought it "looked suspiciously like a 'rig' by the great General Staff trades union". Thereupon the scene shifted to Walton Heath, to which Lloyd George had retired to nurse his cold; and on the evening of 15th Milner, Wilson and Hankey joined him there. The latter now regarded the position as "very critical for the Government"; but on the way down he prophesied that Lloyd George would be found "rising to the occasion and full of fight". And so it proved. For the Prime Minister quickly decided that Wilson "should become C.I.G.S. and, if Derby resigned (as we all hoped he would) Milner should become Secretary of State for War".[3]

Hankey to Lloyd George. 2 Whitehall Gardens 15th February 1918. Postscript Holograph[4]
Confidential
My dear Prime Minister,
    Since I saw you I have had an invitation to lunch from Asquith! After some cogitation I have decided to accept. I think you can trust me! In fact, I might manage to allay trouble, and shall do my utmost. I think it possible, however,

[1] Diary 14th Feb. 1918.
[2] Almost all the remainder of this day's entry is in *Supreme Command*, II, pp. 778–9.
[3] Diary 15th February 1918. [4] Lloyd George papers F/23/2/15.

that you might prefer that I did not lunch with him; if so, perhaps you would ask your housekeeper to send me a telephone message saying: "The Prime Minister suggests that you do not keep your appointment to-day." In this case I will get out of it . . .

Yours ever,

P.S. Esher tells me that Lansdowne and Asquith have agreed that you must be kept in office.

Diary 16th February 1918

Ll. G. saw the King in the morning to obtain his approval to the above changes. The King however insisted on another final offer being made to Robertson, and Lord Stamfordham was, I believe, sent to try and induce him to change his mind. The War Cabinet met at 12.30 and confirmed this. Robertson's reply was merely a repudiation of the whole system. We therefore issued a notice that he had resigned and had been replaced by Wilson, the notice being on the lines of the one I had drafted the previous evening. As Lord Curzon had gone away to Kedleston and had not attended the War Cabinet and was suspected of resigning tendencies, I took [it] on myself to send a telegram and Longhurst as a special messenger to Derby, so that he should not have the first notice of Robertson's resignation in Sunday's newspapers. I had lunched alone with Ll. G. and he had asked me to be "on tap" at Walton Heath, where Sir George Riddell entertained me at the golf club.

On 17th, a Sunday, Hankey's walk around the golf course at Walton Heath was interrupted by a summons from Lloyd George to come to his home. There he found Derby and Haig, the latter having been called in "to consult about filling the Versailles [i.e. Wilson's] appointment." Derby once more made a pitiful impression, appearing to be "on the point of resigning for the 28th time or thereabouts"; and Hankey forbore to discourage him from doing so. But in the end Lloyd George decided that it was "better to keep him, as he insisted that, in his statement of reasons for resignation, he must give away that Haig and Plumer disapproved of the Versailles arrangement". Bonar Law was therefore commissioned "to see the flabby jelly [Derby] and prevent him from resigning, which he did".[1] Hankey returned to town and drafted a statement for the Press, to be issued next day; but in fact it was not issued immediately, because the dismissal of Robertson was to be debated in the House of Commons in the near future. He therefore returned to Walton Heath to coach Lloyd George for his speech, a

[1] Diary 17th Feb. 1918.

task made no easier by the fact that the Prime Minister was "seedy but truculent".

Robertson to Hankey. War Office. 17th February 1918. Holograph
My dear Hankey,

Many thanks for your kind letter. During our association you have been splendid. You could have caused very much mischief and trouble, had you been built that way. But, on the contrary, you have been of the greatest assistance to me, and I have always felt convinced you were a loyal friend. And I always shall.

What a pity, indeed, all this trouble at this particular time. And it could *so* easily [have been] avoided, or remedied.

Believe me
Yours very truly

On 18th Davidson wrote to Hankey about the draft of a statement on the establishment of a Supreme Allied Commander which the latter had "left with the Chancellor" (Bonar Law). The final paragraph read "When finally offered the choice either of becoming British Military Representative at Versailles or of retaining the post of C.I.G.S. under the conditions I have set forth, General Robertson replied with deep regret that he was unable to acquiesce *in a system of control, by which the C.I.G.S. is not on the Executive Committee, and that he regarded the proposed system as dangerous.* This was tantamount to resignation, and he has consequently been replaced as C.I.G.S. by General Sir Henry Wilson". Hankey amended the italicised sentence to read "in the system decided on, which he regarded as unworkable and dangerous".[1] But in fact the official announcement took a somewhat different form, merely stating that the extension of the functions of the Permanent Military Representatives decided on by the Supreme War Council "has necessitated a limitation of the special powers hitherto exercised by the Chief of the Imperial General Staff"; that the government had offered Robertson the choice stated above, but that as he "did not see his way to accept either position" the government "have with much regret accepted his resignation", and Sir Henry Wilson "has accepted the position of Chief of the Imperial General Staff".[2] On the following Monday (19th) Lloyd George made his promised statement in the House. *The Times* described it as "a very convincing review", and members of all parties showed impatience over Asquith's sceptical probing about Robertson's dis-

[1]Bonar Law papers. BL. 84/7/3.   [2]*The Times*, 18th Feb. 1918.

missal.[1] But for Lloyd George to declare that he and the General had "parted with expressions of great kindliness" was surely a remarkable extension even of his outstanding capacity for rhetorical tergiversation.

Diary 19th February 1918
War Cabinet at 11.30. I lunched with the P.M. alone. He was in good fettle for his speech, though still seedy. I heard his speech in the House of Commons, when he completely disposed of the whole business. His speech was on the lines of the statement I had written on Sunday and he avoided the pitfalls I had feared he would slip into. I had tea with him afterwards . . . He was in great spirits, and walked up and down imitating "Wully's" heavy walk. Thus I hope ends the Robertson crisis. He is gone, and Henry Wilson reigns in his stead . . . He was a poor strategist, a splendid organiser and administrator, but suffered from "swelled head". He would not subordinate himself as a public servant must to the Government, and this brought him down. To me personally he was a good friend, and, though I always disagreed with his policy, as he had the responsibility I did my best to support it . . .

We may here return to the story of the prosecution of the *Morning Post* for publishing Repington's article—which Lloyd George has described as "malignant and treasonable".[2] The Cabinet, as stated in Hankey's diary, considered the matter on the day of publication and decided to suppress the paper. However, after consulting the Law Officers and the Director of Public Prosecutions, that decision was modified in favour of prosecution. The difficulty was to frame charges in such a way as avoided making revelations regarding the recent decisions of the Supreme War Council which would be of assistance to the enemy. Although Lloyd George evidently wanted to take very drastic action the final decision was merely to bring charges under the Defence of the Realm Act.[3] Gwynne and Repington were convicted of disobeying the censorship regulations, and both were fined £100 plus costs. But it is surely beyond doubt that Repington's action formed part of a conspiracy against Lloyd George and his government —and that Generals Robertson and Maurice were, at the very least, privy to it. For the former wrote Repington a letter of condolence,[4] and the latter expressed "the greatest admiration for your [Repington's] courage and determination . . . you have been the victim of political

[1] *loc. cit.*, 20th Feb. 1918. [2] *Lloyd George*, V, p. 2796. [3] *ibid.*, p. 2804.
[4] *ibid.*

persecution such as I did not think was possible in England".[1] Small wonder that the whole incident aroused Lloyd George's fury—with which Hankey certainly sympathised.

Once the Robertson crisis was over Hankey turned his energies to a very different matter—the constitution of a League of Nations. On 20th he gave evidence before a Foreign Office committee under the chairmanship of Sir Walter Phillimore.[2] But as we have already recorded Hankey's view that the League should be based on the organisation of the Supreme War Council,[3] and his evidence followed the same general lines, it will not be repeated. It was however typical of his constant foresight that, realising he could not escape involvement in the proposal for a League of Nations, he spent the days following his appearance before the Phillimore Committee in reading up the history, geography and ethnography of the smaller European countries.[4]

Despite Hankey's vast preoccupations he always replied promptly to requests for information or help from Lord Fisher—who was by this time chiefly concerned in proving that his pre-war policies and prophecies had been correct. On 21st he sent the old Admiral a document he had requested—probably relating to Fisher's forecast that submarines would be used to attack merchant ships—and accompanied it with a long letter reviewing the lessons of the war, the opportunities lost and the misuse of our military power.[5] A few days later the Admiral enlisted Hankey's aid in refuting a statement made by Bonar Law in the House to the effect that he had not been a member of the C.I.D. after he had left the Admiralty in January 1910. The flurry evidently arose from the word "not" having been wrongly inserted in Bonar Law's answer to a question, and a correction was promised. But to Fisher's fury ("I think

[1]Quoted in Repington's diary for 24th Feb. 1918. *The First World War*, Vol. II, p. 234.
[2]1st Baron Phillimore 1918 (1845–1929). Ecclesiastical and international jurist. Judge of Queen's Bench Division 1897–1913. Lord Justice of Appeal 1913–16. Chairman, Committee on a League of Nations 1917–18. A member of the family referred to in the couplet—

> When God Almighty made the bores
> He started with the Phillimores . . .

The other members of the Phillimore Committee were Sir Eyre Crowe and Sir Cecil Hurst (Foreign Office), and Sir Julian Corbett and J. Holland Rose, the historians.
[3]See pp. 471 and 482.
[4]Diary 21st Feb. 1917.
[5]Hankey to Fisher 21st Feb. 1918. Marder, *Fisher*, III, pp. 512–14.

Bonar Law is a cad of the first water") the correction was never made publicly, and the offending "not" still stands in the bound volume of Hansard.[1]

On 23rd February Hankey joined Lloyd George "in a gloomy, lonely old house" above Goring-on-Sea, Sussex. But as Milner, Henry Wilson and Philip Kerr were in the party, and other Ministers and officials soon joined them, it was very much a busman's holiday for Hankey.

Diary 24th February 1918

After a walk on the downs we had a conference on Palestine. Then we were joined by the Q.M.G. (General Cowans[2]), [and] Mr. Andrew Weir,[3] director of supplies at the War Office, for lunch, after which we had a long conference on food. The result of this was that Lloyd George, as he told me later in the afternoon, practically made up his mind to sack Lord Rhondda,[4] from the food control office, with his staff, and to put in Weir. Then we drove to Littlehampton to tea with Sir Edward and Lady Carson. The former was in an unhelpful frame of mind about Ireland, as was his wife . . . Driving back Ll. G. told me his plans for reconstituting his Govt. Lord Derby to go as Paris ambassador. Lord Milner to the War Office. He wanted to bring in Austen Chamberlain, and I suggested he should put him in the War Cabinet with control of all the Committees and Departments dealing with supply. Milner and Wilson had gone home and we had a cosy, domestic evening. But I am tired of week-ends away from home.

25th February

. . . War Cabinet at noon, Bonar Law in the chair. They made two thoroughly stupid decisions: firstly to withdraw our embassy from Petrograd owing to the Bolshevists having made peace; secondly to let the Japs loose into Siberia, which, in my opinion will do no good, and may result in the starting of the "Yellow Peril". I spent the afternoon putting the first right, seeing Mr. Balfour, Lord Hardinge, Lord Robert Cecil, and Sir George

[1] See Marder, *op. cit.*, pp. 515 and 519 and Parl. Deb., Commons, Vol. CIII, Col. 1094.
[2] Sir John S. Cowans (1862–1921). Director-General, Territorial Force, 1910. Quartermaster-General 1912–19. A very able administrator on the supply side of the Army.
[3] 1st Baron Inverforth 1919 (1865–1955). Shipowner. President, Andrew Weir Shipping and Trading Co. Surveyor-General of Supply, War Office, and member of Army Council 1917–19. Minister of Munitions 1919–21.
[4] David A. Thomas, 1st Viscount Rhondda 1918 (1856–1918). Politician (Lib.), coal owner and financier. President Local Government Board 1916. Food Controller 1917–18.

Cave.[1] I pointed out to each that to withdraw our Embassy would be to lose all first-hand knowledge of what was going on in Russia, and to lose our cipher communication, and eventually they agreed that someone responsible with a proper cipher should remain. I determined however, as I am not responsible for policy, not to touch the Japanese question, beyond giving Balfour my views. The P.M. rang me up later and expressed himself very dissatisfied with the Cabinet's decisions.

A few days earlier Hankey had in fact produced for the Cabinet a Memorandum on "Policy relative to the Revolutionary Governments at Petrograd". He "thought it would be useful to have a survey made of the more recent decisions on policy", starting from the breach between Korniloff and Kerensky.[2] But his foresight evidently did not deter the Cabinet from making a decision which he had to work hard to get reversed.

Diary 26th February 1918
No War Cabinet until afternoon, so spent useful morning interviewing a number of people including Gen. Delmé-Radcliffe,[3] just home from Italy. War Cabinet 4 p.m. Bonar Law in chair. Saw Lord Beaverbrook, the new Minister of Propaganda in the evening. I had had a row with him, as, without permission he "squatted" in Carson's former room in my office and wrote hundreds of letters on my notepaper. Consequently I wrote him a rude letter. Made up row on basis of my giving him temporary accommodation until permanent accommodation [is] available. Of course it was a "plant" on his part, a first step towards trying to get into the War Cabinet. He was very down on his luck. "Until I took office," he said, "I was the most powerful man in England outside the Govt. Now, instead of being able to order the War Office and [Admiralty?] about I have to say 'Will you please do this and that?' and to take what they give me." This is a measure of his conceit, as his seizure of Carson's room is a measure of his want of tact. He is a Canadian, who made a fortune in a fortnight, came to England and by various obscure methods obtained first a baronetcy and then a peerage. He owns the Daily Express and there is intense feeling against his appointment in the Govt., the House of Commons, and the country. I can only suppose that Ll. G. put him in the Govt. in order to induce him to finance the new party machine, which,

[1]1st Viscount Cave 1918 (1856–1928). Lawyer and politician (Cons.). Solicitor-General 1915. Home Secretary 1916–19. Lord Chancellor 1922–24 and 1924–28. Chancellor of Oxford University 1925. Served as Chairman of many commissions and committees.
[2]GT. 3705 of 23rd Feb. 1918. Cab. 24/43.
[3]Later Brigadier-General Sir Charles Delmé-Radcliffe (1864–1937). Chief of British Military Missions at Italian G.H.Q. 1915–19 and in Austria 1919–20.

as he tells me, he is about to found. A shady business! I found him closeted with Lord Rothermere, owner of the Daily Mirror etc., and a very shady looking personage.

We have already seen how Hankey believed that the frequent Austrian peace feelers were genuine, and should be followed up energetically— despite Italian and French opposition. He also considered that a compromise peace could be obtained in 1917 and might well prove advantageous to the Allies. When at the beginning of March the acceptance by the Russians of the harsh terms of the Treaty of Brest Litovsk brought about the final dissolution of the eastern front Hankey went into action.

Diary 1st March 1918
War Cabinet in afternoon. I went to meet Gen. Smuts on his return from Palestine and drove him to the Cabinet. The subject was "Austria". I was appalled at the slackness of the Foreign Office in dealing with this subject. Nearly 2 months have elapsed since Czernin offered to meet the P.M. and no reply has been sent, although all sorts of hints continue to come to us and to the U.S.A. that Austria is getting into the frame of mind for a separate peace. The War Cabinet sanctioned action 6 weeks ago; but, for one reason or another—first owing to Orlando's visit, and then, when his consent was given, owing to the Austrian approaches to President Wilson—no action has been taken . . . As long as Balfour and Cecil remain at the F.O. peace is utterly impossible, owing to their ultra-caution and laziness and lack of drive. We ought to be in close and continuous contact with Austria now, always stroking her towards breaking away from Germany, but the Foreign Office, what with fears of Italy and fears of America, do absolutely nothing . . .

Hankey to Lloyd George. 2 Whitehall Gardens, 2nd March 1918[1]
Very Secret. Not to be printed
My dear Prime Minister,
    I want to make a suggestion about an improvement in our communications with Austria. I admit I felt rather scandalised at the way the Foreign Office have havered about this business. For one reason or another they have allowed nearly two months to elapse without vouchsafing any reply to the suggestion that Czernin should meet you. In fact, I believe that a particularly favourable epoch for pushing and persuading Austria to detach herself from Germany has been allowed to slip by. In theory we all talk big about a peace offensive. In practice, the moment a concrete suggestion is made, the Foreign Office are found to fear their own shadows. I don't believe they would have agreed to Smuts's visit, if they could have stopped it, though it was the

[1]Cab. 23/16.

finest bit of political propaganda we have ever done, and its effects are daily discernable. As to the idea of letting our political and diplomatic lead pass to Wilson, it is preposterous. We have all at stake; Wilson very little. But we shall automatically lose it if we don't look out. I suspect that Baker,[1] who is described in the letters circulated by Lord Milner as "a well meaning pacifist" is over on this very game. After this preliminary explosion I will outline my plan. It is based on the belief that spasmodic efforts, like Smuts's great exploit, are not enough. They must be accompanied by a regular and systematic liaison designed with two objects:—

1 To enable us to judge the psychological moment to arrange more formal meetings, like the Smuts-Mensdorff meeting.
2 For political propaganda purposes.

To accomplish this I would suggest I select two very brainy and reliable people, not too well known, as King's messengers in the Berne service. They could come and go quite regularly and their movements would attract no attention. Through Skrzynski we should arrange for Austria to have a corresponding messenger. The British and Austrian messengers should arrange a rendezvous and should meet regularly sometimes to gossip, sometimes to do business.

Philip Kerr would be an admirable selection if he could stand the travelling.

I believe that through the establishment of a regular liaison of this kind we should be able in time to detach Austria and perhaps Bulgaria and Turkey from Germany. At any rate we should get a direct channel and should avoid these hopeless delays, which will make us miss our tide every time. With apologies for the length of this.

Yours ever

Diary 2nd March 1918[2]
Spent morning in the office over the dreary job of writing (owing to secrecy) a manuscript account of yesterday's meeting . . . I forgot to mention that I had a talk last night with Eric Geddes, the First Lord. He is very cheerful about submarines and says the Adty. have absolutely certain, but very secret information that they are destroying 10 a month, and he believes they will master this terrible menace in 6 months.[3] They are having tremendous

[1]Newton D. Baker (1871–1937). American lawyer and politician. Secretary of War in President Wilson's Cabinet 1916–21. Member of Permanent Court of Arbitration, The Hague 1928.
[2]The first part of this entry is in *Supreme Command*, II, p. 656.
[3]This "absolutely certain" information, presumably derived from cryptographic sources, was actually incorrect. Eight U-boats were destroyed in January and only four in February 1918.

success with their mining policy (which I have advocated since the first days of the war) and have sunk or damaged 14 German ships in the last day or two, upsetting the Huns dreadfully, so that they got up steam in their main fleet. I lunched with Gen. Smuts. He suggest[ed] Bonar Law for the F.O. and Balfour for Cabinet. I rubbed into him the need for aeroplanes for anti-submarine work until Adty. mining policy [was] fully developed. . . . I forgot to say that Smuts told me that Robertson attached a Col. Kirk[e][1] of the General Staff to him for the trip, and all the time the Colonel was doing his utmost to queer the pitch and prevent Smuts from reporting in favour of an advance.[2] Moreover Robertson sent a letter to Gen. Allenby by Col. Kirk[e], in which he warned Allenby against encouraging Smuts. But Allenby, who was favourable to an advance showed the letter to Smuts!

6th March 1918
War Cabinet 11.30. Austrian question again discussed owing to receipt from a very secret source of information as to gist of President Wilson's reply to Austrian advances through King of Spain. F.O. as usual wanted to make this an excuse for delay in our own negotiations with Austria, but the War Cabinet wasn't taking any, and adhered to their decision to send Philip Kerr. Wilson's reply greatly pleased the F.O.; it contained some 28 points on which the Empress of Austria's views were asked for before conversations could take place. Much too complicated to be helpful, I thought. We also know from a very secret source that, if Austria breaks off from Germany, U.S A. will take over her financial liabilities. I had to see Mr. Balfour about this in the afternoon. Gen. Wilson authorised to instruct Allenby to push on at his discretion in Palestine.[3]

7th March 1918
I believe Philip Kerr has left for Switzerland. War Cabinet at 11.30 attended by all the aerial experts and a full investigation was made of the aerial position. To my regret they decided against the proposal that we should offer the enemy to desist from bombing raids beyond a limited and defined distance from the front. Personally I think we should gain more than we

---

[1]Though Hankey wrote his name as "Kirk" it is almost certain that it should read "Kirke" and was the officer who later became General Sir Walter M. St. G. Kirke (1877–1949). Deputy Director of Military Operations 1918–22. Deputy C.I.G.S. in India 1926–29. G.O. C-in-C, Western Command, 1933–6. Inspector-General, Territorial Army 1936–9 and of Home Defence 1939. C-in-C, Home Forces, 1939–40. See pp. 505 and 546 regarding Kirke's part in the events leading to the "Maurice Debate" of May 1918.
[2]This refers to Smuts's mission to Switzerland to meet Count Mensdorff in December 1917. See p. 470.
[3]General Allenby entered Jerusalem on 9th Dec. 1917.

should lose. In the afternoon Trenchard, the aerial Chief of Staff,[1] called and asked to be placed in the same position *vis à vis* the War Cabinet as the C.I.G.S. and First Sea Lord and I promised to support his request at the War Cabinet. Later, I saw Lord Milner about a new Committee the P.M. is setting up to overlook and co-ordinate reconstruction.[2] General Delmé-Radcliffe also called. I also brought to tea Heseltine,[3] the Secretary of Lord Haldane's Ctee. on Reconstruction of Govt., before which I am due to give evidence to-morrow.[4]

8th March 1918

War Cabinet at 12.30 . . . In the afternoon a big meeting at 10 Downing St. on the subject of tanks. After that I gave evidence for 2 hours before Lord Haldane's Ctee. on the future reconstruction of Government. Then to Churchill at the Ministry of Munitions to discuss a wonderful scheme he has worked out for a tremendous development of mechanical warfare to smash the Germans on the western front next year! . . . I omitted to mention that Lord Curzon called on me before the Cabinet by special appointment and at once started to complain about the inefficiency of the Foreign Office under Balfour's régime, which, he said, was losing us the war. I told him that, to the best of my knowledge, the P.M. and all his colleagues shared this view. He then asked why the P.M. did not make a change. I replied that I understood it to be a difficulty about finding a suitable successor without taking someone out of the War Cabinet. Curzon then said that he himself would be willing to sacrifice his position in the War Cabinet to go to the Foreign Office. Lord Salisbury, he said, had trained him in this work and had always designated him as his successor! I reported this conversation to the P.M. who said "I wonder what sort of a Foreign Secretary he would make?" Hitherto, in discussing this question he has always refused to look at Lord Curzon for the post.

12th March 1918

War Cabinet as usual at 11.30. Got through a lot of civilian business—

[1]1st Viscount Trenchard 1936 (1873–1956). G.O.C., Royal Flying Corps 1915–18 and Commander, Independent Air Force 1918. Chief of Air Staff Jan.–April 1918 (resigned) and 1919–29. Chief Commissioner, Metropolitan Police 1931–35.
[2]The original Reconstruction Committee had been set up in March 1916, but was reconstituted on 15th February 1917. The Ministry of Reconstruction under Mr. C. Addison took over its functions in the following August. The new committee referred to here by Hankey appears never to have come into being.
[3]Michael Heseltine (1886–1952). Civil Servant. Assistant Secretary, Ministry of Health 1928–33. Registrar of General Medical Council 1933–51.
[4]This was the "Machinery of Government Committee", of which Haldane was Chairman. It reported in December 1918. (Cd. 9230). See Dudley Somers, *Haldane of Cloan* (Allen & Unwin, 1960), pp. 346–7 regarding Haldane's work in this field.

Housing for the Working Classes; Maternity; and [?] food . . . In afternoon we received a most important telegram from Philip Kerr, in which, as the result of conversations with Sir Horace Rumbold,[1] our Minister at Berne, and Dr. Parodi, he expressed the view that Czernin was really anxious for a separate peace, as he is growing more and more apprehensive about German domination, and even foreshadowing the possibility of getting Turkey, Bulgaria, and Austria out of the war at once. I pressed for an immediate War Cabinet, but Ll. G. . . . decided to act at once; so I sat down and drafted a telegram authorising Kerr, if he shared their opinion after seeing Skrzynski, to arrange a meeting between Smuts and Czernin. We then sent for Drummond and Ll. G. sent him to Balfour with the draft. Drummond, whom I saw later, told me he had a fearful tussle with Balfour, whom he only persuaded to send the telegram on condition that he was allowed to tell President Wilson . . . Immediately after this I went to see Smuts to let him know what was in the wind for him, and found him quite agreeable. Later in the evening I had to see Lord Robert Cecil about coal for Italy. He told me that to-day the Allied Maritime Transport Council had agreed to commandeer the 600,000 tons of Dutch shipping in the allied ports, but the Americans insisted that they required the whole of it to enable them to carry out their programme of transport of troops etc. to France. On the other hand some part of it was urgently needed to convey to Italy the coal which is essential to the maintenance of that country in the war. I arranged with him, as Chairman of the Transport Conference, to state a case for the Supreme War Council, which meets on Thursday.

Though Hankey got his way over sending Philip Kerr to Switzerland to continue negotiations with the Austrians the result was not what he had hoped for—almost certainly because the Germans were nearly ready to launch their great offensive in the west, and so were able to exert decisive pressure on their hesitant Ally.[2] None the less in the calmness of retrospect it is surely the case that Hankey was right to press the Foreign Office and Lloyd George to follow up the Austrian peace feelers; and if success had been achieved it would have been of vast benefit to Europe—as Lloyd George himself evidently realised later.[3] As to Hankey's appearance before Lord Haldane's committee,

[1] 1869–1941. Minister at Berne 1916–19 and in Poland 1919–20. High Commissioner and ambassador at Constantinople 1920–24. Ambassador at Madrid 1924–28 and at Berlin 1928–33.
[2] See *Lloyd George*, V, pp. 2496–8.
[3] *ibid.*, pp. 2503–4. On Kerr's missions to Switzerland see also J. R. M. Butler, *Lord Lothian* (Macmillan, 1960), pp. 66–8, and W. K. Hancock, *Smuts*, Vol. I (Cambridge U.P. 1962), pp. 466–8.

its chairman wrote "We were as delighted as we were impressed with what you said to us this afternoon".[1] Evidently Hankey showed himself once again to be an admirable witness before a body charged with investigating a complicated issue.

On 12th March, the same day that Hankey went into action over Kerr's telegram from Switzerland, he circulated two memoranda to the War Cabinet. The first was an exposition of the legal position regarding the bombing of open towns—a measure which Hankey regarded with horror, but which the extreme advocates of air power believed would prove decisive.[2] The second one dealt with the programme for the production of tanks in 1918–19, over which the War Office and the Ministry of Munitions were in dispute about the allocation of steel.[3] And all the time he was also preparing for the forthcoming meeting in London of the Supreme War Council, at which trouble was certain to arise with Haig on the old issue of the General Reserve.

Diary 13th March 1918[4]

War Cabinet 11.30, Bonar Law in chair. Afterwards I saw the P.M. for a minute or two. He had spent the morning preparing his discourse to Free Church Ministers at the City Temple and I found him closeted with a very handsome Minister, whom I evicted during our conversation. The P.M. was very worried at the prospect of being heckled about *la maison tolérée* etc. After lunch I went to see Gen. Wilson who was bothered because Haig won't give up his quota to the Allied General Reserve. In the circumstance he advocates a suspension of the whole scheme, which is tantamount to allowing Haig to flout the Supreme War Council. To-day, however, probably on the eve of the enemy's greatest effort in the west, it appears inevitable. Both Milner, whom I saw afterwards, and the P.M. take this view, though the latter, whom I saw at 6.30, vowed he would bring Haig to his bearings eventually. Then I had to rush off to Victoria to meet Clemenceau and Orlando on behalf of the P.M., and thence back to the office with Mr. Balfour, to whom I gave tea. Then a succession of interviews with Lord Milner, Amery, Storr, and the P.M. about the arrangements for the Supreme War Council, and home late. Old Maclay, the Shipping Controller, has been at me all day about the rumour that Lord Pirrie[5] is to be in charge of shipbuilding . . .

[1]Haldane to Hankey 8th March 1918. Holograph.
[2]GT. 3883. Cab. 24/44. Copy in Milner papers, Bodleian Box 123.
[3]GT. 3890. Cab. 24/44.
[4]A small extract from this day's entry is printed in *Supreme Command*, II, p. 782.
[5]1st Viscount Pirrie 1921 (1847–1924). Shipbuilder. Chairman, Harland and Wolff, Belfast. Comptroller-General of merchant ship building 1918.

17th March 1918

For three solid days I have been employed as Secretary of the meetings of the Supreme War Council and the important contemporaneous political conference. We held 5 meetings in all and three of these I had to take single-handed, *procès-verbaux* and all . . . The foreign secretaries, who attended the S.W.C. but not the political conferences were, as usual, absolutely useless and did not function. I drafted practically all the resolutions of both conferences. Some of these were extremely tricky, and it was only my drafting that saved a complete *impasse* on the questions of the Allied General Reserve and the retaliation for air raids. The General Reserve was the most thorny problem for the Supreme War Council. Haig (who was present) had refused to supply the quota demanded of him by the Executive War Board at Versailles. Nominally his reason was that the enemy concentration on his front did not justify him in surrendering it. This however was not really a valid reason, because of course the Executive War Board would, on his representations have put this part of the reserve again at his disposal. I have no doubt at all that the real reason was that he wants to smash the whole idea. Anyhow, he told Henry Wilson he would resign if he were ordered to surrender it, and neither H.W. nor Ll. George were prepared to face that in present circumstances, with the Robertson incident only just over and a great attack threatening. I have nevertheless no doubt that, if the war is prolonged, this stupid act of a stupid man will bring Haig down. Possibly, in fact probably, Haig was in collusion with Pétain, who refused to surrender his quota if Haig didn't give his, and naturally the Italians followed suit. Thus the S.W.C. were faced with the complete breakdown of the scheme they had approved at their last meeting. After some palaver we got over it, as the result of a lunch on Thursday between Ll. George, Henry Wilson, and myself, by putting the whole of the Anglo-French forces in Italy into general reserve—thus maintaining the principle—and by sending a special Ctee. from Versailles to the Italian front to investigate how many of these divisions could be spared for the western front, and how many Italian divisions could go into general reserve. I did a very masterly draft on this (though I say it who shouldn't). Orlando said to Lloyd George—"that is very ingenious indeed", and Clemenceau added "and if an Italian says that you may know that it is". Ll. G. looked knowing, as though he had done it . . . On the whole it was not a sound or satisfactory conference. There was too much finessing and insufficient reality. Ll. George, in supporting Haig's refusal to co-operate in the scheme of a General Reserve, was finessing and dissimulating, because it was inconvenient politically to deal with Haig. On the first day there was a serious outburst between Clemenceau and Foch, which indicates quite clearly what I have suspected, that Foch is Clemenceau's "Wully" (nickname for Robertson). On the following day Clemenceau came out strongly in favour of Foch's

proposal that the transport of American troops to France should be a claim
on the requisitioned Dutch shipping prior to Italy's urgent needs for coal
and the vital need for railway trucks without which the American troops are
merely congesting the French railways. Clemenceau, I felt almost sure, was
finessing and dissimulating, in order not to show the rift between himself and
Foch. Again, on insisting that a special Committee and not the Executive
War Board, of which Foch is chairman, should go to Italy over the question
of the Reserves, I felt Clemenceau was finessing to give Foch a bit of a
knock. Somehow that was my impression of the conference . . .

The remainder of the diary entry for 17th March, part of which is
printed in Hankey's memoirs,[1] dealt with the Political Conference. The
chief issue was Japanese intervention in Siberia, and "after a tussle" and
a proposal from Balfour to delay action, a telegram was sent to
President Wilson "urging him to encourage Japan to go in". As always
Hankey watched the participants in the conferences closely, and recorded
his impressions of them. Clemenceau—"steady, independent, honest,
sincere, witty"—won his admiration; Pichon, the French Foreign
Minister—"very light weight". Lloyd George whispered to Hankey
that "he looks at Clemenceau just like my Welsh terrier looks at me".
Orlando he considered "a decent commonsense politician", while
Bissolati was "a nice quiet fellow but took little part. His French is
execrable".

Diary 19th March 1918
. . . The War Cabinet report for 1917 came out to-day and was very well
received.[2] Curiously enough the only part quoted in the papers was from the
portion I had written in regard to the War Cabinet system. Many people
spoke to me about it in terms of interest and admiration. Mr. Barnes spoke
to me yesterday about my work during the international conferences last
week, and said he was much struck at the way in which I managed every
evening to supply the War Cabinet with a full account of all that had happened
. . . The War Cabinet are so accustomed to having the whole of the Minutes
dished out regularly every evening, that I sometimes wonder whether they
realise the immense amount of work and organisation involved.

The report on the War Cabinet's work for 1917, to which Hankey
had devoted so much time and which finally comprised over 200 closely
printed pages, had a very cordial reception in Parliament and the Press.

[1]*Supreme Command*, II, pp. 783–4.
[2]Cd. 9005. "War Cabinet's Report for the Year 1917". The editors were Hankey and
Philip Kerr. Hankey to Sir James Butler, 10th Nov. 1955.

The Times devoted a first editorial and a leading article to it on the day of its publication, describing it as "A Novel Blue-Book" and "a very wonderful story, for it describes the greatest effort ever made by this nation, or perhaps by any nation in a single year . . .". But in the long view it did more than inform the British people in sober, restrained language regarding what they had accomplished in the prosecution of the war. Because no other body except the Cabinet Secretariat could have produced such a work it placed the organisation for which Hankey bore so great a share of the responsibility on a much firmer footing than formerly; and Hankey himself was to exploit that fact when, in the early 1920s, the Secretariat came under heavy fire and its abolition, or at least its absorption into the Treasury, became a very real possibility.[1]

On 21st Hankey recorded that "the long awaited Hun attack began on the very front where we had expected it, and on ground that I had been over with Gen. Smuts some 7 weeks ago. It is one of the decisive moments of history". Though the second sentence was true enough Hankey was not correct in saying that the attack took place "on the very ground where we had expected it"; but his implication that the Germans did not achieve strategic surprise was true.[2] In fact Ludendorff's onslaught fell between Arras and St. Quentin; and, greatly helped by an early morning mist, the Germans broke right through the comparatively thinly held front of Gough's Fifth Army south of the Somme. Fortunately progress was much less on the German right wing south of Arras; but by 27th the advance had penetrated nearly 40 miles and had reached Montdidier, cutting one railway to Paris. The extent and nature of the crisis soon became apparent in London. On 22nd Hankey wrote that "Although terrific fighting is going on . . . and some bulges have been made in our battle zone, especially on Fifth Army front, there appeared to be no cause for alarm". However, he continued, "during the day the news became worse. The Fifth Army was obviously giving way, and the situation was menacing". Next day he wrote that "we could not but fear a *débâcle*".[3]

On 24th, a Sunday, Hankey went to London, but as "there was nothing doing and little news" he returned home. At 6.30 p.m., when

[1] See Hankey's *Diplomacy by Conference* (Benn, 1946), pp. 69–82.
[2] See *Liddell Hart*, pp. 503–4.
[3] Nearly the whole of the diary entries for 22nd and 23rd are produced in *Supreme Command*, II, pp. 785–6.

he was "singing part songs with the children in the garden", he received "an imperative call from Downing Street that the P.M. wanted me". So off he went back to London where he found "the news was about as bad as it could be", with the likelihood of a complete breach being made between the Third and Fifth Armies. Haig had reported "the situation is serious"; while Churchill, supported by Henry Wilson, was "heavily bombarding the P.M. with demands for a *levée en masse*". Lloyd George wisely slipped off to Walton Heath; whereupon, wrote Hankey, "the bombardment was transferred to me". Though he was resentful about being recalled from a much needed day of rest, and critical of Lloyd George's lack of consideration for his staff, he added philosophically "still one must take the rough with the smooth".[1] It is hardly surprising that he "slept very badly" that night; and the following day he described as "terrible". The War Cabinet held "an anxious meeting" and decided to have a Bill drafted extending conscription to Ireland and raising the age limit for military service.

After dinner on the evening of 26th Hankey and Lloyd George went back to Downing Street where they were joined by Henry Wilson and Milner, who had come straight from the conference of French and British military leaders held at Doullens. There Foch had been made "co-ordinating authority" over the whole western front. But Hankey's description of his new authority as being "practically generalissimo" was in fact exaggerated, and another meeting, held at Beauvais early in April, was necessary before a genuine Supreme Command came into being.

On 27th March things looked a little brighter to Hankey. He wrote in his diary that both British and French reserves were moving up in the most threatened sector, and "attacks were repulsed during the day". The Cabinet was still debating the vexed question whether conscription should be applied to Ireland.[2]

On Good Friday, 29th, the Cabinet decided to press President Wilson "to send over 100,000 men a month for the next three months to fight in American battalions in British brigades". The situation south of the Somme still caused anxiety, and the great communication centre of Amiens was endangered. In the afternoon Lloyd George insisted on Hankey going with him to St. Anne's church, Soho, to hear Bach's Passion Music. "He would hardly let me out of his sight", wrote

[1] Diary 24th March 1918. Part reproduced in *Supreme Command*, II, p. 786.
[2] *ibid.*, p. 788.

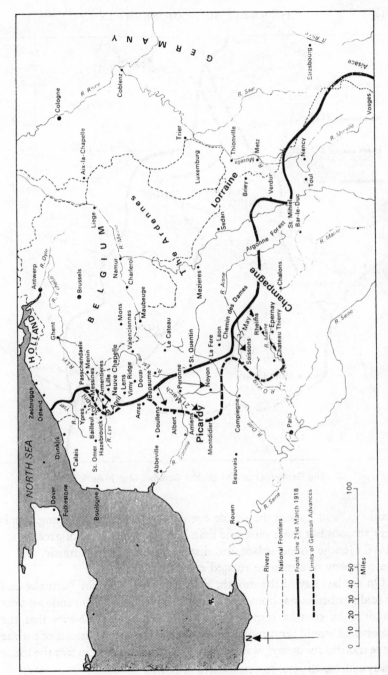

4 The Western Front showing the German Offensives, March-May 1918

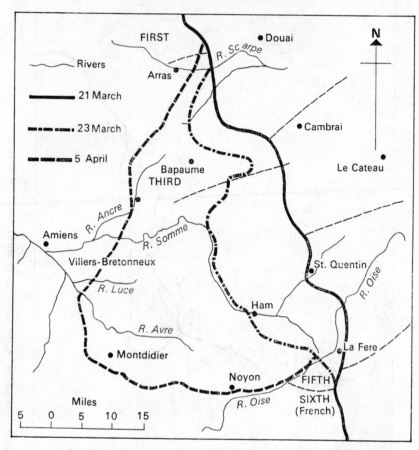

5 The German Offensive on the Somme, March-April 1918

Hankey, "and I spent the whole evening smoking and chatting. He is very anxious but more sanguine than I".[1] Plainly in times of great stress Lloyd George found solace and distraction in religious music, and in the company of a man he trusted completely.

On the last day of the month, Easter Sunday, Hankey "actually had an undisturbed day at home", though he stayed in uniform and had a car standing by to take him to London if a call came. News that the Americans would send 100,000 men for four months, instead of for the three months requested, was extremely heartening; and in fact the totals

[1] Diary 29th March 1918. Part reproduced in *Supreme Command*, II, pp. 788–9.

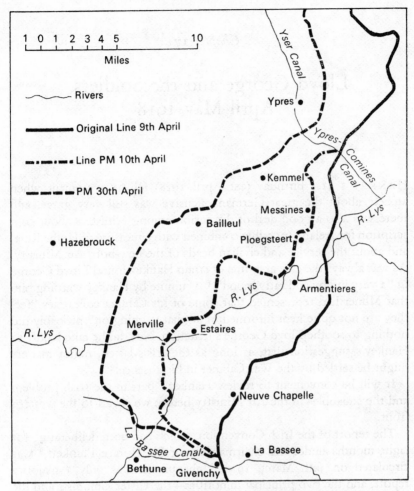

6   The German Offensive in Flanders, April 1918

sent reached about 120,000 men per month. "This is a good Easter egg", wrote Hankey in his diary, "and it seems that the prayers I mumbled at early Communion this morning are already in a fair way to be answered. Nevertheless I doubt not the future has many terrible things in store for us, and that we shall need stout hearts and firm faith for many a day to come".[1] After ten very anxious days, he was at least able to end on a note of hope blended with confidence.

[1] Diary 31st March 1918. Complete entry is in *ibid.*, p. 789.

Chapter 17

Lloyd George and the Soldiers.
April-May 1918

HANKEY'S 41st birthday (1st April 1918) fell at a moment when anxiety about the great German offensive was still very grave, and there was also a good deal of dissension among Ministers about conscription for Ireland (possibly combined with a measure of Home Rule) and about the service and civilian heads of the new-born Air Ministry. As was always the case at a time of strain Hankey found Lloyd George in "a very jumpy and ratty mood".[1] A minute by Hankey warning him that Milner had represented that some of his Cabinet colleagues "feel they are not quite kept informed of all that is going on" probably did nothing to soothe Lloyd George's irritation. Nor did he take kindly to Hankey's suggestion that, as long as the crisis lasted, minor matters might be settled by the War Cabinet in his absence.[2]

It will be convenient to review Hankey's part in the Irish problem and the squabbles in the Air Ministry before we revert to the western front.

The report of the Irish Convention, which had been deliberating for eight months under the chairmanship of Sir Horace Plunkett,[3] was circulated on 30th March 1918. Unhappily it was only a majority report, and the two principal minorities—the Ulster Unionists and the Irish Nationalists—issued dissenting views.[4] Thus a compromise settlement of the Home Rule and conscription issues was obviously no nearer achievement. On 10th April Hankey followed up a suggestion

---

[1]Diary 1st April 1918. Most of the entry is in *Supreme Command*, II, p. 789.
[2]Lloyd George papers F/23/2/20.
[3]1854–1932. Irish politician (U.). Became converted to Home Rule but opposed partition of Ireland. Chairman, Irish Convention 1917–18. Founded Irish Dominion League 1919. Senator, Irish Free State 1922–23.
[4]The report was issued as a Blue Book and is well summarised in *The Times* of 13th April 1918. The report was adopted by 44 votes to 29.

originated by his assistant Lieut-Colonel Leslie Wilson[1] to gain the co-operation of as many Irishmen as possible by forming a committee which Carson, Dillon,[2] O'Brien[3] and Labour Party representatives in Ireland would be invited to join. Hankey, with his instinctive desire to avoid any measure likely to lead to open conflict, vastly preferred this approach to the War Office's claim that they and the Ministry of National Service should be responsible for Irish recruiting.[4] Ten days later he passed to Lloyd George the somewhat similar views of Sir Mark Sykes, who "attached the utmost importance to the War Office not having control of the [Irish] recruiting", and had put forward moderate and sensible proposals whereby some 50–80,000 volunteers might be obtained for "the old Irish regiments", or for "an Irish army composed of Irish divisions", or through enlistment in the American army. "I confess", concluded Hankey, "that I was very much taken by his proposals".[5] In spite of the united front presented by the Cabinet Secretariat Lloyd George refused to accept that conscription for Ireland should be linked with a measure of Home Rule. Though Hankey kept up the pressure he finally wrote despairingly in his diary that the Prime Minister remained "absolutely adamant". "He said", the entry continues, "that the Irish were in the same condition as the southerners before the American civil war, dictating the policy of the government and unwilling to help in any way. They must first be brought to a reasonable frame of mind, and this could only be done by severe measures. He gave no heed to my remonstrances and pleas for a conciliatory policy".[6] Thus did Lloyd George, fortified by a false historical analogy, adhere stubbornly to the old policy of repression. In his defence it should, however, be said that the opposition of the Ulster Unionists and the Irish Nationalists was equally stubborn, and caused Home Rule to be dropped once again. Nor was conscription ever applied to Ireland. In mid-May reports of a German plot to raise

[1]Later Sir Leslie O. Wilson (1876–1955). Soldier and politician (U.). Parliamentary Assistant Secretary to War Cabinet 1918. Parliamentary Secretary to Ministry of Shipping 1919 and to Treasury 1921–23. Chief Unionist Whip 1921–23. Governor of Bombay 1923–8 and of Queensland 1932–46.
[2]John Dillon (1851–1927). Irish politician (Nat.). Several times imprisoned by British. A close ally of O'Brien (see below). Chairman of Irish Party 1918.
[3]William O'Brien (1852–1928). Irish nationalist leader. Several times imprisoned by British. Founded "All for Ireland" League.
[4]Hankey to Lloyd George 10th April 1918. Lloyd George papers F/23/2/24.
[5]Same to same 20th April 1918. ibid. F/23/2/29. [6]Diary 22nd April 1918.

a new insurrection led to the arrests of de Valera and other Irish Nationalist leaders. Despite this depressing development in June Lord French, the Lord Lieutenant, issued a proclamation calling for 50,000 volunteers—very much on the lines proposed by Sykes and Hankey.[1]

While the crisis in France was at its height the trouble which had long been brewing between Lord Rothermere and General Trenchard, the first holders of the new offices of Secretary of State for Air and Chief of the Air Staff, came to a head. This is not the place to adjudicate on the rights and wrongs of the breach, but Hankey's diary places it in a different light from that recorded by Trenchard's biographer.[2]

Diary 11th April 1918[3]

... I lunched with Smuts and Lord Hugh Cecil ... in order to discuss the question of Trenchard, whom Lord Rothermere has decided to get rid of from the post of Chief of Staff of the Air Ministry. The P.M. has delegated the question to Smuts. Hugh Cecil ... was violently opposed to the removal of Trenchard, who, he says, is a very good man, and has the confidence of the Air Service. If he goes the only alternative is Gen. Brancker.[4] He [Cecil] is altogether opposed to Sykes.[5] Smuts is much perplexed ...

Next day Hankey recorded that the War Cabinet had approved the appointment of Sykes in Trenchard's place. But that very evening Smuts came round to Whitehall Gardens to tell Hankey that Rothermere had suddenly got "cold feet" about the change. This led to the discussion being renewed.

Diary 12th April 1918

... After a great palaver we all went off to the P.M. at the House of Commons, where we gradually collected Gen. Wilson and Lord Rothermere. I was asked my opinion, and did not conceal that I thought it a mistake to make a change. Trenchard, whatever his faults, has created the greatest air force in the world, and it is absurd to remove him during a great battle, . . . Sykes, whatever his merits, (and they are many) is unpopular with a part of the air force, and, rightly or wrongly, was superseded in the command in France

---

[1]Lloyd George papers F/23/3/8. See also *Lloyd George*, V, pp. 2664–72.

[2]A. Boyle, *Trenchard. Man of Vision* (Collins, 1960), pp. 266–70.

[3]This date is amended in Swinton's hand from 12th to 11th. Hankey actually wrote it on 13th.

[4]Later Air Marshal Sir W. Sefton Brancker (1877–1930). Director of Air Organisation 1916–17. Controller-General of Equipment and Master-General of Personnel on Air Council 1918. Killed in disaster to airship R.101 5th Oct. 1930.

[5]General Sir Frederick H. Sykes (1877–1954). Chief of Air Staff 1918–19. M.P. (Cons.) 1922. Governor of Bombay 1928–33.

early in the war,[1] and later on in the command in Gallipoli. Eventually they decided that, before confirming the appointment of Sykes, they must clear up the mystery of why he had been got rid of from France in 1915, and I was sent off to see Gen. Robertson, who had been C.G.S. in France at the time, and might be expected to know the facts . . .

Hankey's talk with Robertson threw no light on Sykes's earlier supersession; but next day Smuts telephoned to say that, having consulted the Adjutant-General, who had been on French's staff at the time, "he considered Sykes to be the best man available, and that accordingly Rothermere was to make the appointment".[2]

The Cabinet's decision did not, however, prove quite the end of the Trenchard affair for Lloyd George or Hankey.

Diary 15th April 1918

. . . To-day Lord Stamfordham came to the P.M. to protest on behalf of the King about Trenchard being superseded. The P.M., according to his own account, got very angry and sent Stamfordham away with "a flea in his ear", telling him that the King was encouraging mutiny by taking up the cause of these officers (e.g. Trenchard and Robertson) whom the Government had decided to get rid of. Later Stamfordham rang me up from Windsor to say that the King had not received the Minutes about Trenchard and had only learnt of the affair from Lord Rothermere on Saturday afternoon. He was in a great fuss about the King not having received the Minute. As a matter of fact the King did not receive the Minute until this morning through a slip in the office, but in any case he would not have got it until Saturday night or Sunday morning . . . and by that time he had heard all particulars from Rothermere. So he really hadn't a leg to stand on. However, I wrote a note of apology.[3]

On 2nd April Hankey left London in company with Lloyd George, Henry Wilson and their personal staffs for a military conference at Beauvais. Clemenceau himself met the British delegates, according to Hankey "looking rather worried . . . but he was full of courage and very splendid". The old "tiger" proceeded to turn out of the conference

---

[1] In fact the replacement of Sykes by Brooke-Popham in 1915 arose partly from a clash of personality between the former and Trenchard which dated back to August 1914, and partly from the allegation that Sykes had been "actively scheming to replace" General Sir David Henderson (see p. 251) as Director of Military Aeronautics. See Boyle, *op. cit.*, p. 139, which of course gives Trenchard's side of the story. For Sykes's side see his autobiography, *From Many Angles* (Harrap, 1942), Ch. VI (esp. pp. 143–8).

[2] Diary 13th April 1918.   [3] The note in question is in RA. GV K.1291/13.

room at the Hôtel de Ville all the French and American secretaries. He then asked "Is Colonel Hankey here?", and on finding him present "got to business". The chief subject was the co-ordination of Allied strategy, which was "eventually put into the safe hands of General Foch"— largely at the initiative of the Americans Pershing and Bliss. "It was easy to see", commented Hankey, "that Foch and Pétain did not like each other".[1] Nor did Foch like the restriction of his powers to mere "co-ordination". "What am I?" he remarked to Hankey. "If I co-ordinate I am still Monsieur Foch. If I were General-in-Chief then I could tell Haig, Pétain etc.".[2] Lloyd George, as well as the American Generals, strongly supported Foch, with the result that the Doullens agreement[3] was superseded by the formula that "the British, French and American Governments . . . entrust to General Foch the strategic direction of military operations". But his powers did not yet extend beyond the western front.

The least satisfactory outcome of the Beauvais meeting was that, in Hankey's words, "From our generals we were unable to obtain any coherent reason for the defeat of our Fifth Army". But the inquest into that disaster was to be very prolonged.

Hankey got back to London in the small hours of 4th April, and at once settled down to writing the *procès-verbal* of the conference. That evening he insisted on going down to Highstead "to get a long night in bed". But he always showed remarkable powers of recuperation, and a night under his own roof in Adeline's care quickly restored his vigour.

Though no one realised it at the time 5th April marked the end of the first phase of Ludendorff's great offensive. True he had made a very deep penetration on the British front; but he had failed, though only by a narrow margin, to capture Amiens or to sever the main railway communications from the Channel ports to Paris. And, most important of all, he had not succeeded in dividing the British and French armies. After Hankey and Smuts had visited the front in January they drew attention to the likelihood, and the danger, of a German attack in the valley of the river Lys between Armentières and La Bassée, with the object of cutting off the whole of the Allied armies in the north and

[1]Diary 3rd April 1918. Almost the whole entry is in *Supreme Command*, II, pp. 790–1.
[2]Quoted Dr. Thomas Jones in letter of 9th Feb. 1936 to Lady Grigg. *A Diary with Letters 1931–1950* (O.U.P., 1954), p. 173.
[3]See p. 512.

forcing them back on to the sea coast.[1] With the drying out of the swampy ground in that sector after the winter rains Hankey's mind reverted to this possibility; and it was precisely there that Ludendorff struck his next blow. During the short interlude that followed the end of the first phase of his offensive and the beginning of the second the Cabinet reverted to the old problems of man power and the Irish question.

Diary 6th April 1918
Though [to-day is] a Saturday we had a meeting of War Cabinet at 11 a.m. followed at 11.30 by a meeting of the whole Ministry to give Ll. G. an opportunity of explaining the mil. sitn., the man-power bill, and Irish policy i.e. gilding the conscription pill with the Home Rule Bill . . .

8th April
War Cabinet at noon as usual. Very short. Afterwards Bonar Law, Henry Wilson, Lord Curzon and I went upstairs and Ll. G. rehearsed his speech for parliament to-morrow. We also discussed the desirability of getting rid of Haig. The latter has written a private letter to Lord Derby saying that he is prepared to fight on, but that, if the Govt. prefer it, he is willing to resign. Derby read it at the War Cabinet, but it was not placed in the Minutes.[2] The difficulty is that there is no very obvious successor, Plumer, in whom the troops are said to have confidence, being about as stupid as Haig himself. In fact Ll. George's difficulty is that we have no general of very outstanding merit. I am afraid the future looks black (or is it the east wind?) Foch refused to put any substantial reserve behind our forces. I fear an overwhelming attack from Arras to Armentières which may practically knock us out. I lunched with Balfour, Bob Cecil, Drummond and Tyrrell.[3] Then I went to see Gen. Neill Malcolm,[4] who commanded the 66th Divn. in the late battle and was through the retreat of the Fifth Army, until he was wounded in the right leg . . . He was bitter against Ll. George and Henry Wilson, and appeared to attribute our misfortunes to Robertson being superseded. He made out this is the general view of the army. Later on Mark Sykes called on me, in great perturbation about the Govt.'s Irish policy, which he says will lead to revolution in Ireland. I agree, but believe this is difficult to avoid anyhow.

---

[1] See pp. 484–6. [2] See John Terraine, *Douglas Haig*, p. 427.
[3] William G. Tyrrell, 1st Baron Tyrrell 1929 (1866–1947). Diplomat. Assistant Under-Secretary, Foreign Office 1919–25, and Permanent Under-Secretary 1925–28. Ambassador in Paris 1928–34.
[4] Major-General Sir Neill Malcolm (1869–1953). G.O.C., Malaya 1921–4. High Commissioner for German refugees from the Nazi régime 1936–8.

9th April 1918[1]

Very short War Cabinet in morning. Ll. George, as usual, sent for me to lunch with him before making his big statement introducing the new man-power bill, including compulsory service for Ireland. He was rather depressed and nervous and ill at ease. I went to the official gallery to hear the speech. It was not a great success—too long—and he got involved in the details, which he did not understand very well.[2] The house was sullen and un-responsive—uncongenial circumstances to one of his temperament. It was not the trumpet call of a leader to the nation, which the moment demands. The whole thing lacked crispness. The Irish part was interrupted constantly by the declamations of the Irish party. Asquith was much better, a good patriotic speech. I could not help noticing how terribly Ll. G. has aged in the last twelve months. His hair has turned almost white . . . While I was writing this at home I received a message from the office to say that our front has been stove in north of La Bassée and that the Portuguese have been completely overrun. I have always been anxious about this section (see my visit to France in January) but military opinion was opposed to me, because they thought the ground too marshy and that the enemy would only get into a sort of *cul-de-sac* bounded by the river Lys and the La Bassée canal.

Hankey's critical assessment of Lloyd George's speech was entirely justified; for he did get himself tied into knots over "details which he did not understand very well". As he later admitted to Hankey in a different context "facts and figures were not his strong point, and his Celtic temperament made him unable to resist stretching them to their extreme limits".[3] Events were to show that he would have been far wiser to stick close to Hankey's sober and straightforward brief, and only allow his Celtic temperament to take charge when he came to sound "the trumpet call of a leader to the nation" for which Hankey and others waited in vain. But what neither Lloyd George nor Hankey could foresee was the very far-reaching consequence of the former's statements that the British Army in France had been stronger at the beginning of 1918 than it had been twelve months earlier; and, secondly, that all except three of the divisions in Egypt and Palestine contained a very small proportion of white (as opposed to Indian) soldiers. For the

[1] The last few lines of this entry are in *Supreme Command*, p. 793.
[2] The speech was to move for leave to bring in the new "Military Service Bill". Lloyd George also announced the government's intention "to invite Parliament to pass a measure for self-government in Ireland". But he said that "Both questions will not hang together. Each must be taken on its merits". Parl. Deb., Commons, Vol. 104, Cols. 1337–65.
[3] Diary 9th May 1918. See p. 544.

former statement could only be justified by including non-combatants such as Labour battalions[1]; and the latter was, quite simply, incorrect.[2] It seems likely that when Hankey heard Lloyd George's misstatements he realised that he was going to be put to a great deal of trouble to save him and the government from the consequences, and that the critical comments in his diary were inspired by apprehensions of that nature.

On the very day that Lloyd George made his ill-considered speech Ludendorff launched his new offensive in the north. Though actually intended as a diversion its quick success caused him gradually to convert it into a major effort. The British army was now desperately close to the sea, but resistance was strong enough to halt the German advance just short of the important railway junction of Hazebrouck. Thus although Ludendorff had achieved a big tactical success, causing some 300,000 British casualties, it fell short of a strategic victory. Fresh drafts were now being rushed out from England, and divisions were recalled from Italy, Palestine and Salonika. And, best of all, twelve American divisions had now arrived in France as harbingers of an ever-increasing flood. Though the Germans held the advantage of "interior lines" British sea power was able to restore the balance— albeit slowly.

[1] The student who wishes to follow up these statistical puzzles will not find enlightenment in the Official History, *Military Operations, France and Flanders 1918*. Appendices, Vol. I (Appendix 7, p. 33) of that work shows that whereas "Total Strength" on 1st Jan. 1918 was greater by 302,400 than it had been a year earlier, "Fighting Troops" had decreased by 94,762, and claims that the decrease in fighting strength *accelerated* between 1st January 1918 and the start of the German offensive on 21st March. Yet the text of the same work (Vol. I, p. 52, fn. 1) states that Haig received 167,020 more fighting troops between those dates. Liddell Hart in *The Fog of War* (Faber, 1938), Ch. XXIV, pointed out these discrepancies, and the Liddell Hart papers contain a letter (3rd Oct. 1938) from the Chief Military Historian Brigadier-General Sir James E. Edmonds virtually admitting that the statistics in the official history are no more reliable than the contemporary figures provided by the War Office. Hankey's diary for 6th Dec. 1917 (see p. 469) shows that he completely, and justifiably mistrusted the latter.

[2] On the eve of the great German offensive of 21st March 1918 there was in Egypt one Indian division (7,000 white and 13,000 native troops approximately), and in Palestine there were seven infantry divisions comprising about 100,000 white and only 6,000 native soldiers. There was also a substantial force of white cavalry. Arrangements were, however, in train to replace in all but three of the white divisions in Palestine a number of British battalions by native battalions from India. It was perhaps this knowledge that caused Lloyd George to make his incorrect statement.

Diary 10th April 1918[1]

Short War Cabinet at 11.30. Afterwards I took part in a conference on the question of the incorporation of United States troops with British brigades, the P.M. being in the chair . . . The news is very bad. The enemy has attacked with success from La Bassée to the Messines Ridge; has established a bridge-head across the river Lys, and has penetrated both sides of Armentières, which we shall have to abandon. Further, our divisions in this area are all divisions used up on the Somme, filled with inexperienced drafts. I fear for the Channel ports.

On Thursday 11th April Haig issued his famous "Backs to the Wall" order to the B.E.F.[2] No doubt the situation was serious, but by an odd coincidence Hankey received a letter bearing the same date from his old friend General Seely, who was commanding a Canadian Cavalry Brigade in Rawlinson's Army and had just come through some of the hardest fighting. He told Hankey that a dangerous myth was being built up by newspaper reports "about Hindenburg's hammer blows, Ludendorff's vast hordes, the necessity to give ground to 'organise in depth' " and so on. All that he had seen with his own eyes on various fronts contradicted the view "that some quite new and fearsome onslaught" had fallen on our army. He insisted that the bombardments had been less heavy than on earlier occasions, that the poison gas was "a great inconvenience but nothing more", and that the German soldier was no more redoubtable than formerly and in most respects inferior to our own men. "Now, please dear Maurice", he concluded, "get the P.M. and all concerned to DISPEL THE MYTH", which could, he considered, produce devastating effects on morale. Though Seely had of course a more restricted view than was obtainable at G.H.Q., this splendidly staunch letter from a man who, after a brief respite ordered by Rawlinson because of "a slight touch of gas shell", had just returned to the front, does give a very different impression from the almost panic-struck wording of Haig's order.[3] Hankey evidently replied urging Seely to make a speech in the House of Commons on the lines of his letter; but Seely was doubtful whether that would produce the necessary effect, since on 1st May he wrote again asking "whether on full consideration you think I should do good that way".[4] He was probably still hoping that Lloyd George

[1]Part reproduced in *Supreme Command*, II, p. 793.
[2]The original draft is reproduced in facsimile in *Churchill*, IV, opp. p. 434.
[3]Seeley to Hankey 11th April 1918. 14 pages in holograph (pencil).
[4]Same to same, 1st May 1918. 4 pages in holograph.

himself would undertake the task; but in the event the crisis had passed before anything was done on the lines proposed by Seely.

Diary 12th April 1918
Another long and useful War Cabinet devoted mainly to the question of Japanese intervention in Siberia. After a long discussion, the P.M., on my initiative, pointed out that, while we had discussed different aspects of Russian policy in some detail e.g. Archangel, Siberia, trans-Caucasia etc., we had never presented either President Wilson or Trotsky with a comprehensive scheme of policy, and the Foreign Office were instructed to draft one . . . The P.M., I found, like myself, had passed a good part of the previous night in thinking out our position if we are driven out of the Channel ports. Both of us had been rather under the influence of Gen. Wilson, who had obviously been very disturbed by the news that Bailleul was threatened, and had been decidedly jumpy . . .

Next day Hankey recorded that he was "less pessimistic than General Wilson and some of the War Cabinet" about the situation in France. Though the Germans had "knocked us about badly and gained important ground" he considered that they "must nearly have exhausted their reserves". Though he was sure that "our men are good stickers", despite unskilful leadership, the next month was bound to "be an anxious one".[1]

We saw earlier how Lloyd George, for all that he despised Derby and wished to replace him at the War Office, had in the end decided to hold his hand because the almost simultaneous replacement of the C.I.G.S. and the Secretary of State for War was bound to give his opponents in Parliament the chance to stir up trouble. By the early days of April, however, his determination to get rid of Derby had evidently hardened, and he must have discussed the problem with Milner. But it did not prove easy to decide who Derby's successor should be, and at one stage Bonar Law told Hankey that "the P.M. is flirting with taking it [the War Office] himself", but that Milner would probably do so.[2]

Milner to Lloyd George 13th April 1918. Holograph[3]
A last word about the War Office. Hankey or I? There is a great deal to say for both. I see the point about "new blood", also Hankey has of course in some respects far greater qualifications. On the other hand I should, I think, be more generally acceptable to the Army, [and] could if necessary, take

[1]Diary 13th April 1918. See *Supreme Command*, II, pp. 793–4.
[2]Diary 17th April 1918. [3]Lloyd George papers F/38/3/2

drastic action with greater resoluteness and authority . . . Hankey would not, I think, be a good man in the Commons, and he might not care to be fired into the Lords. Personally I have absolutely no feeling one way or the other . . . But if you do decide to have Hankey I strongly urge you to have a word with [General] Wilson first. I don't think he would object, but clearly it might be a bit of a shock to him and to others . . .

The foregoing letter makes it appear that Milner "wanted the job"— as Hankey later said in explanation of Lloyd George's acceptance of political power at a time of great difficulty.[1] Hankey certainly did not want it, and it seems that Milner did not know that he had already twice headed Lloyd George off from appointing him to Ministerial office. Five days later Milner replaced Derby, who was consoled with the Paris embassy—from which he continued to send Hankey the prolix and circumlocutory letters for which he was noteworthy.

Derby to Hankey 21st April 1918 G.H.Q. British Armies in France. Holograph *Private and Confidential*
My dear Hankey
. . . How I hate leaving the War Office but the P.M. was determined really for some time to [?] press Milner—"the Boche"[2]—into my place. I can't help feeling very bitter, but I look on A.J.B. [Balfour] as my master—and he is the only man I really trust and for his sake I shall do all in my power to assist. I daresay the present "soreness" will wear off, but it is very sore at the moment. This of course is only for your private eye.
Ever yours v. sincerely.
P.S. I go to Paris this afternoon.

Diary 15th April 1918
No particular war news except loss of Neuve Chapelle. Discussion at War Cabinet about the Austrian Emperor's letter [brought] by Prince Sixte of Bourbon.[3] The P.M. had a copy made by him at Folkestone when he met M. Ribot there early in 1917, and a translation given to J.T. Davies by Prince Sixte. He also had a second letter from Emperor Karl to Prince Sixte handed to J.T. Davies by Prince Sixte. These letters made it quite plain that the Emperor Karl did really express sympathy with the French aspirations in Alsace-Lorraine. It was decided to avoid discussion on the subject in

[1] See C. P. Snow, *Variety of Man* (Macmillan, 1967), pp. 104-5.
[2] This is obviously an oblique reference to Milner having received his early education at Tübingen in Germany.
[3] See pp. 377 and 390. By a slip of the pen Hankey wrote "Belgium" instead of "Bourbon".

Parliament as long as possible. Indeed, it was feared that there might be an outburst in this country, particularly when it became known that Italy had stood in the way of our following up this matter. I spent the afternoon delving into the Austrian negotiations with a view to a précis; but it is only after getting home and by the aid of this diary (first volume) that I have been able to trace the essential dates . . .

There is an element of high tragedy in Hankey's recapitulation of the Austrian peace feelers almost exactly a year after they were initiated, since he had always believed them to be genuine and had steadily pressed for them to be followed up. If Lloyd George was to blame for accepting Ribot's demand for absolute secrecy and for yielding to Italian intransigence, he surely aggravated the offence by concealing what had passed from Parliament. No mention of the decision to keep quiet on the matter will be found in the Cabinet minutes for 15th April[1]—or, more expectedly, in Lloyd George's *War Memoirs*. Esher's view was identical to Hankey's, and early in May he wrote that "This Austrian business gets worse and worse. What a show-up of Poincaré . . . But think of our unfortunate country being dragged at the heels of Sonnino and Ribot". None of the people of the British Empire had, he rightly protested, been told that "these peace overtures were disliked because Poincaré wanted a Rhine frontier and the coal fields of the Saar"; all of which was only a slight exaggeration.[2]

Diary 16th April 1918
I saw Adeline and Robin off to Lynton for a holiday. Adeline has had . . . so many disappointments about getting away *with* me, that I have at last persuaded her to go without me. The news is again bad, the enemy having made progress towards the vital Kemmel-Mont des Cats ridge, at the foot of which he now stands. He has also captured Bailleul, through which I have so often and so recently motored in peace and security. War Cabinet at 11.30, devoted mainly to the Irish question. I lunched with Sir Eric Geddes. He tells me that the Admiralty are building a barrage across the Channel consisting of towers, constructed of a mass of vertical tubes, which will be floated out, sunk, and filled with sand, and then joined up by nets etc. forming a complete obstruction to the passage of submarines.[3] The trouble is, as I pointed out to him, that we are in imminent danger of losing the Channel ports of France,

[1] WC. 391. Cab. 23/6.
[2] Esher to M. V. Brett 5th May 1918. *Journals and Letters*, IV, p. 199.
[3] These towers were not completed in time to fulfil their purpose. One of them was moved after the war to mark the eastern entrance to the Solent, and named the Nab Tower.

in which case his scheme will be useless. I proposed something on these lines earlier in the war but the Admiralty would not look at it.

On 18th the reshuffle of offices was finally settled. Austen Chamberlain joined the War Cabinet, as Hankey had long advocated, in Milner's place, since the principle that members of the War Cabinet should not hold departmental responsibilities was by this time firmly established;[1] and in any case the honeymoon period between two such disparate characters as Lloyd George and Milner was rapidly drawing to a close. But trouble was brewing for the government in a new direction—as part of the inquest into the cause of the defeat sustained by the Fifth Army. Too many rumours for comfort were circulating to the effect that drafts of men had been deliberately withheld from Haig lest he should squander them in a repetition of Third Ypres, and that the Prime Minister's statement in his speech on 9th that "the British Army in France was considerably stronger on 1st January 1918 than on the 1st January 1917" was at the very least open to challenge. Nor was a challenger long in appearing.

On 18th, the very day when Milner took over the War Office, Sir Godfrey Baring[2] asked the Prime Minister whether in making that statement he was "including the Labour battalions and other non-combatant units; and whether the combatant strength of the British Army was greater or less at the beginning of this year than at the beginning of last year?"[3] These questions were of course very much to the point, since it was combatant strength, and not total figures, that really indicated the Army's fighting capacity. The question was answered by Ian Macpherson,[4] the Under-Secretary for War, using figures supplied by the Adjutant-General's department, whose responsibility it was to produce such statistics, to the Director of Military Operations—General Sir Frederick Maurice. Unfortunately a clerk in the A.G.'s department included in the figure giving the total strength on 1st January 1918 86,000 men of the British Army in Italy; and Colonel Walter Kirke, the D.M.O.'s deputy, sent the figures across to Downing Street without questioning them or having them checked.

[1]The only exception to this rule was that Bonar Law remained Chancellor of the Exchequer. [2]1871–1957. Politician (Lib.). [3]Parl. Deb., Commons, Vol. 105, Col. 563. [4]J. Ian Macpherson, 1st Baron Strathcarron 1936 (1880–1937). Politician (Lib. then Lib.-Nat.). Under-Secretary of State for War and Member of Army Council 1916– 19. Vice-President of Army Council 1918. Chief Secretary for Ireland 1918–20 Minister of Pensions 1920–22.

General Maurice, it should be remarked, left for France on 13th April, returning three days later. On 22nd General P. de B. Radcliffe[1] succeeded him as D.M.O. The change of office could hardly have taken place at a more unfortunate moment, since a landmine was in process of being laid right in the government's path. We will return to its explosion shortly.

Diary 19th April 1918
War Cabinet postponed until afternoon, the P.M. being at Walton Heath. In afternoon Cabinet sat from 3.30 until nearly 7.30 without a break. Main subject was a recruiting proclamation, but the more important thing was approval [given] to the telegram to President Wilson re policy in Russia. The P.M. has very stubbornly and adroitly resisted the pressure from Foreign Office and War Office to rush the Japs in to "down" the Bolshevists. He has always trusted Lockhart, our agent in Russia, whom F.O. and W.O. mistrust. Now Lockhart has actually received an invitation from Trotsky for the allies to put up a scheme, and, as a first step, we are putting one up to President Wilson. Balfour was very "sniffy" about it, and eventually sent it beginning "I am asked by the War Cabinet to send the following" instead of treating it as though it were sent from the whole Government, including F.O. . . . The war news is much better, a heavy attack southwards against La Bassée canal having been repulsed, and considerable reinforcements having been sent by the French.

Next day most of Hankey's time was taken up in preparing Bonar Law's budget statement for consideration by the War Cabinet and the King. As he was sure the monarch would "want to know all about the new taxation" he at once sent a copy of the minutes of the previous day's Cabinet and of the budget proposals to Stamfordham.[2] He replied gratefully, but represented that the increase of Income Tax from 5/- to 6/- in the pound "will hit very hardly the man with an income just over £500 a year [the limit below which the increase would not apply] with children to educate and the price of living just double what it is in peace".[3] Presumably this regard for the man of very moderate income with family responsibilities derived from the King himself.

[1] Later General Sir Percy de B. Radcliffe (1874–1934). Director of Military Operations, War Office, 1918–22. G.O.C. Scottish Command 1930–33. Generally referred to in the Army as "P. de B." to distinguish him from General Sir Charles Delmé-Radcliffe (see p. 502).
[2] Diary 20th April 1918.
[3] Hankey to Stamfordham 20th April 1918 and reply by latter of 21st. RA. GV. K1296/3 and /4. Also Cab. 23/16. In the light of taxation 50 years later it is interesting to remark that surtax was raised from 3/6d to 4/6d and the starting point

Diary 22nd April 1918[1]

... At 7.30 Lord Milner, who has just taken on as S. of S. for War, came to see me. He told me that he had decided to have an Under S. of S., just as Lord Kitchener had Lord Derby to look after the administration and all matters of detail. He would be a peer. The P.M., he said, had strongly pressed him to take *me*. I at once protested that I was the last person in the world for such a post. My experience was entirely in the field of large questions of policy, and I had no knowledge of or liking for questions of administrative detail. I had no desire to be a peer or to defend the War Office in either House. He agreed with me, but gave as his reason that I was the only person who had any influence over the P.M., and that my encyclopaedic general knowledge of the war and of all that had happened, made me irreplaceable where I was. He asked my opinion between Lord Lovat,[2] Lord Sydenham,[3] and Lord Stanhope,[4] and selected the second.[5] I then pressed him, as I had pressed the P.M. about Irish recruiting . . . Spent a very long time this afternoon and evening in getting out for the Prime Minister a long summary of all the proceedings of the War Cabinet and international conferences and [meetings of] Supreme War Council in regard to the extension of the British line in France, which some of the newspapers are alleging was forced on Haig by the British Government and was the cause of the defeat of the Fifth army.

The gathering storm about the strength of the B.E.F. at the time of the great German offensive was of course inextricably linked with the extension southwards of the British line, since unless Haig's armies were reinforced they were bound to have to spread their strength more thinly. The debate of 9th April and the "Baring Question" of 18th gave ample warning of what was in the wind, and on 22nd Hankey sent Lloyd George a comprehensive history of the negotiations, starting with Henry Wilson's very secret warning to the War Cabinet of June

---

lowered from £3,000 to £2,000 per annum. The total increased yield from the 1918 budget was estimated at £114 millions; that of 1968 at some £800 millions.

[1] A small part of this entry is in *Supreme Command*, II, p. 794.

[2] Simon J. Fraser, 14th (sometimes reckoned 16th) Baron Lovat (1871–1933). First chairman of Forestry Commission 1919–27.

[3] See p. 71.

[4] 7th Earl Stanhope (1880–1967). Parliamentary Secretary to War Office 1918–19. Civil Lord of Admiralty 1924–9. First Commissioner of Works 1936. President, Board of Education 1937. First Lord of Admiralty 1938. Lord President of Council 1939–40.

[5] Sydenham did not become Under-Secretary. Ian Macpherson continued as Parliamentary Secretary until Jan. 1919.

1917 regarding the mutinies in the French army, and ending with the actual extension to Barisis in February of the following year, as had been agreed between Haig and Pétain.[1] This was a masterly recapitulation of an involved story, and Lloyd George certainly had it all at his finger tips before the end of April.[2]

Rather surprisingly Hankey did not mention in his diary that on 23rd three Members of Parliament—Mr. G. Lambert, Colonel C. R. Burn and Mr. W. N. R. Pringle—asked awkward questions of the Prime Minister about the extension of the British line, whether this matter had aroused protests from Robertson and Haig, and whether it had been referred to the Supreme War Council. Bonar Law, answering for Lloyd George, assured the House that the extension of the line had been agreed between the British and French military authorities, that the British leaders had not made any protest, and that "this particular matter was not dealt with at all by the Versailles Council".[3] It was, perhaps, significant that although Lambert and Pringle were "Asquithian" Liberals, Burn was a Unionist. The land mine referred to earlier was now primed.

Diary 24th April 1918
War Cabinet 11.30. I lunched with the McKennas. McK. told me that Asquith could upset Ll. G. any day, but was very reluctant to do so, and that his followers in Parliament were very restive on that account. Esher came to tea in the afternoon. He thinks that Ll. G. will come down over the Irish question, and that I ought to be thinking of the machinery by which Asquith is to run the war, as his followers will not allow him to retain the War Cabinet system as it stands.

In truth McKenna and Esher both greatly underestimated Lloyd George.

After the War Cabinet on 24th Hankey wrote to Geddes, who had not been present, that "a general and unforeseen discussion had taken place on a matter affecting the Admiralty"—notably "the use of labour under Admiralty control". He went on to specify the criticisms made against Geddes's department with regard to the release of men and dilution of labour—which amounted to an accusation of "hoarding" skilled men. "I have put nothing of this talk in the Minutes", he continued, "but I thought it right to let you know *privately* the lines of the

---

[1]See p. 486. [2]Dated 22nd April 1918. Lloyd George papers F/23/2/31.
[3]Parl. Deb., Commons, Vol. 105, Cols. 851-2.

discussion . . . I hope you will treat this letter as private and not quote it". He then added, apparently as an afterthought, that "the suggestion was made in several quarters that the Admiralty, ever since the first days of the war, had lacked a spirit of co-operation and good will in regard to labour matters and recruiting . . .". In short Geddes was warned that his department was likely to come under heavy fire in Cabinet in the near future. Small wonder that Ministers appreciated such intimations of impending trouble, and trusted Hankey the more for the discretion and tact with which he conveyed them.[1]

Diary 25th April 1918
War Cabinet . . . Lunched with the Asquiths, the old boy being in great form . . . In the evening however I received a note from Lord Islington (U.S. for India)[2] enclosing a telegram from the Indian Govt. which put in doubt the decision reached by the War Cabinet in the morning about granting commissions to Indians. The Indian Govt. want to give 200 King's commissions, which enable Indians to command British officers according to seniority, but the soldiers and Indian experts here only want to give Viceroy's commissions, which give no such authority. The War Cabinet decided in favour of the latter view. The new telegram however says that the Indian view emanates from the C. in C. (Monro) who has hitherto taken a cautious line. After getting the views of Lord Curzon and Chamberlain, I saw the P.M., who decided that the question must come before the Cabinet again to-morrow. . . .

26th April 1918[3]
. . . Rather bad news from France as Mont Kemmel has been captured, though Villers Brettoneux (where I slept 3 months ago on my visit to Gen. Gough) has been recaptured. Lunched with Mr. Balfour at Carlton Gardens. In the course of lunch I made a very strong case about the comparative uselessness of aircraft during this war, pointing out that, whether for reconnaissance, bombing, or spotting for artillery, they are only an entirely subsidiary arm, and have achieved but meagre results, and that a great deal too much fuss is made about this arm, which certainly does not deserve a Ministry all to itself. Aerial supremacy, I pointed out, has never made the difference between failure and success in any action of this war, great or small.

[1] Hankey to Geddes 24th April 1918.
[2] John P. Dickson-Poynder, 1st Baron Islington 1910 (1866–1936). Politician (Lib.). Under-Secretary of State for Colonies 1914–15. Parliamentary Under-Secretary of State for India 1915–18.
[3] A small part of this entry is in *Supreme Command*, II, p. 794, but Hankey omitted his strictures on the Air Ministry.

Though Hankey's opposition to the concept of a "unified air service", mentioned earlier, was understandable in the context of 1916–17 his strictures about the influence of air power provide a most unusual example of short-sightedness on his part. For by the spring of 1918 there could be no doubt that command of the air was exerting tremendous influence on both naval and military operations. The truth seems to be that Hankey was unduly influenced by the dislike of the Admiralty and of many senior naval men for the newly created Air Ministry and Air Force—a prejudice which was to culminate in the bitter controversies of the 1920s.[1]

Diary 27th April 1918[2]
I went down this morning to Pearson's works close to the Albert Docks, with Sir Ernest Moir[3] of the Ministry of Munitions, to see a new "pill-box" blockhouse, which he is turning out in great quantities for use in France. I drove down with Col. Allanson[4] of the General Staff and a gas expert, Professor Baker.[5] The former is a conceited but highly intelligent officer. He told me that he was in command of the Ghurkas who occupied Sari Bair during the Suvla Bay battle. He was able to overlook the whole of the Turkish communications and was there for approximately 48 hours.[6] He said it was true that a big shell from a monitor exploded among his troops, but it made no difference, because they held the summit for 36 hours after that. He could see all over the low country behind Suvla Bay, and there were not more than 2,000 Turks in front of us. Our failure to push on was incredible. He firmly believed the war was won, but in spite of message after message of entreaty, he could not get proper support, and was driven out. He also said that in the recent offensive by the enemy on March 21st our failure was largely due to our neglect to supply nucleus garrisons in the third line, with the result that our forces, shattered in the front line, and shaken in the second line by artillery fire, were rushed over the third line, where there was not even

[1]See Roskill, *Naval Policy*, I.
[2]Part reproduced in *Supreme Command*, II, p. 795.
[3]Sir Ernest W. Moir (1862–1933). Civil Engineer and Contractor. Partner in S. Pearson & Son, Lord Cowdray's firm. Member of Council, Ministry of Munitions 1915–19.
[4]Hankey wrote this officer's name as Alanton in his diary, and reproduced that error in *The Supreme Command*. It was obviously Colonel C. J. L. Allanson. But Allanson's story, as quoted here by Hankey does not entirely correspond with that given in *James*, pp. 269–74, 283–92 and 297–301.
[5]Professor Herbert B. Baker (1862–1935). Professor of Chemistry, Imperial College of Science and Technology 1912–32. Was called in to advise the government on protective measures immediately the first poison gas attack took place.
[6]See pp. 197–8.

a nucleus force to rally them. Thus, between Armentières and La Bassée the great mass of wire protecting the third line remains intact to this day. There were no guards at the points where the roads pass through the wire; it was no-one's responsibility to join up the gaps, or destroy the roads, [and] the Germans in the mist simply marched through in fours, and this immensely strong line was abandoned without even a struggle. A truly appalling indictment of our generals . . .

On the same day that Hankey talked to Allanson about the causes of the March defeat he sent Milner a long letter on the subject, repeating almost word for word what he wrote in his diary except that he added the suggestion that "pill-boxes" with permanent garrisons should be established in the third defence line. "I hope you will not mind my writing to you about this", he concluded, "as it is written in no captious or critical spirit, but only to try and help. If you think it worth looking into, I think it would be as well if you left my name out of it". Hankey knew well enough the prickly jealousy of many British generals over intrusion by an outsider into what they regarded as their private province. Milner replied "Thank you for your excellent letter and suggestion", whereupon Hankey sent a copy of the whole correspondence to Lloyd George.[1] It provides an interesting example of the way he was always adding to his encyclopedic knowledge, and how he then put it to use by feeding his information to the appropriate Ministers.

Diary 30th April
War Cabinet at noon. Discussion on subject of possible evacuation of Channel ports, in the course of which I raised the question of the resulting risk of invasion and suggested that Germany's recent diplomatic pressure on Holland is designed to enable her to pick a quarrel and seize the mouths of the Scheldt, when convenient to her. With Holland and the east side of the Channel in her hands the menace of invasion would become serious. Lunched with P.M., Smuts, and Josiah Wedgwood.[2] The latter pleased me much by urging the P.M. not to run amuck [sic] in Ireland . . .

Hankey's next visit to France produced some interesting impressions of Clemenceau's ruthless methods.

[1] Hankey to Lloyd George 29th April 1918. Lloyd George papers F/23/2/32.
[2] 1st Baron Wedgwood 1942 (1872–1943). Politician (Lib., then Lab.). A member of Mesopotamia Commission 1917. Joined Labour Party 1919 and became its Vice-Chairman 1921–4. Chancellor of Duchy of Lancaster 1924.

Diary 1st May 1918

Started at 7.30 a.m. for France—the P.M., Lord Milner, Henry Wilson, Adl. Wemyss, Gen. Radcliffe (new D.M.O.), Gen. Wells[1] of A.G.'s Dept., Col. Allanson, J.T. Davies, Sylvester and self . . . Moderate passage in the destroyer *Broke* to Calais whence I motored to Abbeville in company with Adl. Wemyss. After lunch at the officers' club the conference began and continued until dinner time. During a short interval for tea Gen. Pétain came in to the officers' club. He was less optimistic than Foch had shown himself to be. His estimate of casualties is 3,500 for every German division withdrawn from the fight. Gen. Spears[2] said he must have been sent to remove the impression of optimism Gen. Foch had created at the conference. After dinner Adl. Wemyss and I had a long conversation with Spears, our liaison officer in Paris. He says that Clemenceau has created a regular reign of terror in France. He says that my friend Helbronner, for example, has been hunted out of his staff appointment back to his regiment because he came to Beauvais a few weeks ago to shake me by the hand. I wanted to speak to Clemenceau myself about it, but was warned that I should do more harm than good. Professor Mantoux, according to Spears, has been taken on by Clemenceau as a spy on us . . . But Spears is jealous of Mantoux, who is his successful rival as interpreter . . .

When in 1968 the author of this biography consulted Sir Edward Spears about the foregoing diary entry he strongly denied that he ever felt any jealousy towards Mantoux. He was also able to throw interesting light on both Helbronner, whom he had introduced to Hankey, and on Mantoux. Rather curiously both were Jews, but Helbronner was much the superior of the two in both intellect and character. Spears confirmed that Clemenceau introduced a "reign of terror" in Paris, and that the "high priest of his autocracy" was Georges Mandel, also a Jew, who was murdered by the French during the Vichy régime. Helbronner's end was also tragic. In 1940 he was head of the Jewish community in Paris, and refused every opportunity to leave the country during the German occupation, believing it to be his duty to stay and help his co-religionists. He and his wife were both seized by the Germans and done to death in a concentration camp.[3]

[1]This must have been Brigadier-General John B. Wells (1881–1952).
[2]Hankey wrote this officer's name as "Spiers" throughout this entry. Although Sir Edward Spears, as he later became (see p. 432) did spell his name that way in 1918, and changed it a short time later, it seems less confusing to adhere to the spelling by which he is widely known.
[3]Sir Edward Spears to the author 10th October 1968.

Diary 2nd May 1918[1]

Abbeville is swarming with troops—British, French with some Americans. Before breakfast I had a walk with Ll. G. and we dropped into a church where low mass was being celebrated. He seemed fascinated and remarked as we came out "If I were going to the trenches, I might be brought to believe in it." At 10 a.m. we had a very secret conclave at the Préfet's private house —Ll. G., Haig, Wilson, Wemyss, Lawrence, and self, Clemenceau, Foch, Pétain, and Adl. de Bon. The subject was as to whether, in the event of an unavoidable retirement we should fall back on the Channel ports, the armies separating, or whether we should let go of the ports with our left [wing] and retire behind the Somme. Foch said stoutly *"Ni l'un, ni l'autre"*, but when pressed and cornered said that the loss of the ports was not fatal and that we should have to [?] cover the battle field of the allies. "But it will not come to that—*jamais, jamais, jamais*". After this the Supreme War Council again, with a mob of people including of course Orlando. Lord Milner, in Sylvester's hearing, afterwards described it as a "dog fight", in the intervals of which *I* drafted the decisions they ought to have arrived at. This was not an inaccurate description. The conference was mainly occupied with interminable discussions and arguments about the incorporation of American battalions in British brigades. The U.S. Govt. accepts our point of view but leaves a wide discretion to Gen. Pershing, who hates the whole scheme as detrimental to the building up of an American army under his command. He is very obstinate and we had great difficulty in reaching a not very satisfactory agreement. Gen. Rawlinson (Fourth Army commander) came to lunch, and in the evening we motored out to see Gen. Byng (commanding Third army)[2] in a beautifully situated château at Hesdin. Byng was tired but confident. I remarked that on our last meeting, some 3 months ago, we walked from St. Leger to Mory, now in possession of the enemy, and he reminded me that he had forecasted exactly the method of the enemy's attack, viz. up the valleys. The German artillery preparations on March 21st had been stupendous, about double in intensity the heaviest that we had ever employed in our attacks. He had only dared reply to it with half his guns, for fear of counterbattery work, and had reserved the remainder of his fire for the infantry attack barrage. Even so he had himself seen 100 German dumps set on fire. The number of German dumps had been colossal, every shell hole containing one, and these had been revealed by aeroplane photos., thereby infallibly showing that an attack was coming. This is the most useful bit of work I

---

[1] Parts of this entry are in *Supreme Command*, II, p. 795.

[2] Julian H. G. Byng, 1st Viscount Byng 1928 (1862–1935). Commanded IX Corps at Suvla 1915, Canadian Corps 1916–17, and Third Army 1917–19. Governor-General of Canada 1921–6. Chief Commissioner, Metropolitan Police 1928–31. Field-Marshal 1932.

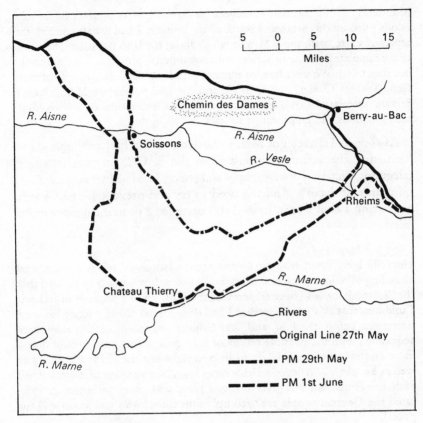

7   The German Breakthrough to the Marne, May 1918

heard of aeroplanes doing. He was convinced the German losses had been colossal, and British privates, who had escaped after being employed to bury the dead, all said they had buried 5 Germans for one Englishman. At present, he said, the enemy were ostentatiously inactive, making him suspect some ruse. A big attack, however, would be very difficult and take long to prepare, as the enemy had the battlefields of the Somme and Ancre behind him, and these were traversed by very few roads. This is why, on my visit with Gen. Smuts, I ventured to say that the enemy would not attack on this front. Personally therefore I incline to the view that the enemy will push his attack in the north, and that the accepted professional view that he will attack between Arras and the Somme may be wrong. He will however probably continue to push S. of the Somme. After this we motored on to G.H.Q. at

Montreuil . . . We met many refugees on the road, carrying their household goods piled up on carts away south of the Somme. I had a walk, during the repair of a tyre, with the P.M. and talked about the Irish question. He seems to contemplate a massacre almost with equanimity, provided the English do not shoot first. We were late for dinner (with Haig) at G.H.Q. I sat between Gen. Travers Clarke,[1] the Q.M.G. and Sir Philip Sassoon M.P.,[2] Haig's private secretary. I rubbed into the latter the importance of avoiding recriminations and he promised to back me up in this . . .

As soon as Hankey got back to London on 3rd he was immersed in "initiating the action resulting from the S.W.C. meeting, drafting telegrams, dictating *procès-verbaux* and seeing Lord Milner and the P.M. on points of detail". And the need to try and prevent Lloyd George provoking a civil war in Ireland still occupied a prominent place in his mind.

Diary 4th May 1918

Horribly busy again reading up the accumulations of telegrams etc. and attending to office affairs. Saw Mark Sykes before lunch. He is convinced that the "Curragh crowd" have (?) screwed the P.M. up to a pogrom in Ireland. I told him that as a public servant I had done all I could in putting his own letters etc. before the P.M. and War Cabinet and to ensure that they were acquainted with the possible results of their policy; that now I could do no more and my duty was clearly to help to carry out the Cabinet's policy as well as I could. . . . Alleged reliable news from Norway says that up to April 18th the Huns had lost over 600,000 men, and other information indicated the German people are "fed up" with their losses and anxious [? for peace].

In truth, however, the German losses between 21st March and 18th April had not amounted to anything like the total quoted by Hankey[3]; and although the German people as a whole probably were longing

---

[1]Later General Sir Travers E. Clarke (1871–1962). Deputy Quartermaster-General and Q.M.G. in France 1917–19, then Quartermaster-General and Member of Army Council 1919–23.

[2]1888–1939. Politician (Cons.) and patron of the arts. Private Secretary to Sir Douglas Haig as C-in-C, B.E.F., 1915–18. Under-Secretary of State for Air 1924–9 and 1931–7.

[3]At the Cabinet meeting on 15th April 1918 the C.I.G.S. reported that in Madrid the Germans were "talking openly" of the loss of 500,000 men and "admitting privately" to 600,000. W.C. 391, Minute 5, Cab. 23/16. However, the German Official History, *Der Weltkrieg 1914-18*, Vol. 14, Appendix 42, gives the total casualties in the whole of March and April 1918 as only 423,900.

for peace there was not the slightest chance of the military leaders accepting such a proposal until they had suffered a severe defeat in the field.

Diary 6th May 1918
War Cabinet 11.30. Mostly "hush" which means I was singlehanded. In the afternoon I wrote a long letter to Mr. Balfour protesting against the atmosphere of intolerance created by the Foreign Office and the press every time there is even a mention of the word peace.

It must have been on 5th or 6th May that General Maurice apparently called to discuss his future prospects with Hankey, and the latter told him that he was *bien vu* by Lloyd George, and suggested several appointments he might get.[1] This conversation makes the action which Maurice took a day or two later the more puzzling; certainly it took Hankey completely by surprise.

Hankey himself has printed the diary entry for 7th May, when the "veritable bombshell" of the notorious "Maurice Letter" appeared in the all important morning newspapers to whom it was sent—except the *Daily Telegraph*.[2] In it General Maurice claimed that statements made by Lloyd George on 9th April and by Bonar Law on 23rd with regard to the strength of the British Army and the extension of the line in France formed part "of a series of misstatements which have been made recently in the House of Commons by the present Government". He assured the public that "this letter is not the result of a military conspiracy", but was written "in the hope that Parliament may see fit to order an investigation into the statements I have made".

Hankey was of course immediately, and deeply involved. The Cabinet devoted most of its time that day to considering what action should be taken; and while the Cabinet was not in session he was constantly in conference with Lloyd George. The decisions of the Cabinet were, firstly, that the "military offences" which had been committed by Maurice should be dealt with by the Army Council; and, secondly, that Bonar Law in reply to a question to be put by Asquith that afternoon should say that the Government "proposed to ask two of His Majesty's judges to act as a Court of Honour to enquire into the charge of misstatements alleged to have been made by Ministers".[3] Hankey at

[1] "Talk with Sir Maurice Hankey at United Services Club 8th Nov. 1932". Liddell Hart papers.
[2] *Supreme Command*, II, p. 798.   [3] W.C. 406 of 7th May 1918. Cab. 23/6.

once realised that "the objection to the latter procedure is that many aspects of the subject are so confidential that their report could not be published during the war and no-one will be satisfied".[1] At 5 p.m. Lloyd George sent for Hankey again and said that he had decided to reject the proposal for a Select Committee "and to make it a question of confidence". He himself "would make a great speech in which he would tell as much as possible". Luckily Hankey had already put in hand "an immense précis of the whole affair", and he worked on it "with relays of stenographers" until 8.30 p.m. An hour later it was put into Lloyd George's hands at Downing Street—which Hankey justly described as "a great performance". Realising that "the issue is of course immensely wider than the small [sic] charges in Gen. Maurice's letter"—in that the fate of the government hung in the balance—he, like Lloyd George, was obviously very much on his mettle.

Unfortunately no complete copy of Hankey's monumental brief for Lloyd George's use appears to have survived. There is no copy in the Cabinet papers, and the one in Lloyd George's papers is obviously incomplete. However we can gain a good deal of information from that extract.[2]

The first statement challenged by Maurice, wrote Hankey, was Bonar Law's answer to Pringle's question (23rd April) about whether the extension of the British line had been discussed by the Supreme War Council. Maurice had written "I was at Versailles when the question was decided by the Supreme War Council to which it had been referred"; which flatly contradicted Bonar Law's answer. Hankey recapitulated the history of the extension of the line "first to the Oise and afterwards to Barisis".[3] This extension "was never discussed by the Supreme War Council", he wrote, "which was dealing with a further extension for which the French government were pressing[4] . . . It is

---

[1] Diary 7th May 1918.

[2] Lloyd George papers F/235. It is endorsed in an unknown hand "Copy extracted from Hankey's *magnum opus*" and "There was no copy of this with P.M's file". Hankey used to refer to the files containing his personal papers and correspondence as his "*magnum opus*", and it therefore seems probable that the office copy was placed in them. Unfortunately they seem to have been destroyed during the process known in the Civil Service as "weeding" the official records before transfer to the P.R.O.

[3] See p. 486.

[4] This presumably referred to the French request for the British to take over a further 23,000 yards south of Barisis, to the River Ailette, a tributary of the Oise. On 10th January the Supreme War Council recommended this should be done, but

clear, therefore that General Maurice has confused the discussion on the further extension of the line, which was discussed at the Supreme War Council, but was never carried out, with the extension to Barisis, which had been arranged some months previously . . . Mr. Bonar Law's statement, therefore, . . . is perfectly correct".

The second statement challenged by Maurice was, Hankey continued, Macpherson's answer to Sir Godfrey Baring's question (18th April) to the effect that "the Army in France was considerably stronger on 1st January 1918, than on 1st January 1917". Maurice had not challenged the statement itself, indeed "to do so would be impossible" remarked Hankey, "since the British Army, as a whole, was greater by [277,873] on the later date".[1] On the other hand Maurice was plainly referring to "Sir Douglas Haig's fighting strength on the eve of the great battle". "I frankly admit", Hankey continued, "that the rifle strength of the Army had been decreased by [100,548][2] bayonets", and "the number of battalions in each division had been reduced from 12 to 9". But this was "precisely the same number as in the German and French Armies, although the British battalions remain stronger than the German or French". "But is rifle strength the only criterion of fighting strength?", he went on to ask, rather rhetorically. Lord Kitchener had always held a contrary view, and had "considered rifle strength a dangerous measure for comparison". "Do heavy and field guns, aircraft, machine guns, tanks, trench mortars, gas, railways,

---

Haig told Milner (27th April) that he would "request that he might be relieved of his command if this course were adopted". John Gooch, *The Maurice Debate 1918*. *Journal of Contemporary History*, Vol. 3, No. 4 (Oct. 1968).

[1] The figure is omitted from the copy, obviously for insertion by the War Office. If one takes the figures first supplied by the A.G. the increase in "Ration Strength in France" between 1st Jan. 1917 and 1st Jan. 1918 was 301,000, and the increase in "Combatant Strength" 43,000. But Hankey presumably had the corrected figures (A.G.I.C. dated 7th May 1918), which gives the figure shown in square brackets for "British Forces in France". If "Dominion Contingents" were included the increase became 324,785.

[2] Again the figure is omitted. But the fact that Hankey mentioned a *decrease* in "rifle strength" confirms that he was using the return of 7th May, which gives the figure inserted in square brackets. The earlier, and incorrect, return used by Macpherson in answering Baring's question showed an *increase* of 45,000 in "Combatant Strength in France". (Gooch, *op. cit.*, p. 221.) Again if "Dominion Contingents" and "Coloured Troops" (Indian cavalry), were included the *decrease* in "Fighting Troops" became 85,664.

roads and entrenchments count for nothing in the fighting strength of the Army?" he asked. If account was taken of all of the foregoing the comparison between 1917 and 1918 took on a very different hue, since all increases in material involved an increase in man-power. Thus did Hankey produce the argument which Lloyd George was to use in the House to great effect.

Next he turned to Maurice's challenge to the Prime Minister's statement (9th April) about the number of "White divisions" in Mesopotamia, Egypt and Palestine—which was in fact where the General stood on firmest ground. Hankey recalled that on 23rd March the C.I.G.S. had informed the War Cabinet, Maurice being present, that there were only three "White divisions" in Egypt; and Maurice, who had seen the minutes of the meeting, was thus "given an opportunity to correct any wrong statement he [the C.I.G.S.] had made".

Finally Hankey returned to the question of the extension of the line, and could find "no trace that pressure of any sort or kind was put on Field-Marshal Haig" after 25th September when the British government had accepted in principle that their army would have to take over more line. "Every time the French Ministers tried to put pressure on the British Government", he went on, "the latter replied that it was a matter for the Generals"; and the pressure "was getting greater and greater" after 25th September, culminating in the request of Clemenceau that the matter should be referred to the Supreme War Council. However at the meeting on 2nd February Haig reported that the extension to Barisis had been agreed between him and Pétain, and that it had been carried out. During the four months between the Boulogne conference, where the decision was taken in principle, and the actual execution of the agreement "the Government had continuously supported Field-Marshal Haig's objections for taking over more line"— that is to say beyond Barisis.

This was an extremely able brief, but not by any means a watertight one—especially with regard to the mistake, now acknowledged, over the number of "White divisions" in the Middle East. For example Hankey said nothing about the error made in the Adjutant-General's department, and passed on by the D.M.O., which Macpherson had used in answering Baring's question in the House.[1]

[1] See p. 528.

Diary 8th May 1918[1]

. . . Mark Sykes called before the War Cabinet and told me in confidence "from one Chinovnik to another"[2] that Robertson had lunched with Asquith on the previous day. Later I learned from Davies, who got it from Ll. G.'s valet (!) that a few days ago Robertson gave a dinner to Trenchard, Repington and Gwynne of the Morning Post and Maurice, and that after dinner the party were joined by Asquith and Jellicoe; that the Maurice letter was discussed, and that at the end Robertson said he would have nothing to do with it, but Maurice said he was going on with it. This looks rather like a conspiracy. War Cabinet 11.30. I was working most of the day on material for Ll. G.'s speech, looking up past records etc. At 6 p.m. Ll. G. rehearsed his speech to Lord Milner, Chamberlain, Kerr, and self and we cut it about a good deal. Earlier in the afternoon Balfour, who had promised to speak to-morrow, came to the office and cross-examined me for an hour in regard to the facts . . .

At the War Cabinet meeting on 8th Lloyd George informed his colleagues that he was entirely opposed to the demand by the opposition for a Select Committee instead of a Judicial Enquiry, since the former would be "constituted on Party lines", and so "perfectly useless". He then went on to give his colleagues his intended riposte to Maurice's triple challenge, on the broad lines of Hankey's brief, but bringing in with great emphasis that the reply to Baring's question had been "based on figures supplied by the Director of Military Operations, in fact by General Maurice's own department". Though the General Staff, and not the Adjutant-General, are the constitutional advisers of the government, and it is therefore the responsibility of the former to ensure the accuracy of information supplied, it was surely disingenuous of Lloyd George not to make clear where the mistake had actually originated. It can definitely be said that Hankey had no hand in propagating this equivocation, though he does not appear to have drawn attention to it when Lloyd George first produced it. The Prime Minister next consulted his colleagues as to whether he should confine himself to answering Maurice's charges or should deal with the wider issue of "the whole history of the extension of the British line". Several Ministers expressed strong feelings against giving figures which were bound to be useful to the enemy. "It was generally agreed",

[1] Only the second part of this entry is in *Supreme Command*, II, p. 798.
[2] "Chinovnik" is Russian for "official" or "civil servant". Under the Soviets the word came to have a pejorative signification, e.g. "bureaucrat". But Sykes was probably using it in the original sense.

state the minutes, "that the Government had in fact a complete answer to their critics, but that the statement of the Parliamentary answer was difficult, owing to the obligation not to give information to the enemy". In the end Lloyd George asked Milner and Chamberlain to meet him that afternoon "to consider in more detail the character of the statement which he should make in the House of Commons".[1] We have no record of what took place at that meeting.

A crucial document on the Maurice affair is Hankey's diary entry for 9th May; and it is noteworthy that in his memoirs he omitted the passage which was most telling about Lloyd George's suppression of awkward facts. They are italicised below, and prove beyond doubt that Lloyd George saw the Adjutant-General's *corrected* statement of fighting and total strength (of 7th May), but chose to ignore it. One must, however, remember that the War Office had produced so many sets of confusing, and in some cases contradictory statements of the Army's strength that even someone who was more careful than Lloyd George in his use of "facts and figures" can be forgiven for getting muddled.

Diary 9th May 1918[2]
In town betimes. War Cabinet postponed. Sent in Storr's name for a C.B. Tom Jones refused to let me send in his name for a C.B.E. because the Welsh miners would say "Here's Tom Jones, whom we thought such a good democrat, being bought like the rest". I told him I respected him for it. At 1 p.m. I went to 10 Downing St. and read the notes of P.M.'s speech and made some alterations. He was walking up and down in the sun on the terrace with Bonar Law. The latter said "the case seems so strong that I cannot help feeling that Maurice, who is a clever man, has something up his sleeve." I have done my best, and only hope there is nothing I have over-looked! I lunched alone with the P.M., as I always do before his big speeches. He was cheerful but in rather a chastened mood. He admitted that speeches dealing with facts and figures were not his strong point, and that his Celtic temperament made him unable to resist stretching them to their entire limits. I thought the moment favourable to improve the occasion about Ireland, as he was in a much less truculent frame of mind than usual. I actually got him to agree that he should get Lord French, the new Viceroy, to try and form an Irish Cabinet to prepare the way for Home Rule and to try a voluntary recruiting effort before enforcing conscription! This was a great triumph and in the afternoon I told Professor Adams of the Garden

[1] W.C. 407 of 8th May 1918.
[2] See *Supreme Command*, II, pp. 798-9.

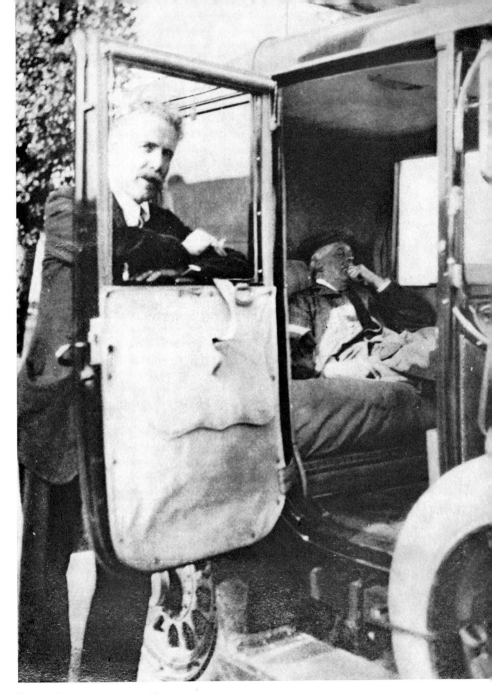

Ian Malcolm and Mr. Balfour

The Imperial War Cabinet, second session June 1918. Taken in the
garden at 10, Downing Street
First row (*left to right*): Mr. W. F. Massey (New Zealand), Maj.-Gen.
H.H. the Maharajah of Patiala (India), Mr. Bonar Law, Sir Robert Borden,
Mr. Lloyd George, Mr. W. M. Hughes, Mr. A. J. Balfour, Mr. Joseph
Cook (Australia), Dr. W. E. Lloyd. *Second row*: Admiral Sir Rosslyn
E. Wemyss, Sir Joseph Ward, Mr. N. W. Rowell (Canada), Mr. Walter
Long, Mr. G. N. Barnes, Earl Curzon of Kedleston, General Smuts,
Mr. Austen Chamberlain, Mr. J. A. Calder (Canada), Mr. H. Burton
(South Africa), Mr. E. S. Montagu, Sir Joseph Maclay, General Sir G. M.
Macdonogh. *Back row*: Sir William Weir, Maj.-Gen. F. H. Sykes, Col. G.
Lambert, Col. Amery, Lt. Col. Sir Maurice Hankey, Mr. A. Meighen
(Canada), Sir S. P. Sinha (India), Col. Storr

Suburb, who was delighted. The speech was a superb parliamentary effort. I was very glad I had got him to insert some passages to give Haig satisfaction, though he might have gone a step further in this respect. Practically all opposition was crushed. Runciman, who was to have wound up for the opposition, looked miserable, and never rose. Ll. G.'s whips asked him to speak earlier "because Balfour is to follow", and this finished him. *Nevertheless I felt all the time that it was not the speech of a man who tells "the truth; the whole truth; and nothing but the truth." For example, while he had figures from the D.M.O.'s Dept. showing that the fighting strength of the army had increased from 1st Jan. 1917 to 1918, he had the Adjutant-General's figures saying the precise contrary, but was discreetly silent about them. This knowledge embarrassed me a little when M.Ps of all complexions kept coming to the official gallery to ask me what was the "real truth".* There was a general recognition of the fact that Ll. G.'s speech was magnificently got up and that this was due to me . . . Lawrence Guillemard,[1] by the way, whom I met in the official gallery, declared that Asquith was privy to the Maurice letter, and that there was a dinner attended *inter alios* by Bongy, Asquith, and Maurice. I don't believe it.

10th May[2]

War Cabinet 11.30. General congratulations to P.M. on his speech and general recognition that it was only rendered possible by my system of records. Sir Reginald Brade,[3] (Secy. War Office) whom I met at lunch, told me that three weeks ago, someone suggested to him that Gen. Maurice was not *compos mentis*. I fear this must be true. Spent whole afternoon on a précis *re* the Austrian peace overtures in 1917. I am very tired of these précis. But in the affair of the Maurice letter so much turned on matters of minute detail that I have decided to re-organise my private office, bringing in Captain Burgis to collate my records, and keep files on all the most secret questions, such as are kept in the office registry on less secret questions, in which every scrap of information will be found. This diary has proved priceless in these investigations.

On 11th Hankey sent Lloyd George the first part of his historical summary of the Austrian peace negotiations which covered the period from the creation of the War Cabinet to June 1917, in which month the idea was dropped because of Sonnino's "insuperable objections". Four

[1]Sir Lawrence (not Laurence as written by Hankey) N. Guillemard (1862–1951). Civil Servant and Colonial administrator. Chairman, Board of Customs and Excise 1909–19. Governor, Straits Settlements and High Commissioner, Federated Malay States 1919–27.
[2]The first sentence only is in *Supreme Command*, II, p. 799.
[3]1864–1933. Civil Servant. Assistant Secretary, War Office 1904–14 and Secretary 1914–20.

days later he followed this up with the second part, which dealt with the discussions with the Italians on "smashing Austria, obtaining Trieste and then reopening negotiations". The final part, which was to cover the Smuts-Mensdorff and Kerr-Skzrynski conversations, mentioned earlier, was not ready until a short time later.[1] Taken as a whole it was an authoritative and admirably clear account of a very complicated story, and on it Lloyd George undoubtedly based the version given in his *War Memoirs*.[2]

Early in May Stamfordham wrote to Hankey, presumably at the instigation of the King, to ask whether he saw any chance of Robertson being re-employed. "It really is wicked", continued Stamfordham, "that he should be performing ceremonies for the Church Army at such a time of national crisis". Hankey replied that he fully shared those views and had "made several suggestions on the subject, but they have not been acted on".[3] In the middle of the month the question came before the War Cabinet.

Diary 15th May

War Cabinet at 11 a.m. to clear up arrears. P.M. not present. Soon after the beginning I was called away to attend meeting the P.M. was having at War Office with Milner and Sir H. Wilson. At the end of this meeting the question of the command of Home Defence vacated by Lord French was raised. Ll. G. was opposed to Robertson's appointment on the ground that he was still intreaguing [sic] with Maurice and others. In fact he said that only last night there had been a dinner at Robertson's house (J.T. Davies told me later it was attended by Maurice, Repington and Gwynne, at which it had been decided that Maurice should write a book against Ll. G. All this, I suspected, is got through Ll. G.'s valet by backstairs espionage. Disgusting!) After much discussion I suggested that Robertson should be sent to India and Monro brought back for the home command, which was greeted with acclamation.[4] . . .

Within a few days of the discovery of the mistake made in the Adjutant-General's department in the figures provided for use by Macpherson in answering Baring's question on 18th April Colonel Kirke of the D.M.O.'s department apparently informed Philip Kerr and

[1] Lloyd George papers F/23/2/33.
[2] IV, pp. 1983–2035 and 2169–77. V, pp. 2462–3.
[3] Stamfordham to Hankey (undated) and reply by the latter of 4th May 1918. RA GV.Q1287/4 and 5.
[4] Nonetheless Robertson became G.O. C-in-C, Home Forces in June 1918.

Macpherson about the error.[1] Indeed it seems likely that the D.M.O.'s department knew the truth even earlier, since a War Office return bears a note that the A.G. telephoned the D.M.O. on 6th April that the figures of Army strength for 1st January 1918 included the troops in Italy.[2] But although Downing Street knew the truth, and had the A.G.'s return of 7th May, Lloyd George again used the incorrect figures in the debate of 9th; and Milner was evidently not told about it until after that occasion. As Hankey recorded in his diary that Lloyd George had the corrected A.G.'s return the responsibility for Milner being left in ignorance must surely lie between Kerr, Macpherson and J. T. Davies. No matter what Milner's faults may have been, he was a strictly honourable man, and as soon as he learnt about the mistake he felt obliged to tell the Prime Minister. That he did at the meeting in his room at the War Office on 15th, which Hankey mentioned only cursorily in his diary. In fact that meeting was extremely important, and gave rise to the institution by Hankey of the "X Series" of minutes recording specially secret discussions outside the War Cabinet. The record shows that General Macdonogh, the Director of Military Intelligence, first made a report on the situation, and was then asked to withdraw, leaving only Lloyd George, Milner, Henry Wilson and Hankey in the room. Milner then said "that a mistake had been discovered in the figures given by Mr. Macpherson as the basis of his statement in the House of Commons [in answer to Baring's question on 18th April] that the fighting strength of the British Army on the western front was greater on January 1st, 1918, than on January 1st, 1917". As a matter of fact, he said, it was less. "It had transpired" continued Milner "that the figures given to Mr. Macpherson included British troops on the Italian front. As the Prime Minister had used Mr. Macpherson's statement in his speech on May 9th, he felt bound to let him know". The record then states that Lloyd George pointed out "that he could not be held responsible for an error which had been made in General Maurice's Department". At this point General

[1]Duke of Northumberland to Maurice 19th June and 12th July 1922. See John Gooch, *op. cit.*, where he states that Macpherson offered to make an explanatory statement in the House, but according to the recollections of the Duke of Northumberland, written four years after the event, "Lloyd George prevented him from doing so".

[2]WO.106/368. I am indebted to Mr. John Gooch for drawing my attention to this note.

Hutchison (Director of Organisation)[1] entered the room and reported on the flow of American reinforcements; so the questions raised by Milner were not pursued.[2] Why, one may well ask, did not he, or for that matter Hankey, point out that the mistake had originated in the Adjutant-General's, and not in Maurice's department as stated by Lloyd George? And why did neither of them draw attention to the significance of the Adjutant-General's return of fighting strength of 7th May, mentioned in Hankey's diary entry for 9th? We cannot answer such questions; but it does seem surprising that Milner, having decided to take up the cudgels with his chief, did not use all the ammunition at his disposal. For it is surely reasonable to suppose that, in raising the matter, he had it in mind that a public recantation or admission of error was desirable.[3] Be that as it may the result was that Lloyd George was able to evade the issue that Macpherson and he himself had both misinformed the House. One deduction at any rate seems clear, namely that a clue to the growing coolness between Lloyd George and Milner is to be found in the meeting at the War Office on 15th May 1918.

Next day, 16th, another "X Meeting" took place, and Lloyd George accepted Milner's draft letter to Maurice "impressing on him the great importance . . . of not giving information to the enemy" in his journalistic work; for on the day of his retirement from the Army Maurice had accepted the post of Military Correspondent to the *Daily Chronicle*.[4] At another X Meeting on 17th Milner read Maurice's reply that "he would not indulge in any recriminations or attempt to re-open the case unless officially asked to do so". He would indeed "regard the Censor as a help and not an enemy".[5] Even Lloyd George cannot have hoped for a more complaisant adversary.

Although Lloyd George displayed great rhetorical skill and political acumen in the debate of 9th May, he was aided by Asquith's inept handling of the opposition's case. But, as Hankey remarked, Asquith was probably reluctant to embarrass the government, let alone bring it

[1]Major-General Robert Hutchison, 1st Baron Hutchison 1932 (1873–1950). Soldier and Politician (Lib., then Nat. Lib., then Lib. Nat.). Director of Organisation, War Office 1917–19. Chief Liberal Whip 1926–30. Paymaster-General 1935–8.
[2]"Note of a Conversation in the room of the Secretary of State for War", 15th May 1918. X1. Cab. 23/17.
[3]Liddell Hart's view (letter to the author of 5th Nov. 1968) that Milner's action was "merely for information and caution" appears unconvincing.
[4]Cab. 23/17. X2 of 16th May 1918. [5]*ibid.* X3 of 17th May 1918.

down at such a time of crisis. Yet it is surely the case that Lloyd George not only gave the House a good deal less than what Hankey called "the whole truth", but knew that he was doing so.

It is interesting here to recall a statement made by Lloyd George many years later about the truthfulness of politicians. In 1932 he told Liddell Hart that he had "never known first-rate politicians tell a deliberate lie". "They colour and exaggerate", he went on, "but they avoid a lie because of the heavy risk of being tripped up".[1] In fact the only prevarication which can be found in Lloyd George's speech of 9th May 1918 is his statement that "The figures I gave [on 9th April] were taken from the official records of the War Office, *for which I sent before I made the statement.* If they were incorrect, General Maurice was as responsible as anyone else. *But they were not inaccurate* ... (italics supplied).[2] Intentionally or not the italicised words were untrue—as Maurice himself was quick to remark.[3]

On the other hand Maurice did consult with senior Army officers in London, and almost certainly also with Haig during his visit to France in mid-April. And he certainly corresponded with, and several times met Robertson to discuss publication of his letter after Bonar Law had answered the critical questions by Lambert, Burn and Pringle on 23rd.[4] Hankey's diary entries show that Lloyd George, with his widespread network of informants, was well aware of these transactions; and they do of course lend support to his theory that a "Generals' Conspiracy" was in progress with the object of bringing down his government.

Maurice always realised that publication of his letter was almost certain to end his Army career, and after that had happened he behaved, as we have seen, with dignity and restraint.[5] True enough he showed

---

[1]Notes on "Talk with Lloyd George at Criccieth, 24th Sept. 1932". Liddell Hart papers.

[2]Parl. Deh., Commons, Vol. 105, Col. 2359.

[3]In his diary. Letter to the author from Mr. F. M. P. Maurice, the General's son, 29th November 1968.

[4]Gooch, *op. cit.*, p. 218. Robertson answered a letter from Maurice on 25th April, agreeing that "some action should be taken 'but it is difficult to know what to do' ". On 30th he wrote again leaving it to Maurice "to decide in your own mind what the right timing is, and to do it irrespective of what the results may be". In other words Robertson was not prepared to implicate himself publicly in Maurice's proposed action. For an apologist's view of Robertson's part in the affair see V. Bonham Carter, *Soldier True*, pp. 357–72.

[5]Maurice was placed on the retired list on 13th May 1918.

considerable immaturity, not to say artlessness, in believing that his letter would right what he regarded as the wrongs inflicted on the Army; but like most service men he was completely lacking in political experience. As Esher wrote to Hankey "Soldiers are so stupid. They never understand that politics are not a battle. Maurice will be let down by all those who have used him . . .":[1] and again "If Frederick Maurice and Wully Robertson wished to make a protest, the moment was in November 1916. Either they should have got the men or stopped the operations of 1917 . . . All this letting off of squibs after the event is futility".[2] Clemenceau put the matter in a nutshell when he remarked *"Pourquoi est-ce que les militaires tâchent de faire l'escrime avec les politiciens?"*[3] At any rate Maurice cannot be accused of lack of moral courage.

Whatever conclusions one may reach with regard to Maurice's conduct, and for a soldier publicly to attack the veracity and actions of his political masters in time of war is, to put it mildly, unusual, Lloyd George's reaction may reasonably be described as vindictive. And when he came to write his version of the affair he showed that the anger aroused at the time had not in any way subsided.[4] Nor did he admit that there could have been any error on the part of himself or other government spokesmen such as Macpherson and Bonar Law, or that any relevant information had been withheld. But the mills of history, though they may grind slow, grind exceedingly small; and the truth is now known—in large part thanks to Hankey's diary and his system of records.

Hankey himself seems to have judged Maurice with unusual harshness, though he was of course in duty bound to make the best case he could for Lloyd George. After the war Maurice wished to enter the academic world, and in 1925 he applied for the Chichele Professorship of the History of War at Oxford. The Chairman of the C.I.D., or his representative, was at that time *ex officio* one of the Electors, and on 20th June Hankey attended a meeting of the Board of Electors to choose a successor to Spenser Wilkinson. The decision, taken "on a vote", was to select Sir Ernest Swinton out of the seven applicants; and it seems very probable that Hankey preferred his friend and colleague

---

[1] 9th May 1918. *Journals and Letters*, IV, p. 199.
[2] Journal, 10th May 1918. *ibid.,* p. 200.
[3] "Why do soldiers try fencing with politicians". Quoted by Esher to O. S. Brett 14th May 1918. *ibid.*
[4] *Lloyd George*, V, pp. 2972–95.

of the war years to Maurice.[1] The latter apparently believed that Hankey's voice had been decisive. It is at least good to record that Maurice finally achieved his academic goal as professor of Military Studies in the University of London in 1927, and as Principal of Queen Mary College of the same university from 1938-44.

One other fascinating conundrum concerned with the Maurice Debate remains to be considered. In 1956, five years after Maurice's death, Lord Beaverbrook published an extract from Frances Stevenson's diary, dated 5th October 1934, in which she described how "a few days after" Lloyd George's speech of 9th April 1918 J. T. Davies found in an unopened War Office despatch box at 10 Downing Street "a paper from the D.M.O. containing modifications and corrections of the first figures they had sent". She wrote that she and Davies "examined it in dismay", and the latter then "put it in the fire, remarking 'Only you and I, Frances, know of the existence of this paper'."[2] But Davies, when consulted by Miss Stevenson, could recall no such incident.[3] Furthermore there are discrepancies between Miss Stevenson's diary entry of 1934 and a letter which she (now Lady Lloyd George) wrote to the *Spectator* (23rd November 1956) arising out of Lord Templewood's review of Beaverbrook's book. Whereas in the former she stated that the "burnt paper" incident occurred "a few days after" Lloyd George's speech of 9th April 1918, in the latter she wrote that "the paper was only found *some time afterwards*"—that is after the "Maurice Debate" of 9th May. Taking account of the evidence in Hankey's diary, the balance of probability seems to lie with the identification of the Adjutant-General's return of 7th May as being both the "amending paper" forwarded by the D.M.O. (though it lacks any covering note by that Department) and the "burnt paper" referred to by Lady Lloyd George. In that event her letter to the *Spectator* is nearer the mark than her diary entry of 1934. Though the identity of those two documents is unlikely ever to be established beyond doubt it does not seem unfair to describe J. T. Davies as an accomplice of Lloyd George in suppressing information which the House of Commons was entitled to have. And one is left wondering, with Hankey, why Lloyd George did not tell the "whole truth", admit the mistake which had turned a decrease in "Fighting

[1] Sir Folliott Sandford, Registrar of Oxford University, to the author 25th June 1968.
[2] *Men and Power* (Collins Ed.), pp. 261-4.
[3] See Frances Lloyd George, *The Years that are Passed* (Hutchinson, 1967), p. 133.

Strength" on 1st January 1918 of 41,000 into an increase of 45,000, and hang his whole case on Hankey's argument that the British army in France was *as a whole* stronger at the beginning of 1918 than a year earlier. It is difficult to believe that a frank admission of that nature would have resulted in the fall of the government. But perhaps such a simple and straightforward line would have been too much out of character for a man of Lloyd George's temperament.

Chapter 18

The Crisis Overcome. May-July 1918

As soon as the passions aroused by the Maurice letter had calmed down, Hankey returned to the routine grind of the daily War Cabinets and Inter-Allied meetings.

Diary 16th May 1918
Our P.M. has invented a new and most tiresome method of doing business. He puts the War Cabinet at noon and has a private meeting of his own with Lord Milner and C.I.G.S. at 11 a.m., when I have to attend and am expected to keep a record. He really is a trial. Just as I have got the War Cabinet system in good working order so as to relieve myself of overwork he overburdens me again. For this means an hour extra in the morning and an hour in the afternoon dictating, a really terrible inroad on my limited time for office business. Luckily he is sure to tire of it soon, but anyhow he ought not to rely so entirely on me . . .

Lloyd George's new system resulted in an extension of Hankey's "X Series" meetings, the third of which took place at Downing Street on 17th with the Prime Minister, Milner, Wilson, Hankey and Amery present. Apart from accepting Maurice's reply to Milner's letter, already mentioned, the meeting considered a proposal by Lloyd George to send a Canadian force to Vladivostok to combine with the "Czech Legion" of former prisoners-of-war of the Russians and with the Japanese to deny the Germans access to "the produce of Siberia, as well as copper, zinc etc. from the Urals".[1] Thus was the purpose of Allied intervention in Russia—which originally had the strategic object of keeping an eastern front in being—widened to include economic objectives. That evening Hankey wound up affairs in his office and went home for the Whitsun holiday—"the longest leave since last autumn".[2] But it was, as usual, broken into by Lloyd George.

[1] X3 of 17th May 1918. Cab. 23/17. [2] Diary 17th May 1918.

Diary Dated 22nd May but probably 21st

. . . Ll. G. summoned me to Walton Heath, where I spent the night. I found him rather "low" about the Irish proclamation issued last Saturday, to the effect that a plot had been discovered between the Sinn Feiners and the Germans. There has since been an outcry for the production of the evidence and Walter Long and the Irish Executive (who forced the Cabinet to approve the proclamation by putting a pistol to their head) have only produced evidence of the most flimsy and ancient description. So the Government are put in a hole, as I expected they would be by their vacillatory and rather insincere Irish policy. Ll. G. practically admitted to me that he was done with Home Rule.

22nd May 1918

Left Walton Heath about noon. No War Cabinet. Worked all day at office. Lunched with Seely, who came back to my office. He gives a most appalling account of the army in France and of the recent battle. According to him there was simply a universal movement to the rear directly the German advance began. No one could be induced to stand and no one would stand, even when it was proved to them that no Germans were in front of them. It was a psychic [sic] catastrophe. According to him there is an entire lack of confidence in Haig and his staff, and until they are cleared out, confidence will not be restored. He is of course to some extent prejudiced, as he has been very badly treated by Haig, but I thought it worth while to arrange for the P.M. to dine with him. War Cabinet at 6.30 . . .

May 26th was a Sunday, and Hankey spent "a quiet day at home . . . tuning up the P.M.'s draft Memo. on the A.G.'s paper" about man-power. He had, he wrote, somewhat tautologically, made it "a horribly biting, mordant document . . . I hate wasting time on it as this sort of thing doesn't win the war, except in so far as maintaining the P.M. in office tends to win the war".

On the following Monday Ludendorff launched a fresh attack— between Soissons and Rheims—in a superiority of about two to one. It was actually a diversion, intended to draw reserves away from the north and so pave the way for a decisive blow against the British. But the degree of surprise achieved, and the depth of the initial penetration caused Ludendorff to throw in some of his own reserves—though not enough to turn a success into a victory. The Germans swept across the Aisne and reached the Marne on 30th; but there the impetus died away in face of strong Allied resistance—notable for the appearance of American divisions at Château-Thierry. Ludendorff had now created two very large and one smaller bulges in the Allied front, and his next blow was designed to pinch out the Compiègne "tongue" between the Amiens bulges.[1] But that did not come until early in June.

Diary 27th May 1918[2]

The P.M. sent for me before 11 a.m. and demanded to know what I had done about the Adjutant-General's Memo., so it was as well that I had pressed on with it, and he took my draft down to Walton Heath in the afternoon in his pocket. Soon after 11 a.m. the C.I.G.S. came in. He had bad news about the German attack on the Chemin des Dames. As usual they seem to have gone through our strong positions like paper. Afterwards we discussed plans for 1919. Wilson thinks we are in for 2 months of great anxiety; these will be followed by 2 months of diminishing anxiety; after this, if we survive, we shall have a long interval before we are in a position to strike the tremendous blow which alone can overcome the enemy (No more Passchendaeles!). That interval should be used for striking some blow in the outlying theatres . . .

28th May

At 11 a.m. I had to take a conference with M. Pichon on the Czecho-Slovak question. War Cabinet at noon. Lunched with Richmond, now Adty. Director of Staff Duties, at Club. He says there is a great improvement at the Adty. since he was last there. News from the Chemin des Dames deplorable, but the British seem to have fought fairly well.

In fact Hankey's former shipmate Herbert Richmond, who for all his ability was never an easy man to work with, was dismissed from the Admiralty by Admiral Wemyss, the First Sea Lord, in the following December—though not before he had done valuable work in placing the Naval Staff organisation on a firm footing. However, thanks to Beatty's good offices he received another command in 1919, and ended his time in the Navy as a Vice-Admiral.[3]

Diary 30th May 1918

The usual 11 a.m. meeting followed by War Cabinet at 11.30 and another War Cabinet at 5 p.m., a very heavy day . . . Very bad news this evening, the Germans having entered Château-Thierry. J.T. Davies asked me to-day if I would like a G.B.E. or any other honour, but I replied that in present circumstances and anxieties as regards the war I could not contemplate it.

There now took place a series of "specially secret" meetings, which Hankey recorded in his "X Series", on the progress of the German offensive and the need to make plans for the abandonment of the

---

[1]*Liddell Hart*, pp. 476–8.   [2]Part of this entry is in *Supreme Command*, II, p. 808.
[3]See A. J. Marder, *Portrait of an Admiral* (Cape, 1952), pp. 327–32.

Channel ports, or even a complete withdrawal from France.[1] They were held before the normal War Cabinets, as Hankey recorded in his diary; but he discreetly gave no inkling of the subjects discussed. Fortunately the German offensive was halted before the withdrawal projects had progressed beyond the stage of preliminary planning.

On the last day of May Hankey crossed to France again in company with Lloyd George, Balfour and the naval and military leaders for another meeting of the Supreme War Council. On the way over the party held informal discussions about whether Dunkirk should be abandoned, as Henry Wilson wished, in order to shorten the line and release ten divisions. The naval representatives were strongly opposed to any such idea, because it would render the Dover anti-submarine barrage ineffective. Hankey told the company that "to give the Germans a new pawn on the vital Channel coast was most undesirable". That evening they reached Versailles, and Hankey had a long conversation with General Du Cane,[2] the head of the British mission at Foch's headquarters, who took a gloomy view of the future, and feared that the British army of some 2½ million men would be hopelessly trapped if the French suffered a decisive defeat. Du Cane also reported on the disagreement between Haig and Foch over whether the size of divisions should be cut, in accordance with Foch's ideas, or whether the number of divisions should be reduced in order to maintain their numerical strength—as Haig was engaged in organising. There was also a clash of opinion between those who, like General Lawrence, Haig's Chief of Staff, wanted to abandon the Channel ports and fall back behind the Somme while it was still possible, and Foch, who "refused to give up anything". Hankey reported all these disagreements to Lloyd George and Milner, and the former was "very indignant" at the idea of sacrificing the Channel ports in order to shorten the line. "I am sure he means to get rid of Haig as soon as there is a lull in the fighting", wrote Hankey in his diary.[3] He went to bed in an anxious frame of mind—the

[1]X6 meeting on 30th May and X8 on 5th June 1918. Cab. 23/17.
[2]Later General Sir John P. Du Cane (not du Cane as written by Hankey) (1865–1947). Commanded XV Corps 1916–18. British Representative with Marshal Foch 1918. Master-General of Ordnance 1920–23. G.O. C-in-C, Western Command, 1923–4 and British Army of Rhine 1924–7. Governor and C-in-C, Malta, 1927–31.
[3]Except for this sentence almost the whole entry for 31st May 1918, summarised above, is in *Supreme Command*, II, pp. 809–10. The officer referred to there as "General X" was Major-General Guy Dawnay (see p. 201), who was serving on Haig's staff at the time. Presumably Hankey suppressed his name for fear of libel

more so because they had been thirteen at dinner! Evidently he was not entirely free from superstition.

June 1st—"a really glorious day"—began with informal talks between Lloyd George, Henry Wilson, Haig, Milner and Du Cane, for which Hankey had previously coached the Prime Minister; but he tactfully absented himself, because he felt it would "be wiser to leave them to talk quite freely and informally, without any notes being taken of their conversations". In the afternoon however he was the sole secretary present when the British and French delegates met in Clemenceau's room to discuss how the American troops should be integrated into the Allied forces.[1] The conferences and discussions continued throughout the following day, a Sunday.

Diary 2nd June 1918[2]

No meeting of the S.W.C. in the morning. I breakfasted alone with the P.M. who was very bitter against Gen. Lawrence's attitude towards American co-operation, which did not give him the impression of a man who was doing his utmost to meet a great national emergency. He was also particularly bitter about Guy Dawnay, who, according to Du Cane is obstructive to Gen. Foch's wishes. . . . At 11 o'clock Gen. Lawrence turned up and we had a long confab. with the P.M., Milner, C.I.G.S., and self. At first his attitude was not helpful, but the P.M. (whom at breakfast I had implored to deal reasonably and not drastically with Lawrence, as he first proposed) handled him well. His attitude steadily improved until at last he declared roundly that Haig was only too anxious to put the Americans in the fighting line as soon as possible, but that he was prevented by Pershing, who insisted on rigid adherence to a schedule (pronounced by Pershing "skedule") of training. The conversation then switched entirely on to the "skedule" and the means to get Pershing to relax it. It was decided to ask Foch's aid, and Gen. Du Cane was sent off to try and square Foch, while Milner undertook to see Pershing (which unfortunately he failed to do as P. arrived too late). Meanwhile I drafted an agreement. The urgency for using these Americans is extraordinarily great. The French reserves are all being drawn south to meet the threat on Paris. We have few reserves, and want men "to stem a rush", which the Americans

---

over the story of his having torn up Haig's orders accepting Foch's scheme to use the Americans to re-form the ten divisions which Haig had "rolled up", instead of using them to increase the size of his divisions to 12 battalions, as Haig had originally wished to do. See *Liddell Hart*, p. 467; Terraine, *Haig*, p. 393.

[1]Diary 1st June 1918. Mostly reproduced in *Supreme Command*, II, p. 810.

[2]Part of this day's entry is in *Supreme Command*, II, pp. 811–12.

could do, if only Pershing would let them be used and Haig and Lawrence would hustle a bit . . . The old idea of having an American battalion in each British brigade has been dropped, and the Americans are all being put into the British Divisions [which are] reduced to cadres for want of drafts . . . At 2 p.m. we met in Clemenceau's room at the Trianon. . . . Pershing was frightfully obstinate and would not look at our proposal to make Haig the authority for deciding when the American troops were to go into the line, and eventually the question was left to Foch and Pershing. Foch was very rude about our breaking up divisions and kept re-iterating that he could not conduct the war unless we maintained our divisions, and Ll. G. repeated the offer accepted by Clemenceau on the previous day to allow a French expert access to all our man-power figures. Eventually they agreed to a declaration to President Wilson by the three P.M.s to be accompanied by a technical agreement signed by Milner, Foch, and Pershing, who were left to arrange it. Then we adjourned for tea and afterwards to the big conference chamber to discuss again the question of the Admiralissimo in the Mediterranean.[1] We had thought this to be settled the previous day, but Sonnino was extraordinarily obstinate and insisted that the Italians must retain command of the Adriatic . . . I am bound to say that Geddes was just as difficult and uncompromising as the Italians. On the one hand he would concede nothing to Italian *amour propre* and on the other he would insist on Jellicoe's dispositions being subject to the Allied Naval Council, which the Italians would not accept. The reason for this was that he doesn't really trust Jellicoe sufficiently to place him in the same position as Foch. The end of the *séance* was screaming farce. Orlando, Sonnino and the Italian Admiral de Revel[2] were all shouting at the top of their voices at once, and gesticulating like monkeys. Sonnino's brick-red face looked like apoplexy, his eyes were bulging out of his head and flashing fire-real sparks, and his body was lolling about with his gesticulations. All this was provoked because Ll. G. said the Italians wanted to make his proposal for an Admiralissimo a sham, that he would not insult Jellicoe by offering him the job on such terms, and that his proposal was withdrawn. Admiral de Revel was an altogether contemptible person. Yesterday he distinguished himself by saying that he could not join the Italian fleet at Taranto with the French fleet at Corfu, because the voyage between the two ports was too dangerous for ships going to and fro to dock. To-day he still further distinguished himself by boasting that the Italian fleet had not been

[1]Hankey had been pressing for Jellicoe's appointment to this post. Diary 1st June 1918.

[2]Admiral Paolo C. Thaon de Revel (not Reval as Hankey wrote and as appears in many British official documents of the period) (1859-?). Chief of Naval Staff and C-in-C Naval Forces 1917-19. Senator 1917. President of Committee of Allied Admirals 1920. Created "Duke of the Sea" 1923. Minister of Marine 1922-25.

to sea for 18 months and consequently, had not lost a ship! The meeting broke up in some confusion. We dined again 13 at table" . . .

3rd June[1]

. . . Albert Thomas lunched with us at the Villa Romaine and gave a depressing account of the fighting. The French were run over at the start. After a very short bombardment, and then, by the infiltration of machine guns through and behind their lines, were forced to retreat. They lost heavily, without themselves inflicting heavy casualties. During lunch Henry Wilson took me outside on to the balcony, to tell me that, as he is off to a conference at Pétain's G.H.Q., I must get the P.M. to speak to Clemenceau and insist on Foch shortening his lines in the north, and obtaining his reserves by uncovering Dunkirk and retiring behind the floods. He evidently anticipates a disaster to the French. After lunch Gen. Hutchison[2] told me that Gen. Weygand had been greatly depressed yesterday and had admitted that the French are not fighting properly and (?) won't attack.

The Supreme War Council met again at 3 p.m. and had a comparatively amicable meeting, which calls for no comment. Thus the session came to a close. It was, on the whole, rather a dog fight. Perhaps it was best described by the American general Bliss, who, when asked how the Conference was getting on said "Well, they are all at sea, except the Italian Admiral and he won't go there". One amusing incident occurred on the last day during a discussion on "Jugo-Slavs". M. Pichon explained what had been agreed to at a conference of Foreign Ministers in the morning. Balfour followed with a very typical speech 20 minutes long, nicely balancing the arguments. Clemenceau replied "Very well—are you for or against?"—a very shrewd commentary on Balfour's character . . .

After the end of the conference Hankey went shopping with Lloyd George "to buy some trinkets for his family". "The saleswoman", he recorded, "was a pretty girl who attracted Lloyd George". Evidently the Prime Minister's coquetry did not pass unobserved by such a constant companion as Hankey. Then the party had a peaceful dinner in the idyllic setting of a lake-side restaurant.[3] One cannot but contrast the enjoyment of such diversions by the Supreme Command with the lot of the soldiers then struggling desperately to hold the German thrust for the Channel ports. Early next morning the British delegates

[1] The first part of this entry is in *Supreme Command*, II, pp. 812–13.
[2] Hankey wrote this officer's name as Hutchinson, but it must have been General Robert Hutchison (later 1st Baron Hutchison of Montrose), the Director of Organisation in the War Office. See p. 548. The same mistake appears in some Cabinet records of the same period, e.g. XI of 15th May 1918.
[3] Diary 4th June. See *Supreme Command*, II, p. 813.

returned to London, Hankey taking with him a somewhat sombre view of the progress of the battle and of Allied prospects. "I cannot exclude the possibility of a disaster" he wrote in his diary. At the next day's War Cabinet the discussion was again centred on the question of shortening the line by abandoning Dunkirk, for which Henry Wilson was strongly pressing but which Foch resolutely refused to countenance, and also on the possible need to withdraw the whole army from France "if the French crack". "It was a very gloomy meeting" was Hankey's comment.[1]

Diary 6th June 1918
Usual meeting at 11 a.m. Milner and C.I.G.S. are off to France to try and arrange that Haig's reserves should be withdrawn. The proposal is that the French troops shall be withdrawn to reinforce Foch, and that we shall keep the new divisions, which have been filled up with American infantry, to replace them, instead of carrying out Foch's proposal to send them to Alsace, which involves a very long journey and weeks of delay before the French divisions they are to replace become available for the battle. War Cabinet at noon. Discussion on Russia and outburst by Lord Robert Cecil against the War Cabinet's conduct of the negotiations for Japanese intervention. Milner and C.I.G.S. are also to press for a retirement in the north from Ypres to the St. Omer–Dunkirk line . . .

Next day Hankey was greatly troubled by Lloyd George telling him that William Pringle, the opposition Liberal M.P.[2] had been overheard talking on the terrace of the House of Commons about the possible abandonment of northern France and the Channel ports, and saying that "he had got his information from a secretary of the War Cabinet". Hankey, who was "very jealous of the integrity of my secretariat, which must be like Caesar's wife 'above reproach' ", at once set himself to trace the source of the report which had reached the Prime Minister's ears—actually at third hand through Bonar Law, Talbot the Chief Unionist Whip[3] and Ronald McNeill.[4] His investigations showed that

[1]Diary, 5th June. [2]See p. 240.
[3]Lord Edmund Bernard Talbot, 1st Viscount Fitzalan (1855–1947). Second son of 14th Duke of Norfolk. Took name of Talbot 1876 and of Fitzalan-Howard 1921. Joint Parliamentary Secretary to Treasury 1915–21. The last Lord Lieutenant of Ireland 1921–22.
[4]1st Baron Cushenden 1927 (1861–1934). Politician (Cons.). Parliamentary Under-Secretary for Foreign Affairs 1922, 1924 and 1925. Financial Secretary to Treasury 1925–27. Chancellor of Duchy of Lancaster with special responsibility for League of Nations affairs 1927–29.

all Pringle had said on the authority of the secretariat was that the Germans had been in Rheims for a week, and Hankey then remembered that he himself had mentioned to Mrs. Asquith that they were in the suburbs of that city—as their own newspapers had claimed—when he had lunched at her house on 30th May. The rumour about the evacuation of the Channel ports Pringle had probably got from Sir Robert Houston,[1] a shipowner and M.P., who knew that certain stores were being shipped back from France.[2] Having traced the sources of Pringle's remarks Hankey at once set about allaying Lloyd George's suspicions with regard to the integrity of the secretariat.[3] But the whole incident must have impressed him still more deeply with the need for absolute discretion—the more so because in this case he himself could be said to have been slightly at fault.

There now followed for the Hankeys a "delightful week-end, walking, bathing and lazing in a lovely country house"—the Seelys' home Brooke in the Isle of Wight. There he met two Canadian officers (one of whom, Lieutenant Harvey, had recently won a Victoria Cross) who were very outspoken about the causes of the German breakthrough on 21st March. According to them the British "compulsory service men" were "not as good as the volunteers of earlier days", and they had seen thousands of them "bolting in no sort of formation". The Canadians (who may well of course have been voicing usual Dominion prejudices) "did not conceal their dislike and contempt of 'brass hats' in general and G.H.Q. in particular", and held that they were "completely out of touch with the realities of the campaign as seen from the front line". This was a view Hankey himself had frequently expressed, and he now recorded his intention to "use much of their [the Canadians'] material"—especially about the need to disband the cavalry and improve communications between the various headquarters and the fighting units.[4] He seems to have forgotten that Seely had quite recently urged on him the view that the British soldier was just as good as his adversary.[5]

[1] 1853-1926. Shipowner and politician (Cons., not Lib. as stated in Hankey's diary) Chairman of the Houston Line. Husband of Dame Fanny Houston, who inherited most of his great wealth, purchased the *Saturday Review* and financed the British Schneider Trophy 1931 and the flight over Mount Everest 1933.
[2] Diary 7th June 1918.
[3] Hankey to Lloyd George 7th June 1918. Lloyd George papers F/23/2/37.
[4] Diary 8th-9th June 1918.   [5] See p. 524.

On his return from Brooke Hankey found "a very handsome letter of apology" from Pringle awaiting him—which doubtless brought him a sense of relief.[1] Then he once more turned his attention to the long-gestating report on man power.

Meanwhile the members of the Imperial War Cabinet had been gradually arriving in London for the second session of that body. With the Allied armies very much on the defensive in the west, and the crushing defeat sustained by Gough's Fifth Army fresh in everyone's minds, the auguries for such a gathering were not exactly favourable. For the Dominion statesmen, and especially those from Canada and Australia, were bound to seek explanations for the *débâcle* in which some of their troops had been involved; and they were also certain to demand a greater voice in the formulation of war policy. On 10th Lloyd George, Auckland Geddes, Henry Wilson and Hankey met in secret to discuss the military situation and man power problems—presumably to get their own ideas clear before facing the Dominions' representatives.[2]

The Imperial War Cabinet, though not yet complete, held its first meeting on 11th June, to hear what Hankey called "a rather depressing statement" from Lloyd George. At a very secret "British only" meeting that afternoon Henry Wilson and Auckland Geddes discussed with the Prime Minister much more wide-ranging problems than the current situation. According to Hankey's diary they included launching a combined peace-cum-military offensive against Austria, Japanese intervention in Siberia, a separate peace with Bulgaria, the encouragement of anti-German revolts by the Poles and Czechs, and the resuscitation of Roumania.[3] Though the official records are silent about such issues it seems fair to conclude that it was on this day that the seeds of an offensive military and political strategy were prepared for sowing.

Diary 13th June 1918[4]

Usual 11 o'clock meeting [of the "X" series]. Imperial War Cabinet at 11.30 Sir Robert Borden came out with some very plain speaking about the Higher Command in France. Lunched with Sir Eric Geddes, who criticised the Versailles Council rather severely and is very keen about establishing a member of the War Cabinet there, to co-ordinate the various departmental

[1] Diary 10th June 1918.
[2] X10 "Notes of a conversation at 10 Downing Street", 10th June 1918. Cab. 23/17.
[3] Diary 11th June 1918. Intervention in Russia was also discussed on 13th, 14th and 19th June. X12, 13 and 15. Cab. 23/17.
[4] Part of this entry is in *Supreme Command*, II, pp. 815–16.

missions in France. In the afternoon the P.M. sent for me. He is sending the Report of the Cabinet Committee on War Policy to the Prime Ministers of the Dominions and had that afternoon seen Borden and Gen. Currie[1] about the former's indictment of our military methods in France. He wished my advice as to the way he should handle the question to-morrow. I replied that I should in his place merely thank Borden for his frankness; and say that the question could not be settled until the arrival of Hughes from Australia, but that vital issues were raised, which must be probed *au fond*; that the question could not conveniently be discussed in a "Duma"; and that the best method would be to deal with it in a Committee of Prime Ministers only. He agreed. He told me that he had ascertained that Smuts had prompted Borden . . .

That evening Hankey had a long session with Curzon to coach him for a speech he was to make in the House of Lords in defence of the War Cabinet. To Hankey's evident pleasure Curzon was "extraordinarily complimentary", and assured him that after the war he would be "indispensable to every Prime Minister". One wonders whether Curzon was visualising having Hankey as his own right-hand man when, as he certainly anticipated would happen some day, he achieved the highest office in the land. Hankey's cautious reply, that he "always lived on a knife edge" and might at any time "make a false step and be engulfed", suggests that he grasped what was in Curzon's mind, but wished to warn him that he might well not survive to serve as secretary of his Cabinet.[2]

Diary 14th June
Invited myself to breakfast with my great pal Col. Charley Fisher[3] and his wife at the Regent Palace Hotel. He is back from E. Africa and full of the most extraordinary yarns. One of them is that Smuts and van Deventer[4] have never really tried to catch von Lettow,[5] but have deliberately herded him

[1]Though Hankey spelt this officer's name Curry it must have been Lieutenant-General Sir Arthur W. Currie (1875–1933). Commanded 1st Canadian Division 1916–17 and Canadian Corps in succession to General Byng 1917–18. Principal and Vice-Chancellor of McGill University, Montreal 1920–33.
[2]Diary 17th June 1918.
[3]An officer who joined the R.M.L.I. at the same time as Hankey joined the R.M.A.
[4]Later Lieutenant-General Sir Jacob L. van Deventer (not Van der Venter as written in Hankey's diary) (1874–1922). Second-in-Command to Smuts on side of Boers in South African war 1899–1902, and as C-in-C, East Africa, on side of British 1917–19.
[5]General Paul von Lettow-Vorbeck (1870–1964). As C-in-C, German forces in East Africa 1914–18, he managed to maintain them in the face of great odds right through to the Armistice. A Nationalist member of Reichstag 1929–30.

down south into Portuguese East Africa, because the Dutch want to get a footing in Delagoa Bay. This is apparently the common talk out there. He also said that all the officers out there are simply after K.C.Bs etc.—that is their one aim—not to earn a black mark. He was very critical of Smuts and van Deventer . . . His contempt of the Indian army officers, especially the senior ones, was scathing. He is off to Archangel or Murmansk. On my way to the office I met Graeme Thomson[1] the shipping man, who said he would have shipping for 320,000 men a month from U.S.A. in July, and he didn't believe the men would be ready to fill the ships . . . Imperial War Cabinet at noon preceded by the 11 o'clock military meeting. At the Imperial War Cabinet Gen. Smuts made an impressive statement justifying the Government's caution about Flanders etc. [i.e. Third Ypres] last year. Unfortunately he made an allusion to the Report of the Cabinet Committee on War Policy, which he referred to as having been circulated to the Prime Ministers. This led to a demand for this paper from all sorts of other people such as Walter Long, Churchill etc., and this put me in an awkward position, as I had to refuse it . . .

18th June

Military meeting at 11 a.m. Imperial War Cabinet at noon at War Office. Weighty statement by C.I.G.S. on our military position, rather marred by a certain flippancy. After the meeting Walter Long told me he hears that Borden and Hughes are both inclined to stop on. Lunched with Montagu, who wants to put all eastern military operations from Palestine eastwards, under the C-in-C, India.

19th June

. . . Went to House of Lords to hear debate on the War Cabinet system. Lord Midleton, who was attacking the Govt., made a nice reference to me in his speech, and Lord Curzon, in winding up for the Govt. paid a high tribute to me and said I should have "a niche in history to myself".[2] His speech was mainly my speech and was a great success. It should form a landmark in constitutional history. He had rehearsed it to the P.M., Bonar Law, Smuts, and myself immediately after lunch at 10 Downing St. Tom Jones told me that the P.M. had told Professor Adams that my Memo. (signed by him) in reply to the Adjutant-General was the most powerful paper he had ever read. Asquith said that my evidence for the Dardanelles Commission was the best State Paper he had ever read—so I seem to have pleased my masters. Rather a "buttery", day altogether . . .

[1]Sir Graeme Thomson (1875–1933). Civil Servant and Colonial Administrator. Director of Shipping, Admiralty and Ministry of Shipping 1917–19. Colonial Secretary, Ceylon 1919–22. Governor and C-in-C, British Guiana 1922–25 and of Nigeria 1925–31.

[2]Parl. Deb., Lords, Vol. 30, Cols. 242 and 271–2.

The "usual 11 o'clock conversation" mentioned above was conducted between Lloyd George, Milner, Auckland Geddes and Henry Wilson, and was recorded by Hankey in his "X Series".[1] It was concerned chiefly with the progress of the German offensive and the provision of additional troops for the western front.

Hankey's diary makes clear how quickly intervention in Russia took on an overtly anti-Bolshevik hue in London. Lloyd George had instructed him to consult Balfour about whether he should meet Alexander Kerensky,[2] the head of the Russian Provisional Government, who had arrived in London; and also whether a talk could be arranged with the Japanese ambassador about the participation of his country's troops in the campaign in Siberia. Balfour was doubtful about the wisdom of the former proposal—as was Hankey—because it was bound to become known and would make British relations with the Bolsheviks still more difficult. None the less the meeting did take place a few days later—though Lloyd George shooed Hankey out at the last moment and took Philip Kerr instead—because he thought "that the uniform might put him [Kerensky] off".[3] Thus we have no record of the conversation. As to the proposed meeting with the Japanese ambassador, Lloyd George thought that if he himself rather than Balfour conducted it "he might get a move on" about intervention in Siberia. Hankey persuaded Balfour to agree; and thus was initiated the arrangement which finally resulted in Japan sending large numbers of troops.[4]

On 21st June the Dominion Prime Ministers met with Lloyd George, Milner and Henry Wilson to consider the transfer of further troops from Palestine to France. Hankey noted that Massey was "the only out and out Westerner"; but it was finally agreed to transfer only one more division. "Billy" Hughes then made "a fiery statement demanding a greater voice in the war"—to be gently told by Borden that "if he had no voice it was because he neglected to attend the Imperial War Cabinet last year". Hankey also recorded that "there was a good deal of criticism of our generals, and some valid criticism of Haig"; but it "did not amount to much". That evening at a big dinner given by the Empire Inter-Parliamentary Association Hankey noticed that a lot of

[1]Cab. 23/17.
[2]1881–1968. Russian lawyer and politician. Became Minister of Justice, then of War after March revolution. Fled to U.S.A. after October revolution.
[3]Diary 24th June 1918.   [4]ibid. 20th June 1918.

important people got themselves introduced to him. He attributed this to Curzon's recent speech, and to a complimentary mention in *The Times*—for which he wrote to thank Dawson, as he considered it had helped him with the Dominions' representatives. At the same dinner Hankey's old shipmate Lord Charles Beresford told him that "his ears must be tingling with what people were saying of me". "I shall get *tête montée* if I don't look out!" he confided to his diary.[1]

Diary 22nd June

C.I.G.S. leaves this morning for Italy, where he hopes to (?) binge up the organ-grinders to biff the Austrians. Saw P.M. at noon. He decided not to circulate any Minutes of the meeting of the P.Ms; He is afraid that they "will talk for the Minutes, instead of what they really think." But he wants a record, which I shall have to style "Secretary's Notes". I am sending copies of them to Smuts, Milner, and C.I.G.S. to check. The P.M. is particularly anxious for some reason that the King should not see the notes. While I was there Sutherland[2] brought in a letter from Thomson[3] of Scotland Yard to the effect that he has evidence that Pemberton Billing, the author of a "purity campaign" was living during the recent trial in illicit relations with one of his chief witnesses, who, by the way, has been charged with bigamy.[4] The P.M. also had another letter from Kerensky, asking for an interview, and, on my advice, sent Philip Kerr to reconnoitre first . . .

Esher to Hankey. Roman Camp, Callander N.B. 23rd June 1918. Holograph
My dear Hankey,

Curzon did not say a word too much. No-one could.

I am not flattering, but no-one will ever know the true value of the service you have rendered our country.

I am sending to-morrow through Lawrence Burgis some articles from the Swiss papers which you should turn over to some of your young men. They

[1]Diary 21st June 1918. [2]See p. 329.
[3]Sir Basil H. Thomson (1861–1939). Barrister, Colonial administrator, prison Governor and Police officer. Assistant Commissioner, Metropolitan Police, 1913–19. Director of Intelligence 1919–21.
[4]Mrs. Villiers-Stuart, a principal witness for the defence in the trial of Pemberton Billing for criminal libel, was prosecuted for bigamy (*The Times*, 20th June 1918). The action against Billing arose out of publication in a paper called *The Vigilante* remarks to the effect that the private production of Oscar Wilde's play *Salome* by Maud Allen and Jack Grein "ministered to sexual perverts" etc. Billing's trial took place at the Central Criminal Court before Mr. Justice Darling and a jury. It lasted 6 days and aroused enormous interest. On 4th June, after a summing up which was very hostile to the plaintiffs, the jury acquitted Billing on all counts. There were enthusiastic scenes outside the court, and Billing became something of a national hero—for a short time.

contain phrases and suggestions which, coming from a neutral observer of the highest intelligence, are worth noting.

Yours ever

Diary 24th June 1918[1]

... The news from Italy is admirable, the Austrians having been driven back across the Piave. I have been trying to persuade Ll.G. that this is the psychological moment to make a speech for propaganda purposes in Austria, pointing out how Austrian soldiers were driven to the shambles by Germany; how Austria is almost starving; how Germany the Robber State, will only give such doles of food from the Ukraine as will keep Austria in vassalage; and how solution is only to be found by Austria throwing off the German yoke and joining herself to the society of free nations that has banded itself together to overthrow Prussian militarism. I cannot get him to catch on, and unfortunately he did not read the draft of a speech on the subject, which I sent him on Saturday ... At 6 p.m. we had the meeting of Prime Ministers at the House of Commons. The P.M. was $\frac{3}{4}$ hr. late, as he was speaking in the House, and during this time they pilloried Milner, Smuts, and self with questions, to which we were able to give more or less satisfactory replies. The questions referred to the Air Service, Inventions, and the defeat of the Fifth Army, the latter being a subject on which they, and especially Mr. Hughes, felt strongly. The P.M. carried out my suggestion and asked them to come to Versailles to meet M. Clemenceau and General Foch . . .

25th June

... At 3.45 called on Churchill in his room at the Ministry of Munitions by appointment to read a paper he is circulating to the Imperial War Cabinet. Advised him as to some alterations in form, in order to bring it constitutionally within the sphere of activity of the Ministry of Munitions, a point of view in which he did not altogether agree, as he thinks a Minister of Cabinet rank has a right to address his colleagues at large on strategy or any other subject. Beaverbrook came in while we were talking, which handicapped discussion.

26th June

Usual X meeting at 11.30. War Cabinet at noon ... Spent afternoon drafting some resolutions to be put before the conference of Prime Ministers on the subject of allied intervention in Russia, which, subject to minor alterations, was accepted at their meeting at 6 p.m. It was also decided to suspend the decision to withdraw the 54th Divn. from Palestine, as the new situation in Italy is held to justify relying on our forces in Italy for any reinforcement that may be required. Moreover, before the meeting, Sir Mark Sykes had tackled first me, and then the P.M. in my presence on the subject. He told us, firstly that an officer from Allenby's General Staff had been told by an officer at the War Office General Staff that he would probably eat his Xmas dinner

[1] A short extract from this entry is in *Supreme Command*, II, p. 819.

in Gaza, instead of in Damascus, as he had hoped: secondly that an officer on Allenby's General Staff had said in the presence of M. Picot, the French political agent, that we should probably be back soon at Gaza: thirdly that Picot, who is just back from Palestine is disturbed about the military situation there, and does not trust our Indian Moslem troops. Sykes wanted preparations made now to evacuate the Christian population of Palestine. Picot told him that the raids across the Jordan had been a very great mistake politically, and had turned the Arab population of that region against us, as they "get it in neck" from the Turks—but apparently, Allenby won't listen to political considerations. On the whole I am much relieved by the decision not to withdraw the 54th Division. In the evening there was a huge banquet given by Lord Curzon in true viceregal style to the Dominions' representatives. I sat between Lord Selborne and Lady Midleton[1] (there were a few ladies present), the latter of whom annoyed me by "crabbing" our pre-war preparations, and rather drew me out, until Montagu, on the other side of her rescued me. There were many most distinguished people present and after dinner I had a long talk with Lord Bryce[2] about the League of Nations
. . .

27th June

Imperial War Cabinet 11.30. My draft resolution on allied intervention accepted with modification. Lunched with P.M., or rather he and Mr. C. P. Scott,[3] the editor of the Manchester Guardian, lunched with me at the club. The P.M. and Scott told me that Lord Northcliffe, at the P.M.'s instigation, had bribed the military correspondent of the Manchester Guardian by a huge salary to go on *The Times*. After lunch I went to see Lord Northcliffe on the question of propaganda in Austria. I found him looking ill and flabby and unfit for work. At 5 p.m. I had a conference in Lord R. Cecil's room at the F.O. on the subject of my final draft of the resolution in regard to intervention in Russia. Afterwards Sir William Weir and Gen. Sykes of the Air Ministry called on me and remained for over an hour, first reading the statement made by C.I.G.S. to the Imperial War Cabinet, and then discussing with me the statements they propose to make themselves to-morrow . . .

1st July 1918

X meeting at 11 a.m. P.M., Bonar Law, Gen. Harington, Gen. P. de B. Radcliffe and self. The P.M. was in an extraordinary perverse and irritable

---

[1] Wife of 9th Viscount and 1st Earl Midleton. See p. 406.

[2] 1st Viscount Bryce (1838–1922). Barrister, politician (Lib.), educationist and diplomat. Chancellor of Duchy of Lancaster 1892; President, Board of Trade 1894; Chief Secretary for Ireland 1905–7. A very successful ambassador at Washington, U.S.A., 1907–13.

[3] 1846–1922. Politician (Lib.) and journalist. Editor, *Manchester Guardian* 1872–1929.

frame of mind, and, before leaving for France, left them a "holiday task" of enormous dimensions; demanding Memoranda on a vast range of subjects— tactics, training, campaign of the winter of 1918, and of 1919, full details as to the utilisation of American troops etc. etc. War Cabinet at 11.30. A lot of time was wasted in gossiping, and the main business, concerning the Indian reform scheme, was consequently not transacted. Adl. Wemyss told me that the influenza is rife in the Navy [and] that many destroyers have been unable to go to sea, so that the loss of several merchant ships is directly attributed to this issue. Nevertheless for the last month our mercantile losses were down to 156,000 tons,[1] compared with a building, I imagine, of over 200,000 tons, and for the last 6 months, the world's output of shipping exceeds the world's losses by 10,000 tons. At 12.45 we had to leave the War Cabinet, as we were leaving at 1.15 for France . . .

As Hankey has reproduced the remainder of the foregoing diary entry, describing the tedious and uncomfortable journey to Versailles we will not repeat it here.[2] It was 1 a.m. on 2nd before the Anglo-French party reached their destination, and even the indefatigable Hankey described himself as "dead tired". Nor was his normally rapid recovery aided by the discovery in the morning that his box of very secret papers had got parted from Sylvester during the journey and was apparently still cruising about France in a motor car unattended.

The Supreme War Council's meetings did not go well. Lloyd George was still in a tiresome and difficult frame of mind; and Hankey had trouble in preventing him proposing a message to President Wilson on the question of intervention in Russia which took no account of the recently expressed views of the Dominion Premiers. However, as usual, Hankey got his way in the end. He did not attend the actual meetings of the S.W.C. because he thought it would "be better to leave them to discuss without record". But of course he heard all that had passed, including the "violent outburst of the P.M. against M. Tardieu[3] for interference in the shipment of American troops".[4] Next day the discussions brought to the surface the fundamental cleavage between British and French opinion over future strategy. Whereas the

[1]Actually in June 1918 British shipping losses were 162,990 tons and total Allied losses 255,587 tons. C. E. Fayle, *Seaborne Trade*, Vol. III, Appendix C.
[2]See *Supreme Command*, II, pp. 819–20.
[3]André Tardieu (1876–1945). French politician (Centre and Republican). High Commissioner for Franco-American affairs 1917–19. Held many Ministerial offices. Prime Minister 1929–30 and 1932.
[4]Most of the diary entry for 2nd July is in *Supreme Command*, II, p. 820, but is there misdated 1st July.

former wanted to take the offensive in Palestine in the autumn, which would mean withdrawing troops from the western front, Foch and Clemenceau were utterly opposed to any such proposal. Yet the French had given General Franchet d'Esperey,[1] the new Allied C-in-C on the Salonika front, authority to take the offensive—contrary to the decision of the previous meeting of the S.W.C. This provoked an "extremely violent attack by Lloyd George on the French". Milner apparently wanted to call a halt to the discussions, which could in his view only exacerbate inter-Allied differences; but Lloyd George was in no mood to allow the French to have their way. A further trouble arose from the Belgians declining to place their forces under Foch. Hankey's remark at the beginning of the session that "Versailles does not work smoothly" was proving a classic understatement. He himself suspected that the French had their eyes chiefly on post-war spheres of influence, and for that reason were "making to take charge of every phase of the war". "As their material resources decrease", he concluded, "their ambitions doubly increase".[2]

Next day, 4th, Hankey first accompanied the Allied political leaders to a review of American and French troops in the Place d'Jéna. Such an occasion at least had the advantage of enabling an outward show of unity to be maintained. Most of the Americans he thought "as fine a set of ruffians as you would wish to see fighting for you", and he was struck by the contrast between those "eager and fresh" men and the "war-worn but determined" French. In the afternoon the S.W.C. held the final meeting of its seventh session, with the Dominion Prime Ministers present for the first time. It was, according to Hankey, "relatively tame". He believed he had "a pleasant and quiet evening" ahead of him, when round came Clemenceau and Foch, with the latter in a state of indignation and threatening resignation because he considered that a resolution passed at the very end of the session "compromised his independence as General-in-Chief". "A rare old wrangle" followed, but Clemenceau showed himself at his best and sided with the British. *"Ils me font fou"* he said of the obstinacy of Foch and Weygand; and "when I am 'fou' I usually try and kill someone—a

---

[1]Louis F. M. F. Franchet d'Esperey (1856–1942). Commanded Army Group in east 1916 and in north 1917. June 1918 Allied C-in-C on Salonika front. Marshal of France 1921. Inspector-General of forces in North Africa 1923–31.

[2]Diary 3rd July 1918. Most of this entry, except the passages quoted here, is in *Supreme Command*, II, p. 820.

General if possible". So Hankey had to turn Clemenceau's almost illegible redraft of the resolution into comprehensible English.[1] Early in the morning he took the paper to Paris, and got Clemenceau and Foch to agree to it. Then the British party set off by car for Boulogne.[2] Unfortunately Hankey's view that he had got the matter settled satisfactorily quickly proved optimistic.

Diary 6th July 1918
In the train last night Drummond showed me a letter from Sir George Cave,[3] written from The Hague where he is at the head of the Prisoners of War Mission, to Mr. Balfour showing that the German diplomatist attached to the German mission, has, as we anticipated, asked for a talk on the subject of peace terms. Cave replied, as instructed, that he was willing to hear what the Germans had to say, but was not empowered to discuss. The German has gone back to Berlin for instructions and Cave has come home for other business (aliens etc.) . . . I was sent for by the P.M. in the middle of lunch at the club and found him closeted with Bonar Law. Curzon came in immediately after. They gossiped for a long time about Clynes,[4] who is to be the new Food Controller; about the King of the Belgians who is in England; about the Supreme War Council, and other matters before I could get to business. I then explained that the resolution on the Versailles organisation, in regard to which I had taken so much trouble at Versailles, was not finally settled, as that morning I had received the French text in which was interpolated words which might be used to compel the Military Representatives to consult Foch about any theatre of the war, whereas the intention was to limit his right of consultation to the Western front. Henry Wilson, whom I had seen in the morning considered that, in the present temper of the French this was dangerous. The P.M. agreed, and said he had never consented to this. Personally I believe he did consent, without realising what it meant, and that I made a mistake in translating from the much altered, erased, and amended

---

[1]Diary 4th July 1918. Most of the entry is in *Supreme Command*, II, pp. 821–3.
[2]*ibid.* 5th July 1918. See *op. cit.*, p. 823.
[3]Sir George Cave, the Home Secretary (see p. 502), was in fact recalled from the conference at The Hague by Lloyd George on account of a violent agitation in the Press against all aliens and against negotiating with the Germans over exchange of prisoners-of-war and civilian internees. The conference continued in his absence and reached an agreement; but the German government refused to ratify it. See Sir Charles Mallett, *Lord Cave: a Memoir* (Murray, 1931), pp. 207–10.
[4]John R. Clynes (1869–1949). Trades Unionist (General and Municipal Workers' Union) and politician (Lab.). Parliamentary Secretary, Ministry of Food 1917–18. Food Controller 1918–19. Chairman, Parliamentary Labour Party 1921–22. Lord Privy Seal 1924. Home Secretary 1929–31.

French translation of our original text. Both agreed however that it was a very useful mistake on my part, if it was indeed a mistake. Anyhow I had to send a telegram disavowing it.

Diary 8th July 1918[1]

War Cabinet at noon. I handed a chit to the P.M. suggesting it was very dangerous for Sir George Cave not to return to The Hague. The Germans had asked if he would discuss peace terms, and he had replied that he was only empowered to listen. The German delegates had then gone to Berlin. What I asked, would the public say, if it afterwards transpired that this had happened and that, on their return from Berlin the Germans found that the British Govt. had withdrawn Cave before he had had an opportunity of hearing what they had to say! Also, if the prisoners-of-war negotiations broke down in Cave's absence, what would the British public say? The P.M. spoke to Cave in this sense after the meeting in my presence, and I hope he is to return. Balfour, with whom I lunched and to whom I told the whole story, agreed with me. In the afternoon I had a long talk with Batterbee,[2] Walter Long's secretary, about the intreagues [sic] going on against the Dominions Dept. of the Colonial Office, and the relation thereto of Sir R. Borden's letter to the P.M. asking that in future communications should pass through the P.M. and not through the Colonial Secretary.

10th July[3]

War Cabinet noon on the Aliens question . . . At 4 p.m. I had an hour's conversation at the Colonial Office with Walter Long and Sir George Fiddes[4] (Permanent Under Secy.) about Borden's letter. I brought them to the same view as I had brought Kerr the previous evening, that the proper step now is to allow direct communication between the P.M. of the U.K. and the P.Ms of the Dominions, on the understanding that it is confined to business of Cabinet importance or of an intimately secret nature, all other business continuing as at present through the Colonial Office. The analogy is the direct communications that pass between the P.M. and his colleagues, as distinct from the business done through official channels—or the communication between the P.M. and Clemenceau for example. Immediately afterwards

---

[1] The last sentence of this entry is in *Supreme Command*, II, p. 833.
[2] Later Sir Henry F. Batterbee (1880–   ). Civil Servant. Private Secretary to Walter Long as Secretary of State for Colonies 1916–19. Assistant Secretary, Dominions Office 1925–30 and Assistant Under-Secretary of State 1930–38. Deputy Secretary for Imperial Conferences 1930 and 1937. High Commissioner for U.K. in New Zealand 1939–45.
[3] Part of this entry is in *Supreme Command*, II, p. 833.
[4] 1858–1936. Civil Servant. Secretary to Milner as High Commissioner for South Africa 1897–1900. Assistant Under-Secretary for Colonies 1909–16 and Permanent Under-Secretary 1916–21.

I had to see the P.M. who had just received Woodrow Wilson's half-fledged acceptance of the Supreme War Council's proposals for allied intervention in Siberia, but only proposed to send 7,000 men, the Japanese sending only man for man i.e. another 7,000. Ll. G. was furious with Wilson and most sarcastic, comparing him to Gladstone and the inadequate Gordon relief expedition. Balfour, Milner, Smuts, and C.I.G.S. were sent for and the P.M. and Balfour both undertook to draft replies . . .

11th July

This morning's batch of telegrams contained characteristic replies to President Wilson's intervention proposals from both Balfour and the P.M. The latter was very direct and rather scathing in its criticism. War Cabinet at 11.30 on aliens. Before the War Cabinet I had a talk with Chamberlain, who has become very meticulous and rather tiresome about Cabinet Minutes . . .

Actually on 10th Hankey wrote at length to Chamberlain about a note he had made on the minutes of the Imperial War Cabinet, to the effect that "minutes ought to follow some consistent rule as regards giving the suggestions and opinions of members of the Cabinet". There was, replied Hankey, "no subject which has given me greater difficulty than evolving a rule which could be followed in all circumstances". He recapitulated the story of the evolution of Cabinet Minutes, and then went on to explain the rules to which he tried to work. These were that the individual views of Ministers were not usually recorded, except in the case of a summing up by the Prime Minister or an expression of opinion by a Minister or Head of Department who was the expert in that particular subject. But he admitted that experience had taught him that it was not always possible to adhere to such principles. "Broadly speaking, therefore", he concluded, "I aim at giving not an accurate account of what everyone said, but a general synopsis of the expert evidence on which the Conclusion was based, and a general summary of the arguments for and against the decision taken, preserving as far as possible, the principle of collective responsibility of the Cabinet". He ended by claiming that, despite constant requests for *précis* on various subjects "I have never yet had a case in which I have not been able to reconstruct the reasons for the policy of the Government".[1] This letter is of interest because, to the best of my belief, the system introduced by Hankey of producing a "general synopsis" of Cabinet discussions has endured to this day.

The letter from Borden referred to by Hankey in his diary for 10th

[1] Hankey to Chamberlain 10th July 1918. Cab. 21/97.

July had proposed that all communications between the Dominions and the Mother Country should pass through an office directly under the Prime Minister. Next day Hankey wrote to Lloyd George explaining his objections to such a proposal. The chief one was that "the Prime Minister would become overwhelmed with detail from which he ought to be kept free" (40,000 communications had, he said, been received from the Dominions in the previous year, and in addition there had been innumerable formal or informal calls, contacts and conversations). As an alternative he proposed that, while ordinary communications should continue to pass through the responsible departments, the Dominion Prime Ministers should, as members of the Imperial War Cabinet, be granted the same right of direct access to the British Prime Minister as was enjoyed by British Ministers—but only on questions of Cabinet importance".[1] In effect this proposal was adopted, though relations with the Dominions, and the channels of communication with them, continued to evolve throughout the next two decades.

Diary 12th July 1918[2]
Imperial War Cabinet 11.30. Statement on munitions by Churchill. At 4 p.m. I was summoned to a conference at 10 Downing St. between the P.M. and Haig, Milner and C.I.G.S. also being present. As a result I was commissioned to draft a letter for the P.M. to send to Clemenceau, C.I.G.S. sending at same time a letter to Foch, urging that 5 more American divs. be put for training behind our lines, available to reinforce in case of necessity . . .

13th July[3]
P.M. tried to catch me for breakfast, but failed, as I was at Limpsfield. After getting agreement of C.I.G.S. to the letter to Clemenceau I spent most of the morning with the P.M., tuning it up. It was a very strong letter in the end. Lunched with Montagu, Mrs. M., the Duchess of Rutland, Lady Diana Manners[4] (exquisitely beautiful in Nurse's costume) and Lord Beaverbrook. In the afternoon motored home to pick up Adeline, en route to Danny Park, Hurstpierpoint, Sussex, where Sir George Riddell is entertaining Lloyd George. Arrived just before dinner and found Ll. G. very rampageous still about getting more Americans, and meditating sending Borden over to bally-rag Clemenceau about it. As Borden knows nothing about the matter

[1]Hankey to Lloyd George 11th July 1918. Lloyd George papers F/23/3/4.
[2]See *Supreme Command*, II, p. 826.   [3]Part reproduced in *ibid*.
[4]3rd daughter of 8th Duke of Rutland. Married 1919 Duff Cooper, 1st Viscount Norwich 1952. A famous society beauty of the war and post-war years. Worked as a nurse at Guy's Hospital 1914–18, and took leading part in Max Reinhardt's production of *The Miracle* in the 1920s.

I rather feared that I should be sent with him, so suggested that Smuts should go too. The P.M. jumped at this idea. P.M. was very fussy and fidgety all the evening . . .

Next day, 14th, news came that Foch was confident that a new German attack was imminent between Château Thierry and the Argonne, and had ordered four British divisions as well as French reserves to that sector. This worried Lloyd George, who had been convinced by Henry Wilson that the main attack would once again be on the British front. He wanted to get Milner, who was at his home Sturry Court near Canterbury, over to discuss the matter. Hankey, "partly in order to get away from him [Lloyd George] in his irritated state",[1] volunteered to go over and fetch Milner. On arriving at his "quaint bachelor house" he sensed a romance, as the "business" Milner was engaged on involved "carrying a basket of roses to a lovely neighbour". However he finally got the Secretary of State for War away, and after dinner a conference took place. Lloyd George was still in a difficult mood "suspecting Clemenceau of using unfair political influence on Foch to save the French army and Paris at all costs". Such suspicions conflict oddly with Lloyd George's enthusiasm for appointing Foch Supreme Commander; but Smuts and Borden supported him, while Milner, Wilson and Delmé-Radcliffe "were inclined to support Foch as we had appointed him Allied C-in-C". In the end a telegram was sent to Haig reminding him of his right under the Beauvais agreement to appeal to the British government if he believed his army was endangered by a decision of the Supreme Commander. It was also decided to send Smuts over to France to watch developments. In fact Foch's prevision was quickly proved correct.

Diary 15th July 1918[2]
The storm has burst. The Germans have attacked from Château Thierry to the Argonne, exactly where Foch had expected. Gen. Clive,[3] who came to see me in the afternoon said the French were completely prepared with all reserves on the spot, and knew the very date of the attack. There was no

[1]Diary 14th July. Hankey deleted these words, but the deletion appears to have been made much later. Most of that day's entry is in *Supreme Command*, II, pp. 826-7.
[2]The first part of this entry is in *Supreme Command*, II, p. 827.
[3]Later Lieutenant-General Sir G. Sidney Clive (1874-1959). Military Attaché, Paris 1924-7. Military Secretary to Secretary of State for War 1930-4. Marshal of Diplomatic Corps 1934-45.

surprise. Prisoners, deserters, agents, aircraft, "dumps" had all agreed. I motored up just in time for the Cabinet at noon, which was attended by the Dominion P.Ms. Lunched with the P.M. and Winston Churchill. Busy afternoon. Am staying in town, as we may get news from Smuts, who went to Haig's G.H.Q. this afternoon, or from the battle, requiring a Cabinet late to-night. After dinner at the club I strolled round to the P.M. at Downing St. to get the latest news, and stayed there until after 11 p.m. The news of the battle was uniformly good, but we did not get much out of Smuts, who could not be induced to say much on the telephone.

In truth that day was of immense importance to the outcome of the war, since the system of "elastic defence", for which the real credit must be given to Pétain, was then given full play for the first time on the Allied side. In essence this consisted of absorbing the first shock of an attack with lightly held forward positions, and then awaiting the next advance in strongly held positions further back, where the attacking troops would be beyond the range of most of their supporting artillery. These tactics were so successfully applied in the Second Battle of the Marne in July 1918, that the assault against the British in Flanders, which Ludendorff had planned to launch on 20th never got off the ground.[1]

Diary 16th July 1918[2]
Delmé-Radcliffe called at about 10.45 a.m., but I had to go off almost immediately for an X meeting. The P.M. was, I thought, very rude to Milner about Borden's criticisms of the higher command, and Milner's apparent inaction in regard to it. Milner rather poured fuel on the flames by suggesting that it was mere newspaper talk. The War Cabinet took place at noon, and afterwards General Delmé-Radcliffe and I lunched with the P.M. After lunch the P.M. asked me to come into his drawing room to talk. He told me to see Milner and insist on his reading Borden's statement at the Imperial War Cabinet in order to realise how serious it was. He said that, if Milner was not prepared to realise this, he would find someone else for the job. He said he had had great misgivings about putting Milner there, but had yielded to Milner's own desire.[3] He himself had thought of and intended "another man altogether" for the post. I could see that he meant *myself*, but I rapidly changed the conversation. I have not the slightest desire to become S. of S. for War. This afternoon therefore I set to work to try and smooth

[1]See *Liddell Hart*, pp. 531 ff. for a succinct account of the defeat of the German offensive of 15th July and the launching of the Allied counter-blow three days later.
[2]A small part of this entry is in *Supreme Command*, II, p. 827.
[3]Evidently Lloyd George had in mind Milner's letter of 13th April 1918. See p. 525.

BEAUVAIS, le 3 Avril 1918.

Le Général FOCH est chargé par les Gouvernements Britannique , Français et Américain de coordonner l'action des Armées Alliées sur le front occidental; il lui est conféré à cet effet tous les pouvoirs nécessaires en vue d'une réalisation effective. Dans ce but, les Gouvernements Britannique, Français et Américain co fient au Général FOCH la direction stratégique des opérations militaires.

Les Commandants en Chef des Armées Britannique, Française et Américaine exercent dans sa plénitude la conduite tactique de leur Armée. Chaque Commandant en Chef aura le droit d'en appeler à son Gouvernement, si dans son opinion, son Armée se trouve mise en danger par toute instruction reçue du Général FOCH.

The Beauvais Agreement. By courtesy of the Beaverbrook Foundation

L.G., Smuts and Hankey in Paris in the closing days of the war

Meeting of the British Empire Delegation at Mr. Lloyd George's flat in Paris, Rue Nitot, Sunday 1st June, 1918 to discuss the German Peace Treaty. Hankey directly behind Churchill

matters out between Milner and the P.M. and sent Amery to see Milner, with whom he is extremely intimate, in order to urge him to tell the P.M. that he did not want to decide the question of the higher command in France until Cavan came back from Italy and to beg him to keep the question in the background until then. At 6 p.m. we had the meeting of Prime Ministers, and Smuts made rather a reassuring statement of his visit to G.H.Q. Haig and Lawrence now say that the 123 German divisions *in line* are "crocked" and useless for offensive purposes and that the enemy relies entirely on his reserve divisions for the offensive, so that Rupprecht[1] cannot now put up a very great attack against us. After the meeting the P.M. kept me until about 7.45 talking on the terrace. He told me that Eric Geddes had informed him that the Scotland-Norway anti-submarine mine barrage is now complete; that a German order to submarines has been captured saying that they must go out through Norwegian territorial waters; that this neutral passage is to be watched, and if submarines are seen in it the Norwegians are to be told that, if they don't close it, we shall. The Channel net barrage, supported by piers building at Shoreham,[2] has been delayed, and will not be completed until the end of the year.

In the early hours of 18th July General Mangin's[3] Tenth French Army, supported shortly afterwards by the left wing of General Degoutte's[4] Sixth Army, struck back at the western flank of the bulge which the Germans had created in the Allied line west of Rheims. Tanks were used by Mangin on the Cambrai model, but the initial impetus was soon lost and the Germans had time to withdraw the bulk of their imperilled forces from the salient. This counterstroke, conceived by Pétain but amended by Foch, has, according to Liddell Hart, received too great acclaim. But it did none the less bring "the first taste of victory after such deep and bitter draughts of defeat"[5]; and, perhaps

---

[1]Crown Prince Rupprecht (1869–1955). Eldest son of Ludwig III of Bavaria. Commander, Sixth Army in Alsace-Lorraine and northern France 1914. Field-Marshal and C-in-C of group of armies on right wing of western front 1916.

[2]This refers to the "towers" being built to link up the net barrage. See p. 527.

[3]Charles Mangin (1866–1925). Made his name as Divisional Commander in Verdun counter-offensive April 1917. Commander French Sixth Army in Nivelle offensive April 1917, which checked his career. Recalled to command an Army Corps Dec. 1917 and Tenth Army 1918. Commanded Army of Rhine 1919. Inspector-General of Colonial Forces 1921–5

[4]Jean M. J. Degoutte (1866–1938). French General. Commanded Moroccan Division on Somme and in Champagne 1916, XXI Corps 1917 and Sixth Army 1918, which conducted offensive in Champagne in July. C-in-C, Allied occupation forces in Rhineland 1920–25. [5]*Liddell Hart*, pp. 535–40.

T

more important, British and American Divisions had been present in time to support the blow. At any rate Foch had been proved right, and Henry Wilson and Lloyd George wrong in their reluctance to concentrate Allied strength in that sector at the expense of the Flanders front.

Diary 18th July 1918[1]

X meeting 11 a.m. Imperial War Cabinet 11.30 ... At 3.30 Seely called to consult me as to accepting Churchill's proposal that he should become Deputy Minister of Munitions; he wants to go back to fight in France, and fears that if he accepts a political office, he may be unable to do so. In the circumstances I advised him to ask Winston to delay his offer for a month or 6 weeks. I did not say so, but he no doubt understood, that by that time Haig and his crowd may have gone, and an atmosphere less hostile to the citizen officer may be created at G.H.Q. Or, alternatively, Haig may not have gone; but in that case he will be more strongly entrenched than ever, and Seely can take the political appointment ... Then Kerr and Christie (Borden's private secretary) came in to talk over Borden's proposals for more direct communications between the Dominion P.Ms and our P.M. and I gave him my proposals, which he agreed with. I dined alone with Smuts to-night to discuss the same question. He was not quite satisfied with my proposal and obviously wants more, particularly the elimination of the Governor-General as a channel of communication with the Home Govt., but accepts my ideas as an immediate step—my idea being the establishment of direct communication between Dominion P.Ms and our P.M. on Cabinet questions, each Dominion P.M. being at liberty to nominate an Asst. Sec. [to] my office ...

19th July

... Considerable jubilation over the French counter-attack between the Aisne and the Marne, but Wilson is inclining more and more to the view that the Germans intend to put in a big attack elsewhere, probably near [Mount] Kemmel. Lunched with the P.M. and Smuts. P.M. explained his intention to shunt Haig and make Cavan C-in-C. He also broached the idea of a visit to America during the parliamentary recess. Seely has just lent me a letter from Lord Fisher, dated Excelsior Hotel, Naples, Feb. 27th, 1912, from which I quote the following: "The reason I am writing to you is that I hear Ottley has gone to Elswick from the C.I.D. and I beseech you to use all your influence to get Captain Hankey put in his place! He is Napoleonic in his ideas and Cromwellian in his thoroughness!—Won't you take my word for it? He has been years and years with me. Have I ever failed to substantiate my statements? Am I a d——d fool?"[2] The poor old boy, who was always a

[1] Parts of this entry are in *Supreme Command*, II, pp. 827 and 833.
[2] This letter is not reproduced in Marder, *Fisher*, II. But Fisher wrote in identical

good friend to me, lost his wife yesterday. Fisher did much to get me my job. First as Assistant Secretary of the C.I.D. in 1908; then as Secretary in 1912 I built up, almost entirely by my own initiative, the system of war preparation incorporated in the War Book, by which I would be willing to stand or fall before any tribunal on earth or in heaven. Then came the war. As Secretary successively of the War Council, the Dardanelles Committee, the War Committee, and lastly of the War Cabinet and Imperial War Cabinet, in addition to innumerable inter-allied conferences, I have had an experience that is unique in the world. As confidant and intimate friend of two Prime Ministers and of innumerable Cabinet Ministers, Admirals, and Generals, I suppose my influence must have been considerable. But I have always tried and shall continue to aim at preserving my constitutional status, my aim being not to thrust forward any policy of my own, but by friendly criticism and helpful suggestion to forward the policy of those whom I serve. I desire to be neither a Cromwell nor a Napoleon. I close this volume of my diary, as I opened it, with a few general observations. The situation, take it all round, though sufficiently obscure, is, I think, a little brighter than when the volume opened. The submarine warfare, which then was giving me sleepless nights, has, for the moment at any rate, passed into a less acute phase. So long as we can maintain our general command of the sea; so long as we can build ships as fast as we lose them, I for one will remain confident of ultimate victory. Moreover, given undiminished actual and relative sea-power I care not if we sink to third place among our allies as military power. I would sooner have our man-power alive in our dockyards and factories, than dead in some stricken battlefield, however glorious and fateful for the history of the world. Russia, since these pages opened, has gone through every phase of degeneracy and degradation, but there are not lacking signs that President Wilson, even though grudgingly, may allow the Japanese sun to rise in the Far East and bring its vitalising rays to revivify what remains of life in the frozen steppes of Siberia, recreating for Germany an eastern front. Should this happen, Germany with her failing man-power, with her dying allies, will be hard put to it to hold her position against the ever growing volume of fresh American troops in the west. Meanwhile the blockade, the dreadful weapon of our sea power is accomplishing gradually and unseen its inevitable purpose; gnawing the vitals and relentlessly sapping the strength of our foes. Germany is hungry; Austria starving! We have great difficulties of our own, but nothing to compare with these, Thank God!

(Finis)

---

terms about Hankey to Mrs. Reginald McKenna (2nd March) and to Esher (2nd April 1912). *loc. cit.*, Nos. 353 and 356.

Chapter 19

The Scent of Victory. July–August 1918

THE last days of July 1918 produced the climacteric of World War I, since on 20th Ludendorff, having dissipated his reserves in subsidiary blows further south, was forced to postpone the renewal of his offensive in Flanders, which might have brought victory to Germany. From Hankey's point of view the following months proved something of an anticlimax; since with the U-boats beaten, the offensive in the west held and the stream of American reinforcements becoming a flood the scent of victory was soon in the air. This resulted in all the disputes in which he had been involved receding into the background, since inter-Allied differences, and even the long-standing quarrel between Lloyd George and the generals, were no longer very relevant; while the difficult political issues, such as Man Power and Conscription for Ireland, also lost their urgency. Instead of coping with the day-to-day problems of conducting the war he was soon immersed in such matters as the terms on which the Allies would grant each of the Central Powers an armistice, the principles which should govern a peace settlement, and the priority of the various measures necessary to transform Britain from a nation totally mobilised for war into one prepared to meet the social and industrial problems of peace. The need to hold a General Election for the first time since 1910 also soon became an issue of cardinal political importance. The re-orientation of his work did not of course take place overnight, or even in a matter of weeks. Rather does it become increasingly discernible during the period covered by this chapter.

Within a few days of Hankey sending Admiral Fisher a letter of sympathy over the death of his wife he had tactfully to tell his old friend and supporter that the recall to office for which he was still hankering must be regarded as finally and irrevocably ruled out. Fisher replied resignedly that he had expected such news "and was not disappointed" though he still "yearned for work in the bow" (presumably of the ship of state).[1] Though his long correspondence with

[1]Fisher to Hankey 22nd July 1918.

Hankey, covering more than twenty years, continued almost to the Admiral's death on 10th July 1920 he fades out of our story in the summer of 1918. Though Hankey was fully aware of Fisher's faults he always retained his affection for the man who had not only played a large part in giving him the great opportunity of his life, but whose naval reforms had transformed that service just in time to meet the German challenge; and Fisher's confidence in and liking for Hankey never wavered.

On 11th July the War Cabinet formed a Post War Priorities Committee, consisting of five Ministers under the Chairmanship of General Smuts.[1] Its functions were "to consider the methods to be followed to effect the gradual removal of controls over materials, manufacture and production", and Hankey was at once involved in making all the necessary administrative and secretarial arrangements.[2] In the following December its functions were transferred to the Demobilisation Committee, whose decisions were to produce serious troubles and arouse much criticism.

Despite the great change which had come over the battle with the U-boats since the introduction of convoy, shortage of shipping continued to cause anxiety, and indeed to dictate in some degree Allied strategy. The French were now pressing for Britain to make up the U.S.A.'s tonnage deficiency in order to increase the flow of American troops to Europe. Hankey considered this impossible, taking account of French and Italian pressure for greater imports—especially of coal. He therefore sent Lloyd George a tactfully worded refusal of Clemenceau's request, and the Prime Minister promised to bring the matter before the Supreme War Council.[3] Actually between April and July 1918 943,000 American soldiers were brought to Europe, 516,000 of them in British ships. It is interesting to remark how exactly the same problems arose again in World War II when, after suffering immense, and largely avoidable losses in 1942–3, the Allies were faced with such a critical shortage of shipping that their strategy in all theatres was cramped and restricted. It will be told in due course how Hankey's long memory and wide experience led him into conflict with Churchill's government on this same issue in the later struggle.

[1]W.C.444. Minute 15. Cab. 23. Minutes of Committee in Cab. 33.
[2]Hankey-Smuts correspondence, July–August 1918. Smuts Archive.
[3]Hankey to Lloyd George 27th July 1918. Lloyd George papers F/23/3/7.

Diary 22nd July

War Cabinet at noon. News still very good, the French having re-captured Château-Thierry and pushed on beyond. Two enemy submarines sunk—one curiously enough by the destroyer *Marne* on the very day that the Germans were driven across the Marne.[1] The Dominions' P.Ms came to the meeting to-day, in order to discuss the reply to President Wilson's refusal of any big intervention in Russia . . . Saw the P.M. in the afternoon and got his decision about a number of points of detail. This can only be effected by a peculiar process of twisting the conversation round in a manner that will interest him —otherwise he will invariably avoid the issue.

Next day Lord Cavan[2] arrived from Italy "nominally to tell the Committee of P.Ms about the Italian front but actually to enable the P.M. to 'vet' him with a view to his replacing Haig". Hankey had to coach Cavan for his encounter with the politicians, but was not greatly impressed by him, partly because "he had not thought out his problem very deep" and partly because of his vagueness regarding where the projected Italian offensive should take place.[3] Hankey's diary shows that at this time there was a clash between the advocates of private enterprise on the railways and the government, the former fearing the continuation or extension of state control after the war.

Diary 25th July 1918

. . . At 5 p.m. we had a conference at 10 Downing St. mainly about railway trucks, large quantities of which are required for Italy. The P.M. is trying to get control of all the private-owned trucks—nearly half the total we possess, but Albert Stanley,[4] Sir Sam Fay,[5] Calthrop[6] and the other railway

[1] This was correct. U.110 was sunk on 19th July and UB.124 by the *Marne* on 20th.
[2] 10th Earl of Cavan (1865–1946). Commanded Guards Brigade (later Guards Division) 1914–15, and XIV Corps in Italy 1917. Took command British troops in Italy 1918. C-in-C, Aldershot 1920–22. C.I.G.S. 1922–26. Field-Marshal 1932.
[3] Diary 23rd July 1918. All except the criticism of Cavan is reproduced in *Supreme Command*, II, pp. 828–9.
[4] Sir Albert H. Stanley, 1st Baron Ashfield 1920 (1875–1948). General Manager of American electric railways for 12 years. Managing Director, Metropolitan District, Central London, City and South London, and London Electric Railways; also of London General Omnibus Co.
[5] 1856–1953. General Manager, Great Central Railway 1902–22. Member of Ports and Transit Executive Committee 1913–21. Director of Movements, War Office, 1917–18 and member of Army Council 1918–19.
[6] Sir Calthrop G. S. Calthrop (1870–1919). General Manager Buenos Aires and Pacific Railway 1910 and London and North Western Railway 1914. Coal Controller 1917.

managers now doing Government work, funk it because so many of these private owners of trucks are on the Board of Directors of railways and will have a leverage over them after the war. After the meeting the P.M. sent me to see Sir Joseph Maclay to "rig" him in regard to an American application for tonnage to help in their military programme in France. The P.M. wants to use our shipping position as a lever to force Foch to put some of the American divisions to train behind our line and to take over part of our line in winter. He therefore wanted Maclay to take up an absolutely *non possumus* attitude, even in the War Cabinet. It was a delicate suggestion to have to make, but Maclay made no bones about it and said he could do it with a clear conscience—the canny old Scot! Very late in the office checking Amery's interminable minutes on the constitutional discussion. Home very late.

Intervention in Russia still stood high on the War Cabinet's agenda, though its original purpose of maintaining an eastern front against Germany, which was strategically sound, had lapsed since the signature of the treaty of Brest Litovsk, and the purpose of the western Allies was becoming more and more overtly anti-Bolshevik. President Wilson was showing very marked reluctance to be involved in any way, but in February an American warship was sent to Vladivostok, and in May another arrived at Murmansk. Though small contingents of American troops were finally despatched to both the northern front and to the Far East their contribution was brief and ineffective.[1] On the other hand Hankey recorded on 27th July that Borden had agreed to the despatch of a Canadian contingent.[2]

Diary 29th July 1918
War Cabinet at noon. Discussion on Ireland and Indian reforms. Lunched at club with Adl. Slade, who told me some interesting things about the oil outlook from which I deduce that we ought to make it a first class war aim and peace aim to acquire oil fields in Persia and Mesopotamia.

That evening Hankey dined in very august company at Gray's Inn, and was flattered when Sir Edward Goulding, the chairman of the Constitutional Club,[3] "specially asked to be introduced to me, because, he said, he had been told that I was the person who managed all the business of the War Cabinet and kept the whole thing together". With engaging vanity he added that this was "true, though I say it who shouldn't".

[1]Roskill, *Naval Policy*, I, Ch. III. [2]Diary 27th July 1918.
[3]1st Baron Wargrave 1922 (1863–1936). Politician (Cons.). Hankey incorrectly described him as Sir Robert Goulding.

Diary 30th July 1918[1]

Imperial War Cabinet at 11.30. Very important decision giving P.Ms of Dominions the right of direct communication with our P.M. and the right of nominating a minister to remain in London to attend meetings of the Imperial War Cabinet held between the regular sessions. I drafted both these decisions (one of them 4 weeks ago) and, in spite of the constitutional difficulties involved, they were accepted without alteration. They refused altogether however to accept a proposal for an informal Ctee. to examine future relations. After the meeting I had a talk with the P.M. about General Wilson's important Memo. on future military policy. He was bitterly disappointed with its purely "Western front" attitude, and described it as simply "Wully redivivus". He told me that he had received a very important report of an interview between an American agent in Switzerland called Herron[2] and a Bavarian Dr. [Foerster],[3] an emissary of the German Govt., in which the latter had endeavoured to induce President Wilson in favour of peace, and had shown the utmost apprehensions of British economic policy. He had also made startling statements about the decrepitude of Austria and the importance of smashing the Austrian army. The document had been given to us on the distinct understanding that only the P.M., Mr. Balfour, and Cecil were to see it, but he thought that, as his confidential assistant [I] ought to see it. I got Drummond to lunch and he agreed that I ought to see it . . .

31st July[4]

Most important meeting of the Dominions' P.Ms at 11.30 to consider C.I.G.S's Memo. on Future Military Policy. A very strong anti-western-front bias was shown by all, but especially by Milner, Smuts, and the P.M. The strong feeling was that we were running the risk of shattering the American army next year, as we shattered our own army in 1916 and 1917, without achieving a decision. Admiral Sims[5] was so impressed with Lord Curzon's

[1]Part reproduced in *Supreme Command*, II, pp. 830 and 834.

[2]George D. Herron was an American Congregational Minister married to a rich woman. They settled in Switzerland, and he conducted unofficial negotiations with the German and Austrian pacifists. The U.S. Legation in Berne resented his activities and asked President Wilson to recall him to U.S.A. But Wilson, who thought very highly of him, refused. See Mitchell Pirie Briggs, *George D. Herron and the European Settlement* (Stanford, 1932).

[3]Hankey wrote this man's name as "Fiore", but it was almost certainly Dr. F. W. Foerster, a professor at Munich. He was an active pacifist in World War I and a strong opponent of Hitler later. He was the author of several remarkable books on German history, in which he argued that Germany should have retained the pattern of the old Federation. I am indebted to Mr. A. J. P. Taylor for information about Herron and Foerster.

[4]A small part of this entry is in *Supreme Command*, II, pp. 830-1.

William S. Sims (1858-1936). A very able and far-sighted officer whose anglophilia

speech the other night,[1] for which I supplied most of the material, that he has asked for the figures on which it was based for a speech of his own and the P.M. gave his consent for him to have part of them, though he kept the remainder for use in his own speech at the end of the session. I lunched with Seely, who told me what he is doing about developing the tank programme—now seriously in arrears. . . .

1st August 1918

Sir Eric Geddes called at 10.30 and told me that the P.M. had practically decided that he must go to France as head of the administrative services with the B.E.F.[2] The P.M. intends to get the appointment confirmed by the Committee of P.Ms now sitting. Geddes was not very keen, but said he would take it on, provided Milner agreed. His object in coming to me was to ask that I should let him know what Milner's and C.I.G.S's attitude was towards the appointment. I promised to do this, but told him that I personally was strongly opposed, as he had made such a success of the Adty. and ought not to leave it. The Adty., I added, was by far the most important post. He told me the P.M. was thinking of Sir Robert Horne,[3] who looks after Admiralty man-power, as First Lord. I don't know Horne well, but he is said to be good. Anyhow it relieves me of the anxiety I had that the P.M. might want to send me to the Admiralty! . . . I forgot to mention that on the 30th I had a most important discussion with Adl. Wemyss about Slade's paper on oil in Mesopotamia. I got him to send the paper to the Imperial War Cabinet with a covering Memo., which he dictated in my presence, urging the importance of these oil wells as a war aim. At my request he directed Slade (through me) to prepare a new paper on the importance of the oil deposits in Mesopotamia north of our present lines. I have written to the P.M. [and] Balfour, and seen Geddes about this. It is supremely important for our future to get this oil . . . The P.M. is in a curious frame of mind. I believe at bottom he is supremely jealous of the position Clemenceau has won in consequence of the recent French successes. He is also jealous of the position President Wilson will achieve when the peace comes, with enormous American armies on the western front. He feels that between Wilson and Clemenceau, between

---

and indiscretions frequently led him into conflict with his superiors. Commanded U.S. Naval Forces in Europe 1917–19. President of Naval War College 1917 and 1919–22.

[1] This refers to Curzon's speech at the dinner at Gray's Inn on 29th July.

[2] This appointment did not take place. Geddes remained First Lord of the Admiralty until 14th Jan. 1919.

[3] 1st Viscount Horne 1937 (1871–1940). Businessman and politician (U.). 3rd Civil Lord, Admiralty, 1918. Minister of Labour 1919. President, Board of Trade, 1920–21. Chancellor of Exchequer 1921–22.

American success and French prestige, he and Great Britain will at the peace conference cut a poor figure. He has never understood and never will understand the importance of our naval and maritime effort. To-night he made it quite clear to me that his aim is to cut down our forces on the western front to a relatively low figure (30 divisions or so), so that we will quite deliberately cut a small figure there, and meanwhile use our surplus strength elsewhere—in Italy, Salonika, Turkey, or Persia. This of course will get us into great difficulties with our allies.

2nd August 1918

Started from home at 7.15 a.m. in my office car and motored to the Savoy where I breakfasted alone with Sir Robert Borden. We discussed the detailed arrangement as to the future communications between the Dominions' P.Ms and our P.M. He undertook to leave a private secretary with the Canadian representative, who should have a seat in my office and eventually be available for use as an Assistant Secretary. Imperial War Cabinet at 11.30. After lunch I saw the C.I.G.S. (about 4.45), as the P.M. had requested me to do, in regard to the War policy. I told him the P.M. found him too much "western front" in his ideas, and too much like Robertson. "It is Irish instead of Scotch, but it is still whisky". He admitted he was dominated by the idea of not quarrelling with our allies and more especially with Foch, but explained a scheme he had for concentrating 12 divisions this winter on the Italian front. On the whole my interview was satisfactory . . .

3rd August

Spent morning working in office. Lunched with Mr. Balfour, who was in a very bad temper because he had been called to read a very unimportant telegram at 4 a.m. I spoke to him about the importance of securing the Persian and Mesopotamian oil wells, but he only replied that this was a frankly imperialistic war aim. Fancy allowing such humbug to stand in the way of our vital national needs! This morning Admiral Slade called on me to protest against his "oil" paper going to the Oil Executive, as approved by the Imperial War Cabinet on Walter Long's suggestion. His reason was that he doubted the discretion of Cadman,[1] the principal man on the oil executive, and believed him to be too much in with the Dutch oil people, through whom he believes information might reach Germany. All I would do was to ask Walter Long to hold the matter up until he could see Admiral Slade.

Though Hankey's views on post-war oil policy were without doubt as overtly "imperialist" as Balfour stated, the British government's

[1]Sir John Cadman, 1st Baron Cadman 1937 (1877–1941). Mining and petroleum engineer and executive. Professor of Mining and Petroleum Technology, Birmingham University 1908–20. Member of Royal Commission on Persian Oil fields 1912. Chairman Anglo-Iranian Oil Co. and Iraq Petroleum Co.

aims after the war did in fact follow closely the lines proposed by Hankey.[1] The story of the intrigues between the international oil companies during and after the war is fascinating, and as Hankey was involved in them through Slade, the Admiralty's adviser on oil policy, it is not irrelevant to summarise the main points here. The basic conflict derived from the bitter rivalry between Anglo-Persian, in which the British Government had acquired a controlling interest in 1913,[2] on the one side and the Royal Dutch Shell and Standard Oil Company of America on the other. Early in the war Sir Charles Greenway, chairman of Anglo-Persian, disclosed that a number of oil distributing companies registered in Britain were in fact controlled by German interests. In 1916 the Admiralty adopted proposals put forward by Slade to form a British National Oil Company with the object of breaking the near monopoly of Shell and Standard Oil and eliminating the German interests. Sir Reginald Hall, the very astute Director of Naval Intelligence, seems to have been the moving figure, after Slade, on the Admiralty's side, and on 29th July 1918 it was he who circulated the paper by Slade to which Hankey refers.[3] Geddes, the First Lord, added a covering memorandum urging that British policy should be to adopt as war aims keeping the enemy out of Persia, developing the Persian and Mesopotamian oil fields "as purely British interests", encouraging and assisting the colonies to obtain control of oil-bearing lands, but only to sell through British companies; and, lastly, to exclude all foreign interests from British oil businesses.[4] Besides these sweeping proposals Hankey's own aims appear relatively moderate. The end of the war by no means terminated the rivalry between the international oil companies, and the involvement in them of the British government through the powerful interest of the Admiralty. And British policy did for many years take a shape which differed but little from Geddes's proposals of 1918[5]; but it would anticipate future events to carry the story further at this stage.

Hankey spent the August Bank Holiday at home "writing up a preliminary draft of the report of the P.Ms on War Policy", in case he was suddenly asked to produce such a document at short notice. This obviously referred to the deliberations of the Committee of Prime

[1]Roskill, *Naval Policy*, I, pp. 219–20.
[2]See Cd. 7419 of 1914 "Agreement with the Anglo-Persian Oil Company".
[3]Adm. 3/8537.   [4]Adm. 116/1810.
[5]Roskill, *Naval Policy*, I, pp. 219–20.

Ministers, to whom the Imperial War Cabinet had delegated responsibility for meeting the crisis on the western front.[1] It sat from 21st June to 16th August, but as by the latter date the crisis had been overcome Hankey's customary foresight proved supererogatory, and his sacrifice of the brief holiday unnecessary.

Diary 6th August 1918

. . . Scarcely had I finished the minutes of the [Prime Ministers'] meeting, when I was sent for by the P.M., and I spent an hour and a half with him, helping him to prepare his speech for the vote of credit. He insisted on my returning to dinner, and I spent the rest of the evening with him over his speech. The P.M. was extraordinarily nervous all the evening about the possibility of an air raid, more especially because his daughter Megan had gone to a theatre. There has been no air raid for months, beyond an approach by the Zepps. to the coast last night, when they lost one; and, except for a still, starry night there was not the slightest foundation for any probability of a raid. Nevertheless he fussed and fidgeted all the evening, going every 5 minutes to the window, and unable to get his mind on his speech. There was no raid—and I only mention this as an example of his extraordinary nervousness of raids and bombardments, on which I have often commented. I disagreed with the portion of his speech dealing with peace, particularly with his refusal to make peace with those Prussians who made the war. I told him I did not believe there were any other Prussians and that he was prolonging the war indefinitely. We also had a wrangle on a subject we have often discussed—he holding that victory to be of any use must be a military victory, while I prefer a "blockade sea-power" victory, in which alone the British can hope to have the principal share.[2]

August 8th 1918 was the day that Ludendorff later called "the black day of the German army in the history of the war", and caused the Kaiser to declare that "The war must be ended". After the offensive of 18th July on the Marne Ludendorff had not lost hope; but the surprise attack in front of Amiens by Rawlinson's Fourth and the French First Armies, in which 456 tanks were used and complete surprise was achieved, was a very different matter. Furthermore it was quickly followed by a succession of other blows further south and on the Flanders front, which prevented the Germans switching their reserves to meet the most dangerous threat. By the end of the month the Third

---

[1] I.W.C. Minutes in Cab. 23.
[2] See Parl. Deb., Commons, Vol. 109, Cols. 1412–28 for Lloyd George's speech on 7th August.

Army had reached the forward defences of the Hindenburg Line.[1] At last the Allies had achieved the long-deferred but essential factors of strategic and tactical surprise.

Hankey was actually busy with the usual War Cabinet and Imperial War Cabinet meetings at the beginning of this crucial week; but on 9th–10th he and Adeline and two of their children enjoyed a short holiday at Oxford. Lloyd George went off to Wales for the Eisteddfod on 8th. Thus some days passed before they appreciated the full significance of the successes achieved by Foch and Haig. On 12th the Imperial War Cabinet began to break up, and Hankey was required "to draft a report for their consideration . . . in a most frightful rush".[2] The Dominion Prime Ministers, who had arrived at a time of acute anxiety and of bitter recriminations in the Allied camp, at least left for their home countries with the scent of victory in their nostrils.

Diary 13th August 1918[3]
Imperial War Cabinet—or rather a meeting of the Prime Ministers of the Dominions with the War Cabinet, raising most complicated constitutional difficulties for the unfortunate secretary!—at 11.30. Important statement by Balfour on War Aims. Very able, but simply a summary of our *desiderata*, entirely divorced from realities. Locked myself up with shorthand writers all the afternoon and until late in the evening drafting the report for the P.Ms . . . Lunched with P.M., who does not take a very sanguine view of our military prospects, in spite of recent success. Nor do I—very.

14th August
. . . Continuation of war aims—peace terms discussion by War Cabinet and Prime Ministers in the afternoon. Sober, sensible speech by Smuts pointing out realities of situation. Most of them, I think, dubbed it as pacifist. In the evening I had to go off with the P.M. to Danny Park,[4] near Brighton, to spend the evening going through my draft report. Our party was small but select—the P.M., General Smuts, Lord Reading, and myself. My draft report was acclaimed as a huge success, but they made a good many alterations, and I sat up until after midnight inserting them.

15th August[5]
Up at 6 a.m. after a very good if short sleep, and off with Gen. Smuts by car

[1]See *Liddell Hart*, pp. 478–80 and 541–51.
[2]Diary 12th Aug. 1918. The second session of the I.W.C. actually ended on 16th. I.W.C. Minutes. Cab. 23.
[3]A small part of this entry is in *Supreme Command*, II, p. 831.
[4]Sir George Riddell's house. See p. 428.
[5]Part reproduced in *Supreme Command*, II, p. 831.

to London. In office at 8.30 to get the report re-cyclostyled in part and circulated to give the P.Ms time to read it before the afternoon. The reason for this colossal hustle is that Borden is due to leave to-morrow. Imperial War Cabinet in morning. Continuation of discussion on war aims . . .

That day Hankey wrote to Adeline that Lloyd George "had decided to fly off to Criccieth to-morrow night" and had insisted that he should go with him. Once again prospects of a real holiday with his family had faded, though he had told the Prime Minister "I must have some private leave in September, and he agreed". "But", he added with the caution gained from long experience of Lloyd George's methods, "God alone knows whether I shall be able to take it, as he returns here in September, and will be full of beans and out for meetings of the Supreme War Council etc. etc.".[1]

Hankey now circulated the draft of an announcement regarding the work of the Imperial War Cabinet during its recent session, and the arrangements agreed for the Dominion Prime Ministers to communicate direct with the British Prime Minister "whenever they see fit to do so".[2] But at almost the same time he was troubled by a leakage of information to *The Times* on these very subjects. Premature disclosure of discussions in Cabinet was a matter on which Hankey was always very sensitive, as it invariably produced difficulties for him. On this occasion he at once saw Geoffrey Dawson, the editor, and asked for the source of the information to be traced. Dawson admitted that it had come from "Dominion sources", and Hankey's memorandum to the Cabinet on the subject expressed his concern about the Dominion premiers' close relations with journalists. He refrained from mentioning that Lloyd George himself maintained very regular and intimate contact with Press magnates; but this was a matter on which the politicians and the civil servants who were responsible for the security of Cabinet documents were never likely to see eye to eye.[3]

Sir Robert Borden had pressed that all important papers circulated to the War Cabinet should be sent to the Dominions "for information", and Hankey sought approval to forward copies of all except "papers of extreme secrecy" to the Dominions' representatives in London.[4] During the final months of the war and the first phase of peace this became the normal practice, so admitting the Dominions into full

[1] To Lady Hankey 15th August 1918.
[2] GT. 5411 of 15th August 1918. Cab. 24/61.
[3] GT. 5440 of 17th August 1918. *ibid.*   [4] GT. 5458 of 20th August 1918. *ibid.*

partnership with the Mother Country. Borden was generous in his acknowledgement of Hankey's part in achieving this very desirable re-interpretation of Dominion status.

Sir Robert Borden to Hankey. Prime Minister's Office, Canada. 2 Whitehall Gardens. 16th August 1918.

My dear Sir Maurice Hankey,

May I be permitted to express the thanks of myself and all my colleagues for the invaluable assistance which we have received during the present visit from the Secretariat of the War Cabinet, and especially yourself. All the members of the staff have been most considerate and helpful in every way; and our task would have been much more difficult except for this unfailing aid and co-operation.

Perhaps you will permit me also to add a word with regard to yourself. In 1912 it was largely [due] to your indefatigable effort that my attention became concentrated upon the need of preparing a War Book for Canada, which, indeed, was completed only a few weeks before hostilities broke out. The fine capacity and zeal of which you gave evidence, and the sound judgment then displayed have unbounded scope in the tremendously responsible duties now devolving upon you. I send my heartfelt congratulations upon the unfailing efficiency with which they are discharged.

Faithfully yours,

In the event Hankey did not accompany Lloyd George to Criccieth when he "flew off" there on 17th, but joined him about a week later. He spent the interval in London consulting Lloyd George's colleagues about his draft report on the discussions of the Committee of Prime Ministers, and then, during a week-end spent at his home, putting it into what he hoped would be its final form with the assistance of Amery and Sylvester.[1] On 20th he was back in London, where the final meetings of the Imperial War Cabinet were to take place.

Diary 22nd August

Travelled to Criccieth with Lord Milner, Amery, and Sir Bertrand Dawson (the King's doctor)[2] . . . Milner told me the American divisions had been taken from our front and put under Pershing's command. He rather funks telling the P.M. and doesn't want to, as it is clear that Foch means to use the

[1] Diary 16th–19th August. See *Supreme Command*, II, pp. 831–2.
[2] 1st Viscount Dawson 1936 (1864–1945). Physician extraordinary to Edward VII 1907–10, to George V and Queen Mary 1914–36, and to Edward Prince of Wales 1923–36 and as Edward VIII 1936. Hankey erroneously described him as Sir Bertram Dawson.

Yankees for a big push somewhere, and he fears the P.M. may butt in and insist on the Divisions being brought back to our front. Arrived at Criccieth about dinner time. P.M. fit and in good form. Very interesting discussion in the evening about future arrangements for looking after the health of the nation, in which Bertrand Dawson, and Dr. Addison took the main part.

At Criccieth Hankey found himself one of "a huge party", and the purposes of the gathering appear to have been two. The first was to prepare for a General Election (hence the presence of Dudley Ward, a Government "Whip"); while the second was to review means of improving the health of the people after the war (which explains the presence of Dawson and Dr. Addison). Hankey was much more enthusiastic about the second than the first purpose, and told Adeline, for the benefit of a relation, that the Public Health course was going to be extremely important "in the medical world of the future".[1] The discussions on the future of the Coalition Government while the war was still far from won irritated him.

Diary 24th August 1918
Spent morning exactly as yesterday. There have been great conferences by the political wire-pullers,—the P.M.: Addison: Norman[2]; and Dudley Ward.[3] Much talk of a general election. The war is forgotten! I pointed out to Milner that the "cat is out of the bag" about the American divisions, as it can be inferred from some of our official returns that 3 out of the 5 American divisions have been taken from the British front. But, as compensation, the French First Army has relieved the Canadian Corps on our right. It is clear from the distribution that Foch intends to concentrate all the American divisions for a biggish push east of St. Mihiel, where the German line forms a sharp salient.

Hankey's assessment of Foch's strategic purpose in shifting the American divisions from the British front was soon proved correct; but in any case as Foch had been accorded the powers of a Supreme Commander there was nothing the British Government could do about it—unless Haig appealed against the decision, which he did not do.

[1] To Lady Hankey from Criccieth 23rd August 1918.
[2] Sir Henry Norman, Bart. (1858–1939). Politician (Lib.), journalist and businessman. Director of colliery companies. Member of Inventions Panel, Ministry of Munitions 1917. Chairman, Imperial Wireless Telegraphy Committee 1920 and of Broadcasting Committee 1923.
[3] As Hankey referred to Dudley Ward as "the Whip" in his diary it was probably William Dudley Ward (1877–1946). Barrister and politician (Lib.); and not Dudley Ward (1885–1957). Economist and journalist.

Hankey described Lloyd George as being "in very good form" during this house party;[1] and, as always when he was in high spirits, there was plenty of music. Lily Elsie was "the star turn" one evening, though Hankey was more impressed by the playing of Cyril Scott, whom he described as "a young composer of great promise".[2] If, as is apparent from his letters to Adeline, the music brought him solace, he also derived amusement from observing the manœuvres of the politically interested at such a gathering. For example Amery ("a queer fish") had invited himself, yet "settled down as though he were an invited guest".[3] Hankey evidently sensed that Amery was hoping to be included in a new government.

Rumours of a General Election had also reached Esher who, as always, had his ear close to the political ground. He viewed the prospect with alarm, but thought that if Lloyd George played "a bold game", asking outright for a mandate to finish the war and set the country on the road to peace, he would get it. "It is Lloyd George *contra mundum*", he concluded. "He may win or lose, but his colleagues are an incubus . . . Let the Curzons and Co. beware". More alarming than an election was, in Esher's view, the prospect of a cold winter combined with an acute fuel shortage; and he urged that, now the Americans were reaching France in great numbers, we should recall and release sufficient coal miners to stave off the crisis he foresaw.[4] Esher, though he was much addicted to backstairs methods and could be malicious in his judgements, had a way of cutting through undergrowth to see the main issues clearly.

Diary 26th August 1918
. . . At dinner we had a discussion on war aims, and Lloyd George, under the stimulus of our present remarkable military successes showed a very hard attitude, talking of judgments and penalties. I fear he may over-rate our power and miss securing a good peace, if he is not careful. My share in the conversation was to suggest a peace which would as far as possible remove the bones of contention. I proposed the creation of two new federated states, both under the suzerainty of the League of Nations. One would be composed of Switzerland, Alsace-Lorraine, Luxembourg, Belgium, and perhaps

[1] To Lady Hankey 25th August 1918.
[2] Diary 23rd Aug. 1918. Cyril Scott (b. 1879) had his first symphony performed at the age of 20, and composed many orchestral, piano and violin works.
[3] To Lady Hankey, 25th August 1918.
[4] Esher to Hankey 21st August 1918. 8 pages, holograph.

Holland: the other of greater Serbia, Roumania, Poland, with perhaps Esthonia, Courland, and Lithuania. Or alternatively a third group composed of Norway, Denmark, Sweden, Finland, and the Baltic provinces. Then I would create a new colonial power, viz. Switzerland, which would administer some of the German colonies under the suzerainty of the League of Nations. All the states in the above federations would be autonomous. The object is to create a barrier between the contending, jealous powers, and to remove causes of friction. Switzerland, being an inland power with no seaboard would be harmless as a colonial power from a maritime point of view. This of course is only a rough outline. I would give Palestine to U.S.A. to administer under the suzerainty of the League of Nations with the object of creating a buffer state to cover Egypt. Ll. G., however, is out for blood, and wants to give Germany a thorough hiding—in fact he actually used the term "destroy Germany" as a punishment for her atrocities by land and sea.

Though Hankey's suggested war aims, and his idea for new federations of states under the League, can hardly be described as politically practicable they did at least recognise the principle of "self-determination" on which President Wilson had laid so much stress; and it is interesting to find that, whereas he recognised at an early stage the evil consequences of a vindictive peace, Lloyd George, who was later to oppose the French desire to hold Germany in permanent subjection, should initially have favoured draconian peace terms. The explanation probably lies in Hankey's possession of a far stronger sense of history than Lloyd George; and in his recollection of the favourable results of the comparatively lenient Treaty of Paris which ended the Napoleonic War, and of the settlement of Europe by the Congress of Vienna of 1814–15—a subject which he had studied intensively earlier in his career.

On 27th Hankey recorded that Lloyd George was becoming "hourly more restless" and by the evening he was determined to return to London—because he was "disturbed at a visit by M. Tardieu[1] whom he loathes". Hankey considered that "there is really no particular reason why he should come back to town either on account of M. Tardieu or for any other reason, but he is a restless beggar . . ." Anyway he had to conform, and next day the whole party motored to Shrewsbury whence they took the train for London.[2] On 29th Hankey was back in the office "picking up the threads". But on the Prime Minister's return the Cabinet encountered a crisis of a totally unexpected nature, which obviously caught them all unawares. The absence from London

[1]See p. 569. [2]Diary 27th and 28th August 1918.

of the Minister and civil servants responsible for the Police Service recalls the similar absence of most of the Board of Admiralty when the mutiny of the Home Fleet at Invergordon in September 1931 shook the whole nation to the core.

Diary 30th August 1918
The Police Strike came this morning like a "bolt from the blue".[1] The Home Secretary, Permanent Under-Secretary, and Commissioner of Police were all away on a holiday. Only a few hours' warning of the strike were received. When I reached London there was not a "Bobby" to be seen. Although the P.M. saw Blackwell[2] of the Home Office before the Cabinet, the matter did not come up formally at the War Cabinet in the morning. It came up in the afternoon however at a meeting of the War Cabinet called at 5 p.m. to consider the coal question. The P.M. decided to stay in town and asked me to do ditto . . . After dinner I went back to Downing St. with the P.M., who saw Mr. Charles Duncan, M.P.[3] the Chairman [Secretary] of the Workers' Union . . . which has been working with the Police. Duncan admitted to the P.M. that the police had behaved badly, and contrary to his advice in going out without warning. As [a] result of the conversation the P.M. said he would see the police, and personally investigate their grievances, provided they would go back to work, and at about 11.30 p.m. Charles Duncan went off to convey this message. The P.M. saw Sir Frederick Wodehouse,[4] who, in Sir Edward Henry's absence[5] is in charge of Scotland Yard. He struck me as a nervous, rather broken man, quite unfit for the present emergency. My personal view is that the opportunity of this strike should be taken to sweep away the anomaly of our present police force with its semi-independent metropolitan commissioner, city police, borough police, county police, watch committees etc. and to replace it by a unified state police under proper discipline. I would put London temporarily under military control, pending the passage of a police law directly parliament meets; allow the old police to return temporarily as military police in order to maintain their pension rights and to re-enlist in the new national police; redress their quite legitimate

[1]For a recent study of this event see G. W. Reynolds and A. Judge, *The Night the Police went on Strike* (Weidenfeld and Nicolson, 1968).
[2]Later Sir Ernley R. Blackwell (1868–1941). Barrister and civil servant. Legal Assistant Under-Secretary, Home Office 1913–33.
[3]1865–1933. Trades Unionist and politician (Lab.). Secretary of Workers' Union from 1900.
[4]Major Sir E. Frederick Wodehouse (1851–1934). Assistant Commissioner, City of London Police 1890–1902 and of Metropolitan Police 1902–18.
[5]Sir Edward R. Henry (1850–1931). Assistant Commissioner, Metropolitan Police 1901–3 and Commissioner 1903–18. Replaced as a result of Police Strike.

pay grievances; and cancel the exemption from military service of those who do not at once return. I doubt if the Govt. will have the courage to do this . . . The London streets seemed very strange without any police protection. We had arranged for a military guard on the Government offices, and as I went to sleep at the Club I heard the assembly sounding in the Guards' Barracks.

31st August

After breakfast I strolled round to Downing St. meeting Sir Eric Geddes . . . on the Horse Guards parade. He told me that the Germans had made a complete sweep of the whole Staff of the High Sea Fleet and Admiralty.[1] What this portends our Admiralty do not know, but there are certain portents which indicate the adoption of a more active policy. He mentioned that some of our sources of secret information were less effective than in the past,[2] and he was evidently slightly uneasy about it all. I was in and about Downing St. most of the morning. First at a conference between the P.M., Cave, Milner, and Wilson, and the Adjutant-General. Then Cave and the A.G. withdrew and we discussed military matters. Wilson had just heard that Foch had changed his plan. Without being certain he believed that, instead of attacking the St. Mihiel salient he intended to put in the Americans just north of Verdun, to threaten the German railway communications at Mezières. He mentioned that there was trouble between Foch and Pershing, the latter wanting all the Americans grouped under his own command, and the former believing that the American staff work was not good enough for a big attack, and that better value would be obtained by giving the American Divisions to Haig and Pétain. After this the P.M. saw the strikers' representatives. He did not want anyone in khaki to be present, but he made C.I.G.S.

[1] On 11th August 1918 Admiral H. von Holtzendorff, Chief of Naval Staff since February 1915, was replaced by Admiral Reinhard Scheer (1863–1928), who had handed over command of the High Seas Fleet to Admiral Franz von Hipper (1863–1932) on 7th. Holtzendorff was retired on 27th August and promoted Grand Admiral. Scheer at once obtained from the Kaiser a greater degree of independence than his predecessor had enjoyed; and that appeared to presage a more energetic policy in the employment of the fleet. He at once created a new Operations Department in the Naval Staff, with Captain Magnus von Levetzow as its head, and moved that department from Berlin to Spa. In Berlin Captain F. von Bülow stayed on as Scheer's deputy. Hipper's assumption of command of the High Seas Fleet necessitated changes within the fleet itself, for example Rear-Admiral von Reuter (1869–1943) took Hipper's own place as Flag Officer, Scouting Groups. It was he who later led the fleet at its "surrender" in the Firth of Forth.

[2] This must refer to Intelligence from cryptographic sources. In April 1918 the Germans adopted counter-measures against the highly skilled cryptographers of the Admiralty's Room 40 OB. See W. M. James, *The Eyes of the Navy* (Methuen, 1955), pp. 171–2.

and myself come out of the room somewhat ostentatiously among the strikers . . .

In fact Henry Wilson's forecast of Foch's plan was wrong, and the Americans, grouped under Pershing as he had long insisted, were to attack each side of the deep St. Mihiel salient just south of Verdun, which for two years had proved both a serious handicap and a strategic threat to the entire French position in this part of the line.[1] But the attack on the salient was not actually launched until 12th September. Meanwhile since the great counter blow of 8th August progress had been most satisfactory further north—and for once fairly economical in lives. The new strategy "of successive attacks at different but closely related points", each being "broken off and succeeded by a fresh [attack] as soon as its initial impetus was spent"[2] had proved entirely successful. By the middle of September the British First, Third and Fourth Armies had all advanced right up to the Hindenburg Line, whence Ludendorff had launched his great offensive on 21st March.

Despite the good news from France in August 1918 Hankey did not escape involvement in the inter-departmental strife which was such a marked feature during the 1914-18 war—and indeed long afterwards. This time the angry protests came from Sir William Weir, the recently appointed Secretary of State for Air; but it seems almost certain that they were inspired by General Trenchard,[3] the commander of the newly created Independent Air Force. On 29th August Weir wrote to Hankey "to record most strongly" his protest against the Military Representatives on the Supreme War Council having anything to do with the conduct of the projected bombing offensive against Germany. This new campaign should, he held, "be entirely independent of the control of the Generalissimo commanding the Allied armies on the Western front". Weir (and without doubt Trenchard) regarded this matter "as of fundamental importance . . . as striking at the root of the constitution of the R.A.F. as separate and distinct from the Naval and Military Forces of the Crown". Hankey forwarded Weir's complaint to the Cabinet with a covering note quoting the functions of the Military Representatives, showing that they were entitled to submit plans to the Supreme War Council as the technical advisers to that body.[4] The controversy is of interest in marking the origin of the long dispute over

[1]*Liddell Hart*, pp. 563 ff. [2]*ibid.*, p. 550. [3]See p. 506.
[4]GT. 5536 of 29th August 1918. Cab. 24/62.

Strategic Bombing and Independent Air Strategy, which was to endure right through World War II, and in showing how touchy were the new-born Air Ministry and R.A.F. over any measures which in their view vitiated their "independence" from the older services. Hankey, it will be remembered, had always opposed the formation of a third service ministry—at any rate while the war was in progress; and although he offered no comment of his own on Weir's protest there is no doubt that he believed in the complete integration of the new arm with the older ones—not in its separate development and application.

Chapter 20

Victory at Last. September-November 1918

DESPITE 1st September being Adeline's and Henry's birthday Hankey
had to go off again to Danny Park to join the politico-journalist party
assembled there. From Danny he went on to Shoreham to inspect the
"towers" being built by Sir Alexander Gibb's firm to make the Channel
anti-submarine barrage virtually impenetrable. He was greatly impressed by what he saw and heard; but in fact the crisis in the U-boat
war had already been overcome and the towers were never used for
their designed purpose.[1] Two days later at an "X Meeting" Geddes and
Wemyss, the First Sea Lord, reviewed the submarine situation for
Lloyd George's benefit.[2]

Diary 3rd September 1918
X Meeting at 11 a.m. Present the P.M., Geddes, Ad. Wemyss and self. The
Adty. think it is no longer worth-while for the enemy to stick to the Flanders
coast. 24 out of 42 submarines based there have been sunk and 50% of their
destroyers. It is very costly to hold owing to the constant bombing and
bombarding. They seem to think the Hun may eventually hook it. Wemyss
described our vast system of mines in the N. Sea . . . War Cabinet at 11.30.
Baku is said to have fallen, and it is believed our forces there will be scuppered.[3]
A bad business, which I never liked. I am, and have long been concerned
about our whole position in Persia, which is in my opinion a very perilous
one. Splendid news from the western front again. A private telephone
message from G.H.Q. to the War Office says that the Germans are everywhere running like hares,[4] but Sir George Perley,[5] Canadian High Com-

---

[1]Diary 1st September 1918. [2]X.28 of 3rd September 1918. Cab. 23/17.
[3]Baku did fall to the Turks in the middle of September, despite reinforcements
being rushed to defend it. See Roskill, *Naval Policy*, I, pp. 161–2.
[4]This message was too optimistic. In fact the follow-up to the victory of 8th August
(see p. 588) had shown that the Germans, though shaken, were still capable of
stubborn resistance. By mid-October Haig himself had lost his earlier confidence
that 1918 would bring victory.
[5]1857–1938. Canadian politician (Cons.). Minister of Overseas Forces 1916–17.
High Commissioner in London 1917–22. Secretary of State 1926. Minister without
Portfolio 1930–35.

missioner, whom I met at lunch, says that the Canadian losses in this last affair were heavy.

Hankey's family now went to Totland Bay in the Isle of Wight, and he was most anxious to join them for his long-postponed holiday; but as Lloyd George still had not approved the report of the Committee of Prime Ministers he could not get away at once.[1] On 4th he sent the Prime Minister a tactful letter pressing him "to sign the short covering note" to the report he had drafted, and adding a postscript which combined a neat touch of flattery with a strong argument for his own release. "Thanks to the 'Unified Command', which you so boldly adopted a year ago", he wrote, "I feel for the first time in the war that I can go on leave with an easy mind".[2] And so it came to pass that from 5th–21st September the whole family was united to enjoy a holiday which even bad weather could not spoil. But Hankey evidently kept his finger on the pulse of Downing Street from the Isle of Wight.

Diary 5th–21st September 1918
. . . The only incident that occurred, which deserves recording, was a letter I wrote to Bonar Law (who was in charge of the War Cabinet during the P.M's absence) urging that the reply to the Austrian Peace Note offered a most admirable opportunity for propaganda in the enemy countries, since it would be bound to be read by everyone. I indicated the lines of the propaganda. The P.M's illness at Manchester gave me an opportunity to prolong my leave for several days, but I thought it wise to return on the evening of 21st (Saturday) as the P.M. himself was returning.

While Hankey was on leave Allenby struck at the Turkish armies in Palestine, and, aided by "two comparatively novel tools—aircraft and Arabs"[3] he won the brilliantly conceived and executed battle of Megiddo. This led to the annihilation of the Turkish armies and the capture of Damascus on 1st October. Meanwhile on 15th September the Allied armies under General Franchet d'Esperey at last took the offensive on the Salonika front. These two victories plainly marked the collapse of the Central Powers in the Near East and Balkans, and so the beginning of the end. Here at last was the vindication of the maritime or "peripheral" strategy which Hankey had always favoured, and for

[1]Diary 4th September 1918.
[2]Hankey to Lloyd George 4th September 1918. Holograph. Lloyd George papers F/23/3/13.
[3]*Liddell Hart*, p. 556.

which Lloyd George had so long and so vainly pressed. On the western front too there was good progress, though the cost in lives was in that case comparatively heavy. On 12th September Pershing's Americans eliminated the St. Mihiel salient and, although the success was not exploited, the event merits remembrance as the first independent blow by the U.S. Army.

On 23rd September Mark Sykes called on Hankey "with many proposals for exploiting the victory in Palestine". Hankey passed him on to Henry Wilson who later in the day described the victories in Palestine and Salonika as "most glaring examples of 'amateur strategy' ". Though Hankey recorded that the C.I.G.S. "was very pleased all the same" one feels that he would vastly have preferred the Allies' successes to have been confined to the western front.[1]

While Hankey was on leave he received what he described as "a very tiresome letter" from General Radcliffe, the Director of Military Operations, proposing that as the former C.I.D. Sub-Committees on Overseas Defence and Home Ports Defence were "defunct" they should be replaced by new committees with himself as chairman and an officer from the War Office as secretary. This was an obvious threat to the revival of the C.I.D. in its pre-war form, towards which Hankey had long been working; so he went into action firmly and promptly. He first telegraphed to Radcliffe "on the lines of Mark Twain's telegram on the announcement of his death—that 'the report is grossly exaggerated' ". Then he got Ian Malcolm and Lambert[2] of the Colonial Office to agree to Brigadier-General S. H. Wilson[3] being brought home to restart the Overseas Defence Committee. Finally he saw Radcliffe, who evidently realised that his proposal had been untimely and withdrew it unconditionally.[4] Plainly when it came to handling a complicated question involving several departments he was no match for Hankey who, in the words of his successor as Secretary of the Cabinet "showed

[1]Diary 23rd September 1918.
[2]Later Sir Henry C. M. Lambert (1868–1935). Civil Servant. Assistant Under-Secretary of State, Colonial Office and Secretary to Imperial Conferences 1916–21. Acting Under-Secretary of State for Colonies 1924–25. Senior Crown Agent for Colonies 1921–32.
[3]Later Sir Samuel H. Wilson (1873–1950). Assistant Secretary C.I.D. and Secretary Overseas Defence Committee 1911–14. Principal Assistant Secretary C.I.D. and Secretary of I.D.C. and H.P.D.C. 1918–21. Governor of Trinidad 1921–4 and Jamaica 1924–5. Permanent Under-Secretary of State for Colonies 1925–33.
[4]Diary 23rd September 1917.

extraordinary skill and adroitness in getting proposals adopted and pushed through".[1]

At this time Esher sent Hankey two letters discussing Lloyd George's political future and his relations with Henry Wilson. Rumours had reached Esher "that he [Lloyd George] is getting tired of Henry Wilson; that he—like Henry VIII—wants a new wife every six months". We have already seen how Hankey had warned the C.I.G.S. that his relations with the volatile Prime Minister were not what they had been. As for Lloyd George himself, his illness had made Esher anxious about his stamina, and he viewed with alarm his readiness to throw over old friends and supporters. "Ll. G. has so many enemies", he wrote, "that he should husband his resources of friendship. He must not (indeed cannot afford) to get the reputation of being what the French call a *lâcheur*—a man who lets go of those who help him! Your influence is the only disinterested influence about the little man", he went on, "and perhaps instinctively he feels this". Esher evidently distrusted Churchill's influence on Lloyd George, and hoped that Hankey would act as a sedative when relations between the Prime Minister and his colleagues became difficult.[2] Though there was more than a grain of truth in the rumours picked up by Esher's ever-attentive ear, Hankey was himself fully aware of all that went on in Lloyd George's entourage, and stood in no need of coaching on what should be done to smooth out difficulties.

Diary 22nd September 1918
The P.M., who has been very seriously ill, went off before 11 a.m. to Danny [Park] for a week, saying he would see no-one for two or three days. I did not see him, but had an hour's talk with Bonar Law, whom I found very cheerful after the victories on the western front, Salonika and Palestine and his success in settling the threatened railway strike, on which I warmly congratulated him. He was in a very confidential mood and told me that Cave was threatening to resign and that he himself felt he could not keep on the Treasury as well as his other duties, and he was pre-occupied as to how to fill these posts.

Diary 24th September 1918
Long War Cabinet at noon. Bonar Law in chair. Mainly about railway strike. In the afternoon Campbell,[3] Lord Hardinge's private secretary, brought me,

[1] Lord Bridges to the author. Dec. 1968.
[2] Esher to Hankey 16th and 18th Sept. 1918. Both holograph.
[3] Later Sir Ronald H. Campbell (1883–1953). Diplomat. Private Secretary to Lord

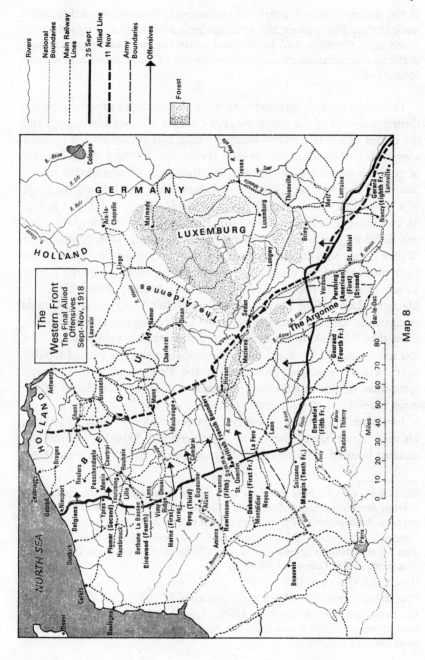

The Western Front
The Final Allied
Offensives
Sept.-Nov. 1918

Rivers
National Boundaries
Main Railway Lines
25 Sept
11 Nov Allied Line
Army Boundaries
Offensives
Forest

Map 8

at Mr. Balfour's request, a series of very secret intercepted despatches which made it clear that Austria had acted on her own initiative in regard to the peace note. Germany had known and consented, but did not approve. I drafted an important Memo. about distribution of War Cabinet Minutes and Memoranda.

The memorandum referred to above was an attempt to rationalise the thorny question of the distribution of Cabinet Minutes and papers, and the duties of the Secretary—matters which had always caused Hankey a great deal of trouble. However in the present instance the differences of outlook of various Ministers, and their lack of unanimity, totally frustrated his purpose. The memorandum never got beyond the stage of a preliminary draft, heavily amended in Hankey's hand; and in fact he continued to run his office on pragmatic lines—which quite often got him into trouble with touchy Ministers like Edwin Montagu or Walter Long, who considered that they had been unjustifiably excluded from meetings of the War Cabinet or denied copies of high-level papers which concerned them.[1] A short time later Hankey issued an Office Memorandum telling his assistants that Walter Long, who had made complaints, should normally receive Cabinet papers, and reminding them that "the rule of the office is to distribute too widely rather than too narrowly".[2] However, this discretionary principle caused trouble later, when "leakages" occurred to the Press, and a very drastic restriction of the distribution of papers had to be introduced in the early 1920s.[3]

Just when Lloyd George was getting over an illness which Newnham, his valet, described to Hankey as "touch and go",[4] Hankey himself had another bout of what he called "my old throat and stomach trouble";

Carnock 1913–16, to Lord Hardinge 1916–19 and to Marquess Curzon 1919–20 as Foreign Secretaries. Counsellor, 1928. Minister at Paris 1929–35 and at Belgrade 1935–39. Ambassador to France 1939–40 and to Portugal 1940–45.

[1] Montagu to Hankey, "Private and Confidential" letter of 24th Sept. 1918 deals with his complaint as Secretary of State for India over his exclusion from regular attendance at War Cabinets. Cab. 23/29.

[2] Dated 16th Oct. 1918. Cab. 21/100.

[3] The leakage occurred in March 1922. Cab. 23/29.

[4] To Lady Hankey 22nd Sept. 1918. Hankey here spelt the name of Lloyd George's valet "Nuneham", but a later entry (1st Nov.) gives it as Newnham, which seems more likely to be correct.

and moreover he was sleeping badly.[1] The truth must surely be that, in both cases, the long months of strain and overwork were beginning to tell.

On 27th September Hankey learnt that Bulgaria had requested an armistice, which was actually signed on 29th.[2] Then he briefed Eric Geddes, who was about to leave for U.S.A. to discuss with President Wilson the general terms on which an armistice might be granted to Germany. Geddes was also to ascertain the American attitude on the thorny issues of "Freedom of the Seas" and "Belligerent Rights", about which the Admiralty—and Hankey—held strong views. The moment chosen for the mission was not very happy, as the British Admiralty was becoming apprehensive about the enormous 1916 building programme of the U.S. Navy which, if completed, would deprive Britain of her centuries-old dominance at sea; while American navalists were showing increasing determination to challenge that dominance, and were profoundly suspicious about British policy and purposes. However, Geddes seems to have succeeded in keeping off the treacherous ground of naval rivalry. He reported back to London that President Wilson's opinion was that the terms of an armistice should not be so humiliating as to risk Germany rejecting them, and that his views on Freedom of the Seas "appeared to be unformed"; which, bearing in mind that Wilson had pronounced this dogma as the second of his Fourteen Points, was a little disingenuous.[3]

Hankey had planned to return to his family at Totland Bay after his talk with Geddes; but a railway strike was in progress, and when he found Waterloo station in a state of chaos he returned sadly to his "lonely bachelor life".[4] One feels that, after more than four years of constant separation from Adeline and his children, and of repeatedly interrupted periods of rest and constantly postponed holidays, he was getting near to the end of his tether. The following week produced hectic discussions on the strategic advantages to be reaped from the Bulgarian armistice in order to increase the pressure on Turkey and Austria; but as the sequence of events is well known, and Hankey has

[1]Diary 25th Sept. 1918.
[2]ibid. 27th Sept. 1918. Part reproduced in Supreme Command, II, p. 837.
[3]Lloyd George, VI, pp. 3289–91. On Anglo-American naval rivalry at this time see Roskill, Naval Policy, I, Ch. I.
[4]Diary 27th Sept. 1918.

reproduced the greater part of his diary entries for 28th September–2nd October they will not be repeated here.[1]

Meanwhile Ludendorff had insisted on the necessity for an immediate armistice, and Prince Max of Baden[2] had replaced Count Hertling[3] as Imperial Chancellor of Germany. During the night of 3rd–4th October the German Government sent a telegram to President Wilson accepting the Fourteen Points and requesting "an armistice on land and sea and in the air". Though Ludendorff changed his opinion a fortnight later, "the mind and morale of the German Supreme Command" had, in Liddell Hart's words, been "unhinged".[4] With events moving so fast it was obviously essential to hold another Inter-Allied meeting as soon as possible, and Hankey was of course at once involved in making the necessary arrangements. Unhappily the portents of serious disagreements between the Allies were becoming more ominous as the prospect of victory improved.

Diary 3rd October 1918
. . . War Cabinet at noon . . . At 5 p.m. a second War Cabinet, the P.M. having returned from Danny, to consider the line to be taken at his forthcoming conferences with Clemenceau and Orlando. Very interesting, but discursive and ill-ordered discussion. P.M. is very strongly in favour of eliminating President Wilson from these discussions, which concern Bulgaria and Turkey, with whom America is not at war. Balfour however is apprehensive of doing this, as President Wilson came into the war for great world objects. He is anxious lest Ll. George should identify himself too closely with a rude message on this subject which Clemenceau sent to President Wilson.[5] Much discussion also as to whether, if the approaches from Turkey take shape, we should demand peace, or merely an armistice. Ll. G. rather favours the former in order to keep President Wilson's finger out of the Turkey pie, but others point out that we are almost bound to quarrel with the French over

[1] *Supreme Command,* II, pp. 839–40.
[2] Prince Maximilian of Baden (1867–1929). The last Chancellor of Imperial Germany. Took office 3rd October 1918. Dismissed Ludendorff and negotiated the Armistice. Announced abdication of Wilhelm II 9th November and resigned in favour of Friederich Ebert, the Social Democrat leader.
[3] Georg, Count von Hertling (1843–1919). German politician (Centre). Bavarian President of Council and Foreign Minister 1912. Succeeded Michaelis as Imperial Chancellor 1917, but resigned in October 1918 after a struggle with the military leaders.
[4] *Liddell Hart,* p. 541.
[5] The message is printed in *Lloyd George,* VI, p. 3273.

the Sykes-Picot agreement[1] and with Italy over her outrageous claims in Asia Minor. By the way Balfour and Cecil have practically re-confirmed the Sykes-Picot agreement by entering into negotiations on this basis for the temporary administration of Syria . . . This came out at the Cabinet, and Ll. G. and Curzon are furious, as the Eastern Ctee. were trying to think out a plan to dodge the agreement, which gives all Syria and a stretch of country eastwards to Lake Urmia,[2] including Mosul, to the French . . .

On 4th Hankey set off for Paris with Lloyd George and Lord Cavan. The ill-humour, no doubt brought on by fatigue, from which he was suffering, was aggravated by a heavy cold which he accused Balfour of having passed on to him. From Paris the party went straight to Versailles, where they were met by Henry Wilson, who gave them "the news and gossip".[3] Next day they heard that the British left wing of the Allied offensive had broken through the last defence of the Hindenburg line to emerge at last into open country, "with only natural obstacles and a devastated area to hinder its advance".[4] But a brief pause was now necessary to organise supplies and improve communications before the advance eastwards could be resumed.

Next day the British delegates first considered the French proposals to crush Turkey finally, which were utterly different from their own. Hankey commented in his diary that whereas the French wanted "to isolate Turkey" and "cut her off from the Black Sea", the British plan was for "an immediate advance on Constantinople, either direct or first opening the Dardanelles". The French also objected, in Hankey's opinion with reason, to the British proposal to make Allenby rather than Franchet d'Esperey Supreme Commander for the next offensive.[5] The outcome of these preliminary manœuvres was that Lloyd George visited Clemenceau and Orlando for private talks. Hankey was not present, but learnt from Lloyd George that Clemenceau "was much put out at our proposal". On the command issue Hankey was wholly on the side of the French, and told Lloyd George so whilst driving back

[1]See p. 270.   [2]Just inside the north-west Turko-Persian frontier.
[3]Diary 4th October 1918. Part reproduced in *Supreme Command*, II, p. 840, but Hankey omitted Cavan's strictures on the Italian army of which he had "the poorest opinion". "In all seriousness and without a smile on his face", continued Hankey, "he [Cavan] said that if the Duc d'Aosta, their best general, were put in charge and were allowed about a year to train them they would be about as good as the Belgian army. The material is good, but the officers cannot or will not train them".
[4]*Liddell Hart*, p. 583.
[5]Diary 5th October 1918. Most of the entry is in *Supreme Command*, pp. 840–1.

to Paris; but on the strategy to be adopted he supported the British soldiers. They lunched with Lord Derby at the British Embassy, and while walking in the garden the arrival of one of the staff of the American Embassy produced a comment in Hankey's diary which reveals very nicely the British attitude to the Americans at this stage of the negotiations leading to an armistice.

Diary 5th October 1918

... Presently in came Frazier[1] of the American Embassy, who is Col. House's man, and usually attends the meetings of the Supreme War Council as an "ear" of President Wilson, but not as a "voice". He was all agog to know what we were discussing at these conferences, and why we did not have a Supreme War Council. We could hardly tell him point blank that we were holding conferences, instead of the S.W.C., because President Wilson would not declare war on Turkey and Bulgaria ... and that we do not feel obliged to consult him either as to our military operations or peace discussions in regard to these regions. But we had to give Frazier a hint of it. However, we did not comment to him on the unreasonableness of President Wilson's attitudes in refusing on the one hand to call himself an "ally" or to speak of us as more than "associated nations", in sending no accredited representative to speak with authority on his behalf, and yet on the other hand expecting to be told everything, and [be] consulted on everything. Meanwhile ... the P.M. and Orlando were closeted together. The P.M. told me afterwards that Orlando, who had seemed serene and smiling at the meeting with Clemenceau, was really seething with indignation against the old boy, and poured it out in this conversation at the Embassy in a veritable torrent. Ll. G.'s observation was that "these Latins are very odd people". After this we drove back to Versailles ... At 5 p.m. we had a conference at the Villa Romaine between the P.M., Clemenceau, Orlando, Foch, Wilson, Adml. Hope[2] and self. Clemenceau sprang upon us the announcement that the Central Powers had asked for an armistice.[3] Most of the discussion however related to the operations in the Balkans, and Marshal Foch delighted the P.M. and annoyed Clemenceau by "plonking" for our project for an attack on Constantinople.

Sunday 6th October began quietly for Hankey at the Versailles headquarters, but around noon London telephoned that a Turkish

[1] Hankey wrote this man's name as Frasier, but it was almost certainly A. H. Frazier. See p. 464.
[2] Later Admiral Sir George P. W. Hope (1869–1959). Director of Operations, Admiralty War Staff 1917. Deputy First Sea Lord 1918–19. Admiralty representative at signing of Armistice and at Paris Peace Conference.
[3] This must refer to the German Government's telegram of 4th October to President Wilson.

envoy was en route to Athens to open negotiations with the British Minister, Lord Granville.[1] Hankey at once drafted a telegram of instructions to the latter.[2] In the afternoon discussions took place at the Quai d'Orsay on the terms for a Turkish armistice, and also for an armistice with Germany and Austria—if one were requested. Hankey already had a draft of the former ready, and although it was amended in some respects both by the political conference and the military drafting committee, he had Lloyd George's support throughout and encountered no very serious difficulties—except with Sonnino who tried hard to get his country's full claims inserted.[3] That evening Bonar Law and Lord Robert Cecil joined the British delegation.

Diary 6th October 1918
... After dinner there was a very interesting discussion about the cutting up of Turkey. Ll. G. took a very *intransigeant* attitude and wanted to go back on the Sykes-Picot agreement, so as to get Palestine for us and to bring Mosul into the British zone, and even to keep the French out of Syria. He also had some subtle dodge for asking America to take Palestine and Syria, in order to render the French more anxious to give us Palestine, so that they might have an excuse of [for] keeping Syria. He was also very contemptuous of President Wilson and anxious to arrange the division of Turkey between France, Italy and G.B. before speaking to America. He also thought it would attract less attention to our enormous gains in this war, if we swallowed our share of Turkey now, and the German colonies later. Lord R. Cecil was for sticking to the Americans at all costs, and for bringing them into the controversy at once, as he thought they would pull the chestnuts out of the fire for us with the French and Italians ...

Next day, despite Hankey's cold being now "in full fury", proved extremely busy and trying. He had the *procès-verbaux* of two conferences to prepare and the memorandum on the Turkish armistice to finalise. At the outset Lloyd George clashed furiously with Clemenceau over

---

[1] 3rd Earl Granville (1872–1939). Diplomat and courtier. Diplomatic Agent, Salonika 1917. Minister at Athens 1917–21, Copenhagen 1921–6, and The Hague 1926–8. Ambassador in Brussels 1928–33. A Lord in Waiting 1895 and 1905–15.
[2] Diary 6th October 1918. Mostly reproduced in *Supreme Command*, II, pp. 841–2. This Turkish representative proved not to be properly accredited, and on Lord Granville's recommendation negotiations through him were never opened. Diary 7th October 1918.
[3] In his diary Hankey wrote that Sonnino "*was up to an intreague* to wedge in some Italian claims". In *Supreme Command*, II, p. 842 he amended the italicised words to read "wanted".

British strategy and the command of the Allied armies in the Near East; but by the evening he had given way about placing Milne's Salonika army under Allenby, while Clemenceau had sent a very strong telegram to Franchet d'Esperey "rapping him on the knuckles" for adopting what Lloyd George called "a political not a military plan" aiming at French aggrandisement in the Balkans.[1] Hankey commented that "as usual he [Clemenceau] took the big line and behaved very well". Then the conference turned to the terms for an armistice with Germany, which were referred to the Military and Naval representatives at Versailles.

Hankey spent the morning of 8th exploring the park of Versailles with Henry Wilson and Lord Duncannon[2] until the conference re-assembled. However, little business could be conducted because President Wilson's reply to the German request for an armistice had not yet arrived. They did, however, consider the draft terms proposed by the Military Representatives at Versailles, which Hankey thought "much too extreme".[3] His view received general support, and the question "was adjourned for further consideration". That evening Hankey dined at the British Embassy and picked up a lot of amusing, and possibly malicious gossip about the American army from Hall,[4] correspondent of *The Times*. He had been present during the American attack in the Meuse-Argonne sector on 26th September, which Liddell Hart has aptly called "The Battle of a Nightmare".[5] According to Hall there was a complete breakdown of the commissariat arrangements, and when the Australians relieved the Americans they opened up recruiting offices for the latter in the trenches with the advertisement "at any rate you will be fed". Perhaps it was only human for the British and French, who had learnt so much the hard way in 1916–17, to gloat a little over the mistakes made by their very confident new Allies.

President Wilson's reply to the German approach came in next day, 9th, and irritated Lloyd George considerably—firstly because Wilson had not consulted the Allied nations, and secondly because, as Hankey

---

[1] Diary 7th October 1918. Long extracts are in *Supreme Command*, II, pp. 842–3.
[2] Viscount Duncannon, 9th Earl of Bessborough 1920 (1880–1956). Politician (Cons.), barrister and author. A.D.C. to Haig 1916–18. Governor-General of Canada 1931–35.
[3] Diary 8th October 1918. Long extracts are in *Supreme Command*, II, p. 854.
[4] Henry N. Hall (1872–1949). Journalist. War Correspondent with American Expeditionary Force 1918–19.
[5] *Liddell Hart*, Ch. VIII, Scene 8.

remarked, he seemed to assume that the British accepted his Fourteen Points. And, as regards "Freedom of the Seas" this certainly was not the case. That afternoon and evening Hankey had to draft a message from the Allies to the President, and a "secret despatch" from the three Foreign Ministers to Washington setting out the Allied nations' views on the armistice terms.[1]

On 10th Hankey set off for Boulogne and London, passing through Amiens on the way. He observed with interest the defences of the recently threatened city, and that for many miles on the *Paris* side "barbed wire, trenches and deep dug-outs" had been prepared. He also recorded his impression of Paris as "a changed city". "The feeling of strained endurance . . . has disappeared", he wrote, and "great hope and confidence has taken its place". But the most remarkable feature was, in his view, that the Americans, who on his last visit had been "all in all to the Parisians" were now "almost out of the picture". This, he considered, was because they had "over-advertised" themselves. "We, on the other hand", he added, with more than a touch of smugness, "who never advertised at all . . . are at the zenith of a well-deserved popularity".[2]

Diary 11th October 1918
. . . Lunched alone with Smuts, who is very keen that we should make peace this year when the victory is due mainly to British arms, and not next year when it may be due mainly to American [arms]. He also does not wish to grant an armistice, but to discuss peace terms and hustle the Hun all the time. At 3.15 had long discussion [with] Mr. Stanley Baldwin[3] of the Treasury on the subject of my application for increased pay for my subordinates. The Treasury refuse to admit that the War Cabinet Secretariat has become a permanent institution, and to give us an "establishment" . . . I made an impassioned appeal for my office from a "stony-hearted" Treasury. He did not commit himself, but said my office had a very powerful advocate. I had already "got at" Bonar Law, when driving with him and the P.M. from

[1] Diary 9th October 1919. Mostly printed in *Supreme Command*, II, pp. 854-5. The American reply to Germany of 8th October and the messages referred to here by Hankey are printed in *Lloyd George*, VI, pp. 3279-83.
[2] Diary 10th October 1919. See *Supreme Command*, II, p. 843, where Hankey slightly modified his strictures on the Americans.
[3] This appears to be Hankey's first encounter with the future Earl Baldwin (1867-1947), whose Cabinets he was to serve for so many years in between the wars.

Versailles to Paris, so I am hopeful. I put Sylvester first; the clerks second, and Longhurst third in my demands . . .

Hankey's first encounter with Baldwin foreshadowed what was to prove perhaps the hardest battle of his whole career—to preserve the Cabinet Secretariat as an independent organisation against the insistent demands of the all-powerful Treasury that it should be placed under its own aegis. But that was not to come to a head until after the fall of Lloyd George in October 1922. The foregoing diary entry also spotlights one of the most attractive facets of Hankey's character—namely his loyalty to his staff. On issues of status and salary, and over the recognition of their work by the award of honours, he was always prepared to go to battle in their interests; and that of course won him a handsome return in devoted service. On 12th he passed to Lloyd George, as was his wont, the information he had gleaned from Smuts over lunch about the latter's views on armistice terms.[1] That same day Lord Robert Cecil, then Chancellor of Birmingham University, told Hankey that he was putting his name forward for the honorary degree of Doctor of Laws—a proposal which he accepted with pride and pleasure.[2] In between the wars, when Cecil was a leading advocate for disarmament and for basing British foreign policy entirely on the League of Nations, he and Hankey came into conflict, and Cecil then wrote some unkind things about him[3]; which makes his support for Hankey receiving an academic honour in 1918 the more eloquent. Another high personage with whom Hankey was on very cordial and intimate terms in 1918, as the diary entry below shows, but with whom he later came into conflict was Winston Churchill.

Diary 13th October 1918[4]
On my way home from lunch I was met by Adeline with a message that the P.M. wanted me at Danny [Park], so I started off immediately after lunch, arriving about 2.30. I found that, already in conference over their cigars, [were] the P.M., Bonar Law, Balfour, Churchill, Lord Reading, 1st Sea Lord, [and] C.I.G.S. with Philip Kerr. We conferred for three hours on the subject of the German acceptance of President Wilson's conditions. The

[1]Hankey to Lloyd George 12th Oct. 1918. The wording is almost identical to the diary entry for 11th October. Lloyd George papers F/23/3/16.
[2]Diary 12th October 1918. Also Cecil to Hankey 16th Oct. 1918.
[3]See for example Cecil to Philip Noel Baker 8th April 1934. BM. Addl. MSS. 51108.
[4]The first part of this entry is in *Supreme Command*, II, p. 856.

Germans have assumed, as we expected they would, that in his message President Wilson intended the evacuation of occupied territories to be the sole condition of armistice. After much rather unnecessary palaver it was decided to ask President Wilson to disillusion the Germans even before he consults us about the conditions of an armistice. Another difficult point is that President Wilson's 14 points are by no means clear; that we do not accept them all, e.g. "Freedom of the Seas" . . . A telegram giving President Wilson a hint of this was also sent. I motored home with Winston Churchill, who was very friendly. He wants me to become the High Commissioner for Mesopotamia after the war. This morning however I had a "vision" that my destiny is to become the Secretary-General of the Allies at the Peace Conference, and by a transition to become the first Secretary of the League of Nations. Churchill also told me, what I had forgotten but now well remember, that on the Wednesday preceding the outbreak of war, I came to him and urged that the "Precautionary Arrangements" should be put in force. He then put the matter next day before the Cabinet, who approved, hardly realising how much action their decision implied. He told me many other interesting facts about the early days of the war.

Though Hankey believed that his troubles over the distribution of Cabinet papers, mentioned earlier, had been solved he was soon disillusioned; and the next diary entry explains why his memorandum on the subject was never circulated to the Cabinet.[1]

Diary 14th October 1918
. . . This morning I tackled the P.M. about giving permission for Walter Long and Montagu, Secretaries of State for the Colonies and India respectively, to receive the "Special Distribution" telegrams. I pointed out that, if the Prime Ministers of the Dominions were to be properly posted in what was going on . . . it was essential this should be done. He replied that it was his responsibility and not Walter Long's to keep the Dominions' Premiers informed. My rejoinder was that, even so, he ought constitutionally to be advised by the S. of S. for the Colonies. He did not admit this, but he asked me not to raise the question at present, because he did not trust Montagu. This places me in a difficult position because I am always being badgered by these people about not getting enough information. I had intended to raise the whole question of distribution of papers, but this incident deters me from doing so.[2]

[1] This problem seems to have defeated the authors of the Public Record Office's admirable pamphlet on the subject. See *The Record of the Cabinet Office to 1922* (H.M.S.O. 1966) p. 8.
[2] See p. 604.

15th October 1918

President Wilson's reply to the German acceptance of his previous note on an armistice was received to-day.[1] The P.M. sent for me at 11 a.m. and I found him on the terrace at Downing Street with Lord Reading, and we were immediately joined by Lord Milner and Gen. Wilson. All were very sarcastic about the note, which seems a complete *volte face*, flying from excessive leniency to austere strictness. There was a good deal of talk at the ensuing War Cabinet, but it was decided to take no action. In the afternoon I had many visitors, including Lord Esher. I consulted him about my own future! He begged me not to think of becoming a "Pro-Consul", involving banishment to Mesopotamia or some other abominable climate. His advice to me was to hang on here for all I am worth. If some "Bolshevik" (he referred to Smillie),[2] should become Prime Minister, as he agreed may well happen, he said that none the less he could not govern without a machine, and would probably be only too glad to use me. In fact, he said that I was the supreme safeguard against extreme Bolshevism. A cheerful prospect for me! If, however, I saw a chance of doing better work as Secretary of a League of Nations, he advised me just to jump into it. Meanwhile to sit tight and do my job. I think he is right.

16th October

Last night I had got out an Agenda paper on the assumption that Ll. G. would not be at the War Cabinet meeting to-day. Rather late in the evening I learnt that he *would* be present, and put down a number of important questions which were awaiting his presence after his long absence through illness and his visit to Paris, arranging for the attendance of great numbers of ministers. Five minutes before the meeting I heard that he was not coming up from Walton Heath, and had to cancel half the programme. This sort of thing is disastrous to the proper functioning of the War Cabinet system! . . .

17th October

X Meeting at 11 a.m., followed by a War Cabinet at 11.30. I lunched with the Asquiths—Venizelos, Lord Reading, Jack Tennant,[3] and Professor Gilbert

[1] See *Lloyd George*, VI, pp. 3288–9.

[2] Robert Smillie (1857–1940). Politician (Lab.) and Trades Unionist. President, Scottish Miners' Federation 1894–1918 and, after 1921, President, Miners' Federation of Great Britain 1912–21.

[3] Presumably Harold John Tennant (1865–1935). Politician (Lib.). Parliamentary Secretary, Board of Trade 1909–11. Financial Secretary to War Office 1911–12. Under-Secretary for War 1912–16. Secretary for Scotland 1916. But it may have been John Richard Tennant (1890–1941). Sailor, soldier and airman who served with distinction in the R.F.C. and R.A.F. in World War I and returned to the Air Staff early in World War II. Hankey spelt the name Tenant, which must surely be wrong.

Murray.[1] A very jolly party, everyone being in great spirits . . . Venizelos was very fluent in abominable French, and was deliciously indiscreet, describing General Franchet d'Esperey's plans for an attack on Turkey in great detail. Luckily they are wrong, having been upset by the Paris conference, and I expect Venizelos knew it . . . It had been arranged at this morning's Cabinet that there should be a Cabinet to-morrow, solely for the consideration of the preparations to be made for an armistice and peace, should this be sprung on us. After the meeting I had followed Ll. G. to his drawing room to warn him that Hughes, Walter Long and Montagu would all expect to be there. As he didn't want Hughes or Montagu he determined not to have a Cabinet, but merely an informal conference of Ministers. Obviously, however, he was reluctant to hold the conference at all. At this same interview I asked him to approve a decision of the War Cabinet, made *ad referendum* to him that, as a preliminary to the discussion of the question of a Bill to redeem the pledges to Trade Unionists, the Minister of Labour should informally consult certain employers who had been on Mr. Justice McCardie's Committee.[2] He flatly declined. I fear he will get in a mess over this. The Trades Unions required it as an obligation of honour on him to redeem pledges, for which he was responsible. He replied that the conditions have entirely changed, and that the great mass of unskilled workers and women workers, whom the war has produced, would regard it as dastardly. Further, it is of course generally admitted that a return to pre-war conditions would be disastrous to industry. My opinion is that the Govt. should produce their Bill as an obligation of honour, but explain the circumstances from a national point of view, and invite the Trades Union to reach an accommodation. At present the P.M. is steering straight to disaster over it . . .

18th October
War Cabinet at noon under Bonar Law. After the meeting there was an outburst on Curzon's part about the postponement of the discussion on armistices etc., about the conference at Danny last week, [and] about the P.M's failure to circulate the report of the Prime Ministers' Ctee. to the Imperial War Cabinet. It is all described in a letter I wrote to the P.M., of which I enclose a copy. My opinion is that the P.M. is assuming too much the rôle of a dictator and that he is heading for very serious trouble. I simply

[1]Gilbert A. Murray (1866–1957). Classical scholar and writer of great distinction. Regius Professor of Greek, Oxford University 1908–36. Chairman, League of Nations Union 1923–38.
[2]Sir Henry A. McCardie (1869–1933). Judge of the High Court 1916. Described as "the greatest master of case-law in our time". But he aroused strong passions in a libel action of 1924 by holding that Brigadier-General R. E. H. Dyer had been wrongly removed from the Army for his part in the notorious "Amritsar massacre" of 1919.

cannot run the machine on these lines. I lunched with Mr. Balfour and Lord R. Cecil who were fairly chuckling over what the latter described as "all my colleagues in their most characteristic attitudes". In the afternoon I saw Chamberlain, to explain to him the position about the report of the P.Ms, and generally to try and stroke him down. I had also seen Bonar Law before lunch and given him most solemn warning of the trouble that was brewing. He took it fairly lightly.

In the letter to Lloyd George ("Strictly Personal and Confidential") to which Hankey referred above he explained in tactful terms exactly what had passed when, after the conclusion of normal Cabinet business, Curzon asked Bonar Law, Montagu, Long, Balfour, Chamberlain and Cecil to stay behind. Reading, who was intending shortly to return to the embassy in Washington, was also present.[1] Curzon then protested about the manner in which discussions on the armistice terms had been handled—notably at Danny Park a few days earlier, when only a few members of the War Cabinet had been present; and Chamberlain supported the Lord President. Balfour and Bonar Law, remarked Hankey, "had pretty well disposed of any suggestion that the conference ought not to have taken place"—because of the urgent need to consider the German reply to President Wilson's Note and the difficulty of assembling Ministers at short notice. Then Walter Long intervened to "make a very strong plea" that "Billy" Hughes of Australia should be invited to Cabinets at which such matters were to be discussed; and Montagu had followed in rather similar vein. But, as Hankey very well knew, Long and Montagu were always complaining about insufficient consultation; and Hughes was using them as a useful mouthpiece for his own opinions. However, Hankey pressed the Prime Minister to take a placatory line and devote a whole morning's Cabinet to the matter—with Montagu, Long and Hughes present—on the following Monday. He also admitted that he himself might have erred in circulating his "Note" of the previous Sunday's conversations, and thereby stirring up a hornets' nest. But he had been unable to get hold of Lloyd George to obtain his approval, and desired to show Ministers that there had not been "any hole-in-the-corner arrangement behind their backs". "If I

[1]Reading had been appointed ambassador at Washington in January 1918. He came home to take part in these consultations in the middle of August, but did not carry out his intention of returning to U.S.A. because Lloyd George pressed him to join the British delegation to the Paris Conference on armistice terms. See H. Montgomery Hyde, *Lord Reading* (Heinemann, 1967), pp. 286–303 and 310–12.

erred", he concluded, "I deeply regret it, but I want you to understand that I was trying to act as I thought in your best interests". This was an extremely clever letter—in part information, in part gently reproving, and in part apologetic.[1] Lloyd George, however, was habitually ill-disposed towards Montagu and Long, and was not likely to accept that all the trouble arose from his habit of holding highly important discussions in the remote country houses of his friends.

Next day armistice terms were discussed at an "X Meeting", at which Haig spoke about the prospects for an Allied victory in 1919, and described the French army as "very weak and of low morale". Hankey then told Lloyd George about his conference with Balfour and Cecil, and enlarged on the need "to hold gauges as security for the payment by Germany" of reparations for the damage done to Belgium and France. Milner suggested holding the left bank of the Rhine above Coblenz, and Bonar Law agreed. At this date the general view was that Germany had not sustained a sufficiently crushing defeat to concede the terms put forward by Haig, which included the evacuation of France and Belgium and the cession of Alsace-Lorraine. A strong anti-American prejudice is also to be remarked in these discussions—notably in Lloyd George's remark that House should be told "that the Americans were making a mess of it", and "the absurdity of there being any shortage of men in the American army", when we were "bringing over 250,000 of their soldiers a month". There was even talk of withholding our shipping from such purposes. Wemyss and Beatty represented the Navy's views on armistice terms, which were very draconian and included the surrender of virtually the whole High Seas Fleet.[2] The discussion was continued on 21st,[3] and two days later Beatty sent Hankey his views "to help you in compiling the Minutes of the Meeting"—which was not a task over which he ever required assistance.[4] Meanwhile Hankey was still experiencing great difficulty over handling his temperamental master.

Diary 19th October 1918
Last night I received instructions from the P.M. to warn his colleagues to hold themselves in readiness for a meeting of the War Cabinet to-day

[1] Rather oddly the original has not survived in the Lloyd George papers.
[2] X29 of 19th Oct. 1918. Cab. 23/17, esp. pp. 119 and 120–1. See also Roskill, *Naval Policy*, I, Ch. I.
[3] X30. Cab. 23/17.
[4] Beatty to Hankey 23rd Oct. 1918. Circulated as CP. 6107. Cab. 23/14.

(Saturday). Chamberlain came up from East Grinstead, Barnes postponed a journey to Glasgow, and Lord Curzon postponed any visit to the country. At 10.45 I was summoned to a conference at 10 Downing Street where I found Haig, Bonar Law, Milner and Wilson with the P.M. . . .—Balfour and Admiral Wemyss joining us later. Haig was for very moderate terms for an armistice. Although I warned the P.M. of the inconvenience to which he had subjected his colleagues by issuing a warning for a Cabinet, he flatly declined to summon them, even though there was ample time. He told me afterwards that "this is my reply to their remarks yesterday", which he had been made acquainted with first by Bonar Law . . . and afterwards by my letter. While I was with him on the terrace he received a letter from Montagu asking him to see him on Sunday at Walton Heath. I warned him that Montagu is in a disgruntled frame of mind, and he only replied by saying that he had no political following. I said that if he was not carefully handled he would resign, and Ll. G. said he would accept his resignation without seeing him. He then instructed me only to ask the War Cabinet to meet Haig on Monday, and not Walter Long, Montagu, or Hughes. Bonar Law came out and added his persuasion to mine. But we could do nothing with him. I told him that I thought it was a great pity, at the very moment of victory, to offend his colleagues, when a very little consideration would rally them to him, but I could not influence him. I cannot understand him except on one of two hypotheses, either that he is bent on grasping the reins of power more and more in his own hands, thus virtually becoming dictator, or that, before the General Election, he means to reconstruct his Ministry and get rid of all those whom he does not want. I lunched with him to-day and after lunch he talked General Election with Captain Guest,[1] his chief whip. There seems to be some idea of a rapprochement with Asquith, and they discussed such an eventuality on the basis of a bargain by which the party machine would be handed over to Ll.G. When asked my view I bluntly opposed it, by pointing out the harm of having no effective opposition, which alone will keep a Govt. up to the mark. Then back to the office to dictate the morning's minutes, and to try and arrange a "hush" meeting of the War Cabinet without outraging the feelings of Walter Long and Montagu, to say nothing of Hughes, all of whom want to be in [on] all the secrets. I am between the hammer and the anvil and in daily difficulties of an acute kind in regard to the distribution of papers etc. to meet these very peculiar conditions. Ll. G. most friendly to me personally.

Diary 21st October 1918

A most trying day, which left me nearly dead beat. At 11.15 there was an X

[1] Captain Frederick E. Guest (1875–1937). Politician (Lib., then Cons. from 1931). Patronage Secretary, Treasury 1917–21. Secretary of State for Air 1921–22. Joined Conservative Party 1930.

meeting at 10 Downing Street, attended by the P.M., Bonar Law, Balfour, Milner, Wilson, Wemyss, Beatty, Haig and Davidson,[1] his D.M.O. The object was to consider the naval and military conditions of an armistice. The War Cabinet joined at noon. Suddenly there arrived a telegram announcing that General Townshend[2] accompanied by the A.D.C. of the Turkish Minister of (?) Marine had been released and had arrived via Mytilene at Lemnos with definite overtures of peace from Turkey. This of course caused the other questions to be brushed aside, and there was a tremendous discussion, resumed again and again during the day with intervals for drafting telegrams etc., as to what should be done. Eventually a telegram was sent to the Admiral at Mudros[3] telling him to reply that the British Govt. were prepared to discuss with properly accredited Turkish representatives the question of the measures for throwing off the German yoke; peace could not be discussed without our Allies, which would take time; but we would consider an armistice, the conditions of which would be communicated to him to-morrow. The question is complicated by the fact that the French have flatly declined to accede to our request that the command of any fleet proceeding up the Dardanelles shall be British, and are constantly trying to get all these matters into their hands. The P.M. gave a big lunch to those who attended the Cabinet, which was resumed immediately afterwards. The discussion was again interrupted at an early stage by the receipt of the German reply to President Wilson's second note, which of course again side-tracked the discussion of terms of [an] armistice. Thus Haig and Beatty, though given an opportunity to air their views, were not quite the central figures of the picture, which they might reasonably have expected to be. Haig put forward relatively moderate conditions, based on the assumption that we would not crush the Huns this year, and only asked for the evacuation of all territory west of the pre-1870 frontier of Germany. Beatty, on the other hand, basing himself on the principles that we were out to destroy Prussian militarism, and that hostilities would never be renewed once an armistice had been entered into, demanded the greater and more modern part of the German fleet, including all submarines. I think the general view was

---

[1]Later Major General Sir John H. Davidson (1876–1954). Soldier, politician (U.) and business man. Served on General Staff and as D.M.O. at British G.H.Q. 1914–18. Director of many industrial companies and banks.

[2]Major-General Sir Charles V. F. Townshend (1861–1924). Commanded Mesopotamian Forces 1914–16 and surrendered at Kut-el-Amara 29th April 1916 after siege of nearly 5 months. (See p. 269)

[3]This was Admiral Sir S. A. Gough-Calthorpe (1864–1937). Second Sea Lord 1916. C-in-C, Mediterranean 1917–19, also High Commissioner, Constantinople 1918–19. C-in-C, Portsmouth 1920–23. Admiral of the Fleet 1925.

that by considering the situation in the east as well as in the west, Haig's terms might be screwed up, and that the naval conditions might be screwed down, both being brought to a common denominator. The less said about the discussion on the German note the better, as it was long and desultory, but it resulted in a fairly good telegram to President Wilson, warning him of the dangers of the position, and asking him not to act without consulting us. The Cabinet ended at 6.15. I had been sitting continuously since 11.15— including lunch—taking notes single-handed . . .

22nd October

. . . At noon the War Cabinet met, continuing yesterday's discussion in a desultory sort of way. I smuggled in Tom Jones as Asst. Secy, without asking permission. They at least finally settled the telegram to be sent to our Admiral at Lemnos in regard to the Turkish armistice. He was to try and get the Paris conditions, but was authorised, if he couldn't get the whole to close on the free passage of the Straits. French and Italian Govts. informed . . . In the late afternoon Montagu called in a great fury because he was not being sent the telegrams about the Turkish overtures for peace, nor being invited to the meetings of the War Cabinet on this subject. He talked of threatening to resign. Bonar Law had "blown the gaff" on it to him on the bench in the House of Commons, and when he flared up passed him on to me. I said I had no authority to tell him anything officially, but told him privately exactly how matters stood. I hinted that the P.M. would not give in to him and asked whether, if he resigned he could explain his reasons to the House of Commons at such a time as this. I told him that the P.M. was not very strong yet, after his recent illness, and that I was doing my best to save him from being bothered about minor questions, and did all I could to smooth things . . .

23rd October

Saw Bonar Law at 10.15 and told him of my interview with Montagu. Also impressed on him the need of a Cabinet Ctee. to deal with demobilisation. No War Cabinet, though there is a fearful lot of business piling up for them. I suspect the P.M. is to be immersed in General Election business . . . At 7 o'clock I was sent for to an X meeting with the P.M., Balfour, Milner, Reading, [and] C.I.G.S., the P.M. being in a great ferment about a telegram from Washington indicating that the President intended to reply at once to the German note. However, Lord Reading calculated that there was no time for us to do anything, so nothing was done . . .

24th October

. . . I lunched with the P.M. and Sir Eric Geddes, who has just returned from the U.S.A. Geddes was full of the point, which I have always suspected, that there is too much diplomacy and too little plain speaking with President Wilson. The glib-tongued Reading and the sycophant Wiseman merely flatter and turn their phrases to tickle the President's ear. The President, Geddes says, golfs every morning, motors every afternoon and goes to a picture palace every evening. He really knows very little of the war, and was astounded when Geddes showed him the real comparative figures as regards British and American naval war effort. It is the same throughout the U.S.A., where it is universally believed that they are doing the whole thing . . .

After a quiet Sunday (20th October) at home Hankey was almost overwhelmed by the pace at which events came to a climax.

That day Hankey wrote to Smuts, the chairman of the Demobilisation Committee, that a hurried conference on Industrial Demobilisation had taken place, and that Lloyd George had directed that it should be treated as a Cabinet meeting. Hankey thus hoped to forestall Smuts's "surprise" at receiving Minutes of a meeting which plainly concerned him but which he had not attended.[1] But the whole incident underlines the muddled way in which Cabinet business was, despite all Hankey's efforts, conducted at this crucial period; and it may also help to explain why the preparations for demobilisation were so badly organised in 1918.

Diary 25th October 1918 [actually written on 28th]
I am writing in the train en route to Versailles. On the evening of Oct. 25th the P.M. called a "hush" meeting of the War Cabinet at 5 p.m. to discuss the attitude to be taken up by him and Mr. Balfour at the forthcoming Paris Conference. The meeting lasted until 7.30 and covered a wide range— desirability of an armistice (similar to the Danny conference), naval conditions of an armistice, League of Nations, and at the end Lord Curzon practically asked for a reversal of the decision re the conditions of an armistice. One puzzle is that no-one knows from Pres. Wilson's last note with whom the next move lies. Eventually it was decided to arrange a conference at Versailles next Tuesday 29th, and an immediate meeting of the Allied Naval Council to precede it to consider the Naval Conditions of an armistice . . .

26th October [also written on 28th]
Continuation of yesterday's discussion at 11 a.m. Satisfactory. Instructions to the P.M. in Paris to get "a peace" if he can, rather than to continue the war with the object of "strafing" Germany. Freedom of Seas to be repudiated before the peace conference. Naval conditions of armistice to correspond to military. After the meeting I tackled Balfour in Wiseman's presence and told him W[iseman] and Drummond were very bad advisers about Freedom of the Seas . . .

[1] Hankey to Smuts 24th Oct. 1918. Smuts Archive.

Shortly before Hankey left for Paris the Allied armies under Cavan on the Piave front attacked, and by 27th their complete success, culminating in the battle of Vittorio Veneto, which split the Austrian armies in two, was plain. Another important prop of the Central Powers' position was about to be knocked away. Furthermore on 26th Ludendorff resigned as German C-in-C in the west—a consequence of the utter failure of the great offensive launched in March.

Diary 28th October 1918

Left home 6 a.m. and motored to Victoria. Left there 7.35 for Folkestone. Balfour with us. At Folkestone the P.M. joined us from Sandwich where he has been staying with Astor. Sent telegram from Folkestone authorising the Admiral at Mudros . . . to agree that the forts of the Dardanelles and Bosphorus shall not be occupied by Italians, but only by British and French. Amusing telegram from the Admiral describing how the French admiral under instructions from his Govt. tried to take part in armistice negotiations,[1] but was told that the Turks only had credentials to negotiate with the British . . . P.M. in great form on the good news, viz. capture of Aleppo (most timely,) German note (practically conceding everything) and Ludendorff's dismissal. The F.O. telegrams say that Austria will sue for peace without conditions to-day. Uneventful journey up to Paris and Versailles except for a long and very interesting gossip Philip Kerr and I had with the P.M. in the train. We covered a vast field, but the following points stood out:—I am to go to the peace conference as one of his personal entourage; he wants the peace conference to be at Geneva and not Brussels. In this he was moved mainly by my argument that Brussels would probably be unhealthy and the food beastly. In some form or another he wants to keep the War Cabinet system after the war. I suggested a Cabinet of 2 Ctees. dealing respectively with internal and external affairs—the latter Imperial—and the P.M. chairman of both . . .

29th October 1918[2]

. . . I drove to Paris [from Versailles] at about 11.30 with Ll. George, Geddes and Wemyss. They told us that the negotiations with Turkey are going well, and that the Admiral at Lemnos is continuing to prevent the French Admiral from butting in to the armistice negotiations with Turkey. We drove to Col. House's temporary residence on the S. side of the river, and left the P.M. there . . . At 3 p.m. I went to the Quai d'Orsay and spent the afternoon

---

[1] See p. 624 regarding the French Admirals Amet and Gauchet. Henry Newbolt, *Naval Operations*, Vol. V (Longmans, Green, 1931), pp. 351-7, gives the official version of the Turkish armistice negotiations.

[2] A small part of this entry is in *Supreme Command*, II, p. 861.

taking notes of a conference of the P.M., Balfour, Clemenceau, Pichon, Sonnino, and Col. House. The meeting was mainly conspicuous for an outburst by Ll. G. against Freedom of Seas (for which I had coached him). He made it perfectly clear that the British Govt. would have nothing to do with it. Even after the League of Nations had become an effective reality, they would only begin to discuss it. House looked very sick. There were many criticisms of the 14 pts. At last Col. House declared that it amounted to this, that the President in his next communication to Germany and Austria would have practically to clean the slate. In this case America would have to consider whether [they] would take up these matters with the German and Austrian Govts. only. Clemenceau—"Do you mean that you will make a separate peace?" House—"It might amount to that—it depends on how far your criticisms go". Ll. G.—"We shall be very sorry if you won't—but we shall fight on". Sensation! After that, Ll. G. having made it clear we were not to be bullied, things went better, and eventually we agreed to put up a draft. Clemenceau said few specially witty things, but looked unutterable things when Col. House spoke in hushed tones of what the President thinks . . .

In the evening Hankey wrote to his wife that "one or two interesting things had emerged from his conversations with Lloyd George. The first was that "he means me to be with him at the Peace Conference"; and another was that "if he remains in office after the war, he means to keep the War Cabinet system in some shape or form, and evidently intends that I shall work it for him". Obviously Hankey was pleased, and probably relieved, to feel that his own future was reasonably secure. He added the joyous note that he "felt sure it is peace".[1]

On 27th Austria sought an armistice, which was granted on 4th November.

Diary 30th October 1918[2]
. . . At 11 a.m. motored with the P.M. and Kerr to the French War Office, where he had a meeting with Clemenceau and House—a meeting specially designed to dodge Sonnino and Balfour, who waste a lot of time. These three in twenty minutes agreed to our comments on the 14 pts. viz. "that the freedom of the seas is liable to various interpretations, some of which we cannot accept", and reparation for damage; also to the heads of military terms of an armistice with Austria, which C.I.G.S. had drafted . . . [After lunch at the Embassy] the conference re-assembled at the Quai d'Orsay.

[1] To Lady Hankey 29th Oct. 1918.
[2] Short extracts from this entry are in *Supreme Command*, II, pp. 845–6 and 861.

During the discussion of naval terms of an armistice with Austria Clemenceau commented on the Allied Naval Council's propositions as follows "They have not asked for the Kaiser's trousers, but that is about all"! Fearful row between the French and ourselves because Adl. Calthorpe conducted the armistice negotiations with Turkey without calling in the French Adl. at Lemnos (Adl. Amet[1]) to represent Adl. Gauchet[2] the French C-in-C. Ll. G. quoted Franchet d'Esperey's conduct of the Bulgarian negotiations, and gave more than he got. In the end the French gave in and accepted the *fait accompli*, as we heard during the meeting that the armistice is to be signed to-day ... Orlando, who arrived to-day, brings news of a Flag of Truce on the Italian front. Drove back alone with the P.M. He tells me House has a letter from Pershing saying that the German is beat stiff and ought not to be conceded an armistice. Ll. G. says it was written for political purposes to discredit President Wilson later on—Pershing being a Republican ...

31st October[3]

... Drafted some resolutions for Ll. G. to submit to the Supreme War Council in the afternoon. Drafted a telegram to London giving an account of the proceedings of the conference up to date. Had my usual half hour's walk in the forest. Then motored with Lloyd George, Geddes and Wemyss to House's residence in Paris, where Ll. G. had a conversation with House, Clemenceau and Orlando. This meeting was specially arranged to keep Sonnino and Balfour out, and had just that suspicion of intreague [sic] that Ll. G. loves. ... Motored back to Versailles to lunch, the P.M. having invited M. Venizelos. Immediately after lunch I went off to the Supreme War Council taking with me as usual typewritten draft conditions for Ll. G. to put before the Supreme War Council. These proved valuable, and were eventually adopted without the alteration of a syllable. [Here Hankey, who had not been present at the morning conversation, described at length the "inextricable confusion" which resulted from Geddes acting as British secretary and Mantoux, the French interpreter, having nothing but "a lot of untidy rough notes". The result was that no one knew what Military and Naval Armistice terms had been agreed.] Henry Wilson told everyone that the trouble was all due to my not being present at the meeting. "If you once lose hold of Hanky-Panky you are done, absolutely done" I heard him saying. I pointed the moral to Auchincloss, House's private secretary, and to Aldrovandi, and they faithfully promised it should not occur again, if they

[1]Vice-Admiral Jean F. C. Amet (1861–1940). Commanded Allied naval forces at Dardanelles and French forces in Black Sea 1917–19. Minister of Marine, Inspector-General of Matériel and member of Naval Council 1920–2.
[2]Vice-Admiral Dominique M. Gauchet (1857–1931). C-in-C, French Naval Forces 1916 and of Allied Naval Forces in Mediterranean 1916–19.
[3]Small parts of this entry are in *Supreme Command*, II, pp. 846–7.

could influence their chiefs. During the day we heard that the armistice with Turkey was signed, and hastily telephoned a communiqué to London to be read out in the House of Commons, explaining clearly that the *British* Admiral had made the armistice. After the Supreme War Council Ll. G., Bonar Law, Geddes, Wemyss, Lord Duncannon, Philip Kerr and I motored up to Paris, dined at the Meurice and went on to *La Fille de Madame Angot*. Bonar Law made the characteristic remark "It would be less intolerable if only they wouldn't sing". Thus we celebrated the exit of Turkey from the war . . .

1st November
Up betimes. Olivier[1] the artist sketched me for his big picture of the Supreme War Council, while I was writing this diary. At 10.30 . . . I started with the P.M., Geddes and Wemyss to House's residence, where there was a meeting of the "hush frocks"[2]—Ll. G., Clemenceau, House, Orlando, with Geddes, Foch and Weygand. This time I forced my way in. Interesting discussion on military terms of an armistice with Germany and afterwards on naval terms. Ll. G. made a good representation of Haig's appeal for moderation, but Foch with his claim for bridge-heads on the Rhine prevailed. His clinching argument was that the soldiers would fight all right, should the peace negotiations fail, if they could start fair and square the other side of the Rhine, but not otherwise.

As though at this juncture Hankey had not got enough on his hands in trying to create order out of the turmoil of the inter-Allied conference in Paris, he was again bothered by a Ministerial complaint about exclusion from Cabinet deliberations. This time the complainant was Sir Joseph Ward, Massey's running-mate in the New Zealand government. Batterbee of the Colonial Office reported that Ward claimed to have been "cut out of the Imperial War Cabinet" after 2nd August, and Hankey at once sent the letter on to Lloyd George. But the latter had plenty of bigger fish to fry, and appears to have ignored the protest.[3]

Diary 2nd November 1918
. . . Short meeting of P.Ms., Generals and Admirals in the morning at which it was decided to remit to the soldiers and sailors the question of the future military policy to be adopted as to advance across Austria into Germany on the assumption that Austria either collapses in chaos, or alternatively accepts

[1]Herbert A. Olivier (1861–1952). Portrait painter, and painter of the Supreme War Council in session at Versailles 1918.
[2]Henry Wilson's nickname for the top politicians.
[3]Lloyd George papers F/23/3/18.

or rejects the armistice terms. Decided also that the answer must be delivered by to-morrow (Sunday) at midnight. After that the "Hush-Frocks" managed to slip off by themselves into Clemenceau's private room. I was called in and found a wrangle going on as to whether the Austrian fleet, which has been handed over to the Jugo-Slavs was or was not to be invited to come to Corfu and place itself under the Allied command. Orlando was being bullied by Clemenceau and "wangled" by Ll. George. Suddenly they turned to me and said "now draft telegrams". I did my best, but, not having heard the whole discussion I got the wrong end of the stick, and Mantoux the interpreter, produced a better draft than mine . . . Eventually two telegrams were decided on—one to the Allied Admirals in the Adriatic telling them not to attack the Austrian ships in harbour or en route to Corfu and to arrange by wireless for their safe passage, and one signed by the four P.Ms. to the Jugo-Slav Committee inviting them to send the fleet to Corfu . . . Meeting of the Supreme War Council at 3 p.m. Lot of useful business in tuning up the terms of armistice with Germany—but no final decisions will be taken until we know whether Austria has accepted. During the meeting Col. House was asked questions about the 14 points, but replied he could not undertake to explain them without his notes. Even the arch-priest cannot explain them without the official commentary! . . . Ll.G. had a private dinner with Bonar Law, Balfour, Milner, and fixed up the general election and Coalition programme.

By this time Hankey was able to foresee the future trend of events clearly enough to warn Adeline that for some time he would be "more in Paris than in London", and was therefore organising a branch of his office in the French capital. He intended to arrange for her to join him for at any rate part of the time; but he offered no suggestions regarding how that could be combined with the children's education and need for a home. No doubt he felt sure that Adeline would produce a workable solution.[1]

Diary 3rd November 1918[2]
. . . Lunched at the Ritz in Paris with Philip Kerr and young Stein.[3] Then to a conference of Prime Ministers at Col. House's residence, 78 Rue de l'Université, M. Hymans[4] the Belgian foreign minister being present. We

[1] To Lady Hankey 3rd Nov. 1918.
[2] The last part of this entry is in *Supreme Command*, II, p. 848.
[3] Probably Leonard J. Stein (1887–   ). President Anglo-Jewish Association 1939–49. Served on Political staff E.E.F. in Jerusalem and at G.H.Q., Cairo 1918–20. Political Secretary, World Zionist organisation 1920–29.
[4] Paul Hymans (1865–1941). Belgian diplomat and politician (Lib.). Ambassador at

settled for a moment the question of Freedom of the Seas on which Lord
Reading and Sir W. Wiseman had led us to expect serious trouble. I think
they are both frauds and make things out to be worse than they really are to
give the impression that they are functioning usefully. Ll. G. said bluntly
that neither he nor any other P.M. could accept the principle of Freedom of
the Seas. But he agreed that it should not be excluded from discussion and,
after the meeting, we went to the Embassy, and after discussion with
Balfour, he sent a letter to Col. House in this sense. Just as we were breaking
up Orlando received a telegram to say that the armistice with Austria had
been signed. I shall not easily forget the scene of enthusiasm. All stood up
and shook hands and the utmost cordiality and jubilation prevailed . . . The
P.M. was curiously piano. He said that as a Celt he was superstitious about so
much success. However, he determined to get back to-morrow night, so as
to be able to read the Austrian terms of armistice in the House of Commons
on Tuesday afternoon . . .

Diary 4th November[1]
Conference at Col. House's place at 11 a.m. I drove up with the P.M. and
Lord Milner. Dr. Beneš[2] of the Czecho-Slovak Ctee. was present. We decided
on the plan of operations against Germany through Austria, and on measures
to prevent Germany getting oil and coal, from Galicia and Bohemia; put
Foch in command of all operations against Germany; on naval terms of
German armistice; and on the procedure for the armistice viz. President
Wilson to tell Germans to send a white flag to Foch. Ll. G. and I ran the
conference as usual. I brought most of the resolutions typed out and handed
round copies, drafting others *currente calamo* and [?] plonked them in front of
Ll. G. at the psychological moment. I drafted every resolution. We really are
an ideal combination because our understanding is so complete . . . Eric
Geddes was not invited to the conference, because the P.M. had the hump
with him for lobbying Balfour and Bonar Law behind the P.M's back for
stiffer terms of naval armistice than the P.M. wanted to give. As it was, Foch
protested against the naval terms as too harsh. Then to the Embassy to
lunch . . . Told Geddes why the P.M. had the hump with him. Had to rush

---

London 1915–17. Belgian delegate to Paris Peace Conference 1919. President of
first session of League of Nations 1920. Foreign Minister 1918–20, 1924–5 and
1927–34.
[1] The last sentence of this entry is in *Supreme Command*, II, p. 864.
[2] Eduard Beneš (1884–1948). Czecho-Slovak statesman. The creator with Masaryk
of the Republic of 1919, and its first Foreign Minister. Member of Council, League
of Nations 1935. Succeeded Masaryk as President of Republic 1935, dismissed after
Munich agreement 1938. President of Czecho-Slovak government in exile 1940.
Returned to Prague 1945, but was overthrown in Communist coup of 1948.

off in the middle of lunch to the train as we are off this afternoon leaving Balfour, Milner and Geddes to represent Great Britain at the formal meeting of the Supreme War Council this afternoon. I write in the train en route to Boulogne . . . It has been an amazing week. Turkey, Bulgaria and Austria are out of the war. Germany is isolated and suing for peace. British prestige is higher than it has ever been before. So is Lloyd George's. So is mine! . . .

The party's return to England was a good deal less enjoyable in the event that it had been in anticipation when Hankey wrote up his diary in the train. They had "a fearful passage" by destroyer, which brought on his usual sea-sickness, and the sea was so rough that they had to disembark by boat at Dover. This proved a long ordeal, and it was 2.30 a.m. on 5th before Hankey reached his home.

Dr. Thomas Jones to Lady Hankey. 2 Whitehall Gardens, 5th November 1918.
Holograph
Dear Lady Hankey,

Can you keep a Cabinet secret and from your husband? Here is a Minute passed to-day with enthusiasm—"and so say all of us". If I thought it would "turn your heads" I should not send it, but I don't think you *both* want to retire to the House of Lords just yet!

Anyway he is a wonderful Man is the Secretary and a great example to his devoted staff.

Yours sincerely

The Minute sent by Tom Jones read as follows[1]:—

5. Mr. Chamberlain stated that he wished, on behalf of himself and his colleagues, to pass a formal vote of thanks to the Secretary of the War Cabinet for the expeditious circulation of the papers giving an account of the recent meetings at Paris and Versailles. He desired that this appreciation of Sir Maurice Hankey's services should be recorded in the minutes.

The Prime Minister added that he welcomed such a proposal and that, in his opinion, the thanks of the War Cabinet to the Secretary were most thoroughly deserved.

The War Council decided—

To record upon their minutes their warm appreciation of the remarkable work done by their Secretary, Sir M. Hankey, K.C.B., in producing for their information, within so short a time and in the midst of such heavy labours, the notes which he had circulated of the Versailles deliberations and conversations.

[1]W.C. 497 of 5th Nov. 1918, Minute 5. Cab. 23/8.

Diary 5th November 1918[1]

Went up late to town viz. by the 9.50. I am afraid I must have looked very haggard after my trying experiences. Even my lady shorthand writer enquired in tones of real anxiety after my health. The War Cabinet, on Chamberlain's suggestion passed a formal minute thanking me for the way I had kept them posted on all that happened in Paris. The P.M. said very nice things and remarked that it was really a great physical feat on my part; at the end of a meeting he himself was dog tired, but my work was only begun. This was gratifying. Heard P.M. read terms of Austrian armistice in House of Commons in afternoon. Got away 5.30. As it turned out, this was the last occasion on which I was to see my office until after the armistice was signed . . .

Hankey must in fact have already been ill when he returned to the office on 5th and, despite a double inoculation against the prevalent epidemic of influenza, it smote him with all its virulence that evening. From 6th–17th November he was completely *hors de combat*, and so took no part in the celebration of the Armistice signed at Compiègne on 11th. Furthermore Adeline also was desperately ill at the same time, and one of the family's domestic props actually died. While Hankey was ill he confided his most intimate thoughts on the grave crisis through which his family was passing, and the terrible ordeal from which his country had emerged victorious, to his diary. In the circumstances his self-satisfaction, even boastfulness, about his contribution to victory may be forgiven. Moreover what he wrote was soon to be amply confirmed from the most authoritative sources.

Diary [Probably written about 16th/17th November 1918]

Adeline nursed me—but, as I only learnt afterwards, had influenza herself all the time! . . . A hectic week! On Monday November 11th at 11 a.m. the armistice came into operation. They telephoned it from the office a few minutes before. Adeline threw open the windows for a minute, [so] that, lying in bed, I might hear the joy bells! I missed by my illness the Lord Mayor's dinner, for the second year in succession: the installation of LL.D. at Birmingham,[2] all the interesting Cabinets over the later stages of the

[1]Mostly in *Supreme Command*, II, p. 872.

[2]On 12th November Lord Robert Cecil conferred the Honorary Degree of Doctor of Laws *in absentia* on Hankey at Birmingham University. The Public Orator, Sir Oliver Lodge, made the following presentation speech:—

"Some there are who stand in the glare of the footlights, some who work behind the scenes, and on the labour of these the responsibility for smooth running may largely depend.

armistice, and all the public rejoicings. But I think I was happier at this supreme moment to be alone with Adeline, even though I was on a bed of sickness, which she ought to have been; even though the house was full of sickness; short of coal and no fuel but logs. For Adeline knows all that this war has meant to me and what my share has been in it. She knows that I initiated and forced through all our preparations for war; that half the structure of our innumerable War Depts. has arisen out of my conceptions; that the War Cabinet itself is my design and my conception; and my creation; that I have been the confidant and consultant first of one great war Prime Minister and then of another; that I have steered the great ship of state round one dangerous headland after another into a port of security. Thus I can claim that the War machine of the British Govt. is as much my creation as the German machine was von Moltke's[1] (? or was it von Roon's[2]). All this Adeline knows. In all of it she is my sympathiser and confidant. If some others realised, there might be envy. Thus I am happy at home, and I avoid the dangers of too great prominence in the hour of my overwhelming triumph. Thanks be to God who giveth us the victory. It is strange that He gave me strength to bear up through $4\frac{1}{4}$ years of strenuous war, and that it was only in the last 4 days that I fell ill.

To have been Secretary of the War Committee and later of the War Cabinet through the whole period of the War, whichever Government was in power, must have been an experience fraught with anxiety and at times overburdened with dangerous knowledge.

Such a high servant of the State I present for the Honorary Degree of Doctor of Laws in the person of

Lt. Col. SIR MAURICE PASCAL ALERS HANKEY"

On the same day Lodge wrote to Hankey expressing regret at his illness and absence, and enclosed a copy of the order for the ceremony and of the speeches made. Lady Hankey preserved these in her scrap book.

This was the first of the four Honorary Degrees conferred at various times on Hankey.

[1]Presumably Hankey meant to refer to Count Helmuth von Moltke (1800–91) and not to his nephew of the same name (1848–1916) who was Chief of German General Staff 1906–Sept. 1914. The elder von Moltke was the initiator of the strategy employed in the victorious campaigns of 1866 and 1870, and after the Franco-Prussian war the creator of the united German, as opposed to the former Federal army. Chief of General Staff until 1888, he was dismissed by Wilhelm II at the same time as Bismarck.

[2]Count Albrecht von Roon (1803–79). German soldier, politician and military historian. Minister of War and of Marine 1861, and a staunch supporter of the elder Moltke. Organiser of the mobilisations of 1866 and 1870, and moderniser of the Prussian army. Field-Marshal 1873.

Later—probably 18th November

These days of illness have been days of great trial. For most of our household of 10 fell ill at once. I had to get up from my bed of sickness to nurse Adeline night and day. Her temperature was 105° and she developed septic pneumonia. At last the office got me, first one, and then two nurses. But we could get no [domestic] help and right up to to-day Nov. 17th I am doing a lot of housemaiding, log carrying, making beds, cleaning the nursery etc. etc. All the world is rejoicing, but I cannot yet rejoice. However Adeline is out of danger, the children are convalescent, and the outlook better. Yesterday (Sunday. 17th) I motored over to lunch with Ll. George. He was alone with Mrs. Ll. G. and the two girls, and extraordinarily friendly, thanking me again and again for all that I had done to help him win the war. He asked if I would like to go into political life and offered me a post in his new Reconstruction Ministry. I think he was relieved when I declined, and he agreed that I might prove rather sensitive foᵣ the rough and tumble of the House of Commons. He told me that last week he had an hour and a quarter's conversation with Asquith, who was very anxious to be friends, but not to take office, though he wanted to be at the peace conference. I urged this all I could, but Ll. G. said he could not ask Bonar Law, or Balfour, or Barnes, who had been loyal to him to give place to Asquith. He says Clemenceau proposed 5 representatives each at the Conference, and this will enable him to include the three above-mentioned and one Dominions' representative. I suggested he should ask for an extra place for Asquith and he promised to consider it. He told me he was going to make a big speech about Henry Wilson and myself. Yesterday also I had an extraordinarily kind and generous letter from Asquith saying that he and the King had agreed that so far as our success in the war could be attributed to any individual, Sir John Cowans[1] and I had done most; he also called me the "organiser of victory". I also had a note from F. S. Oliver the pamphleteer and bitter opponent and critic of Asquith, saying that in his view Ll. George, Milner, Henry Wilson, and I are the four people mainly responsible for our victory. So I am rather up in the stirrups . . .

Asquith to Hankey. 20 Cavendish Square, London, W.1. 15th November 1918.
Holograph[2]
Personal

My dear Hankey,

I was lunching *en famille* at the Palace to-day, and the question was propounded as to whom we owed most for the success of the war. I replied

---

[1]Quartermaster-General of the Forces throughout the war. See p. 501.
[2]Hankey printed this letter 45 years later in *The Supreme Control at the Paris Peace Conference 1919* (Allen and Unwin, 1963), p. 10.

without any hesitation; to yourself and Cowans. And I am glad to say that the King heartily assented to my opinion.

None knows as well as I how much we owe to you for our (ignorantly derided) pre-war preparations; nor the extent and value of your daily, and almost hourly contribution, during the first two-and-a-half years, to every measure, in all spheres, that was thought out and done. I know that you have continued to the end, under a constant strain that cannot be measured, to render the same invaluable service.

I should like you to know that, in my judgement, you have been in a true sense (what Carnot[1] was called) "the organiser of victory".

Yours always sincerely

It would be tedious to reproduce all the tributes from politicians and service men received by Hankey at the time of the Armistice. Though it is probably fair to say that their warmth may be attributable, at any rate in part, to the euphoria aroused by victory and by the end of what Wilfred Owen has aptly called "the carnage incomparable, and human squander"[2] of World War I. Yet there is a unanimity in the letters written by Curzon, Milner, Balfour, Haldane, Smuts, Esher and by many of the leading soldiers and sailors which cannot be disregarded. Furthermore the golden opinions expressed in those letters find echoes in all the biographies and autobiographies of the famous men of the period.[3] Nor was it only the great who appreciated Hankey's qualities. He undoubtedly won the loyalty and admiration, though rarely the affection, of his staff. Thus A. J. Sylvester, his private secretary for many years, writes[4]:—

"In my judgement he was the finest 'Civil Servant' who ever functioned in Whitehall. He was solely dedicated to his work, which he performed with

[1] Lazare N. M. Carnot (1753–1823). French soldier, joint victor with Jourdan at Wattignies, which probably saved the Revolution in 1793. A member of the Directory 1795, but under suspicion of Royalist sympathies was forced to flee the country. Returned after revolution of "18th Brumaire" (9th–10th November 1799) and became Minister of War 1800. Minister of Interior during "the hundred days" 1815.

[2] "Mental Cases". *Collected Poems of Wilfred Owen*, Ed. C. Day Lewis (Chatto and Windus, 1963), p. 69.

[3] See for example Roy Jenkins, *Asquith*, p. 412; Lloyd George, *War Memoirs*, III, p. 1081; Lady Lloyd George, *The Years that are Passed*, p. 100; Sir Evelyn Wrench, *Alfred, Lord Milner*, pp. 334–5 and 350–1; Kenneth Young, *Arthur James Balfour*, p. 397 and Blanche Dugdale, *Arthur James Balfour*, II, p. 242; Sir Almeric Fitzroy, *Memoirs*, II, p. 708; Dudley Sommer, *Haldane of Cloan*, pp. 254–5.

[4] To the author 8th Oct. 1968.

machine-like efficiency and integrity. He had a most amazing memory, never spared himself and did not spare others. In his work he was ruthless, had very little consideration; little if any humour, and little or no sentimentalism in his nature . . . He was very abstemious, hated the limelight, avoided most kinds of social engagements and distractions, and disliked the Press. He was a very happy family man, and very simple in all his tastes . . . I really grew up with him. I was with him from 1914 till 1921, through the fateful years of the First World War, including the Allied Conferences at home and abroad, the Peace Conference, and the aftermath—including the Great Strike of 1919 . . . Then for the first time in the history of this country records were kept of the proceedings of the Cabinet, made by Hankey . . ."

Such a view, coming from such a quarter, must obviously command respect—even though Hankey was far more relaxed, and showed both more sentiment and more humour in the seclusion of his family circle than Sylvester and his colleagues at 2 Whitehall Gardens realised. Although it dates to a few months later than the stage now reached in this biography it will be appropriate here to introduce the impression Hankey made on Professor Arnold Toynbee. "Though I was only a junior Foreign Office clerk [at the Paris Peace Conference]", he wrote, "and Hankey was already a grandee, he did not make me feel the difference. He had no pomp or selfconceit".[1] It would probably be truer to say that he confided his ambitions, and his pride in his position and accomplishments only to the securely locked volumes of his diary —and, of course, to his devoted wife.

Perhaps the best description of Hankey when he was at the height of his power and influence in World War I comes from the pen of that very shrewd observer Sir Edward Spears, who saw a great deal of him during his many visits to France. Referring to the time of the notorious Calais Conference of February 1917 he wrote as follows:—

"Mr. Lloyd George . . . was flanked as usual by Lieutenant-Colonel Sir Maurice Hankey, the Secretary of the War Cabinet.

"That extraordinary man, who played so important a part behind the scenes of British politics for two decades, looked then . . . [like] a small, cherubic d'Artagnan. A high forehead, hair brushed round to conceal a seemingly premature but never increasing baldness, a slight moustache, apple cheeks, blue eyes, an air of candour. Such was the Secretary of the War Cabinet, of all Cabinets, of all Prime Ministers, equally trusted and relied upon by all. I think it was Mr. Asquith who described him as the cement that

[1]Letter to the author 7th Aug. 1968.

bound all Cabinets together, and it was true. Attending every meeting, where he took down everything in longhand, prepared minutes and dealt with every conceivable matter with the industry of a continental housemaid, he was never ruffled, never out of temper, only a little in a hurry sometimes, rushing off with a roll of the upper body, torso well forward, using his elbows as if he were pushing his way through a wood. His voice was musical, his sentences balanced. He has probably never said a foolish thing in his life, betrayed a secret, made a tactless remark or spoken out of turn. I have often thought that in the next world he will certainly be selected to help St. Peter in his arduous duties. He will put difficult questions so as to cause the minimum of embarrassment, and always he will be writing, in longhand, in an enormous book".[1]

And there, at the peak of his power, influence and success we will take temporary leave of Lieutenant-Colonel Sir Maurice Hankey, K.C.B., LL.D.

[1] *Prelude to Victory* (Cape, 1939), pp. 136–7. Quoted by kind permission of the author.

Appendix A

Specimen of Hankey's rough notes for Minutes of a Cabinet Meeting

FOR some reason there has survived in the Cabinet records the original notes taken by Hankey of a Cabinet meeting held at 1 a.m. on 14th August 1917.[1] The notes are in pencil and in his own peculiar shortened longhand, which has made transcription difficult. But as they show his methods, and the type of material from which he could produce a complete and authoritative record of proceedings, they are reproduced below.

[Present]	P.M.	Milner	Barnes	Balfour
	B.L. [Bonar Law]	Curzon	Smuts	Hankey
P.M.	French rec'd [? information of a reliable character] that Austria is anxious for peace and willing to pay price of a break with Germany.			
	Have contact in Switzerland.			
	Telegram from Paris indicating progress of negotiations.			
Balfour	Great advance. Austria wants peace. [Doubts?] if previous con[versations] intimated Austria prepared to quarrel with G[ermany]			
P.M.	Indicates Austria wants to come out of this war is dominating factor instead of Germany. Prefers document obviously based on Austrian terms. Particularly in reference to Poles. Austrians want to put Germany in fix.			
Balfour	French told Austrians we don't want to break up Austrian Empire. At worst (?) Italy would be content with Trieste and some islands. Roumania (?) hard case. Incompetent to the verge of a crime (?)			
Smuts	Idea of bribing Roumania with Bessarabia and Thessally [sic]			
P.M.	Austria wants to make peace with us. We ought to move swiftly.			
Balfour	Difficulty as regards Roumania. What is your feeling?			

[1]Cab. 23/16.

[The next note was probably jotted down during a pause in the discussion. Hankey obviously had the agenda for the following day's meeting in mind.]

To-morrow   Amm^n for Palestine.
            Brewing and resumption of malting
            Guns for Russia.

P.M.   To get best terms you can from Roumania. If Austria is to get
            back position in Europe.
Balfour   If Austria refuses Transylvania. You cannot keep secret.
            Roumania goes to Germany.
Smuts   Get as far as you can without bringing in Roumania.
P.M.   Pictures (?) Conference.
            Begin with Italy; then Serbia; if you have agreement you put
            up your fight on Roumania. If it comes to pt [point] would
            have no hesitation.
Curzon   R[ussia] cannot expect to get much. If she gets back where she
            was and gets something on R [? Roumanian] side. Not so bad.
P.M.   Bulgaria not in negotiation. Roumania might get D [? Do-
            brudja] afterwards.
Balfour   Reverts to Rumbold's [deleted] telegram (s.d.) [probably
            No. 39 of 11/1/18]
P.M.   They [Austria] want economic (?) support.
            Didn't reveal details of budget.
            Hopelessly bankrupt. More and more getting in grip of
            Germany.
            Would rather owe money to us.
Milner   Doesn't believe Austria is prepared to break with Austria
            [sic. Presumably Hankey meant Germany]
P.M.   Thinks Milner underrates extent to which Austrians disgusted
            with Germany, whose vassal they are becoming.
            Not first time Austria has sold her Allies.
            Cannot altogether ignore religious considerations.
            They would like Bavaria.
P.M   Decided that no record of this meeting be kept.

Appendix B

List of Administrative Staff who served in the Cabinet Office

Including the Committee of Imperial Defence 1908–1938. In Alphabetical Order. Ranks and Titles as at the time of service in Cabinet Office

Captain E. G. F. Abraham (1918–20)
Commander C. C. A. Allen, R.N. (1931–4)
Lieutenant-Colonel L. C. M. S. Amery (1916–20)
Major-General Sir George Aston, K.C.B. (1918–19)
Mr. E. Beck (1917–23)
Mr. W. J. O. P. Bland (1917)
Sir Edward E. Bridges, K.C.B., M.C. (1938–45)
Mr. L. F. Burgis, C.M.G., C.V.O. (1918–49)
Major A. M. Caccia (1918–22)
Sir John Chancellor, K.C.M.G. (1922–3)
Mr. C. G. Clark (1930–1)
Captain A. W. Clarke, R.N. (1934–7, 1939–40)
Major L. A. Clemens, O.B.E., M.C. (1922–6)
Lieutenant-Colonel W. Dally Jones (1914–23)
Major J. A. Davies (1937–40)
Mr. P. K. Debenham (1930–41)
Mr. H. d'Egville (1918–19)
Brigadier V. Dykes, C.B.E. (1935–40, 1942)
Wing Commander W. Elliot, D.F.C. (1937–41)
Mr. G. M. Evans (1919, 1941–2)
Colonel J. Gorton (?1908–14)
Major A. Grant Duff (1908–13)
Commander R. L. Hamer, R.N. (1920–1)
Sir Maurice P. A. Hankey, G.C.B., G.C.M.G., G.C.V.O., LL.D. (1908–39)

Mr. A. F. Hemming, C.M.G., C.B.E. (1925–41)
Mr. H. D. Henderson (1930–4)
Commander The Hon. C. P. Hermon-Hodge, D.S.C., R.N. (1924–8)
Sir T. St. Quintin Hill, K.C.M.G., O.B.E. (1919–23, 1941–2)
Major N. G. Hind (1930–4)
Wing Commander E. J. Hodsoll (1929–35)
Mr. H. V. Hodson (1930)
Lieutenant-Colonel H. W. L. Holman (1918–19)
Major-General Sir Leslie C. Hollis (1936–46)
Sir Rupert B. Howorth, K.C.M.G., C.B. (1920–42)
General Sir Hastings L. Ismay, G.C.B., CH., D.S.O., C.B.E.
    (1926–30, 1936–47)
Major-General E. I. C. Jacob, K.B.E., C.B. (1938–46)
Mr. F. W. C. T. Jaffray (1918–19)
Captain Bulkeley Johnson (1918–19)
Captain C. Jones (1916–20)
Mr. T. Jones, CH. (1916–30)
Mr. F. W. Leith Ross (1920)
Wing-Commander Sir Norman R. A. D. Leslie, Bart., C.B.E. (1924–9)
Mr. C. Longhurst, C.B. (1914–42)
Lieutenant-Colonel K. G. McLean (1938–9)
Lieutenant-Colonel G. N. Macready, C.M.G., D.S.O., O.B.E., M.C.
    (1926–32)
Commander L. E. H. Maund, R.N. (1928–31)
Commander H. R. Moore, D.S.O., R.N. (1921–4)
Lieutenant-Colonel The Right Hon. Sir Matthew Nathan (1918–19)
Captain A. D. Nicholl, R.N. (1937–41)
Major The Hon. W. Ormsby-Gore (1917–18)
Mr. J. H. Penson (1934–5)
Lieutenant-Colonel H. R. Pownall, D.S.O., M.C. (1932–6)
Mr. D. H. F. Rickett, C.M.G. (1931–42, 1945–7)
Sir Arthur Robinson (1937–?)
Paymaster-in-Chief P. J. H. L. Row, R.N. (1916–18)
Mr. C. F. M. N. Ryan (1937–9)
Mr. H. H. Sellar (1936–9)
Mr. J. C. Stobart (1918–19)
Lieutenant-Colonel L. Storr (1916–20)
Lieutenant F. Storrs, R.N.V.R. (1918–19)
General E. D. Swinton, C.B., D.S.O. (1913–17)

Colonel Sir Mark Sykes, Bart., M.P. (1916–19)
Mr. A. J. Sylvester, C.B.E. (1920–21)
The Hon. C. H. Tufton, C.M.G. (1921–2)
Mr. H. G. Vincent (1936–9)
Lieutenant-Colonel C. W. G. Walker, D.S.O. (1923–6, 1943–7)
Squadron-Leader P. Warburton (1935–7)
Lieutenant-Colonel F. B. Webb (1934–9)
Mr. P. Wicks (1918–22)
Mr. W. D. Wilkinson (1930–4, 1935–42)
Lieutenant-Colonel L. Wilson, C.M.G., D.S.O. (1918–19)
Colonel Sir S. H. Wilson, K.B.E., C.B., C.M.G. (1918–21)
Mr. G. M. Young (1916–17)

Index

Compiled by The Rev. S. B-R. Poole

Where a footnote outlines the career of a person, this is indicated in brackets after the first entry.

demands knowledge of Calais Conference, 364; conveys George V's resentment of attacks on Admiralty, 380; concern for Robertson, 497, 546 (and Lloyd George's abrupt treatment of, 519); sent cabinet minutes on budget proposal (1918), 529

Stanhope, Rt. Hon. 7th Earl, 530 (and note 4)

Stanley, Sir Albert H. (later 1st Baron Ashfield), 582 (and note 4)

Stanley, Venetia (Mrs. Edwin Montagu), 216

Stanley, Admiral the Hon. Sir Victor, 53 (and note 1)

Steel-Maitland, Sir Arthur H. D. R., 342 (and note 2), 343-5

Stein, Leonard J., 626 (and note 3)

Stevenson, Frances (later Countess Lloyd George), 421 (and note 1), 551

Stockholm Peace Conference (1917), 419-20, 424

Stopford, General Sir Frederick, 198 (and note 1), 199

Storr, Major L., Military Assistant Secretary to H, 343, 371, 458 (and note 4), 508, 544

Strachey, J. St. Loe, Editor of *Spectator*, 245 (and note 1), 458

submarine menace, 171, 180-1, 242, 247, 253, 295, 315, 335-6, 354, *et seq.*, 366, 372, 379 *et seq.*, 389, 404-5, 409-10, 411-12, 424-5, 442, 446, 473, 476, 478, 500, 504-5, 527, 569, 580, 581-2, 599

Sueter, Admiral (later Sir) Murray F., 146 (and note 4)

Supreme War Council, decided upon at Rapallo Conference, 453 *et seq.*; conferences to establish, 464 *et seq.*; first meeting of, 468; teething troubles of, 471, 479; second meeting of, 487, 489-93; third meeting of, 508-10; subsequent meetings of, 535-6, 556-9, 569-71, 581, 590, 597, 608-10

Sutherland, Sir William, Private Secretary to Lloyd George, 329 (and note 1), 566

Swinton, General Sir Ernest D., part played in development of tank warfare, 146 (and note 3), 256, 268, 291, 304-5. Mentioned, 179, 205, 211, 217, 250, 343, 398, 412, 461, 550

Sydenham, 1st Baron (formerly Sir George Clarke), Secretary of C.I.D. 1904-7, 71 (and note 1), 84, 91, 116, 396, 530

Sykes, Colonel (later Major-General Sir) Frederick, 202 (and note 3); becomes Chief of Air Staff, 518-19, 568

Sykes, Sir Mark, Assistant Secretary in War Cabinet Secretariat, close association with H, 270 (and note 2), 328; his position under H in Cabinet Secretariat, 344-5, 352, 423, 424, 543; relations with Picot, 446, 567-8; policy in Palestine, 450, 601; concern for state of Ireland, 517, 521, 538

Sykes-Picot Agreement (1916), 270 *note* 2, 446 *note* 4, 607, 609

Sylvester, A. J. (H's private secretary), 345 (and note 1), 363, 535, 536, 569, 591, 612, 632-3

Talaat Pasha, 159 (and note 2), 417 (and note 2)

Talbot, Lord Edmund (later 1st Viscount Fitzalan of Derwent), 560 (and note 3)

tank warfare, H's part in development of, 146-7; his ideas about, 268, 286, 297; present at trials of, 256, 291; interests Lloyd George in, 270; first use of by English, 298 and by French, 377 *note* 3; successful action at Cambrai, 462

Tannenberg, Russian defeat at (1914), 151

Tardieu André, 569 (and note 3), 594

Templewood, Rt. Hon. 1st Viscount, 551

Tennant, Jack, 614 (and note 3)